Minitab®

DeMYSTiFieD®

DeMYSTiFieD® Series

Minitab®
DeMYSTiFieD®

Andrew Sleeper

New York   Chicago   San Francisco   Lisbon   London   Madrid   Mexico City
Milan   New Delhi   San Juan   Seoul   Singapore   Sydney   Toronto

The McGraw-Hill Companies

Cataloging-in-Publication Data is on file with the Library of Congress.

McGraw-Hill books are available at special quantity discounts to use as premiums and sales promotions, or for use in corporate training programs. To contact a representative please e-mail us at bulksales@mcgraw-hill.com.

Minitab® DeMYSTiFieD®

1 2 3 4 5 6 7 8 9 0   DOC/DOC   1 9 8 7 6 5 4 3 2 1

ISBN   978-0-07-176229-8
MHID   0-07-176229-9

Sponsoring Editor Judy Bass	**Production Supervisor** Pamela A. Pelton
Editing Supervisor David E. Fogarty	**Composition** Cenveo Publisher Services
Project Managers Ranjit Kaur and Ridhi Mathur, Cenveo Publisher Services	**Art Director, Cover** Jeff Weeks
Copy Editor Bev Weiler	**Cover Illustration** Lance Lekander
Proofreader Eina Malik, Cenveo Publisher Services	

Trademarks: McGraw-Hill, the McGraw-Hill Publishing logo, Demystified, and related trade dress are trademarks or registered trademarks of The McGraw-Hill Companies and/or its affiliates in the United States and other countries and may not be used without written permission. All other trademarks are the property of their respective owners. The McGraw-Hill Companies is not associated with any product or vendor mentioned in this book.

Information contained in this work has been obtained by The McGraw-Hill Companies, Inc. ("McGraw-Hill") from sources believed to be reliable. However, neither McGraw-Hill nor its authors guarantee the accuracy or completeness of any information published herein, and neither McGraw-Hill nor its authors shall be responsible for any errors, omissions, or damages arising out of use of this information. This work is published with the understanding that McGraw-Hill and its authors are supplying information but are not attempting to render engineering or other professional services. If such services are required, the assistance of an appropriate professional should be sought.

To Lady Công Huyền Tôn Nữ Xuân Phương,
my love and my inspiration

About the Author

Andrew Sleeper is a statistical consultant and trainer who runs his own company, Successful Statistics LLC. His industrial career includes work as a design engineer, reliability engineer, project manager, and Six Sigma Black Belt. Mr. Sleeper has presented numerous papers and articles on statistical tools in the quality industry. He is the author of *Design for Six Sigma Statistics* and *Six Sigma Distribution Modeling*.

Contents

Acknowledgments

I am very grateful for the assistance of Judy Bass, Senior Editor at McGraw-Hill. Her vision for this book and her ideas for its organization and content have been essential. I also acknowledge the help and advice of Edward Jaeck and Jim Martin, who reviewed the manuscript and suggested important improvements.

The many fine people at Minitab, Inc. continue to provide excellent customer service, while dealing with a large number of my inquiries, as I prepared this book. I am grateful that they provide both good software and good support.

Finally, and most importantly, I could not have completed a project like this without the love and support of my wife and my family.

Introduction

If you need to use Minitab for school or work, and you're worried about it, this book is for you. In recent years, statistics has become a required skill for students and professionals in all fields. For many of those people, math and statistics are not their favorite activities.

The good news is that Minitab handles the hard math of statistical analysis quickly and easily. The better news is that new tools in Minitab 16 help explain and interpret those results with color-coded graphs, sentences in plain language, and neatly formatted reports. The best news is that this book will guide you gently and quickly to find the best features of Minitab and apply them to solve your problems.

This book is organized informally into four parts:

- Chapters 1–3 are for newcomers to Minitab who want to quickly come up to speed. Chapter 1 introduces common Minitab features using one extended example. Chapter 2 explores many types of Minitab graphs. Chapter 3 provides a thorough tour of the Minitab interface.

- Chapters 4–7 describe tools to make better decisions from data. These chapters cover distribution models, intervals for making decisions, hypothesis testing, and sample size calculations.

- Chapters 8–9 are for modelers and experimenters. Chapter 8 discusses regression tools. Chapter 9 covers the powerful design of experiments (DOE) toolbox in Minitab, including factorial, response surface, and mixture designs, plus an important new feature of Minitab 16 that handles split-plot designs.

- Chapters 10–14 introduce the most important tools used in process control, quality improvement, and Six Sigma initiatives. These tools include measurement systems analysis, control charts, capability analysis, acceptance sampling, and reliability analysis.

NEW IN 16 — In release 16, Minitab introduced an impressive array of new and improved features. The revolutionary Minitab assistant offers sound advice about collecting and organizing data, selecting the right analysis tool, and interpreting analysis results with plain language and consistently formatted reports. Throughout this book, new features of Minitab 16 are flagged with the distinctive logo shown here.

How to Get the Most from This Book

Feel free to jump around in this book, as you need to. Each chapter is written without assuming a thorough familiarity with preceding chapters. The first example of each chapter is explained down to the keystroke level. When you need to solve a particular type of problem, jump to that chapter and start reading. Here are some other tips for readers:

- **Work the examples.** Almost all the datasets used in this book are included with Minitab in the Sample data folder. Follow along with the examples, and explore the results you see on your computer. You will learn much more by working on your computer than by merely reading a book.

- **Refer to other books.** This book explains Minitab, with explanations of statistical terms and concepts required to understand Minitab reports. Other books have more space to define and illustrate statistical tools more thoroughly. Most chapters in this book list good references in the "Find Out More" section.

- **Do the quizzes.** Each chapter ends with a 10-question quiz. The quiz reinforces concepts in the chapter and sometimes introduces new variations on Minitab tools. For most questions, the answer is explained at the end of the book.

- **Work your own problems.** After reading the examples here, try them on your own data, and use Minitab to solve your problems.

- **Take the final exam.** After some time passes, come back and take the final exam. The exam has several questions relating to each chapter, more or less in order. These questions provide more opportunities to practice your statistical and Minitab skills, using Minitab example data files. Answers to most questions are explained.

Not every Minitab tool and function is covered here. Most people will find their first, second, and hopefully third set of Minitab tools explained in this book. By that time, the Minitab help files will hopefully suffice for learning more Minitab skills.

Trademarks

MINITAB® and all other trademarks and logos for the Company's products and services are the exclusive property of Minitab Inc. All other marks referenced remain the property of their respective owners. See www.minitab.com for more information on Minitab products.

Microsoft®, Windows®, Word®, Excel®, and PowerPoint® are registered trademarks of the Microsoft group of companies.

chapter **1**

Getting Started with Minitab Statistical Software

In this chapter, we will explore a dataset by using Minitab® statistical software to create graphs, statistical summaries, and a report. If you are new to Minitab, working through the sections of this chapter will guide you through a variety of commonly used functions, including some of the exciting, new features of Minitab 16.

CHAPTER OBJECTIVES

Here's what you'll learn in this chapter:

- How to create, open, and save Minitab projects and worksheets
- How to create histograms
- How to combine multiple graphs in panels of a single graph
- How to calculate descriptive statistics
- How to reveal relationships between variables with scatterplots and matrix plots
- How to use brushing to select and analyze certain data values from a graph
- How to organize a Minitab project and navigate through it using the Project Manager
- How to quickly create a printed report from a Minitab analysis

1.1   Opening a New Minitab Project

To start Minitab statistical software, either double-click the Minitab icon on the Windows® desktop, or select Minitab > Minitab 16 Statistical Software from the Start menu. Minitab opens a window displaying a new, empty Minitab project, as shown in Fig. 1-1.

In the Minitab window, below the menus and toolbars, are three parts of this new Minitab project:

- The Session window displays messages and reports from all Minitab commands as you execute them.
- The data window named Worksheet 1 *** can hold and display data of many types, arranged into columns. Data values may be entered directly

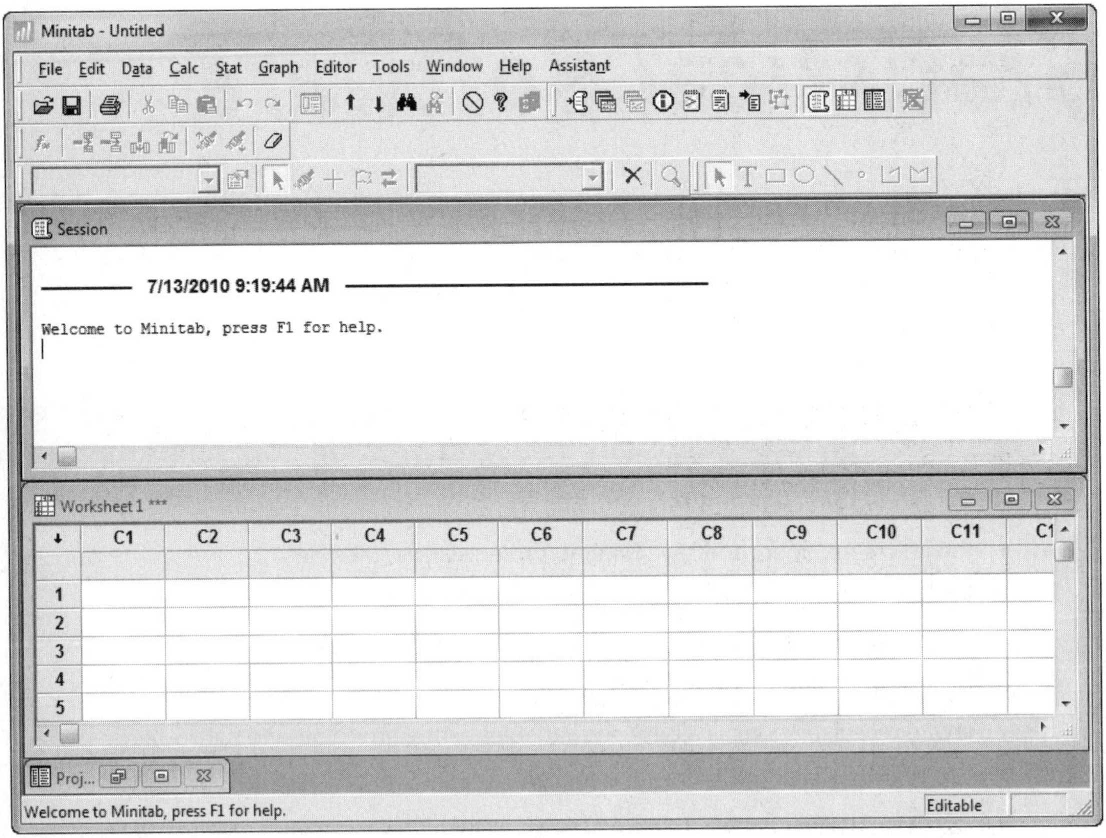

FIGURE 1-1 · New, empty Minitab project.

into the data window, imported from other files, or copied and pasted through the Windows clipboard. Navigation around the data window is similar to navigation in a Microsoft® Office Excel® spreadsheet. A Minitab project may hold any number of worksheets, but this new project holds only one. The *** indicates that Worksheet 1 is the current worksheet. If many worksheets are open in the project, all Minitab commands operate only on data contained in the current worksheet.

- The Project Manager window is minimized at the bottom of the Minitab window. The Project Manager window and toolbar allow quick navigation between the components of a Minitab project.

Chapter 3 provides more details about the windows, toolbars, features, and capabilities of the Minitab interface.

At this point, if we wanted to continue working with a saved Minitab project, we could use the File > Open Project menu command. Since we have no project to continue, we will build up a new project from this empty template.

1.2   Loading Data into the Project

In the Minitab File menu, select Open Worksheet. This command is located below the group of commands for Minitab projects in the File menu. The Open Worksheet dialog appears, as shown in Fig. 1-2. Near the bottom of the dialog, click the ▣ icon, labeled Look in Minitab Sample Data Folder. Since most of the datasets used in this book are stored in the Minitab sample data folder, this is a convenient shortcut.

Open the Student14 folder in the Sample Data folder, select the worksheet file named OldFaithful, and click Open. A box appears to advise that a copy of the data in the worksheet file will be added to the current project. Click OK in the warning, and the dataset appears in a new data window named OldFaithful.MTW ***. MTW is the file extension for Minitab worksheet files, and the *** is a reminder that this is now the current worksheet. The empty Worksheet 1 is still in the project, but it is no longer current.

Figure 1-3 shows the data window for the OldFaithful.MTW worksheet. The worksheet contains three columns with names Duration, Interval, and Height. Columns in Minitab worksheets always have identifiers C1, C2, and so on, but entering more descriptive names in the name row below C1, C2, …, is always a good idea.

How many numbers are in each column of data? Scrolling through the data window is one way to see the size of a dataset, but Minitab provides an easier

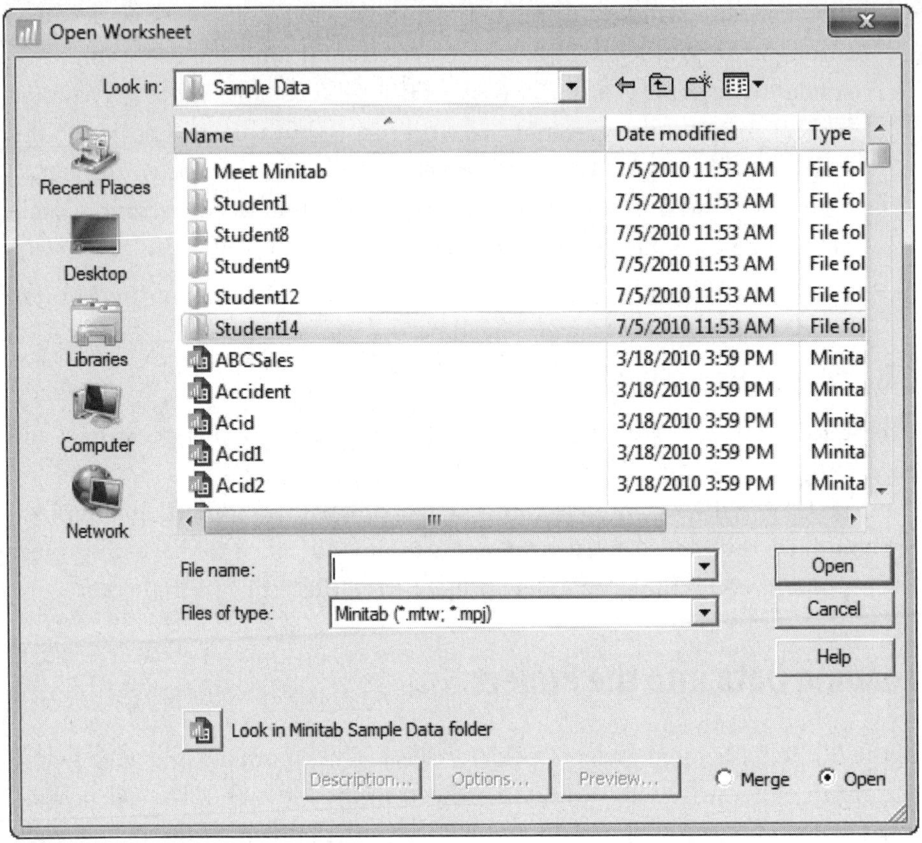

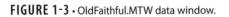

FIGURE 1-2 • Open Worksheet form.

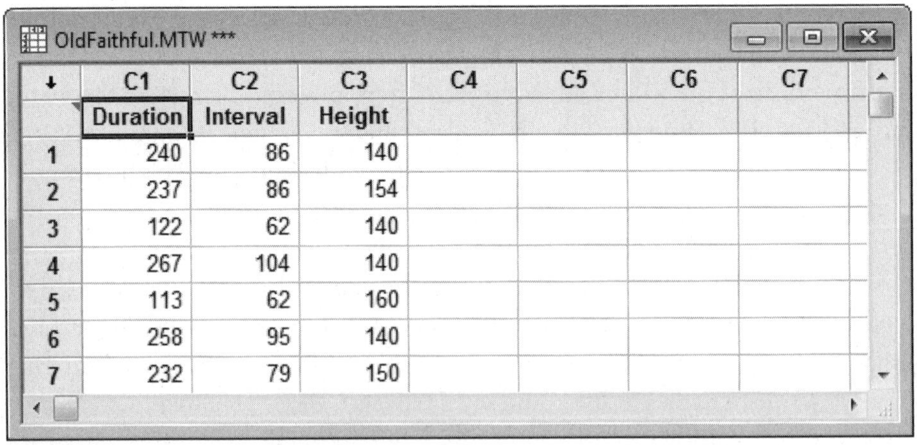

↓	C1	C2	C3	C4	C5	C6	C7
	Duration	Interval	Height				
1	240	86	140				
2	237	86	154				
3	122	62	140				
4	267	104	140				
5	113	62	160				
6	258	95	140				
7	232	79	150				

FIGURE 1-3 • OldFaithful.MTW data window.

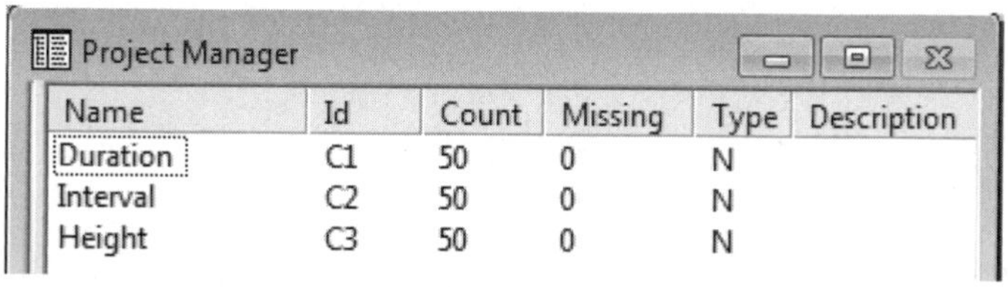

Project Manager					
Name	Id	Count	Missing	Type	Description
Duration	C1	50	0	N	
Interval	C2	50	0	N	
Height	C3	50	0	N	

FIGURE 1-4 • Project Manager information on OldFaithful.MTW.

way to display information about all the columns in the worksheet. In the toolbars, look for the ① button, and click it. The Project Manager window appears on the left, tiled with the worksheet data window on the right. Figure 1-4 shows the Project Manager information for this worksheet, listing column names, ids, counts, the number of missing values, and data types.

If you cannot find the ① button, this could be because the Project Manager toolbar is hidden. To see a menu of all the available toolbars, move the cursor over any of the menus or toolbars, then right-click the mouse. When there is a check next to Project Manager in the toolbar menu, the Project Manager toolbar should be visible. This toolbar contains many other buttons for quickly navigating to different parts of the Minitab project. An alternative to clicking the ① button is to use the Ctrl+Alt+I keyboard shortcut.

In statistical analysis, it is important to identify missing data values. These are different from the empty cells in the data window below the end of the data in each column. Minitab identifies missing data values with the * symbol in the data window. In the OldFaithful.MTW data window, click on any cell and delete the value with the delete key, followed by enter. Now, the deleted value is replaced by *, and the Project Manager reports one missing value. Restore the missing value with Edit > Undo or use the keyboard shortcut Ctrl+Z.

At this point, it is a good idea to save the new Minitab project using File > Save Project As from the Minitab menu. Choose any convenient file name and location. The file will be saved with the MPJ extension reserved for Minitab projects. Note that the worksheet loaded from the OldFaithful.MTW file is only a copy of the data, and this copy will be saved as part of the new MPJ file. The original MTW file is unchanged unless the Save Current Worksheet command in the File menu is used. It is good practice to preserve any datasets in their original, unchanged form, in case the analysis needs to be repeated later.

Many users of Microsoft Office have come to expect programs to automatically save their work at regular intervals and to recover unsaved files in the event of a crash. Autosave and recovery are convenient features of Microsoft Office, but these features do not exist in Minitab. Also, like many other complicated Windows applications and Windows itself, Minitab does occasionally crash. For these reasons, savvy Minitab users save their work frequently. If they don't, they will soon learn why they should.

1.3   Creating a Graph

Now it is time to explore this data by creating some graphs. The OldFaithful.MTW dataset contains measurements of duration in seconds, interval in minutes, and height in feet for 50 eruptions of the Old Faithful geyser in Yellowstone National Park. How are duration, interval, and height distributed?

In the Minitab menu, click Assistant > Graphical Analysis. The assistant appears as shown in Fig.1-5. Starting in version 16, Minitab provides a variety of assistants

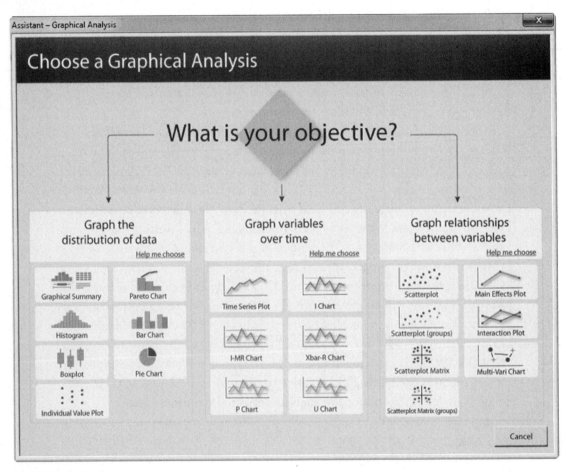

FIGURE 1-5 • Graphical analysis assistant.

to help people choose the most appropriate tool for their situation and then interpret the results. The graphical analysis assistant offers three categories of graphs: to graph the distribution of data, to graph variables over time, and to graph relationships between variables.

Clicking on any of these categories shows a flow chart with decisions to help identify the best tool. Clicking on any diamond-shaped decision box in the flow chart displays examples and explanations for this decision. Next to each tool in the flow chart is a *more...* hyperlink. Clicking *more...* shows guidelines for collecting data and interpreting the results of any tool you choose.

For the OldFaithful.MTW worksheet, many of these graphs could be appropriate. For a first graph, select a histogram from the assistant. Figure 1-6 shows the histogram assistant dialog. This dialog is only used to create a simple histogram of one variable. In this dialog, click on the field labeled Y column. The column listbox is the large white space near the left edge of the dialog. This listbox lists all the columns in the current worksheet which may be selected. If this listbox is empty, be sure to click on the Y column field first. Double-click on C1 Duration in the column listbox, and Duration appears in the Y column field. Alternately, you may directly enter C1 or Duration into the Y column field. Click OK, and the histogram appears, as shown in Fig. 1-7.

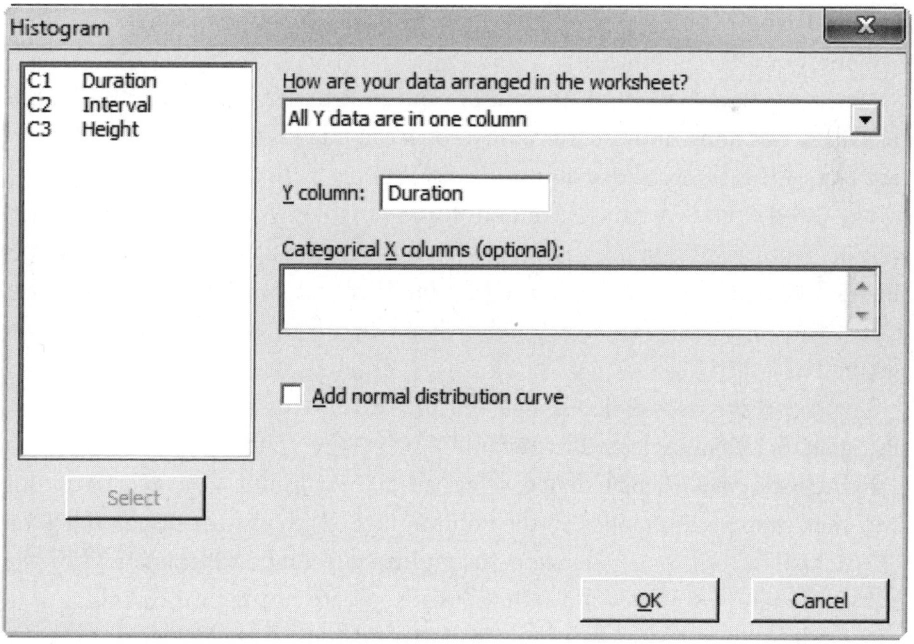

FIGURE 1-6 · Histogram assistant.

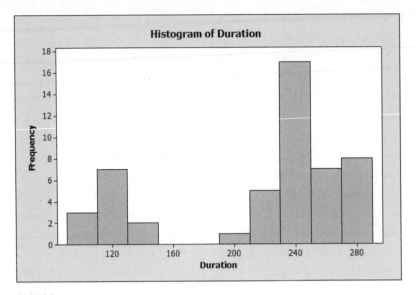

FIGURE 1-7 · Histogram of eruption duration.

The histogram shows what is often called a bimodal distribution for duration. Some eruptions have a short duration, around two minutes (120 seconds), while others have a long duration, around four minutes. Between these two groups of eruptions is a gap. There are no eruptions in this dataset with a duration of around three minutes.

Statistics offers many tools to describe and summarize datasets with numerical values. But none of these numerical tools can adequately convey the important fact of this bimodal distribution as effectively as this one simple graph.

The OldFaithful.MTW dataset contains three variables. With a little more effort, we can create a single graph displaying the distribution of several variables. This time, select Graph > Histogram in the Minitab menus. Compared to the Assistant menu, the Histogram function in the Graph menu offers more options and flexibility.

The first Histograms dialog is a gallery of available histogram styles. A Simple histogram is already selected by default. Click OK to continue.

In the Histogram – Simple dialog, select all three columns. One way to do this is to click first on C1 Duration in the column listbox, then shift-double-click on C3 Height. This will enter Duration–Height into the Graph variables field of the dialog. Clicking OK now will produce three separate histograms. Try this.

Now, look for the ▣ button in the Standard toolbar and click it. This is a shortcut to recall the last dialog used, which is the Histogram – Simple dialog.

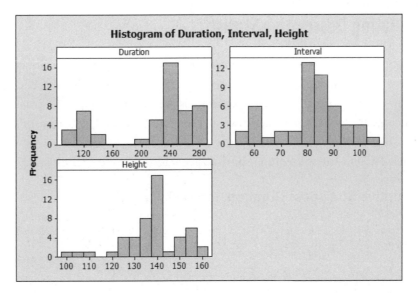

FIGURE 1-8 · Histogram with panels.

Two other ways to access the last dialog used are to click Edit > Edit Last Dialog, or to use the keyboard shortcut Ctrl+E. For many people, this is their favorite Minitab function!

Back in the Histogram - Simple dialog, click the Multiple Graphs button. Under Show Graph Variables, select the option labeled In separate panels of the same graph. Click OK in the two open dialogs. Figure 1-8 shows the resulting histogram graph with three panels, one for each column of data.

The default arrangement of panels in a paneled graph may or may not be the most appropriate. To try a different arrangement of panels, right-click on the graph, and select Panels. In the Edit Panels dialog, select the Arrangement tab. Here, we can override the automatic arrangement and specify any number of rows and columns for the panels. Alternate arrangements for this example include one row with three columns and three rows with one column. Try alternate arrangements for the panels to find the one you like best.

Many graphs are possible, but which one is best? In general, the best graph makes it easy to see the most important features or stories of the dataset with a minimum of clutter and distractions. This comes down to a set of judgments made by the analyst. The first judgment is to decide what the big story in the data is, and next, to decide which graphs best reveal that story to the viewer.

As a reminder, now is a good time to save the Minitab project file by clicking the 🔲 button in the Standard toolbar, or by using the Ctrl+S keyboard shortcut.

1.4 Calculating Descriptive Statistics

A typical statistical report on a dataset includes both graphs and descriptive statistics to summarize the data. To prepare a table of descriptive statistics, click Stat > Basic Statistics > Display Descriptive Statistics. In the Display Descriptive Statistics dialog, select all three variables using the column listbox as before, or simply enter C1-C3 in the Variables field.

Click OK, and the following report appears in the Session window:

Descriptive Statistics: Duration, Interval, Height

Variable	N	N*	Mean	SE Mean	StDev	Minimum	Q1	Median	Q3
Duration	50	0	216.64	8.25	58.32	102.00	187.25	238.00	264.25
Interval	50	0	80.66	1.69	11.98	56.00	73.75	82.00	88.25
Height	50	0	138.08	1.79	12.65	100.00	134.00	140.00	146.25

Variable	Maximum
Duration	276.00
Interval	104.00
Height	160.00

This table lists selected descriptive statistics for the three variables in the dataset. This table is helpful, but perhaps not ideal for a report. The overflow onto a second row is awkward, and perhaps other statistics are needed, such as coefficient of variation. The coefficient of variation, defined to be standard deviation divided by the mean and expressed as a percentage, is a useful way of comparing variation between variables with very different mean values.

Recall the Display Descriptive Statistics dialog with the ▣ button or the Ctrl+E keyboard shortcut. Click on the Statistics button to display a dialog listing the available statistics. To make room in the report, clear the checkboxes for SE of mean and N missing. Set the checkbox for Coefficient of variation. The dialog should now look like Fig. 1-9. Click OK in the two open dialogs, and the following report appears in the Session window.

Descriptive Statistics: Duration, Interval, Height

Variable	N	Mean	StDev	CoefVar	Minimum	Q1	Median	Q3	Maximum
Duration	50	216.64	58.32	26.92	102.00	187.25	238.00	264.25	276.00
Interval	50	80.66	11.98	14.85	56.00	73.75	82.00	88.25	104.00
Height	50	138.08	12.65	9.16	100.00	134.00	140.00	146.25	160.00

The Display Descriptive Statistics command is convenient for generating a neat table for a report. However, reports of statistical summaries often require greater flexibility. When more significant digits are required, or fewer, these options are not available in this Session window report. Also, the fixed-width

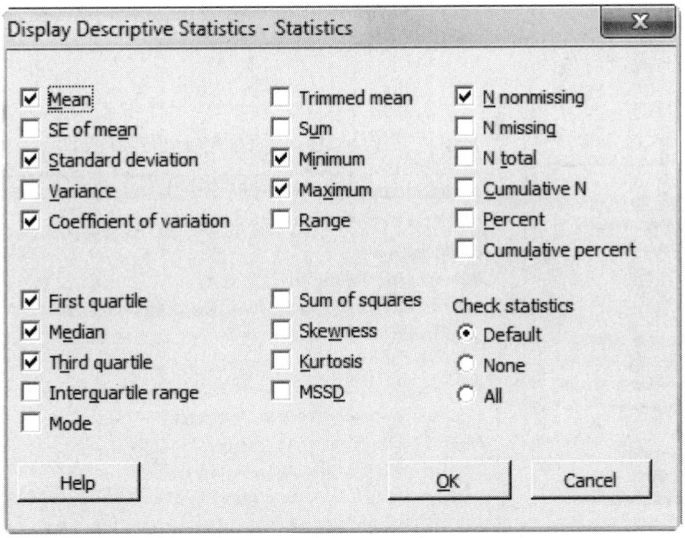

FIGURE 1-9 • Descriptive statistics.

Courier New font of the Session window helps to align columns of numbers in the table, but it looks old-fashioned.

The Stat > Basic Statistics > Store Descriptive Statistics command is similar to Display Descriptive Statistics, except that the statistics are stored in new columns of the current worksheet, with all available significant digits. From here, the statistics may be copied and pasted into a report for further formatting.

Still Struggling

If you ever have questions about Minitab features or functions, the Minitab help files should be your first reference. Now is a good time to explore the Minitab help features. Most dialogs have a Help button leading to explanations of the available features and functions. Back in the Display Descriptive Statistics – Statistics dialog shown in Fig. 1-9, click the Help button. This displays a Minitab Help window similar to Fig. 1-10. In the right pane, each statistic listed has an underlined hyperlink, which, when clicked, displays a definition and explanation of that statistic. The left pane shows the outline structure of the Minitab Help file, with quick links to help on almost any Minitab topic.

Before proceeding, now is a good time to save the Minitab project file.

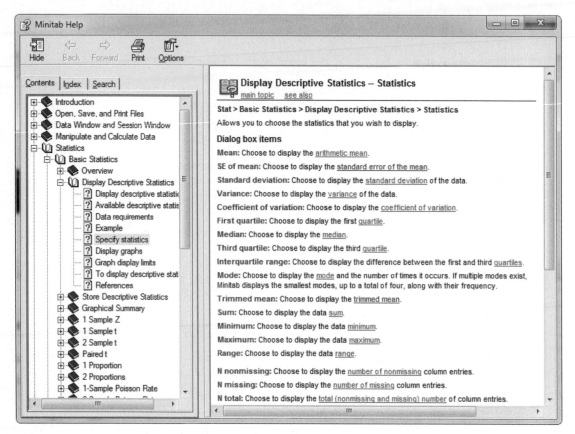

FIGURE 1-10 · Minitab help for descriptive statistics.

1.5   Exploring Relationships between Variables

The histograms and descriptive statistics created in the preceding sections consider each column as a separate, disconnected dataset. This section continues the exploration of data in the Minitab sample dataset OldFaithful.MTW by examining connections and relationships between the three variables.

The values in each row of this dataset are connected because of the way the data were collected. Each row lists the duration, interval before, and height of the same eruption. We can explore the possibility of relationships between these variables using scatterplots and correlation coefficients. In particular, we might wonder if the duration or height of each eruption can be predicted by measuring the interval before the eruption.

The scatterplot is the fundamental graph for visualizing relationships between two variables. Start the graphical analysis assistant shown in Fig. 1-5, by selecting

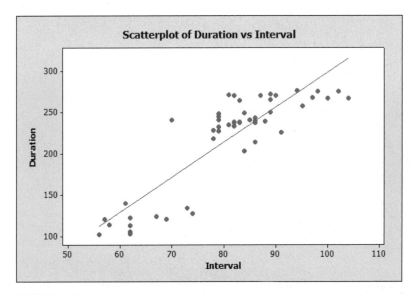

FIGURE 1-11 · Scatterplot of eruption duration vs. interval.

Assistant > Graphical Analysis, and then click on Scatterplot. In the Scatterplot dialog, select Duration for the Y column and Interval for the X column. The quickest way to do this is to double-click first on C1 Duration and next on C2 Interval in the column listbox. Click OK, and the scatterplot in Fig. 1-11 appears.

In a scatterplot, each dot represents one row of values in the worksheet. In this example, each dot represents the interval before and the duration of one geyser eruption. The dots form two obvious clusters. One cluster of eruptions has shorter intervals and shorter durations; the other cluster has longer intervals and longer durations.

Visually, it appears that interval is a good predictor of duration. If an eruption starts in less than 75 minutes after the preceding eruption, it will probably be a two-minute eruption. If the interval is longer than 75 minutes, the eruption will probably be a four-minute eruption.

With three variables in the dataset, six different scatterplots are possible by choosing different variables for the Y column and the X column. Each choice of variables provides a different view of potential relationships between variables. For example, to explore whether the height of an eruption can be predicted by measuring the interval before the eruption, a useful scatterplot would plot Height on the Y axis versus Interval on the X axis.

In Minitab, a matrix plot can display many scatterplots in a single graph. To create a matrix plot, select Graph > Matrix Plot from the Minitab menu. The first

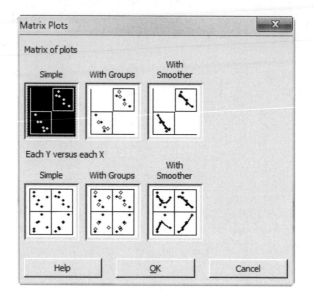

FIGURE 1-12 · Matrix plots gallery.

dialog to appear is the Matrix Plots gallery, as seen in Fig. 1-12. This dialog offers six versions of matrix plots. The top row, labeled Matrix of plots, produces a matrix of scatterplots containing all possible pairs of variables. The second row, labeled Each Y versus each X, produces a matrix with any number of Y variables and any number of X variables.

Select the Simple matrix plot in the top row of the dialog, and click OK. Then select all three variables Duration-Height in the Graph variables field of the following dialog. After clicking OK, the matrix plot in Fig. 1-13 appears. This matrix shows all six possible scatterplots made from the three variables in this dataset.

Do the scatterplots we have created provide any evidence of a relationship between interval and eruption height? In Fig. 1-13, the bottom-center panel shows **Height** versus **Interval**, and the center-right panel shows **Interval** versus **Height**. Both of these scatterplots show a square, random pattern of points, with no evidence of correlation or trend. Visually, it is easy to see that eruption height cannot be predicted by interval, or vice-versa.

Correlation coefficients are measures of linear relationships between pairs of variables; the most common type of correlation coefficient is known as a Pearson correlation. In an Excel worksheet, this is easily calculated using either the CORREL or PEARSON worksheet functions. Minitab can also calculate and display Pearson correlations for many variables using the Stat > Basic Statistics > Correlation function in the Minitab menu.

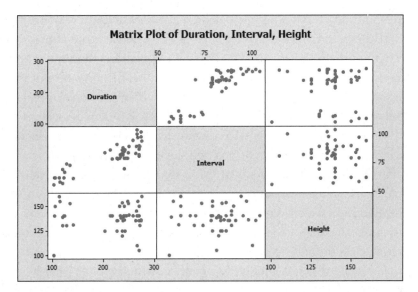

FIGURE 1-13 · Matrix plot.

To try this Minitab tool, select Stat > Basic Statistics > Correlation. Select all three columns in the OldFaithful.MTW worksheet and click OK. The following report appears in the Session window:

Correlations: Duration, Interval, Height

```
          Duration   Interval
Interval     0.870
             0.000

Height      -0.019    -0.010
             0.898     0.946

Cell Contents: Pearson correlation
               P-Value
```

This table displays two numbers for each pair of variables. For `Duration` and `Interval`, the first number is `0.870`, the Pearson correlation. The second number, `0.000`, is a *p*-value for a test of significance. Since this *p*-value is small, less than 0.05, we can be very confident that these two variables are positively correlated. This is consistent with the appearance of the scatterplot.

The other two pairs of variables have a Pearson correlation close to zero, and a high *p*-value, indicating no evidence of a linear relationship between them.

Scatterplots reveal relationships between variables. If these relationships are linear, linear correlation coefficients, such as the Pearson correlation, measure the strength of that relationship. The Pearson correlation is a number between −1 and +1. When the Pearson correlation is positive, higher values of the two variables tend to be associated with each other. When the correlation is negative, higher values of one variable are associated with smaller values of the other. Extreme values of −1 or +1 indicate that all points in the dataset fall along a straight line of negative or positive slope, respectively.

But in real life, we usually want to know something about cause and effect. Do changes in X cause changes in Y? Correlation does not answer this question. The correlation between eruption interval and duration does not say which variable causes the other variable to be more or less. It is possible that an unseen third variable causes both variables to change together.

Correlation alone is not enough to prove cause and effect. Only when correlation is a result of a carefully designed experiment, in which other variables are controlled and measured, is a conclusion about causality justifiable. Regression and experimental tools, which can detect and prove a causal relationship, are discussed in Chapters 8 and 9.

1.6   Brushing Data

This section introduces brushing, a powerful technique to identify a subset of data in one plot and explore features of that subset in additional plots and analysis steps. The example in this section uses scatterplots created from the OldFaithful.MTW dataset in the preceding section.

Using the OldFaithful.MTW dataset, find or create a scatterplot of Duration versus Interval as shown in Fig. 1-11. Can we learn something about the group of 12 eruptions with short, two-minute durations? To find out, look for the brush 🖊 icon in the Graph Editing toolbar, and click it. Alternatively, select Editor > Brush from the Minitab menu.

The brush function is only available if a Minitab graph window containing certain types of graphs is active. If the brush icon is gray or unavailable, click anywhere in a Minitab scatterplot. This should activate the graph and enable brushing.

When brushing is on, and the cursor is over a scatterplot, the cursor becomes a pointing hand ☜. To select or brush a data point, point the hand to any data symbol on the graph, usually a red dot, and click it. The data symbol changes

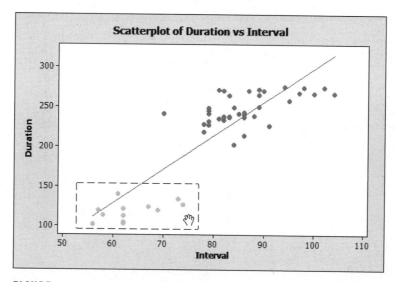

FIGURE 1-14 · Scatterplot with data brushed.

to a different color, and the brushed data value is also highlighted in the data window and in other graphs, where brushing is on.

To brush a cluster of data on a graph, click the mouse and drag to define a rectangular region, as shown in Fig. 1-14. After releasing the mouse button, all data symbols in the box are selected, and they are said to be brushed. Now, when the cursor is over a region of brushed data, the cursor changes to a flat hand ☝. By clicking and dragging, the region can be moved to brush a different set of data values.

When brushing is on for the current graph, a small window appears called the Brushing Palette. This can be seen at the left of Fig. 1-15. This figure shows several Minitab windows after brushing a subset of data values. The Brushing Palette is the top left window in Fig. 1-15, and lists the row numbers of the brushed data points in the worksheet. The data window includes • symbols to highlight brushed rows.

One of the most powerful features of brushing is the ability to see the same brushed points highlighted in every plot which shows data points with individual symbols. The bottom graph in Fig. 1-15 is a time series plot displaying Duration measurements in time order. This important type of graph can be selected from the graphical analysis assistant, or by using the menus and selecting Stat > Time Series > Time Series Plot.

In Fig. 1-15, both the scatterplot and the time series plot show the same set of brushed data points highlighted. To highlight brushed points in multiple

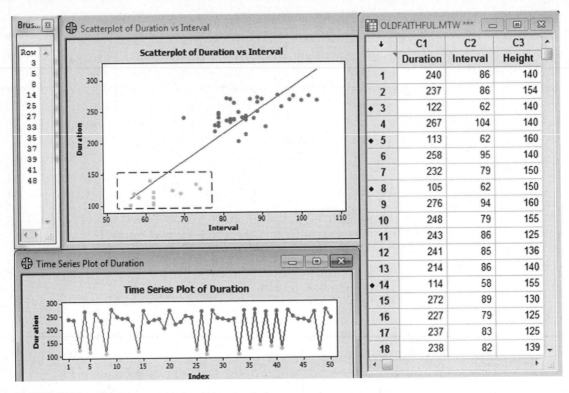

FIGURE 1-15 • Brushed data highlighted in many windows.

plots, brushing must be turned on for each graph separately by selecting each graph and clicking the ✐ button. After this is done, points brushed in one graph are highlighted in all graphs.

In this example, brushing allows us to quickly see that the shorter two-minute eruptions are not clustered together in time, but are scattered throughout the dataset. Further, the time series plot shows that a two-minute eruption was always preceded and followed by a four-minute eruption, at least during the time this dataset was collected.

After brushing a subset of data, it is useful to see values of certain variables only for that subset. For a large dataset, it is not practical to scroll through a large data window, picking out only the brushed values. Another way is to select what Minitab calls ID variables, which will appear in the Brushing Palette.

With a graph window active, select Editor > Set ID Variables from the Minitab menu. Then choose any or all columns and click OK. Up to ten columns may be chosen as ID variables. Figure 1-16 shows the Brushing Palette with ID variables Interval and Duration.

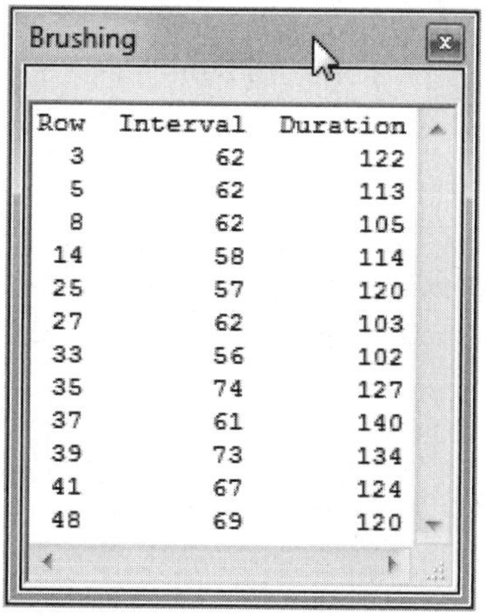

Row	Interval	Duration
3	62	122
5	62	113
8	62	105
14	58	114
25	57	120
27	62	103
33	56	102
35	74	127
37	61	140
39	73	134
41	67	124
48	69	120

FIGURE 1-16 • Brushing palette with ID variables.

Suppose we want to calculate the mean, standard deviation, and other descriptive statistics separately for the short eruptions and for the long eruptions. To do this quickly, first brush the short eruptions in a scatterplot graph. Then, with the scatterplot still active, select Editor > Create Indicator Variable from the Minitab menu. In the Column field, enter a name for a new column, such as Short. Then, select the Update now option, and click OK.

Now look in the data window, and notice there is a new column named Short containing 0s and 1s. In this column, 1 indicates the short eruptions from the brushed data, and 0 indicates the long eruptions.

Now select Stat > Basic Statistics > Display Descriptive Statistics from the Minitab menu. In the Variables field, enter Duration-Height, and in the By variables field, enter Short. If you wish, click the Statistics button and select which statistics to display. After clicking OK, a table like this appears in the Session window.

Descriptive Statistics: Duration, Interval, Height

Variable	Short	N	Mean	StDev	CoefVar	Minimum	Median	Maximum
Duration	0	38	247.58	19.11	7.72	203.00	242.00	276.00
	1	12	118.67	11.93	10.06	102.00	120.00	140.00
Interval	0	38	86.05	7.42	8.62	70.00	84.50	104.00
	1	12	63.58	5.93	9.33	56.00	62.00	74.00
Height	0	38	137.79	11.70	8.49	105.00	139.50	160.00
	1	12	139.00	15.85	11.40	100.00	140.00	160.00

In this table, the rows where `Short = 1` display the descriptive statistics for the short eruptions with a mean duration of 118.67, and the rows where `Short = 0` correspond to the long eruptions with a mean duration of 247.58.

This section illustrated the use of brushing with a scatterplot and a time series plot. In Minitab, brushing is available for any type of graph where one data symbol represents one row in the data window. Graph types where one data symbol represents many data values, such as a histogram, do not have brushing available.

1.7   Navigating with the Project Manager

After creating many graphs and analyzing data in many ways, a Minitab project can become quite large. With dozens or hundreds of graphs and analysis results, it can become difficult to find one particular graph or to remember what options were chosen for a particular analysis. The Project Manager makes these navigation and organization tasks much easier.

The fastest way to use the Project Manager is through the Project Manager toolbar, shown in Fig. 1-17. If this toolbar is not visible, place the cursor over any menu or toolbar and right-click. In the toolbar menu, be sure that Project Manager is selected. Here is a quick description of the buttons on this toolbar, along with the associated keyboard shortcuts.

- The ⌐ button or the Ctrl+Alt+M keyboard shortcut shows the Session window, which contains a list of graphs and analytical reports in the order they were created. In this view, the Project Manager window shows an outline view of the Session window, listing only the title lines of sections in the Session window. Click any of these titles to jump directly to that section. Right-click on any section title to append it to the Minitab project report or to send that section directly to Microsoft Office Word® word-processing software or PowerPoint® presentation software.

- The ⌐ button (Ctrl+Alt+D) shows the data window of the current worksheet with the Worksheets folder of the Project Manager listing all the worksheets in the project. Right-click on any worksheet in this window to rename it, bring it to the front, or to enter a description for the worksheet.

FIGURE 1-17 · Project Manager toolbar.

- The ▣ button (Ctrl+Alt+G) shows the most recently viewed graph with the Graphs folder of the Project Manager listing all the graphs in the project. Right-click on any graph title in this window to append it to the Minitab project report or to send it directly to Microsoft Word or PowerPoint.

- The ① button (Ctrl+Alt+I) displays the data window of the current worksheet, along with information about each column in the worksheet. Right-click on any column name in the Project Manager to change its name, width, or format.

- The ▣ button (Ctrl+Alt+H) displays the History folder, containing all the Minitab session commands for the project. This command history is normally hidden from view, but it documents all actions performed by the user since the project was created. The command language seen in this window is used to write macros to automate Minitab tasks. When viewing the History folder, the left pane displays all folders of the project in outline format.

- The ▣ button (Ctrl+Alt+R) displays the ReportPad™, a simple word processor designed to hold the Minitab project report. The ReportPad is a convenient place to organize graphs and analysis results into a report without using any other software. Appending an analysis report from the Session window or a graph from the Graphs folder adds these items to the Report-Pad. From here, the report can be saved in rich text format (.RTF extension) or as an HTML web page.

- The ▣ button (Ctrl+Alt+L) displays the Related Documents folder. To add a link to files or web pages relevant to the project, right-click in the folder and select Add Link.

- The ▣ button (Ctrl+Alt+E) displays information about the experimental design attached to the current worksheet. This option is grayed out until a design has been defined using the Stat > DOE menu. These features are covered in Chapter 9.

- The ▣ button (Ctrl+M) brings the Session window to the front, without resizing or tiling any windows.

- The ▣ button (Ctrl+D) brings the data window of the current worksheet to the front.

- The ▣ button (Ctrl+I) brings the Project Manager window to the front.

- The ▣ button will close all graph windows, after asking for confirmation.

1.8   Creating a Report

After analyzing data and creating graphs, Minitab makes it easy to create a report. If you use Microsoft Office Word or PowerPoint, Minitab can export graphs and analysis reports directly to those programs using the Project Manager shortcuts mentioned in the preceding section. Even without Microsoft Office or any other program, Minitab's ReportPad is a simple word processor for preparing reports.

Continuing the analysis of the OldFaithful.MTW worksheet featured in this chapter, follow these steps to build a report, using ReportPad.

First, click the 🔳 button in the Project Manager toolbar to see the ReportPad window. If the report is empty, it will only contain this default title:

Minitab Project Report

Edit the title to something descriptive, and add some brief introductory text, such as this:

Eruption Characteristics of the "Old Faithful" Geyser

This is an analysis of measurements of eruption duration (seconds), interval before eruption (minutes), and height (feet) of 50 eruptions of the "Old Faithful" geyser in Yellowstone National Park.

The title of the report is centered by default. To left-justify the text below the title, select Editor > Align Left from the Minitab menu.

Start the report with a histogram of the three variables, either as three histograms or as one histogram with three panels. After creating and adjusting the histogram to be satisfactory, open the Graphs folder of the Project Manager by clicking the 🔳 button. Then right-click the title of the histogram and select Append to Report. Swich back to ReportPad by clicking the 🔳 button, and the histogram is there.

Now add a table of descriptive statistics. Using Stat > Basic Statistics > Display Descriptive Statistics, create a table of selected statistics of the three columns in the worksheet. Open the Session folder of the Project Manager by clicking the 🔳 button. Right-click the Descriptive Statistics section title, and select Append to Report.

Next, add a scatterplot matrix showing relationships between the three variables. If not already part of the project, this can be created with the Graph > Matrix Plot tool. Right-click the graph and select Append Graph to Report. Notice that the report can be built either from the Project Manager window or directly from the graph windows.

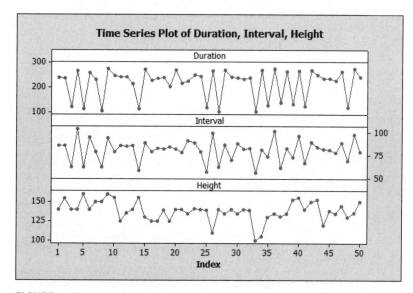

FIGURE 1-18 • Time series plot with three panels.

Next, add a table of Pearson correlation coefficients, prepared with the Stat > Basic Statistics > Correlation function. In the Session window, right-click the correlation table and select Append Section to Report.

A time series plot provides another interesting view of this data. Figure 1-18 shows a plot made with the Graph > Time Series Plot function. In the gallery, select a Simple time series plot. In the next dialog, select all three variables Duration-Height in the Series field. Click the Multiple Graphs button, and select In separate panels of the same graph. After clicking OK, the plot shown in Fig. 1-18 appears. Append this new graph to the report.

If printed, the report created so far would look something like Fig. 1-19. Using ReportPad, the report can be enhanced with additional graphs, analysis or blocks of text discussing the findings.

From ReportPad, Minitab offers options to share the report with the rest of the world, including these:

- Print the report directly with File > Print Report.
- Save the report in rich text file (.RTF) format, or as a web page (.HTM)
- Copy the report to the default word processor. In the Project Manager window, right-click ReportPad, and select Copy to Word Processor.

As always, save the Minitab project often. The Minitab project file includes all worksheets, graphs, history, ReportPad, and other objects together in one .MPJ file.

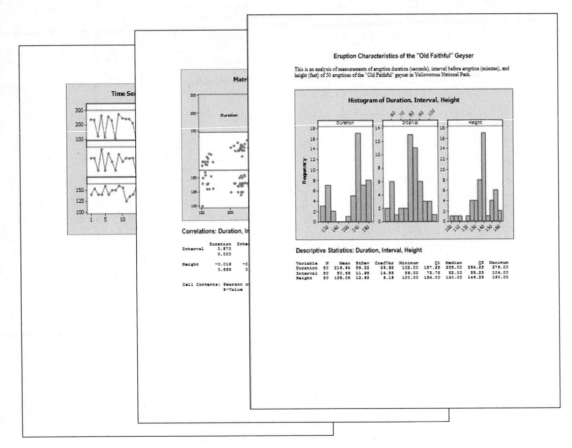

FIGURE 1-19 • Example report.

It is not necessary to save worksheets and graphs in separate files, if they are already included in a project file.

1.9   Find Out More

To learn more about any topic in this chapter, keep reading. The following chapters explore many popular types of Minitab functions in depth. The documentation that comes with Minitab software is also quite thorough and useful. Here are the major parts of the online documentation package:

- *Meet Minitab* is an introductory tutorial which guides the reader through a variety of simple Minitab tasks, using a single case study which evolves through several chapters. This guide can be downloaded in .PDF format for free from the Minitab Web site at www.minitab.com.

- *Minitab Help* provides instructions for every Minitab function, including a glossary, examples, methods, formulas, and references. Click the 💡 button or Help > Help to access the help files using the Windows help viewer. Or, from almost any Minitab dialog, click the Help button to jump directly to the relevant page in the help file. The Minitab assistant dialogs are supposed to be self-explanatory, so these dialogs have no help files.

- *Minitab StatGuide™* provides guidance about when, why, and how to apply the tools in Minitab, and how to interpret the results of Minitab analysis. This guide goes beyond how to use the software and explains some statistical concepts in concise language. In Minitab, click the 📖 button or Help > StatGuide to access the StatGuide using the Windows help viewer. The 📖 button is context-sensitive, and is only available when a graph or Session window report with an associated topic in the StatGuide is active. Clicking 📖 will open the StatGuide directly at the relevant page.

- *Methods and Formulas* is a separate help file containing all the methods and formulas used by Minitab functions. This can be accessed directly through the Help menu. Or, from the help page for any function, click the see also link at the top, and then click Methods and formulas.

In this chapter, we explored many Minitab features by analyzing an example dataset. We created graphs using both the new graphical analysis assistant and the traditional menus. The assistant provides a friendly interface for selecting the most appropriate Minitab graph, while the traditional menus offer more flexibility and options. The next chapter introduces many other types of Minitab graphs and illustrates the powerful features of the Minitab graphical engine. Chapter 3 provides an in-depth survey of the Minitab environment, including windows, toolbars, and customization features.

QUIZ

1. Which Minitab window holds analytical reports and tables generated by functions such as Display Descriptive Statistics?
   A. History window
   B. Session window
   C. Data window
   D. Project Manager window

2. Which Minitab menu provides access to interactive guides and flow charts for choosing the most appropriate Minitab tool for a specific situation?
   A. Editor menu
   B. Tools menu
   C. Help menu
   D. Assistant menu

3. What does the ⓘ button do?
   A. Displays general information about the Minitab project
   B. Displays information about columns in the current worksheet
   C. Displays information about the last analysis performed
   D. Displays information about graphs

4. The top of a Minitab window includes this: [Shaft.MTW ***] What does *** mean?
   A. It means that Shaft.MTW is the current worksheet in the project.
   B. Three stars means that the data in Shaft.MTW has been used in three different analyses.
   C. Three stars means that there are three missing data values in the Shaft.MTW worksheet.
   D. It is simply part of the file name.

5. A file created by Minitab with the .MPJ extension may contain what:
   A. Data
   B. A graph
   C. A report
   D. All of the above

6. Open the file Shaft.MTW in the Minitab sample data folder, and create a histogram of the data.

7. Using the data in the file Shaft.MTW, use Minitab to create a table with the count of nonmissing data, mean, median, standard deviation, skewness, and kurtosis of the data.

8. **Open the file** Poplar1.MTW **in the Minitab sample data folder. This file contains measurements of diameter, height, and weight for several poplar trees. Create a matrix plot containing scatterplots for all pairs of variables in this file.**

9. **In the file** Poplar1.MTW, **the diameter and weight of all the trees, except for one, fall along a curved line. Using brushing, identify which row in the worksheet contains measurements of the outlying tree.**

10. **Use Minitab to calculate the Pearson correlation of tree diameter and weight in the** Poplar1.MTW **worksheet.**

Analyzing and Comparing Variables with Graphs

Graphs are among the most powerful statistical tools. A good graph is the easiest and fastest way to reveal key features of a dataset, to detect significant changes, and to communicate complicated concepts with clarity. Chapter 1 used simple graphs like histograms and scatterplots to visualize simple datasets. This chapter introduces a wider variety of Minitab graphs for many more interesting and challenging situations.

CHAPTER OBJECTIVES

Here's what you'll learn in this chapter:

- How to create graphs of the distribution of one variable, specifically: stem-and-leaf displays, dotplots, individual value plots, boxplots, and interval plots

- How to use graphs to compare the distributions of several variables

- How to graph quantitative data or sample statistics by categories

- How to create and manipulate 3D scatterplots, contour plots, and surface plots

2.1   Graphing the Distribution of One Variable

This section introduces several types of graphs designed to display the distribution of one set of data. Besides the histogram seen in Chapter 1, these graphs include the graphical summary, stem-and-leaf display, dotplot, boxplot, interval plot, and individual value plot. Simple versions of most of these graphs may be selected from the graphical analysis assistant. All graph types have separate menu commands, most located in the Graph menu. The graphical summary may be selected either from the graphical analysis assistant or from the Stat > Basic Statistics menu. For all of these functions, the observed values of the variable need to be arranged in one column of a Minitab worksheet.

Open the Minitab sample worksheet file Pres.MTW. For 19 presidents of the United States, from Andrew Johnson through Lyndon Johnson, this file lists the number of years the president lived after his first inauguration, and also the life expectancy of a man of the same age as the president at the time of his first inauguration.

A graphical summary is a good first step to evaluate a new, unfamiliar dataset. Open the graphical analysis assistant by selecting Assistant > Graphical Analysis from the Minitab menu. Select the first option in the first column, Graphical Summary. Click in the Y column field to activate it. Here, type C2 or Actual, or simply double-click C2 Actual in the column listbox. Click OK. Figure 2-1 shows the resulting graphical summary for actual survival years for these 19 presidents.

An alternative to the graphical analysis assistant is to select Stat > Basic Statistics > Graphical Summary from the Minitab menu. As with most graphs, the individual menu command uses a slightly different dialog and offers more options, but the resulting graphical summary is the same by either route.

The Minitab Graphical Summary presents a standardized analysis with several parts:

- At the top left is a histogram of the data, with a blue line representing a normal (Gaussian) distribution model, fitted to the data. Chapter 4 discusses distribution models in more detail.

- Below the histogram is a boxplot of the data, using the same scale as the histogram. A boxplot shows the minimum, maximum, and quartiles of a dataset. Boxplots are explained later in this section.

- Below the boxplot is a drawing depicting two intervals. One interval is a 95% confidence interval for the mean, and the other interval is a 95%

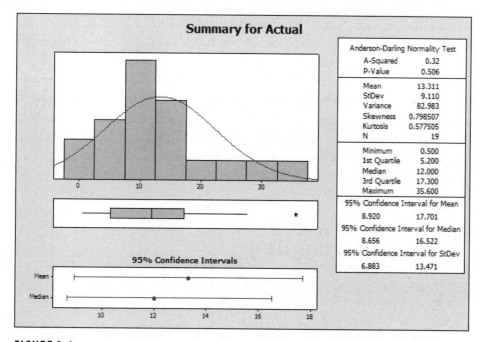

FIGURE 2-1 ·. Graphical summary.

confidence interval for the median. These intervals are ranges which contain the true values of the population mean and median with 95% probability, based on the data in this sample. Chapter 5 discusses confidence intervals in greater detail.

• At the right is a table listing the results of a normality test, various sample statistics, sample quartiles used to create the boxplot, and confidence intervals for the mean, median, and standard deviation.

Many statistical tools rely on the assumption of an underlying normal distribution, so a test of normality is often a good test to perform before applying other procedures. The histogram provides a visual estimate of how well a distribution model fits the data. For the Actual variable in the Pres.MTW dataset, the histogram does not look very normal. However, with only 19 values in this dataset, a normal distribution could possibly produce a histogram like this, by random variation. Is the normal distribution a reasonable model for this variable?

The Anderson-Darling test is a popular type of goodness-of-fit test, which is a tool used to evaluate the fit of a proposed distribution model. Goodness-of-fit tests consider both the distribution shape and the size of the dataset. The p-value provides an easy way to interpret the results of the test. If the data truly comes from a normal distribution, the *p*-value is the probability that a sample of this size would look at least as nonnormal as this sample. If the *p*-value is small (usually less than 0.05), we can confidently reject the normal distribution model.

In this example, the *p*-value is 0.506, meaning that a random sample of size 19 from a normal distribution would look at least as nonnormal as this data about half the time. Because the *p*-value is greater than 0.05, we cannot reject the normal distribution based on this sample of 19 values. Chapter 4 explains goodness-of-fit tests and distribution models in more detail.

? Still Struggling

Many people are confused by confidence intervals. Since this graphical summary presents three confidence intervals, for mean, median, and standard deviation, now is a good time to discuss them.

A sample of data generally represents some larger population. In the example of Pres.MTW, the life expectancy of 19 presidents represents the population of life expectancy of all presidents, past, present, and future. If the sample is a fair, random sample of the population, then confidence intervals provide a way to infer conclusions about the population with a known degree of confidence. In this example, the 95% confidence interval for the mean life expectancy is between 8.920 and 17.701 years. The probability that mean life expectancy of all presidents is between 8.920 and 17.701 years after their first inauguration is 95%, or 0.95. Mean life expectancy could be less than 8.920 years with probability 0.025, or greater than 17.701 years with probability 0.025.

Confidence intervals do not provide information about the distribution of individual values. It would be incorrect to say that 95% of presidents survive between 8.920 and 17.701 years after taking office. A quick look at the histogram shows that this statement cannot be true.

Confidence intervals all involve assumptions which may or may not be true, including the randomness of the sample, and the normality of the population distribution. If the assumptions are not valid, then the confidence intervals may not be reliable. Chapter 5 discusses these issues in more detail.

Minitab produces two broad categories of graphs. The first category includes packaged analytical graphs, such as the graphical summary, which provide a lot of information in a small space. With few options and a consistent format, these graphs are popular tools for reports and presentations. When managers and readers become comfortable with a consistent format, like the Minitab graphical summary, they can quickly find the information they require to make decisions. Most Minitab graphs fall into the second category of single-purpose graphs with many options for customization. These individual graphs provide endless choices for an analyst to explore and view data from different angles, cross-sections, and perspectives.

The stem-and-leaf display, arguably, is not a graph at all, but a type of histogram made of numbers. To create a stem-and-leaf display of the presidential survival years, select Graph > Stem-and-Leaf from the Minitab menu. In the Graph Variables field, select Actual from the Pres.MTW worksheet. Click OK. The following appears in the Session window, not as a separate graph window.

Stem-and-Leaf Display: Actual

```
Stem-and-leaf of Actual N = 19
Leaf Unit = 1.0

  4    0   0224
  7    0   599
 (4)   1   0022
  8    1   5667
  4    2   13
  2    2   7
  1    3
  1    3   5
```

This display has three columns, representing counts, stems, and leaves, from left to right. The leaves, in this example, are the ones digits of the data values. The stems are the tens digits. Combining the stems and leaves, the first row represents the values 0, 2, 2, and 4, and the last row represents the value 35. In this example, the increment between rows is five years. Since each digit in the leaf column represents one value in the dataset, the shape of the leaf column forms a histogram. The stem-and-leaf display is a unique statistical tool in that at least two significant digits are preserved in the visual display of the data. In this example, tenths of years are lost to rounding.

In the counts column, the row containing the median of the data has a count of values in that row enclosed by parentheses, (4) in this example. Counts above the median row are cumulative counts of values from the minimum value to that row. Counts below the median row are cumulative counts of values from that row to the maximum value.

By default, Minitab chooses an increment between rows based on the range and size of the dataset, but this can be changed in the Stem-and-Leaf dialog. Increments may be 1, 2, or 5 times any power of 10. With an increment of 10, the stem-and-leaf plot changes to this:

```
 7   0   0224599
(8)   1   00225667
 4   2   137
 1   3   5
```

Because the next four types of graphs are typically long and skinny, they are frequently used to compare distributions of many variables side-by-side. Before using them for comparisons, let's see how they work for one variable.

Select Graph > Dotplot from the Minitab menu. The Dotplots gallery shown in Fig. 2-2 appears offering many optional versions of dotplots. Many of these dotplot versions are used to compare variables in different columns, to compare subsets of one column according to values in another column, or to do both at once. For now, select a Simple dotplot of One Y, and click OK. In the next dialog, select the variable to plot in the Graph Variables field, and click OK.

Figure 2-3 shows a dotplot of the Actual variable from Pres.MTW. This figure is shortened to save space. In this graph, one dot represents one observation in the dataset. Minitab will attempt to create every dotplot with one observation

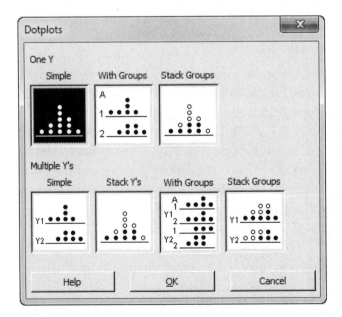

FIGURE 2-2 · Dotplots gallery.

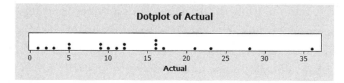

FIGURE 2-3 • Dotplot.

per dot, but if the dataset is too large to do this, a note appears on the graph saying, for example, Each symbol represents up to 20 observations. The dotplot may be brushed only if each symbol represents one observation. For more on selecting subsets of the data by brushing, see Section 1.6.

To make a dotplot, Minitab sorts the data into a number of bins, one bin for each column of dots in the plot. Because of this procedure, a dotplot is actually a kind of histogram with stacks of dots instead of bars. In a dotplot, each stack of dots represents close but not necessarily identical numerical values.

Figure 2-4 illustrates an individual value plot, a boxplot, and an interval plot, all made from the same Actual variable in Pres.MTW. Each of these three plots

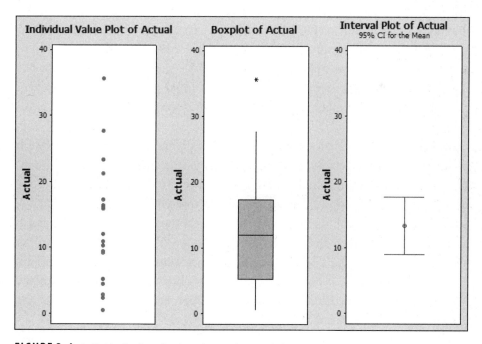

FIGURE 2-4 • Individual value plot, boxplot, and interval plot, combined with the Minitab Layout tool.

can be made using functions in the Minitab Graph menu, in much the same manner as the earlier dotplot. The graphical analysis assistant also includes short-cuts to make simple versions of the individual value plot and the boxplot.

The individual value plot is one of the simplest plots, with one dot represent-ing each individual value. Unlike the dotplot, values are not sorted into bins, and each symbol on the individual value plot always represents one value. If the dataset includes repeated values, the dots are offset side by side, so the viewer always sees one symbol for each value.

Often for large datasets, the individual value plot provides too much informa-tion. A boxplot is a more concise display of a dataset, by summarizing the data in five statistics: minimum, first quartile, median, third quartile, and maximum. These five numbers divide the dataset into four quartiles with equal numbers of values. In the standard boxplot, the box extends from the first quartile to the third quartile, with a line drawn to represent the median. The length of the box from top to bottom represents the interquartile range, a popular measure of variation. Lines extend out the ends of the box to the minimum and maximum values. If any values lie more than 1.5 times the interquartile range outside the box, Minitab represents these potential outliers with ＊ symbols. The ＊ symbols represent individual values that are unusually far from the middle part of the distribution. These may represent data collection errors, changes in the process that produced the data, or just values that are extreme for no particular reason.

Of these three plots, the least information is conveyed by the interval plot, which by default shows only the mean and a 95% confidence interval for the mean. Based upon the sample data and an assumed normal distribution, you can be 95% confident that the population mean is somewhere within the inter-val as shown on the plot.

To make the interval plot seen here, the Y scale has been adjusted to match the other two plots. To adjust the Y scale or any other part of a Minitab graph, first click on the graph to make it active. Be sure the cursor is in select mode by clicking the ▧ button in the Graph Editing toolbar, or by selecting Editor > Select from the Minitab menu, when a graph is active. Then click in the graph to select an element of the graph like the Y scale. The Graph Editing toolbar also has a dropdown box containing a list of all objects in the active graph. This dropdown box can be used to select any object in the graph. With the object selected, click the ▧ button in the Graph Editing toolbar, or use the Ctrl+T (for ediT) keyboard shortcut.

To prepare Fig. 2-4, three graphs were combined into one graph using the Minitab Layout tool, which is available in the Editor menu any time a graph is active. The Layout tool creates a new Minitab graph from an array of other, previously created Minitab graphs. This tool is often used to create customized, combination graphs for reports or presentations. The new Layout graph contains copies of the original graphs. Objects in any part of a Layout graph may be edited without changing the original graphs.

2.2   Comparing Distributions of Multiple Variables

Now that we have seen a variety of graphs for viewing distributions, this section shows how they may be used to compare distributions of multiple variables.

First though, let's consider how variables are organized in Minitab. People familiar with spreadsheet software such as Microsoft Office Excel may expect to store variables in rows, columns, or rectangular tables, perhaps assigning different formats to each cell in a worksheet. Although the Minitab data window looks like an Excel worksheet, Minitab does not provide the degree of flexibility found in modern spreadsheet software.

In Minitab, each column may be formatted as a whole to contain numbers, text, or date/time values; to display values in a variety of formats in the data window; or to hold values calculated from other columns by a formula. Individual cells or values within a column may not have individual formats or formulas different from the column as a whole. Each column has a total length, which is the sum of counts of missing and nonmissing values. In the data window, a column is always displayed with its first value on row 1, with missing values represented by *. Users familiar with Excel spreadsheets may find this restrictive, but Minitab worksheets provide more than enough flexibility for statistical analysis. Further, the consistent structure of Minitab worksheets makes it easier to navigate through large or unfamiliar Minitab projects.

In Minitab, we have two ways to arrange multiple variables in a worksheet—in the same column (stacked) or in different columns (unstacked). Variables of different data types, different units of measure, or representing different physical quantities must be unstacked, in different columns. However, variables representing the same physical quantity measured in different conditions, on different objects, or at different times, may be either stacked or unstacked.

- Stacked is the more traditional format used to test variables for differences between groups. Many Minitab testing tools require data to be in stacked format. The groups to be tested are identified by values in other columns in the worksheet.

- Unstacked format may be used for any situation, with the different variables identified by column names or column descriptions. To add descriptive comments to any column, right-click anywhere in the column, then select Column > Description from the popup menu.

In Minitab, data may be converted between stacked and unstacked format using the Stack and Unstack Columns tools in the Minitab Edit menu.

For an example of unstacked data, open the Minitab example data file Maple.MTW. Samaras are winged fruit created by maple and some other trees. Leif, an arboriculturist, is studying the dynamics of maple samaras in a laboratory environment. For several samaras from three maple trees, Leif measured the fall velocity and also the calculated disk loading, a function of the samara size and weight. This worksheet lists the loading and velocity in six columns, two for each tree studied. One samara from tree 2 was damaged during testing, resulting in a missing value in two columns.

To see how velocity varies between trees, Leif creates an individual value plot. He selects Assistant > Graphical Analysis from the Minitab menu and chooses an Individual Value Plot. In the Individual Value Plot dialog, shown in Fig. 2-5, the first field is a dropdown box labeled How are your data arranged in the worksheet?

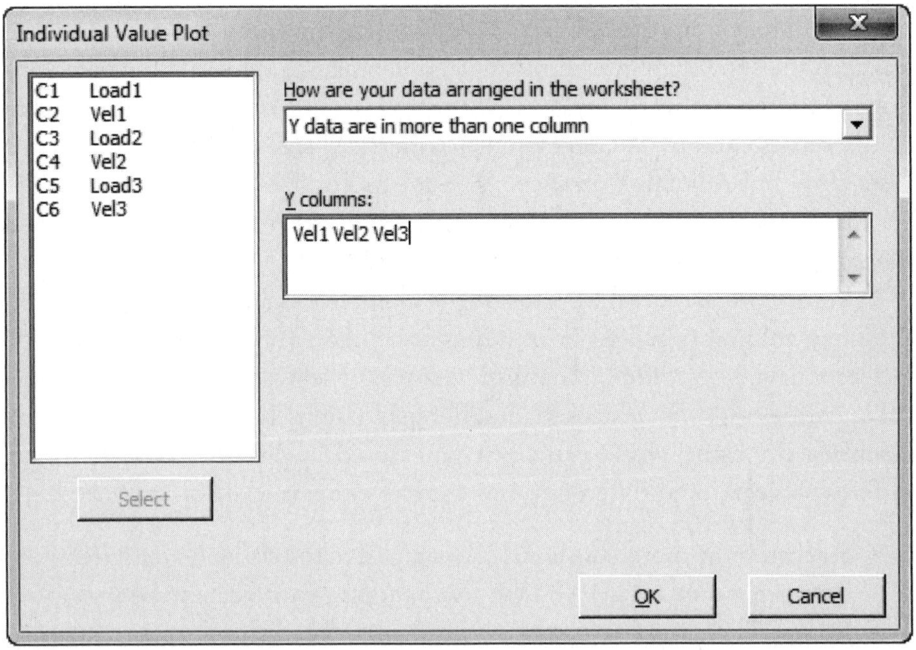

FIGURE 2-5 · Individual value plot assistant dialog.

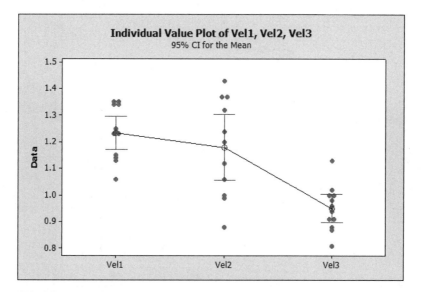

FIGURE 2-6 · Individual value plot of samara velocity by tree.

Using the dropdown box, Leif selects Y data are in more than one column. Then, in the Y columns field, Leif double-clicks columns Vel1, Vel2, and Vel3 in the column listbox. After Leif clicks OK, the plot seen in Fig. 2-6 appears.

When Minitab creates an individual value plot from the graphical analysis assistant, the graph combines individual data symbols with intervals representing 95% confidence intervals for the group means. Also, the means of the groups are connected by a line.

Notice that the confidence interval for tree 3 does not overlap the confidence intervals for trees 1 and 2. This provides strong evidence that samaras from tree 3 have less mean velocity than from the other two trees. The confidence intervals for mean velocity of trees 1 and 2 overlap, so there is no evidence that trees 1 and 2 have different mean velocities. Leif can safely conclude that tree 3 is different from the other two, but so far, he has no evidence of a difference between trees 1 and 2.

Hypothesis tests, covered in Chapter 6, provide a more powerful way of reaching this conclusion, but it is faster and easier to look for non-overlapping confidence intervals on an interval plot. If the confidence intervals for the means do not overlap, this provides strong evidence that the population means are truly different.

Now try to create the same plot by another route. First, stack the velocity data into a single column. From the Minitab menu, select Data > Stack > Columns. Fill out the dialog as shown in Fig. 2-7. After you click OK, notice the worksheet

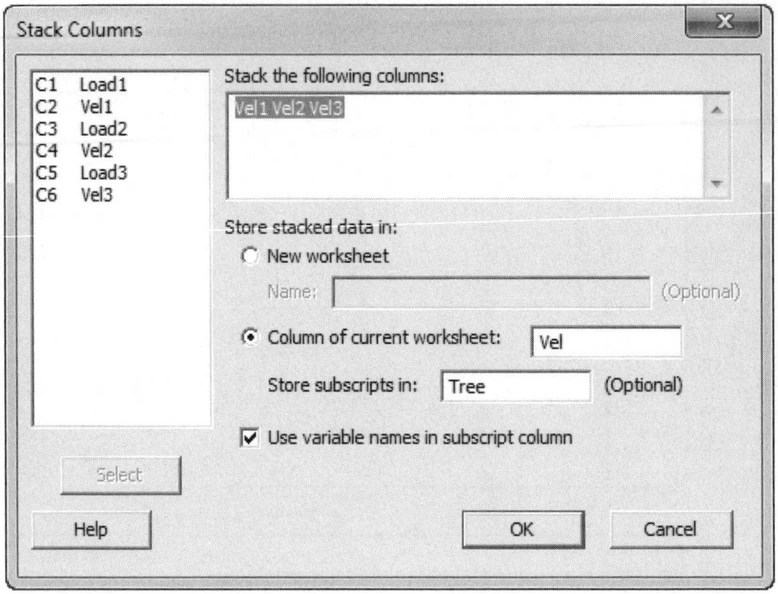

FIGURE 2-7 · Stacking columns of data.

now has two new columns, named Vel and Tree. At the top of the Tree column, notice the header is C8-T, with the T denoting text format for this column.

Click the ⓘ button in the Project Manager toolbar to see information about the current worksheet. The Project Manager window should look like Fig. 2-8. Notice that the new columns Vel and Tree are the combined length of Vel1, Vel2, and Vel3. Also, the missing value from Vel2 is represented by a missing value in Vel.

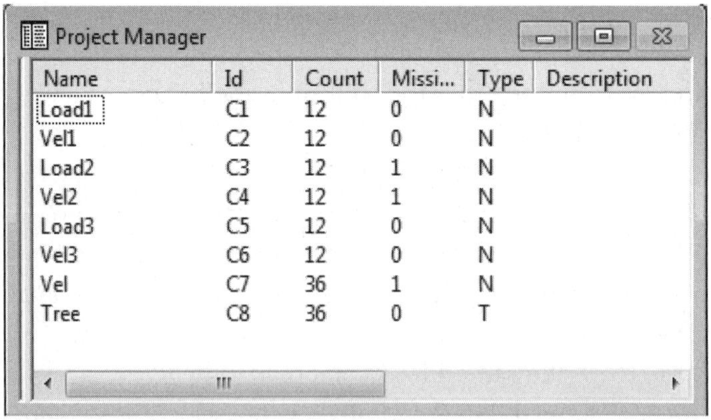

FIGURE 2-8 · Project Manager after stacking data.

Here's how to create the same plot seen in Fig. 2-6 from the Minitab Graph menu:

- Select Graph > Individual Value Plot from the Minitab menu.
- In the gallery, select One Y, With Groups, and click OK.
- In the next dialog, in the Graph variables field, enter Vel. In the Categorical variables for grouping field, enter Tree.
- Click the Data View button. In the Data View dialog, select Interval bar, Individual symbols, Mean symbol, and Mean connect line. Click OK, and click OK in the main dialog. The resulting plot should look like Fig. 2-6.

Starting from an Interval Plot in the Minitab Graph menu, the same plot can also be created by adding individual symbols in the Data View dialog for Interval Plots.

Data from experiments are frequently recorded in stacked format. For an example, open the Minitab sample data file FishWeights.MTW. This worksheet lists the weights of several fish which were raised in different water temperatures, but otherwise similar conditions. Does temperature significantly change the weights of these fish?

Starting from the graphical analysis assistant, choose a Boxplot. The Y column is Weight, and the Categorical X variable is Temp. Figure 2-9 shows the resulting boxplot. For each of four temperatures in the dataset, this graph shows the

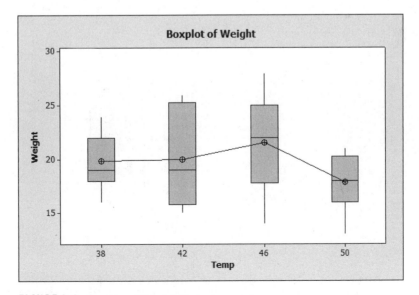

FIGURE 2-9 · Boxplots of fish weights by temperature.

five-number summary of the distribution of fish weights. In addition to the standard boxplot, the graphical analysis assistant adds symbols at the mean of each group, plus a line connecting the means. For this dataset, there is no apparent trend or relationship between temperature and weights.

Many analysts like to add mean symbols to their boxplots, so the graph shows both mean and median. Comparing the mean and median tells us something about skewness in the dataset. Skewed distributions typically have one long tail, with a few observations much farther from the median than in the other tail. These extreme values tend to pull the mean in the direction of the long tail, without affecting the median. When the mean is above the median, the distribution is said to be "skewed to the right," and when the mean is below the median, it is said to be "skewed to the left."

When creating a boxplot from the Graph menu, mean symbols, mean connect lines, and other optional features can be selected by clicking the Data View button and using the Boxplot – Data View dialog.

Open the Minitab sample data file Cap.MTW. In this dataset, provided to Minitab from Proctor & Gamble, the Torque column lists the measured torque required to remove caps from bottles of hair conditioner. A second variable, Machine, lists the ID number of the capping machine. Using the graphical analysis assistant, create both a boxplot and an individual value plot of Torque by Machine. Your plots should look like Figs. 2-10 and 2-11.

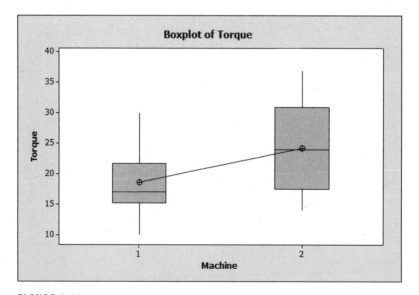

FIGURE 2-10 · Boxplot of cap torque by machine.

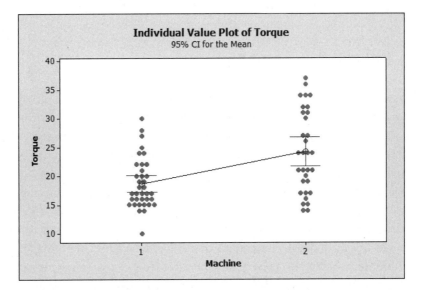

FIGURE 2-11 · Individual value plot of torque by machine.

Looking at the individual value plot for torque from machine 1, notice how many values are clustered together just below the mean, while values above the mean are more spread out. This is typical of a distribution that is skewed to the right.

In Fig. 2-10, the boxplot for machine 1 shows three signs of skewness to the right. First, the mean symbol is above the median. Second, the upper half of the box is longer than the lower half, indicating that the third quartile is longer than the second quartile. Third, the upper line representing the fourth quartile is longer than the lower line representing the first quartile. The boxplot for machine 2 shows only one of these signs, that the fourth quartile is longer than the first. Seeing these signs of skewness in a boxplot helps to understand potentially important features of a process distribution.

Since the graphical analysis assistant adds confidence intervals for the means, mean symbols, and a mean connect line to the individual value plot, Fig. 2-11 allows us to look for a significant difference between group means. The confidence intervals do not overlap in this example, providing strong evidence that machine 2 has higher mean torque than machine 1.

The significant difference between means may be confirmed by more sophisticated tools like the two-sample t-test, covered in Chapter 6. However, these simple graphs make this conclusion visually apparent, and they also reveal the skewness of machine 1. Understanding the causes of the mean shift and the skewness will help the manufacturer reduce variation and produce a more consistent product.

? Still Struggling

With so many graph types to choose from, you might wonder which one is best. Since every graph shows some information while concealing other information, no graph can ever provide a full and complete presentation of the data. The examples in this chapter showed some of the strengths and weaknesses of various Minitab graph types.

For an analyst facing an unfamiliar dataset, a smart strategy is to create all possible graphs, to look for whatever messages may be hidden within the data. Once the most important message is understood, the simplest graph that reveals that message most directly is often the best choice for a report or presentation.

Presenters should also consider the comfort level of their audience. If the audience is most familiar with one style of graph, such as a graphical summary or a histogram, choosing that style will usually be best. Choosing a graph which requires lengthy explanation will distract from conveying the message.

2.3   Graphs of Quantitative Y Versus Categorical X Variables

The previous section showed how to graph the distribution of a Y variable over several groups. In all these cases, the X variable was categorical, representing the groups of Y data. Instead, if we wanted to plot single numbers or summary statistics for the Y values versus a categorical X variable, other types of graphs are more often used. In Minitab, these graphs include the bar chart, pie chart, time series plot, and area graph. All of these may be created using the Minitab Graph menu, and the first three types are also available through the graphical analysis assistant.

These types of graphs are similar to graphs available in Microsoft Excel. However, Minitab offers advantages that Excel does not. One advantage of Minitab graphs is the ability to visually summarize the data by plotting counts of unique values or functions of the data rather than the data values themselves. Also, when preparing a statistical report, keeping all graphs in Minitab format gives the report a consistent look and feel.

To create examples of these graphs, open the Minitab example data file ComputerSoftware.MTW. This dataset lists the sales volume and count of on-site visits over 26 weeks for a software company. In the data window, Week in column C1 is the categorical X variable with values from 1 to 26. The sales data are sums of individual sales orders, and the on-site visits are counts of visits for

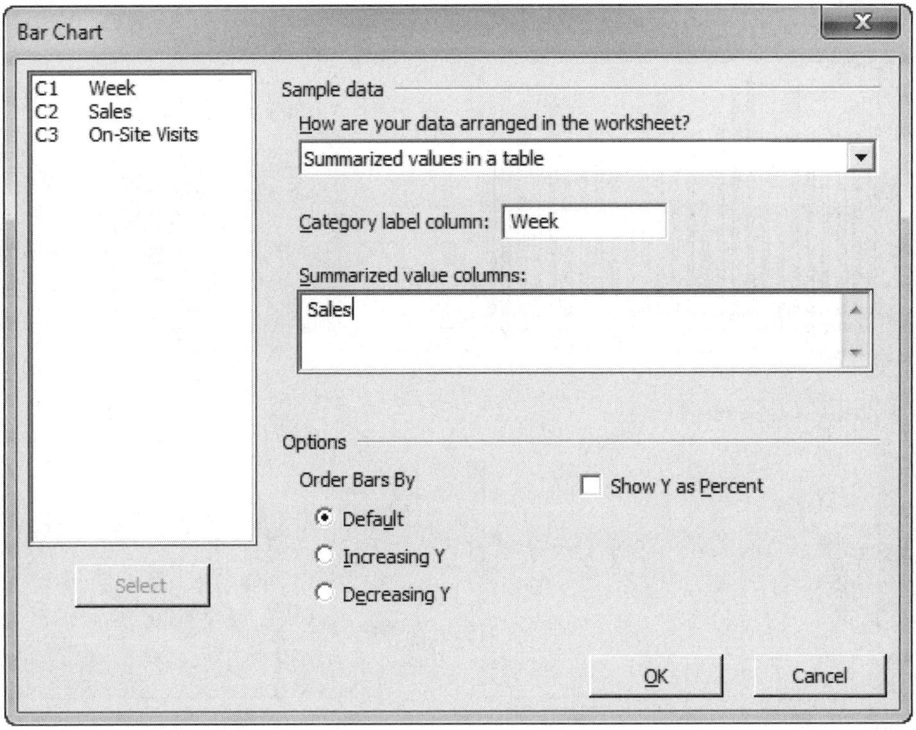

FIGURE 2-12 · Bar Chart assistant dialog.

each week. The **Sales** and **On-Site Visits** columns have already been summarized from another database.

Select Assistant > Graphical Analysis from the Minitab menu. Select Bar Chart from the assistant. The Bar Chart dialog, seen in Fig. 2-12, asks: How are your data arranged in the worksheet? Select Summarized values in a table. The column of category labels is Week, and the summarized values are in Sales. After clicking OK, a bar chart of Sales by Week appears.

Figure 2-13 shows the bar chart in the upper left corner of the figure. For comparison, Fig. 2-13 also shows a pie chart, a time series plot, and an area chart of the same data. These charts can all be created using their respective functions in the Graph menu.

But which graph is best? The answer depends on the data itself, and on the objectives of the analyst. Here are some of the benefits of each type of graph:

- The **bar chart** emphasizes the size of the values more than the trend from time to time. Since the Y scale goes to zero, the shading in each bar is directly proportional to the value represented by each bar.

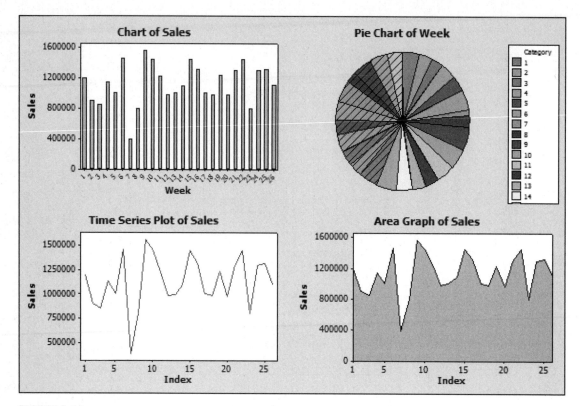

FIGURE 2-13 · Bar chart, pie chart, time series plot, and area graph.

- The **time series plot** emphasizes the trend from time to time while deemphasizing the size of the values. The Y scale is based on the range of values, and may not include zero. Notice how the bad sales in week 7 appear to represent a more significant drop in the time series plot than in the bar chart.

- The **area graph** combines the shading of the bar chart with the trend line of the time series plot. This is a balanced presentation of both the trends and the values represented. Like the bar chart, the Y scale goes to zero, so the amount of shading is directly proportional to the values.

- The **pie chart** is popular with businesspeople, but generally unpopular with statistical analysts. The pie chart only shows the relative proportion contained in each category, without providing any clue about how much the total pie represents. It is also difficult or impossible for the viewer to infer any quantitative conclusions from a pie chart. The fact that week 7 had low sales is barely noticeable on this chart.

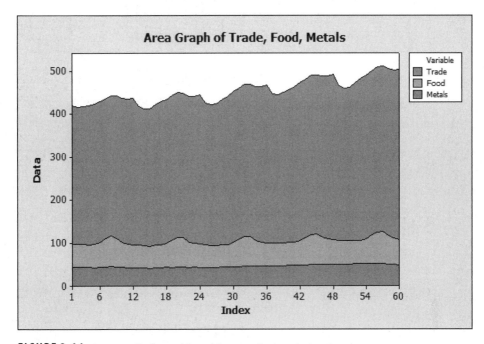

FIGURE 2-14 • Area graph of monthly employment in three industries.

For another example of summarized data, open Employ.MTW from the Minitab sample data folder. This file lists the number of employees in Wisconsin in three industries, measured every month for five years. Select Area Graph from the Minitab Graph menu, and make an area graph of the three variables: Trade, Food, and Metals. Figure 2-14 shows the completed area graph.

Notice how easily seasonal employment patterns in food and trade industries can be seen in the wavy patterns of Fig. 2-14. However, it is important to realize that an area graph of multiple variables stacks the areas in the graph. Whenever a graph involves shaded data areas, the amount of shading must be proportional to the values represented to provide a fair display of the data. Therefore, area graphs should always be stacked like this one. But for this dataset, stacking causes confusion. The wavy seasonal patterns in the Trade variable, plotted at the top, are the sum of the seasonal patterns in all the variables. If it is important to see the seasonal patterns of each industry separately, this area graph is an inappropriate choice for this dataset.

Instead, Fig. 2-15 is a time series plot of the same data. This graph is easy to create using either the graphical analysis assistant or the Time Series Plot command in the Graph menu. Since this graph represents data with lines and dots,

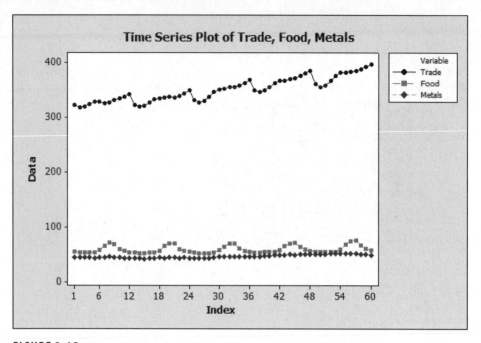

FIGURE 2-15 · Time series plot of monthly employment in three industries.

not shading, the three variables are plotted separately and independently on the same scale. On this graph, the seasonal patterns can be fairly compared between the three variables.

One convenient feature of Minitab is the ability to graph and compare statistical functions of variables. Earlier in this chapter, Fig. 2-6 compared individual measurements of samara velocity from three maple trees. Looking at this graph, it seems that tree 2 has more variation between samaras than the other trees. A different way to illustrate this observation is to graph the standard deviation of velocity for the three trees.

Open the Maple.MTW worksheet file from the Minitab sample data folder, and select Graph > Bar Chart from the Minitab menu. In the Bar Charts gallery seen in Fig. 2-16, use the Bars Represent: dropdown box to select A function of a variable. Then, select a Simple plot of Multiple Y's, and click OK.

In the next dialog, not shown here, the Function dropdown box lists the available functions for this plot. Select StDev to plot the standard deviation. Then select the velocity variables Vel1, Vel2, and Vel3, and click OK. The finished graph is shown in Fig. 2-17. This graph highlights that the sample standard deviation of velocity of samaras from tree 2 is almost double that of samaras from the other two trees.

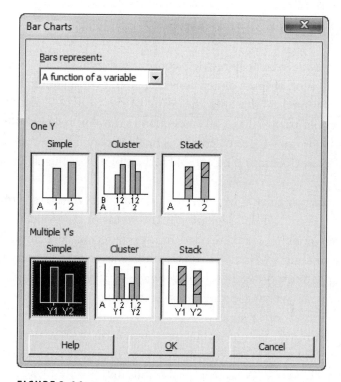

FIGURE 2-16 · Creating a bar chart of functions of variables.

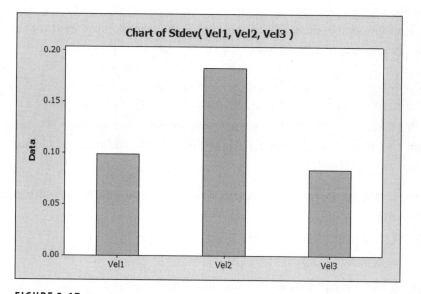

FIGURE 2-17 · Bar chart comparing standard deviations of three variables.

2.4   Graphing in Three Dimensions

Although today's technology restricts computer displays to a two-dimensional surface, the illusion of three dimensions is created by projecting the features of a three-dimensional model onto the plane of the display. These "3D" graphs make it possible to visualize and understand complex relationships between variables which other types of graphs cannot display. This section introduces the 3D scatterplot, contour plot, and 3D surface plot, all available in the Minitab Graph menu.

Many datasets involve a large number of variables measured from a set of things. These empirical datasets are not the result of controlled experiments, where some variables are controlled in a predetermined manner and other dependent variables are observed. Here, all the variables are observed in hopes of detecting patterns or relationships between variables. To successfully detect these patterns, an analyst typically must create many graphs, both 2D and 3D, on different subsets of variables.

For an example of this type of dataset, open Furnace.MTW from the Minitab sample data folder. This file lists a variety of measurements on the heating systems of 90 homes in Wisconsin. For details on the variables in this dataset, open the Minitab help system by clicking on the ? button or Help > Help in the Minitab menus. Then click the Search tab, and search for Furnace.MTW. Many of the sample data files have explanatory entries in the Minitab help system.

A good way to explore this dataset is to make scatterplots of pairs of the variables, or a matrix plot of several of the variables. Both of these graphs were introduced in Section 1.5. A 3D scatterplot is used to display relationships between three quantitative variables. Using grouping to display additional categorical variables by distinctive symbols can add even more variables to the plot.

With Furnace.MTW as the current worksheet, select Graph > 3D Scatterplot from the Minitab menu. Select a plot With Groups and click OK. In the next dialog, select variables as follows:

- For Z Variable, select BTU.Out, the average energy consumption with damper out.
- For Y Variable, select Age, the age of the house.
- For X Variable, select CH.Area, the area of the chimney.
- In the Categorical variables for grouping box, select House, the type of house.

After clicking OK, the graph shown in Fig. 2-18 appears. This 3D scatterplot actually represents four variables, one on each axis, and a fourth grouping variable. Up to three categorical grouping variables can be specified to represent up to six variables in a single plot.

When looking at a cloud of dots from one viewpoint, it is not possible to see whether individual dots are near to or far from the viewer. To visualize this third dimension, the plot must be rotated. Whenever a 3D graph is active, Minitab shows the 3D Graph Tools toolbar, which Fig. 2-18 shows floating over the graph. Clicking and dragging this toolbar to the top of the Minitab window will cause it to dock with the other toolbars.

The first six buttons in the 3D Graph Tools toolbar are used to rotate the graph back and forth around the X, Y, and Z axes of the graph. When the cursor hovers over any of these buttons, as in Fig. 2-18, a diagram of the three axes appears in the lower left corner of the graph, with an arrow illustrating the direction of rotation for that button.

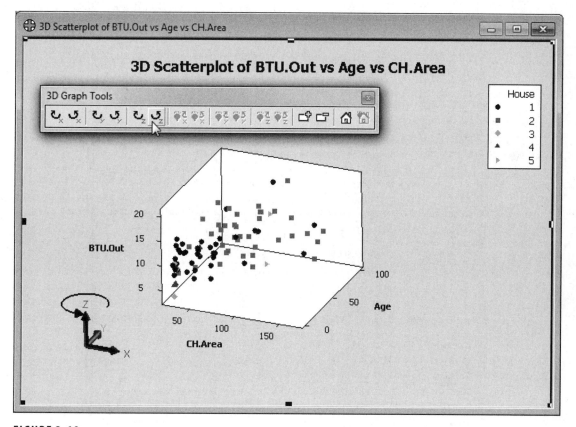

FIGURE 2-18 · 3D scatterplot with the 3D graph tools toolbar.

Try rotating this graph in different directions, looking for interesting patterns or clusters of dots in the data. For example, rotating this graph can show that almost all the houses older than 30 years are of type 2, two-story houses. This correlation between house type and age will make later analysis more difficult. If regression analysis shows that age is related to some effect of interest, this effect could also be explained by house type. Minitab tools for regression analysis and issues with correlated variables are discussed in Chapter 8.

To explore the usefulness of contour plots and surface plots, it is helpful to create our own Minitab dataset where Z is a mathematical function of X and Y. In this dataset, X and Y should vary over a rectangular grid of values. Here are the steps to build this example dataset:

- Open a new worksheet with File > New. Select Minitab worksheet and click OK.
- Select Calc > Make Mesh Data. Fill out the dialog as shown in Fig. 2-19 and click OK. This will create in the first two columns, labeled X and Y, all combinations of the series of 101 equally spaced numbers from –6.3 to +6.3.
- Verify, using the ⓘ button, that the worksheet has two columns, X and Y, both of length 10,201.

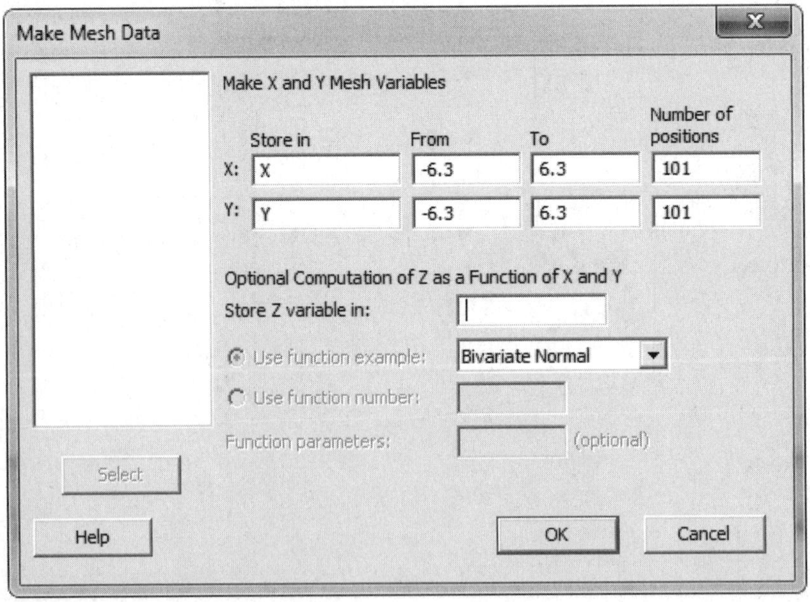

FIGURE 2-19 • Making mesh data.

- Assign the name Z to an empty column, like C3. To do this in the data window, click on the empty name space between C3 and the first data row, type Z, and enter.

- Right-click on the Z column. In the popup menu, select Formulas > Assign Formula To Column.

- In the calculator dialog that appears, enter the formula sin(X)*cos(Y)*exp(–sqrt(X^2+Y^2)/2) and click OK. This creates the functional relationship $Z = \sin X \times \cos Y \times e^{-\sqrt{X^2+Y^2}/2}$ between the columns of the worksheet, and Minitab will automatically perform these calculations, updating them if the X or Y columns change. In the data window, note that $\boxed{\text{C3} \ \blacksquare}$ appears at the top of the Z column. The $\blacksquare$ denotes that this column has a formula assigned to it.

Now, create a 3D surface plot with Graph > 3D Surface Plot in the Minitab menu. The gallery offers two styles of plots, a Surface plot and a Wireframe plot. Select the Surface plot and click OK. Enter the three variables Z, Y, and X into the spaces provided and click OK to create the graph. Figure 2-20 shows the surface plot along with the 3D Graph Tools toolbar.

As created, this surface plot shows the wavy nature of this function, although some of the features are hidden or not well-lighted. As with the 3D scatterplot, the 3D Graph Tools toolbar offers six buttons to rotate the 3D surface plot in various directions. In addition to this feature, the rendering of surface plots involves lighting and reflections of light sources off the surface. By default, surface plots have two lights, one above and one below the surface. Up to three lights may be used, and these may be varied in location, intensity, and color.

In the 3D Graph Tools toolbar, the second set of six buttons is used to rotate the set of light sources around the X, Y, or Z axes. While any of these buttons are clicked, the lights may be seen as orbs rotating around the surface plot. To edit the lighting in other ways, double-click on the surface of the plot. In the Edit Surface dialog, click on the Lights tab. Here, the number, location, color, and intensity of the lights may be entered directly into the dialog.

Wireframe is an alternate style for the 3D surface plot, in which lines are drawn through a regular mesh of points and hidden surfaces are concealed. A surface plot may be changed to wireframe style by double-clicking on the surface, clicking the Attributes tab, and selecting the Wireframe option. In this example, with a 101 x 101 mesh of X and Y values, Minitab will draw 101 lines in each direction. This creates a rather busy plot, where the lines blend

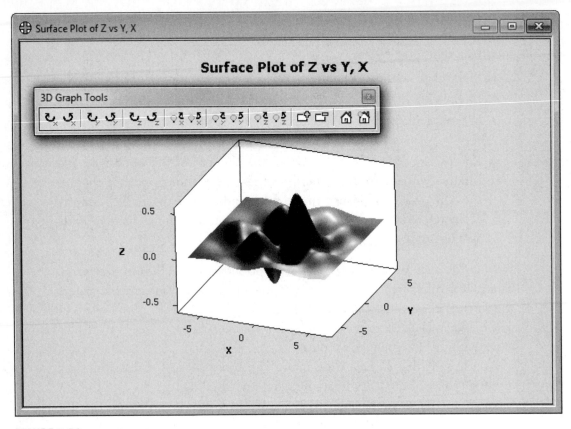

FIGURE 2-20 · 3D surface plot.

together. To reduce the number of mesh lines, double-click on the surface, and click on the Method tab. In the frame labeled Mesh for Interpolating Surface, select Custom, and enter the desired number of lines in the X-Mesh Number and Y-Mesh Number boxes. Figure 2-21 is a wireframe surface plot of this example with 51 mesh lines.

A contour plot is actually a 2D plot used to visualize 3D surfaces using shades of color. Contour plots may be created in much the same way as surface plots, from the Graph menu. Figure 2-22 is a contour plot of the same example where shades of color represent values of the Z variable. The number of levels in a contour plot may be changed, up to 11 levels, by double-clicking on the contour plot, and then selecting the Levels tab.

In this example, we created a regular mesh of X and Y values and specified Z for every value, using a functional relationship. The Calc > Make Mesh Data tool also provides several interesting built-in functions for 3D plots.

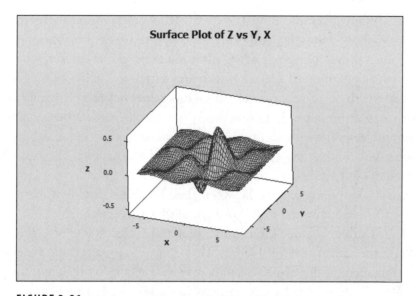

FIGURE 2-21 · Wireframe surface plot with 51 X and Y mesh lines.

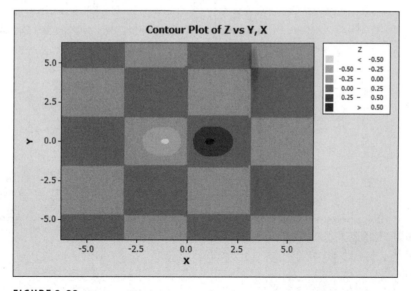

FIGURE 2-22 · Contour plot.

A regular mesh of X and Y values in the worksheet is not required for 3D surface plots and contour plots. In creating the plots, Minitab will create a regular mesh of values and, if necessary, interpolate between the points available in the dataset to estimate the Z value at mesh points. Up to 101 mesh lines in each direction can be specified by the user in the Edit Surface or Edit Contour dialogs.

The Minitab example data file Cereal.MTW contains measurements of calories, carbohydrates, fat, and protein for twelve types of breakfast cereals. Figure 2-23 shows four types of 3D plots made from this dataset, where the Z axis is Calories, plotted against Protein and Carbo.

Clearly, with only twelve cereals, this dataset does not form a regular grid of Protein and Carbo values. In fact, as the 3D scatterplot shows, there is only one cereal with low Protein and low Carbo. Predictably, this cereal also has low Calories, but it is the only one in this corner of the dataset. The rest of the products fill out the "plateau" in the other corner. Even with very little data, Minitab is able to interpolate between the available values and extrapolate outside the range of values to create a graph that looks reasonable.

It is debatable whether the contour plot and surface plots of Figure 2-23 represent the data in a reasonable way. They appear to predict the Y variable for all combinations of the two X variables over the rectangular region of the plot, even if there are no nearby observations to support such a prediction. These predictions may be precise in areas where there are observed values and wildly

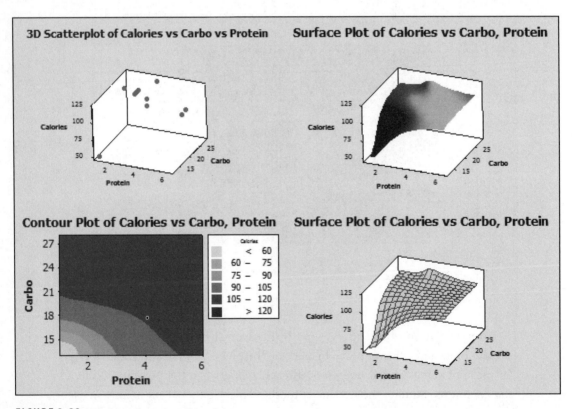

FIGURE 2-23 · 3D plots of cereal nutritional data.

incorrect where they represent extrapolations. The presence or lack of precision in the prediction is not represented on these plots. Whenever a contour or surface plot is created from an empirical dataset without a regular grid of X values, it may be useful in visualizing patterns or trends in the dataset, but it is unwise to use such a graph for predicting values outside the range of experience.

2.5   Other Graphs in Minitab

This chapter introduced some important types of graphs, but Minitab can produce many, many others. A few important graphs are briefly mentioned here. Other graphs used for specialized analysis will be introduced later in this book.

Main Effects Plot

The main effects plot uses symbols to represent the mean of a response (Y) variable over each level of a categorical explanatory (X) variable. The means are connected by a line to help visualize the trend. Figure 2-24 is a main effects plot made from the data in the Minitab sample data file Carpet.MTW. In this

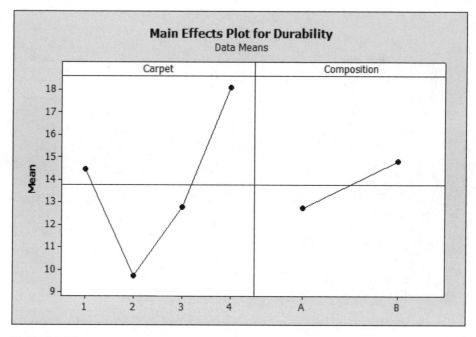

FIGURE 2-24 · Main effects plot.

dataset, carpet durability has been measured for four types of carpet and two compositions. The main effects plot shows the mean durability for each type of carpet and for each composition.

Main effects plots have long been used to analyze the results of a designed experiment. After an experiment has been defined in the Minitab Stat > DOE menu, main effects plots may be produced for that experiment. But now in Minitab 16, main effects plots may be created directly through the graphical analysis assistant, without setting up an experiment first. This is a great convenience for analyzing datasets with categorical X variables, whether they come from a designed experiment or not.

Interaction Plot

Like the main effects plot, the interaction plot is a graph from the design of experiments (DOE) toolbox, which Minitab 16 now makes available in the graphical analysis assistant. The interaction plot shows the mean value of a Y variable over all combinations of two categorical X variables. Figure 2-25 is an interaction plot made from the Carpet.MTW dataset. Each line on the plot represents a different level of the second X variable.

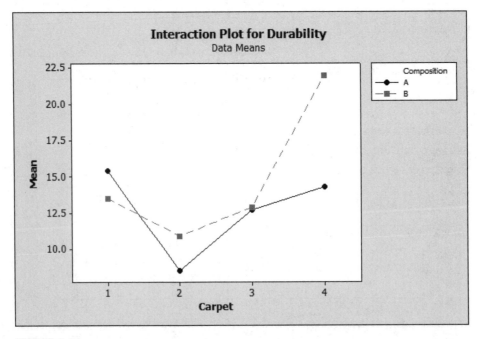

FIGURE 2-25 · Interaction plot.

Interaction plots can show effects from combinations of variables which do not appear on the main effects plot. Figure 2-25 shows that composition B improves the durability of carpet type 4 much more than any of the other carpet types. This is an interaction between composition and carpet type that only appears when all combinations of the two variables are plotted.

Multi-Vari Chart

The multi-vari chart has long been a popular problem-solving tool for identifying the biggest source of variation in a set of data. Minitab offers the multi-vari chart in the Stat > Quality Tools menu, and now also in the graphical analysis assistant. The multi-vari chart shows the mean value of a Y variable over all combinations of up to four categorical X variables. On a multi-vari chart, the X variables are nested within each other. One line shows how the first X variable affects the mean of Y. Then, for each level of the first X variable, a separate line shows how the second X variable affects the mean of Y. This is different from the interaction plot, and it makes more sense in certain situations.

Figure 2-26 shows a multi-vari chart made from Carpet.MTW. The outer X variable is carpet, so one line shows the overall effect of carpet type on durability, as on the main effects plot. Then, for each of the four carpet

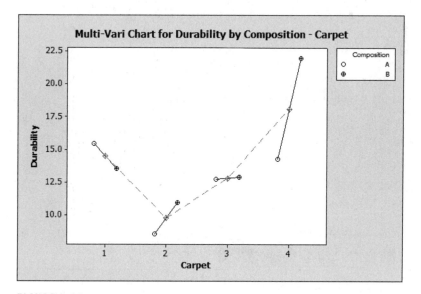

FIGURE 2-26 · Multi-vari chart.

types, a separate line shows how composition affects durability. Although this multi-vari chart contains the same information as the interaction plot, this nested format may be better for visualizing how variation happens in this system.

To make a multi-vari chart, Minitab requires Y values for at least 40% of all combinations of the X variables. Ideally, a multi-vari chart should have a completely balanced dataset, where all combinations of X variables have the same number of observations. Any departure from this perfect balance creates the possibility of misinterpretation. Multi-vari charts on unbalanced datasets need to be interpreted with some caution.

Marginal Plot

The marginal plot is a powerful way to visualize both the marginal and joint distributions of two variables on a single plot. Among major statistical programs, Minitab is the only one to offer this type of graph. Figure 2-27 is a marginal plot made from two variables in the OldFaithful.MTW sample dataset. This graph combines a scatterplot with histograms of each variable. Marginal plots can also be made with box plots or dotplots on the sides of the scatterplot. To make a marginal plot, select Graph > Marginal Plot from the Minitab menu.

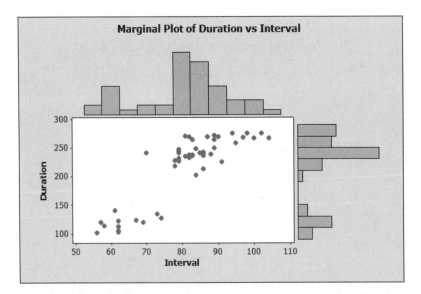

FIGURE 2-27 · Marginal plot.

Probability Plot

A probability plot is used to test whether a set of data fits a particular family of distribution models. On a probability plot, dots following a straight diagonal line indicate a good fit. For more information on this plot, see Chapter 4.

Empirical CDF Plot

The cumulative distribution function (CDF) is a function of x representing the cumulative probability of observing smaller values than x. The CDF is a monotone nondecreasing function representing the distribution of a variable. The empirical CDF is the same concept applied to a set of data, resulting in a stairstep function. Like a probability plot, an empirical CDF plot can be used to test whether a distribution model fits a set of data. If the stairstep empirical CDF follows the smooth curve of the distribution model, then the model is a good fit. For more information on this plot, see Chapter 4.

Control Charts

Control charts are a family of time series plots with limit lines called control limits. Control charts are commonly used in quality control applications to test an ongoing process for changes in the behavior of the process. In the Minitab graphical analysis assistant, the middle section under the label Graph variables over time includes five varieties of control charts. Minitab also offers a control charts assistant to help in selecting and creating a variety of popular control charts for statistical process control (SPC) applications. Many more types of control charts can be found in the Stat > Control Charts menu. For more information and examples of control charts, see Chapter 11.

2.6   Find Out More

Most good books on statistical tools emphasize graphs. Any book on analysis without graphs should be avoided. But what is a good graph? When does a good graph turn bad? The seminal book in this field is *The Visual Display of Quantitative Information*, by Tufte (2001), now in its second edition. All of Tufte's books are entertaining, enlightening, and informative.

This chapter introduced a wide range of Minitab graphs, using both the graphical analysis assistant and the traditional Minitab menus, including the many options for customizing and combining these graphs. The wide variety of these graphical tools is valuable in describing and understanding the huge variety of real datasets. The next chapter provides a detailed tour through the many facets of the Minitab interface. The following chapters delve into specific types of problems that Minitab can solve quickly and efficiently. Almost all of these solutions involve both graphs and a text report. As a general rule, always look at a good graph before the text report. Graphs convey knowledge and understanding more efficiently than any table of numbers.

QUIZ

1. In Minitab, which type of graph represents the distribution of a variable using one dot for every value placed along a numerical scale?
    A. Stem-and-leaf display
    B. Individual value plot
    C. Boxplot
    D. Interval plot

2. The simple version of which plot represents the distribution of a variable using a five-number summary? Bonus: What are the five numbers?
    A. Dotplot
    B. Histogram
    C. Stem-and-leaf display
    D. Boxplot

3. Using Minitab, what is the fastest way to create a one-page report about one variable in a dataset, where the report includes a histogram, a boxplot, a confidence interval for the mean, and a selection of descriptive statistics?
    A. Create a histogram, boxplot, interval plot, and descriptive statistics summary, then combine this information using ReportPad.
    B. Create a histogram, boxplot, interval plot, and descriptive statistics summary, then copy and paste these items into a word processor for formatting onto one page.
    C. Create a graphical summary from the Minitab Graph menu.
    D. Create a graphical summary from the Minitab Stat > Basic Statistics menu.

4. The same exam is given to four sections of an introductory statistics class. After grading the exams, the instructor wants to create one graph to look for significant differences between sections in the mean exam grades. Which would be the best choice of graph?
    A. An interval plot
    B. A boxplot
    C. A histogram
    D. A scatterplot

5. Which type of graph uses shades of color to represent values of a Z variable over a rectangular grid of X and Y variables?
    A. Surface plot
    B. Wireframe plot
    C. Contour plot
    D. 3D scatterplot

6. The Minitab sample dataset Cholest.MTW contains cholesterol measurements on 28 heart attack victims, measured two days, four days, and 14 days after the attack. For comparison, the Control variable in this dataset lists the cholesterol

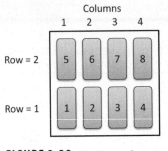

FIGURE 2-28 · Positions of meat loaves in the oven.

measurements of 30 people who have not had a heart attack. Create a single graph which shows all individual cholesterol measurements for these four variables, and also allows comparisons of the mean cholesterol between groups.

7. Using the graph created for question 6, is there a significant difference between the mean cholesterol in the control group and heart attack victims two days after the attack? How can you determine from the graph whether the difference is statistically significant?

8. Create a graph that can be used to compares the variation of the four variables in the Minitab sample dataset Cholest.MTW.

9. The Minitab sample dataset Meatloaf.MTW lists the measured drip loss for 24 loaves, cooked in eight oven positions, over three cooking batches. Create a single graph which shows how drip losses vary both between batches and between oven positions. If you create a 3D graph, rotate the graph until you feel the graph shows the data best.

10. In the Meatloaf.MTW dataset, suppose you know that the eight oven positions are configured in two rows and four columns as shown in Fig. 2-28.

   A. Using one of the methods in this chapter, add two columns to the worksheet named Row and Column, containing the row and column numbers.

   B. Create a suitable plot showing the average drip losses by row and column in the oven.

chapter 3

Exploring the Minitab Environment

The first two chapters presented a wide variety of graphs and analytical tools provided by Minitab. This chapter provides more details about how Minitab inputs, stores, and outputs data, and about what happens behind the Minitab user interface. Since so many Minitab users also use Microsoft Excel for data storage and to communicate with non-Minitab users, this chapter provides some details of compatibility and the interface between Excel and Minitab. Later sections cover the Minitab menus, toolbars, and customization features.

CHAPTER OBJECTIVES

Here's what you'll learn in this chapter:

- How to enter data so that Minitab assigns the correct data type
- How to transfer data between Minitab, Excel, and other programs
- How to examine the Minitab session commands behind the menu commands
- How to use columns and constants in calculations and display the results
- Which types of files can be opened and saved by Minitab
- Where to find Minitab commands in the many menus and toolbars
- How to rearrange commands on toolbars and create custom Minitab toolbars
- How to store options and customization settings in profiles

3.1   Data Types in Minitab

In Minitab, variables are represented by columns within a worksheet. Columns have one of three data types: numeric, date/time, or text. A column must be of the correct type before it can be used for analysis or graphs.

By now, you have seen the column listbox, a large field which appears in the left half of most Minitab dialogs. The column listbox lists only the columns or variables in the current worksheet which are eligible to be selected, based on the active field and the data types of the columns.

Figure 3-1 shows an example Minitab worksheet created by Tom to keep track of his grades in his Introductory Statistics class. Minitab automatically assigns data types to each column based on the first value entered into that column. When Tom types "HW1" into the first cell of column C1, Minitab does not recognize this as a valid numeric or date/time value, so C1 becomes a text column. At the top of the column, C1-T denotes that C1 is a text column.

For the date column, Tom types "8/31/11" into the first cell. Minitab interprets this as a date and assigns date/time data type to column C2, denoting this by C2-D at the top of the column.

It is important to note that conventional date formats vary around the world. Minitab refers to the Regional and Language Options of the Windows Control

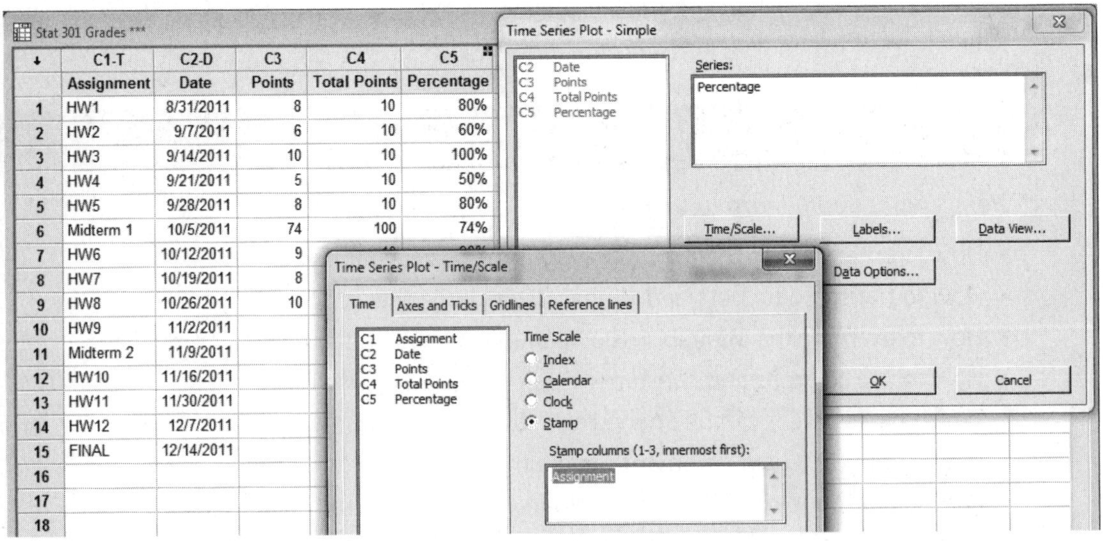

FIGURE 3-1 · How the column listbox reacts to data types.

Panel to interpret and display dates correctly. Depending on your part of the world, August 31, 2011 could be represented by 8/31/11, 31/8/11 or 11/8/31. Entering "8/31/11" into Minitab on a computer configured for the United Kingdom, where d/m/yy format is standard, will result in text data type being assigned to that column, rather than date/time data type.

Also, instead of the slash (/) separating the components of a date, Minitab will recognize the hyphen (-) or period (.) to separate parts of the date, as long as the same separator is used in both places.

In the example shown in Fig. 3-1, Tom has decided to create a time series plot to display his grades as a percentage. Column C3 lists Tom's grade, C4 lists the total points, and C5 calculates the percentage using a formula C5 = C3/C4, displayed in percentage format. As a reminder that C5 is calculated from a formula, Minitab displays the ▓ symbol at the top of the column. Since C3, C4, and C5 have no suffix after the column ID like text or date/time columns, this denotes that these columns all have numeric data type.

To create a time series plot, Tom selects Graph > Time Series Plot from the Minitab menu. At the top right of Fig. 3-1 is the dialog for this graph. In the Series field, Tom selects C5 Percentage from the column listbox. Notice that the column listbox only lists date/time and numeric columns, since a time series plot of text data is not possible.

Next, Tom clicks the Time/Scale button to define labels for the X axis of the graph. On the Time tab, he selects the Stamp, and then clicks his mouse in the Stamp Columns field. As soon as this field is active, all columns of the worksheet appear in the column listbox, since a column of any data type may be used as a label. Figure 3-2 shows the finished graph. Notice that the labels on the Y scale have the same percentage formatting as the column being graphed.

It is important to understand the difference between the internal representation of a number and the display formatting for that number. Internally, Minitab stores numeric values in a floating point representation containing a sign, a mantissa, and an exponent. Minitab can display these numeric values in many different ways, but changing the display formatting does not change the values as stored internally.

In the example shown in Fig. 3-1, the calculated value in column C5, row 1, is stored as 0.8, or the closest possible binary representation of 0.8. When Tom set up this column, he right-clicked on the column and selected Format Column > Numeric. Figure 3-3 shows the numeric format dialog, where Tom selected Percentage format with 0 decimal places.

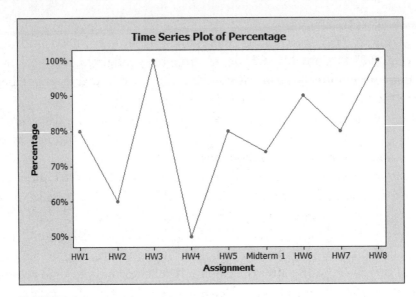

FIGURE 3-2 · Tom's grades.

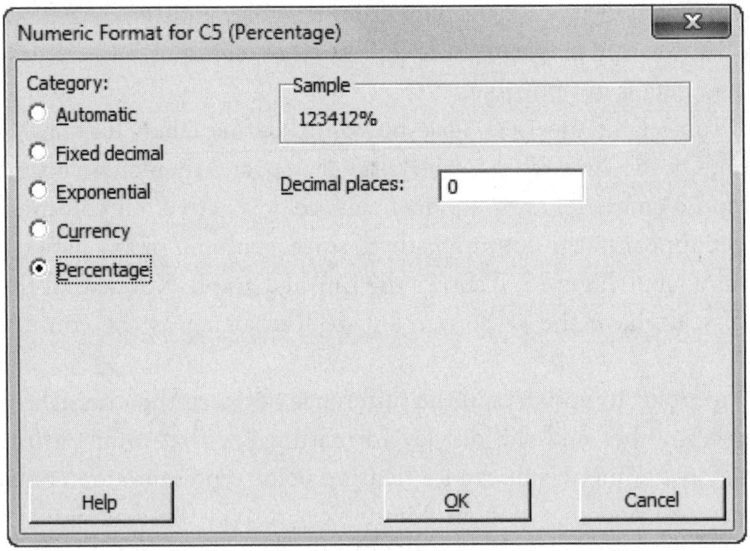

FIGURE 3-3 · Numeric format dialog box.

If, instead, Tom had selected Exponential format with 2 decimal places, the value 0.8 would be displayed as 8.00E-01, where E represents a power of 10. In this notation, 8.00E-01 represents $8.00 \times 10^{-1} = 0.8$. In Minitab, and in this book, "E" is shorthand for "times 10 to the power of." Note that Microsoft Excel refers to this display format as "scientific," and the term "scientific notation" is a common phrase to describe this notation.

Like numeric values, date/time values in Minitab are also stored as numbers, representing the number of days since December 30, 1899 at 0:00:00 AM. To see the equivalent numeric value for a date, first type a date like "August 31, 2011" into the first row of an empty column. Minitab detects this as a date and assigns the date/time data type to this column.

To see or change the display format, right-click on the column and select Format Column > Date/Time from the popup menu. Minitab has assigned the "mmmm d, yyyy" format to this column, causing the date to be displayed exactly as entered. This dialog also shows a wide variety of other date/time formats. Click the Help button for an explanation of these formats. However, this dialog cannot be used to change the data type of a column.

To convert a date/time column to numeric and see the number used to represent a particular date or time, select Data > Change Date Type > Date/Time to Numeric from the Minitab menu. Fill out the dialog to convert the date column to numeric in another column. After doing this, the date August 31, 2011 is converted into the numeric value 40,796, representing the number of days between December 30, 1899 and August 31, 2011.

After Minitab has assigned a data type to a column, the only way to change data type is to use one of the commands in the Data > Change Data Type menu. The reformatted data can be written into a new column to preserve the old data format, or into the same column to overwrite it.

The display format of any column may be changed at any time using the Format Column menu which appears in the column popup menu, or in the Minitab Editor menu whenever any part of the data window is active. Changing the display format has no impact on the internal representation of any values.

The key to avoiding incorrect data types in Minitab is to pay attention to the first value entered in each empty column. Minitab uses that first value to assign data type and display formatting. Additional values in that column which do not comply with that data type will be replaced with *, the missing data symbol.

3.2   Working with Excel and Minitab

Microsoft Office Excel is undoubtedly the world's most popular software for organizing and storing numerical data. Like most other statistical and spreadsheet programs, Minitab can read and write worksheets directly in Microsoft Excel formats. While not everyone has access to Minitab, virtually everyone with a computer can edit or at least view an Excel spreadsheet in .XLS format, and more recently in .XLSX and .XML formats.

Importing data from Excel into Minitab is the most common task involving these two programs. Here are three ways to do this:

- **Windows clipboard.** With both Excel and Minitab open, select the data in Excel and copy to the clipboard with Ctrl+C or by clicking the ⧉ button. Then switch to Minitab and open a new worksheet. If the first row of the copied data includes headers naming each column, then click in the name row below C1 and above row 1. If the copied data does not include headers, then click in row 1 of an empty column. Paste the data to Minitab with Ctrl+V or by clicking the ⧉ button. The same procedure also works to copy data from Minitab and paste it into Excel.

- **Open the file in Excel format.** In Excel, save the file with .XLS, .XLSX, or .XML file extensions. In Minitab, select File > Open Worksheet from the Minitab menu. In the Files of type: dropdown box, select Excel (*.xls; *.xlsx) or Spreadsheet XML (*.xml), as appropriate. Locate the Excel file, and click Open. Minitab will open the Excel file, storing the data in a new Minitab worksheet. Minitab can also save worksheets in Excel format.

- **ODBC.** Open DataBase Connectivity (ODBC) is a computing standard which allows access to data in any database management system (DBMS), on any platform or operating system, as long as that DBMS has an ODBC driver. Minitab can access any available DBMS through the File > Query Database (ODBC) menu command. To use ODBC to query an Excel file, click on the Machine Data Sources tab, and then double-click Excel Files. From there, you can select the file to query, select a table within the file, and specify which columns and rows to import. If you want to import all the data from an Excel file into Minitab, it is easier to simply open that file as a Minitab worksheet. However, if you only need to import a subset of a large database in an Excel file, ODBC can be very convenient and a great timesaver. The same procedure works to query other types of ODBC-compliant databases directly from Minitab.

Data imported into Minitab by any of the above methods is a static copy. Any changes made in the Excel data source after the import will not be reflected in the Minitab copy. There is one way to create a dynamic link from Minitab to a data source in an Excel file, which is by using Dynamic Data Exchange (DDE). To do this, select the data in Excel and Copy to the clipboard. Then, in Minitab, use Edit > Paste Link. Now, any change in the Excel data source will be instantly reflected in the linked data in Minitab, as long as the file containing the source data is open in the source application. Data can also be dynamically linked from Minitab back to Excel, or from Minitab to another place in Minitab.

If you use DDE linked data in Minitab, the Edit > Worksheet Links > Manage Links dialog will be useful. Here, you can add, change, or deactivate DDE links for the current worksheet.

Although Excel and Minitab are generally compatible, not every dataset can be freely exchanged between these programs without losing information. Here are some of the features of an Excel worksheet which do not transfer to Minitab:

- **Formulas**. In Excel, each cell may have a formula which calculates its value from other cells. Also, in Minitab, columns may have a formula which calculates values from other columns. But these formulas do not transfer between Excel and Minitab, in either direction. Only the calculated values in each cell can be transferred between Excel and Minitab.

- **Multiple data types in a column**. In Excel, each cell may be completely different in data type and format from every other cell. But since Minitab organizes variables into columns, each column must have the same data type, which may be text, date/time, or numeric. When an Excel column is pasted into a Minitab column, Minitab uses the contents of the first cell to assign a data type to the entire column. If any of the remaining values are not compatible with this data type, Minitab replaces those values with *, the missing data symbol.

- **Special values**. Excel worksheets have many special values, including #NULL!, #DIV/0!, #VALUE!, #REF!, #NUM!, #N/A, and #NAME? to indicate various types of errors. However, Minitab only has one special value, *, representing a missing value in a numeric or date/time column. All special values, text, or blank cells in an Excel column will be replaced by * in a numeric or date/time Minitab column.

- **Most cell formatting**. Minitab does not support cell borders, fill colors, different fonts, font colors, and all the many kinds of pretty formatting introduced in recent versions of Excel. Therefore, this information does not transfer from Excel into Minitab.

On the other hand, many kinds of numeric and date formatting do transfer successfully between Excel and Minitab. For an example of this, see "Excel

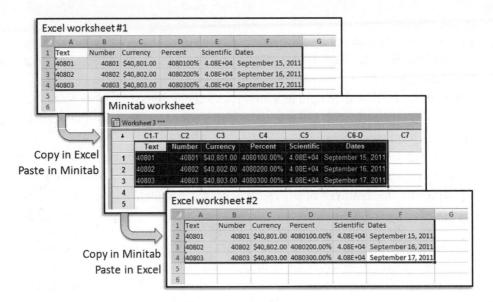

FIGURE 3-4 · Display formatting copies between Excel and Minitab.

worksheet #1" in Fig. 3-4. Each column has the same values, except that column A is text and the other columns are numeric, with various types of display formatting. Columns B through F have general, currency, percentage, scientific, and date formats, respectively.

Suppose you select the highlighted range in Excel, including the labels in the first row, and copy to the clipboard with Ctrl+C or by clicking the ⧉ button. Then switch to Minitab, click in the name cell at the top of C1, and paste with Ctrl+V or by clicking the ⧉ button. Minitab will put the first row of the range in the name cells, and then correctly sense both the data type and display format of each column. The only difference is two digits displayed after the decimal in the percentage format. Copying the same data from Minitab and pasting into Excel worksheet #2 results in an almost identical copy of the original Excel data.

Very large datasets may be too large to be completely compatible. Table 3-1 lists limitations on the size of worksheets in Excel and Minitab. All of these limits are subject to the availability of resources on the computer.

Excel and Minitab both use the same internal representation for numerical data, which has a maximum absolute value of ± 1.7976931348623158 E+308 and a minimum absolute value of ± 2.2251 E-308, with at least 15 digits of precision. However, Minitab imposes an artificial limit on values entered into

? Still Struggling

Before transferring a large dataset from Excel, Access, or any other database into Minitab, it is smart to wonder whether all the values, data types, and formats will transfer correctly. Here are some suggestions to prevent unexpected problems:

- Carefully examine the data types of all values in the first row. If text headers are to be copied, the first row of values may be the second row of the table. Minitab uses the first row to assign data types to all columns. Any missing, blank, or special values in this row may cause an inappropriate data type to be assigned.
- Numbers stored as text values, like Column A in Fig. 3-4, will become text values in Minitab. If any numerical analysis of this column is required in Minitab, the data type must be changed to numeric.
- Long identification or account numbers, stored as numbers, may not appear correctly in Minitab. These numbers may be rounded or even replaced by *, the missing data symbol, if they do not fit within the constraints of the Minitab numeric data type.
- In the source data application, copy a section of the data with the largest, smallest, or most unusual values into the clipboard, and then paste the data into Minitab. Inspect each column for correct data type and appropriate numeric format before copying the entire database.

the worksheet, which can be no larger than ± 1.001 E18. In Minitab, any value larger than this is replaced by *, the missing value symbol. If your data involves counts of atoms in the universe or Zimbabwean currency, this restriction may be important to remember.

TABLE 3-1 Size Limitations in Excel and Minitab				
Limitation	Excel 5.0/95	Excel 97-2003	Excel 2007-2010	Minitab 16
Maximum number of rows	16,384	65,535	1,048,576	10,000,000
Maximum number of columns	255	255	16,384	4,000
Maximum characters in a cell	255	32,767	32,767	80 for text data type

3.3   Minitab Session Commands

Every action in Minitab, whether creating a graph, calculating statistics, or analyzing data, is specified by a set of commands in the session command language. The windows, menus, and dialogs most people use to control Minitab are simply a convenience that writes session commands based on the user's choices. Any Minitab task may be performed either through the usual menus or by entering session commands directly into the Session window.

Normally, session commands are hidden from the user. To see the session commands for any menu command, and to enter session commands directly, first activate the Session window by clicking the [image] button in the Project Manager toolbar, by using the Ctrl-M keyboard shortcut, or by selecting Window > Session from the Minitab menu. Next, select Editor > Enable Commands from the Minitab menu. If the Editor menu is empty or does not have Enable Commands, then click in the Session window first to activate it.

Now, in the Session window you will see this prompt:

```
MTB >
```

The Session window will now show all the session commands for any Minitab commands performed. To see how this works, enter some numbers into column C1 of a worksheet, using the data window, and then make a histogram with Graph > Histogram. Now, the Session window will show these commands:

```
MTB > Histogram C1;
SUBC>   Bar.
```

Histogram of C1

The first line, Histogram C1; tells Minitab to make a histogram of column C1, but the semicolon (;) says wait, there is a subcommand on the next line.

The second line, Bar., tells Minitab to make the histogram as a bar chart, and the period (.) ends the command. Finally, **Histogram of C1** is the confirmation that the histogram was made. Any new graph produces a line like this in the Session window.

To learn more about the Histogram session command, type the following in the Session window:

```
MTB > ? Histogram
```

The ? command opens a help window for session commands, which displays a different set of help files than are normally displayed with the 🛈 button. The Histogram session command has a dizzying array of subcommands and options, all listed with hyperlinks to their own help pages.

Histograms of the same data can look very different as the number and width of the bins change. Minitab chooses bin width and count automatically, but to override the automatic choice, use the Midpoint subcommand:

```
MTB > Histogram C1;
SUBC > Midpoint 1:19/2.
```

This command will create a histogram where the middle of the bins are at 1, 3, 5, up to 19. In Minitab, 1:19/2 is shorthand for "count from 1 to 19 in steps of 2." By default, histograms are made with bars, so the Bar subcommand is not required.

The Cutpoint subcommand is another way to specify the bins by listing the numbers on the boundaries between bins. For example, Cutpoint 0:20/2 specifies the same set of bins as Midpoint 1:19/2.

Now, try these session commands to see what happens:

```
MTB > New
MTB > Set C1
DATA> 51(0:5/.1)
DATA> end
MTB > Name C1 "X"
MTB > Set C2
DATA> (0:5/.1)51
DATA> end
MTB > Name C2 "Y"
MTB > Formula C3 = sin(X)*cos(Y)
MTB > Name C3 "Z"
MTB > Surfaceplot Z*Y*X
```

These commands will complete the following actions:

- Open a new worksheet.
- Enter into C1 numbers from 0 to 5, counting by 0.1, with the whole sequence repeated 51 times. This is equivalent to the Calc > Make Patterned Data > Simple Set of Numbers menu command.
- Enter into C2 numbers from 0 to 5, counting by 0.1, with each number repeated 51 times.

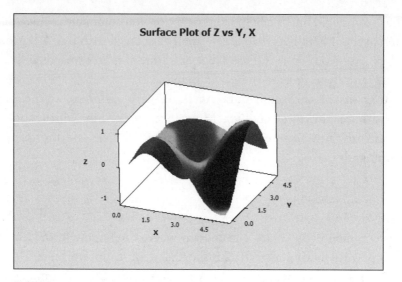

FIGURE 3-5 • Surface plot of Sin(X)Cos(X).

- Name C1 "X", C2 "Y", and C3 "Z".
- Enter a formula into C3 representing Z = sin(X)cos(Y).
- Create a 3D surface plot, as shown in Fig. 3-5.

Note that the shorthand notation a(b:c/d)e means "starting with b, count up to c in steps of d. Then, repeat each number in the sequence e times, and repeat the whole sequence a times."

Minitab session commands provide more commands and options than are available through the menus and dialogs, including some historical curiosities from the olden days before graphical user interfaces. For example, try this:

```
MTB > Gstd
* NOTE * Standard Graphics are now enabled, and Professional
          Graphics are
        * disabled. Use the GPRO command when you want to re-enable
        * Professional Graphics.

MTB > Histogram C3
```

Histogram

```
Histogram of Z    N = 2601
Number of observations represented by each * = 15
```

```
Midpoint          Count
    -1.0            100   *******
    -0.8            187   *************
    -0.6            211   **************
    -0.4            246   ****************
    -0.2            341   **********************
     0.0            555   ************************************
     0.2            307   *********************
     0.4            210   **************
     0.6            180   ************
     0.8            168   ************
     1.0             96   *******

MTB > Gpro
```

Many types of graphs are available in these character graph versions. For another interesting display, try `Contour Z Y X` in `Gstd` mode. To return to the now-standard professional graphics mode, use `Gpro`.

This book only provides a brief introduction to Minitab session commands, and casual Minitab users may never use them. However, familiarity with this layer of Minitab provides a level of flexibility and power unavailable through the menus. It also opens up endless opportunities to write macros for automating Minitab. Macros are beyond the scope of this introductory book, but for those who want to learn this powerful skill, exploring the session commands used to write macros is an excellent place to start.

3.4   Constants, Columns, and Matrices

In Minitab, a worksheet can hold three different types of variables.

- **Constants** are scalars, or single values. A constant may be of numeric or text data type. Constants have unique IDs of K1, K2, and so on, but constants may also be assigned more descriptive names. Each worksheet may contain up to 1,000 constants. There are three special constant values in Minitab. If not otherwise assigned in a worksheet, K998 = *, the missing data symbol; K999 = 2.7183... (e); and K1000 = 3.1416... (π). In many programming languages, a "constant" is assigned a value only once, and cannot change. But in Minitab, "constants" are true variables and may be assigned new values at any time. Like columns, constants may also be assigned a formula to update the constant any time some other variables change.

- **Columns** are vectors, or one-dimensional arrays of values. The data window for each worksheet displays all the columns in a spreadsheet format. A column may be of numeric, date/time, or text data type. Each worksheet may contain up to 4,000 columns, and each column may contain up to 10,000,000 values, although limited system resources will prevent almost everyone from approaching these limits. Columns have unique IDs of C1, C2, and so on, but columns may also be assigned descriptive names.

- **Matrices** are rectangular, two-dimensional arrays of numeric values. Each worksheet may contain up to 100 matrices. Matrices have unique IDs of M1, M2, and so on, but they may also be assigned descriptive names.

Many Minitab users have no idea that constants and matrices exist in Minitab. The data window makes it easy to view and edit columns, but it is not quite as easy to access constants and matrices. Even so, with skillful use of all three types of Minitab variables, a huge variety of problems can be solved, beyond what is available in the Minitab menus.

For a simple example, open a new Minitab worksheet and enter the numbers 1, 2, 3, and 4 into column C1. Suppose we wanted to calculate the sum of squares of the numbers in C1. Open the calculator dialog with Calc > Calculator in the Minitab menu. Figure 3-6 shows the Calculator dialog. Enter K1 in the Store result in variable box. The drop-down box labeled Functions: lists several categories of the available functions. In the Statistics category, find and select Sum of Squares. This enters the functional form SSQ(number) in the Expression: box. Type C1, check the Assign as a formula check box, and click OK.

Now where is the answer? One way to see all the constants in the worksheet is with the project manager. Click ① to show information about all the columns in the worksheet. At the left edge of the Project Manager window is a divider bar. Hover the mouse over this bar until the cursor changes to ↔ and drag the divider to reveal the folder view in the left pane, as shown in Fig. 3-7. Click on the Constants folder within the current worksheet, and the Project Manager window shows that the constant with ID K1 has value 30, which is $1^2 + 2^2 + 3^2 + 4^2$. If you change a value in column C1, the constant K1 should also change, since it has been assigned a formula. In the Project Manager constant listing in the right pane, right-click on *** Unnamed ***, and select Rename from the popup menu to assign the constant a more descriptive name, perhaps SumSqC1.

Another way to display variables is with the Data > Display Data menu command. With this dialog, any constants, columns, or matrices can be printed in the Session window.

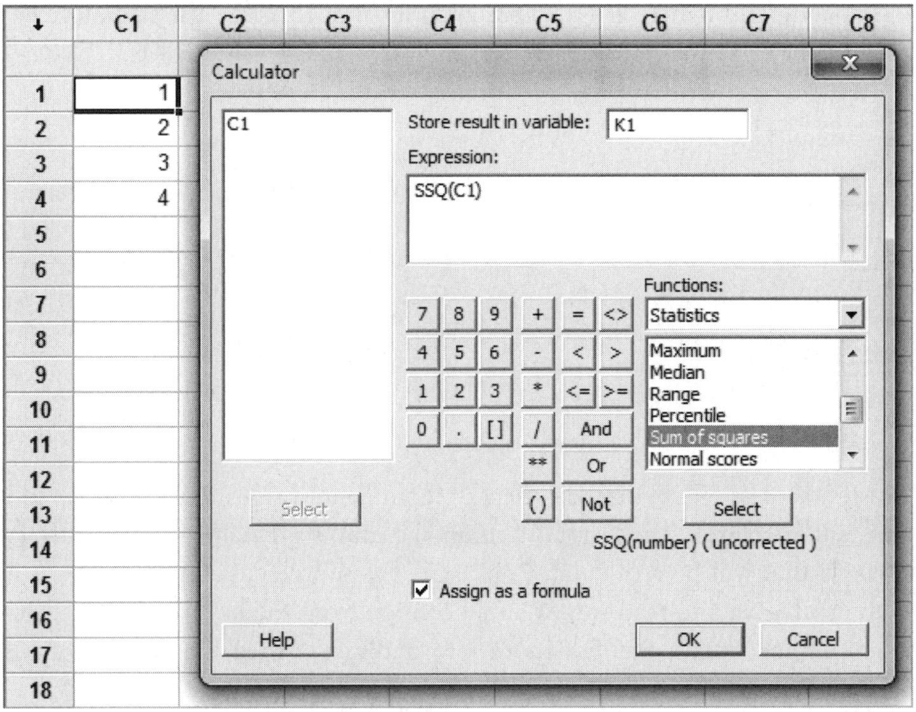

FIGURE 3-6 · Assigning a formula to constant K1.

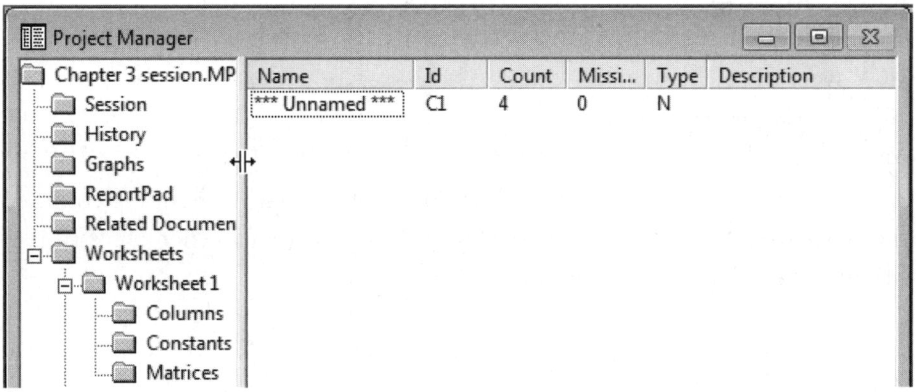

FIGURE 3-7 · Project Manager window with folder view.

For comparison, here are the session commands to assign the same formula to constant K1 as was done above, and then display the value of K1:

```
MTB > New
MTB > Set C1
DATA> 1:4
DATA> End
MTB > Formula K1 = SSQ(C1)
MTB > Name K1 "SumSqC1"
MTB > Print K1
```

Data Display

```
SumSqC1    30.0000
MTB >
```

In Minitab session commands, the Let command assigns a static value to a constant or column. The Formula command makes a dynamic assignment of a formula that will be recalculated any time the source data changes. The Set command is used to read values into a column from the keyboard, as in these examples, or from a file. For more information on these commands, use ? followed by any command from the MTB > prompt.

Matrices can also be read into a matrix variable from a file or from column variables, and then manipulated with various matrix functions. The Calc > Matrix menu lists the matrix calculations provided by Minitab. Matrices may be displayed with Data > Display Data. Matrix math is not a common application for Minitab, so it is not covered further in this book.

3.5   File Types in Minitab

Through the examples in this book, you have already seen the most common file types used by Minitab. Table 3-2 lists these and many other types of files Minitab can either open or save.

3.6   Menus in Minitab

Like most Windows applications, Minitab uses a mixture of familiar menus, like File, with specialized menus, like Stat. One Minitab menu, Editor, has four versions, which appear depending on the context. Here is a quick tour

TABLE 3-2 File Types Used by Minitab

Extension	Description	Minitab Can Open or Save	File Stores What
.MPJ	Minitab project	Open/Save	All information in current project, including worksheets, graphs, output, and history
.MTW	Minitab worksheet	Open/Save	All information in one Minitab worksheet
.MTP	Minitab portable worksheet	Open/Save	Columns, constants, and matrices, but no DOE design objects, formulas, or settings
.TXT, .DAT, or .CSV	Text files; CSV = comma separated values; either ANSI (ASCII) or Unicode characters may be selected	Open/Save	Column data only
.TXT	Text files	Save	Session window, ReportPad, or History folder
.RTF	Rich text format	Save	Session window or ReportPad
.XLS, .XLSX, .XML	Microsoft Excel	Open/Save	Column data only
.WK1, .WKS, .WR1, .WRK, .WB1, .WQ1, .DBF	Lotus 1-2-3, Symphony, Quattro Pro, dBASE/ FoxPro	Open/Save	Column data only
.HTM, .HTML	Hypertext markup language	Open (only a table of data, not full web pages)/Save	Column data only
.HTM, .HTML	Hypertext markup language	Save	Session window, ReportPad
.MGF	Minitab Graphics Format	Open/Save	Minitab graph
.JPG, .PNG, .TIF, .BMP, .GIF, .EMF	Various graphic formats	Save	Minitab graph
.MTB	Minitab exec file	Save/Open	Minitab macro file, limited to commands that can be run from the command prompt in the Session window
.MAC	Minitab macro file	Save/Open	Minitab macro file including control statements, arguments, and more flexibility than .MTB files

through the menu structure, highlighting a few useful commands you may not have seen before:

- The File menu contains commands to create, open, save, or print Minitab projects, worksheets, and other Minitab components, like graphs or the Session window. Some commands only appear in the File menu in the right context. For example, commands to print or save the Session window only appear when the Session window is active.
  - The File > Other Files submenu has commands to import or export data in text format, or to run macros stored in the form of an exec file.
- The Edit menu contains commands to Undo or Redo, plus commands to Clear, Delete, Copy, Cut, and Paste, which should be familiar to most users of other Windows programs. In addition to the usual clipboard commands, Minitab offers these:
  - Edit > Paste link pastes a dynamic link to data already copied from another place in Minitab, or from Excel or another outside data source. Unlike the other methods of importing data, this link will automatically reflect updates in the source data, as long as the source application is open.
  - Use Edit > Worksheet Links > Manage Links to add, change or remove links to external data.
  - The popular Edit > Edit Last Dialog command recalls the last dialog for you to make changes.
  - Edit > Command Line Editor opens a small text window for editing and submitting Minitab session commands. Unlike the MTB > prompt in the Session window, this command line editor allows many commands to be composed and submitted in one batch.
- The Data menu contains many commands for moving, coping, converting, and organizing data stored in worksheets.
  - Commands to Subset Worksheet, Split Worksheet, or Merge Worksheets are convenient ways to filter, split, or combine large datasets.
  - The Data > Copy menu has commands to copy data between constants, columns, and matrices, or to copy whole worksheets.
  - The Data > Unstack Columns command and Data > Stack menu are used to rearrange columns into different formats. Most Minitab analysis commands require stacked data.

- Data > Transpose swaps rows for columns. When importing Excel data organized in rows, this command is helpful to rearrange the data into columns for Minitab analysis or graphs.

- The Data > Code menu creates a new column with coded versions of data in an existing column.

- The Data > Change Data Type menu contains commands to change columns from one data type to another.

- The Data > Extract from Date/Time menu is used to pull a part of a date, like the month or week, into a numeric or text column.

- The Calc menu includes the Calculator, seen earlier, plus these useful tools:

  - Calc > Column Statistics and Calc > Row Statistics calculate summary statistics by column or by row.

  - The Calc > Make Patterned Data menu contains commands to quickly generate columns with repetitive patterns of values.

  - Calc > Make Mesh Data creates a two dimensional mesh of X and Y variables and optionally calculates a Z variable with several types of functions. This is helpful to build data for contour or surface plots.

  - The Calc > Random Data menu is used to generate random numbers from a wide variety of distribution models. Use Calc > Set Base to reset the random number generator if it is important to generate the same random numbers on multiple occasions.

  - The Calc > Probability Distributions menu is used to calculate probabilities and quantiles from a wide variety of distribution models. These tools are discussed further in Chapter 4.

  - The Calc > Matrix menu lists matrix calculations.

- The Stat menu is where all the analytical tools of Minitab are organized into several submenus. Most of these submenus will be discussed in separate chapters. Chapter 6 covers the hypothesis tests in the Stat > Basic Statistics menu. Chapter 8 discusses the Stat > Regression menu and the Stat > ANOVA menu. Chapter 9 discusses the Stat > DOE menu. Chapter 11 covers Stat > Control Charts. The Stat > Quality Tools menu includes many important tools such as distribution identification (Chapter 4), capability analysis (Chapter 12), and acceptance sampling (Chapter 13). For convenience, many types of graphs associated with these tools are located in submenus of the Stat menu instead of in the Graph menu.

- The Graph menu is where the most common types of graphs can be created. This is a very flat menu without submenus, and each type of graph has an icon in the menu as a tiny reminder of what that type of graph looks like.

- The Editor menu has four different versions which appear, depending on which Minitab window is active.

  - When the Session window is active, the Editor menu has commands to navigate up or down through the Session window, to enable the MTB > command prompt, to find text, and to change fonts in the Session window. Right-clicking on the Session window brings up a popup menu with the same set of commands, plus some from the Edit menu.

  - When the data window is active, the Editor menu has commands to find and replace, to navigate around the data window, to insert or move selected cells, to assign formats, to manage formulas, and to take a variety of other actions regarding column variables. Most of these commands are also on the data window popup menu.

  - When a graph is active, the Editor menu is used to select or edit any of the elements of the graph. There are also five cursor modes, Select, Brush, Crosshairs, Plant Flag and OptiPlot Interactive. These modes will only appear in the Editor menu when appropriate to the active plot. Select is the usual mode where elements of the graph are selected by clicking on them. Brushing was illustrated in Chapter 1. In Crosshairs mode, the coordinates of the cursor are displayed on the plot. The other two modes are for special plots used in the analysis of designed experiments. The Editor menu also starts the Layout tool, which can create a new graph containing an array of existing graphs. Another convenience is the ability to duplicate a graph or to make a similar graph directly from the Editor menu. Many, but not all of these commands are also on the graph popup menu.

- The Tools menu contains some convenient links to the Microsoft Calculator, Notepad, and Windows Explorer. The Tools menu also contains many options for reorganizing Minitab tools and changing the way they work. With the Tools > Toolbars menu, any of the available toolbars may be shown or hidden. Tools > Customize allows the user to move menu items and toolbar icons around to be more convenient, to create new toolbars, or to assign keyboard shortcuts. Tools > Options opens a dialog with many pages of options affecting both the functioning and display of information in Minitab. Tools > Manage Profiles offers a convenient way to create, save, and load profiles, which combine the options and customization settings.

- The Window menu contains commands similar to other Windows programs, including Cascade, Tile, Minimize, and Restore, plus a list of all open windows. When a project becomes hopelessly cluttered with dozens of graphs, the Window > Close All Graphs command both cleans up the project and reduces the space and time required to save it.

- The Help menu is one of the best features of Minitab. Compared to other statistical software, the Minitab help files are remarkably comprehensive and helpful. All help files have search and index capabilities. Here are some of the links available in the Help menu.

  - Help > Help provides a description of every Minitab menu function, organized as they are in the menus. Every field in every dialog is explained, often with links to resources in other help files, plus references to textbooks.

  - Help > Meet Minitab links to www.minitab.com, where the introductory guide *Meet Minitab* can be downloaded.

  - Help > StatGuide opens a detailed explanation of the statistical tasks and tools available in Minitab. Some practitioners use this as a general purpose statistical reference book, but the StatGuide is limited to tools supported by Minitab.

  - Help > Tutorials opens a selection of tutorials explaining many of the tools in the Stat menu, each with a story, data to analyze, and an explanation of the results. Many of these tutorials are new and improved for Minitab 16.

  - Help > Glossary opens a thorough dictionary of statistical terminology.

  - Help > Methods and Formulas lists equations and methodology behind the Minitab analysis tools.

  - Help > Knowledgebase / FAQ links to www.minitab.com, where many questions have been already asked and answered by the staff at Minitab, Inc.

  - Help > Keyboard Map lists keyboard shortcuts currently assigned. These may be changed using Tools > Customize.

This is far from a complete explanation of the Minitab menus, but this listing features the most often used or the most distinctive functions in the menus. For more help finding a particular function, search the help files.

3.7   Toolbars in Minitab

Minitab contains 12 toolbars. Some of these are always visible by default, while others will appear in the right context. Toolbars can be individually shown or hidden in the Tools > Toolbars menu. Toolbars are normally docked at the top of the Minitab window, but by clicking and dragging the ⌐ bar at the left end of any toolbar, it can be changed to a floating toolbar. To reveal the function of any toolbar button, hover the cursor over the button, and in most cases, a description will appear.

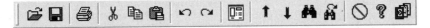

The Standard toolbar, shown above, contains buttons to open and save a project; to print; to cut, copy, and paste; to undo and redo; to recall the last dialog; to navigate up and down through the Session window; to find and replace; to cancel an operation; or to invoke the Help file or the StatGuide. The StatGuide button, at the right end of the toolbar, is context sensitive. When viewing a graph or a report where the StatGuide has a relevant topic, this icon will light up, and clicking it will open the StatGuide to the correct section.

The Project Manager toolbar, shown above, contains buttons which navigate to various parts of the Minitab project. Section 1.7 discussed this toolbar in detail.

The Worksheet toolbar, shown above, contains buttons to assign a formula, insert cells, insert rows, insert columns, or move columns. When brushing data in a graph, two buttons navigate to the previous or next brushed row in the data window. The final button clears contents from cells in the data window.

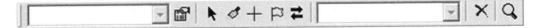

The Graph Editing toolbar, shown above, is the toolbar version of the Editor menu when a graph is active. The first dropdown box is used to select one element of the graph, which can be edited by clicking the 🖻 edit button. The next five buttons change the cursor mode between select, brush, crosshairs, plant flag, and OptiPlot interactive modes, depending on the type of plot. The second dropdown box adds or edits optional features of the plot such as gridlines, subtitles, and so on. The final two buttons are to delete the plot and to zoom in or out.

The Graph Annotation Tools toolbar, shown above, contains another instance of the select cursor mode button, plus tools to add text, boxes, lines, markers, or other geometric figures to annotate graphs.

The 3D Graph Tools toolbar, shown above, normally appears as a floating toolbar whenever a 3D graph like a surface plot or contour plot is active. This toolbar contains six buttons to rotate the graph in various directions, six buttons to rotate the lighting in various directions, two zoom buttons, and two buttons to restore the graph rotation and lighting rotation to their initial settings. For examples of using these tools, see Section 2.4.

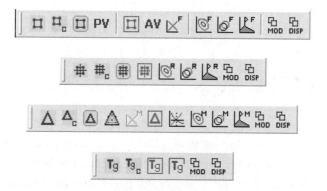

The Factorial Designs, Response Surface Designs, Mixture Designs, and Taguchi Designs toolbars, shown above, contain tools for designing and analyzing different types of experiments. These tools will be discussed in Chapter 9.

The OptiPlot toolbar, shown above, is used to control a special kind of interactive plot used to optimize results of a model derived from a designed experiment.

Define ▾ Measure ▾ Analyze ▾ Improve ▾ Control ▾

The DMAIC toolbar, shown above, is new in Minitab 16, and is part of the DMAIC profile. If the DMAIC toolbar is not listed in the Tools > Toolbar menu, go to Tools > Manage Profiles. Select the DMAIC profile in the Available Profiles box, and click the ⟩ button to move it to the Active Profiles box. After clicking OK, the DMAIC toolbar will become available.

In the Six Sigma system for improving business processes, people typically follow a five-phase model for improvement: Define, Measure, Analyze, Improve, and Control (DMAIC). The DMAIC toolbar has five controls, each of which opens a menu listing several Minitab tools typically used during that phase of a Six Sigma project. These tools are all available elsewhere in the Minitab menus, but the DMAIC toolbar organizes them in a format convenient for Six Sigma practitioners.

The DMAIC toolbar is an example of a custom toolbar that anyone can make for themselves using the customization features of Minitab, discussed further in the next section.

3.8   Customizing Minitab

Minitab offers great flexibility to customize both the user interface and the way analysis is performed. These customizations can be personal, affecting only your work with Minitab, or they can be integrated into a profile to be exported and shared with other Minitab users.

This section describes three levels of customization, by changing options, by customizing menus and toolbars, and by creating profiles. All of these customization options are accessed through the Minitab Tools menu.

Figure 3-8 shows the Options dialog. To see this, select Tools > Options. This is a dialog with many pages, which are chosen using the large box on the left side. Click on any ⊞ to expand a category of pages and see options pages within that category. Figure 3-8 shows the Graphics > Regions page, which explains the three regions within a graph, labeled Graph, Figure, and Data. Click on the Graph page, Figure page, or Data page within the Regions category to change default fill and border settings for each region.

It is worth the time to browse through the different options pages available. If you create a lot of graphs, you need to be aware of the settings on the Graphics > Graph Management page. Graphs in Minitab can use a significant amount of memory, and projects with many graphs take much time and space to save. Because of this, Minitab limits the maximum number of graphs to 100 by default. On the Graph Management page, this limit can be changed, up to 200,

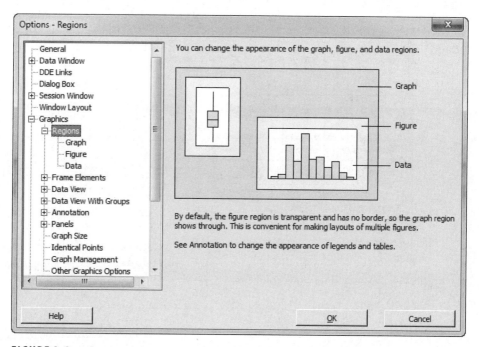

FIGURE 3-8 • Options dialog.

and options also control the action taken when this limit is reached. If your system has limited resources, you may need to lower this limit, if you find that having a lot of open graphs bogs down your system.

The next level of customization is accessed through the Tools > Customize menu command. When the Customize dialog is open, all items on the menubar and toolbars are in a special mode where they can be dragged and dropped to new locations, or simply deleted by dragging them off the toolbars. For example, if you want the Help menu to be at the end of the menubar, instead of behind the new Assistant menu, simply click and drag it where you want it. You can drag and drop items onto other toolbars to reorganize them. To make a copy of an item, hold the Ctrl key down while clicking and dragging.

Minitab has many commands which do not appear on the toolbars. For example, the Standard toolbar is missing the New command and commands to open and save worksheets. To find a list of all available menu items, the Commands tab lists all Minitab commands organized into 25 categories. In the File category, the New, Open Worksheet, and Save Worksheet commands can be dragged onto the Standard toolbar or any other toolbar, as desired.

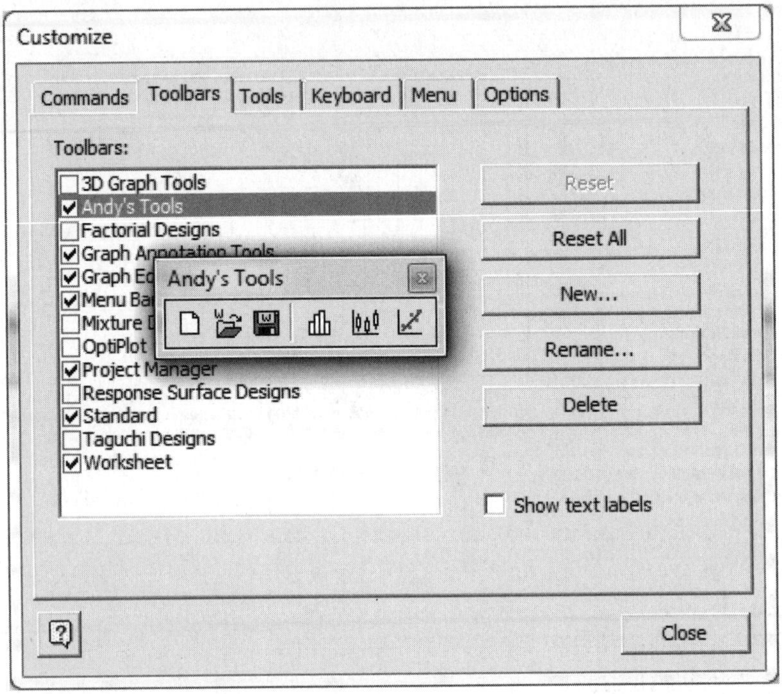

FIGURE 3-9 · Using Customize to create a new toolbar.

Another option is to create a new toolbar. Figure 3-9 shows the Toolbars tab of the Customize dialog, with a new toolbar I created in a couple of minutes. To do this for yourself, click the New button, and assign the new toolbar a name. A small, empty toolbar appears on the screen, ready to be filled. In this example, I added New, Open Worksheet, Save Worksheet, plus three of my favorite graphs, Histogram, Boxplot, and Probability Plot. After dragging the Histogram command from the Graph menu into my new toolbar, it first appears like this: ⬛ Histogram... To save space and show the command as an image only, without text, right-click on the item and select Image from the popup menu. Finally, to separate the file commands from the graph commands, I right-clicked on the Histogram icon and selected Start Group. This adds a vertical bar to the left of that item.

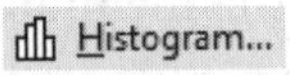

The DMAIC toolbar is an example of a custom toolbar with multiple levels of menus. To add a menu to a new toolbar, click on the Commands tab, find the New Menu category, and drag New Menu to the custom toolbar. Once added to the toolbar, it can be renamed and populated with any collection of tools, commands, or other new menus.

The Customize dialog provides even more ways to customize Minitab. The Tools tab lists the three Windows programs included on the Tools menu by default. More can be added. For example, to add a menu item to start Microsoft Excel, click on the ☐ new icon. Enter E&xcel in the Menu Contents box. Then enter excel.exe in the Command box and click Close. The & precedes the letter, x in this case, that will be used as a keyboard shortcut. With this setting, Alt+T for Tools, followed by Alt+X will start Excel.

The Keyboard tab of the Customize dialog allows the user to specify or change keyboard shortcuts for commonly used operations.

All customization changes are stored in the Windows registry so your custom menus, toolbars, and shortcuts will still work every time you start Minitab. If you are using Minitab under a shared network license, your changes will not affect any other user, since they are saved for your user name on your individual computer.

If you wish to reset your choices to Minitab defaults, the Toolbars, Keyboard, and Menu tabs have Reset buttons which will reset some settings. Another way to reset everything will be explained shortly.

In Minitab, a profile stores all settings chosen in the Tools > Options or Tools > Customize dialogs, including custom menus and toolbars. To import, export, activate, or deactivate profiles, select Tools > Manage Profiles.

Figure 3-10 shows the Manage Profiles dialog. This dialog contains a list of Available Profiles, and a list of Active Profiles. Use the ▷ or ◁ buttons to move profiles from one list to the other. Use the ↑ ↓ buttons to move active profiles up or down in the list. The profile listed on top will take precedence over any profiles below. In this figure, a new profile has been created with the ☐ button.

One quick way to reset Minitab to all default settings, while preserving your custom settings for later use, is to click the ◁◁ button to move all profiles to the available list. When you click OK, Minitab will create a new active profile with all default settings and activate this profile. Your previously used profile can be reactivated at any time.

In this chapter we toured the Minitab environment. We saw all the commonly used features, plus many that are rarely seen. It should be clear that the Minitab user interface offers great flexibility to those who wish to tweak and customize it for their individual needs. Also, for those who prefer writing text commands over using the graphical interface, Minitab session commands offer even greater flexibility and power.

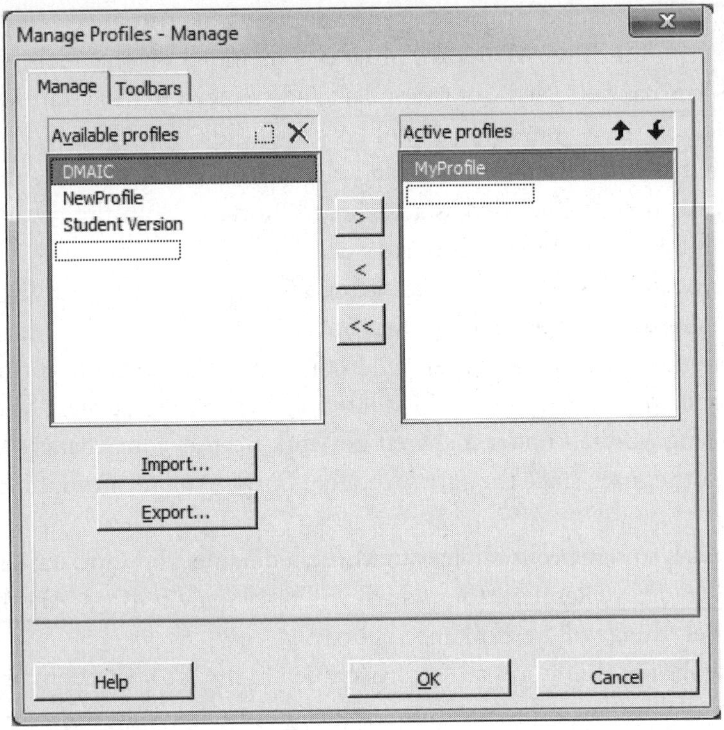

FIGURE 3-10 • Manage Profiles dialog.

This chapter ends the first part of this book, which introduces Minitab. Each of the following chapters explains a group of statistical functions for solving one type of problem. These chapters are not cumulative, as far as Minitab skills are concerned. Feel free to jump to whichever chapters are needed for your classes and to advance your career. Most importantly, when your friends ask how you became such a Minitab power user, be sure to recommend this book!

QUIZ

1. **In the data window fragment shown below, column C1 has what data type?**

   A. Time
   B. Integer
   C. Numeric
   D. Text

2. **Suppose you type "October 12" into the first cell of an empty column in the Minitab data window. How does Minitab assign a data type to the column?**
   A. Since the entry is text, Minitab assigns text data type to the column.
   B. Minitab sees 12 as a number, and assigns numeric data type to the column.
   C. Minitab recognizes "October 12" as a date and assigns the date/time data type to the column.
   D. Minitab does not recognize this and produces an error message.

3. **When filling out a Minitab dialog, you click on an empty field and expect to see a list of columns in the column listbox, but the column listbox is empty. What does this mean?**
   A. The current worksheet has no data.
   B. All of the columns in the current worksheet are of the wrong data type to be selected for that field in the dialog.
   C. The empty field in the dialog requires a number or text entry from the keyboard, and cannot accept a column name.
   D. All of the above are possible explanations for an empty column listbox.

4. **In an Excel worksheet, Columns A and B contain measured data, and column C contains formulas to calculate the sum of the values in columns A and B. If you copy columns A, B, and C from Excel and paste them into columns C1-C3 of an empty Minitab worksheet, what is true about column C3?**
   A. Column C3 will have a formula calculating the sum of values in columns C1 and C2.
   B. Column C3 will have values copied from Excel, but no formulas.
   C. Column C3 will have missing values because the formula is not recognized by Minitab.
   D. Column C3 will have a formula calculating the sum of values in columns A and B of the Excel worksheet.

5. You need to work in Minitab with selected rows and columns of a large database stored in an Excel file. What is the most direct way to create a Minitab worksheet containing only the desired rows and columns?

A. From Minitab, use ODBC to query only the columns and rows needed and put the results in a new Minitab worksheet.

B. In Excel, make a copy of the database, delete rows and columns not required, and then copy and paste the reduced table into Minitab.

C. From Minitab, open the entire Excel database into a new worksheet. Then, using the tools in the Data menu, create a new worksheet containing only the rows and columns required.

D. In Excel, use the filtering tools to show only the required columns, and hide unneeded columns. Then copy and paste the filtered data into Minitab.

6. In Minitab session commands, what does 10:15 mean?

A. A time, like 10:15 AM
B. A sequence of two numbers, 10 and 15
C. 10:15 is a ratio which is equivalent to the fraction 2/3
D. A sequence of six numbers, 10, 11, 12, 13, 14, 15

7. In a Minitab worksheet, a variable with ID of K1 refers to what?

A. K1 is a constant which can be assigned a value once and may never be changed.

B. K1 is a constant or scalar variable which can have only a single numeric or text value, but K1 can be assigned a new value at any time.

C. K1 refers to a column in the data window.

D. K1 is a matrix.

8. To save all information in a Minitab worksheet to one file, including all variables, formulas, and formatting choices, what file type can be used?

A. .XLS
B. .TXT
C. .MTW
D. All of the above

9. Commands to split worksheets and to stack columns are found in which Minitab menu?

A. Data
B. Calc
C. Editor
D. Assistant

10. **Suppose you need to use the** Project Manager **toolbar, but it is not visible in Minitab. How can you show the** Project Manager **toolbar?**

   A. Right-click in the toolbar area of the Minitab window, and select Project Manager.

   B. In the Minitab menu, select Tools > Toolbars > Project Manager.

   C. Select Tools > Customize, click the Toolbars tab, select the Project Manager toolbar in the list, and click OK.

   D. Any of the above methods work.

chapter 4

Selecting and Using Distribution Models in Minitab

Distribution models are fundamental tools of statistics. Many types of analysis assume that populations follow a particular distribution family, usually the normal distribution. A much wider variety of problems can be solved by selecting an appropriate distribution model and applying that model to predict future behavior. Minitab offers graphical tools to help identify which distribution model fits best, and goodness-of-fit tests to quantify that fit. After a model is selected, Minitab can perform many calculations for 24 different families of distribution models.

CHAPTER OBJECTIVES

Here's what you'll learn in this chapter:

- How to create graphs to illustrate and compare distribution models
- How to calculate densities, cumulative probabilities, and quantiles for a distribution model
- How to generate random numbers according to a distribution model
- How to select the best distribution model
- How to select the best normalizing transformation
- When to apply different families of distribution models

4.1   Graphing Probability Mass Functions and Density Functions

There are basically two types of distribution models, discrete and continuous. Random variables following a discrete distribution can only have values in a discrete set of values. For simplicity, most discrete distribution models are limited to integer values. Random variables following a continuous distribution may have any real number value.

A discrete random variable X is often described by a probability mass function (PMF) $f(x)$, where $f(x)$ is the probability that X will have value x.

A continuous random variable X is often described by a probability density function (PDF) with the same symbol as a PMF, $f(x)$, where the area under $f(x)$ between A and B is the probability that X will have a value between A and B.

For either continuous or discrete distributions, Minitab can graph $f(x)$ using Graph > Probability Distribution Plot. This graph is a handy way to learn about distribution models and to compare different ones.

For a first example, consider the binomial distribution. The binomial distribution is based on a set of simple experiments called Bernoulli trials. Bernoulli trials are experiments with two outcomes, like pass or fail, win or lose, conforming or nonconforming. In a set of Bernoulli trials, we assume that the probability of one outcome is always the same, p, and we assume that all trials are independent of each other. Bernoulli trials are a convenient model for many real problems, including games of chance and inspections of parts.

Let's say the probability of a "pass" is p. In a series of n pass/fail Bernoulli trials, what is the probability that x trials will pass and $n - x$ trials will fail? The answer is given by the binomial distribution, with this PMF:

$$f(x) = \frac{n!}{x!(n-x)!} p^x (1-p)^{n-x} \text{ for } 0 < p < 1,\ x \in \{0,\ 1,\ ...,\ n\}$$

For example, suppose Sarah flips a fair coin 12 times. How many heads will Sarah see out of 12 flips? The answer has a binomial distribution with $n = 12$ and $p = 0.5$. To see this PMF, select Graph > Probability Distribution Plot, and then select a View Single plot from the gallery. From the dropdown box, select Binomial, and enter 12 for Number of trials and 0.5 for Event probability.

After Sarah made this graph, she decided that it was difficult to read probabilities from the graph. To make this easier, she turned on gridlines by right-clicking on the graph and selecting Add > Gridlines from the popup menu. Sarah selected Y major ticks and Y minor ticks and clicked OK. Sarah's finished graph is

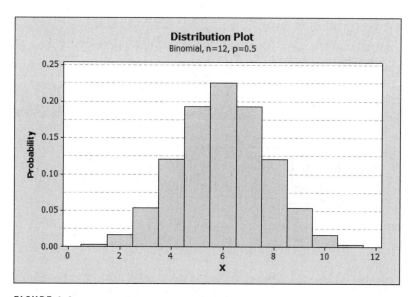

FIGURE 4-1 · Binomial PMF with gridlines.

shown in Fig. 4-1. Gridlines are a helpful addition to any graph where the viewer needs to make a quantitative assessment.

The most likely outcome of 12 flips of a coin is 6 heads, but how likely is this? Reading from the graph, this probability is approximately 0.225.

Then Sarah actually flips a coin 12 times and records 9 heads. She looks at the coin wondering how fair it really is. Is it highly unusual to have at least 9 heads out of 12?

To answer this, Sarah makes another graph. After selecting Graph > Probability Distribution Plot, she selects View Probability from the gallery.

In the next dialog, she again selects a Binomial distribution with $n = 12$ and $p = 0.5$. She clicks the Shaded Area tab, shown in Fig. 4-2. In this tab, Sarah opts to Define Shaded Area By X Value. She selects Right Tail, and enters 9 for the X value.

Figure 4-3 shows the finished distribution plot. This graph illustrates visually that the probability of 9, 10, 11, or 12 heads out of 12 coin flips is 0.073. This means that 7.3% of the time, or about 1 time in 14, flipping a fair coin 12 times will result in 9 or more heads. This is an unusual outcome, but probably not unusual enough to prove that the coin is unfair. More trials and stronger evidence would be required to reach that conclusion.

A different way to look at a set of Bernoulli trials is to count the "loss" outcomes until the first "win." When the probability of a win is p, the number

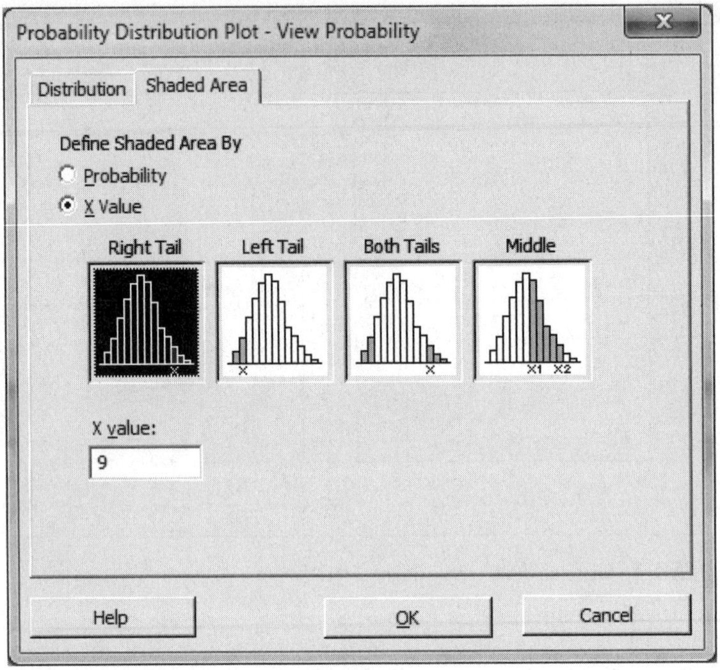

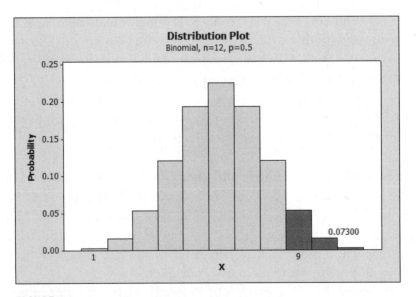

FIGURE 4-2 • Settings to view a probability.

FIGURE 4-3 • Probability of at least nine of twelve heads.

of trials up to and including the first win has a geometric distribution, with this PMF:

$$f(x) = p(1-p)^{x-1} \text{ for } 0 < p < 1, \ x \in \{1, 2, 3, ...\}$$

Note that the geometric distribution has an infinite number of possible values. There is no absolute guarantee that continually flipping a coin will ever result in heads, or that continually playing the lottery will ever produce a win. The geometric distribution has a "lack of memory" property which is unique among discrete distributions. Regardless of the history of past wins and losses, the distribution of trials before your next win is always the same.

To see what the geometric distribution looks like for different values of p, create a probability distribution plot, but this time select Vary Parameters in the gallery. Select Geometric from the dropdown box, and enter a range of p values in the Event Probabilities box. To create the graph shown in Fig. 4-4, enter 0.2:0.5/0.1, which is Minitab shorthand for 0.2, 0.3, 0.4, 0.5. Instead of using the shorthand version, you could enter the numbers directly, separated by spaces: 0.2 0.3 0.4 0.5. Then, click the Multiple Graphs button. The default setting of Overlaid on the same graph does not work well in this case, because the bar charts hide each other. Instead, select In separate panels of the same graph. After the graph appears, add X and Y gridlines.

Notice in this graph that 0 is not a possible outcome. This version of the geometric distribution is defined to model the total number of trials, which

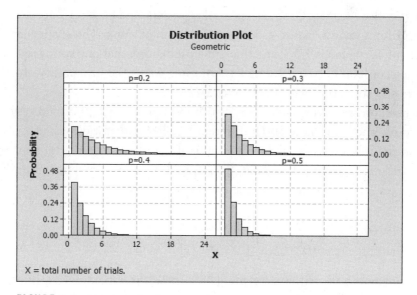

FIGURE 4-4 • Geometric distribution.

must be 1 or more. Some books define a different version of the geometric distribution that models the number of losses before the first win, which can possibly be 0. Minitab supports both versions. In the Probability Distribution Plot form, after selecting Geometric, click the Options button to change this setting.

For continuous distributions, the PDF uses the same symbol $f(x)$ as the discrete PMF $f(x)$, but these are two very different functions. The discrete PMF is zero everywhere except at integer values where $f(x)$ equals the probability of observing that exact value. But the continuous PDF defines probabilities by the area under $f(x)$ and above zero.

For example, the normal distribution, also known as the Gaussian distribution, has this PDF, where the mean is μ and the standard deviation is σ:

$$f(x) = \frac{1}{\sigma\sqrt{2\pi}} \exp\left[\frac{-1}{2}\left(\frac{x-\mu}{\sigma}\right)^2\right], \text{ for } \sigma > 0$$

For an example, suppose Greg is a mechanical engineer investigating problems with a spring. According to the specification for the spring, the spring constant should be between 1.20 and 1.40 Newtons per meter. Measurements of actual springs show that the spring constant has a normal distribution with a mean $\mu = 1.330$ and standard deviation $\sigma = 0.035$ Newtons per meter. What is the probability that any one spring will fail to meet its specification?

In Minitab, Greg creates a distribution plot of a normal distribution with the View Probability option. He enters $\mu = 1.33$ and $\sigma = 0.035$ in the Distribution tab. In the Shaded Area tab, Greg selects X Value, Middle, and enters 1.2 for X value 1 and 1.4 for X value 2. Figure 4-5 shows the finished graph. The shaded area on the graph is labeled 0.9771, and this is the probability that one spring will have a spring constant between 1.2 and 1.4. If Greg wants the probability of failing the specification, this is $1 - 0.9771 = 0.0229$.

When you are learning statistics, distribution plots are a quick and easy way to explore and learn more about different families of distributions.

For example, the Weibull distribution family contains many different shapes of distributions. Here is the Weibull PDF, with three parameters: a threshold parameter λ, a scale parameter α, and a shape parameter β:

$$f(x) = \frac{\beta(x-\lambda)^{\beta-1}}{\alpha^\beta} \exp\left[-\left(\frac{x-\lambda}{\alpha}\right)^\beta\right], \text{ for } x > 0, \ \alpha > 0, \ \beta > 0$$

Different books use different symbols for these three parameters, but these symbols are used in the Minitab help files.

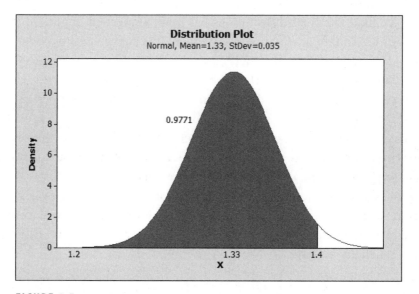

FIGURE 4-5 · Normal density plot with shaded probability.

Figure 4-6 is a distribution plot showing the Weibull distribution with four different shape parameters, 0.5, 1, 2, and 4. All four distributions have the same scale parameter, 1, and the same threshold parameter, 0. For Minitab practice, try to duplicate this plot for yourself. To improve legibility, this plot has a modified X scale and increased font size in the legend.

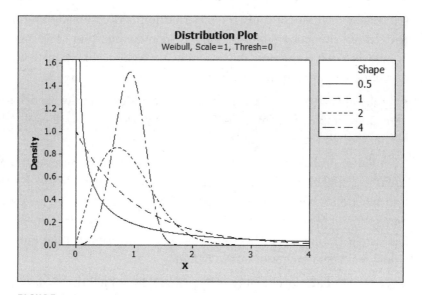

FIGURE 4-6 · Weibull densities with different shapes.

The Weibull family of distributions has many important applications, particularly in reliability or survival theory, where it is convenient to model many different shapes of distributions with a single family. Also, certain special cases of the Weibull family are important families of their own.

With a shape parameter of 1, a Weibull random variable becomes an exponential random variable. The exponential distribution is unique among continuous distributions in having a "lack of memory" property, like the discrete geometric distribution. Because of this property, the exponential is a popular model for many natural processes, including radioactive decay.

With a shape parameter of 2, a Weibull random variable becomes a Rayleigh random variable, another distribution with many important applications in science and engineering. Chapter 14 has examples applying the Weibull distribution to reliability analysis.

4.2   Probability and Quantile Calculations

Every problem related to distribution models can be answered by one of three calculations, and Minitab provides all three of these in the Calc > Probability Distributions menu. Here are the three calculations:

- **Probability mass** or **probability density.** This calculation is different for discrete and continuous distribution models.

  - Probability mass for a discrete distribution is occasionally useful. For example, suppose an intersection has an average of four accidents each month. What is the probability of exactly eight accidents at that intersection in one month?

  - Probability density for a continuous distribution is rarely used, except to draw graphs, and this function can be performed more easily from the Minitab Graph menu.

- **Cumulative probability** is the probability of observing a value less than or equal to a specified value x. This is often called the cumulative distribution function (CDF) with symbol $F(x)$. For an example, if the height of a population of people is normally distributed with a mean of 70 inches and a standard deviation of 3 inches, what is the probability that one individual will be 65 inches or less in height?

- **Inverse cumulative probability** is the value x for which the probability of observing a value less than or equal to x is a specified value p. This is the inverse CDF with symbol $F^{-1}(p)$. For example, if the height of a population of people is normally distributed with a mean of 70 inches and a standard deviation of 3 inches, what height is taller than 95% of the people?

Sarah, from the previous section, made a graph of a binomial PMF (Fig. 4-1), and she showed it to her Statistics professor, Andy. Andy was not happy with this graph, because it is not like PMF graphs in the class textbook, or like the PMF sketches Andy draws on the board. Andy prefers a graph like Fig. 4-7, with dots at every probability mass point, and vertical lines down to the axis. The PMF $f(x)$ equals 0 almost everywhere, except when x is an integer. Figure 4-7 is a more correct representation of a discrete PMF than bar charts like Fig. 4-1.

Sarah discovered how to make Fig. 4-7 using these steps:

- In a new Minitab worksheet, Sarah entered the integers 0, 1, ..., 12 into C1 using Calc > Make Patterned Data > Simple Set of Numbers.
- Sarah calculated binomial probability masses using Calc > Probability Distributions > Binomial. In the Binomial Distribution dialog box, Sarah selected Probability, entered 12 for Number of trials and 0.5 for Event Probability. Then Sarah specified C1 for the Input column and C2 for Optional storage. After clicking OK, Sarah saw that column C2 now contained the binomial PMF values.

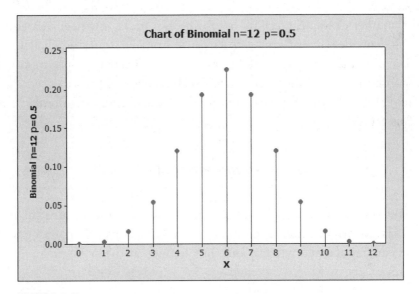

FIGURE 4-7 · Binomial mass function with symbols and project lines.

- To make the graph, Sarah selected Graph > Bar Chart. In the gallery, Sarah selected Values from a table in the dropdown box and a Simple graph. Then she clicked OK.

- In the next dialog, Sarah specified C2 as the Graph variable, C1 as the Categorical variable, and clicked the Data View button.

- In the Data View form, Sarah unselected Bars, and selected Symbols and Project Lines. Then clicking OK produced the plot in Fig. 4-7. Andy was much happier with this graph.

This procedure for making a PMF graph is clearly more work than the Probability Distribution Plot in the Graph menu, but it made Andy happy, and that's important. This example also illustrates how to customize bar charts for different purposes.

All the dialog boxes in the Calc > Probability Distributions menu require an input number and provide an output number. There are two options for each. To read one or many input numbers from a worksheet column, enter that column in the Input column box. If, instead, you want to enter a single number directly, select the Input constant option, and either enter the number or a constant name (like K1) into the Input constant box.

The example above illustrated using the Optional storage option for putting the output numbers in a worksheet column. Instead, to print the output number(s) in the Session window, simply leave the Optional storage box blank.

For another example, consider Seth, who is a traffic engineer in a growing city, Medianville. (It just changed its name from Firstquartileville.) One of Medianville's main intersections has a mean of 4.0 accidents per month, but last month, there were eight. Seth wonders how unusual this is.

The Poisson distribution is a good model for accidents per month. Here is the Poisson PMF:

$$f(x) = \frac{e^{-\lambda}\lambda^{x}}{x!}, \text{ for } \lambda > 0, \ x \in \{0, 1, 2, ...\}$$

The Poisson distribution only has one parameter, λ, which is also the mean. The Poisson distribution applies to many situations when independent events can happen at any time, and they happen at the same mean rate per unit time.

Using the Poisson model, what is the probability of experiencing eight accidents per month, when the mean is only 4.0? To find out, Seth selects Calc > Probability Distributions > Poisson. He selects the Probability option and enters 4 for the Mean. Then, he selects the Input constant option and enters 8. After Seth clicks OK, the result appears in the Session window:

Probability Density Function

```
Poisson with mean = 4

x   P( X = x )
8   0.0297702
```

According to Minitab, the probability of experiencing exactly eight accidents per month at the intersection is about 0.03 or 3%.

Sadly, this is the wrong way to approach this problem. Seth wants to know if it is unusual to have eight accidents in a month. To answer this question properly, Seth needs to also consider the probability of nine, ten, or more accidents, and then add all those probabilities together. Seth needs to calculate the probability of *eight or more* accidents per month. If the probability of eight or more accidents sums up to, say, 0.25, then eight is not very unusual.

Minitab calculates cumulative probabilities, but these are always in the form of *X or less*. Seth needs to calculate the probability of *seven or less* accidents per month, and subtract this from one.

Again in the Poisson probability distribution form, Seth selects Cumulative probability, with a Mean of 4, and Input constant of 7. Here is the result:

Cumulative Distribution Function

```
Poisson with mean = 4

x    P( X <= x )
7    0.948866
```

Subtracting this result from 1, the probability of eight or more accidents is $1 - 0.948866 = 0.051134$. Therefore, this intersection should expect to see eight or more accidents about 5% of the time, or one month in twenty. Seth decides that this is unusual and launches an investigation to look for causes of the increase in accidents.

Still Struggling

Are you confused about how eight became seven in the above example? Take a look at Fig. 4-8. These two distribution plots show the same Poisson distribution with two areas highlighted. Combined together, these two shaded areas are the whole distribution, with probability one. On these two graphs, it should be clear that seven-or-less is the complement of eight-or-more. If an integer is not seven or less, then it must be eight or more. In the above problem, if we had incorrectly calculated the probability of eight-or-less and subtracted that from one, the result would have been nine-or-more.

Most statistics students are confused by this aspect of discrete probability distributions, and teachers know it. Watch out for tricky words like "at least," "or less," "no more than," "no less than," and so on. It's always a good idea to sketch the problem, either by hand or with Minitab, to check if your interpretation matches the wording of the problem.

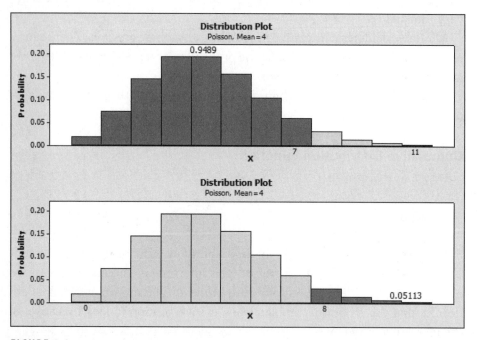

FIGURE 4-8 · Poisson cumulative probabilities.

With continuous distribution models, probabilities are always assigned to a range of values, not to a single value. In fact, the probability of observing any exact value of a continuous random variable is always zero.

For a continuous probability example, suppose Linda is designing the interior of a sports car intended for males having a mid-life crisis. The interior needs to be comfortable for the vast majority of this population. Automotive seating is designed around the H-point, which is roughly where the hip joint is located when seated. Linda refers to an extensive dimensional database of males having a mid-life crisis, and finds that the distance between the H-point and the top of the head is normally distributed with a mean of 33 inches and a standard deviation of 1.50 inches.

Marketing data suggests that the typical customer for this car does not want to feel short, even if he is short. Under the current car design, visibility starts to be impaired when the H-point to the top of the head is less than 29 inches. How likely is this?

In Minitab, Linda selects Calc > Probability Distribution > Normal. In the Normal Distribution form, Linda selects Cumulative probability, Mean of 33, Standard deviation of 1.5, and an Input constant of 29. Here are the results printed in the Session window:

Cumulative Distribution Function

```
Normal with mean = 33 and standard deviation = 1.5

  x    P( X <= x )
 29     0.0038304
```

Based on this calculation, about 0.0038 or 0.38% of the target population has less than 29 inches between their H-point and the top of their head. Therefore, 0.38% will have impaired visibility when they first enter the vehicle, without adjusting the seat. This is an acceptably small probability.

On the other hand, tall men don't like to have their head bump into the top of the car when seated. Linda wants to be sure that 99.5% of men will not bump their heads. What distance between H-point and the top of the head is greater than 99.5% of the target population?

This is the inverse of the cumulative probability problem. Here, we start with a probability and we need to calculate a measurement value x so that the probability of observing a smaller value than x is 0.995. In symbols, $P[X \leq x] = F(x) = 0.995$. To find x, we need the inverse CDF: $x = F^{-1}(0.995)$.

Minitab makes it easy to calculate this, in the same dialog box, by selecting Inverse Cumulative Probability. To solve this particular problem, Linda selects Calc > Probability Distributions > Normal. She selects Inverse Cumulative Probability, Mean of 33, Standard deviation of 1.5, and Input constant of 0.995. Here is the report:

Inverse Cumulative Distribution Function

```
Normal with mean = 33 and standard deviation = 1.5

P( X <= x )        x
     0.995   36.8637
```

If Linda designs the car interior with at least 36.9 inches between H-point and the headliner on the inside surface of the roof, this will accommodate 99.5% of the target customer population without bumping heads.

As another example, consider George, a real estate broker. George only gets paid when a deal closes, so he keeps records of when closings happen. George has found that the time between closings has an exponential distribution with a mean time of 11 days.

What is the probability that George will have two closings within one week, or seven days? In statistical terms, what is the probability that an exponential random variable with mean 11 will be less than 7?

The exponential distribution has its own dialog in the Probability Distributions menu. In this dialog box, there are two parameters, Scale and Threshold. Threshold is the minimum possible value, which in this case is zero. When Threshold is zero, the Scale parameter is equal to the mean.

In this box, George selects Cumulative probability and enters 11 for Scale, 0 for Threshold, and 7 for Input constant. The cumulative probability report is:

Cumulative Distribution Function

```
Exponential with mean = 11

x   P( X <= x )
7     0.470787
```

Therefore, George has a 47% probability of having his next closing in less than seven days after his previous closing.

In planning his cash flow, George wants to be 99% confident that he has enough cash to last between closings. What time is longer than 99% of the times between closings?

This question provides a probability and asks for a time, so the answer requires an inverse cumulative probability. Using the same form with Inverse cumulative probability selected, George enters 0.99 in the Input constant box. Here is the report:

Inverse Cumulative Distribution Function

```
Exponential with mean = 11

P( X <= x )        x
      0.99  50.6569
```

According to this calculation, 50.7 days is the 99th percentile of time between George's closings. George needs to plan cash flow to last at least this long between closings, to cover 99% of the possible situations.

4.3   Generating Random Numbers

Another common use for distribution models is to generate random numbers that follow a specified distribution. There are two major reasons for generating random numbers. The first is to create some fake data to test how a statistical tool, graph, or analysis reacts to that data. This is a widely used technique to build an understanding of how statistical tools react to simulated typical or atypical data. With this understanding, real data can be analyzed and interpreted with more confidence.

The second major use for random numbers is in Monte Carlo analysis, a tool used to predict how variation flows through products or processes. In Monte Carlo analysis, randomly generated input values are passed through a mathematical function representing some real system. Output values from the function, representing how the system would react to real values, are collected and analyzed.

Minitab generates random numbers from dozens of distribution families, using functions in the Calc > Random Data menu. Each distribution listed in the Probability Distributions menu is also listed in the Random Data menu.

Two of the most common families of distribution models are normal and exponential. How do these distributions look different on a time series plot? It is easy to find out.

In a new Minitab worksheet, generate 100 normal random numbers with mean 100 and standard deviation 10. To do this, select Calc > Random Data > Normal. In the Normal form, enter 100 in Number of rows of data to generate, and enter a name, like Normal in the Store in column(s) box. Enter a mean of 100 and a standard deviation of 10. After clicking OK, the normal random data appears in the worksheet.

When comparing two distributions with different shapes, a fair comparison requires that both the mean and standard deviation be the same. In the exponential distribution, the standard deviation is equal to the scale parameter, and the mean is equal to the sum of the scale and threshold parameters. If you need to know this later and forget it, look at the Exponential page in the Methods and Formulas help file. This helpful page lists the PDF, mean, and variance of the exponential distribution.

To generate exponential random numbers with a mean of 100 and a standard deviation of 10, set the scale parameter to 10 and the threshold parameter to 90. In the Minitab menu, select Calc > Random Data > Exponential and use the Exponential Distribution form to generate 100 rows of data with Scale = 10 and Threshold = 90, putting the data into a new column called Exponential.

To make a time series plot for comparison, select Graph > Time Series Plot and then a Simple plot from the gallery. Select both columns of data. Click the Multiple Graphs button. Select the In separate panels of the same graph option, and also select the option to use the Same Y scale for both graphs. After creating the graph, add gridlines for the Y major ticks.

Your graph will NOT look exactly like Fig. 4-9. The form of the graph will be similar, but your data will be different. It is, after all, random. But the general

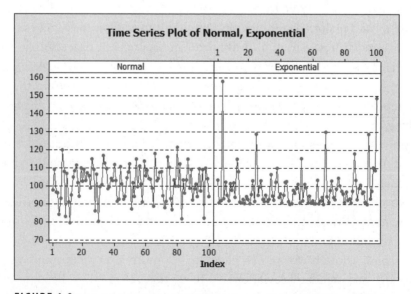

FIGURE 4-9 · Time series plot comparing normal and exponential random data.

pattern of the dots provides some insight into the nature of the two distribution families. The normal data is roughly symmetric around the mean 100, but the exponential data is not symmetric around the mean.

The dashed gridlines in Fig. 4-9 are spaced 10 units, or one standard deviation, apart. In your graph, with different data, the spacing of gridlines might be different. Using these gridlines as a reference, the normal data spreads out about two standard deviations on either side of the mean, sometimes more. The exponential data extends below the mean one standard deviation, to 90, and then stops. We specified 90 as the threshold parameter, which is the absolute minimum value for the exponential data. It is rare to see normal data more than three standard deviations away from the mean on either side, but in this sample of 100 values, the exponential data may extend to six or even more standard deviations above the mean.

Now right-click your graph and select Update Graph Automatically. Select Calc > Random Data > Normal and generate some new normal random data, in the same column. Then generate some new exponential data. How does your graph change? Repeating this process helps to build your understanding of the differences between distribution families.

The coefficient of skewness measures the skew or lack of symmetry of data and distribution models. For the normal and exponential models, the coefficients of skewness are 0 and +2, respectively. If you calculate the sample skewness of your random data, using Stat > Basic Statistics > Display Descriptive Statistics, your skewness should be close to these values. Viewing these graphs in conjunction with the sample skewness is also a good method to build your understanding of what skewness looks like.

Similarly, the coefficient of kurtosis measures the heaviness of the tails of a distribution, relative to the normal distribution. The normal and exponential distribution models have kurtosis of 0 and 6, respectively. How closely does your random data approach 0 and 6?

Most people who do this exercise find that the skewness and kurtosis of 100 normal random numbers is within a few tenths of zero. But the skewness and kurtosis of 100 exponential random numbers may be far from the theoretical values of 2 and 6. In real life, 100 measurements is typically a lot of data. But 100 measurements is not a lot to learn about the shape of a distribution, skewness, or kurtosis, especially when that distribution is very different from the normal distribution.

For an example of Monte Carlo analysis, consider Pat, a mechanical engineer. Pat is designing a piece with a triangular cross-section as shown in Fig. 4-10.

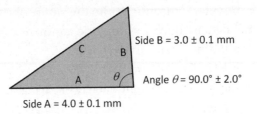

Side B = 3.0 ± 0.1 mm

Angle θ = 90.0° ± 2.0°

Side A = 4.0 ± 0.1 mm

FIGURE 4-10 • What is the distribution of Side C?

Side A has a length specification of 4.0 ± 0.1 mm, Side B has a length specification of 3.0 ± 0.1 mm, and Angle θ has a specification of 90.0° ± 2.0°. Based on these assumptions, what is the distribution of the length of Side C?

The law of cosines provides a formula to calculate the length of Side C:

$$C = \sqrt{A^2 + B^2 - 2AB\cos\theta}$$

The exact distributions of A, B, and θ are unknown, except for the specification limits. Pat decides to assume that A, B, and θ are uniformly distributed between their specification limits. That is, Pat assumes that A has a uniform distribution between 3.9 and 4.1 mm, B has a uniform distribution between 2.9 and 3.1 mm, and θ has a uniform distribution between 88.0° and 92.0°.

Pat decides to perform a Monte Carlo analysis with 1,000 trials, by generating 1,000 random values for A, B, and θ, and then calculating C for each of those trials.

In a new Minitab worksheet, Pat selects Calc > Random Data > Uniform. Pat asks for 1,000 rows of random data, uniformly distributed between 3.9 and 4.1, in a column named A. Similarly, Pat creates a column B with 1,000 uniform random numbers between 2.9 and 3.1, and a column Theta with 1,000 uniform random numbers between 88 and 92. Then, Pat assigns this formula to an empty column: Sqrt(A^2+B^2-2*A*B*cos(radians(Theta))). Figure 4-11 shows a portion of Pat's worksheet at this point.

Note that θ is specified in degrees, but Minitab trigonometry functions require values to be in radians, not degrees. This is consistent with the trigonometry functions in Microsoft Excel. Radians( ) is a convenient function that converts from degrees to radians. Degrees( ) is also available to convert radians into degrees.

Figure 4-12 is a histogram showing the predicted distribution of the length of Side C. From this graph, Pat can decide if the variation of C is acceptable, and Pat can establish reasonable specification limits for C.

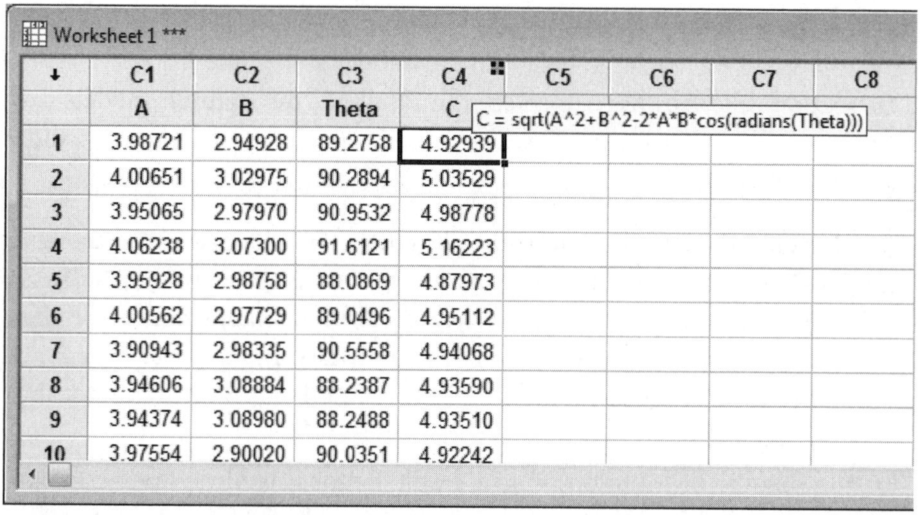

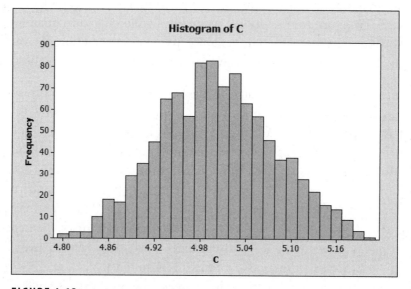

↓	C1	C2	C3	C4	C5	C6	C7	C8
	A	B	Theta	C				
				C = sqrt(A^2+B^2-2*A*B*cos(radians(Theta)))				
1	3.98721	2.94928	89.2758	4.92939				
2	4.00651	3.02975	90.2894	5.03529				
3	3.95065	2.97970	90.9532	4.98778				
4	4.06238	3.07300	91.6121	5.16223				
5	3.95928	2.98758	88.0869	4.87973				
6	4.00562	2.97729	89.0496	4.95112				
7	3.90943	2.98335	90.5558	4.94068				
8	3.94606	3.08884	88.2387	4.93590				
9	3.94374	3.08980	88.2488	4.93510				
10	3.97554	2.90020	90.0351	4.92242				

FIGURE 4-11 • Worksheet with Monte Carlo analysis.

FIGURE 4-12 • Predicted distribution of Side C.

Notice that A, B, and θ all had uniform distributions in the Monte Carlo analysis. So why is the distribution of C more like a triangle? This is because the probability is small that A, B, and θ will all have extremely high or low values simultaneously. But there are more combinations of A, B, and θ values that will result in a middle value for C. Therefore, the final distribution of C has higher probability in the middle than in the tails.

4.4   Selecting a Distribution Model

This section describes how to select the family of distribution models that best fits a random variable or a set of measured data. In general, there are three ways to do this:

- **Matching the distribution to the situation.** This is a process of thought, not computation. Facts known about the system are used to select an appropriate distribution family or to rule out inappropriate families. Minitab cannot help with this matching process. Training and experience does help. The last section of this chapter briefly introduces the distribution families found in Minitab.

- **Viewing the distribution fit on a graph.** Graphs are always powerful statistical tools. Minitab can quickly generate graphs for a variety of distribution families, so the best family becomes easy to select visually.

- **Testing goodness of fit.** Minitab can perform a variety of goodness-of-fit tests. These are computational procedures which measure quantitatively how badly a given distribution family fits a set of data. Using this method, the least bad fitting distribution family is often selected as the best fit.

It is important to realize that any of these methods may be used to select a family of distribution models, but choosing the specific distribution within that family is a separate step automatically handled by Minitab. For example, you might choose the bell-shaped normal distribution family using a combination of distribution matching, graphs, or goodness-of-fit tests. Once this is done, the specific normal distribution is chosen by specifying its mean and standard deviation. In statistics, this step is called parameter estimation. This is performed by a variety of methods which you may study in advanced courses. Since parameter estimation is mathematically difficult, it is best left to Minitab, which will quickly perform this estimation any time it is required.

Minitab offers three types of graphs for selecting distribution families: histograms, empirical CDF plots, and probability plots. A good example dataset to use for learning these graphs is the set of torque measurements in the Minitab sample dataset Cap.MTW. This is an example of real data, where we don't know enough to match a distribution family to the process of applying caps to bottles.

In Chapter 2, various graphs of this dataset suggested that torques applied by the two machines, identified by column C2, are somehow different. For the moment, ignore this issue, and treat all the torque data in column C1 as a sample from one population.

With the Cap.MTW worksheet open, select Graph > Histogram from the Minitab menu. From the gallery of histograms, select With Fit. Enter Torque in the Graph Variables box. Click the Data View button and then click the Distribution tab. Here, a dropdown box presents a library of continuous distribution families. Select Normal and click OK. The resulting histogram, with normal distribution curve, is the top left graph in Fig. 4-13.

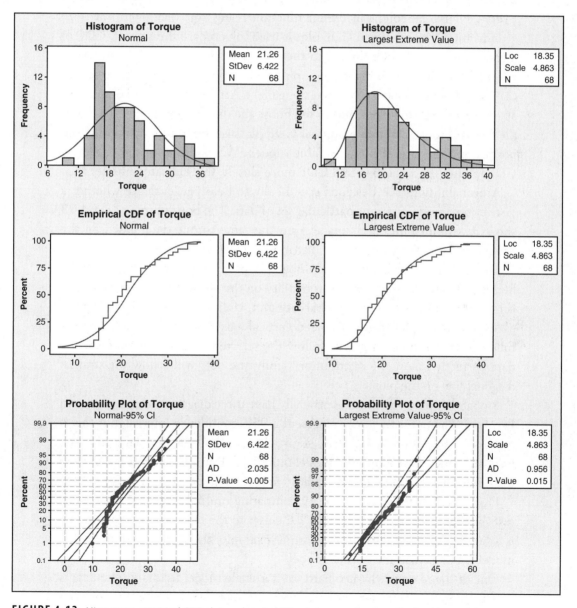

FIGURE 4-13 · Histogram, empirical CDF plot, and probability plot comparing two distribution models.

Now make another histogram, with a fitted distribution, but this time, choose a Largest Extreme Value distribution. This graph is the top right graph in Fig. 4-13. Notice how this probability curve fits the histogram better than the normal curve.

The probability curves in these histograms are probability density functions (PDF). A cumulative distribution function (CDF) is a different way to describe a distribution in terms of the cumulative probability of observing smaller values. Every CDF is a monotone increasing function, rising from 0 at $-\infty$ to 1 at $+\infty$.

In Minitab, the empirical CDF plot is used to compare the smooth CDF of a continuous distribution model to the empirical CDF of the dataset, which resembles a staircase. To make an empirical CDF plot, select Graph > Empirical CDF and choose a Simple plot from the gallery. After choosing the Graph Variables, click the Distributions button to choose the distribution model. The middle row of Fig. 4-13 shows empirical CDF plots of the torque data, using the normal and the largest extreme value models. When the stair-step empirical CDF follows the smooth model CDF more closely, this indicates a better fit.

A probability plot is designed specifically to help you evaluate whether a distribution model fits your particular set of data. The bottom row of Fig. 4-13 shows two probability plots made from the same torque data, based on the normal and largest extreme value distribution families.

Like the empirical CDF plot, a probability plot uses the data values for the horizontal axis, and cumulative probability on the vertical axis. The data itself is represented by dots on the probability plot. Unlike the empirical CDF plot, each probability plot uses a distorted vertical axis designed to make the dots follow a straight line, if the data follow the selected distribution family. If the data perfectly follow the distribution family, the dots will follow the straight diagonal line on the plot.

Probability plots in Minitab optionally have three diagonal lines, as shown in Fig. 4-13. The outer two lines represent a 95% confidence interval, but this is more of a suggestion than a strict statistical test. If all the dots fall inside the lines, then the data follows the model quite well. But if a few dots fall outside the outer lines, this does not necessarily mean the model should be rejected.

Probability plots are best used by comparing multiple plots with different distribution models. When the dots fall closer to the diagonal line, that model is a better fit to the data. In the torque example, the largest extreme value model is better than the normal model.

One of the reasons why it is hard to fit a single model to this torque data is that the data represent a mixture of two different distributions, one for each machine. An interval chart of torque by machine, shown in Chapter 2, visually shows the difference in mean torque. In Minitab, either the empirical CDF plot or the probability plot can be created to fit different models from the same distribution family to different groups in the data.

For example, select Graph > Probability Plot from the menu. Then select a Multiple plot from the gallery. Select Torque for Graph Variables, and Machine for Categorical Variables. Select the Largest extreme value distribution model. Figure 4-14 shows the resulting plot, combining two probability plots for the two groups of data into one plot. In this plot, the dots follow the middle diagonal lines fairly closely for Machine 1, but not so closely for Machine 2. The two machines may be following two different distribution models.

Between histograms, empirical CDF plots, and probability plots, which one is best? The answer depends on what you need to accomplish. For a presentation, histograms are usually best because they are understood by more people, even those without statistical training. However, the best plot for an analyst to compare and select distribution models is the probability plot, because it is very easy to see when dots follow or veer away from a straight diagonal line. However, none of these plots provide a quantitative measure of fit. For this, we need to perform a goodness-of-fit test.

Goodness-of-fit tests are among many statistical tools with odd names, because these tests actually measure how badly a model fits. Each goodness-of-fit test

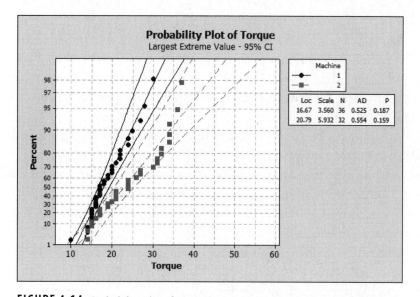

FIGURE 4-14 · Probability plot of torque by machine, with largest extreme value model.

starts with a set of data and a hypothetical distribution model. A test statistic is calculated, which measures how badly the distribution fits the available data. A higher value for this test statistic indicates a worse fitting model.

Many different procedures have been proposed for goodness-of-fit tests, but the one generally used in Minitab for continuous distribution models is called the Anderson–Darling or AD test. Minitab automatically performs this test every time a probability plot is generated. Look at the probability plots in the bottom row of Fig. 4-13. Each one lists an AD statistic in the box to the right of the plot. The AD statistic is 2.035 for the normal model, and 0.956 for the largest extreme value model, indicating that the normal model is the worst fitting model between the two of them. Compare this to the AD statistics for the two groups in this data, listed in Fig. 4-14. Since these AD statistics are 0.525 and 0.554, by this measure, the largest extreme value model fits the torque from Machine 2 less well than Machine 1. These conclusions should be the same as one would conclude by looking at the probability plots.

Minitab provides an additional way to interpret the AD test by converting the test statistic into a p-value, identified by P in the plots. A p-value is the probability, between 0 and 1, that data following the model would be at least as badly fitting as the data tested. As usually interpreted, a small p-value, less than 0.05, means that the model should be rejected because of significant lack of fit. If the p-value is larger than 0.05, then there is no reason to reject the model.

In Fig. 4-13, both the normal and largest extreme value models have very small p-values, meaning that both models have significant lack of fit. But in Fig. 4-14, after fitting separate models to each group of data, the p-values are larger than 0.05, meaning that there is insufficient evidence to reject these models.

You might expect these goodness-of-fit tests to tell you whether to accept a model, but for a variety of reasons, statistical tools do not work that way. Since these tests measure the lack of fit, they can only tell you if the model should be rejected for lack of fit. If there is insufficient evidence for lack of fit, the statistical tools can't advise you to accept the model. The final choice of which model to accept is up to you as the analyst.

Minitab offers another powerful tool which makes it easy to compare many continuous distribution models at once. This is the Individual Distribution Identification tool found in the Stat > Quality Tools menu.

To try this tool on a different dataset, open the Minitab example data file Circuit.MTW. This file lists the age of 80 pressure sensors at the time they failed. The age is measured in weeks and listed in column 1. Is this dataset normally distributed? A normal probability plot, which you can quickly generate from the Graph menu, indicates that the answer is no. In fact, the Anderson–Darling goodness-of-fit test returns a p-value of <0.005, affirming that the normal model is not appropriate for this data.

Which models are more appropriate? To quickly test this dataset against a wide variety of distribution models, select Stat > Quality Tools > Individual Distribution Identification from the menu. Enter Weeks in the Single column box. Select Specify, and use the default four distribution families of Normal, Exponential, Weibull, and Gamma. After clicking OK, the set of probability plots shown in Fig. 4-15 appears.

It is clear from the probability plots that normal and exponential models do not fit the data, but either Weibull or gamma look like good fits for this data. The box to the right of the plots lists results from the Anderson–Darling goodness-of-fit test. The gamma distribution has the lowest AD statistic, 0.201, so this may be the best fitting distribution model.

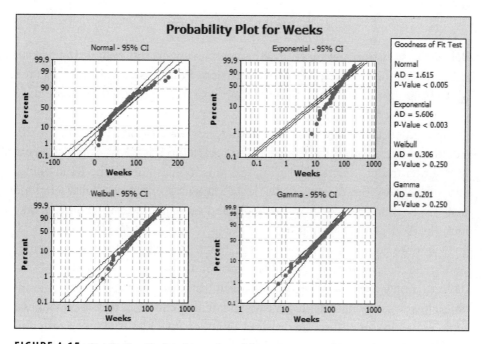

FIGURE 4-15 · Distribution ID plots for weeks to failure.

For more information, the Session window contains this report:

Distribution ID Plot for Weeks

```
Descriptive Statistics

 N N*    Mean   StDev  Median  Minimum  Maximum  Skewness  Kurtosis
80  0  64.125  39.7764      58        7      192   1.07345   1.07890


Goodness of Fit Test

Distribution      AD        P
Normal          1.615  <0.005
Exponential     5.606  <0.003
Weibull         0.306  >0.250
Gamma           0.201  >0.250


ML Estimates of Distribution Parameters

Distribution  Location    Shape     Scale  Threshold
Normal*       64.12500            39.77639
Exponential                       64.12500
Weibull                 1.70722   72.13091
Gamma                   2.57221   24.92988


* Scale: Adjusted ML estimate
```

Below the statistical summary and the goodness-of-fit test results, the Session window lists the parameters of all distributions fit to this data. In this case, the best fitting gamma distribution has a shape parameter of 2.57221 and a scale parameter of 24.92988.

Sometimes, all we care about is whether the data are normal or not. For this situation, Minitab offers the Normality Test tool in the Stat > Basic Statistics menu. In addition to the Anderson–Darling test, this tool also offers the Ryan–Joiner and Kolmogorov–Smirnov normality tests. The subtle differences between these tests are beyond the scope of this book, and most people will choose to stay with the Anderson–Darling test.

One more goodness-of-fit test is available in Minitab. So far, these distribution fitting tools have been designed for continuous data only. When the data are discrete counts, the plots and goodness-of-fit tests described above are not available. However, the Stat > Basic Statistics menu does contain a tool for Goodness-of-fit Test for Poisson, a discrete distribution for counts. This tool uses a different type of test, called a chi-squared test, to test discrete data against a Poisson distribution model.

The Poisson distribution is simple, with only one parameter, λ, and λ is also the mean value. The Poisson distribution is one of the most widely used discrete models. When events happen independently at the same mean rate per unit time, the count of events typically has a Poisson distribution.

For example, open the Minitab sample dataset Accident.MTW. This worksheet lists the accidents per week at one dangerous intersection, over the course of 50 weeks. If each accident is independent of other accidents, this scenario seems to fit the general Poisson template. But does this data follow the Poisson distribution?

To answer this question, select Stat > Basic Statistics > Goodness-of-fit Test for Poisson from the Minitab menu. Select Accidents for the Variable and click OK. The following report appears in the Session window:

Goodness-of-Fit Test for Poisson Distribution

Data column: Accidents

Poisson mean for Accidents = 2.24

Accidents	Observed	Poisson Probability	Expected	Contribution to Chi-Sq
0	7	0.106459	5.3229	0.52839
1	8	0.238467	11.9234	1.29097
2	13	0.267083	13.3542	0.00939
3	10	0.199422	9.9711	0.00008
>=4	12	0.188569	9.4285	0.70136

N	N*	DF	Chi-Sq	P-Value
50	0	3	2.53020	0.470

Minitab first estimates the mean accidents per week, which is 2.24. This is the estimated value of λ. Then, Minitab compares the observed to the expected count of values, over several categories of values found in the dataset. This is analogous to comparing a histogram of the data to the hypothetical distribution model. Minitab then computes a chi-squared test statistic, which is 2.53020, and a p-value, which is 0.470.

Since the p-value of 0.470 is larger than 0.05, there is no evidence in this data to reject the Poisson model.

4.5   Selecting a Normalizing Transformation

The normal, also known as Gaussian, distribution has a special place in statistics. Two hundred years ago, Carl Gauss observed that the means of repeated measurements tend to have a bell-shaped distribution. Today we know this important result as the central limit theorem (CLT). Regardless of the distribution of individual values, the CLT says that the mean of many independent values approaches a normal distribution as more values are included in the mean.

Many important statistical tools, including *t*-tests, analysis of variance (ANOVA), and most control charts are based on the assumption of normality. If the underlying distribution is not normal, the results of these procedures can be incorrect or misleading.

If you need to perform a test which assumes normality, fitting a nonnormal distribution model as described in the previous section may not be helpful. A useful alternative is to find an appropriate normalizing transformation. Minitab can help identify the best function which transforms a set of data into an approximately normal distribution. The transformed data may then be tested with any normal-based statistical methods.

Minitab offers two families of normalizing transformations:

- **Box–Cox transformation.** This family of transformations includes power transformations of the form $W = Y^\lambda$ when $\lambda \neq 0$, and $W = \ln Y$ when $\lambda = 0$. In addition to the log transformation, this family includes the square, square root, and inverse transformations. Many types of skewed distributions can be successfully normalized using this method. Because of the simplicity of the functions involved, the Box–Cox transformation is a widely accepted normalization tool.

- **Johnson transformation.** The Johnson family of distributions is a very large and flexible family with the common property that any Johnson distribution can be transformed into a normal distribution by a function called the Johnson transformation. The Johnson distribution includes three families for different situations: unbounded (Type SU), bounded on the left (SL), and bounded left and right (SB). Minitab uses an algorithm to select the best Johnson transformation based on the Anderson–Darling normality test applied to the transformed data.

For an example of a normalizing transformation, open the Minitab example data file Circuit.MTW. Column C1 (Weeks) lists the time-to-failure of a circuit, measured in weeks. In the previous section, a gamma distribution was suggested as a good fitting model for the Weeks data. This is only useful if the gamma distribution can be used to answer your questions about the reliability of this system. If you want to create a control chart, which many experts say is highly sensitive to the shape of the distribution, a normalizing transformation would be more appropriate than charting the untransformed data. See Chapter 11 for more information on control charts.

To find a good Box–Cox transformation, select Stat > Control Charts > Box-Cox Transformation from the menu. From the dropdown box, select All observations for a chart are in one column. Select Weeks for the column to transform, and enter 1 for the Subgroup size.

Figure 4-16 shows the graph produced by this procedure. The results are listed in the text box. Minitab found the best value of the power λ is 0.43, with a confidence interval of 0.06 to 0.74. The confidence interval means that the best value of λ could be anything between 0.06 and 0.74. Minitab suggests a rounded value of $\lambda = 0.50$ for a final transformation of $W = \sqrt{Y}$. Since it is easier to communicate a simple expression like $\sqrt{Y}$ than $Y^{0.43}$, the rounded value of λ is generally preferred.

The graph in Fig. 4-16 shows the standard deviation of a standardized version of the dataset after raising to various powers. Box and Cox (1964) showed that this quantity is minimized by the best normalizing transformation. This is how Minitab finds the best value of λ. As with all Minitab procedures, more details are available in the StatGuide or by clicking Help > Methods and Formulas.

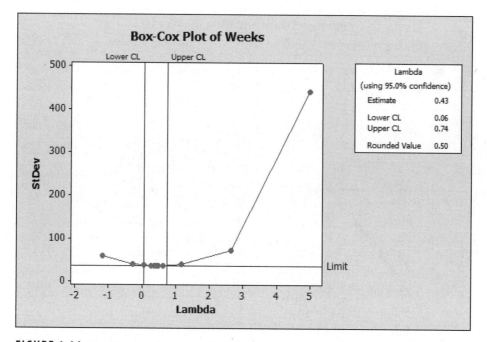

FIGURE 4-16 · Box–Cox transformation of Weeks data.

The Options button in the Box-Cox dialog allows you to calculate and store the transformed data in a new column of the worksheet for further analysis.

The Johnson transformation has become popular in the quality control area, and its Minitab function can now be found at Stat > Quality Tools > Johnson transformation. In the Johnson dialog, select the Single column option, and enter the name of the column.

Figure 4-17 is the graph produced by the Johnson transformation procedure. This graph contains two probability plots, created before and after applying the best-fitting transformation. Minitab selects the best Johnson transformation by looking for the largest p-value for an Anderson–Darling normality test applied to the transformed data. The text box in the graph notes that Minitab has selected a transformation from type SB, which means that the untransformed data is assumed to be bounded on both the left and the right. The selected transformation formula listed in the figure is much more complicated than the Box–Cox transformation, but the normality of the transformed data is impressive.

Perhaps an easier way to apply both transformations at once is using the Individual Distribution Identification tool, also in the Stat > Quality Tools menu. The

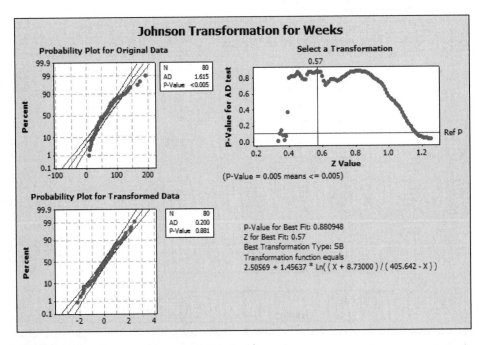

FIGURE 4-17 • Johnson transformation of Weeks data.

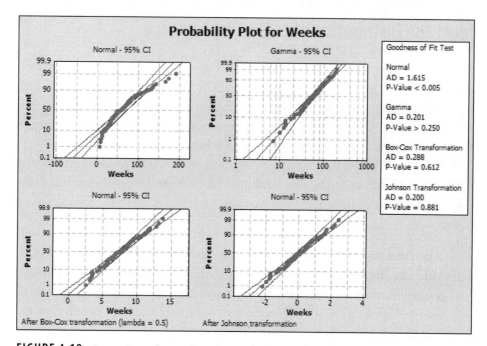

FIGURE 4-18 · Comparison of normal, gamma, and transformation models.

dropdown box listing available distribution families includes both Box–Cox and Johnson transformations. Figure 4-18 shows four probability plots generated by this function:

- a normal probability plot of the raw data
- a gamma probability plot of the raw data
- a normal probability plot of the Box–Cox transformed data
- a normal probability plot of the Johnson transformed data

Except for the first plot, this figure shows three very acceptable models for the Weeks data, one distribution and two transformation models.

But which model is best? It depends on what you what to do with it. Many reliability or survival analysis tools (See Chapter 14) work well with the gamma distribution model. Other tools may require a normal distribution, and for these tools, the square root transformation recommended by Box–Cox may be the best approach. The Johnson transformation is not appreciably better than Box–Cox in this case, and it is certainly more complicated.

In general, the simplest model which meets your needs is the best choice.

4.6   Meet the Distributions

Each distribution in Minitab's arsenal has its uses, and no one is going to need them all. Still, it is good to have some familiarity with the various models. This section gives a very brief introduction to each distribution family, without pictures or formulas. You can create your own pictures using Graph > Probability Distribution Plot. Some formulas are listed in Minitab's Methods and Formulas help file.

If your work frequently involves selecting distribution models, one of the several good distribution catalog books would be a good investment. These are discussed further at the end of the chapter.

Here are the distributions in Minitab, in the order listed in the menu:

- The **chi-square** (χ^2) distribution describes how the sum of squared standard normal random variables is distributed. This distribution is used for a large number of hypothesis tests involving variances, contingency tables, and goodness-of-fit. The chi-square distribution is always positive, and it is a special case of the gamma distribution.

- The **normal** (also known as Gaussian) distribution is the most widely known and applied distribution in statistics, with a familiar bell-shaped probability curve. Because of the central limit theorem, sums and means of independent random variables tend to be normally distributed, regardless of the distribution of the individual data. The normal distribution is symmetric around its mean.

- The *F* distribution describes how a scaled ratio of two chi-square random variables is distributed. The *F* distribution is used in many tests related to variances, including analysis of variance (ANOVA). The *F* distribution is always positive.

- The *t* distribution (also known as Student's *t*) describes how a standard normal random variable divided by the square root of a scaled chi-square random variable is distributed. The *t* distribution is used in tests related to means. The *t* distribution is symmetric around zero, and has heavier tails (higher kurtosis) than a normal distribution.

- The **uniform** distribution is a continuous distribution which may have any value between two limits with equal probability.

- The **binomial** distribution is a discrete distribution with nonnegative integer values. In a set of independent pass/fail trials, where each trial has the same probability of passing, the count of passing trials during a fixed number of trials has a binomial distribution.

- The **geometric** distribution is a discrete distribution with positive integer values. In a series of independent pass/fail trials, where each trial has the same probability of passing, the count of trials up to and including the first passing trial has a geometric distribution. An optional version of the geometric distribution, starting at 0, counts the failing trials before the first pass. Minitab supports both versions.

- The **negative binomial** distribution is a discrete distribution with positive integer values. In a series of independent pass/fail trials, where each trial has the same probability of passing, the count of trials up to and including the kth passing trial has a negative binomial distribution. The minimum possible value is k. An optional version of the negative binomial distribution, starting at 0, counts only the failing trials before the kth pass. Minitab supports both versions. When k is an integer, the negative binomial distribution is also known as the Pascal distribution.

- The **hypergeometric** distribution is a discrete distribution with nonnegative integer values. In a situation where items are selected at random from a finite population containing two types of items, the count of one type of item selected out of a fixed number of selections has a hypergeometric distribution. This model is used to calculate probabilities for games and finite population sampling in quality control.

- The **discrete** distribution in Minitab is a distribution you define yourself by providing a set of values and a set of probabilities in two columns of the worksheet.

- The **integer** distribution in Minitab is a discrete distribution which can have any integer value in a range specified by you, and each integer in the range has equal probability. This is the discrete analog to the continuous uniform distribution.

- The **Poisson** distribution is a discrete distribution with non-negative integer values. A homogeneous Poisson process is a system in which events happen independently with the same mean rate. The count of events per unit time in a Poisson process has a Poisson distribution. This is the most commonly used discrete distribution, with applications in virtually every field.

- The **beta** distribution is bounded on the left and the right, and it can assume a wide variety of shapes between those boundaries, based on its two shape parameters.

- The **Cauchy** distribution is a bell-shaped distribution, symmetric around its location parameter, but the tails of the distribution approach zero less quickly than a normal distribution. The tails of this distribution are so heavy that none of its moments exist, including the mean.

- The **exponential** distribution is bounded on the left by its threshold parameter, which is usually zero. The time between events in a homogeneous Poisson process has an exponential distribution. In some Minitab procedures, the exponential distribution has a fixed threshold parameter of zero, while the **2-parameter exponential** distribution allows the threshold parameter to be nonzero.

- The **gamma** distribution is bounded on the left by its threshold parameter. The gamma distribution is a frequent model for waiting times. Gamma random variables can assume a wide variety of shapes, depending on the shape parameter. Special cases of the gamma family include exponential, Erlang, and chi-square distributions. In some Minitab procedures, the gamma distribution has a fixed threshold parameter of zero, while the **3-parameter gamma** allows the threshold parameter to be nonzero.

- The **Laplace** distribution (also known as double exponential) is symmetric around zero, with a probability curve that looks like two exponential probability curves back to back. It has heavier tails (higher kurtosis) than a normal distribution.

- The **largest extreme value** (also known as Gumbel) is an asymmetric, unbounded distribution with positive (right) skew. In some cases, the largest value in a large set of independent random variables has a largest extreme value distribution.

- The **logistic** distribution is a symmetric, bell-shaped distribution. With a kurtosis of 1.2, the logistic distribution has somewhat heavier tails than a normal distribution.

- The **loglogistic** distribution is bounded on the left by its threshold parameter. The log of a loglogistic random variable follows a logistic distribution. In some Minitab procedures, the loglogistic distribution has a fixed threshold parameter of zero, while the **3-parameter loglogistic** allows the threshold parameter to be nonzero.

- The **lognormal** distribution is bounded on the left by its threshold parameter. The log of a lognormal random variable follows a normal distribution. In some Minitab procedures, the lognormal distribution has a fixed threshold parameter of zero, while the **3-parameter lognormal** allows the threshold parameter to be nonzero.

- The **smallest extreme value** distribution is an asymmetric, unbounded distribution with negative (left) skew. In some cases, the smallest value in a large set of independent random variables has a smallest extreme value distribution. For this reason, this can be regarded as a "weakest link" distribution, and it is important in reliability and survival analysis.

- The **triangular** distribution is a bounded distribution with a triangular probability curve specified by its minimum value, most likely value, and maximum value.

- The **Weibull** distribution is bounded on the left by its threshold parameter. An exponential random variable raised to a positive power has a Weibull distribution. In some cases, the smallest value in a large set of independent random variables has a Weibull distribution. Like the smallest extreme value, Weibull can be regarded as a "weakest link" distribution, and it is important in reliability and survival analysis. Exponential and Rayleigh distributions are special cases of the Weibull distribution. In some Minitab procedures, the Weibull distribution has a fixed threshold parameter of zero, while the **3-parameter Weibull** allows the threshold parameter to be nonzero.

4.7   A Word of Caution

For many, distribution modeling is a fascinating and important topic. But it is easy to get carried away to the point where distribution modeling becomes counterproductive. As one who has been burned by overmodeling, the author offers two pieces of sage advice.

> Sage advice #1: **The model is not the message. The model is the medium through which the message is revealed.**

In the real world, all measured data include both signals and noise, combined together. Signals are the changes, effects, and messages we need to see and measure to make decisions. Noise is the random variation which obscures the signals. Distribution models are tools to model the noise, so that the signals can be detected, separated from the noise, and measured more precisely.

A common trap is to fit an exotic distribution model or transformation model to the combination of signals and noise, so that all signals appear to be noise, and the signals disappear. If occasional unusually large values are seen in a set of data, the first step ought to be to look for causes for those large values, not to seek a skewed distribution model that incorporates those large values into the noise model and masks them.

Sage advice #2: **Always choose the simplest model that works.**

A model that works is one that satisfies the requirements of the science or the business. If Minitab says the best model is a 3-parameter loglogistic distribution, no law says you have to use it. If that specific model allows some vital information to be revealed, it's a good model. But if a simpler exponential or normal model reveals the same information, the fancy model is just showing off.

Keep in mind the requirements of your customers, the history of the system being studied, and the science behind the system. A simple distribution model that crisply models the noise, allowing the right decisions to be made at the right time, is a beautiful thing.

Finally, it is also worth noting that distribution models provide benefits, but they are not mandatory. Many statistical procedures have nonparametric versions which do not assume any distribution model. In Minitab, some of these nonparametric tools are integrated with their parametric cousins in the same tools and dialogs. Minitab also offers a special Stat > Nonparametrics menu which collects many nonparametric tools in one place. For space reasons, these nonparametric tools are not covered specifically in this introductory book, but they represent important additions to the analyst's toolbox.

4.8   Find Out More

The Individual Distribution Identification tool in Minitab has many features not explained in this chapter. It will be revisited in Chapter 14. To learn more about how to interpret the output in the Session window, consult the Minitab help files, or visit the Minitab knowledgebase at www.minitab.com, and search for ID 1724.

A catalog of distribution models is a smart addition to any reference bookshelf. Sleeper (2007) is an excellent choice, providing industrial application examples, with full references to Minitab and Excel functions. It's also great for Father's Day, housewarmings, or any special occasion. Evans, Hastings, and Peacock (2000) is a good paperback catalog with a more academic focus. The encyclopedic reference in this area continues to be the set of several volumes by Johnson, Kotz, et al.

Box and Cox (1964) and Johnson (1949) devised their eponymous transformations, and Chou, Polansky, and Mason (1998) developed the method Minitab uses to select the best Johnson transformation.

This chapter introduced graphical and statistical tools for selecting the most appropriate distribution model. When appropriate, normalizing transformations are also available. The next chapter discusses the popular statistical decision-making tools of confidence intervals, prediction intervals, and tolerance intervals.

QUIZ

1. If you roll five fair six-sided dice, what is the probability of at least three of those dice landing with side #6 on top?

    A. 0.03215

    B. 0.03549

    C. 0.9645

    D. 0.9967

2. In a standard American Roulette game, the probability of any one number winning is $1/38 \approx 0.026316$. If you bet $1 on your lucky number, 9, in every game, what is the probability that you will lose $50 or more before your first win?

    A. 0.2636

    B. 0.2707

    C. 0.7364

    D. 0.7434

3. Suppose the yield strength of a certain type of steel is normally distributed with a mean of 250 and a standard deviation of 10. What is the probability that the strength of one piece of this steel will be less than 220?

    A. 0.00135

    B. 0.0027

    C. 0.01

    D. 0.025

4. For the same piece of steel with normally distributed strength with mean 250 and standard deviation 10, what strength is less than the strength of 99.5% of all samples of this steel?

    A. 215.487

    B. 224.242

    C. 233.551

    D. 275.758

5. The time between calls received at a certain call center has an exponential distribution with a scale parameter (mean) of 30 seconds, and a threshold parameter of 0. What is the probability that no calls will be received for 120 seconds or more?

    A. 0.9817

    B. 0.6321

    C. 0.1553

    D. 0.0183

6. When comparing the Anderson–Darling goodness-of-fit test results between different distribution models, which set of test results indicates the best fitting distribution model?

    A. The highest AD statistic and/or the highest p-value

    B. The highest AD statistic and/or the lowest p-value

    C. The lowest AD statistic and/or the highest *p*-value

    D. The lowest AD statistic and/or the lowest *p*-value

7. **The Minitab example data file** Grades.MTW **lists the SAT scores and grade point averages (GPAs) for a set of students. Which of the following distribution models is the best fit to the GPA data in this file:**

    A. Normal

    B. Weibull

    C. Gamma

    D. Box–Cox transformation

8. **Create a single graph that compares the probability density function (PDF) of the gamma distribution, for shape parameters of 1, 2, 3, 4, and 5, all with scale parameter = 1 and threshold parameter = 0.**

9. **The Minitab example data file** Train.MTW **lists the days between replacements of two types of brake components in trains. The Days are listed in C2, and the Type (1 or 2) is listed in C3. Create a normal probability plot showing how two separate normal models fit to the Days data for each Type of component.**

10. **Open the Minitab example data file** Boxcox.MTW. **Apply the Box–Cox transformation to identify the best normalizing transformation for this data. Then create two histograms showing data before and after the transformation.**

11. **Extra Credit: What distribution family best fits the "Skewed" data in** Boxcox.MTW? **Triple extra credit if you can do this without running any Minitab functions other than what you did for question 10.**

chapter 5

Making Decisions with Intervals

In a world full of uncertainty, statistical tools allow us to make decisions with high confidence. Among the simplest of these tools to understand and apply are intervals. An interval is simply a range of values possessing some property relevant to the required decision, with a known probability that the interval is correct. This probability is called the confidence level. Minitab provides tools and support for three different types of intervals: confidence intervals, prediction intervals, and, new in Minitab 16, tolerance intervals.

CHAPTER OBJECTIVES

Here's what you'll learn in this chapter:

- How to select the right interval for your problem
- How to calculate and interpret confidence intervals for the normal mean, standard deviation, variance, binomial proportion, and Poisson rate
- How to calculate and interpret prediction intervals based on one sample of data
- How to calculate and interpret normal tolerance intervals
- How to download and install Minitab macros to extend Minitab functionality

5.1   Confidence, Prediction, and Tolerance Intervals

The modern statistical toolbox offers several different types of intervals, so it is natural to be confused about which is the appropriate interval for your situation. This section explains the usage of three common types of statistical intervals: confidence intervals, prediction intervals, and tolerance intervals. All of these intervals have a confidence level, so multiple uses of the word "confidence" may cause part of this confusion.

Every statistical interval is a statement about something unknown, based on what is known, a sample of data. Since data always vary randomly, the statement made by the interval may or may not be true. The confidence level is the probability that the statement is true. The confidence level is chosen in advance, and this choice controls the width of the interval.

An alternate way to measure the probability that an interval is true is the error rate α (alpha), which equals 1 minus the confidence level. Alpha is the probability that the statement made by the interval is false.

Figure 5-1 illustrates the distinction between confidence, prediction, and tolerance intervals.

- A **confidence interval** is a range of values that contains the true value of a population parameter such as the mean or the standard deviation. The probability that the selected parameter is inside the confidence interval is the confidence level. When estimating a population parameter, a confidence interval is a good way to quantify the uncertainty in that estimate.

- A **prediction interval** is a range of values that contains a single, future value. The probability that one future value will be inside the prediction interval is the confidence level. When predicting a future value, a prediction interval is a good way to quantify the uncertainty in that estimate.

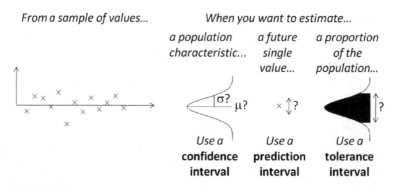

FIGURE 5-1 · Selecting the right interval.

Prediction intervals may also be used to estimate the mean or standard deviation of a future sample of many values from the same population.

- A **tolerance interval** is a range of values that contains a specified proportion of the population of values. The probability that the tolerance interval contains at least the specified proportion of values is the confidence level. When specifying limits that must contain a proportion of the population, a tolerance interval is a good way to quantify the uncertainty in that estimate. Tolerance intervals can be confusing because each interval is described by two percentages: a confidence level and a containment percentage.

For example, suppose Leo has received a set of 30 parts. He measures a critical characteristic of all 30 parts. Leo uses the Minitab graphical summary to prepare an initial summary of the data. The sample mean is $\overline{X} = 100$ and the standard deviation is $s = 10$. Further, the p-value for the Anderson–Darling normality test is about 0.6, indicating that the normal distribution is a reasonable model for this dataset.

Note that this example provides no instructions for calculating intervals. These are given in the following sections of this chapter. This example only illustrates the appropriate uses of different types of intervals in different scenarios.

Which interval does Leo need to use? The correct interval depends on the question Leo wants to answer. Consider four scenarios:

- In the first scenario, suppose Leo has a long history of measurements of this part. Over time, these measurements have been normally distributed with a mean of 105 and a standard deviation of 9. Does this sample of 30 parts provide significant evidence of a change in the population of parts? One way to answer this question is to calculate confidence intervals for the mean and standard deviation.

  - Based on the new sample of 30 parts, a 95% confidence interval for the mean is (96.27, 103.73). Since the historical mean of 105 is outside this range, Leo can be at least 95% confident that the mean has shifted down from 105 to somewhere between 96.27 and 103.73 with this set of parts.

  - Based on the new sample of 30 parts, a 95% confidence interval for the standard deviation is (7.96, 13.44). Since the historical standard deviation of 9 is inside this range, there is no evidence of a significant change in variation.

- In the second scenario, suppose there is no historical data, and this set of 30 represents the first of these parts ever made. The next part, with serial number 31, will be shipped directly to Leo's customer, and Leo will not have the chance to measure it. What can Leo say about the 31st part without seeing it? One way to answer this question is to calculate a prediction interval for one future part.

  - Based on the sample of 30 parts, a 95% prediction interval for one future part is (79.21, 120.79). Leo can be 95% confident that the next part manufactured will measure within this range.

- In the third scenario, suppose there is no historical data. The next 10 parts, with serial numbers 31–40, will be shipped directly to Leo's customer. What can Leo say about the distribution of the next 10 parts? One way to answer this question is to calculate prediction intervals for the mean and standard deviation of a future sample of size 10.

  - A 95% prediction interval for the mean of a future sample of size 10 is (92.53, 107. 47). A 95% prediction interval for the standard deviation of a future sample of size 10 is (5.29, 16.10). Leo can be 95% sure that the mean and standard deviation of the next ten parts will be within these limits.

- In the fourth scenario, suppose Leo is an engineer who needs to establish specification limits for this part, and this sample of 30 provides the only information available. He wants the limits to be wide enough that 99% of all parts will lie within those limits. One way to establish these limits is to calculate a tolerance interval.

  - A tolerance interval providing 95% confidence of covering at least 99% of the population is (66.41, 133.59). Leo can be 95% confident that 99% of the individual units will fall within this interval.

Figure 5-2 compares the width of four of these intervals pertaining to individual values and means. The sample standard deviation in this example is 10, which is also the interval between vertical grid lines in this plot.

All of these intervals have two-sided and one-sided versions. The intervals in the scenarios above are all two-sided intervals. When only one limit is needed to make the required decision, a one-sided interval is more appropriate. Figure 5-3 illustrates a two-sided interval, a one-sided interval with an upper limit, and a one-sided interval with a lower limit. The ends of the two-sided interval are usually called "limits," while the single end of a one-sided interval is usually called a "bound," but these terms are also used interchangeably.

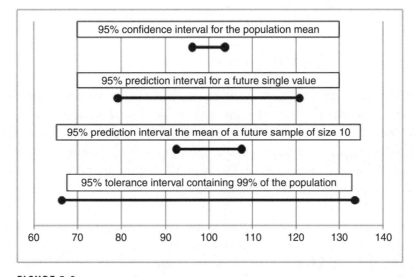

FIGURE 5-2 • Comparison of intervals.

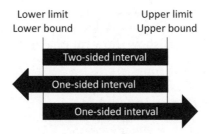

FIGURE 5-3 • Two-sided and one-sided intervals.

Take the first scenario above for an example. Historically, the standard deviation is 9, but this set of parts has a standard deviation of 10. If there is a significant increase in variation, this would be alarming, but Leo might not care if there is a significant decrease in variation. Suppose Leo would only take action if the standard deviation increases significantly.

Using the same data, a 95% one-sided lower confidence bound for the population standard deviation is 8.3. This one-sided interval includes all values between 8.3 and +∞. The lower confidence bound is higher than the lower limit of the two-sided interval. However, since the historical standard deviation, 9, is still within the one-sided interval, there is no evidence of a significant increase in variation.

❓ Still Struggling

All of the intervals have 95% confidence. Why 95% and not some other level? For a variety of reasons, 95% has become a customary default confidence level, but it is not always appropriate. If you calculate a lot of 95% intervals, on average 95% (19 out of 20) will be correct, and 5% (1 out of 20) will be incorrect. In the case of 95% confidence intervals for the population mean μ, 95% of the confidence intervals will contain μ and 5% will not.

To select the best confidence level, think about the impact of making an incorrect decision based on an incorrect interval. In some situations, this is called a "false alarm," with the probability $\alpha = 1 -$ the confidence level. If this impact is unusually severe, the confidence level can be raised to 99% or higher, but not as high as 100%. Increasing the confidence level makes the interval wider. Sometimes the impact of a false alarm is not very bad, but an excessively wide interval makes it hard to ever make a decision. In these cases, the confidence level can be reduced.

The following sections show how to make all these calculations in Minitab 16.

5.2   Calculating Confidence Intervals

Confidence intervals have already appeared in earlier chapters of this book:

- Chapter 2 introduced the Minitab graphical summary, in Fig. 2-1. This summary presents a variety of graphs and numerical statistics in a quick, convenient format. Included in the graphical summary are 95% confidence intervals for the mean, median, and standard deviation, under the assumption that the data follow a normal distribution. A graphical representation of the mean and median confidence intervals appears at the bottom left of the summary.

- Later in Chapter 2, Fig. 2-4 includes an interval plot, a graphical presentation of the 95% confidence interval for the mean.

- Figure 2-6 combines an interval plot with an individual value plot for three categories of data in one dataset. When the confidence intervals do not overlap, this provides strong evidence of a difference in means between categories.

- In Chapter 4, Fig. 4-16 presents a 95% confidence interval for the power λ of the best Box–Cox transformation for normalizing a dataset.

In this section, you will learn other ways to use Minitab to calculate confidence intervals for means, standard deviations, proportions, and rates.

In Chapter 6, which covers hypothesis tests, we will find that every confidence interval is associated with a hypothesis test for the same class of problem. In Minitab, both confidence intervals and hypothesis tests are accessed through the same menu items. Hypothesis tests can be more flexible tools, but they also tend to be more confusing than confidence intervals. For this reason, confidence intervals are presented first.

5.2.1   Confidence Intervals for the Mean of a Normal Distribution

Suppose that the normal (Gaussian) distribution is a reasonable model for a population of data. Many simple and convenient tools are available when this assumption is valid. Among these tools are confidence intervals for the population mean μ, based on Student's *t* distribution.

As an example, consider Gordon, a nutrition science major. For a senior project, Gordon wants to determine if the nutrition information published by a major fast food company matches the actual nutrition content of food sold. According to the company's Web site, the "Gordoburger" (Gordon's personal favorite) contains 15.0 grams of total fat. Gordon goes to all 13 of the company's restaurants in his city and buys one Gordoburger from each. These burgers are submitted to the university lab for total fat measurement. The results may be found in the Minitab example data file Fat.MTW.

Gordon first produces a graphical summary of the data, shown in Fig. 5-4. (This function is found in the Minitab menus as Stat > Basic Statistics > Graphical Summary, or in Minitab 16, the graphical analysis assistant can produce this graphical summary.) Before applying any procedure that assumes normality, Gordon wants to know if the normal distribution is reasonable. Reading from the graphical summary, the *p*-value from the Anderson–Darling normality test is 0.970. With any *p*-value larger than 0.05, there is no reason to reject normality, so this assumption is fine for this dataset. (See Chapter 4 for more information on normality tests.)

The graphical summary lists a 95% confidence interval for the mean, which is between 15.351 and 17.849. The company claims that one Gordoburger

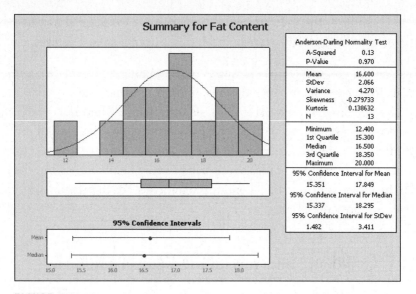

FIGURE 5-4 • Graphical summary of fat.

contains 15.0 grams of fat, and since 15.0 is outside the confidence interval, Gordon can be 95% confident in saying that the mean fat in a Gordoburger exceeds 15.0 grams.

But Gordon wants to be careful before launching such a claim against a large company. Gordon would prefer to be 99% confident in his results. The confidence interval used by the graphical summary can be adjusted if the graph is created from the Stat menu. However, another tool offers even greater flexibility.

In the Minitab menus, Gordon selects Stat > Basic Statistics > 1-Sample t. In the dialog, shown in Fig. 5-5, Gordon selects the column with the data. Then, Gordon clicks the Options button, and the Options dialog in Fig. 5-6 appears. Here, Gordon adjusts the default 95% confidence level to 99%.

After Gordon clicks OK in both open dialogs, the following report appears in the Session window:

One-Sample T: Fat Content

```
Variable      N    Mean   StDev  SE Mean       99% CI
Fat Content  13  16.600   2.066    0.573  (14.849, 18.351)
```

This report lists a 99% confidence interval as being between 14.849 and 18.351. Comparing this to the 95% confidence interval, notice that increasing the confidence makes the interval wider. The claimed fat content, 15.0, is inside the

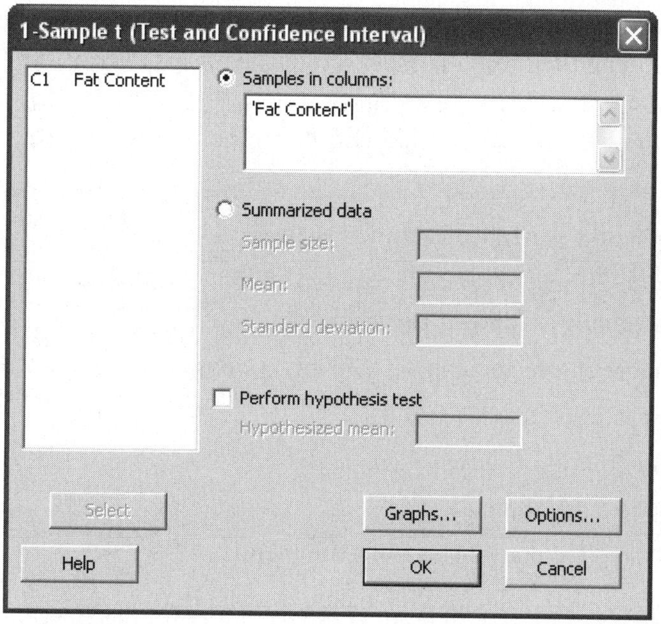

FIGURE 5-5 • 1-Sample *t* dialog.

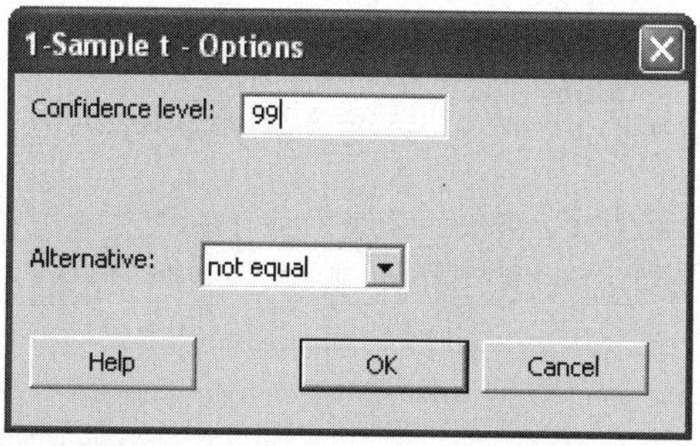

FIGURE 5-6 • 1-Sample *t* Options dialog.

99% interval. Therefore, Gordon cannot say with 99% confidence that the mean fat in a Gordoburger is different from 15 grams.

Ultimately, the decision about what to conclude is up to Gordon. He has more than 95%, but less than 99%, confidence that the mean fat in the product tested exceeds the company's claims.

A good way to understand how confidence intervals work is to run a simulation. Minitab makes it very easy to simulate confidence intervals for many situations. For example, suppose the true mean is 15.0 and the true standard deviation is 2.0. If we calculate a large number of 95% confidence intervals for the mean, 95% of them should contain the true mean, 15.0. 5% of them, 1 out of 20, will not contain the true mean.

Follow these steps to simulate 20 confidence intervals on datasets of size 13:

- Create a new worksheet with File > New.
- Generate 20 sets of random data with Calc > Random Data > Normal. Fill out the dialog as follows, and click OK:
  - Number of rows to generate: 13 (this is the size of each dataset)
  - Store in column(s): C1-C20
  - Mean: 15.0
  - Standard deviation: 2.0
- Select Graph > Interval Plot from the menu.
  - In the gallery, select a Simple plot of Multiple Ys.
  - For Graph Variables, enter C1-C20
- Right-click on the completed plot and select Add > Reference Lines. Enter 15 in the Show reference lines at Y values box, and click OK.

Figure 5-7 shows a plot created using this procedure. Any confidence interval which contains the true mean of 15 is a true statement. In this simulation,

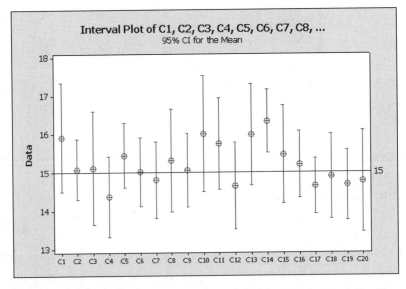

FIGURE 5-7 • Simulation of twenty 95% confidence intervals with true mean = 15.

19 intervals contain 15, and one interval does not. This ratio of 19 correct intervals out of 20 matches the expected probability of 95%.

Since simulation is a random procedure, your results may vary. Out of 20 confidence intervals, all 20 might contain the true value of 15, or perhaps many might not contain the true value. But in the long run, 95% of these intervals will correctly contain the true value.

What if the true mean were different from 15? Here, we want 15 to be outside the confidence interval, leading to the conclusion that the mean is not 15. How many confidence intervals will correctly exclude 15? This question can also be answered by simulation.

Figure 5-8 is another interval plot of 20 confidence intervals where the true mean is 16.0, with a reference line drawn at 15.0. In this simulation, 10 out of 20 intervals did not contain 15.

If you perform the same simulation, your results may vary. In the long run, about 38% of these confidence intervals will correctly exclude the test mean of 15. This value, 38%, comes from a power and sample size calculation discussed in Chapter 7.

The Minitab 1-Sample t tool is based on the assumption of a normal distribution. In practice, sample means tend to be normally distributed even if the individual data are not. Because of this fact, the 1-Sample t function is fairly robust for nonnormal data.

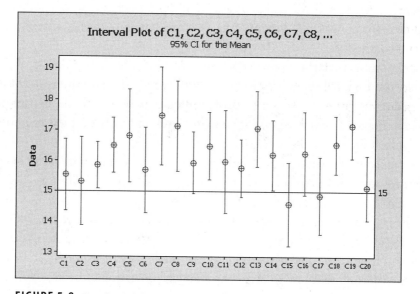

FIGURE 5-8 • Simulation of twenty 95% confidence intervals with true mean = 16.

5.2.2   Confidence Intervals for the Standard Deviation and Variance

Most statistical teachers and textbooks talk about confidence intervals for the variance, not the standard deviation. This is because statisticians are the only people on the planet who prefer to work with variances. For the rest of us, standard deviations are a more natural measure of variation, since standard deviations are measured in the same units as the raw data.

Fortunately for us, Minitab makes this easy by calculating confidence intervals for both standard deviation and variance using one menu command, Stat > Basic Statistics > 1 Variance. It is also very easy to convert one to the other, since the confidence limits for variance are simply the square of the confidence limits for standard deviation.

Minitab also provides two different methods for calculating these confidence intervals:

- The chi-square method is based on normal distribution theory. If the distribution is known to be normal, this is the best method, but it is not accurate for other distributions.

- The Bonett method, published in 2006 and now available in Minitab 16, provides confidence intervals for the standard deviation of any continuous distribution, normal or nonnormal.

In earlier versions of Minitab, an "adjusted degrees of freedom" method was included for nonnormal distributions, but this has now been replaced by the Bonett method.

If the normal distribution is an acceptable model for a population, the chi-square method will generally produce a narrower confidence interval. For nonnormal distributions, or when the distribution is in doubt, the Bonett method is recommended. Some experts are now recommending the Bonett method for all applications, normal or otherwise.

For an example, suppose Lu is testing the reliability of light bulbs by measuring the hours until they burn out. The lifetime of 100 light bulbs is recorded in the Minitab example data file Lightbulb.MTW.

The graphical summary of the data (not shown here) lists a mean of 1248 hours and a standard deviation of 84.1 hours. The Anderson–Darling normality test indicates that the normal distribution is reasonable. Also, the graphical summary lists a 95% confidence interval for the standard deviation of between 73.9 and 97.7 hours.

These results concern Lu, since the specification for these light bulbs specifies a standard deviation of no more than 75 hours. But 75 hours is inside the 95% confidence interval, so Lu cannot conclude that the standard deviation exceeds 75, at least not with 95% confidence.

To verify these results with a report that looks more analytical, Lu selects Stat > Basic Statistics > 1 Variance from the Minitab menu. Lu selects the Hours column to analyze, and clicks OK. The following report appears in the Session window:

Test and CI for One Variance: Hours

```
Method

The chi-square method is only for the normal distribution.
The Bonett method is for any continuous distribution.


Statistics

Variable     N   StDev   Variance
Hours      100    84.1       7076


95% Confidence Intervals

                         CI for        CI for
Variable   Method        StDev         Variance
Hours      Chi-Square  (73.9, 97.7)  (5455, 9549)
           Bonett      (72.6, 99.4)  (5272, 9880)
```

Notice that the final two lines of the report list confidence intervals for both standard deviation and variance, using both chi-square and Bonett methods.

It is not necessary to have the raw data to perform this analysis. Suppose all you know is that the standard deviation of 100 measurements is 84.1 hours. In the same 1-Variance dialog, select Sample standard deviation in the Data drop-down box, then enter the sample size and standard deviation directly in the dialog. Only chi-square results are provided when entering the standard deviation directly. The Bonett method requires the raw data.

In Lu's situation, the chi-square analysis is appropriate, since the normal distribution model fits the data well. Lu can be 95% confident that the true standard deviation is between 73.9 and 97.7.

But this may not be the best analysis for Lu. What if Lu only cares if the standard deviation is too large, and will take no action if the standard deviation is too small? This one-sided business decision requires a one-sided confidence interval.

To calculate a one-sided confidence interval, Lu goes to the same 1 Variance dialog, and clicks the Options button. In the Alternative dropdown box, she selects Greater than. This indicates that we are looking for evidence that the standard deviation is greater than some value. After clicking OK, here is a portion of the one-sided report:

```
95% One-Sided Confidence Intervals

                      Lower
                      Bound
                        for    Lower Bound
Variable   Method      StDev   for Variance
Hours      Chi-Square   75.4          5685
           Bonett       74.4          5532
```

Since the 95% lower confidence bound for standard deviation is 75.4 by the chi-square method, Lu can say with more than 95% confidence that the population standard deviation is greater than the specified 75 hours.

For one more example, consider the data in Hcc.MTW. Column C3 in this file lists the length of stay in days for 58 patients of a Wisconsin psychiatric hospital. Dolores, the administrator of the hospital, first prepares a graphical summary, not shown here. As with most time datasets, the distribution of the length of stay data is skewed to the right. The normality test has a p-value reported as < 0.005, which soundly rejects a normal distribution model. To estimate the standard deviation of length with a confidence interval, the chi-square method is clearly inappropriate.

To estimate the variation in length of stay, Dolores uses the Minitab 1 Variance function. Here is the Session window report from that analysis:

```
Variable   N   StDev   Variance
Length     58  13.1        172

95% Confidence Intervals

                       CI for         CI for
Variable   Method      StDev          Variance
Length     Chi-Square  (11.1, 16.1)   (123, 258)
           Bonett      ( 8.2, 21.8)   ( 67, 474)
```

Using the Bonett method for nonnormal distributions, a 95% confidence interval for standard deviation is between 8.2 and 21.8.

5.2.3   Confidence Intervals for a Proportion

When a variable has only two possible values for each measurement, it is often useful to estimate the probability associated with one of those two values. To do this, we generally make these simplifying assumptions:

- Assume that the measurements observed are a sample from a larger population.
- Assume that each measurement has the same probabilities.
- Assume that all measurements are independent from each other.

Under these assumptions, each measurement becomes a Bernoulli trial. The count of measurements having one value out of a set of Bernoulli trials is a binomial random variable.

In Minitab, it is easy to calculate confidence intervals for proportions using the Stat > Basic Statistics > 1 Proportion function.

For example, consider the Minitab sample data file Hcc.MTW, which lists information about 58 patients at a Wisconsin psychiatric hospital. Column C1 lists the reason each patient was discharged, where 1 indicates a normal discharge, and 2 indicates any other reason (against medical advice, ran away, etc.).

Administrator Dolores wants to estimate the proportion of patients normally discharged, with a confidence interval. To do this, she selects Stat > Basic Statistics > 1 Proportion from the Minitab menu. In the Samples in columns box, she enters C1 and clicks OK. This report appears in the Session window:

Results for: Hcc.MTW

Test and CI for One Proportion: Reason

```
Event = 2

Variable   X   N  Sample p        95% CI
Reason    16  58  0.275862  (0.166625, 0.408964)
```

Among the 58 rows, 42 had Reason = 1 and 16 had Reason = 2. Minitab decided to calculate a confidence interval for the least probable event, which is the abnormal discharge represented by Reason = 2. The estimated probability of abnormal discharge is 16/58 = 0.276. A 95% confidence interval for this probability lies between 0.167 and 0.409.

Since Dolores is more interested in the probability of normal discharge, she can simply subtract these values from 1. A 95% confidence interval for the probability of normal discharge lies between 0.591 and 0.833.

There are different ways to calculate confidence intervals for proportions, and many entry-level statistics books present a different method based on a normal approximation to the binomial distribution. This method is computationally simpler, but as an approximate method, it is inferior to the exact method. When the probability is close to 0 or 1, the normal approximation is particularly inaccurate.

Minitab offers the normal approximation as an option you can select by clicking the Options button in the 1 Proportion dialog. With the normal approximation selected, here is a section of the 1 Proportion report on the Reason variable of Hcc.MTW:

```
Variable   X   N   Sample p        95% CI
Reason     16  58  0.275862   (0.160837, 0.390887)

Using the normal approximation.
```

The "exact" method is always preferred over the normal approximation, as long as Minitab is available to calculate it.

To purists, the "exact" confidence interval is not totally exact, because of the computational difficulties of dealing with a discrete distribution. The "exact" method in Minitab is based on the Clopper–Pearson (1934) method, and it is generally regarded as exact. However, in some cases, this "exact" 95% confidence interval will be wider than it needs to be to have 95% confidence. Therefore, any error in this method will be conservative or safe. The normal approximation to a 95% interval could be either wider or narrower than an exact 95% interval, and its error will exceed the error of the Clopper–Pearson method.

Using the 1 Proportion tool, Minitab can analyze any two-valued column of data, regardless of its data type: numeric, text, or date/time. However, it is more common to have data summarized as a total number of trials (n) and a number of events with the selected outcome (x). These numbers may be entered directly into the 1 Proportion dialog by selecting the Summarized data option.

For example, consider Nick, an engineer who designs robotic toys for a major toy company. A new voice-controlled robot, designed by Nick, was well-received by the public until some disturbing reports surfaced about robots turning around and attacking the robot's owner. Out of 6,050 robots sold so far, there have been six confirmed attacks. The CEO issued a press release saying that, "99.9% of these robots won't attack you," but this did little to quell the public outcry.

Nick first wanted to know how bad the problem might be, given the available information. This can be determined by calculating an upper confidence bound on the proportion of robots with the problem. To answer this question in Minitab, Nick selected Stat > Basic Statistics > 1 Proportion and filled out the dialog as follows:

- He selected Summarized data.

- Number of events: 6.

- Number of trials: 6050.

- Nick then clicked Options, and selected Less than in the Alternative drop-down box.

Nick knew he wanted a one-sided upper confidence bound, but he was unsure whether to select Less than or Greater than in the Options dialog. In this case, Nick wants a number which the true proportion will be less than, so he selects Less than. The result is an upper confidence bound.

After clicking OK, Nick saw this report in the Session window:

Test and CI for One Proportion

```
                                    95% Upper
Sample   X      N   Sample p         Bound
1        6   6050   0.000992        0.001956
```

According to this report, the estimated probability of attack is 0.000992, with a 99% upper confidence bound of 0.001956. Nick can be 95% confident that at least $(1 - 0.002) \times 100\% = 99.8\%$ of the robots will not attack.

Nick set to work investigating the problem. After a costly recall and much engineering work, the attacks were linked to a rare virus which had infected the robots' operating system. Nick fixed the problem with a software upgrade.

Eventually, 4,120 robots were upgraded or sold with the new software, and zero attacks occurred with this group of 4,120. Is the problem fixed for good? There is no way to answer this question with certainty, but we can say with high confidence that the probability of an attack is below a lower confidence bound.

In the same 1 Proportion dialog, Nick entered 0 events and 4,120 trials. Here is the report:

Test and CI for One Proportion

```
                                    95% Upper
Sample   X      N   Sample p         Bound
1        0   4120   0.000000        0.000727
```

After 4,120 trials of the improved software and 0 failures, Nick can be 95% confident that the probability of a defect is less than 0.000727.

But has the probability of a problem really been reduced? This is a different question. To prove that the probability has been reduced, Nick needs to compare the proportion of failed robots before the change to the proportion of failed robots after the change. This requires the 2 Proportions function in Minitab.

The 2 Proportions function will calculate a confidence interval for the difference $p_1 - p_2$, where p_1 is the probability of an event in sample 1, and p_2 is the probability of an event in sample 2. If this confidence interval does NOT include zero, this is proof that the probability has changed between sample 1 and sample 2.

To perform this calculation, Nick selects Stat > Basic Statistics > 2 Proportions and fills out the dialog as follows:

- He selects Summarized data.

- First Events: 6; Trials: 6050.

- Second Events: 0; Trials: 4120.

- Nick then clicks Options and selects the Greater than alternative. Here, Nick wants to know if the difference $p_1 - p_2$ is greater than zero.

Here is the resulting report in the Session window:

Test and CI for Two Proportions

```
Sample   X     N   Sample p
1        6   6050   0.000992
2        0   4120   0.000000


Difference = p (1) - p (2)
Estimate for difference:  0.000991736
95% lower bound for difference:  0.000326107
Test for difference = 0 (vs > 0):   Z = 2.45   P-Value = 0.007

* NOTE * The normal approximation may be inaccurate for small samples.

Fisher's exact test: P-Value = 0.044
```

Minitab estimates that the probability of an event was reduced by 0.000992, with a 95% lower confidence bound of 0.00033. Since this lower bound of the probability decrease is greater than 0, Nick can be very confident that the probability of this problem has been reduced.

But, Minitab includes a warning that the normal approximation may be inaccurate for small samples, and this confidence interval does rely on a normal approximation. With over 10,000 robots before and after, this may not seem like a small sample. However, what matters in this case is the number of robots that passed or failed, whichever count is smaller. There are four possible categories here, and the normal approximation needs at least five items in each of the four categories to be accurate. Here, with zero robots failing after the change, the approximation simply cannot be trusted.

There is a better way to interpret this report, using an exact hypothesis test. This example will be continued in Chapter 6.

5.2.4 Confidence Intervals for a Poisson Rate

When independent events happen at the same rate of events per unit time, the count of events in some length of time has a Poisson distribution. In many common situations, we need to estimate the rate of events with a confidence interval. Minitab provides the Stat > Basic Statistics > 1-Sample Poisson Rate function to perform these calculations.

In Chapter 4, we saw the Minitab sample data file Accident.MTW. This file lists the accidents per week at one intersection, over 50 weeks. We applied the Poisson goodness-of-fit test to this data, and found that the Poisson distribution fits the available data well. What is the mean rate of accidents per week, with a 95% confidence interval?

With the Accident.MTW workbook open, select Stat > Basic Statistics > 1-Sample Poisson Rate. In the Samples in columns box, enter Accident and click OK. This report appears in the Session window:

Confidence Interval for One-Sample Poisson Rate: Accidents

Variable	Total Occurrences	N	Rate of Occurrence	95% CI
Accidents	112	50	2.24000	(1.84441, 2.69530)

"Length" of observation = 1.

Based on this dataset, the estimated rate of accidents per week is 2.24, with a 95% confidence interval of 1.84 to 2.69.

As in the previous section on confidence intervals for proportions, many books teach a method for Poisson rate confidence intervals based on a normal approximation to the Poisson distribution. In Minitab, this method can be selected in the Options dialog, but it is not recommended. The preferred method is based on established distribution theory, and is much more accurate, especially when the rate is close to zero.

For convenience, the Poisson distribution is often presented as a model of events per unit time. However, instead of time, the denominator of the ratio could be a length, a volume, a unit of product, or any other set, as long as the events counted could possibly occur anywhere in that set.

For example, suppose the Gnuon is a new model of all-electric car. One of the business goals for the Gnuon is to have fewer than 2.00 customer complaints per vehicle at the time of delivery. Carl is the quality engineer in charge of tracking this metric, based on direct phone contact with a large sample of customers. Carl decides that the Poisson model is appropriate for complaints per vehicle, because one customer could possibly have many different complaints.

After interviewing 100 randomly selected customers, Carl has counted 185 complaints total. This sounds good, at 1.85 complaints per vehicle, but it is a sample of a larger population. Is the true rate really meeting the management goal of 2.00?

In Minitab, Carl selects the 1-Sample Poisson Rate tool. In the dialog, Carl selects Summarized data and enters 100 for Sample size and 185 for Total occurrences. In the Options dialog, Carl selects the Less than alternative. Carl wants a 95% upper confidence bound, since he only needs to know if the complaint rate is too high, not too low. Here is the report:

Confidence Interval for One-Sample Poisson Rate

Sample	Total Occurrences	N	Rate of Occurrence	95% Upper Bound
1	185	100	1.85000	2.08987

Since the 95% upper confidence bound for the Poisson rate is 2.09, Carl can't say with 95% confidence yet that the rate of defects is less than 2.00. The rate could be higher or lower than 2.00. More customer interviews will help to resolve this question.

5.3 Calculating Prediction Intervals

A prediction interval is a range of values that has a high probability of containing a single future value from a population already sampled. Prediction intervals can also be constructed for the sample mean or sample standard deviation of a future sample of many values of known size.

The prediction interval methods used in this section assume that the data come from a normal distribution. If the distribution is not normal, prediction intervals calculated using this method will be inaccurate.

The most common use of prediction intervals is following a designed experiment or multiple regression analysis, in which a model is constructed to represent how a system performs in response to several variables. After the best settings of input variables are selected, a prediction interval is useful to predict how the system will perform at those settings. In Minitab, prediction intervals are available as part of the regression or design of experiments (DOE) tools.

For a variety of reasons, it is less common to calculate a prediction interval based on one sample of values, which is the scenario for this chapter. This feature is not available in the standard Minitab menus. However, a macro is available at www.Minitab.com which calculates prediction intervals easily.

In this section, you will learn how to locate, download, and install a Minitab macro from the Web, and how to use that macro to extend the functionality of Minitab software. By using that macro, you will also learn how to calculate prediction intervals based on a sample of data.

Minitab, Inc., maintains a large knowledgebase on their Web site, including answers to many questions and macros for adding functionality to Minitab. To find the macro for prediction intervals, follow these steps:

- Go to www.minitab.com.

- Click on the Knowledgebase / FAQ link.

- Search the knowledgebase for "Prediction interval."

- In the search results, locate the article called "Calculate a prediction interval for a future value or mean and standard deviation of a future sample - ID 2510."

- You may wish to either print or save this article on your computer for future reference, since it contains instructions for using the PREDINT macro. However, these instructions are also included as comments in the macro code itself.

- Scroll down in the document and click on this link to related documents: "Prediction Interval for a Future Observation or for a Future Sample."

- This link takes you to a list of all macros, at the spot where the PREDINT macro is located. Click on the link to the macro code.

- When the page with the macro code appears, select all the code starting with macro and ending with endmacro.

- Right-click on the code and select Copy to copy the macro to the clipboard.

- Open Notepad. This can be done from the Minitab Tools menu, or from Windows in the Accessories group.

- Paste the macro code into Notepad. Verify that the file starts with macro on the first line and endmacro on the last line.

- Save the macro to the Minitab macros folder. The location of this folder may vary depending on the configuration, language, and other options of your computer. On the author's computer, this folder is C:\Program Files\ Minitab\Minitab 16\English\Macros.

- Save the macro with file name PREDINT.MAC. For Minitab to find the file as a macro, it must have the .MAC file extension.

If you are interested in learning how to write your own Minitab macros, you may find it interesting to browse through the PREDINT.MAC file. This is an excellent example of how to organize, write, and document a high-quality macro.

Earlier in this chapter, Gordon analyzed the fat in 13 "Gordoburgers" purchased from 13 fast food restaurants. The fat content is listed in the Minitab example data file Fat.MTW. Gordon has already calculated a 95% confidence interval for the mean, which is from 15.351 to 17.849.

If Gordon goes out and buys one more Gordoburger, how much fat will be in that burger? A prediction interval will answer this question.

With the PREDINT.MAC file stored in the Macros folder, and Fat.MTW open as the current worksheet, click in the Session window. Select Editor > Enable Commands in the Minitab menu. Notice that the session command prompt appears in the Session window:

```
MTB >
```

After the prompt, type %predint c1 and the report appears:

```
MTB > %predint c1
Executing from file: C:\Program Files\Minitab\Minitab
16\English\Macros\predint.MAC
```

Prediction Interval for a Single Future Observation

```
Future Sample Size:        1
Estimated Value:           16.6000
95% Prediction Interval:   (11.9277, 21.2723)
```

Based on Gordon's sample of 13 burgers, he can predict with 95% confidence that one future burger will have between 11.93 and 21.27 grams of fat. Notice how much wider this prediction interval is, compared to the confidence interval for the mean. One value always has more variation than a sample mean, and this is reflected in the width of these intervals.

Suppose Gordon decides to collect another sample of 13 burgers from another town. He can use the PREDINT macro to calculate prediction intervals for the mean and standard deviation of that future set of 13 measurements. To do this requires the OBS subcommand to be entered on a second line.

To duplicate the results below, pay attention to the punctuation. In Minitab session commands, when multiple lines are required, end every line except the last with a semicolon (;) and end the last line with a period (.)

```
MTB > %predint c1;
SUBC> obs 13.
Executing from file: C:\Program Files\Minitab\Minitab
16\English\Macros\predint.MAC
```

Prediction Interval for Mean and Standard Deviation of a Future Sample

```
Future Sample Size:          13
Estimated Mean:              16.6000
95% Prediction Interval:     (14.8341, 18.3659)

Estimated Standard Deviation:    2.06640
95% Prediction Interval:_1       (1.1415, 3.7409)
```

The macro has calculated and reported 95% prediction intervals for both the mean and standard deviation of a future sample of 13 burgers.

Notice that the 95% prediction interval for the sample mean of 13, which is from 14.83 to 18.36, is wider than the 95% confidence interval for the population mean, which is from 15.35 to 17.85. This is because the prediction interval starts from the confidence interval and then incorporates more variation to account for the variation in the future, unknown sample of 13.

The PREDINT macro has two other subcommands, oside to generate one-sided prediction limits, and conf to adjust the confidence level. These are documented in the comments at the beginning of the macro file.

5.4   Calculating Tolerance Intervals

NEW IN 16 A statistical tolerance interval is a range with a high probability of containing a specified proportion of the population of individual values. Unlike the other intervals featured in this chapter, tolerance intervals are specified by two percentages: a confidence level and a containment percentage. In some references, the containment percentage is called coverage. In Minitab, this is descriptively labeled "Percent of population in interval."

Earlier versions of Minitab did not have a menu item for tolerance intervals, requiring users to download a tolerance interval macro, much like the prediction interval macro featured in the previous section. But now in Minitab 16, the Stat > Quality Tools menu contains a function for calculating tolerance intervals.

Many students of statistics and even experienced professionals are confused by all these intervals. The first, and sometimes, the only interval taught is the confidence interval for the mean. As a result, some people use a confidence interval when they really need a tolerance interval. Individual values are more familiar to most of us than a statistical abstraction like the mean. Because of this, tolerance intervals ought to be easier and more natural to apply than confidence intervals.

Minitab 16 calculates tolerance intervals using two methods: one method which assumes a normal distribution, and a second method applicable to any continuous distribution, called a nonparametric method. As we will see, the nonparametric method has significant limitations for small samples, and must be interpreted with caution.

For a first example, consider Gordon's burger fat data in Fat.MTW. Suppose Gordon wants to calculate a tolerance interval to contain 90% of the fat content data, with 95% confidence.

Select Stat > Quality Tools > Tolerance Intervals from the Minitab menu. In the Samples in columns box, enter C1. Click Options. In the Minimum percentage of population in interval box, enter 90, and click OK. Here is the report in the Session window:

Tolerance Interval: Fat Content

```
Method

Tolerance interval type           Two-sided
Confidence level                  95%
Percent of population in interval 90%


Statistics

Variable       N    Mean   StDev
Fat Content   13  16.600   2.066

95% Tolerance Interval, Using Normal Method

Variable       Lower   Upper
Fat Content   11.223  21.977
```

```
95% Tolerance Interval, Using Nonparametric Method

                                   Achieved
Variable        Lower    Upper   Confidence
Fat Content    12.400   20.000        37.9
```

Minitab also produces the tolerance interval graph seen in Fig. 5-9.

Since two sets of results are presented, which one should we use? The graph includes a normal probability plot and a text box with the results of an Anderson–Darling normality test. As before, there is no problem with the assumption of a normal distribution for this data. Using the normal method, a 95% tolerance interval containing 90% of the population lies between 11.223 and 21.977. The graph includes a histogram of the data, an interval plot comparing both intervals, and text boxes summarizing the results.

Notice that the nonparametric tolerance interval is much narrower than the normal-based interval. Isn't a narrow interval better? Why not use the narrower nonparametric interval instead of the normal one?

The answer lies in the last line of the report in the Session window. The nonparametric tolerance interval is between 12.4 and 20.0. What can't be seen in this report is that these are the minimum and maximum values in the dataset. Most significant is that the Achieved confidence of this interval is only 37.9%, far short of the desired 95%. Unfortunately, this limitation of the

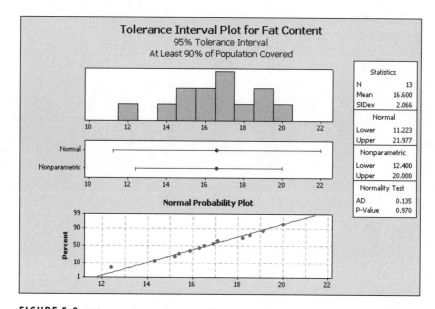

FIGURE 5-9 · Tolerance interval graph of fat content data.

nonparametric interval is not listed in the tolerance interval graph, and as a result, some may misinterpret the graph and incorrectly use the nonparametric interval. Hopefully this will be clarified in future releases of Minitab.

For this dataset, the normal tolerance intervals are the only acceptable and usable results of this report. The assumption of a normal distribution provides the opportunity to extrapolate beyond the range of observed data and predict probabilities of values far out in the tails. Without assuming any distribution family, one cannot make any inference outside the range of available data. As a result, nonparametric tolerance intervals can never exceed the observed range. This is a fundamental limitation, or some would say a benefit, of nonparametric methods.

As another example, consider Lu's light bulb lifetime data in Lightbulb.MTW. Suppose Lu wants to use this dataset to establish a specification for reliability. According to the policy of Lu's company, at least 95% of the light bulbs should last longer than the specified lifetime. Lu chooses a 95% confidence level for this analysis.

With the Lightbulb.MTW dataset current, select Stat > Quality Tools > Tolerance Intervals and enter Hours in the Samples in columns box. Click Options. Select 95 for both Confidence level and Minimum percentage of population in interval. Finally, select Lower bound from the dropdown box. Here is the resulting report:

Tolerance Interval: Hours

```
Method

Tolerance interval type          One-sided (Lower)
Confidence level                 95%
Percent of population in interval  95%


Statistics

Variable    N      Mean    StDev
Hours      100  1248.004  84.118

95% Lower Tolerance Bound, Using Normal Method

Variable      Lower
Hours      1085.947

95% Lower Tolerance Bound, Using Nonparametric Method

                         Achieved
Variable      Lower    Confidence
Hours      1070.700          96.3
```

Figure 5-10 shows the tolerance interval graph for this dataset.

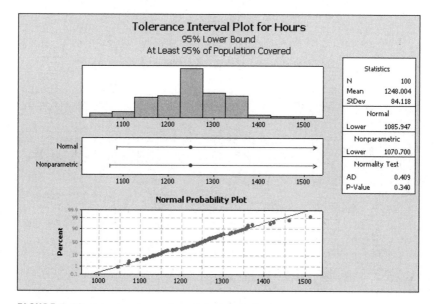

FIGURE 5-10 · Tolerance interval graph for lightbulb data.

The normal distribution fits this dataset well, so the normal method is preferred. Using this method, the 95% lower tolerance bound less than 95% of the population is 1086 hours. Therefore, Lu can establish a lower specification limit 1086 or less, and she can be 95% confident that 95% of the bulbs will exceed that lower limit.

Notice that the nonparametric lower tolerance bound is 1071 hours at an achieved confidence of 96.3%. This nonparametric bound is outside the normal tolerance interval, which is a typical result for large, normally distributed datasets.

For one more example, consider Hcc.MTW column C3, which lists the length of stay for 58 patients at a psychiatric hospital. In many cases, the hospital is paid a fixed price regardless of length of stay, so patients who stay a long time end up costing the hospital a lot of money. Suppose hospital administrator Dolores wants to establish a length of stay after which a high-level review of each patient's case must be conducted. She wants to find a time at which 75% of the patients have already been discharged, with 95% confidence.

Using the Tolerance Interval calculator in Minitab, Dolores calculates a 95% upper tolerance bound on the length of stay, with 75% of the population in the interval. Figure 5-11 is the plot from this analysis.

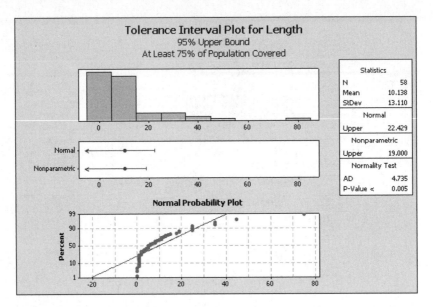

FIGURE 5-11 · Tolerance interval graph for hospital length of stay.

Clearly from the normal probability plot and the AD test, the normal distribution is inappropriate for this data. But is the nonparametric method appropriate? Dolores checks the Session window, which contains this report, in part:

```
95% Upper Tolerance Bound, Using Nonparametric Method

                    Achieved
Variable   Upper   Confidence
Length     19.000       97.1
```

Since the nonparametric tolerance bound of 19 days has achieved 97.1% confidence, greater than the required 95%, this is a reliable tolerance bound. Based on this analysis, Dolores establishes a policy to review each patient's case on the 19th day.

5.5   Find Out More

As usual, the first reference for methods and formulas used by Minitab is the Methods and Formulas section of the Minitab help files. Besides the formulas, these files also list reference books with more information about these tools.

Most of the methods cited in this chapter are so well established that virtually any statistics text like Montgomery, et al, (2010) or Ott and Longnecker

(2010) provides the basic formulas. As a desk reference for professionals, Sleeper (2006) provides formulas and interpretation advice for many types of confidence and tolerance intervals.

Bonett (2006) is one of the newer methods of nonnormal confidence intervals for standard deviation, which is now available in Minitab 16.

Binomial confidence intervals continue be a subject of research and publication. The "exact" method used in Minitab is based on Clopper and Pearson (1934). Two good papers that summarize the strengths and weaknesses of different methods are Agresti and Coull (1998) and Ross (2003).

This chapter presented three families of statistical tools for making decisions based on limited data. Confidence intervals express the uncertainty in the estimate of a mean, standard deviation, proportion, rate, or other population parameter. In later chapters, confidence intervals will be applied to other numerical characteristics of a population. Prediction intervals express the uncertainty in either one or a set of future measurements. Tolerance intervals express the uncertainty in the population of individual values by containing a specified percentage of the population with high confidence.

In addition to these important topics, this chapter showed how to download and install a Minitab macro from the Web. Using the wide variety of Minitab macros available, the functionality of Minitab can be extended in limitless ways.

The next chapter covers hypothesis testing, which is closely linked to confidence intervals. For every confidence interval, there is also a hypothesis test, and many of these are accessed through the same Minitab functions.

QUIZ

1. Mark has measured the diameter of 30 shafts. Based on this sample of data, Mark wants to set limits which will contain 99% of the population of shafts. What kind of interval does Mark need to calculate to set these limits?

   A. Mean ± 3 standard deviations
   B. Confidence interval for the mean
   C. Prediction interval
   D. Tolerance interval

2. Mark is concerned that the variation of diameter among shafts may be too high, and he wonders how large the variation might be. What is the most appropriate bound or interval for Mark to calculate to answer this question?

   A. Lower confidence bound on standard deviation
   B. Prediction interval for standard deviation
   C. Upper confidence bound on standard deviation
   D. Two-sided confidence interval for standard deviation

3. In calculating confidence intervals, Mark generally chooses a 99% confidence level rather than the more customary 95%. Mark's 99% confidence levels will be (wider/narrower) than 95% confidence levels. Also, Mark will have (higher/lower) risk of the true population values lying outside the 99% confidence interval, compared to a 95% confidence interval.

   A. wider; higher
   B. wider; lower
   C. narrower; higher
   D. narrower; lower

4. In Minitab, the 1-Sample t function can be used to calculate what?

   A. A confidence interval for the sample mean
   B. A confidence interval for the population mean
   C. A tolerance interval
   D. A confidence interval for individual values

5. On the International Space Station, a certain guidance computer has failed 5 times in the last 2 years, for a mean failure rate of 2.5 failures per year. Based on this information, what is a 90% upper bound on the rate of failures per year?

   A. 0.75
   B. 1.06
   C. 4.64
   D. 5.26

6. Using the data in the Minitab example data file Airplanepin.MTW, calculate a 90% confidence interval for the population mean.

7. **The measurements in** Airplanepin.MTW **have an intended target value of 15.00. Is there any strong evidence that the mean is above or below 15.00? Why or why not?**

8. **Using the data in the Minitab sample data file** Airplanepin.MTW, **calculate a 90% confidence interval for the population standard deviation. Pay due attention to the shape of the distribution.**

9. **Using the data in the Minitab sample data file** Airplanepin.MTW, **calculate upper and lower limits which should contain at least 99% of the population of parts, with 95% confidence.**

10. **Using the data in the Minitab sample data file** Airplanepin.MTW, **calculate a 99% prediction interval for one future value.**

chapter **6**

Testing Hypotheses

If statistics is the science of data-driven decisions, then hypothesis testing is the essential toolbox of statistics. In a hypothesis test, data are summarized and analyzed with respect to a null hypothesis (also called initial hypothesis or H_0) and an alternative hypothesis (H_A). If the data are inconsistent with H_0, beyond a reasonable doubt, then we decide to reject H_0 in favor of H_A. From this fundamental structure, an endless variety of real-world questions can be answered, with the support of data and sound statistical methods.

CHAPTER OBJECTIVES

Here's what you'll learn in this chapter:

- How to use the Minitab hypothesis tests assistant to select tests for one sample, two samples, and many samples
- How to specify settings for hypothesis tests
- How to interpret Minitab hypothesis test reports
- How to use the traditional menus in Minitab for hypothesis testing

169

Minitab software offers two distinctly different personalities for hypothesis testing—one using the traditional menus, and now in Minitab 16, the hypothesis testing assistant. The traditional menus work very much like the confidence interval functions seen in Chapter 5. These functions produce a text report in the Session window, in some cases with optional graphs.

The hypothesis tests assistant, new in Minitab 16, provides an almost entirely graphical interface. The assistant offers a flow chart to select the most appropriate test and dialog boxes with a consistent look and feel across all tests. The reports produced by the assistant are completely graphical, including a **Summary Report**, a **Diagnostic Report**, and a **Report Card**. Compared to the traditional Minitab menus, the assistant offers less flexibility, but more advice about interpreting test results and warnings about questionable assumptions. The graphical reports can serve either as a report or a presentation, neatly summarizing test results and concerns.

New users of Minitab will almost certainly prefer the hypothesis tests assistant to the traditional menus, because of the plain-text interpretation, helpful advice, and automatic diagnostics offered by the assistant. As one's experience grows, and the computer's advice becomes less important, the traditional menus may be preferred. The traditional menus offer more options, many of which are unavailable in the assistant. Sometimes, the traditional menus analyze data in two ways, printing both results in the Session window. This requires the user to think more about how to interpret the results before making a decision. In the assistant, these choices are hidden or removed from the user, presenting a clean report with a text explanation of the results.

6.1   Hypothesis Testing Demystified

Few statistical tools inspire as much fear and loathing among students as hypothesis tests. The combination of massive formulas, arcane terminology, and doubts about applicability can render this subject nearly impenetrable.

Minitab software helps with the first two objections. Although textbooks are filled with massive formulas, Minitab plows through these in an instant. Terminology may still be arcane, but Minitab's consistent presentation across tests and plain-text interpretive advice reduces this burden to a minimum. Ultimately, the application of hypothesis testing to solve meaningful problems still rests with you.

Here is a quick tour of hypothesis testing terminology which every Minitab user needs to know, using two example tests featured in earlier chapters.

Example A is the Anderson–Darling normality test, a tool to decide whether the normal distribution model fits a set of data.	Example B concerns Gordon's burger fat data in Fat.MTW. In Chapter 5, Gordon asked whether the mean fat was 15 grams, and answered this question with a confidence interval. This question can also be answered with a hypothesis test.

The **null hypothesis** H_0 is the initial theory about the system. H_0 represents "no effect" or "no change." If the data are not consistent with H_0, then H_0 is rejected. Otherwise, H_0 is not rejected. H_0 may be proven false, but H_0 cannot be proven true. As the experimenter, you may decide to accept H_0 as true, but this is your choice.	
Example A: H_0: The population follows a normal distribution.	Example B: H_0: The population mean of fat per burger is 15 grams. H_0: $\mu = 15$.

H_0 has nothing to do with what you want to be true, or what you think might be true. H_0 is a theory which might be proven false by strong evidence, provided by the data.

The **alternative hypothesis** H_A is the alternative theory about the system. H_A is usually the logical complement of H_0 ("H_0 is not true") but H_A could be some subset of the complement of H_0. If the data are inconsistent with H_0, then H_0 is rejected in favor of H_A.	
Example A: H_A: The population follows some other distribution. Here, H_A is the complement of H_0 and includes all other distribution families.	Example B: H_A: The population mean of fat per burger is not 15 grams. H_A: $\mu \neq 15$. This is a two–sided alternative. When the real–world decision is based on being greater than or less than 15, a one–sided alternative, H_A: $\mu > 15$ or H_A: $\mu < 15$ is more appropriate.

Two hypotheses have been defined, H_0 and H_A, so that only one can be true. After the hypothesis test, either H_0 will be rejected in favor of H_A or not. Combining two hypotheses and two outcomes from the test, there are four possibilities. Two of these possibilities represent correct decisions, and two represent errors.

A **type I error** happens when H_0 is true, but H_0 is rejected in favor of H_A. The probability of a type I error is α **(alpha)**. $0 \leq \alpha \leq 1$. In some Minitab dialogs, α is described as alpha level or significance level.

Example A:	Example B:
A type I error happens when the population follows a normal distribution, but the sample looks so nonnormal that the normal distribution is rejected. As a result of this error, the analyst needlessly looks for another distribution model or takes action based on the conclusion of nonnormality.	A type I error happens when the population mean $\mu = 15$, but the sample mean $\bar{x}$ is so far from 15 that the analyst rejects H_0 and concludes that $\mu \neq 15$. As a result, needless action may be taken to respond to a mean shift or to adjust the mean.

The probability of a type I error, α, is always controlled by you, the analyst. A customary value for α is 0.05, but smaller or larger values are also commonly used. When using a confidence interval to make decisions, the **confidence level**, $(1 - \alpha) \times 100\%$, is selected in advance. With a hypothesis test, α is compared to the p-value to decide the result of the test. The p-value is defined later.

A **type II error** happens when H_A is true, but H_0 is NOT rejected. The probability of a type II error is β **(beta)**. $0 \leq \beta \leq 1$. β depends on the size of the effect, or the size of the difference from H_0.

Example A:	Example B:
A type II error happens when the population follows a distribution other than normal, but the sample distribution is not sufficiently nonnormal for the analyst to reject the normal model. As a result, subsequent procedures will assume a normal distribution model when this is not correct.	A type II error happens when either $\mu < 15$ or $\mu > 15$, but the sample mean $\bar{x}$ is so close to 15 that the analyst fails to reject H_0. As a result, action to adjust the mean may not be taken when it is necessary.

The probability of a type II error, β, depends on α, the sample size, and the size of the effect being detected. It is more likely to detect a large shift than a small shift. β can be controlled before data collection by choosing a sufficient sample size.

The **power** of a hypothesis test is the probability of rejecting H_0 when H_A is true. Power = $1 - \beta$. $0 \leq$ Power ≤ 1. Power depends on the size of the effect or the difference from H_0.

Example A:	Example B:
If the population distribution is symmetric and bell-shaped but nonnormal, such as a logistic distribution, the power will be very small, unless the sample size is extremely large. If the population is heavily skewed or heavy-tailed, such as an exponential distribution, the power will be high even at a modest sample size.	If the population mean μ is very close to 15, the power will be very small. If μ is very far from 15, the power will be very large. The Minitab power and sample size functions can draw a graph of power for most hypothesis tests.

Both β and power are functions of sample size, the size of the effect to be detected, and α. Using the Minitab power and sample size functions before collecting data is a good way to explore these tradeoffs and choose a sufficient sample size. After data are collected and analyzed using the Minitab hypothesis tests assistant, the power can be calculated as part of the report.

Minitab 16 is inconsistent in how it presents power. In the Stat > Power and Sample Size menu, power is a probability between 0 and 1. However, in the reports generated by the hypothesis tests assistant, power is expressed as a percentage, sometimes with % and sometimes without %. Be careful in interpreting power values, to avoid confusing percentages with probabilities.

Power and sample size calculations are discussed further in the next chapter.

The **p-value** for a hypothesis test is the probability that random variation could cause a sample to appear at least as far from H_0 as the observed data, when H_0 is true. The calculations are performed so that the p-value is uniformly distributed between 0 and 1 when H_0 is true. If the p-value is less than α, then reject H_0 in favor of H_A. If the p-value is greater than α, then do not reject H_0. If the analyst decides to reject H_0, the p-value is the risk that this is an incorrect decision.

Example A:	Example B:
In Chapter 2, Fig. 2–1 is a graphical summary of the data in Pres.MTW. The normality test p-value is 0.506. Since this is greater than $\alpha = 0.05$, do not reject H_0. The normal distribution is acceptable. In Chapter 4, Fig. 4–15 shows four AD goodness-of-fit tests for data in Circuit.MTW. The normal p-value is < 0.005. Since this is very small, the normal model should be rejected. Both gamma and Weibull models have a p-value > 0.250, so either of these models is acceptable.	The p-value for a 1-sample t-test on Gordon's fat data is 0.016. If Gordon selects $\alpha = 0.05$, then he should reject H_0. But if Gordon selects $\alpha = 0.01$, then he should not reject H_0. If Gordon decides to reject H_0 and conclude that $\mu \neq 15$, he has a 0.016 probability of being incorrect in this decision. Stated differently, Gordon has 98.4% confidence that mean fat is different from 15. $98.4\% = (1 - 0.016) \times 100\%$

Behind the scenes, every type of hypothesis test uses different theory and formulas. But at the end, every hypothesis test performed by Minitab results in a p-value, and the interpretation of p-values is always the same. By comparing the p-value with α, we decide first whether to reject H_0, and next, what this means for our problem. The examples in this chapter will illustrate and explain these decisions further.

6.2 Using the Hypothesis Tests Assistant

New Minitab users may not recognize the revolutionary nature of the Assistant menu in Minitab 16. Other Minitab functions analyze and report, without advising; the Minitab assistant offers advice to help select the most appropriate tool and to interpret the results. Besides performing the selected analysis, the assistant also performs diagnostic tests to evaluate whether assumptions of the analysis are justified, and to identify possible concerns with the data.

It is important to separate analytical results from advice. Since Minitab uses well-established statistical methods, its analytical results are rarely questioned. But advice may always be accepted or overruled, especially when the advice comes from a computer. The human is always responsible for the ultimate decisions.

For a first example, consider Gordon's data in the Minitab sample data file Fat.MTW. In this file are measurements of the total fat in 13 burgers purchased from 13 restaurants operated by one company. The company claims the fat content should be 15.0 grams. Gordon questions whether the fat content is 15.0 grams or not. In Chapter 5, we used confidence intervals to answer this question. Here, we will use the hypothesis tests assistant.

With Fat.MTW as the current worksheet in Minitab, Gordon selects Assistant > Hypothesis Tests from the menu. The assistant asks a series of questions to help identify the correct test procedure. The first question is shown graphically in Fig. 6-1: What is your objective? Three available answers are:

- Compare one sample with a target
- Compare two samples with each other
- Compare more than two samples

In this case, Gordon wants to compare one sample with a target. In the left column of Fig. 6-1 are four hypothesis tests for one sample. If Gordon already

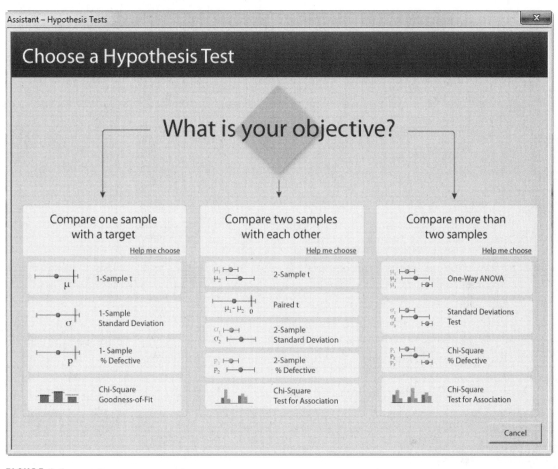

FIGURE 6-1 · Hypothesis tests assistant.

knows which test he wants, he can click it directly here. If not, he can click Help me choose in the "Compare one sample with a target" box. This links to a flow chart shown in Fig. 6-2, with decision boxes leading to each of the four tests.

If Gordon wants step-by-step assistance, he can click on any ◆ decision box for explanations and examples for every choice. Since Gordon's data is continuous, not attribute, and he is comparing the mean to a target, the flow chart leads to a 1-sample *t*-test, with the ⊢–μ⊣ icon.

From the flow chart, Gordon can click on the test icon directly, or he can click *more...*, which links to a list of advice and guidelines for the 1-sample *t*-test, shown in Fig. 6-3. These guidelines provide good advice, but they are not hard and fast rules. For more information on any of the guidelines, click the ⊞ icon for expanded comments.

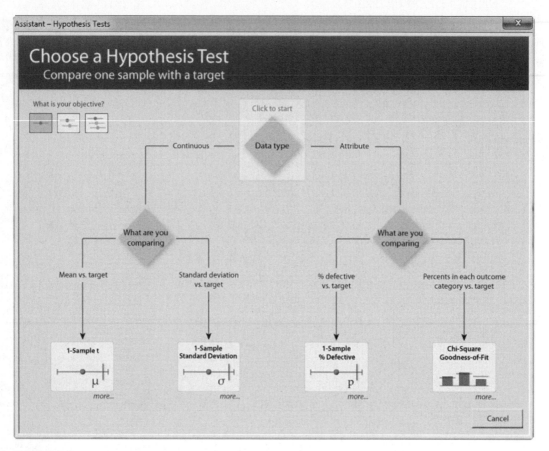

FIGURE 6-2 • Flow chart to select a 1-sample hypothesis test.

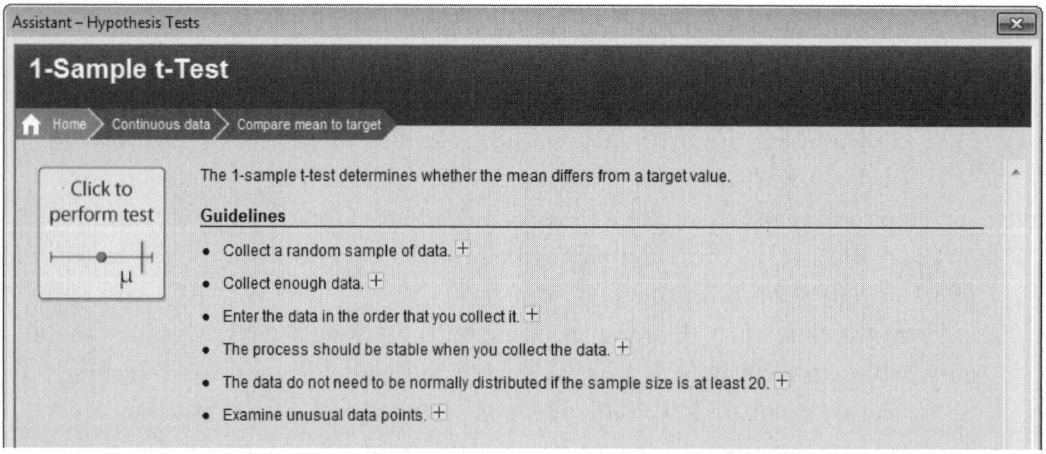

FIGURE 6-3 • Guidelines for a 1-sample *t*-test.

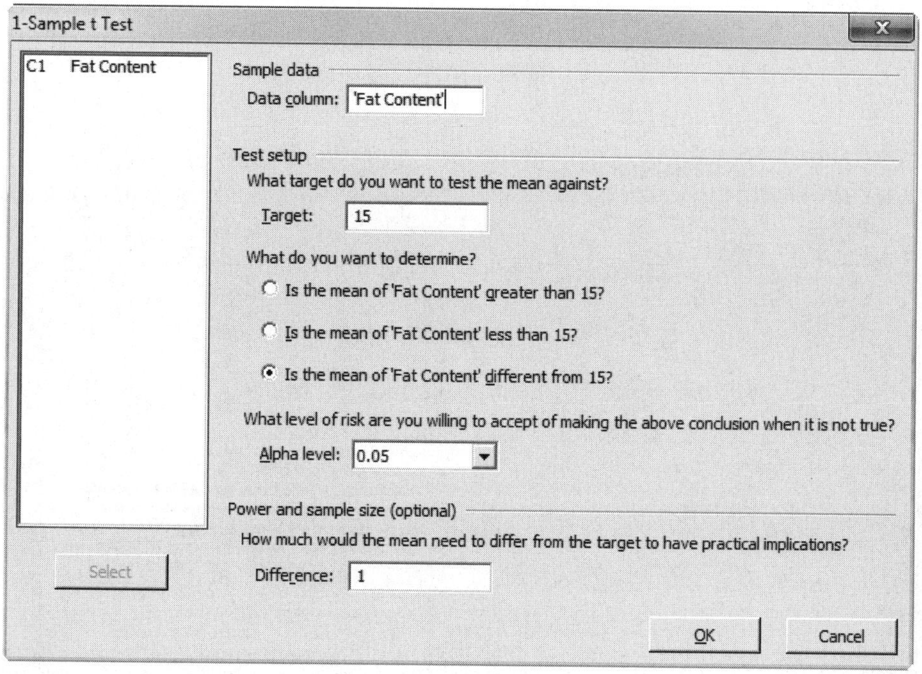

FIGURE 6-4 · 1-Sample *t*-test assistant.

Finally, Gordon reaches the 1-Sample *t*-Test assistant dialog seen in Fig. 6-4. In this dialog, the assistant asks a series of questions to finalize the test:

- Where is the data? Enter the name of the Data column, which is Fat Content.

- What target do you want to test the mean against? Here, the target is 15.

- What do you want to determine? Is the mean 'Fat Content' greater than/less than/different from 15? This choice defines the alternative hypothesis H_A.

- What level of risk are you willing to accept of making the above conclusion when it is not true? Here, the "above conclusion" is the alternative hypothesis H_A. The answer, often 0.05, is α (alpha), the risk of a type I error.

- (Optional) How much would the mean need to differ from the target to have practical implications? This is used to evaluate whether the sample size was adequate. If Gordon thinks 1 gram above or below 15 is a significant difference, he can enter 1 here.

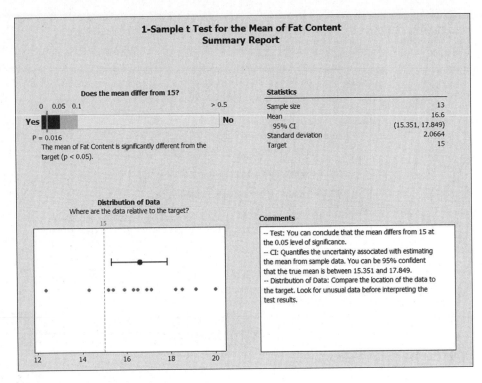

FIGURE 6-5 • 1-Sample *t*-test summary report.

After Gordon clicks OK, the report appears in the form of three graphs. The first one, the **Summary Report**, appears here as Fig. 6-5. The **Summary Report** has four panels listing all the key results from this hypothesis test.

- The top left panel shows the *p*-value as P = 0.016, on a graph comparing it to α = 0.05. Below the graph is one sentence describing the result of the test, that The mean of Fat Content is significantly different from the target of 15. By summarizing the test in one place, this is the most important part of the report.

- The top right panel lists a statistical summary, including a 95% confidence interval for the mean.

- The bottom left panel is a graph showing the individual values as dots, a confidence interval for the mean, and the target value of 15 as a green vertical line.

- The bottom right panel offers advice and comments on how to interpret the results of the test. Double-click the **Comments** box to edit the comments.

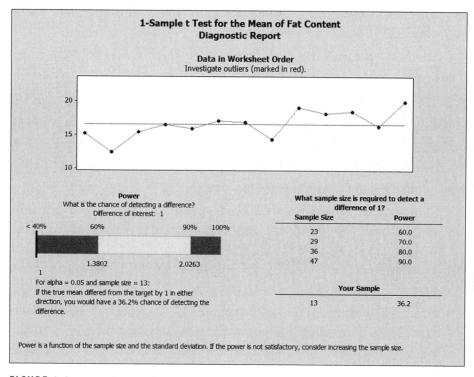

FIGURE 6-6 · 1-Sample *t*-test diagnostic report.

The second graph is the Diagnostic Report, shown here as Fig. 6-6. The Diagnostic Report helps you to evaluate the validity of various assumptions for the 1-sample *t*-test.

- The top panel is a run chart, showing the data in the order listed in the worksheet. If the chart shows clear trends, cycles, or outlying values, this may indicate that the system is not stable. If the system is not stable, the results of this hypothesis test are not a reliable indicator of future performance. Minitab performs an outlier test, and if unusually extreme values are found, Minitab will show these with red dots. In this example, no outliers are found.

- The bottom-left panel shows the power of this test graphically, with a sample size $n = 13$ and $\alpha = 0.05$. With these settings, this test has only a 36.2% power, which is the probability of detecting a shift of size 1. That is, if $\mu = 16$ instead of 15, the test would only have a 0.362 probability of detecting that shift with a sample size of 13. This is quite low, so the graph shows the power in a zone shaded red.

- The bottom-right panel lists sample sizes which would be required to detect a shift of size 1 with different levels of power.

In this example, any concern about power is moot, since the test did detect a shift at $\alpha = 0.05$. The third graph in this report is the **Report Card**, shown here as Fig. 6-7. This graph presents advice that summarizes any potential concerns about the validity of this test. For this example:

- Minitab did not detect any unusual data points.
- Minitab raises a caution about normality with small samples. Normality cannot reliably be tested with small samples, and if the population is not normal, the *p*-value may be incorrect for a small sample. This is only a caution, since the only way to mitigate it would be to collect more data.
- Minitab finds no concern with the sample size, since the shift was detected at $\alpha = 0.05$. If the analysis is repeated at $\alpha = 0.01$, the green icon becomes an X in a red stop sign, indicating a serious concern with inadequate sample size.

The report card uses color coded icons to indicate a variety of different situations.

The check in a green box indicates no problem.

The *i* in a blue circle indicates information only. This may or may not be a concern depending on other information that Minitab cannot know.

		1-Sample t Test for the Mean of Fat Content
		Report Card
Check	**Status**	**Description**
Unusual Data	✓	There are no unusual data points. Unusual data can have a strong influence on the results.
Normality	⚠	Because your sample size is less than 20, normality can be an issue. If the data are not normally distributed, the p-value may be inaccurate with small samples. Because normality cannot be reliably checked with small samples, you should use caution when interpreting the test results.
Sample Size	✓	The sample is sufficient to detect a difference between the mean and the target. Because you entered a difference of interest, the Diagnostic Report provides a sample size evaluation for this difference. You do not need to be concerned that the power is low because the test detected a difference.

FIGURE 6-7 · 1-Sample *t*-test report card.

⚠️   The ! in a yellow triangle indicates a caution. This is a reason why the test results may not be correct. The analyst may or may not have a way to address this concern.

❌   The X in a red octagon indicates a serious concern with the test results, such as clear evidence that an assumption is not satisfied.

As another example of using the hypothesis tests assistant, consider the case of Nick, designer of robotic toys. Out of 6,050 robots sold, six robots had a defect causing them to attack their owners. After a recall and design change to eliminate the defect, 4,120 robots were sold with zero defects. Based only on these numbers, has the probability of a defect been reduced?

This is a two-sample problem, comparing the population of robots before and after the design change. The true probabilities of defects before and after the design change are unknown and will be estimated using the counts of robots and defects.

From the Minitab hypothesis tests assistant, Nick selects the 2-Sample % Defective test with the logo. Nick fills out the assistant dialog as shown in Fig. 6-8.

Notice that this assistant does not offer the option of using data in the worksheet. In this case it is much more common to simply enter counts of units tested and units defective, so the dialog provides a small table to fill out.

After labeling the two groups Before and After, Nick selects the question to answer: Is the the % defective of Before greater than the % defective of After?

Figure 6-9 is the summary report from this test. In the top left panel of this graph, Minitab reports that there is a significant decrease in % defective between Before and After, with $\alpha = 0.05$. The p-value for this test is 0.044, which is less than the selected α risk of 0.05.

The bottom left panel shows an interval plot with a 90% confidence interval for the difference in % defective, Before–After. Zero is outside this confidence interval, which is another reason to conclude there is a significant shift.

Still Struggling

Are you confused why $\alpha = 0.05$ corresponds to a 90% instead of a 95% confidence interval? If so, you are not alone. In Chapter 5, when the confidence level was used to make decisions, the false alarm rate α was defined as one minus the confidence level. In the hypothesis tests assistant, when a two-sided alternative hypothesis is selected with $\alpha = 0.05$, the corresponding two-sided confidence interval is 95%, as shown earlier in Fig. 6-5. But when a one-sided test is selected, the corresponding confidence interval should also be one-sided. If $\alpha = 0.05$, either a 95% upper confidence bound or a 95% lower confidence bound corresponds to the decision required. In the hypothesis tests assistant, Minitab combines the 95% upper bound and the 95% lower bound into a 90% interval, with 5% error above and 5% error below the interval. In doing this, the Minitab assistant is not wrong, but it is needlessly confusing. Hopefully, in a future release, Minitab will change this aspect of the assistant for one-sided hypothesis tests.

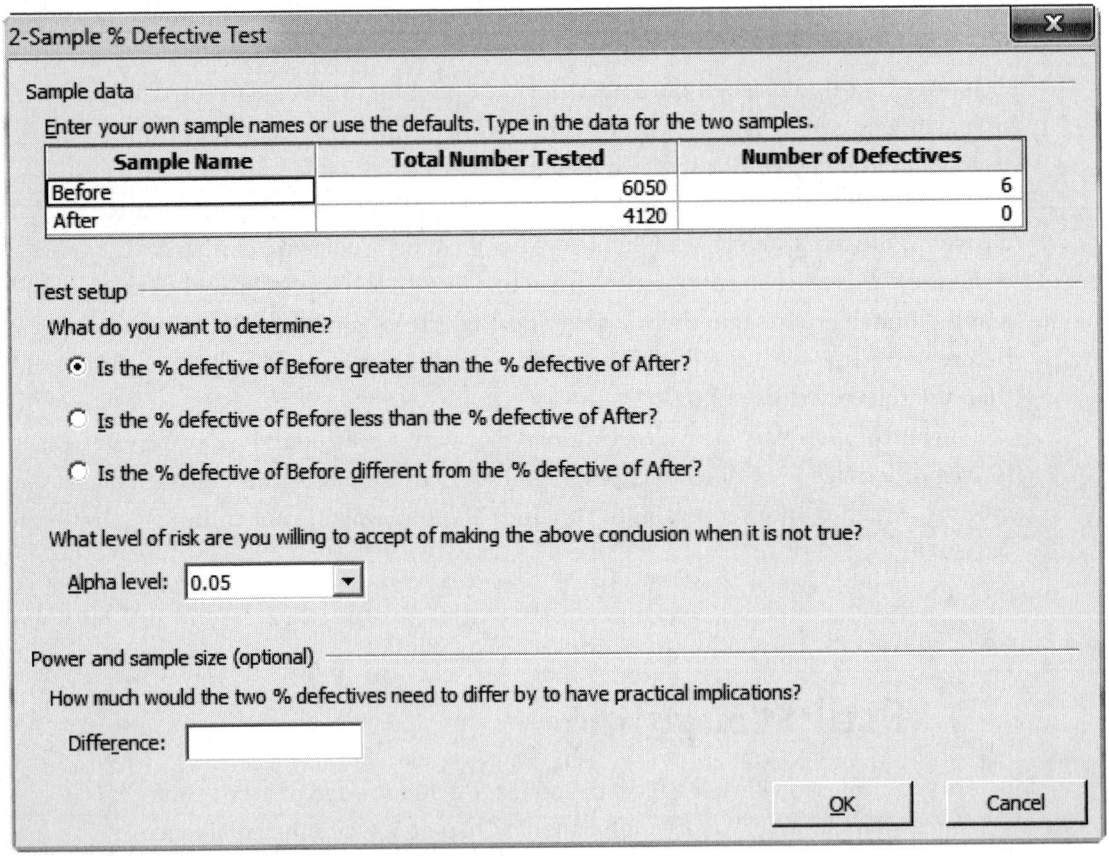

2-Sample % Defective Test

Sample data

Enter your own sample names or use the defaults. Type in the data for the two samples.

Sample Name	Total Number Tested	Number of Defectives
Before	6050	6
After	4120	0

Test setup

What do you want to determine?

⊙ Is the % defective of Before greater than the % defective of After?

○ Is the % defective of Before less than the % defective of After?

○ Is the % defective of Before different from the % defective of After?

What level of risk are you willing to accept of making the above conclusion when it is not true?

Alpha level: 0.05 ▼

Power and sample size (optional)

How much would the two % defectives need to differ by to have practical implications?

Difference: [   ]

OK   Cancel

FIGURE 6-8 · 2-sample % defective assistant.

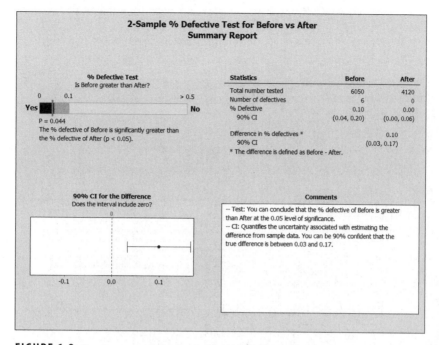

2-Sample % Defective Test for Before vs After
Summary Report

% Defective Test
Is Before greater than After?

Yes [ ] No
P = 0.044
The % defective of Before is significantly greater than
the % defective of After (p < 0.05).

Statistics	Before	After
Total number tested	6050	4120
Number of defectives	6	0
% Defective	0.10	0.00
90% CI	(0.04, 0.20)	(0.00, 0.06)
Difference in % defectives *		0.10
90% CI		(0.03, 0.17)
* The difference is defined as Before - After.		

90% CI for the Difference
Does the interval include zero?

Comments

-- Test: You can conclude that the % defective of Before is greater
than After at the 0.05 level of significance.
-- CI: Quantifies the uncertainty associated with estimating the
difference from sample data. You can be 90% confident that the
true difference is between 0.03 and 0.17.

FIGURE 6-9 · Summary report for the 2-sample % defective test.

This particular example of Nick and the insubordinate robots raises another important issue. Overall, the Minitab assistant is a wonderful tool for organizing and presenting results, but it cannot overcome fundamental limitations in statistical theory. Here, in this silly, simple example, we have bumped into one of those limitations.

To understand this issue, click the 🔲 button or use the Ctrl+E hotkey to recall the last dialog. Complete the 2-sample % Defective dialog as shown in Fig. 6-4, except now, select an alpha level of 0.01 instead of 0.05. Figure 6-10 shows the Summary Report with these settings.

In the top left panel of Fig. 6-10 is the same p-value of 0.044, with a correct statement that the % defective of Before is not significantly greater than the % defective of After, since the p-value > α = 0.01. So far, so good.

Now look at the 98% confidence interval on the difference in % defective, which is (0.01, 0.19). The lower bound of the interval, 0.01, is a 99% lower confidence bound on the difference. Since this lower confidence bound is greater than zero, this proves with at least 99% confidence that the % defective before IS significantly greater than the % defective after.

On two parts of the same graph are two apparently opposite conclusions calculated from the same data. Which one is right?

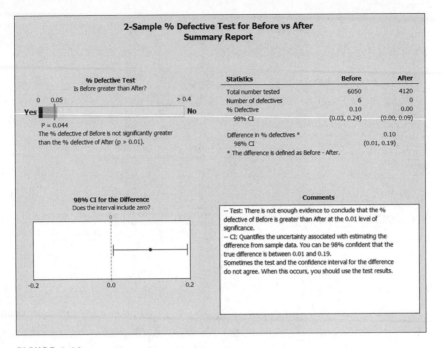

FIGURE 6-10 • Summary report with alpha = 0.01.

The Comments box includes an explanatory note that sometimes the test and confidence interval do not agree. "When this happens, you should use the test results."

In this situation, a 2-sample % defective test, the usual analysis method relies on a normal approximation for the counts in each cell of the table. Based on this approximation, normal distribution theory is used to calculate the confidence interval shown in the interval plot.

However, an exact test is available, called Fisher's exact test. Fisher's test involves more computation than the approximate method, so it may not appear in introductory statistics texts. This exact method produced the p-value of 0.044. Fisher's exact test can calculate p-values, but it cannot calculate confidence intervals. When the exact test gives a different answer from the approximate confidence interval, the exact test should be trusted, as the assistant correctly advises. In the Report Card (not shown here) is a comment that "the confidence interval for the difference may not be accurate."

In Chapter 5, on page 154, is a report from the Stat > Basic Statistics > 2 Proportions tool, using the same numbers as this example. This report lists the p-value from Fisher's exact test of 0.044. Also in the report is a p-value from the approximate test, which is 0.007. This is a significant difference in *p*-values between exact and approximate methods.

If we had at least five failed robots before and after the design change, the approximate method would be very close to the exact method. But this would be a terrible situation in real life. In a real situation, after we fix a problem, we should always have zero failures. With zero failures in one group, statistical tools in Minitab are unable to provide a reliable confidence interval for the change in probabilities. Fortunately, we have an exact hypothesis test which is a reliable way to make decisions.

To end this section on a more upbeat tone, consider the case of Leif, the arboriculturist. Leif collected 12 winged fruits (properly called samaras, not whirlybirds) from each of three maple trees. Leif measured fall velocity and disk loading on all 36 samaras, except for one that he dropped and stepped on. Leif's data is available in the Minitab sample data file Maple.MTW.

When we last left Leif in Chapter 2, he used an interval plot to look for differences in mean velocity between trees. Many people use nonoverlapping confidence intervals as an informal way to look for significant differences between means. But now we have a better tool for this purpose, called analysis of variance, ANOVA for short. ANOVA is an oddly named tool because it tests for differences between means (not variances) of two or more populations.

If Leif looks in the hypothesis tests assistant and follows the advice offered to select the best test, he will select the one-way ANOVA test with the ▦▦▦ logo. The ANOVA dialog has a dropdown box with two options for specifying how the data are organized in the worksheet:

- Choose Y data for each X value are in separate columns when the data are organized as they are in Maple.MTW. In the other Minitab menus, this arrangement is called unstacked.

- Choose Y data are in one column, X values are in another column when the data are in stacked format.

After choosing the first option above, Leif enters Vel1 Vel2 Vel3 in the Y data columns box and clicks OK.

For the ANOVA report, the Minitab assistant produces four graphs instead of three. The **Diagnostic Report** graph has a lot of information for ANOVA. The power calculations have been split into a separate **Power Report**.

Figure 6-11 shows the **Summary Report** for this test. Since the *p*-value is 0.000, this data provides very strong evidence of a difference between means.

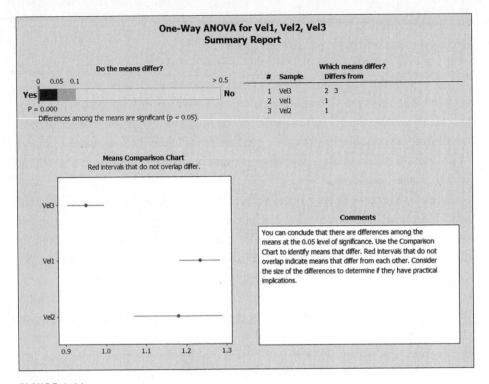

FIGURE 6-11 · ANOVA summary report.

But which means are different? The top right panel is a table listing which population means are different from which others. In this case the mean Vel3 is significantly different from Vel1 and Vel2, but the means of Vel1 and Vel2 are not significantly different from each other.

This is graphically shown using the Means Comparison Chart in the bottom left panel of Fig. 6-11. These intervals look like confidence intervals, but they are not the same as the ordinary confidence intervals shown on a Minitab interval plot or elsewhere in Minitab. These are called simultaneous confidence intervals, specifically designed for an ANOVA test on three groups. When these intervals do or do not overlap, they really do indicate which means are significantly different from which others, based on the overall alpha level selected for the test.

Figure 6-12 is the Diagnostic Report from this test. For each group, this graph plots the same data as dots on an individual value plot, and also on a time series plot in worksheet order. If there were significant outlying values in any group, Minitab would highlight these with red dots. A quick glance at this plot shows if there are trends or other signs of instability. Because of the amount of

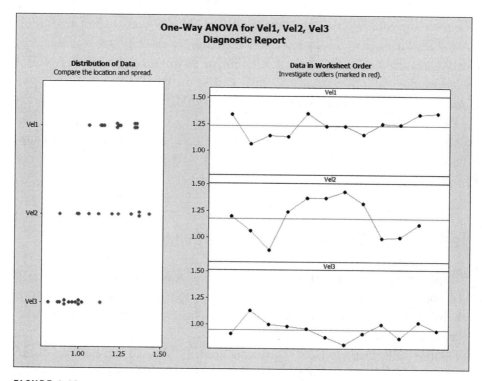

FIGURE 6-12 · ANOVA diagnostic report.

information displayed in a convenient and readable format, this graph may be one of the best features in the Minitab assistant.

As presented in many textbooks, ANOVA has three basic assumptions:

- **Independence of all observed values.** This assumption is very difficult to test, but the Diagnostic Report helps to spot correlated data using the time-series plots.

- **Normality of the population distribution.** If there is enough data, the assistant performs a normality test and reports the results. The assistant also checks for outlying data values.

- **Homogeneity of variance,** which means that the variation is the same in every group. The assistant uses an alternative procedure, called the Welch ANOVA, which does not make this assumption. The Welch ANOVA performs well even if some groups have much more variation than others. The tradeoff for this convenience is that the Welch ANOVA does not have as much power to detect differences in means, when the variation really is homogeneous.

Because the Minitab assistant uses the Welch ANOVA instead of traditional ANOVA, the assistant may provide different numerical results than if the same data is analyzed using the Stat > ANOVA menu. In this case, the Welch ANOVA used by the Minitab assistant is not available in the traditional menus. This omission will hopefully be corrected in a future Minitab release.

What's left for Leif? By analyzing the loading data in the same file, Leif finds that tree 3, with the lowest fall velocity, also has the lowest disk loading. This leads to Leif's Law of the Good Samara, #10: It's aloft last that's loaded least.

6.3　Testing Hypotheses Using the Traditional Menus

The Minitab hypothesis tests assistant is a well-designed tool which most people will use when possible. But the assistant is not right for every test or for every analyst. Minitab offers many tests and other tools in its traditional menu structure that are not provided by the assistant.

Figure 6-13 diagrams how the various tools of Minitab can be used during the whole process of testing hypotheses. In the center column of the figure is a general flow chart for testing, in five broad stages:

- **Planning** involves many tasks, depending on the situation. The Minitab assistant can help the analyst select a statistical procedure for many types

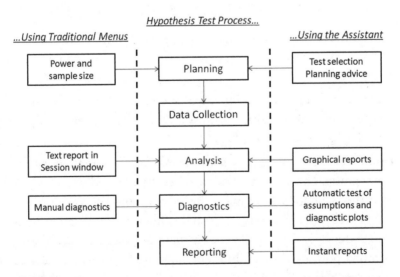

FIGURE 6-13 • Hypothesis tests with the traditional menus or the assistant.

of real-world questions, with its flow chart and illustrated examples for each choice. After selecting a test, the assistant offers general advice about collecting data, how to enter data into the worksheet, and other advice depending on the test. None of this advice is available from the traditional menus. However, power and sample size can be calculated from the Stat menu for most tests. It is awkward to do these calculations in the assistant before data collection, since this requires creating fake data to analyze. Power and sample size calculations are discussed further in the next chapter.

- **Data collection** happens in the real world, not in Minitab.

- **Analysis** involves calculating the hypothesis test statistics, p-values, and confidence intervals as required to answer the question. The testing tools in the Stat menu produce text reports in the Session window. The assistant produces graphical reports in a predefined format.

- **Diagnostics** are evaluations of the validity of assumptions made by the analysis. Using the traditional menus, this is an entirely manual process. The analyst is responsible both for understanding the assumptions and for running additional Minitab tests or creating graphs to validate the assumptions. The Minitab assistant automatically produces graphs and, where possible, tests assumptions, reporting findings and concerns in the Report Card.

- **Reporting** is where people will really love the Minitab assistant. The three or four graphs produced by the assistant form a comprehensive and consistently formatted report, with zero additional effort. These can be easily pasted into Microsoft Word, PowerPoint, or any other convenient format for presentation or archival purposes. Reporting can't be any easier than this.

The Minitab Stat menu is full of hypothesis tests. Many of these are integrated into submenus tailored for specific applications or industrial specialties. Here is a brief listing of how these hypothesis tests are organized in the Stat menu:

- The Stat > Basic Statistics menu contains almost all of the tests featured in the assistant, plus additional tests for Poisson rate (one-sample and two-sample), normality tests, and a Poisson goodness-of-fit test. In some of these dialogs, select the Perform hypothesis test option and specify the parameter value for testing.

- The Stat > Regression menu contains many types of regression tools for fitting models to a set of observed data. Hypothesis tests are used to decide which terms in the model are significant, and which can be removed from the model. Chapter 8 discusses regression tools further.

- The Stat > ANOVA menu contains several types of analyses of variance, plus diagnostic tools and specialized graphs. As with regression, hypothesis tests are used to include or exclude individual terms from ANOVA models. Advanced statistical training is required to understand many of these tools, so they are beyond the scope of this introductory book.

- The Stat > DOE (design of experiments) menu is for designing and analyzing experiments. These tools are very important for scientists and engineers to understand how complex systems function. The analysis of experiments uses hypothesis tests to select which variables in the experiment have significant effects on the system. Chapter 9 introduces the tools in this menu.

- The Stat > Control Charts menu creates control charts used by quality professionals to test processes for stability and causes of variation. Control charts are essentially visual hypothesis tests, without all the confusing terminology. Chapter 11 discusses control charts.

- The Stat > Quality Tools menu includes hypothesis tests for identifying distribution models (Chapter 4), gage studies (Chapter 10), capability analysis (Chapter 12), and acceptance sampling (Chapter 13).

- The Stat > Reliability/Survival menu contains specialized hypothesis tests for fitting reliability models. Some of these tools are introduced in Chapter 14.

- The Stat > Multivariate menu contains advanced hypothesis tests for datasets with many output variables. These tools are beyond the scope of this book.

- The Stat > Time Series menu contains hypothesis tests to help select models to represent how time-dependent processes behave. Time series analysis is also beyond the scope of this book.

- The Stat > Tables menu contains tools and tests for tables of data. The 2-sample % defective test seen earlier in this chapter is an example of the simplest form of this test, the 2×2 table. Much more elaborate tables can be compiled and tested for significant associations using these tools.

- The Stat > Nonparametrics menu contains alternative tests to the tests in the Basic Statistics menu, but without the underlying assumption of a normal distribution, or any other distribution model.

Although hypothesis tests come in endless forms, in Minitab they all end with a *p*-value. If you understand the null hypothesis H_0 for the test, the *p*-value always means the same thing. If the *p*-value is less than your selected value for α, there is significant evidence to reject H_0 and accept the alternative H_A.

To illustrate the process with a perhaps too-familiar example, consider Gordon's burger fat data in the Minitab example data file Fat.MTW. Suppose Gordon wants to test whether the mean fat is 15 grams, as the restaurant claims. This is a 1-sample test for the mean, with null hypothesis H_0: $\mu = 15$ and two-sided alternative hypothesis H_A: $\mu \neq 15$.

With Fat.MTW as the current worksheet, Gordon selects Stat > Basic Statistics > 1-Sample t, and fills out the form as shown in Fig. 6-14. Gordon checks the Perform hypothesis test box and enters the test value of 15 in the Hypothesized mean box. After clicking OK, Gordon sees this report in the Session window:

One-Sample T: Fat Content

```
Test of mu = 15 vs not = 15
```

Variable	N	Mean	StDev	SE Mean	95% CI	T	P
Fat Content	13	16.600	2.066	0.573	(15.351, 17.849)	2.79	0.016

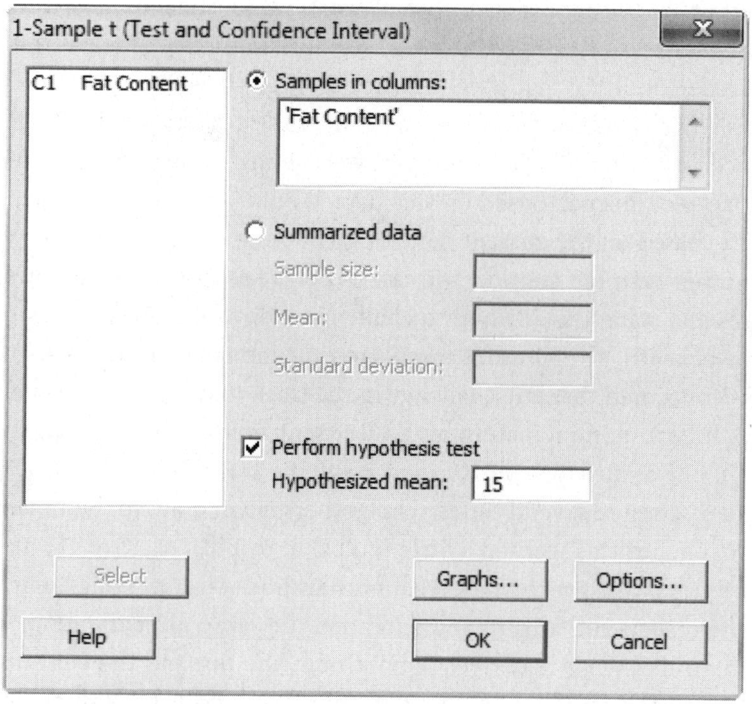

FIGURE 6-14 • Setting up a 1-sample hypothesis test.

Selecting the Perform hypothesis test option adds a T statistic and a P value to the table. The *p*-value for this test is 0.016. If the true mean fat $\mu = 15$ grams, there is a 0.016 probability of observing a sample at least as far away from 15 grams as this sample.

What does Gordon do with this information? He has two choices:

- He can conclude, with $(1 - 0.016) \times 100\% = 98.4\%$ confidence, that the mean fat is not 15 grams, and specifically, the mean fat is above 15 grams.

- If 98.4% confidence is not enough, he can conclude that there is not significant evidence of mean fat being different from 15 grams. If Gordon makes this choice, he could end the experiment with the conclusion of no difference, or he could go out and collect more data to look for stronger evidence.

In Chapter 5, when we used a confidence interval, the risk of an error was selected in advance. If Gordon chooses $\alpha = 0.05$, he concludes that mean fat is greater than 15. But if Gordon chooses $\alpha = 0.01$, he cannot make that conclusion. Earlier in this chapter, using the hypothesis tests assistant, Gordon must select and enter α in the Alpha level box before creating the report.

However, when running tests with Minitab's traditional menus, it is not necessary to choose α in advance. One can simply run the test, look at the *p*-value, and then decide if the evidence is strong enough. It is good practice to think about risk levels and choose α before running the test, but it is not necessary.

Suppose you were Gordon, and you were going to publish your findings in a newspaper or journal. Based on this data, would you decide to reject H_0 and accept H_A based on the current data, or go out and collect more data?

As another example, consider the case of Biff, a rancher whose hobbies include dirt bikes and statistics. Biff built a challenging dirt bike track on his property. On the weekends, he invites his friends to ride and race on the track.

Biff is concerned that one challenge in the track may be a bit too challenging. A jump, followed immediately by a turn, sent many riders skidding into the berm. On one Saturday, with 10 riders using the track, Biff counted 13 crashes. Some riders crashed several times, while others never crashed. Not many bones were broken, but this seemed a little too harsh to Biff.

On Monday, Biff got to work with his backhoe. After moving a fair amount of dirt, he realigned that turn and extended the ramp after the jump. The following Saturday, word had spread about both the fun and the danger of Biff's track. Among the 18 riders on that day, there were only 11 crashes. Was this a significant reduction in the number of crashes per rider?

As an avid statistical hobbyist, Biff knows the key to answering this question is to select the correct distribution model. The number of crashes per rider is a count, so a discrete distribution is appropriate. Biff read in Chapter 4 of this book that the Poisson distribution applies to situations when independent events can happen at any time, and they happen at the same mean rate per unit of time. In this case, events are crashes, and the unit of time is one rider in one day. Since these are reasonable assumptions, Biff decides to adopt the Poisson distribution model. The Poisson rate is the mean crashes per rider in one day.

To test whether the crash rate has significantly decreased requires a 2-sample Poisson rate test. In Minitab, the hypothesis tests assistant does not offer this test, but it is easy to find in the Minitab Stat > Basic Statistics menu.

In Minitab, Biff selects Stat > Basic Statistics > 2-Sample Poisson Rate. The dialog for this test offers three choices for how the data are organized: Samples in one column (stacked), Samples in different columns (unstacked), or Summarized data in the dialog. Biff completes the dialog as follows:

- He selects the Summarized data option.
- For the First sample, Biff enters Sample size: 10 and Total occurrences: 13.
- For the Second sample, Biff enters Sample size: 18 and Total occurrences: 11.
- He clicks the Options button and selects an Alternative of Greater than.

The choice of Greater than seems odd, but Minitab estimates and tests the rate for the first sample minus the rate for the second sample. Biff wants to test whether this difference is greater than zero.

Here is the report in the Session window:

Test and CI for Two-Sample Poisson Rates

Sample	Total Occurrences	N	Rate of Occurrence
1	13	10	1.30000
2	11	18	0.61111

```
Difference = rate(1) - rate(2)
Estimate for difference: 0.688889
95% lower bound for difference: 0.0228742
Test for difference = 0 (vs > 0): Z = 1.70 P-Value = 0.044

Exact Test: P-Value = 0.050
```

According to the table in this report, the Poisson rate is estimated to be 1.3 crashes per rider for the first day, and 0.61 crashes per rider for the second day. As in many other Minitab reports, this report offers both an approximate and an exact test. The approximate test is not labeled approximate, but it is based on a normal approximation for the Poisson distribution. When testing for a zero difference, the exact test is available, and in this case, it is preferred over the approximate test. The exact test, with a p-value of 0.050, gives Biff 95% confidence that the rate of crashes has been reduced between the first day and the second day.

Many people are confused about whether a one-sided or two-sided test is appropriate. The key to understanding this is to understand the real-world question. Think about what action will be taken depending on the result of the test. If action will be taken if the parameter is too high or too low, then a two-sided test is appropriate. If action will only be taken if the parameter has moved in one direction, but not the other direction, then a one-sided test is appropriate.

In the example of Gordon's burger fat data, Gordon may take action if he finds the mean burger fat to be higher or lower than the advertised 15 grams. The action may involve publication or sharing the data with the company. If there is no evidence that the mean is anything other than the advertised 15 grams, then there is no action to take. This situation calls for a two-sided test.

In the example of Biff's crash rate, he is looking for evidence that crash rate was reduced, so he is actually asking a one-sided question. If he finds a significant reduction, he may be satisfied with the new track configuration and do nothing. But if the reduction is not significant, he will take additional action to improve safety on the track. Since the potential action is also one-sided, a one-sided hypothesis test is appropriate.

What is not appropriate is to look at the data, see which way it is leaning, and then run a one-sided test based on the direction indicated by the data. If a two-sided test would be appropriate, using the data to choose a one-sided test will effectively cut the p-value in half without a good reason. This is generally regarded as unethical statistical trickery. It is better to select a one-sided or two-sided test based on the real-world question and potential actions that may result from the test.

The other hypothesis tests in the Stat > Basic Statistics menu all work the same way as the two featured in the above examples. In Chapter 5, many of these were used to calculate confidence intervals. Some of these dialogs have a Perform hypothesis test checkbox, and all have an options button to select the alternative hypothesis.

6.4   Find Out More

For all the functions in Minitab's traditional menus, the help files, in particular the Methods and Formulas file, are full of details on how these functions are performed.

However, the hypothesis tests assistant is not well documented in the Minitab help files. Some of the assistants use different statistical tools or calculations not available in other menus. To learn more about these tools, visit the Minitab Web site, click on the Knowledgebase/FAQ link, and search for "Assistant Methods." This will lead to a web page titled "Methods for Minitab 16 Assistant." Each of the analytical tools in the assistant has a white paper linked to this page. These white papers detail the research, simulations, and conclusions of the Minitab team as they developed the tools in the assistant. The white papers also list references.

Since hypothesis tests are at the core of statistical methods, almost any statistical text, like Montgomery (2010) or Sleeper (2006), covers many of these tools with examples, explanations, and exercises.

This chapter presented some of the most powerful and important statistical tools, hypothesis tests. Minitab 16 provides two platforms for performing hypothesis tests: the assistant offers easy diagnostics and consistently formatted reports, while the Stat menu offers more tests and more flexibility. The next chapter explains how to calculate sample size and power for hypothesis tests. The following chapters show how to use specialized hypothesis tests in regression analysis, the analysis of designed experiments, and many other specialized situations.

QUIZ

1. In a hypothesis test for normality, such as the Anderson–Darling test, what is the null hypothesis?

   A. H_0: The population follows a normal distribution.
   B. H_0: The population does not follow a normal distribution.
   C. H_0: The sample follows a normal distribution.
   D. It depends on the situation and what the analyst suspects might be true.

2. Which of the following is the best definition of what Minitab calls the alpha level or significance level?

   A. Alpha is the probability that H_0 is not rejected, when H_0 is true.
   B. Alpha is the probability that H_0 is rejected in favor of H_A, when H_0 is true.
   C. Alpha equals one minus beta.
   D. Alpha is the probability that random variation could cause a sample to appear at least as far from H_0 as the observed data, when H_0 is true.

3. Minitab reports that the *p*-value for a test is 0.01. With $\alpha = 0.05$, what does this indicate?

   A. There is insufficient evidence to reject H_A and accept H_0.
   B. There is strong evidence to reject H_A and accept H_0.
   C. There is insufficient evidence to reject H_0 and accept H_A.
   D. There is strong evidence to reject H_0 and accept H_A.

4. The Minitab hypothesis tests assistant produces a report in the form of graphs. Which graph contains an overall summary of the test, including a text interpretation of the results and comments?

   A. **Diagnostic Report**
   B. **Report Card**
   C. **Power Report**
   D. **Summary Report**

5. The Session window contains a report from a hypothesis test, including a `p-value = 0.085` and a separate `Exact test: p-value = 0.032`. If $\alpha = 0.05$, what is the best interpretation of this test?

   A. Since $0.085 > 0.05$, there is insufficient evidence to reject H_0.
   B. Since $0.032 < 0.05$, there is strong evidence to reject H_0.
   C. Since $0.032 < 0.05$, there is insufficient evidence to reject H_0.
   D. The test is inconclusive.

6. Load the Minitab sample data file Airplanepin.MTW. Do a hypothesis test to evaluate whether the population mean is different from 15.00. What do you conclude?

7. The university has a goal that 75% of freshman should pass a standardized physical fitness test. A random sample of 30 freshmen take the test, and 24 (80%) pass the test. Based only on this information, can we conclude whether the 75% goal is met for the overall freshman class?

Questions 8 and 9 are based on the Minitab sample data file Billiards.MTW. In this file are measurements of elasticity of billiard balls, made using three different additives. Ten batches were made using each additive, and the elasticity measured on each batch. In the file, column C1: Elastic lists the elasticity measurements, and C3: Additive lists 0, 1, or 2 to identify the additive.

8. Perform an appropriate hypothesis test to look for a difference in mean elasticity between the three additive groups. Is there a significant difference? If so, which additives produced significantly higher or lower elasticity?

9. Perform an appropriate hypothesis test to look for a difference in the standard deviation of elasticity between the three additive groups. Is there a significant difference? If so, which additives produced significantly higher or lower standard deviation?

10. A major industrial plant has a historical record of 3.0 lost-time accidents per month. A major safety initiative is implemented. In the three months following the initiative, there are only 5 lost-time accidents instead of the expected 9.0 accidents. This is encouraging, but is it statistically significant? With $\alpha = 0.05$, decide whether 5 accidents in 3 months is significant evidence that the accident rate has been reduced below 3.0 per month. Hint: use a Poisson model for accidents per month.

chapter 7

Calculating Sample Size

"How many units do I need to measure?"

Perhaps no question is more frequently asked of statistical experts or is more difficult to answer than this one. Part of the difficulty is that a precise answer to this question requires information that cannot be known until after data are collected. But in real life, few experiments are expeditions into the unknown; most are derivations and extensions of past work. Those who know the system best generally have some relevant historical data or educated guesses about how the system will perform in the proposed experiment. Combining such data or guesses with the objectives of the new experiment, an appropriate sample size can be calculated.

Accurate sample size formulas can be dauntingly complex, but Minitab handles these complexities easily for a wide range of hypothesis tests and experiments. Of greater significance is a new sample size interface provided in Minitab 16, called Sample Size for Estimation. This tool extends the sample size functions of Minitab to include a simpler class of experiments, and it does so using friendly, plain language.

CHAPTER OBJECTIVES

Here's what you'll learn in this chapter:

- How to decide whether sample size for estimation or hypothesis testing is appropriate for a particular problem

- How to calculate sample size requirements for estimating means, standard deviations, proportions and Poisson rates

- How to calculate power and sample size requirements for one-sample and two-sample hypothesis tests

- How to create and interpret power curves to explore the tradeoffs between sample size, effect size, power, and risk levels

Questions about sample size typically arise at two critical times: before data collection, and after. Waiting until after data collection to ask about sample size is like buying a length of rope at the store without deciding how much rope is needed. Either the purchased rope will be too short, a total waste, or too long, a partial waste. With careful measurements and advance planning, just enough rope is purchased for the required task, plus a little extra to provide a reasonable margin of error. So it is with sample size calculations. The best time to ask about sample size is before collecting data.

Minitab's new hypothesis tests assistant, featured in Chapter 6, performs a wide variety of sample size and power calculations for a dozen popular hypothesis tests. In an odd twist for an otherwise well-designed tool, these sample size and power reports are only accessible at the same time data are analyzed. Before collecting data, using the assistant to calculate sample size requires the awkward task of generating fake data embodying the educated guesses about how the system will perform. Because of this limitation of the assistant, this chapter illustrates only the traditional Minitab menus, and not the assistant, for all sample size and power calculations.

7.1 Asking the Right Question

Noted inventor Charles Kettering once said that a problem well stated is a problem half solved. Sleeper's corollary to Kettering's law is that a problem badly stated is a problem never solved.

These maxims are especially valid in statistics, where a simple question like "How many?" can lead to mind-numbing discussions of distribution models, risk probabilities, and octosyllabic data disorders like heteroscedasticity. No wonder statisticians are the death of any party.

Let's cut through the clutter. An experiment is the process of planning, data collection, and analysis to answer a question. Depending on the question, there are two broad categories of experiments, as illustrated in Fig. 7-1.

- Some experiments ask "What is it?" The primary goal of these experiments is to estimate something important about a population of items. A representative sample of items is measured. Since the sample is smaller than the population, sampling error is the variation between the sample and population. Sampling error is managed and communicated by a confidence interval, as discussed in Chapter 5. In Minitab, sample size calculations are provided by the Sample Size for Estimation tool.

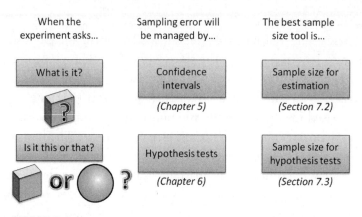

FIGURE 7-1 · Two families of sample size problems.

- Other experiments ask "Is it this or that?" This question can take many forms, including these: "Is it different from … ?" "Is it better than … ?" "Does this factor affect that response?" All of these questions require a decision based on a measured sample of data. Hypothesis tests, discussed in Chapter 6, are the standard tool for making these decisions, although confidence intervals can also be used in some cases. When a data-based decision is required, Minitab provides sample size calculations for many types of hypothesis tests.

As the examples below illustrate, most situations have opportunities for both types of experiments. It is critical to understand the question to be answered before starting any experiment.

Example: A political campaign often uses public opinion polling to gauge the support for a candidate or issue among likely voters.	
Estimation Question: How many voters support candidate X today? The answer will be an estimate with a confidence interval, often expressed as a margin of error.	**Testing Question:** Is support for candidate X today more or less than it was in a similar survey last month? The question will be answered by a hypothesis test.

Example: A machine shop manufactures parts for automobile engines. Before starting production on a new part, a set of parts is manufactured in a capability study. Critical characteristics on these parts are measured to determine whether the parts and process are acceptable.	
Estimation Question: For the population of future parts to be made using the same process, what are the means and standard deviations of all critical characteristics?	**Testing Question:** Are the means close enough to target, and are the standard deviations small enough to meet company standards for quality?

Example: In a sensitive measurement instrument, spurious transients happen occasionally for no apparent reason, even when no signal is present to measure.	
Estimation Question: What is the mean rate of spurious transients per hour?	**Testing Question:** Do different instruments have different rates of spurious transients? Does the rate of spurious transients change with temperature?

Example: Cable By Ed LLC provides cable TV, Internet, and phone services in Edburg. To monitor signal quality, Ed remotely polls his set-top boxes in subscribers' homes to measure signal strength.	
Estimation Question: What is the mean and standard deviation of signal strength?	**Testing Question:** Is signal strength high enough to make it unlikely that customers will experience signal loss problems?

The next two sections will explain how to use Minitab to calculate sample sizes for estimation and hypothesis testing.

7.2 Calculating Sample Size for Estimating Parameters

When the objective is to learn something about a population by measuring a sample, how large should the sample be? Minitab makes it easy to answer this question with a new feature of Minitab 16 called Sample Size for Estimation. This tool can be found at the top of the Stat > Power and Sample Size menu.

There are three interrelated quantities in every estimation sample size problem. These are illustrated in Fig. 7-2, with lines representing the relationships between them as a lever on a fulcrum.

- **Sample size** is the count of individual items to be measured. It is always assumed that the sample is representative of a larger population.

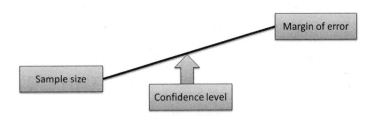

FIGURE 7-2 · Sample size, margin of error, and confidence level are related.

- **Margin of error** is a region of uncertainty around the estimate of an unknown population parameter. Margin of error is the difference between the estimate and the limit of a confidence interval. The margin of error is a result of sampling error caused by the sample being a subset of the population. Therefore, a larger sample size reduces the margin of error. A smaller sample size increases the margin of error.

- **Confidence level** is the probability that the true population value will be no further than the margin of error from the estimate. To increase the confidence level requires an increased sample size, an increased margin of error, or both.

To see how these quantities work together, consider the case of Paul, an aspiring politician. Paul is considering a run for the state Senate. Before launching a campaign, he wants to perform a telephone survey to estimate how much support he would have among likely voters. How many people should be surveyed?

To find out, Paul selects Stat > Power and Sample Size > Sample Size for Estimation from the Minitab menu. This dialog is shown in Fig. 7-3. Using the Parameter dropdown box, Paul selects Proportion (Binomial), since the goal of the survey is to estimate a proportion of likely voters who would support Paul. The proportion is assumed to follow a binomial distribution model.

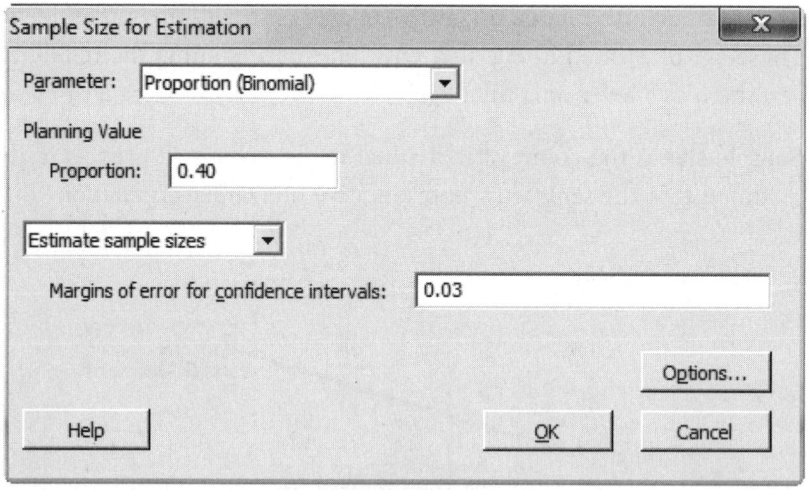

FIGURE 7-3 · Sample Size for Estimation dialog.

Next, Minitab asks for a Planning value for the proportion. This would be a guess about the result of the survey, which Minitab will use to calculate the sample size. Paul guesses that he is reasonably well known in the state Senate district because of his career in local politics. Paul enters a Planning value of 0.40, representing 40% of likely voters.

Finally, Minitab asks for the Margins of error for confidence intervals. Here, Paul enters 0.03. He would like to measure the level of support within ± 3%. After Paul clicks OK, he sees this report in the Session window:

Sample Size for Estimation

Method

Parameter	Proportion
Distribution	Binomial
Proportion	0.4
Confidence level	95%
Confidence interval	Two-sided

Results

Margin of Error	Sample Size
0.03	1075

Minitab reports that to measure his support within ± 3% would require a survey of 1,075 voters. This is far more than Paul's budget will allow. He wonders what he can accomplish with a more affordable survey of 200 voters.

Minitab can reverse this calculation by calculating a margin of error for a given sample size. To do this, Paul uses the ▣ icon in the Standard toolbar to recall the last dialog. He uses the dropdown box in the middle of the dialog to select Estimate margins of error. In the Sample sizes box, Paul enters 200 and clicks OK. Here is part of the revised report:

Results

Sample Size	Margin of Error
200	0.0714643
200	-0.0684537

This report lists two numbers, because the confidence interval for proportion is not symmetric. The upper and lower margins of error are calculated separately.

Minitab calculates that a sample of 200 likely voters can estimate a proportion of 0.40 with a 95% confidence interval of +0.071 and –0.068. If 40% of the 200 voters surveyed give a certain response, the 95% confidence interval on that proportion will be (0.332, 0.471).

Did you notice the plurals in the Sample sizes and Margins of error box labels? Entering multiple values in these boxes produces a table of results. Suppose Paul enters 200:500/100 in the Sample sizes box. This is Minitab shorthand for "count from 200 to 500 in steps of 100." Here is the resulting report:

```
Results

Sample    Margin of
  Size        Error
   200    0.0714643
   200   -0.0684537
   300    0.0578664
   300   -0.0558710
   400    0.0498538
   400   -0.0483629
   500    0.0444282
   500   -0.0432386
```

Paul's survey would need to contact 400 likely voters to have a margin of error of less than 5%.

Now suppose Paul wants to save more money, by calculating 90% confidence intervals instead of 95%. After clicking the ⊞ icon, Paul clicks the Options button. In this dialog, shown in Fig. 7-4, Paul changes the Confidence level from 95 to 90.

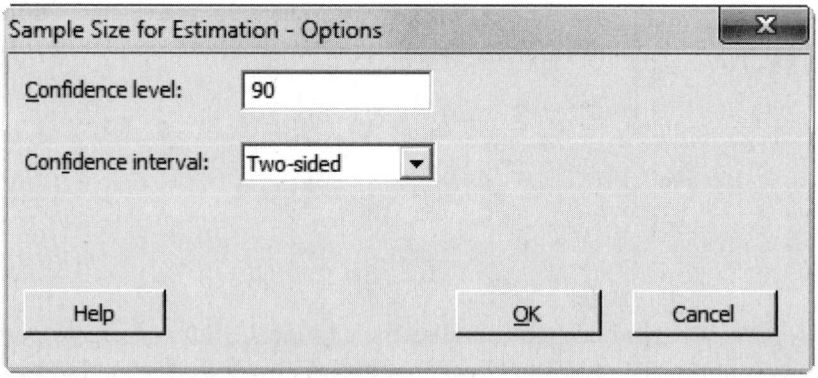

FIGURE 7-4 • Sample Size for Estimation options.

Here is the resulting report:

Sample Size for Estimation

Method

Parameter	Proportion
Distribution	Binomial
Proportion	0.4
Confidence level	90%
Confidence interval	Two-sided

Results

Sample Size	Margin of Error
200	0.0603162
200	-0.0580749
300	0.0487797
300	-0.0472967
400	0.0419963
400	-0.0408894
500	0.0374088
500	-0.0365262

Comparing this report to the previous ones, it is easy to see how reducing the confidence level reduces the margin of error for the same sample size. Or, for the same margin of error, reducing the confidence level reduces the sample size.

For a different example, Max is a manufacturing engineer for a company that manufactures fuel valves. One part of a fuel valve contains a critical orifice with a width tolerance of ± 50 µm. Max plans to manufacture a prototype run of these parts to prove that the process is capable of meeting that tolerance.

Since this is not a new process to Max, there is some historical data from similar parts. The machining process that creates the orifice recently demonstrated a standard deviation of 8 µm, with a fairly normal distribution.

Max would like to manufacture enough parts to estimate the mean with a margin of error of 5 µm. How many parts does Max need to manufacture?

Max selects Stat > Power and Sample Size > Sample Size for Estimation from the Minitab menu. In the Parameter dropdown box, Max selects Mean (Normal). For a Planning value, he enters a Standard deviation of 8. Since Max wants to estimate the mean with a margin of error of 5 µm, he selects Estimate sample sizes from the dropdown box and enters 5 in the Margins of error box.

Max then clicks the Options button, sets the Confidence level to 95, and verifies that the Confidence interval is Two-sided.

Here is the sample size report for the mean:

Sample Size for Estimation

```
Method

Parameter            Mean
Distribution         Normal
Standard deviation   8 (estimate)
Confidence level     95%
Confidence interval  Two-sided


Results

  Margin  Sample
of Error    Size
       5      13
```

With a sample size of 13, and a standard deviation of 8, Max will be able to estimate the mean with a margin of error of ± 5.

Max is also concerned about the standard deviation. He expects the standard deviation to be 8 μm, but if it gets larger than 12 μm, this will be a significant problem. Therefore, he wants to estimate the standard deviation with a 95% one-sided upper confidence bound. If the standard deviation is estimated to be 8 μm, Max wants the upper bound to be 12 μm. This would provide some evidence that problems of excessive variation will be avoided.

To calculate the sample size for standard deviation, Max clicks the 🖳 icon to recall the sample size dialog, and selects Standard deviation (Normal) in the dropdown box. The Planning value for Standard deviation is still 8. Since Max wants to detect if the standard deviation is 12 or higher, he enters a Margin of error of 4, which is 12 – 8.

This is a one-sided problem, since Max only wants to detect if the standard deviation is too large, not too small. Max clicks the Options button and selects Upper bound in the Confidence interval dropdown box. Here is the report:

Sample Size for Estimation

```
Method

Parameter            Standard deviation
Distribution         Normal
Standard deviation   8
Confidence level     95%
Confidence interval  Upper bound
```

```
Results

   Margin   Sample
  of Error    Size
         4      14
```

With a sample size of 14, the one-sided upper confidence bound for standard deviation will be 50% higher than the estimate. Combining these two results, 14 is the largest of the two sample sizes, so 14 is the minimum sample size for Max's prototype run.

For one more example, Eli is an engineer who designs radiation counters. Occasionally, an isolated counter will count, even when there is nothing to count. Eli blames these counts on cosmic rays, although there is no way to know for sure. What is important is to measure the rate of these spurious counts.

Eli estimates that the spurious counts happen once per minute. He connects a counter to a computer which will collect the accumulated counts once every five minutes. How long does this test need to run to estimate the rate of spurious counts within 10%?

Eli selects Stat > Power and Sample Size > Sample Size for Estimation from the Minitab menu. He selects Rate (Poisson) from the Parameter dropdown box, since the Poisson model is reasonable for this situation. He enters 1 for a Planning value of the Poisson rate. He selects Estimate sample sizes and enters 0.1 in the Margins of error for confidence intervals box to specify confidence intervals of ± 10% of the estimate.

Eli clicks Options. He selects a Confidence level of 95 and a Two-sided Confidence interval. When Rate (Poisson) is selected, Minitab adds a field to the Options form labeled "Length" of observation (time, items, area, volume, etc.). Since Eli's computer will collect the counts every five minutes, he enters 5 in this box.

Sample Size for Estimation

```
Method

Parameter           Rate
Length              5
Distribution        Poisson
Rate                1
Confidence level    95%
Confidence interval Two-sided
```

```
Results

  Margin  Sample
 of Error   Size
     1.1     85
```

Based on this report, a total of 85 counts, one every five minutes, for a total of 425 minutes, are required to estimate a Poisson rate of 1 per minute within a margin of error of ± 10%.

In the Sample Size for Estimation dialog, the Parameter dropdown box has both Rate (Poisson) and Mean (Poisson) options. In the Poisson model, the rate is the same as the mean, so these are two versions of the same thing, with one exception. With Rate (Poisson) selected, the Options dialog has the "Length" of observation option, but the Mean (Poisson) does not have that option.

Repeating Eli's example with Mean (Poisson) selected results in a required sample size of 423 minutes.

7.3   Calculating Sample Size for Hypothesis Tests

A hypothesis test is a process of deciding between two hypotheses, called H_0 and H_A for short. The null hypothesis H_0 generally represents equality, no change, or no effect. In terms of population parameters like a mean or a proportion, H_0 represents a single value. In the language of the previous section on sample size for estimation, H_0 could be the planning value for the population parameter. The margin of error is the difference between the estimate and the limit of a confidence interval, if H_0 is true.

But sample size calculations for hypothesis tests focus more on H_A than H_0. H_A represents a larger set of possibilities than H_0. If H_0 represents one value of a parameter, H_A usually represents all other values. To calculate sample size, we pick one alternate value of special interest and specify what power the test should have at that point. In other words, we specify the probability that the test will detect one specific value of the parameter; this will determine the sample size.

Here are the quantities involved in sample size selection for hypothesis tests:

- **Sample size** is the count of individual items to be measured. For two-sample tests, this is the size of each sample. It is always assumed that a sample is representative of a larger population.

- **Effect size** specifies the parameter value which needs to be detected with high probability by the test. Depending on the test, the effect size has different names. The effect size is called a difference for mean tests, a comparison proportion for proportion tests, a comparison rate for Poisson rate tests, or a ratio for standard deviation and variance tests. In general, a larger sample size will detect a smaller effect.

- **Power** is the probability that an effect of the specified size will result in a correct decision to reject H_0 and accept H_A. If beta (β) represents the probability of a type II error, power equals one minus beta. In general, a larger sample size provides greater power to detect a specified effect. A larger sample size will also detect a smaller effect with a specified power.

If the user specifies any two of the quantities above, Minitab will calculate the third quantity. This provides great flexibility to do a variety of what-if calculations before any money is spent to collect real data. If the initial calculation of sample size is too large, the user can enter a smaller sample size and then calculate either the power for a specified effect, or an effect size for a specified power. Minitab can also handle multiple values in these functions, producing a report and power graph with a range of sample sizes, effect, or power values.

Because of differences between hypothesis tests, each hypothesis test in the Stat > Basic Statistics menu has its own power and sample size calculator in the Stat > Power and Sample Size menu. After selecting the correct power and sample size function, these calculations also depend on the following user-supplied settings:

- A **planning value** provides context required to interpret the effect size specified above. Depending on the test, the planning value could be a standard deviation, a proportion, or a Poisson rate. Although it is impossible to know these values with certainty before collecting data, an educated guess or a value from a previous test must be provided here.

- The **significance level** is the value of alpha (α) which will be used to interpret the test. If the p-value is less than the significance level, H_0 will be rejected in favor of H_A. The significance level is often 0.05, although larger or smaller values are sometimes appropriate. A smaller value of significance level will increase the sample size for the same power and effect size. To change the significance level, click on the Options button in the power and sample size dialog.

- The **alternative hypothesis** is either less than, not equal, or greater than. The default choice, not equal, is for a two-sided hypothesis test. Choose either less than or greater than for a one-sided test. If the real-world decision depends only on the parameter being too small or too large, but not both, choose a one-sided alternative. A one-sided test will require a smaller sample size for the same power and effect size. To change this setting, click on the Options button in the power and sample size dialog.

In the last section, we saw how Max calculated a sample size for a prototype run of a new product. He did this by specifying the widths of confidence intervals based on a planning value of 8 μm for the standard deviation. For the mean, Max wanted the confidence interval to have a width of ± 5 μm. This would require a sample size of at least 13 units.

But Max has another concern with this test. If the mean is off target by 5 μm or more, he wants to have a high probability of detecting that shift. Suppose Max wants to have a power of 0.8 for an effect size of 5 μm. Does this require more than 13 units?

To find out, Max selects Stat > Power and Sample Size > 1 Sample t, since the 1-sample *t*-test will be used to test whether the mean is significantly off target. Figure 7-5 shows this dialog. Max leaves the Sample sizes field blank, so Minitab will calculate the required sample size. Max enters 5 in the Differences field, 0.8 in the Power values field, and 8 in the Standard deviation field. In the Options

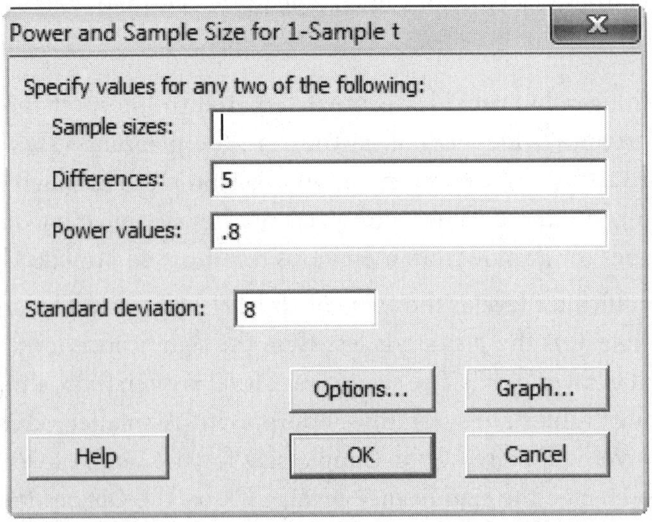

FIGURE 7-5 · Power and sample size dialog for 1-sample *t*-test.

form, the default options of not equal and a Significance level of 0.05 are acceptable here. After clicking OK, Max sees this report in the Session window:

Power and Sample Size

```
1-Sample t Test

Testing mean = null (versus not = null)
Calculating power for mean = null + difference
Alpha = 0.05  Assumed standard deviation = 8


              Sample  Target
Difference      Size   Power  Actual Power
         5        23     0.8      0.817107
```

This Minitab report shows that a sample size of 23 is required to have a power of 0.8 with a difference of 5 units when the standard deviation is 8 units.

Max also sees a Minitab graph displaying a power curve for this test. To duplicate the graph seen in Fig. 7-6, click the Graph button and enter 13 in the Generate additional power curves based on sample sizes box. This option is helpful to compare power curves for two or more different sample sizes.

A power curve plots power, the probability of rejecting H_0, against the effect size. For this 1-sample t-test, the horizontal scale represents the difference between

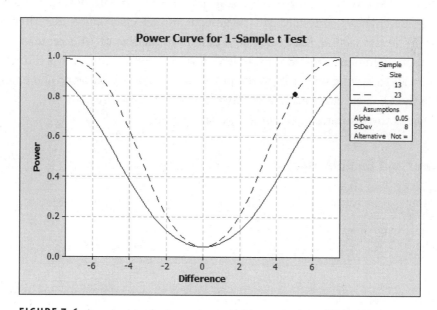

FIGURE 7-6 • Power curves for 1-sample t-test with sample sizes of 13 and 23.

the true population mean μ and the target value. If H_0 is true, and the mean is on target, this difference is zero in the middle of the plot. The probability of rejecting H_0 if it is true is α, which is 0.05. As μ departs from target in either direction, the probability of rejecting H_0 increases along the smooth power curve.

The two power curves shown in Fig. 7-6 are for sample sizes of 13 and 23. With a sample size of 23, and a difference of 5, the power is 0.82, just above the required 0.80. This point is shown by a red dot on the power curve. If Max runs this test with a sample of only 13 units, he will have less than 0.6 power at a difference of 5 μm. If μ is off target by 5 μm, the test will have less than 60% chance of rejecting H_0. Power curves make it easy to visualize the relationship between power and effects for a given sample size.

Max has one more goal for this test, and that is to be able to detect if the standard deviation is too large. Historical data suggests that $\sigma = 8$ μm. But if $\sigma > 12$ μm, this would be a serious concern for quality. Max wants to have a power of 0.8 of detecting $\sigma > 12$ μm.

To calculate this sample size, Max selects Stat > Power and Sample Size > 1 Variance, since the 1 Variance hypothesis test will be used to test for an increase in the standard deviation. In the dropdown box, Max selects Enter ratios of standard deviations. This form asks for Ratios, which would be the ratio of the alternate to the null values of σ. In this example, the ratio is $12 / 8 = 1.5$. Max enters a Power value of 0.8 and leaves Sample sizes blank.

Since Max is only looking for a possible increase in standard deviation, this is a one-sided hypothesis test. Max clicks Options and selects a Greater than alternative. In the last section, Max calculated that a sample size of 14 is required for the upper confidence bound for standard deviation to be 12 when the estimate is 8. To add a sample size of 14 to the power curve, Max clicks Graph and enters 14 in the Generate additional power curves based on sample sizes box.

Here is the resulting report in the Session window:

Power and Sample Size

```
Test for One Standard Deviation

Testing StDev = null (versus > null)
Calculating power for (StDev / null) = ratio
Alpha = 0.05


        Sample  Target
Ratio    Size   Power   Actual Power
 1.5      19     0.8       0.801525
```

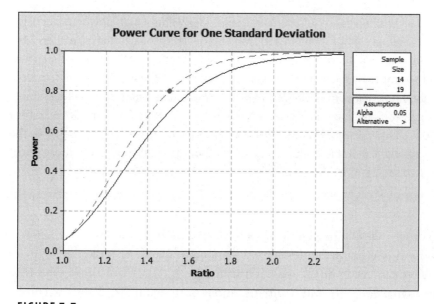

FIGURE 7-7 • Power curves for one standard deviation test.

For this test, Minitab reports that a sample size of 19 is necessary to provide a power of 0.8 for an alternative value of 1.5 times the null value.

Figure 7-7 shows the power curves for this test, with sample sizes of 14 and 19. The horizontal scale for this graph is the ratio of alternative to null values of standard deviation. When the ratio is 1.0, $\sigma = 8$ μm in this example, and the test has a 0.05 probability of falsely detecting a shift. A ratio of 1.5 represents $\sigma = 1.5 \times 8 = 12$ μm. At this ratio, a sample size of 14 provides a power of 0.7, but a sample size of 19 increases the power to over 0.8.

Combining these results, Max needs to run a prototype run of at least 23 units to provide a power of 0.8 to detect either a mean shift of 5 μm or a standard deviation of greater than 12 μm.

Still Struggling

The example of Max has now led to four different sample sizes: 13, 14, 23, and 19. Why are there so many answers to the same question: How many? The answer depends entirely on how the question is asked. If Max only wants to estimate the mean and standard deviation within a specified margin of error,

13 or 14 samples are sufficient. Instead, if Max wants a high power (probability) to detect a change in mean and standard deviation of a certain size, then 23 or 19 samples are required. If Max only cares about the mean and not standard deviation, only the first of these sample size pairs, 13 or 23, are relevant. To learn about the standard deviation, 14 or 19 samples are required. For a real sample size problem, you might only care about one of these four questions, so only one sample size is required. When multiple questions are to be answered by the same data, multiple sample sizes are calculated, and the largest of these calculated sample sizes should be used.

For an example of sample sizes for a two-sample test, consider Larry, who produces and markets one-day seminars on a variety of topics. Larry markets his seminars using direct mail. Typically, 1.5% (0.015) of those who receive Larry's mailers contact him with questions or to sign up for a course. This is the response rate Larry wants to increase.

Larry wants to experiment with a larger, more informative direct mail piece than he usually uses. In this experiment, Larry will print up two sets of mailers, one set of the old style, and a second set of the new style. Since the larger piece costs more for printing and postage, he does not want to send any more than he has to for the experiment.

To calculate sample size, Larry considers the risks of type I and II errors. A type I error would result if there is no difference in response rate, but Larry concludes that there is a difference. Larry decides to accept a 5% ($\alpha = 0.05$) risk of this "false positive" result. This value will be the Significance level in the Minitab Power and Sample Size Options dialog.

A type II error would result if there is a difference in response rates, but Larry falsely concludes there is no difference. This would be a "false negative" result. Larry decides that if one style of mailer has double the response rate of the other, 3.0% instead of 1.5%, he wants less than 10% ($\beta = 0.10$) risk of not detecting this shift. This would be a power of 0.90, with a response rate of 0.030 instead of 0.015.

The required hypothesis test is a two-proportions test, so to calculate sample size, Larry selects Stat > Power and Sample Size > 2 Proportions from the Minitab menu. Leaving the Sample sizes field blank, Larry enters 0.03 in the Comparison proportions field, 0.9 in the Power values field, and 0.015 in the Baseline proportion field. The default options of a Not equal (p1 not = p2) Alternative hypothesis and a Significance level of 0.05 are correct.

After clicking OK, Larry sees this report in the Session window:

Power and Sample Size

```
Test for Two Proportions

Testing comparison p = baseline p (versus not =)
Calculating power for baseline p = 0.015
Alpha = 0.05


               Sample  Target
Comparison p    Size    Power   Actual Power
       0.03     2053     0.9       0.900122

The sample size is for each group.
```

This Minitab report shows that a sample size of 2,053 mailers in each group will have a power of 0.90 of detecting a 3% return rate, compared to the baseline of 1.5%.

Figure 7-8 shows the power curve for this test. If both mailers have the same return rate of 1.5%, the test has an $\alpha = 0.05$ probability of falsely detecting a difference. If one mailer has a 1.5% return rate and the other has a 3.0% return rate, the test with 2,053 mailers in each group will have a power of 0.90, or a type II error $\beta = 0.10$, as designed by Larry.

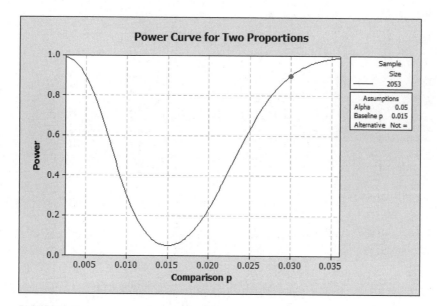

FIGURE 7-8 · Power curve for two proportions test.

In tests with proportions, as the proportion gets closer to zero, a much larger sample size is required to detect the same effect size. In the example shown in Fig. 7-8, notice that if the two mailers have response rates of 1.5% and 0.75%, the power is only about 0.60. A much larger sample size would be required to detect this effect with a power of 0.90.

At the bottom of the Power and Sample Size menu are four sample size calculators for one-way ANOVA and three types of designed experiments with many factors. These calculators work in much the same way as the examples already presented in this section. Designed experiments are discussed further in Chapter 9.

This concludes the informal second section of this book on statistical tools for decision making. This chapter complements the previous chapters on intervals and hypothesis tests by describing how to select the best sample size. The remaining chapters in this book cover Minitab tools for specific types of problems, starting with regression analysis in the next chapter.

QUIZ

1. A sample of college students are going to be surveyed to estimate the proportion who are interested in joining a proposed Statistics Club. Which is the most appropriate Minitab function to calculate the required sample size?

   A. Stat > Power and Sample Size > Sample Size for Surveys
   B. Stat > Power and Sample Size > Sample Size for Estimation
   C. Stat > Power and Sample Size > 1 Proportion
   D. Stat > Power and Sample Size > 2 Proportions

2. A traffic engineer wants to determine if the rate of accidents per month at an intersection has significantly decreased, compared to historical levels, since the installation of a new traffic light. Which is the most appropriate Minitab function to calculate the required sample size?

   A. Stat > Power and Sample Size > Sample Size for Estimation
   B. Stat > Power and Sample Size > 1 Sample t
   C. Stat > Power and Sample Size > 1 Variance
   D. Stat > Power and Sample Size > 1-Sample Poisson Rate

3. If the margin of error for an estimate is 5 units, with a 95% confidence level, which of the following is the most correct statement?

   A. The estimate is within 5 units of the true population value.
   B. The width of a 95% confidence interval is 5 units.
   C. The difference between the estimate and one limit of a 95% confidence interval is 5 units.
   D. The standard deviation is 2.5 units.

4. In the planning of a hypothesis test, you decide to accept $\alpha = 0.10$ risk of a "false positive" or a type I error. How is this specified in the Minitab Power and Sample Size dialog?

   A. Enter 0.10 in the Alpha level field.
   B. Click Options and enter 0.10 in the Significance level field.
   C. Enter 0.90 in the Power values field.
   D. This is the default setting. It is not necessary to enter anything.

5. In the planning of a 1 Sample *t*-test, suppose you want to calculate the differences that can be detected with sample sizes of 10, 20, and 30, and type II error probabilities of 0.10 and 0.20. What is the easiest way to do this?

   A. Perform six separate calculations using all combinations of settings.
   B. In the Power and Sample Size for 1-Sample t dialog, enter "10:20/10" in the Sample Sizes field and "0.10 0.20" in the Significance level field. Leave the Differences field blank.

C. In the Power and Sample Size for 1-Sample t dialog, enter "10 20 30" in the Sample sizes field and "0.10 0.20" in the Type II Errors field. Leave the Differences field blank.

D. In the Power and Sample Size for 1-Sample t dialog, enter "10:30/10" in the Sample sizes field and "0.80 0.90" in the Power values field. Leave the Differences field blank.

6. **What sample size is required to estimate the standard deviation of a normal population with a two-sided 95% confidence interval and a margin of error of 5? For a planning value, suppose the standard deviation is expected to be 10.**

7. **A structural beam in an aircraft has been redesigned to increase strength and decrease weight. Suppose you are planning a test during which a sample of the old design and a sample of the new design will be stressed to failure, so that the strength can be measured. It is expected that the standard deviation of strength is 100 units, and it is also expected that the new design will be stronger than the old design. How large a sample size is required to detect an increase of 50 units in the mean strength of this beam with a power of 0.9 and a significance level of 0.05?**

8. **The calculated sample size in problem 7 would be too expensive. The largest sample size that the budget will allow is 20 beams in each sample. Also of interest is that an engineering model of the new design predicts a strength improvement of 93 units. What can be accomplished with an affordable sample size? Create a relevant graph.**

Questions 9 and 10 refer to Fig. 7-9, a family of power curves for the two-proportions hypothesis test.

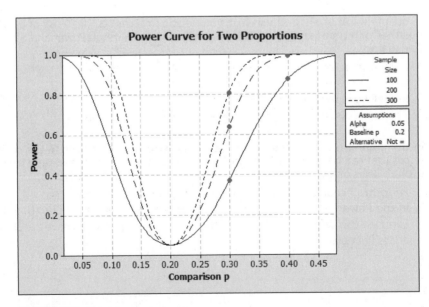

FIGURE 7-9 • Power curves.

9. What sample size provides an approximate type II error of $\beta = 0.36$, when the true probabilities of the two populations are 0.2 and 0.3?

10. With a sample size of $n = 100$ units in each sample, and the true probabilities of 0.2 and 0.4, what is the probability that this test will correctly reject the null hypothesis?

Bonus: When you show this graph at a meeting, someone asks why the power curves do not drop all the way to zero at 0.2. How do you answer this question?

chapter **8**

Fitting Regression Models

Regression analysis is the process of finding the best model $Y = f(X)$ to fit a set of observed data for the X and Y variables. The Minitab Stat > Regression menu has many regression tools for different situations. In release 16, Minitab has upgraded many regression tools and added new ones, including a new regression assistant for fitting polynomial models with one X variable.

CHAPTER OBJECTIVES

Here's what you'll learn in this chapter:

- How to fit polynomial models of one predictor (X) variable
- How to fit models with many predictor (X) variables
- How to diagnose common regression problems
- How to fit nonlinear regression models
- How to fit models with a binary response (Y) variable

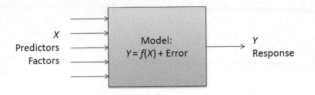

FIGURE 8-1 · Regression terminology.

Figure 8-1 illustrates common regression terminology. The box in the figure represents a system which produces a response (Y) variable. Inputs to the system (X) are called predictor variables. In an experiment where the X variables are controlled and set to specific values, the X variables are often called factors. Designed experiments are discussed further in Chapter 9. This chapter focuses on examples where the predictor (X) variables are observed and measured, but are not controlled.

Inside the box is a model, represented by $Y = f(X) + \text{Error}$. The analyst must select the general form of the model, with a set of unknown parameters. Regression analysis will find the best values of the parameters. Any variation in the data not explained by $f(X)$ is called error. In general, the best model is the one that explains the most variation, leaving the least variation in the error term.

Why use regression analysis? Here are some of the questions that Minitab regression tools can help to answer:

- How should data be gathered and entered into Minitab? The Minitab regression assistant offers good advice for all analysts to collect meaningful data, to analyze it properly, and to diagnose common problems.

- Is there a relationship between X and Y? A scatter plot may suggest that X and Y are related, but the pattern in the plot could be created by random variation. Regression analysis provides a p-value, which is the probability that random noise could cause the pattern when no relationship exists. If the p-value is very small, this is strong evidence that the relationship is significant.

- If there are many X variables, which ones should be in the model? This question can be answered with p-values, but these results can be confusing. The Minitab Best subsets tool helps to identify which X variables explain the most variation in Y.

- What is the best model $Y = f(X)$? Minitab regression analysis finds the best model to fit the available data. Uncertainty in the parameters of the model is quantified using confidence intervals.

- What is the predicted value of Y for future values of X? All Minitab regression functions have the option to predict future values of Y for any specified values of X, with prediction intervals to quantify the uncertainty around those predictions. It is unwise and unreliable to extrapolate outside the range of X values used to fit the model.

This chapter will cover most Minitab regression functions, starting with the new regression assistant.

8.1   Fitting a Polynomial Model

Polynomials are the simplest and most common models used to represent relationships between one predictor (X) variable and one response (Y) variable. Minitab makes it easy to fit any of the following regression models:

- Linear model: $Y = b_0 + b_1 X$
- Quadratic model: $Y = b_0 + b_1 X + b_2 X^2$
- Cubic model: $Y = b_0 + b_1 X + b_2 X^2 + b_3 X^3$

Three Minitab functions are available to select and fit these models. The regression assistant is the easiest tool to use, and like the other Minitab assistants, it provides a neatly formatted graphical report. Another tool, Stat > Regression > Fitted Line Plot provides more options, and a traditional text report in the Session window. Polynomial models may have much higher orders, but cubic is the highest order available in these two Minitab functions. Higher order polynomials may be fit using the Stat > Regression > General Regression tool, which provides the greatest flexibility.

To see an example of how these tools work, load the Minitab sample data file BMI.MTW. This file was created by Lena, a physical trainer. For 77 people, the file lists body mass index (BMI), which is a function calculated from height and weight, % fat based on skin fold measurements, and an activity level based on a survey completed by each person.

Lena wonders if % fat can be predicted as a function of BMI. To find out, she NEW IN 16 selects Assistant > Regression from the Minitab menu. This is a new feature of Minitab 16. The Assistant – Regression dialog presents a collection of good advice on collecting the data, evaluating the results, and using the model. For space reasons, this dialog is not shown here, but it is worth a look. Click on any ⊞ icon for more information on any of the points of advice.

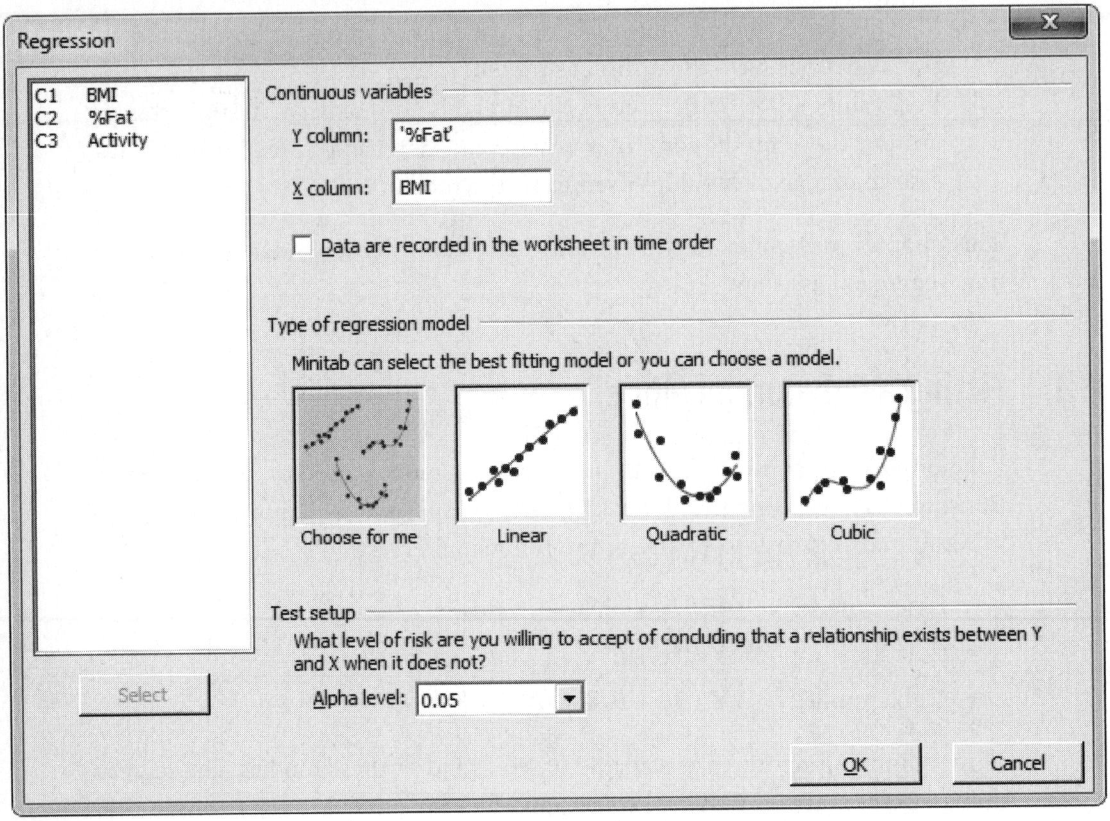

FIGURE 8-2 · Regression assistant dialog.

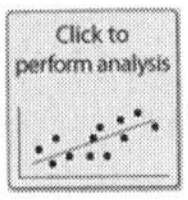

To proceed to the analysis, click the button (shown in the margin) on the left side of the dialog. In the Regression dialog, enter %Fat in the Y column field and BMI in the X column field. The Regression dialog is shown in Fig. 8-2.

Lena checks the checkbox labeled Data are recorded in the worksheet in time order. The dialog also offers a choice of models: Linear, Quadratic, Cubic, or the default and Lena's personal favorite, Choose for me. Lena leaves everything at its default setting and clicks OK.

The Minitab report appears in the form of five new graphs. The top graph, labeled **Summary Report** is shown here as Fig. 8-3. There are four panels in this graphical summary, each with different information.

- The top left panel of the report answers the question of whether there is a significant relationship between X (BMI) and Y (%Fat). With a p-value of 0.000, there is a very significant relationship. Any p-value less than 0.05 indicates a significant relationship.

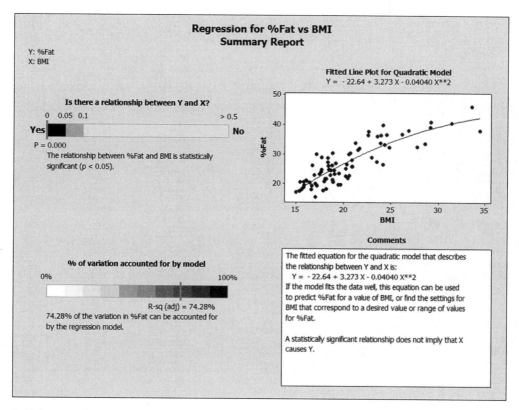

FIGURE 8-3 · Regression assistant summary report.

- The top right panel reports the best fitted model, in this case a quadratic function. In this function, X**2 represents X^2. The fitted line plot shows dots for all observed values, plus a fitted line representing the model.

- The bottom left panel shows the adjusted R^2, 74.28%, with an explanation that 74.28% of the variation in %Fat can be accounted for by the regression model.

- The bottom right panel lists comments explaining the test. These comments are suggested by Minitab, but they can be edited by the analyst. Double-click this panel to edit the text.

The other four graphs are worth studying, as well. Here is a quick summary of the information in the other graphs.

- The Model Selection Report, shown in Fig. 8-4, provides information about the choice of a quadratic model over the linear and cubic alternatives. Minitab fitted all three models, and chose the quadratic for this data

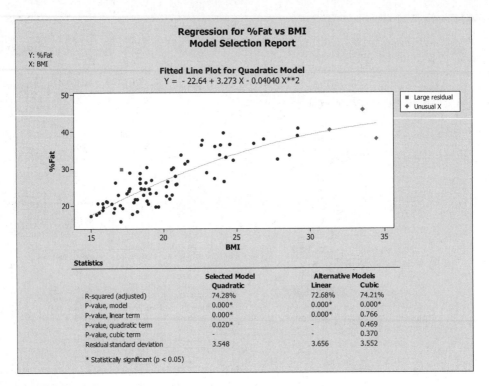

FIGURE 8-4 · Model selection report.

because it has the lowest adjusted R^2, and the highest order term in this model is statistically significant. This report has a copy of the fitted line plot, but on this report, selected points with unusually large residuals or unusual X values are highlighted in red. These highlighted points may be worth investigating.

- The **Diagnostic Report 1** shows a plot of residuals versus fitted values. Residuals are the difference between the observed values of Y and the predicted values of Y. If the model fits well, this plot should appear random without obvious trends, unusual points, clusters, or patterns. The bottom half of this graph offers advice about interpreting the residual plot, including little pictures illustrating conditions that warrant extra caution.

- The **Diagnostic Report 2** shows a plot of residuals versus time order. This report is only produced if the time order option is checked in the regression assistant dialog. This graph should be free of obvious trends, shifts, or other patterns which could indicate an extraneous effect interfering with the system or the data. The bottom half of this graph offers advice about interpreting the residual plot.

- The Report Card lists additional information about the analysis. This information includes potential concerns about sample size, unusual values, normality, and model fit.

Taken as a group, the set of graphs produced by the regression assistant provide a thorough report on the regression analysis, including a set of diagnostic reports and advice on interpretation. If these reports provide enough information, then this is clearly the fastest and easiest way to perform and document a polynomial regression analysis.

But Lena wants more. She would like to add lines to the fitted line plot representing a 95% prediction interval for %Fat. The regression assistant does not offer this option.

Lena turns to the traditional Minitab menus and selects Stat > Regression > Fitted Line Plot. The Fitted Line Plot dialog is shown in Fig. 8-5. After entering the variable names, Lena selects a Quadratic model.

This function is not able to automatically select one model over another. If Lena had not already used the regression assistant, she would start here with the Cubic model. Then, when she finds that the cubic term is not significant, she would proceed to the Quadratic model.

Lena clicks the Graphs button. In the Graphs dialog, shown in Fig. 8-6, Lena selects the Four in one residual plot. When using the Minitab regression functions, this is always a good idea.

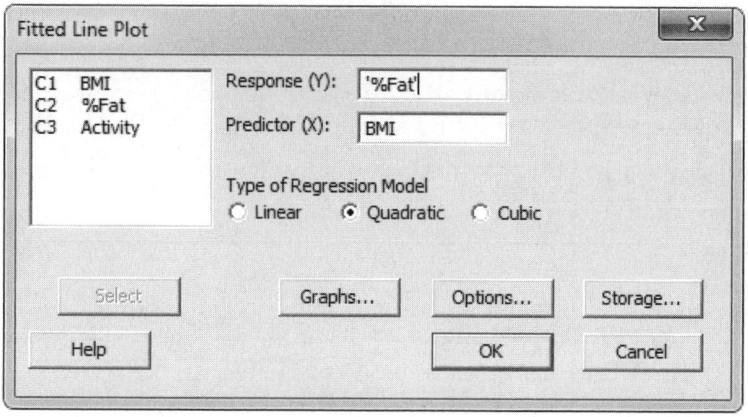

FIGURE 8-5 · Fitted Line Plot dialog.

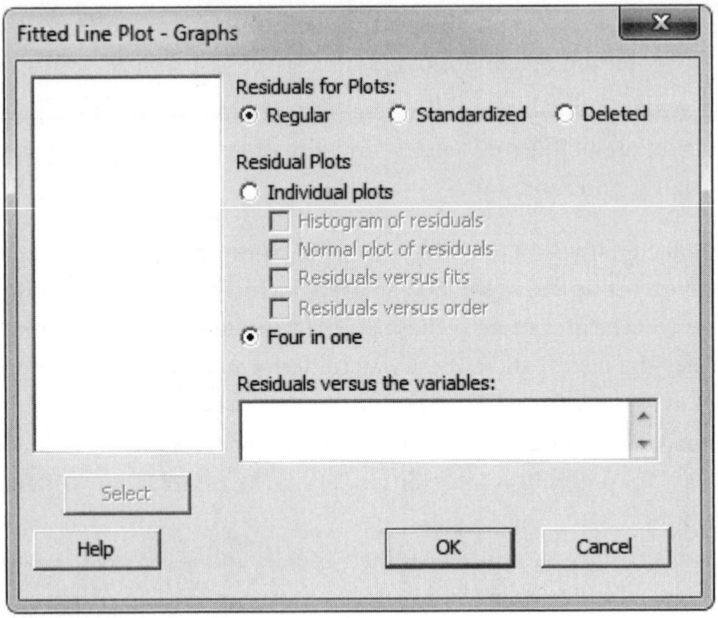

FIGURE 8-6 · Graphs dialog for fitted line plot.

Back in the Fitted Line Plot dialog, Lena clicks the Options button. In the Options dialog, shown in Fig. 8-7, she selects both the Display confidence interval and the Display prediction interval options. Selecting both is unusual because it clutters the plot, but it is done here to compare both sets of intervals.

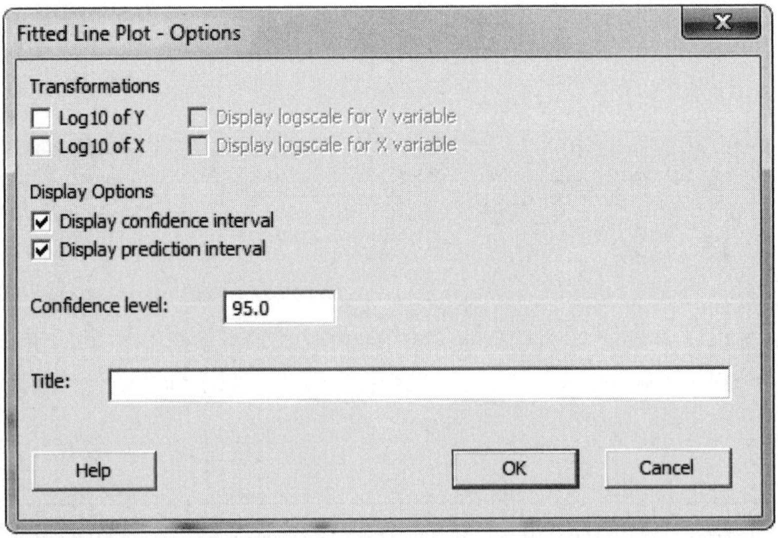

FIGURE 8-7 · Options dialog for fitted line plot.

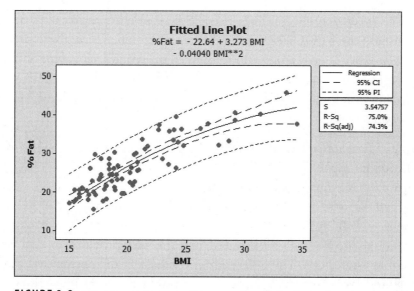

FIGURE 8-8 · Fitted line plot with confidence and prediction intervals.

Figure 8-8 shows the completed fitted line plot, with both sets of intervals drawn with dashed lines. The 95% confidence interval is represented by the lines closest to the middle line. The 95% prediction interval is represented by the outside lines.

Since many people are confused by these intervals, it is critical for an analyst to understand the difference between them. Here is a quick explanation:

- The middle line of Fig. 8-8 represents an expectation. Based on available data, it is expected that the mean %Fat over all individuals with the same BMI will follow this line. One can think of the expectation as a single number at each BMI representing our best guess of mean %Fat.

- The confidence interval lines of Fig. 8-8 represent a region of uncertainty around the expectation or mean line. The mean line is determined by a quadratic equation with three parameters. Each parameter has its own confidence interval. Taking these confidence intervals together, the true mean line might run anywhere within the confidence interval, with 95% confidence. Notice how much the confidence interval flares out at the ends of the plot, reflecting increased uncertainty in those areas.

- The prediction interval lines of Fig. 8-8 represent a region of uncertainty around the individual values of %Fat. This region is a combination of the confidence interval around the mean with the residual variation of individual values, which was not explained by the model. Lena can expect 95% of individuals with a given BMI to have a %Fat somewhere inside this 95% prediction interval.

Chapter 5 has more information about the differences between confidence and prediction intervals.

Figure 8-9 is a four-in-one residual plot, which is a convenient way to visually assess and diagnose common regression problems. In the top left of the plot is a normal probability plot of the residuals. Least squares regression assumes that the residuals are normally distributed, and this plot provides an easy way to assess that assumption. The histogram of residuals in the bottom left can also be used to look for unusually large or small residuals. The residual plots versus fitted values, top right, and versus time order, bottom right, are helpful to spot other concerns with the regression model.

Unlike the reports from the regression assistant, the residual plot in Fig. 8-9 provides neither outlier tests, nor advice, nor help with interpretation. As with

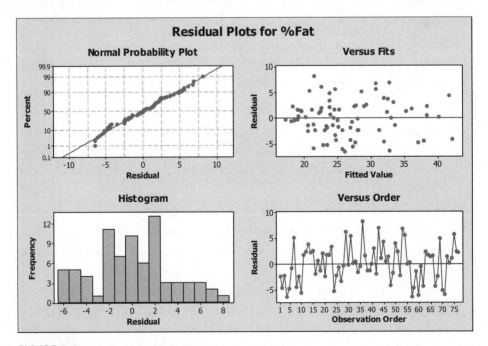

FIGURE 8-9 · Four-in-one residual plot.

all traditional Minitab functions, it is your responsibility to interpret this graph, recognize concerns, and respond appropriately.

But Lena is still not satisfied. She would like to create a table of 95% prediction intervals for BMI values of 15, 20, 25, 30, and 35. To do this, she must use the Minitab General Regression tool.

 The Stat > Regression > General Regression tool, new in Minitab 16, is an expanded and redesigned version of the Stat > Regression > Regression tool. Because of its greater convenience and flexibility, the General Regression is now recommended instead of the older Regression tool.

To prepare for this analysis, Lena needs to enter the BMI values for the prediction table into a new column in the worksheet, as shown in Fig. 8-10. With only five values, Lena could directly type these in, or she could use the Calc > Make Patterned Data > Simple Set of Numbers tool.

Lena selects Stat > Regression > General Regression from the Minitab menu. In the dialog, shown in Figure 8-11, she enters %Fat for the Response variable. In the Model box, enter all the terms required in the model, separated by spaces. For a quadratic model in BMI, Lena enters a model of BMI BMI*BMI, representing a linear and a quadratic term in the model. The constant (or intercept) term is always in the model, unless specifically excluded by an option in the Options dialog.

To create the table of prediction intervals, Lena clicks the Prediction button. In the Prediction dialog, not shown here, Lena enters BMItable, the name of the new worksheet column, in the New observation for continuous predictors field.

After clicking OK, Lena sees the lengthy report below in the Session window. By default, no graphs are created by the General Regression tool.

	C1	C2	C3	C4	C5
↓	BMI	%Fat	Activity	BMItable	
1	22.9642	28.8	312	15	
2	27.7900	32.4	151	20	
3	20.9174	25.8	290	25	
4	19.6575	19.6	340	30	
5	20.6038	22.8	310	35	
6	20.3064	26.4	196		

BMI.MTW ***

FIGURE 8-10 · BMI worksheet with added values for prediction.

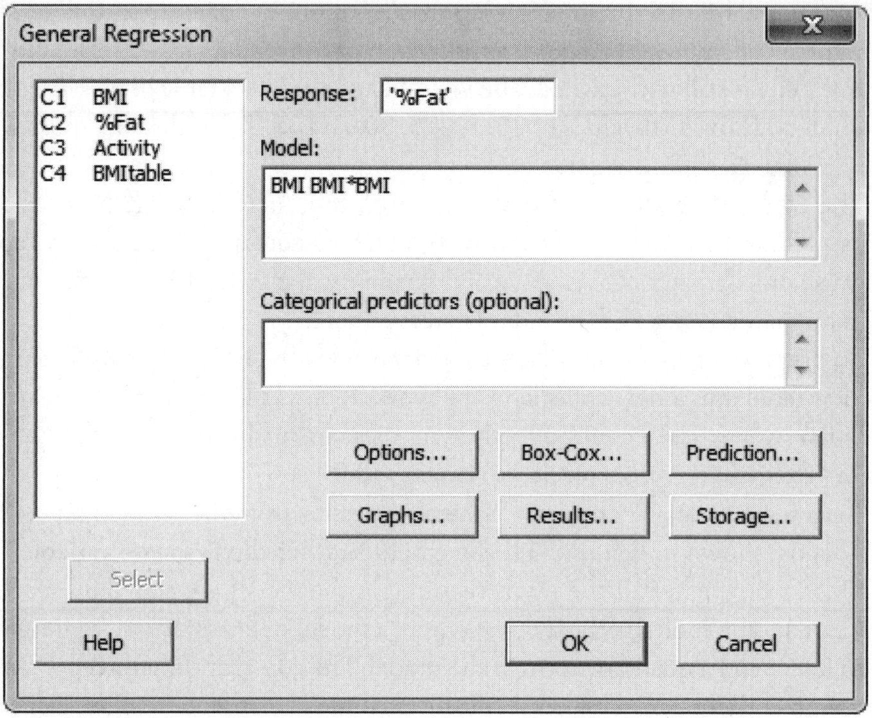

FIGURE 8-11 · General Regression dialog.

General Regression Analysis: %Fat versus BMI

Regression Equation

%Fat = -22.6418 + 3.27346 BMI - 0.040403 BMI*BMI

Coefficients

Term	Coef	SE Coef	T	P
Constant	-22.6418	8.96983	-2.52422	0.014
BMI	3.2735	0.79589	4.11294	0.000
BMI*BMI	-0.0404	0.01700	-2.37672	0.020

Summary of Model

S = 3.54757   R-Sq = 74.96%   R-Sq(adj) = 74.28%
PRESS = 1027.32 R-Sq(pred) = 72.37%

```
Analysis of Variance

Source        DF   Seq SS   Adj SS   Adj MS        F          P
Regression     2  2787.34  2787.34  1393.67  110.738  0.0000000
  BMI          1  2716.25   212.90   212.90   16.916  0.0001002
  BMI*BMI      1    71.09    71.09    71.09    5.649  0.0200544
Error         74   931.31   931.31    12.59
Total         76  3718.65
```

```
Fits and Diagnostics for Unusual Observations

Obs  %Fat       Fit   SE Fit  Residual  St Resid
 36  29.8  21.6227  0.54921   8.17729   2.33316  R
 45  46.0  41.7138  1.89635   4.28618   1.42959     X
 48  38.0  42.1840  2.19645  -4.18404  -1.50190     X
 56  40.5  40.2558  1.29531   0.24421   0.07394     X
```

```
R denotes an observation with a large standardized residual.
X denotes an observation whose X value gives it large leverage.
```

```
Predicted Values for New Observations

New Obs      Fit   SE Fit          95% CI               95% PI
      1  17.3695  0.97573  (15.4253, 19.3137)  (10.0383, 24.7007)
      2  26.6663  0.48169  (25.7065, 27.6261)  (19.5327, 33.7998)
      3  33.9429  0.70275  (32.5427, 35.3432)  (26.7369, 41.1490)
      4  39.1994  1.04602  (37.1152, 41.2837)  (31.8298, 46.5690)
      5  42.4358  2.39255  (37.6685, 47.2030)  (33.9097, 50.9618)
```

```
Values of Predictors for New Observations

New Obs  BMI
      1   15
      2   20
      3   25
      4   30
      5   35  XX
```

```
XX denotes a point that is an extreme outlier in the predictors.
```

This report provides many potentially useful details about the regression analysis and this dataset. Here is a description of the sections in the report:

- The `Regression Equation` matches the model fit by the other Minitab tools.

- The `Coefficients` section provides significance tests for all three parameters in the model, intercept, linear, and quadratic. The p-values in the right column of this table are all smaller than 0.05, therefore, all three parameters are significantly nonzero.

- The `Summary of Model` section lists several statistics that are useful to compare this model with other models. The most commonly used ones are S, the standard deviation of the residuals, and `R-Sq(adj)` (adjusted R^2). In general, the model with the smallest S and the highest adjusted R^2 is the best model. For the other statistics, either search Minitab help or consult a good text on regression, such as Kutner, et al (2004).

- The `Analysis of Variance` (ANOVA) section is a formal significance test for the overall model and for each term. The p-value for the overall model, 0.000, is found on the `Regression` row. Below that are p-values for each parameter in the model except for the intercept.

- The `Fits and Diagnostics` section identifies individual observations which may be of concern. In this case, observation 36 is flagged as having a suspiciously high residual. Observations 45, 48, and 56 are flagged because they are on the tail end of the dataset, and these points have a strong effect on the model, also known as high leverage. These are the same values flagged in the diagnostic reports generated by the regression assistant.

- The `Predicted Values` section lists fits (predicted values), the standard error for each fit, 95% confidence intervals, and 95% prediction intervals for each of the five values requested. Notice the XX flag by the highest value requested 35. This is because the maximum BMI in the file is 34.461, less than 35. Since 35 is an extrapolation beyond the range of observed data, prediction at this point may be unreliable.

In this section, the same regression problem was solved using three different Minitab functions. Each function has its advantages. The regression assistant quickly and automatically chooses the best model out of three polynomial models, and prepares a graphical report ready for presentation. The Fitted Line Plot prepares a plot of the model with optional confidence or prediction interval lines. The General Regression tool provides a thorough text report and maximum flexibility. The well-prepared analyst will learn to use all three tools, depending on the occasion.

8.2   Fitting a Model with Many Predictor Variables

A typical regression scenario involves many potential predictor variables. When we don't know in advance which variables are good predictors, a common planning strategy is to measure and record many variables in hopes of finding enough predictors to build a useful model. As a result, many of the potential predictor variables are correlated, making it difficult to select the significant predictors.

Why does this happen? Consider Lena's BMI data used in the previous section. Figure 8-12 is a matrix plot of BMI, BMI^2, BMI^3, and %Fat. The cubic model considered by the regression assistant attempts to predict %Fat as a function of BMI, BMI^2, and BMI^3. It is obvious in the matrix plot that these three variables are highly correlated with each other. What happens when Minitab tries to fit this model?

Turn back to Fig. 8-4, and look in the bottom right, at the p-values reported for the cubic model. This model has an overall p-value of 0.000, meaning that the cubic model predicts a lot of the variation in the data, and is very significant. But the p-values for the linear, quadratic, and cubic coefficients in this

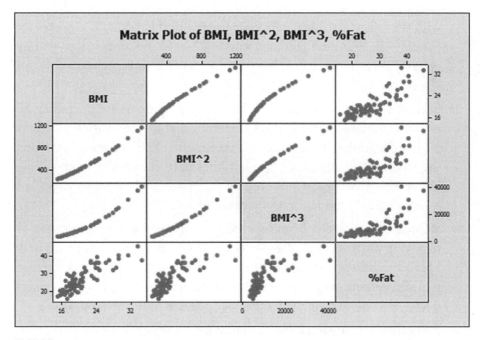

FIGURE 8-12 • Matrix plot showing correlation of BMI, BMI^2, and BMI^3.

model are all large, indicating that they are not significant. Apparently the model is significant, but none of the coefficients are significant.

This apparent contradiction is the result of another octosyllabic data disorder known as multicollinearity. When the predictor variables are strongly correlated, statistical tools are unable to determine which ones are good predictors. The apparent variation of each coefficient inflates to the point that they all appear to be non-significant.

Once multicollinearity is recognized, it can be resolved by removing one or more terms from the model. In Lena's BMI example, the cubic term is removed, leaving a quadratic model. In the quadratic model, BMI and BMI^2 are still correlated, but BMI^2 explains enough variation in the response, beyond the variation explained by the linear model, that both linear and quadratic coefficients are significant, with low p-values.

When many predictor variables are available, good practice is to enter variables into the model, or remove them from the model, one at a time. By comparing models created in this way, the best model can be identified. Several different strategies are used, and the Minitab Stat > Regression menu has tools to help with all of them.

- **Forward selection** starts with the simplest model, a mean only with no predictor variables. All unused predictor variables are tested, and the one with the lowest p-value (or Alpha) is added to the model. The process of entering the best next predictor continues until the model stops getting better. The Minitab Stat > Regression > Stepwise tool performs forward selection, if selected in the Methods dialog.

- **Backward selection** starts with the most complex model including all predictor variables. All variables are tested, and the one with the highest p-value (or Alpha) is removed from the model. The process of removing the worst remaining predictor continues until the model stops getting better. The Minitab Stat > Regression > Stepwise tool performs backward selection, if selected in the Methods dialog.

- **Stepwise selection** combines forward and backward selection, entering or removing variables from the model until no more changes are indicated. This is the default method used by the Minitab Stat > Regression > Stepwise tool. By default, stepwise selection starts with an empty (mean-only) model, but the starting model may be specified in the Methods dialog.

- **Best subsets regression** looks at all possible models. With k predictor variables, this requires 2^k regressions. Large models may take a lot of computing time. The Minitab Stat > Regression > Best Subsets tool performs this task and prints out a summary of the best two models with each number of predictors.

The Stepwise and Best Subsets tools are for model selection only. After using either of these tools, use General Regression to fit the final model.

To see how these techniques work, consider the case of Ursula, the zoologist. When a hunter shoots a bear, he needs to know the animal's weight, but it is difficult to weigh a huge animal in the forest. It would be convenient to have a model that predicts the bear's weight based on simple measurements.

Ursula and her team track and anesthetize fifty wild bears, recording several measurements and weight. The Minitab sample data file Bears2.MTW lists the sex, estimated age in months, head length, head width, neck girth, chest girth, and weight for fifty bears. The age is not something that the average hunter can estimate with accuracy, so age will not be considered in the models.

With Bears2.MTW as the current Minitab worksheet, Ursula selects Stat > Regression > Stepwise. She completes the dialog as shown in Fig. 8-13, specifying weight as the Response and the four head, neck, and chest measurements

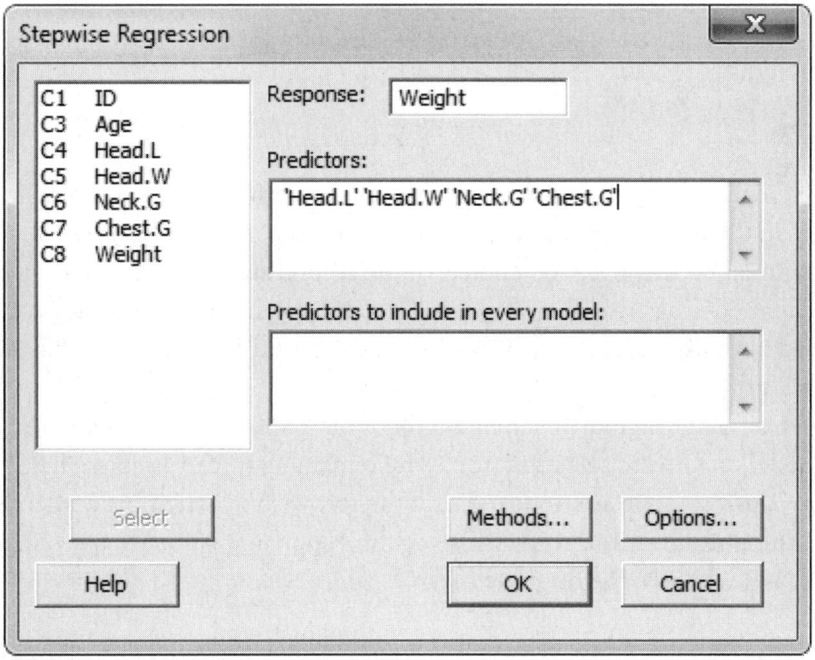

FIGURE 8-13 • Stepwise Regression dialog.

as Predictors. Leaving the Methods and Options in their default settings, Ursula clicks OK. The following report appears in the Session window:

Stepwise Regression: Weight versus Head.L, Head.W, Neck.G, Chest.G

```
   Alpha-to-Enter: 0.15  Alpha-to-Remove: 0.15

Response is Weight on 4 predictors, with N = 50
```

Step	1	2	3
Constant	-293.5	-303.8	-252.8
Neck.G	22.64	13.55	16.32
T-Value	26.41	5.08	5.52
P-Value	0.000	0.000	0.000
Chest.G		5.6	5.6
T-Value		3.56	3.71
P-Value		0.001	0.001
Head.L			-8.5
T-Value			-1.95
P-Value			0.058
S	30.2	27.1	26.3
R-Sq	93.56	94.93	95.32
R-Sq(adj)	93.43	94.72	95.01
Mallows Cp	16.0	4.9	3.1

The stepwise process required three steps, shown in vertical columns in the report. In the first step, Neck.G was entered into the model. Its p-value of 0.000 is very small, so this is a good choice. In the second step, Chest.G was entered into the model, again with a very small p-value. In the third step, Head.L was entered into the model. The p-value for Head.L is 0.058, which is not as small, but still probably significant.

At this point, the fourth variable did not have a low p-value, if entered into the model, so forward selection stops. The remaining three variables all do have low p-values, so none are removed, and the stepwise selection process ends.

At the bottom of the stepwise selection report are statistics assessing the model as a whole. What do these mean?

- S is the standard deviation of the residual variation unexplained by the model. In general, the best model has the lowest value of S.

- R-Sq is R^2, the coefficient of determination for the model. This measures the percentage of variation explained by the model.

- R-Sq(adj) includes an adjustment to R^2 which reduces the adjusted R^2 for every term added to the model. This is a safeguard against over-fitting. A model with too many variables may have high R^2, but be bad at prediction. In general, the best model has the highest value of adjusted R^2.

- Mallows Cp is an attempt to balance the risks of too many variables with the risks of too few variables. The Minitab help file has more information on this. The ideal value of Mallows Cp is equal to the number of parameters, including the constant. In the three models above, the ideal values would be 2, 3, and 4.

For the Bears2.MTW data file, the best model in the report shown above has the lowest S, the highest adjusted R^2, and the Mallows Cp closest to its ideal value. Often these three indicators may point to different models, but in this case, they favor the same model.

To see another method in action, analyze the same data with Stat > Regression > Best Subsets. In the dialog, enter the four predictors in the Free Predictors box. Here is the report:

Best Subsets Regression: Weight versus Head.L, Head.W, Neck.G, Chest.G

```
Response is Weight

                                                     C
                                             H H N  h
                                             e e e  e
                                             a a c  s
                                             d d k  t
                            Mallows          . . .  .
Vars  R-Sq  R-Sq(adj)    Cp         S        L W G  G
   1  93.6       93.4  16.0    30.199            X
   1  92.1       92.0  29.7    33.361               X
   2  94.9       94.7   4.9    27.081          X X
   2  93.9       93.7  14.7    29.675    X     X
   3  95.3       95.0   3.1    26.311    X     X X
   3  94.9       94.6   6.9    27.372        X X X
   4  95.3       94.9   5.0    26.561    X X X X
```

This report looks only at the overall model statistics, not the p-values for each coefficient. This report lists two models with one predictor, two with two, two with three, and one model with all four. Of the seven models listed in this report, the one with the highest R-Sq(adj) and lowest S is the first model with three predictors, using Head.L, Neck.G, and Chest.G.

So what is this best fitting model? The Best Subsets tool identifies which predictors are in or out, without specifying the model itself. To finish fitting this model, Ursula must use the General Regression tool. In the dialog, she selects Weight for the response, and 'Head.L' 'Neck.G' 'Chest.G' for the model. In the Graphs dialog, she requests the Four in one residual plot. Here is the report:

General Regression Analysis: Weight versus Head.L, Neck.G, Chest.G

```
Regression Equation

Weight = -252.843 - 8.52162 Head.L + 16.325 Neck.G + 5.63836 Chest.G
```

```
Coefficients

Term            Coef   SE Coef        T       P
Constant    -252.843   31.2071  -8.10209   0.000
Head.L        -8.522    4.3763  -1.94723   0.058
Neck.G        16.325    2.9556   5.52341   0.000
Chest.G        5.638    1.5184   3.71336   0.001
```

```
Summary of Model

S = 26.3108       R-Sq = 95.32%        R-Sq(adj) = 95.01%
PRESS = 40087.2   R-Sq(pred) = 94.10%
```

```
Analysis of Variance

Source          DF  Seq SS  Adj SS  Adj MS        F         P
Regression       3  648133  648133  216044  312.086  0.000000
  Head.L         1  476847    2625    2625    3.792  0.057627
  Neck.G         1  161740   21119   21119   30.508  0.000001
  Chest.G        1    9546    9546    9546   13.789  0.000552
Error           46   31844   31844     692
  Lack-of-Fit   45   31831   31831     707   56.589  0.105161
  Pure Error     1      13      13      13
Total           49  679977
```

```
Fits and Diagnostics for Unusual Observations

Obs   Weight      Fit   SE Fit   Residual   St Resid
  8       26  -26.509  10.1668    52.5086    2.16377   R
 10      436  371.202   8.3309    64.7976    2.59636   R
 33      446  382.282  12.7003    63.7182    2.76524   R

R denotes an observation with a large standardized residual.
```

The report lists the regression equation at the top. In the Coefficients table, all coefficients have low enough p-values that Ursula decides to accept this model.

At the bottom of the report, the Fits and Diagnostics table lists three observations with unusually large residuals. On the residual plot shown in Fig. 8-14, the dots for these three observations are circled. One of these represents a 26 pound bear, who would be predicted to have a negative weight of −26.5 pounds. The other two are heavy bears whose weight was predicted 64 pounds too light. It is possible that these bears had some unusual condition and ought to be excluded, or it is possible that some other variables should have been measured to better account for the very small and large bears. Whether

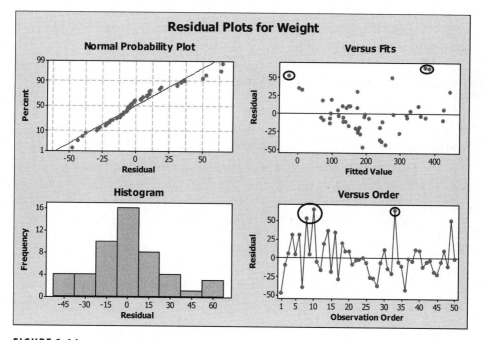

FIGURE 8-14 • Bears2.MTW residual plot.

Ursula chooses to leave the model alone or exclude some of these cases and run another model is ultimately up to her.

As you know by now, Minitab does not flag any unusual cases in the residual plots generated from the Regression menu. The ellipses in Fig. 8-14 were added using the ellipse ⊙ button in the Graph Annotation Tools toolbar. After each ellipse was added, its properties were edited by clicking the edit 🖺 button in the Graph Editing toolbar. Here, the fill and the border of each ellipse can be edited as required.

One important feature of the new General Regression tool needs to be high-lighted here. In the examples above, all the predictor variables have been con-tinuous, numerical variables. Categorical predictors may also be added to the Model box, and Minitab will handle them appropriately. Text columns will automatically be treated as categorical. Numerical categorical columns (for example, company 1, 2, or 3) must also be listed in the Categorical predictors box.

Newcomers to Minitab may not realize the convenience of this new feature. In earlier versions of Minitab, categorical variables had to be converted to indi-cator variables by the analyst, a tedious and often confusing process. Now, Minitab 16 handles all of that behind the scenes.

In Ursula's Bears2.MTW worksheet, Sex is a text column containing either M or F. Does knowing the sex of the bear help in predicting its weight? To find out, recall the General Regression dialog and add Sex to the Model box. Here is a portion of the resulting report:

General Regression Analysis: Weight versus Head.L, Neck.G, Chest.G, Sex

```
Regression Equation

Sex
F    Weight  =   -252.963 - 8.56052 Head.L + 16.2345 Neck.G + 5.68819 Chest.G

M    Weight  =   -251.893 - 8.56052 Head.L + 16.2345 Neck.G + 5.68819 Chest.G


Coefficients

Term            Coef   SE Coef          T       P
Constant    -252.428   31.7282   -7.95595   0.000
Head.L        -8.561    4.4353   -1.93009   0.060
Neck.G        16.235    3.0777    5.27497   0.000
Chest.G        5.688    1.5879    3.58221   0.001
Sex
  F           -0.535    4.3672   -0.12250   0.903
```

```
Summary of Model

S = 26.5971       R-Sq = 95.32%        R-Sq(adj) = 94.90%
PRESS = 41874.7   R-Sq(pred) = 93.84%
```

Apparently not. In this report, the `Coefficients` table has an added row for `Sex = F`. With a p-value of 0.903, this extra term is not helpful in explaining the variation of weight. Notice also that `R-Sq(adj)` went down and `S` went up with the addition of this term in the model. These are all reasons to leave `Sex` out of it.

Notice that this report lists two separate prediction equations for female and male bears. If the categorical variable had been significant, this would be a great convenience to have the equations presented in this form.

To see how Minitab deals with all categorical variables, consider the case of Fat Leoma's Meat Loaf company. Leoma is working hard to reduce variation in everyone's favorite entrée. The Minitab sample data file Meatloaf.MTW contains measurements of drip loss for each of eight oven locations, over three batches of meat loaf. Are there significant differences between batches, or between oven locations?

To find out, Leoma selects Stat > Regression > General Regression from the Minitab menu on her oven-side computer, with Meatloaf.MTW as the current worksheet. Leoma enters Driploss in the Response field, and Batch Position in the Model field. The Batch and Position columns are numeric, so Leoma must tell Minitab to treat these as categorical variables by entering Batch Position also in the Categorical predictors field. Here is the report:

General Regression Analysis: Driploss versus Batch, Position

```
Coefficients

Term            Coef    SE Coef          T       P
Constant     5.56458   0.166278   33.4656   0.000
Batch
  1          -0.95458   0.235152   -4.0594   0.001
  2          -0.09958   0.235152   -0.4235   0.678
Position
  1           2.26875   0.439930    5.1571   0.000
  2          -1.82458   0.439930   -4.1474   0.001
  3          -1.24792   0.439930   -2.8366   0.013
  4           1.37875   0.439930    3.1340   0.007
  5           0.45208   0.439930    1.0276   0.322
  6          -0.91458   0.439930   -2.0789   0.056
  7           0.43542   0.439930    0.9897   0.339
```

```
Summary of Model

S = 0.814591     R-Sq = 85.91%        R-Sq(adj) = 76.86%
PRESS = 27.3007  R-Sq(pred) = 58.60%


Analysis of Variance

Source        DF   Seq SS   Adj SS   Adj MS         F          P
Regression     9  56.6550  56.6550  6.29500    9.4867  0.0001412
   Batch       2  16.2593  16.2593  8.12965   12.2516  0.0008403
   Position    7  40.3957  40.3957  5.77081    8.6968  0.0003462
Error         14   9.2898   9.2898  0.66356
Total         23  65.9448
```

Looking first at the `Analysis of Variance` section, Leoma sees that both batch and position have very small p-values, indicating significant differences between batches and also between oven positions.

At the top of the report, in the `Coefficients` section, are the coefficients for each batch and each oven position. By default, Minitab treats the highest value of a categorical variable as a baseline, and compares each value with that highest value. For example, batch 1 had 0.95458 less drop loss than batch 3, and with a p-value of 0.001, that difference is very significant.

This simple dataset gives Leoma a lot of information to work with. She must reduce both variation between batches and between oven positions, if she expects to win the coveted D. J. Power Meatloaf Quality Award.

 One more convenient new feature in Minitab 16 is worth mentioning here, especially for those who use the Stat > Regression menu to analyze the results of a designed experiment. Typically, the Stat > DOE menu is used, as discussed in the next chapter, but there are occasions when the Regression menu provides features or flexibility not available in the DOE menu.

In the Model box, several abbreviations are available to speed up the process of specifying a complex model with many variables:

- Use the * symbol to denote interactions between variables. For example, A*B includes the interaction or product of columns A and B in the regression model. Note that this symbol does not automatically include the main effects of A and B, as hierarchy would typically require.

- Use the | or ! symbol to denote a complete model, including all interactions between different columns. For example, A|B|C represents an eight-term model including the intercept, specifically: A B C A*B A*C B*C A*B*C.

This abbreviation cannot be used to enter quadratic or higher order polynomial terms involving a single column.

- Use the - symbol to exclude a term from a complete model. For example, use A|B|C -A*B*C to specify a complete model in three variables, but not including the three-factor interaction.

The next section provides an example illustrating the use of these symbols in the Model field.

8.3   Diagnosing Regression Problems

Identifying and resolving issues which arise in regression analysis is a topic worthy of entire books, and many good books are available. This section will highlight Minitab tools for recognizing and reacting to concerns about the validity of regression models.

The regression assistant, seen earlier, automatically prepares diagnostic reports and flags some areas of concern. When using the traditional Minitab menus for regression, this process must be done separately by the analyst. Either way, the analyst is responsible for assessing diagnostic plots and reports with a critical eye, and for reacting appropriately.

Three categories of potential problems deserve attention in most regression problems:

- **Process instability** could take many forms, including shifts, trends, cycles, or individual outliers. If the process is not stable during data collection, then any predictions derived from a regression model are unreliable. Residual plots of various types are used to recognize process instability in its various forms. Minitab regression reports will flag observations with unusual or extreme X or Y values, but other forms of instability require a human eye to recognize.

- **Multicollinearity** is correlation between predictor variables. This is unavoidable in most regression applications, but if these correlations are too strong, they can result in misleading or inaccurate models. In severe cases of multicollinearity, the regression analysis becomes numerically unstable. Variance inflation factors, an optional feature of Minitab regression reports, are helpful to quantify the amount of multicollinearity.

- **Heteroscedasticity** is unequal standard deviation of residuals. Regression analysis assumes that residual variation is the same throughout the range of observed values. Unequal variation can affect the validity of the regression model. Regression plots can identify when this condition exists by a characteristic < pattern. When variation increases in this way, the Box–Cox transformation can sometimes resolve it.

Graphs are key to recognizing these and other problems. To illustrate the importance of using graphs, Frank Anscombe (1973) created four sets of X and Y variables for regression analysis. Figure 8-15 shows four fitted line plots created from the Anscombe dataset. Linear regression fits the same model to each set of X and Y variables, with the same residual standard deviation and R^2. The Session window has the same regression report for all four cases, but only by viewing the graphs can the obvious differences be detected. For your use, this famous dataset is available as a Minitab sample data file FA.MTW.

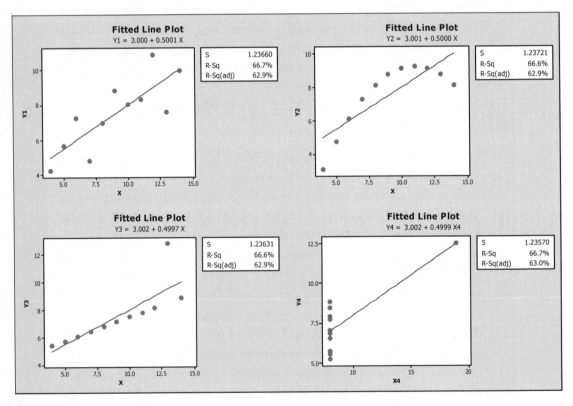

FIGURE 8-15 · The Anscombe dataset.

Outliers have already appeared in earlier examples. For the BMI.MTW dataset, Figure 8-4 highlighted one observation with an unusually large residual, and three observations with unusually large X values. The General Regression tool highlighted the same observations in the Session window report. In Fig. 8-14, three observations with large residuals in the Bears2.MTW dataset are circled after they were flagged in the Session window report.

A large residual could indicate something special or unusual with that individual case, or it might be simple random variation. If an outlying case was somehow defective, or did not represent the overall population, there could be a case for removing that observation from the dataset. However, most experts caution against removing outlying cases without having a clear reason to do so.

When an observation has an unusual X value, this observation has a much higher leverage, or impact, on the model than most other X values. In this region of high leverage X values, the model may be less reliable than one would expect. The only way to fix this issue is either to restrict the model to a smaller range of X values, or to collect more data in the region of high leverage observations.

Multicollinearity is harder to recognize, because it does not show up in residual plots. Scatter plots of predictor variables show correlation, but it can be difficult or impossible to see when the correlation is too much. In severe cases, Minitab will warn of "ill-conditioned data." But far short of this point, analysts should be aware of the potential problems with correlated predictors. For this decision, we need a quantitative measure of multicollinearity, which is provided by variance inflation factors, or VIF.

The effect of multicollinearity is to inflate the variation of coefficients for correlated predictors, and VIF measures the extent of this inflation. In the ideal case, which only happens with orthogonal designed experiments, VIF = 1 for every term in the model. As correlation between predictors increases, VIF increases above 1. The square root of VIF indicates how much larger the standard error of the coefficient is than what it would be if the predictor were uncorrelated.

To use Minitab to calculate VIF, use the General Regression tool, click the Results button, and choose the Display variance inflation factors option. For example, consider the final model chosen above for Ursula's Bears2.MTW dataset. With the VIF option selected, here is a portion of the regression report:

General Regression Analysis: Weight versus Head.L, Neck.G, Chest.G

Regression Equation

Weight = -252.843 - 8.52162 Head.L + 16.325 Neck.G + 5.63836 Chest.G

Coefficients

Term	Coef	SE Coef	T	P	VIF
Constant	-252.843	31.2071	-8.10209	0.000	
Head.L	-8.522	4.3763	-1.94723	0.058	4.9523
Neck.G	16.325	2.9556	5.52341	0.000	15.6561
Chest.G	5.638	1.5184	3.71336	0.001	12.0283

Summary of Model

S = 26.3108   R-Sq = 95.32%   R-Sq(adj) = 95.01%
PRESS = 40087.2   R-Sq(pred) = 94.10%

The VIF option has added a VIF column to the Coefficients table. For this model, the three coefficients have VIF of 5, 16, and 12. Is this too much? Expert opinions vary. Montgomery and Peck (1982) suggest that a VIF of 5 or more is too much. Kunter (2004) suggests that VIF of 10 is too much.

In an orthogonal designed experiment, where predictors are controlled according to a careful plan, all VIFs should be 1. In some experiments, VIF > 1, either because of planned compromise or unplanned missing data. In the context of a designed experiment, a VIF of 5 is unusually high. However, when regression is applied to a dataset where predictors were uncontrolled, it is common for VIF to be greater than 5.

What can be done about excessive VIF? Options are few, and here they are:

- Eliminate one or more correlated terms from the model to lower the VIF.

- Use a multivariate method such as partial least squares regression to predict the response based on a linear combination of predictor variables. This powerful tool is included in the Minitab Regression menu, but its proper use is beyond the scope of this book.

- Collect additional data in such a way as to reduce the correlation between predictors. This is a risky strategy because unexpected changes in the process between data collection events could contaminate the dataset and any resulting model.

- Use the model as is.

One of the dangers of multicollinearity is that the model might fit the available data well, but, at the same time, be a very bad predictor of Y values for new X values. The regression report offers a measure of this risk called predicted R^2, or `R-Sq(pred)`. To calculate this, Minitab removes one value from the dataset, and tries to predict that value using all the other values. After doing this for all values, predicted R^2 is a measure of how well those predictions worked.

For the Bears2.MTW model above, `R-Sq(pred) = 94.10%`, a very good number. Also, the p-values for the highly correlated `Neck.G` and `Chest.G` variables are very small, even with inflated variation. Considering both these factors, this model is probably acceptable as is.

The Minitab sample data file Insulate.MTW provides another example of regression diagnostics in action. In this file, a company measured the times to failure of polymer insulators at four different temperatures and from two different plants.

With Insulate.MTW as the current worksheet, select Stat > Regression > General Regression. In the Response field, enter FailureT. In the Model field, enter Temp | Plant. This is shorthand for a complete model including main effects and the interaction between the two variables. Click the Graphs button and select the Four in one residual plot.

The residual plot in Fig. 8-16 shows several reasons for concern with this model. The normal probability plot and the histogram cast doubt on the normality of the residuals. Perhaps more concerning, the Versus Fits plot shows a

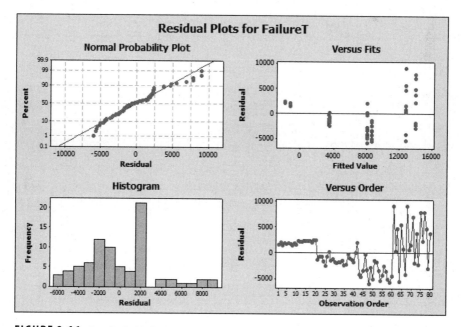

FIGURE 8-16 · Residual plot for insulate dataset.

curve in the residuals and significantly increasing variation with higher fitted values. The dots in this plot are collected in four clusters because of the intentional design of this experiment to collect data at four different temperatures. The clustering does not represent a problem, but the < pattern of the plot is a strong indicator of heteroscedasticity.

Now recall the General Regression dialog with the ▦ button. Click the Box-Cox button. Select the Box-Cox power transformation option with the default Use optimal lambda option. The Box–Cox transformation, first introduced in Chapter 4, is a family of power transformations which can effectively normalize a wide range of skewed datasets.

After the Box–Cox transformation, Fig. 8-17 shows the new residual plot. These plots show similar variation in all four clusters of dots, and a more normal distribution of residuals. After this transformation, the concerns with nonnormality and heteroscedasticity have been effectively resolved.

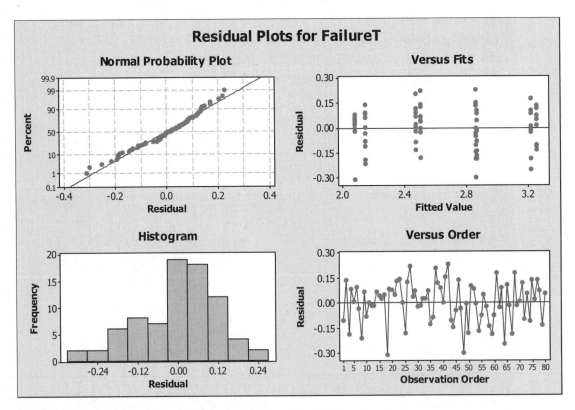

FIGURE 8-17 • Residual plot for insulate dataset after optimal Box–Cox transformation.

? Still Struggling

Regression diagnostics are confusing for even experienced statistical professionals. The best way to deal with data disorders is to prevent them. Whenever possible, a designed experiment with factors carefully planned and controlled is superior to a regression study. Often, predictor variables cannot be controlled, and the resulting datasets are far from ideal. Always look at residual plots, searching for unusual or unexpected patterns. If the process is unstable over time, this is the most serious problem, usually requiring correcting the instability and perhaps collecting new data. Correlated predictors or unequal variation can usually be corrected by one or more of the techniques discussed here. As George Box famously said, "All models are wrong, but some are useful." A useful model is good enough.

8.4   Fitting Nonlinear Regression Models

This section introduces a new feature of Minitab 16 which provides a convenient platform to fit a wide variety of nonlinear models.

To understand this feature, it is vital to understand the difference between linear and nonlinear models. Unfortunately, the phrase "linear model" is frequently used in ambiguous ways. In this book, a linear model is a straight line model, with an equation of the form $Y = b_0 + b_1 X$. Many references refer to this as a "simple linear regression model" to distinguish it from multiple regression models with many predictor variables.

Here, the phrase "linear regression model" refers to any model which is a linear function of the coefficients. Linear regression models comprise a much wider class of models than the simple straight-line linear model. All models seen so far in this chapter, including those with high-order polynomial or interaction terms, are linear regression models. All linear regression models are fit using a well-established technique called least squares regression. Using this method, matrix formulas quickly and reliably estimate the best coefficient values and most other statistics used by regression analysts.

Nonlinear regression models could take any function of the form $Y = f(X)$. Computationally, nonlinear regression models are much harder to fit and require more thinking on the part of the analyst. The new Nonlinear Regression tool in Minitab provides a catalog with dozens of predefined nonlinear models and the facility to create and edit one's own custom models. Once the model is defined, the analyst must specify starting values for all parameters, a step not required for linear regression models. The final model is fit by an iterative procedure, either the Gauss–Newton or the Levenberg–Marquardt algorithm.

For an example of nonlinear regression, consider an alternate approach to the Insulate.MTW data file first used in the previous section. One model for the rate of temperature-dependent chemical reactions is the Arrhenius model, shown here:

$$k = Ae^{-E_a/RT}$$

In this model, k is the rate of the reaction per unit time, A is a prefactor, E_a is called the activation energy, R is the Boltzmann gas constant, and T is absolute temperature.

A dataset like Insulate.MTW measures the time to failure, which is the inversely related to the reaction rate. After inverting the Arrhenius model to express the time to failure instead of a rate, the model can be expressed as $E(t)$, the expected time to failure:

$$E(t) = \frac{\exp(EaOverR/T)}{Prefactor}$$

This model has only two unknown parameters, *EaOverR*, which combines the activation energy and gas constant, and *Prefactor*. T represents absolute temperature. In the collected data, temperature is in degrees Celsius, so 273 must be added to convert Celsius to Kelvin, an absolute temperature scale.

To fit the Arrhenius model to this data, select Stat > Regression > Nonlinear regression. In the Nonlinear regression dialog, click the Use Catalog button to review the set of predefined models provided by Minitab. The Arrhenius model can be entered directly in the large box, as shown in Fig. 8-18, or use the Use Calculator button to enter it with a calculator interface. In the model, temperature must be spelled as Temp to match the column name in the current worksheet. In parsing this formula, Minitab assumes that any name not matching a column name is a parameter of the model.

For the next step, click the Parameters button. The Minitab nonlinear regression algorithms require starting values for each parameter, specified in the Parameters dialog. The starting values do not have to be close to the final values,

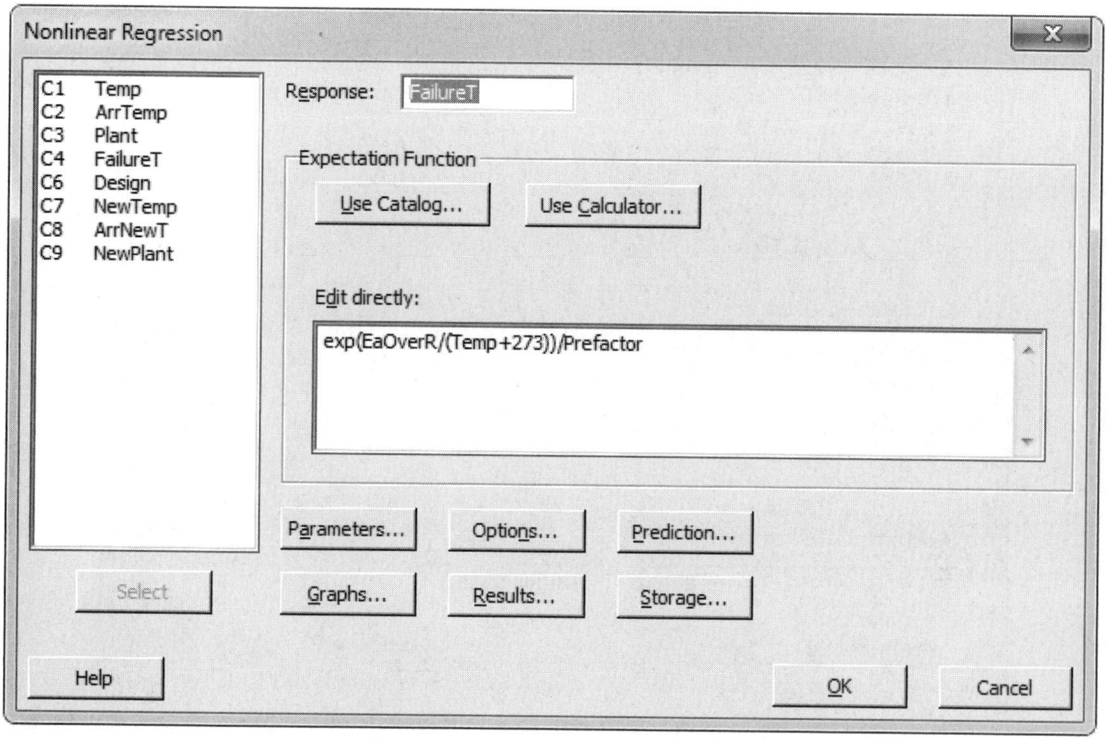

FIGURE 8-18 · Nonlinear regression dialog.

but they do need to produce valid numerical results when applied to the available data. Specifying nonviable values in this form typically leads to an error message like this:

```
* ERROR * No usable rows of data at iteration 1.
```

After some trial and error, viable starting values for this problem are EaOverR = 10,000 and Prefactor = 100,000.

As shown in Fig. 8-19, the Parameters dialog provides a way to specify both starting values and lower and upper bounds to constrain parameters to within a specified range of values.

As is generally good practice, select the Four in one residual plot in the Graphs dialog, and select the Display confidence intervals option in the Results dialog. Click OK to perform the analysis.

Figure 8-20 shows the fitted line plot and the nonlinear regression model fitted by this procedure. The model appears to fit well through the means of each group of observed failure times.

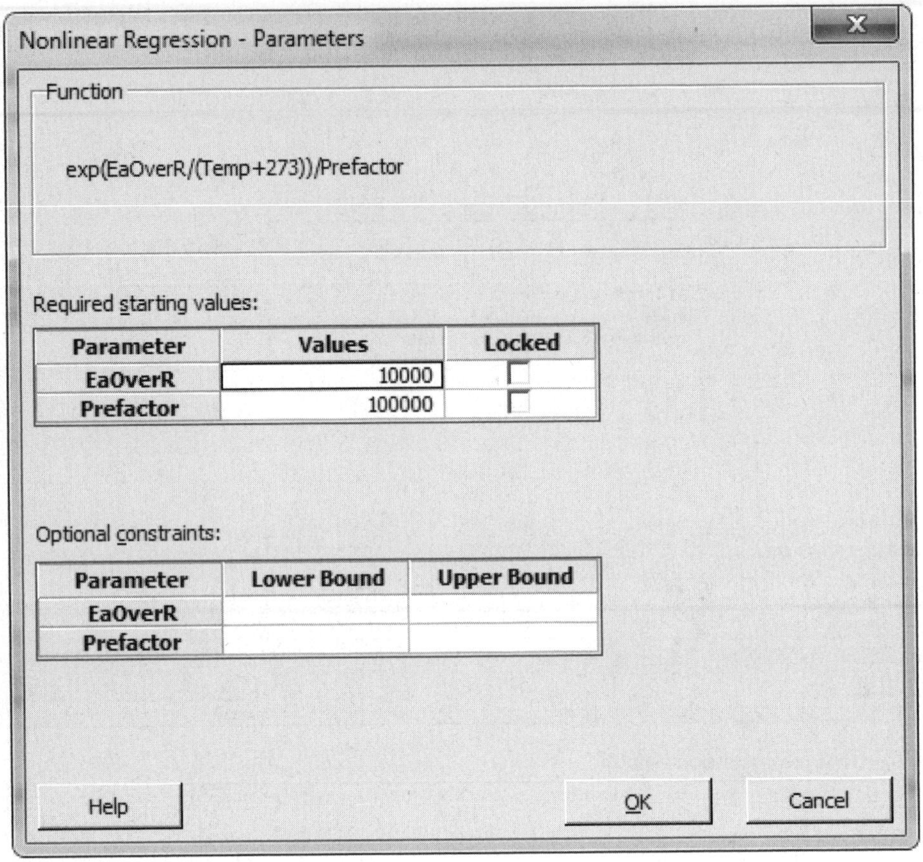

FIGURE 8-19 • Nonlinear regression parameters.

Figure 8-21 is the four-in-one residual plot from the nonlinear procedure. If this were a typical linear model fitted by least squares regression, the appearance of heteroscedasticity would be cause for concern. Here, uniformity of variation is not an assumption of the nonlinear regression procedure, so it is not a concern.

8.5   Fitting Models with Categorical Response Variables

So far, all examples in this chapter have featured continuous response variables. Many problems have categorical response variables, with a small set of two or more discrete possible values. For these problems, the standard least squares regression methods do not work well without some modifications.

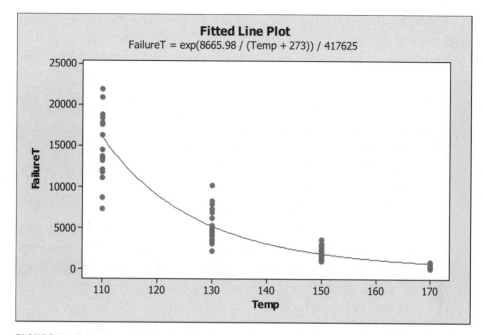

FIGURE 8-20 • Nonlinear fitted line plot.

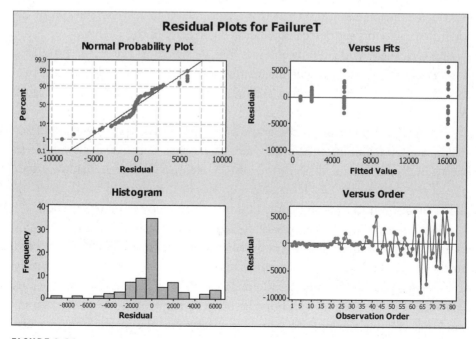

FIGURE 8-21 • Nonlinear residual plots.

These modifications for categorical response variables are collectively known as logistic regression.

The regression menu in Minitab has three logistic regression tools for different types of response variables:

- Use Binary Logistic Regression when the response variable has only two values. The response variable could be any column with numeric, text, or date/time data type. The binary logistic regression model will predict the probability of one of the two response values, called the reference event. Minitab chooses the reference event as the largest of the two response values in numeric or alphanumeric sequence.

- Use Ordinal Logistic Regression when the response variable has three or more values, with a defined ordering. For example, an ordinal response could be a survey response with five values: strongly disagree, disagree, neutral, agree, strongly agree. The ordinal regression model will take the form of parallel lines, one for each response value.

- Use Nominal Logistic Regression when the response variable has three or more values with no particular ordering.

For all three of these tools, the model is specified using the same format as in General Regression, seen earlier in this chapter. Categorical variables must be identified as Factors so they can be handled correctly in the analysis.

Billy is a college student. Billy observes that, for whatever reason, male students seem to perform better in some majors than females, while female students perform better than males in other majors. Or is this just Billy's preconceived notion?

To find out, Billy collects the grade point average (GPA) for 50 Statistics majors and 50 Economics majors, of various genders. Billy's data is available as the Minitab sample data file Department.MTW. Figure 8-22 is an individual values plot of the data in this file. The pattern of dots in this graph is consistent with Billy's theory, but this pattern could also be explained by random variation.

Billy chooses to use binary logistic regression to analyze this data. Using this tool, he will find out whether it is possible to predict a student's major based on their GPA and gender. In Minitab, Billy selects Stat > Regression > Binary Logistic Regression and completes the dialog as shown in Fig. 8-23. He specifies Department as the Response and Gender | GPA as the Model. Using the | shorthand will create a model with two main effects and the interaction between Gender and GPA. Since GPA is a two-valued categorical variable, it must also be listed in the Factors field.

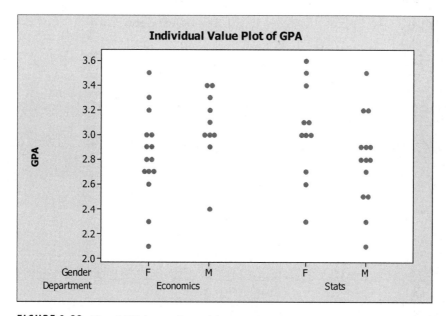

FIGURE 8-22 · Plot of GPA by gender and department.

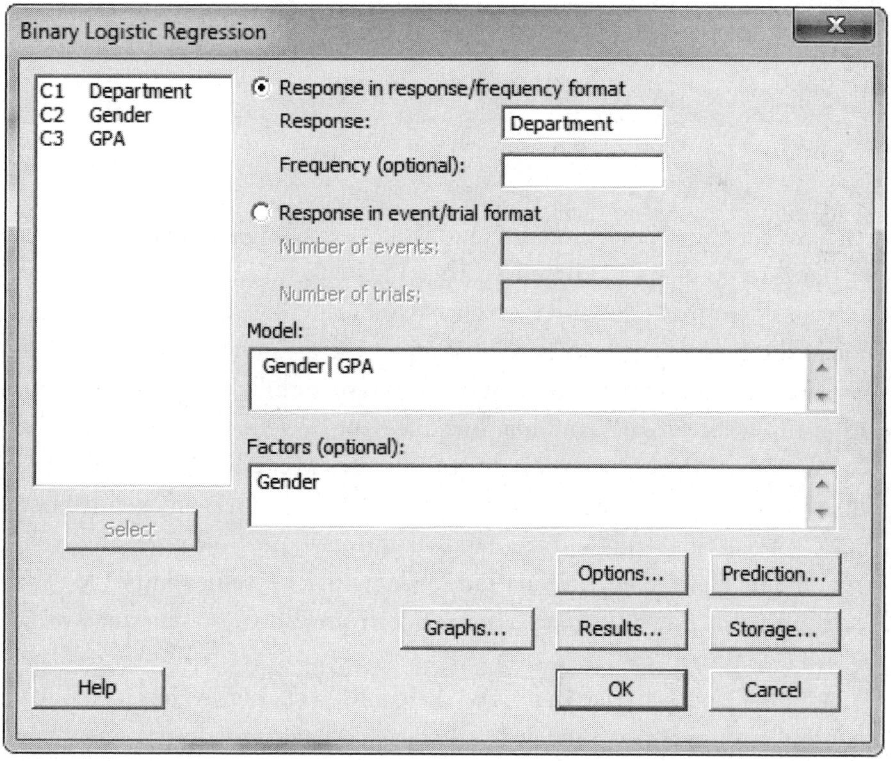

FIGURE 8-23 · Binary Logistic Regression dialog.

Here is a portion of the report in the Session window:

Binary Logistic Regression: Department versus Gender, GPA

```
Link Function: Logit


Response Information

Variable     Value       Count
Department   Stats          25   (Event)
             Economics      25
             Total          50


Logistic Regression Table

                                                              95% CI
Predictor        Coef  SE Coef       Z       P  Odds Ratio  Lower       Upper
Constant     -4.76804  3.52220   -1.35   0.176
Gender
  M           12.9441  5.73595    2.26   0.024   418371.72   5.48  3.19160E+10
GPA           1.52066  1.18711    1.28   0.200        4.58   0.45        46.87
Gender*GPA
  M           -4.18695  1.92584   -2.17   0.030        0.02   0.00         0.66


Log-Likelihood = -31.140
Test that all slopes are zero: G = 7.035, DF = 3, P-Value = 0.071
```

At the end of the report shown above is an overall significance test, with a reported p-value of 0.071. Based on this, Billy can be $(1 - 0.071) \times 100\% = 92.9\%$ confident that GPA and Gender have some ability to predict a student's major. In the `Logistic Regression Table`, the p-value for the `Gender*GPA` interaction is 0.030. This is statistical confirmation of Billy's hypothesis that the relationship between GPA and major is different by gender.

To understand this relationship more, Billy uses Minitab to predict the probability that a student is a Statistics major, based on their GPA and gender. Using the Calc > Make Patterned Data menu, he creates two new columns of X values for prediction. He creates column PredGender with 21 F values and 21 M values. In column PredGPA, Billy puts a sequence from 2.0 to 4.0 in steps of 0.1, repeated two times.

Back in the Binary Logistic Regression dialog, Billy clicks the Prediction button, and enters PredGender PredGPA in the Predicted event probabilities for new observations field. Billy selects the Event probabilities storage option. After clicking OK,

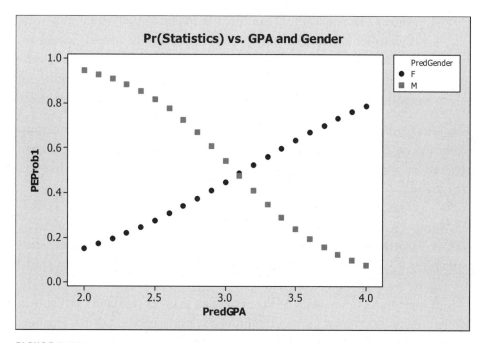

FIGURE 8-24 • Predicted probability of statistics majors.

Billy sees a new column in the worksheet containing predicted probabilities. Plotting this column versus PredGPA results in the graph shown in Fig. 8-24.

The predictive value of this model is limited only to students who are either Statistics or Economics majors. To extend this model to other majors would require much more data and nominal logistic regression, instead of binary logistic regression. But this small study confirms Billy's suspicions about gender differences between majors. Among statistics majors, those with higher GPAs are more likely to be female; among economics majors, those with higher GPAs are more likely to be male.

8.6   Find Out More

This short chapter barely scratches the surface of what can be accomplished using Minitab regression tools. Two additional tools in the Stat > Regression menu are worth mentioning here:

- The Orthogonal Regression tool, new in Minitab 16, can fit a simple linear model between X and Y, where both variables are observed with random variation. This tool can be effectively used to compare the effectiveness of two measurement systems measuring the same set of items.

- The Partial Least Squares tool can identify linear combinations of several X variables which are the best predictors of one or more Y variables. This powerful tool is useful with a large number of correlated X variables, or even when the number of X variables exceeds the number of observations.

The Minitab help files provide a lot of details on how regression functions work, and on how to use them, but not on the appropriate or most effective applications of these tools to your field of study. For this advice, other references are needed.

For regression applications in general, many good books are available, including Montgomery and Peck (1982), Draper and Smith (1998), and Kutner, et al. (2004). Barnett and Lewis (1994) is a well-written reference on how to detect outliers.

This chapter introduced many of the regression analysis functions available in Minitab, including several new and improved features of Minitab 16. The next chapter reviews the Minitab functions for experimenters in the Stat > DOE menu. These functions integrate regression tools within a structure for the design and analysis of experiments. As you will see, proper design and planning of an experiment removes many of the difficulties and complexities of regression analysis on historical data. For this reason, experiments with carefully controlled factors are a more efficient way to develop a good predictive model.

QUIZ

1. If you want to fit a model of the form $Y = b_0 + b_1X + b_2X^2 + b_3X^3$, which Minitab 16 function(s) can be used for this purpose?

   A. Assistant > Regression
   B. Stat > Regression > General Regression
   C. Stat > Regression > Fitted Line Plot
   D. Any of the above functions can be used.

2. For the same model described in question 1, which Minitab 16 function(s) can be used to create a plot with dots for the observed data, a line for the fitted model, and optional confidence or prediction intervals?

   A. Assistant > Regression
   B. Stat > Regression > General Regression
   C. Stat > Regression > Fitted Line Plot
   D. Any of the above functions can be used.

3. To compare a linear, quadratic, and cubic model fitted to the same data, which of the following is the best criteria to compare and select one of those three models?

   A. The best model generally has the highest residual standard deviation S.
   B. The best model generally has the best R-Sq.
   C. The best model generally has the best R-Sq(adj).
   D. The best model generally has the best R-Sq(pred).

4. Which of the following Minitab 16 functions should be used to fit a model of the form $Y = a \times \exp(b \times X)$, where a and b are the unknown parameters?

   A. Stat > Regression > Orthogonal Regression
   B. Stat > Regression > Nonlinear Regression
   C. Stat > Regression > General Regression
   D. Stat > Regression > Exponential Regression

5. Multicollinearity, or correlations between predictor variables, can create what type of problem for regression analysis?

   A. It increases the variation of coefficients in the model.
   B. It may increase p-values in the regression table, so that effects which are actually significant appear to be insignificant.
   C. The model might fit the available data well, but at the same time be a bad predictor for other X values.
   D. All of the above are potential problems with multicollinearity.

6. A cell phone provider wants to determine if the way people use smartphones makes warranty claims more likely. In the data collected to analyze this problem, the response variable is "Yes" if any warranty claim(s) were processed or "No" if there were no warranty claims. Predictor variables included the volumes of calls, texts, web downloads, and other usage information. Which Minitab function is the best to analyze this data?

7. The regression assistant has identified two observations with unusually large residual values. What should be done about this?

Questions 8-10 use the Minitab sample data file Winearoma.MTW. This file contains data on 37 Pinot Noir wines. For each wine, the file lists measured concentrations of 17 elements, and an aroma score from a panel of expert judges.

8. Using stepwise selection, which elements have the greatest predictive value on the aroma score?

9. Choose the best four predictor variables, and fit a regression model using these four predictors. Are there any concerns with diagnostics in this fitted model?

10. From the model fit for question 9, remove the least significant predictor variable. Compare this three-variable model to the four-variable model. Which one is better, and why?

chapter 9

Designing and Analyzing Experiments

Earlier in this book, an experiment was broadly defined as a process of planning, data collection, and analysis to answer a question. This definition includes one-sample experiments, where one set of units, collectively called a sample, is measured to answer a question about a larger population. It also includes experiments with two or more samples, where one controlled factor changes between samples. These one-factor experiments answer questions about the effect of that one controlled factor, and they can be quickly analyzed using the Minitab hypothesis tests assistant.

The phrase "design of experiments" (DOE) generally refers only to experiments with two or more controlled input variables, known as factors. The challenges of identifying which of many factors have significant effects, fitting an appropriate model, and finding optimal settings have inspired the development of a rich and powerful set of statistical DOE tools. In Minitab, the Stat > DOE menu provides a friendly and well-organized interface for experimenters from all branches of science and engineering.

CHAPTER OBJECTIVES

Here's what you'll learn in this chapter:

- How to design a two-level factorial or fractional factorial experiment
- How to analyze the results from a factorial experiment and reduce the model to only significant terms
- How to optimize a system with multiple response variables
- How to fit a model to variation and use the model to minimize it
- How to remove the effects of extraneous variables from an experiment
- How to design and analyze experiments with hard-to-change variables
- How to model and optimize response surfaces
- How to experiment with mixtures

A good experiment requires good planning. Before collecting any data, use the Minitab DOE menu to define the experiment in a new Minitab worksheet. The worksheet provides a form for data collection, with one experimental run on each worksheet row. After data collection is complete, other functions in the DOE menu provide analytical reports, graphs, and optimizers.

Before using any Minitab DOE tools, the experimenter must decide which class of experiments will be applied to the system. Each of these classes has its own submenu in the Stat > DOE menu:

- **Factorial designs** are the simplest class of experiments to understand, and many variations of factorial experiments are available through the Stat > DOE > Factorial menu.

  - **2-level factorial designs** are limited to two levels for all factors, with the optional addition of center points. This class of experiments includes both full factorial and fractional factorial designs. In Minitab, these experiments may have up to 15 factors, and up to 128 runs.

  - **2-level split-plot designs**, a new feature of Minitab 16, have some factors which are harder to change than other factors. These experiments involve tiered randomization and multiple levels of analysis to correctly identify the best model for the system.

  - **Plackett–Burman designs** are a family of experiments often used to screen a few significant factors from a larger number of factors of interest. In Minitab, Plackett–Burman designs can have up to 47 factors, each at two levels. Often, these experiments are unreplicated, except for an optional center point.

  - **General full factorial designs** involve all combinations of factors with two or more levels for each factor.

- **Response surface designs** are intended to fit a quadratic model to predict the response as a curved function of the factors. All factors in a response surface design are quantitative. This quadratic model is often used to identify operating points with less variation or more robustness. Minitab provides two families of response surface designs: central composite designs and Box–Behnken designs.

- **Mixture designs** are used to experiment with components of a blend or mixture. The sum of component proportions are constrained to be 1. Mixture designs involve compromises to gain the most information from a constrained factor space, with specialized graphs and analysis to interpret the results.

- **Taguchi designs** comprise a catalog of experimental designs made popular by engineer and quality guru Genichi Taguchi (1987). Almost all of these designs have equivalent designs available through the Factorial menu. Because of this fact, and the declining usage of Taguchi designs in recent years, Taguchi designs are not discussed further in this book.

Minitab can also create an optimal design, which is the best possible experiment limited to a specified number of runs, to estimate a model with specified terms. To build an optimal design, start with a general full factorial, response surface, or mixture design containing all possible runs to be considered. Then, use the Select Optimal Design tool in the appropriate menu to find an optimal subset of those runs.

Power and sample size calculations for experiments are available in the Stat > Power and Sample Size menu for two-level factorial designs, Plackett–Burman designs, and general full factorial designs. Except for these power and sample size tools, all Minitab tools for designing and analyzing experiments are contained in the Stat > DOE menu.

9.1   Optimizing a System with DOE

This section uses the example of one relatively simple experiment to show how an experimenter interacts with Minitab to plan, design, and analyze an experiment, and then to use the model to find optimal settings. This example will illustrate the following Minitab features:

- Sample size calculations for two-level factorial experiments
- Design of a two-level factorial experiment, including preparation of a randomized worksheet for data collection
- Preparing and interpreting main effects plots, interaction plots, and cube plots
- Analysis of a two-level factorial experiment with a full factorial model
- Reducing the model to hold only significant factors and interactions
- Preparing and interpreting residual plots
- Using the Minitab optimizer to find optimal settings of three factors to simultaneously optimize two responses

Minitab provides toolbars for experimenters to reduce the number of clicks required. This section uses a factorial design. To enable the toolbar for factorial functions, right-click on the toolbar area, and select Factorial Designs. The toolbar appears as shown below:

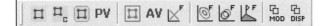

Austin is a process engineer for Acme Petroleum and Energy Products, Inc. For one critical reaction process, Austin needs to identify the optimal process time and temperature, and to select one of two catalyst suppliers. The optimal process will have highest yield and lowest cost.

Figure 9-1 diagrams the process with three factors, or input variables, and two responses, or output variables. Austin has identified two levels for time and temperature, and there are two possible catalyst suppliers, A and B.

Each run in the experiment will involve one choice of catalyst and settings of time and temperature. At the end of the run, Austin measures the yield of the desired product and calculates the cost of the run. Cost includes energy costs and plant resources to support the process for the run, plus raw materials.

One small complication is that raw material for the process is provided in batches, each of which is sufficient for eight process runs. Austin knows from experience that batches of raw material vary from one another, but there is less variation within a batch.

With three factors and two levels each, a full factorial design involves $2^3 = 8$ runs. This is a convenient number of runs, since it matches the size of each batch of raw materials. Therefore, Austin decides to use this 2^3 full factorial design, and to treat each set of 8 runs from one batch as a block in the experiment. In DOE lingo, a block is a set of runs which is expected to have less variation within the block than between blocks. Treating each batch of raw material as an experimental block is both an appropriate and a clever way to reduce the noise, so that signals will stand out more.

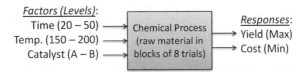

FIGURE 9-1 · Chemical process to be optimized.

How many replications should Austin use in this experiment? In this experiment, each set of eight runs will be one replication. Most experiments require more than one replication to properly measure the noise and detect the signals. Minitab includes a tool to calculate sample size for this type of experiment.

In Minitab, Austin selects Stat > Power and Sample Size > 2-Level Factorial Design and fills out the dialog as shown in Fig. 9-2. This design has 3 factors and 8 corner points. Austin feels that 1 unit of yield would be a significant improvement, and he wants a power of 0.9. In other words, Austin wants to have a probability of 90% that the experiment will correctly identify a difference of 1 unit of yield. To calculate sample size, Austin fills in the Effects and Power values fields and leaves the Replicates field empty.

This experiment will not have any center points, so Austin enters 0 in the Number of center points per block field. Based on earlier experiments, he expects to see a Standard deviation of 0.5 yield units, so this is a reasonable planning value to enter in the form. After clicking OK, Austin sees this report in the Session window:

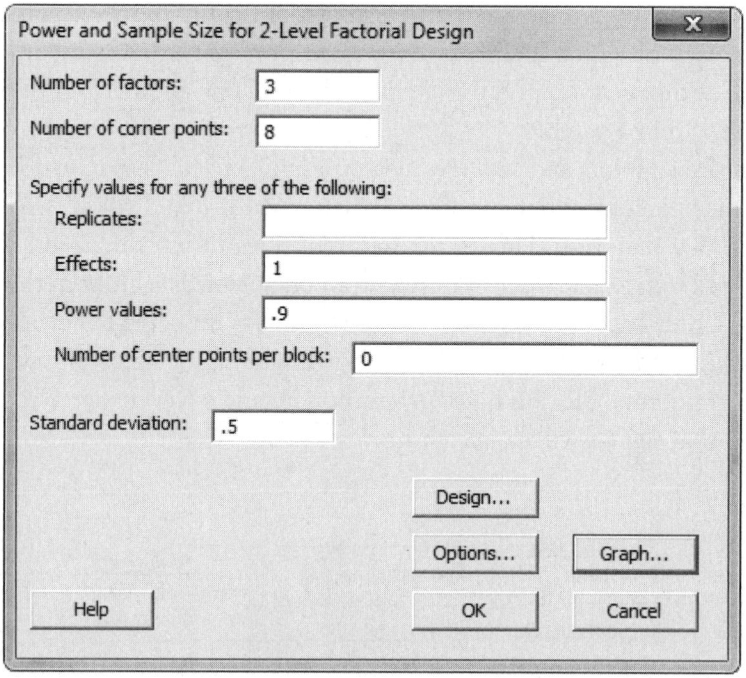

FIGURE 9-2 • Sample size calculation for two-level factorial design.

Power and Sample Size

```
2-Level Factorial Design

Alpha = 0.05   Assumed standard deviation = 0.5

Factors:    3   Base Design: 3, 8
Blocks:  none

Center                Total  Target
Points  Effect  Reps   Runs   Power   Actual Power
     0       1     2     16     0.9        0.936743
```

According to the report, two replications, for a total of 16 runs, will provide a power of 0.937, exceeding Austin's requirement of 0.9. A power curve, seen in Fig. 9-3, shows the probability of detecting effects of various sizes.

This calculation did not consider that the experiment will be divided into blocks of eight runs. For good measure, Austin repeats the sample size calculation to include blocks. This time, he clicks the Design button and enters 2 in the Number of blocks field. The report and graph, not shown here, report the power is reduced to 0.927 by this change, still quite acceptable.

Chapter 7 has more information about power and sample size calculations.

The next step is for Austin to create the design worksheet. He selects Stat > DOE > Factorial > Create Factorial Design, or he could click the  toolbar button.

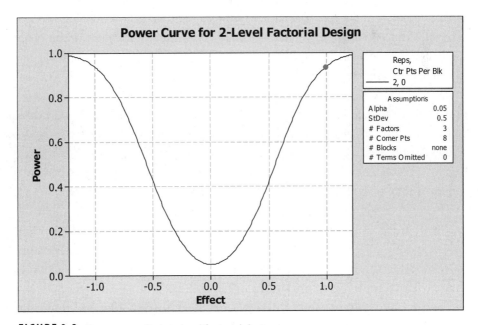

FIGURE 9-3 · Power curve for two-level factorial design.

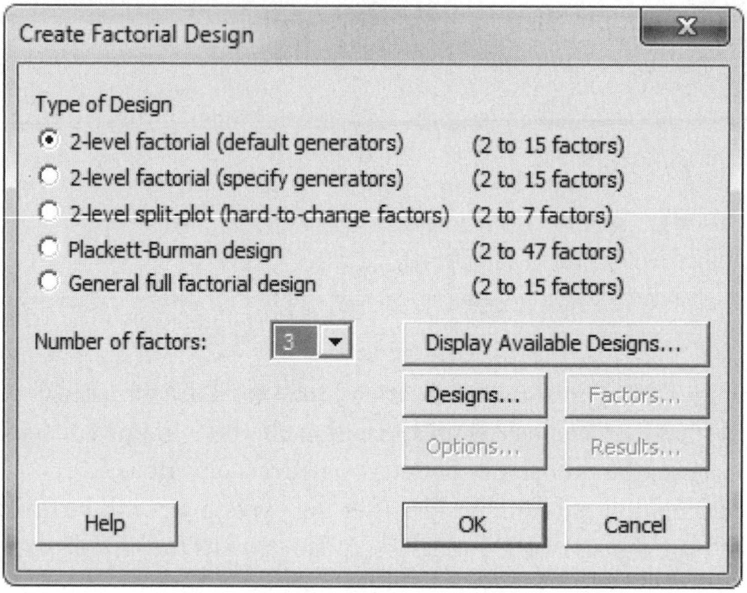

FIGURE 9-4 · Create Factorial Design dialog.

In this dialog, shown in Fig. 9-4, Austin selects the 2-level factorial (default generators) option, and enters 3 for Number of factors.

At this point, only two buttons are available. The Display Available Designs button shows a table listing available designs, but with no clickable buttons other than Help and OK. This table is discussed in more detail later in the chapter. Instead, Austin clicks the Designs button.

The Designs dialog is a mandatory part of this process of creating an experiment in Minitab. Here, Austin makes choices to determine the size and structure of the experiment, as shown in Fig. 9-5. For a two-level factorial design with three factors, two options are offered, a ½ fraction with 4 runs, and a Full factorial with 8 runs. Austin selects the Full factorial option. Austin also uses the dropdown boxes to select 2 replications of corner points and 2 blocks. This defines the experiment to have a total of 16 runs. Austin clicks OK to return to the main dialog.

The next step is to click the Factors button to specify factor names and levels as shown in Fig. 9-6. For the Options and Results dialogs, all the default options are acceptable. After clicking OK in the main dialog, Austin sees a design summary report in the Session window and the design itself appears in a new worksheet, with 16 rows. These are shown in Fig. 9-7.

The first two columns in the design worksheet are StdOrder and RunOrder, with the standard and run orders for all runs. Both of these columns contain the

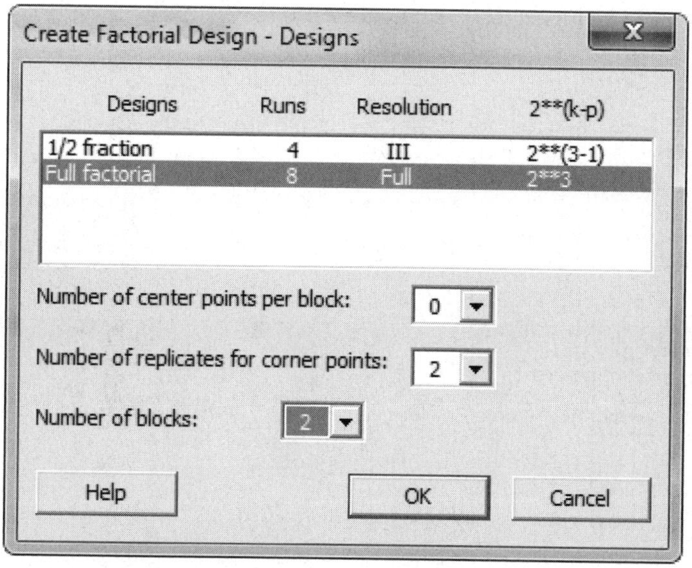

FIGURE 9-5 · Designs dialog.

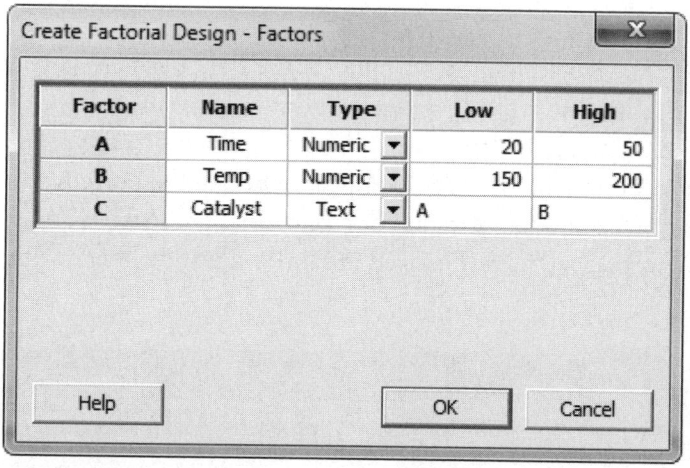

FIGURE 9-6 · Factors dialog.

numbers 1 through 16. To sort the design into standard or run order, use the Data > Sort tool to sort the worksheet by the StdOrder or RunOrder columns. For this design with two blocks, the run order is completely randomized for the eight runs within each block, but the blocks are listed in numerical order.

In a Minitab project, a design is an object stored with a worksheet, along with column, matrix, and constant variables. To see this structure, click on the

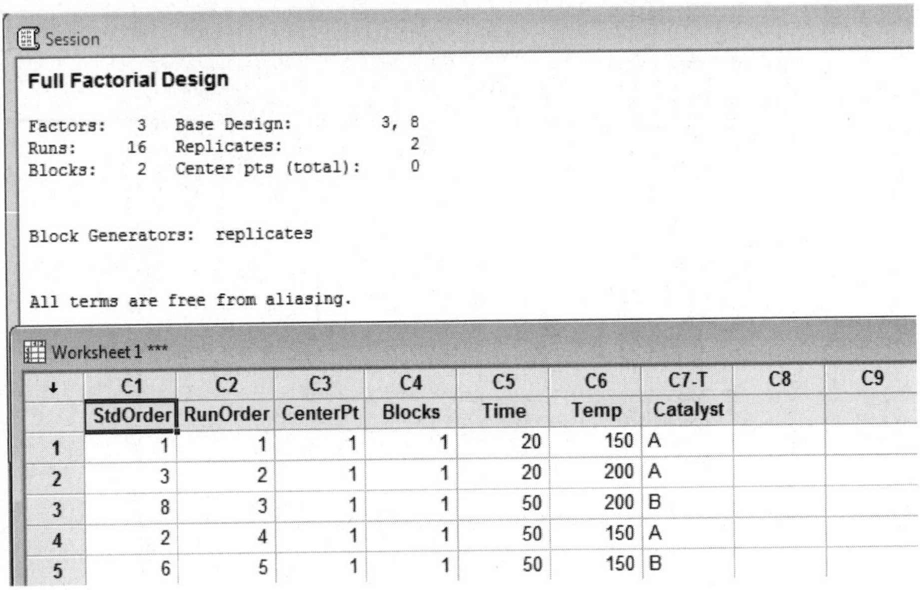

FIGURE 9-7 · Design report and randomized design worksheet.

button of the Project Manager toolbar, or use the Ctrl+Alt+E keyboard short-cut. This will show the Project Manager window. The result will look something like Fig. 9-8. On the left is the tree structure of objects in the project, and on the right is information about the design attached to the current worksheet.

This is a convenient data structure for experimenters. After a design has been defined in a worksheet, it can be saved in a .MTW file and opened with all design

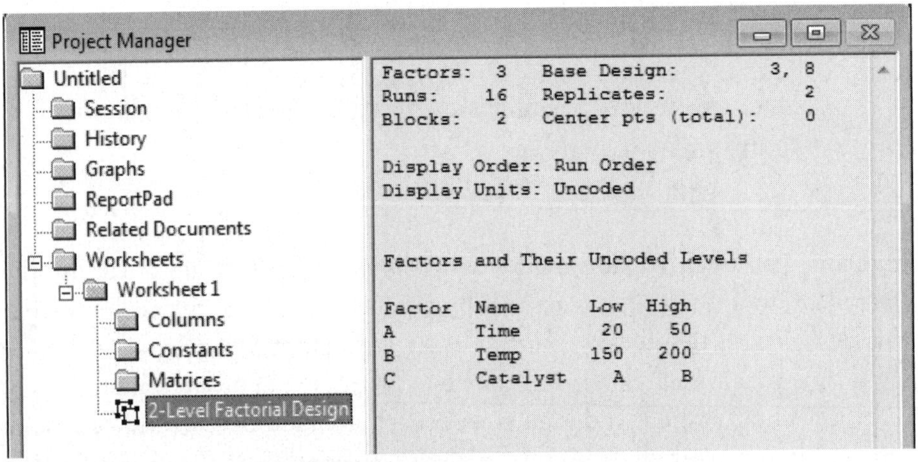

FIGURE 9-8 · Project Manager showing design stored in worksheet.

details intact by anyone else with Minitab. Also, a Minitab project file may contain many experimental designs, one for each worksheet.

To see the data collected by Austin in this experiment, open the Minitab sample data file Yield.MTW. This worksheet contains the same design with response data in two additional columns called Yield and Cost.

Graphs are always better than tables to visualize data. With factorial experiments, we have three popular styles of graphs: main effects plots, interaction plots, and cube plots. All three are available by selecting Stat > DOE > Factorial > Factorial Plots in the Minitab menu, or by clicking the ⬚ᶠ button. Each of the three types of graphs has a checkbox to select the graph and a Setup button to specify the responses and factors to plot.

Figure 9-9 is the main effects plot for Yield. For each factor, this graph shows how the mean value of yield changes between levels. Based on this plot, more time increases yield, and more temp increases yield, but changing the catalyst supplier has little effect. Be cautious interpreting this plot in a vacuum, because it could be deceiving. It is possible that the time and temp effects are caused by random noise, and not a real effect. This question of statistical significance will be answered in the next step.

By default, Minitab arranges the three parts of the main effects plot with two on the first row and one on the second row. This arrangement can be customized by right-clicking on the graph and selecting Panel.

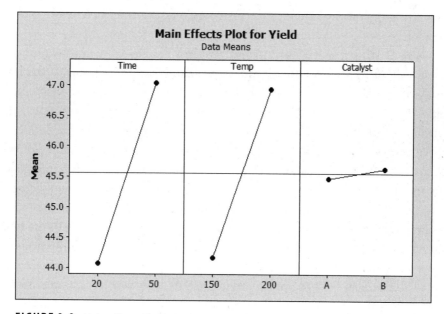

FIGURE 9-9 • Main effects plot for Yield response.

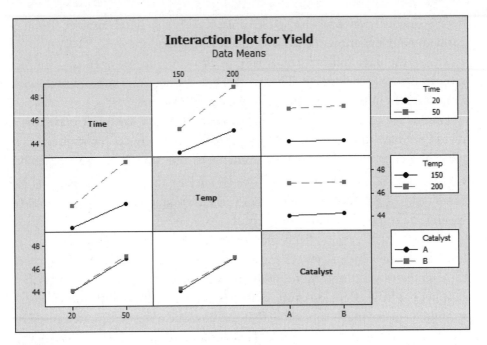

FIGURE 9-10 • Interaction plot matrix for Yield response.

The main effects plot can also be created by selecting Stat > ANOVA > Main Effects Plot, or now in Minitab 16, from the graphical analysis assistant. Neither of these functions require a factorial design to be defined before creating the plot, but in the Factorial menu, a factorial design must be defined before making the plot.

Figure 9-10 is a matrix of interaction plots for Yield. An interaction plot shows the mean response for all four combinations of two factors. If the lines on the interaction plot are parallel, there is no interaction, and the factors are said to be additive. But if the lines are not parallel, there is an interaction, since a change to one factor causes the effect of another factor to change.

With three factors, there are six possible ways to create an interaction plot, and all are shown here in this matrix of plots. The option to plot the full interaction plot matrix is found by clicking Options from the Interaction Plot – Setup dialog.

In this example, there may be an interaction between Time and Temp, because the lines on the Time by Temp interaction plot are not parallel. As with the main effects plot, this apparent interaction could be a result of random variation. Statistical significance will be tested in the next step. Since the other interaction plots have parallel lines, it appears that Catalyst is not involved in any interactions, at least for the Yield response variable.

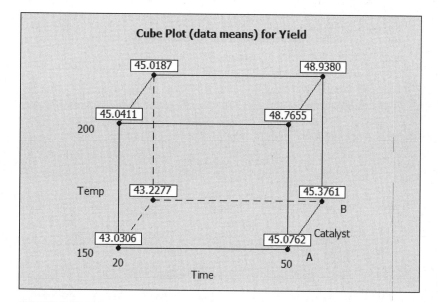

FIGURE 9-11 • Cube plot for Yield response.

Interaction plots may also be created by selecting Stat > ANOVA > Interaction Plot in single or matrix format. The graphical analysis assistant, new in Minitab 16, also provides a tool to create single interaction plots. Neither of these tools requires a factorial design to be defined before making the plot.

Figure 9-11 is a cube plot for Yield. In this plot, the mean yield values are printed at corners of a cube representing the three factors in the experiment. This plot has become a popular feature of DOE presentations, but it is arguably inferior to main effects and interaction plots. The cube plot shows how the experiment varied the three factors over a cube-shaped space. But if one wants to understand how the factors affect the response, this requires reading and correctly interpreting numbers. For this purpose, the cube plot is little better than a straight table of the data.

In this example, a second set of main effects, interaction, and cube plots may be created to help interpret the Cost response.

To analyze this data for statistical significance, Austin selects Stat > DOE > Factorial > Analyze Factorial Design from the Minitab menu, or he could click the ▥ toolbar button. In the Analyze Factorial Design dialog, shown in Fig. 9-12, Austin selects both response columns Yield and Cost.

Next, Austin clicks the Terms button to review the terms selected for the model. In this dialog, shown in Fig. 9-13, selected terms are on the right, and available terms are on the left. The buttons between the windows may be used

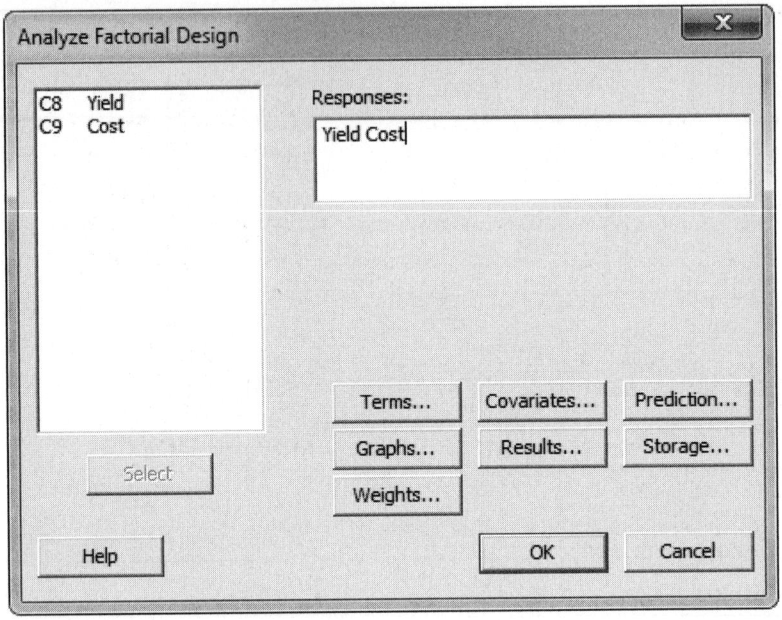

FIGURE 9-12 • Analyze Factorial Design dialog.

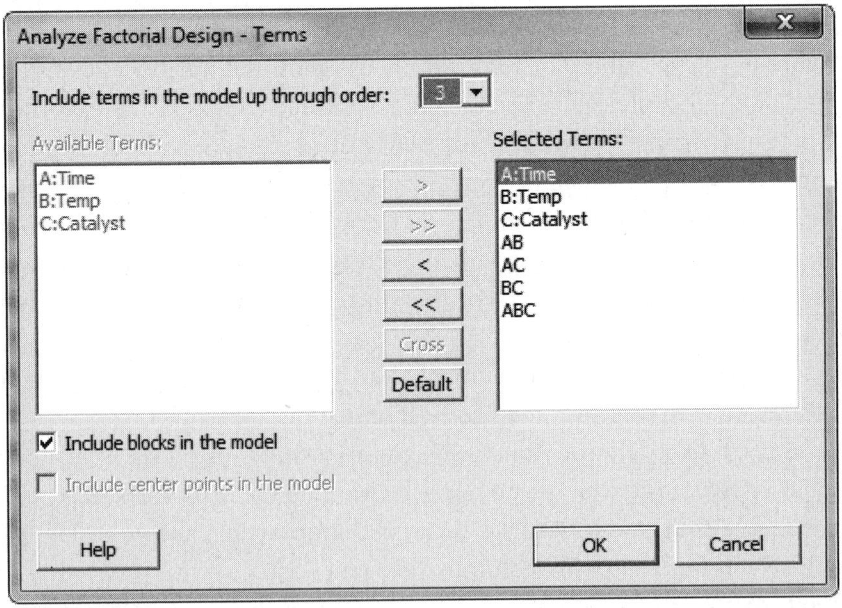

FIGURE 9-13 • Terms dialog.

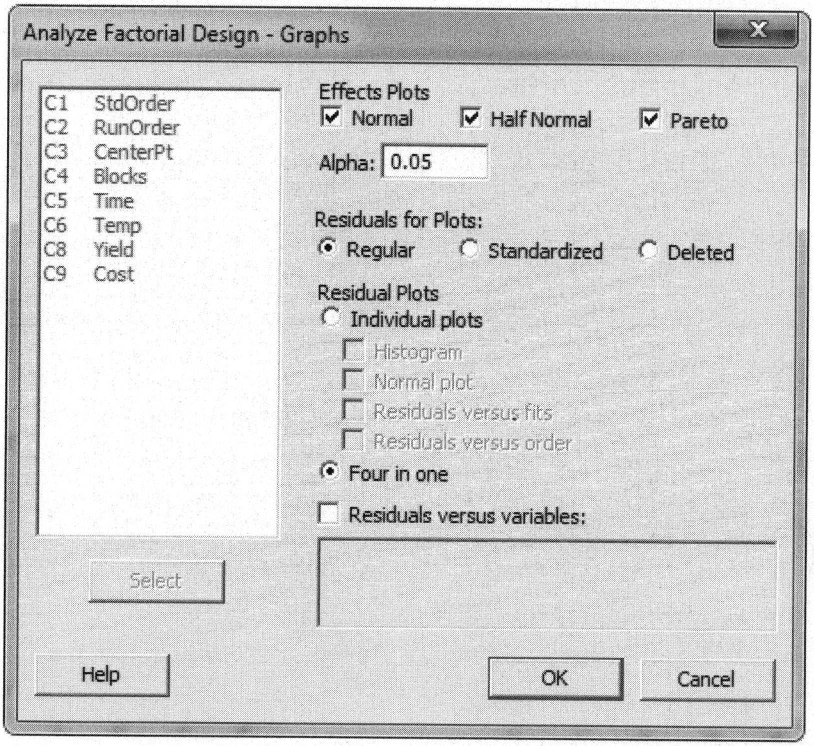

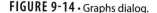

FIGURE 9-14 · Graphs dialog.

to move terms between the available and selected fields. By default, a full factorial model, including the highest-order interaction, is already selected, with the
option to include blocks in the model. No changes are needed here.

Clicking OK now produces a text report with no graphs. To display optional
graphs, click the Graphs button. At the top of this dialog, shown in Fig. 9-14, are
three forms of Effects plots: Normal, Half Normal, and Pareto. All three of these
plots show the same information, which main effects and interactions are statistically significant, in different formats. Selecting all three plots allows the
experimenter to choose the plot format he likes best. It is also a good idea to
request the Four in one residual plots. With these options selected, eight graphs
will be created, four for each response variable.

Figure 9-15 shows the half normal and Pareto effects plots for Yield and
Cost. In the half normal plots, significant effects are shown with square, red
symbols and labels. In the Pareto plot, significant effects are bars extending to
the right of the red vertical line.

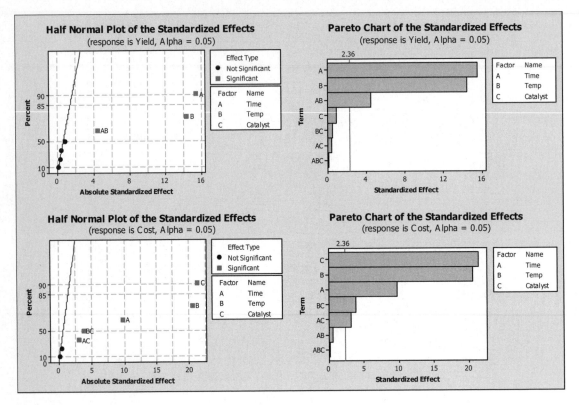

FIGURE 9-15 · Effects plots for Yield and Cost.

In the Session window is a report of the regression analysis used to fit a model to the experimental data. Here is a section of the report for the first response variable, Yield:

Factorial Fit: Yield versus Block, Time, Temp, Catalyst

Estimated Effects and Coefficients for Yield (coded units)

Term	Effect	Coef	SE Coef	T	P
Constant		45.5592	0.09546	477.25	0.000
Block		-0.0484	0.09546	-0.51	0.628
Time	2.9594	1.4797	0.09546	15.50	0.000
Temp	2.7632	1.3816	0.09546	14.47	0.000
Catalyst	0.1618	0.0809	0.09546	0.85	0.425
Time*Temp	0.8624	0.4312	0.09546	4.52	0.003
Time*Catalyst	0.0744	0.0372	0.09546	0.39	0.708
Temp*Catalyst	-0.0867	-0.0434	0.09546	-0.45	0.663
Time*Temp*Catalyst	0.0230	0.0115	0.09546	0.12	0.907

```
S = 0.381847      PRESS = 5.33236

R-Sq = 98.54%    R-Sq(pred) = 92.36%    R-Sq(adj) = 96.87%
```

Analysis of Variance for Yield (coded units)

Source	DF	Seq SS	Adj SS	Adj MS	F	P
Blocks	1	0.0374	0.0374	0.0374	0.26	0.628
Main Effects	3	65.6780	65.6780	21.8927	150.15	0.000
Time	1	35.0328	35.0328	35.0328	240.27	0.000
Temp	1	30.5405	30.5405	30.5405	209.46	0.000
Catalyst	1	0.1047	0.1047	0.1047	0.72	0.425
2-Way Interactions	3	3.0273	3.0273	1.0091	6.92	0.017
Time*Temp	1	2.9751	2.9751	2.9751	20.40	0.003
Time*Catalyst	1	0.0222	0.0222	0.0222	0.15	0.708
Temp*Catalyst	1	0.0301	0.0301	0.0301	0.21	0.663
3-Way Interactions	1	0.0021	0.0021	0.0021	0.01	0.907
Time*Temp*Catalyst	1	0.0021	0.0021	0.0021	0.01	0.907
Residual Error	7	1.0206	1.0206	0.1458		
Total	15	69.7656				

Estimated Coefficients for Yield using data in uncoded units

Term	Coef
Constant	39.4786
Block	-0.0483750
Time	-0.102585
Temp	0.0150170
Catalyst	0.48563
Time*Temp	0.00114990
Time*Catalyst	-0.0028917
Temp*Catalyst	-0.00280900
Time*Temp*Catalyst	0.000030700

This report is similar to regression reports seen in Chapter 8, but it is tailored to the specific needs of experimenters. One difference is that in an experiment, all factors are converted into coded levels, which typically run from −1 to +1, before the analysis. This improves the numerical stability of the analysis and also makes interpretation easier.

The top section of the report is a table listing Estimated Effects and Coefficients for the model, in terms of coded units. Each number listed under the Effect column is the change in the response, Yield, as the factor changes from its low level to its high level. The next column, Coef, lists half the effect for each term in the model. With all the factors expressed in coded form, these would be the coefficients in the regression model.

The rightmost column, under P, lists the *p*-values for each term in the model. If the true value for an effect is zero, the *p*-value is the probability that random variation could cause an effect to be at least as large as this one. If the *p*-value is small, generally less than 0.05, that effect is statistically significant. In this example, the `Constant`, `Time`, `Temp`, and `Time*Temp` interaction are the only significant terms in this model to predict yield.

Below the first table is a list of statistics summarizing the model. These include the residual standard deviation, `S = 0.381847`, and the adjusted R^2, `R-Sq(adj) = 96.87%`. When comparing different models for the same response variable, the best model will generally have the highest adjusted R^2 and the lowest residual standard deviation. Chapter 8 has more information on these statistics and the others listed here.

The `Analysis of Variance` table is a formal hypothesis test for significance of the model and for every term in the model. This table has the same information as the table above, with the addition of combined tests for significant `Main Effects`, `2-Way Interactions`, and `3-Way Interactions`.

At the bottom of the report is a table of `Estimated Coefficients for Yield using data in uncoded units`. To write out a model in terms of time and temperature in their measured units, use these coefficients. For this model, catalyst, as a text variable, is coded so that –1 represents A and +1 represents B.

The next step in the analysis is to reduce the model to contain only significant main effects and interactions. To remove effects, recall the Analyze Factorial Design dialog with the ▣ button, click the Terms button, and move terms from the selected terms to the available terms, with the ⟨ < ⟩ button.

When reducing a regression model, it is good practice to observe the rule of hierarchy. If the model contains a higher-order interaction term, all included lower-order terms must also be included, even if they are not statistically significant. For example, if the `Time*Temp` interaction is significant, both `Time` and `Temp` main effects must be included in the model, regardless of their *p*-values.

It is also good practice to remove terms from the model one at a time. Any change to the model might change the residual error and *p*-values for the remaining terms. This example has two blocks. The two blocks do not have a significant difference, but the block effect should not be removed from the model.

To reduce the regression model, fit models separately to each response variable. After removing higher-order, insignificant terms, the reduced models will have only these terms:

- For the Yield response, the model will have only A, B, and AB terms, plus the blocks.

- For the Cost response, the model will have only A, B, C, AC, and BC terms, plus the blocks.

After reducing the models, double-check that the correct reduced models are stored in the worksheet, by using the 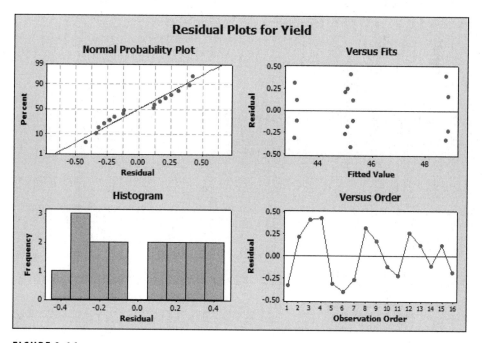 button. At the bottom of the design information in the Project Manager window is a listing of the models most recently fitted to each response variable:

```
Responses and Models

Response:  Yield
Terms:     A B AB
Blocks included in model

Response:  Cost
Terms:     A B C AC BC
Blocks included in model
```

It is also a good idea to view residual plots for all response variables. These are easily produced by selecting the Four in one residual plot option in the Graphs dialog, when the factorial design is analyzed. Figure 9-16 shows the residual plots for the Yield response. Residual plots provide a good way to look for severe nonnormality or heteroscedasticity (unequal variation) in the residuals. Chapter 8 has more information on these and other forms of data disorders. In this example, there is no significant reason to worry about the residuals.

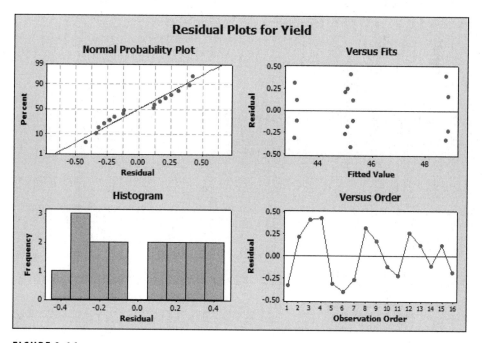

FIGURE 9-16 · Residual plots for yield with reduced model.

Now that a reduced model has been fit to both response variables, Austin can use the Minitab optimizer to find the best values of time, temperature, and catalyst to maximize yield and minimize cost. To start this process, Austin selects Stat > DOE > Factorial > Response Optimizer from the Minitab menu, or he could click the ⬈ toolbar button.

Figure 9-17 shows the Response Optimizer dialog. In the Available field, this dialog shows all the response variables which have a fitted model available to optimize. Austin clicks the >> button to select both Yield and Cost.

Next, Austin clicks the Setup button, and fills out the Setup dialog as shown in Fig. 9-18. For each response variable, the settings in this dialog define a desirability function to reflect these choices. Austin specifies that Yield needs to be maximized, with a target value of 50 and a lower limit of 40. These settings specify a desirability function for Yield that is 0 for values less than 40, 1 for values greater than 50, and a straight line ramp from 0 to 1 between 40 and 50.

For Cost, Austin specifies that this variable should be minimized, with a target of 30 and an upper limit of 40. These settings specify a desirability function that is 1 for values less than 30, 0 for values greater than 40, and a straight line ramp from 1 to 0 between 30 and 40.

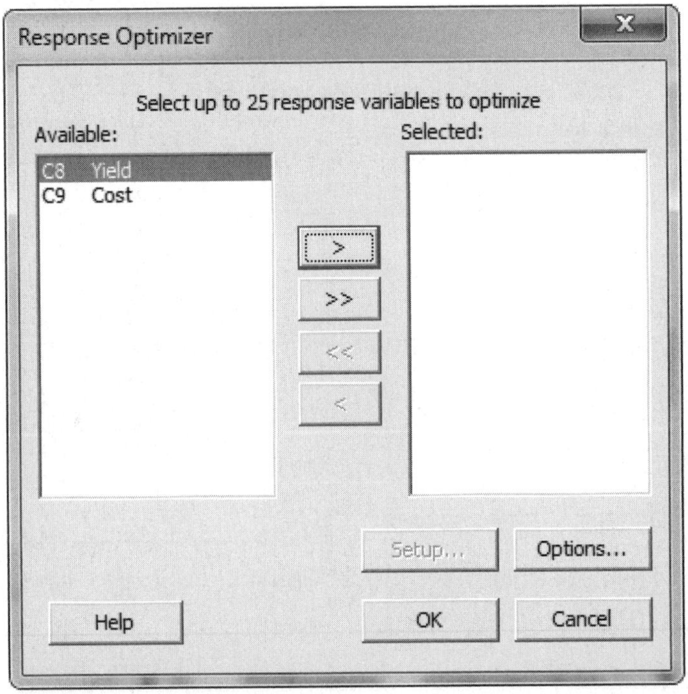

FIGURE 9-17 · Response Optimizer dialog.

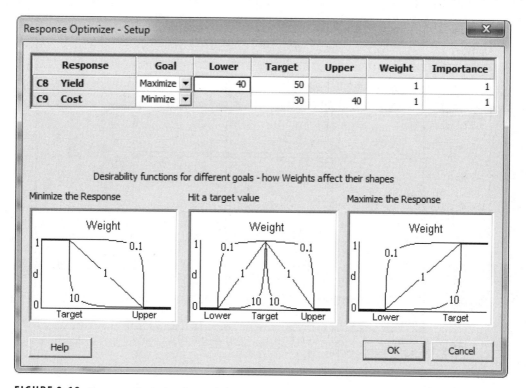

FIGURE 9-18 · Response Optimizer Setup dialog.

The little drawings at the bottom of this dialog illustrate how the desirability functions are drawn, when the goal is to minimize, hit a target, or maximize. The Weight value can be changed if desired to change the shape of the desirability function.

To find the optimal settings, the Minitab optimizer multiplies these two functions together to form a composite desirability. If one response is more important than another, the Importance value can be changed to reflect the relative importance of each response. The composite desirability is always between 0 and 1, where 1 is ideal and 0 represents a setting where at least one response variable is outside its limits.

After clicking OK, Austin sees the interactive Optimization Plot as shown in Fig. 9-19. This special graph has many interactive elements, and a special toolbar is available with these interactive functions. All the toolbar functions can also be accessed by right-clicking on the graph. To enable this toolbar, seen below, right-click in the toolbar area of the Minitab window and select OptiPlot.

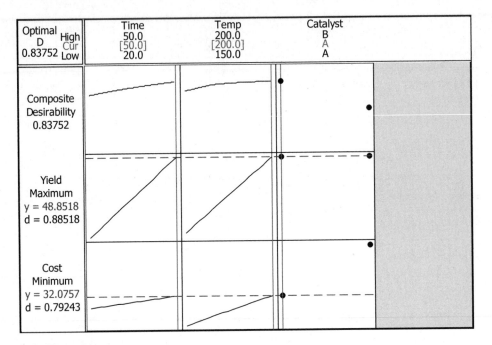

Optimal High D 0.83752 Cur Low	Time 50.0 [50.0] 20.0	Temp 200.0 [200.0] 150.0	Catalyst B A A

FIGURE 9-19 · Optimization plot.

The Optimization Plot shows the optimum settings to maximize yield and minimize cost, which are high time, high temp, and catalyst A. These settings are shown in the middle, red row in the top margin of the plot. Click on any of these red values to change them. Or, click on any of the vertical, red lines in the plot and drag them to explore new values of the three factors.

The bottom two rows of graphs show the main effects of the three factors on the two responses. The top row of graphs shows how the composite desirability changes as the factors change. The OptiPlot toolbar provides options to save multiple sets of settings, scroll through them, return to the optimal settings, or zoom in and out. Hover over the icons in the toolbar to see the functions of each.

The optimizer combines our objectives for all response variables. If one response is more important than another, this may change the optimal settings. For example, suppose that every two units of yield is equivalent to one unit of cost, and therefore, cost is twice as important as yield. Back in the Response Optimizer – Setup dialog, change the Importance to 2 for Cost. Now what are the optimum settings?

The Factorial menu has more powerful tools to explore. When interactions exist, contour and surface plots are very useful to visualize these effects. These

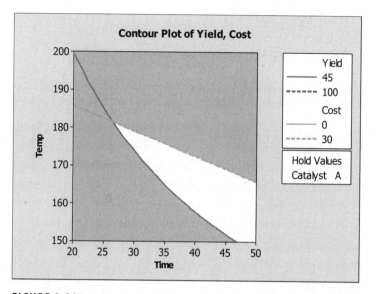

FIGURE 9-20 • Overlaid contour plot.

plots were first seen in Chapter 2. To quickly make these plots from a factorial experiment, select Stat > DOE > Factorial > Contour/Surface Plots or click the 🔲 button in the toolbar.

The above example showed how desirability functions are used to simultaneously optimize multiple response variables. Another popular technique, with two factors, is to use overlaid contour plots. These can be created using Stat > DOE > Factorial > Overlaid Contour Plot or by clicking the 🔲 button in the toolbar.

For this example, Fig. 9-20 is an overlaid contour plot showing the region of Time and Temp which will keep Yield over 45 and Cost under 30, with Catalyst A.

This lengthy example has illustrated all the major Minitab functions for the design, analysis, and interpretation of experiments. The remaining sections of this chapter will show some additional features for different situations.

9.2 Creating a Design from an Existing File

It is often necessary to analyze an experiment that was not designed in Minitab. Perhaps the design was created by some other program, published in a magazine, or distributed in an Excel worksheet. For these situations, each of the four DOE menus has a Define Custom Design tool. Defining a custom design will add the necessary columns and other information to the worksheet, so that Minitab can analyze the data as a designed experiment.

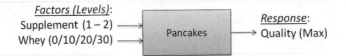

FIGURE 9-21 · Pancake experiment.

Sue's Lodge of Pancakes (SLOP) is experimenting with Sue's classic pancake batter recipe. In one experiment, Sue wants to vary the malt flavor supplement from 1 to 2 tablespoons, and also find the correct level of a whey additive. The response is quality, which will be measured by a panel of Sue's best customers. Figure 9-21 shows the variables for this experiment.

This 2×4 full factorial experiment was replicated 3 times for a total of 24 runs. Suppose Sue asks you to analyze the data, which is in the Minitab sample data file Pancake.MTW.

The Pancake.MTW file has only three columns, with the two factors and one response variable. No information is provided about run order, so there is no way to know from this file whether Sue randomized the runs.

With Pancake.MTW as the current worksheet, select Stat > DOE > Factorial > Define Custom Factorial Design or click the ⬛ button in the Factorial Designs toolbar.

In the dialog shown in Fig. 9-22, select the two factors Supplement and Whey. Since one of the factors has more than two levels, this must be defined as a General Full Factorial design. Click OK to create the design.

When the design is created, Minitab adds the following four columns to the worksheet:

- **StdOrder** lists the standard order for all runs.
- **RunOrder** lists the run order for the runs. In this case, the run order is unknown, but Minitab requires a column for this information anyway. Here, it is set to be the same as the standard order.
- **Blocks** lists block numbers. If there are no blocks in the experiment, this is a column of ones.
- **PtType**, sometimes called **CenterPt**, describes the type of each point in the design, where most points are type 1, center points are type 0, and axial points in a central composite design are −1.

If any of the four required columns are already available in the worksheet, click the Designs button to specify them. Otherwise, Minitab will create four new columns, as in this case.

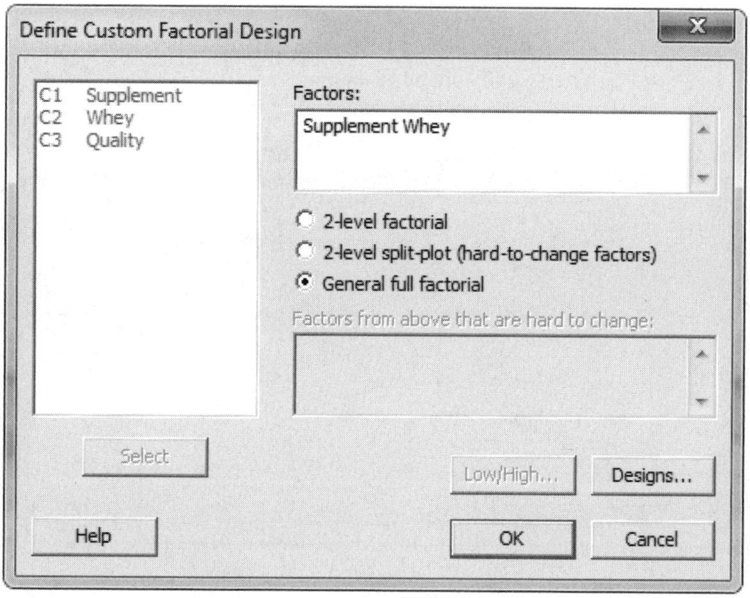

FIGURE 9-22 • Defining a custom design.

To verify that the design was created correctly, click the button in the Project Manager toolbar. As displayed, the design should look like this:

```
Factors:  2    Factor Levels: 2, 4
Runs:    24

Display Order: Standard Order
Display Units: Uncoded

Factors and Their Uncoded Levels

Factor  Name        Levels
A       Supplement  1 2
B       Whey        0 10 20 30
```

Now that the worksheet has a defined design, it can be analyzed like any other experiment. Analysis shows that the interaction between `Supplement` and `Whey` is significant, with a *p*-value of 0.000. Figure 9-23 is an interaction plot made from this data.

Based on the interaction plot, Sue can safely conclude that pancake quality is improved most with Supplement = 2 and Whey = 30.

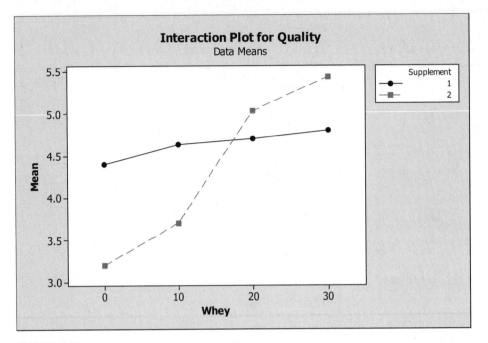

FIGURE 9-23 · Interaction plot for pancake quality.

9.3   Analyzing Variation as a Response

To be successful today, a product must be robust. This means that it must perform consistently over time, between units, and over all usage conditions. This urgent business goal means that engineers and scientists must pay due attention to variation at all levels of product and process design.

With a replicated two-level factorial design, Minitab makes it easy to analyze the variation of replicated runs as an additional response variable. There are two steps in this process:

- Use Stat > DOE > Factorial > Pre-Process Responses for Analyze Variability or click the **PV** button in the Factorial Designs toolbar. This function will calculate the standard deviation across replicated runs and the counts of runs in each standard deviation. The standard deviations and counts will be added to the worksheet as two new columns. If the standard deviations and counts are already in the worksheet, this function must be used to identify them to Minitab.

- Use Stat > DOE > Factorial > Analyze Variability or click the **AV** button in the Factorial Designs toolbar. This function will analyze the standard deviation and help you select effects which significantly reduce variation. Typically, the natural log of standard deviation is treated as a response variable for the regression analysis.

For an example of variation analysis, we return to Austin, of the newly renamed Acme Puppies and Kittens, Inc. Austin is still working on the same process, and he is now conducting a follow-up experiment. Since Austin saw no significant difference between blocks in the last experiment, he is no longer tracking blocks or using them in the design.

This experiment has the same three factors at two levels, with eight full replications, for a total of 64 runs. Yield data for this experiment is contained in the Minitab sample data file Yieldstdev.MTW. The Yieldstdev.MTW worksheet already includes a two-level factorial design, and measured response values are listed in the Yield column. With Yieldstdev.MTW as the current worksheet, Austin selects Stat > DOE > Factorial > Pre-Process Responses for Analyze Variability and fills out the dialog as shown in Fig. 9-24.

This dialog has three options for different situations. If each replication is stored in a different column of the worksheet, choose Compute for repeat

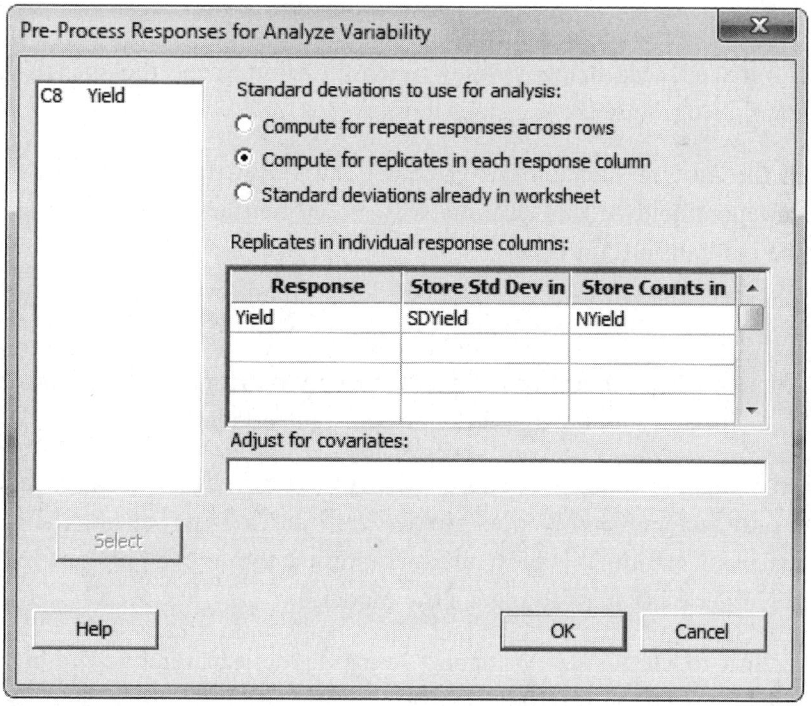

FIGURE 9-24 · Pre-Process Responses for Analyze Variability dialog.

Yieldstdev.MTW ***

↓	C1	C2	C3	C4	C5	C6	C7-T	C8	C9	C10	C11
	StdOrder	RunOrder	CenterPt	Blocks	Time	Temp	Catalyst	Yield	SDYield	NYield	
1	3	1	1	1	20	200	A	45.1931	1.0240	8	
2	24	2	1	1	50	200	B	59.6118	10.0303	8	
3	35	3	1	1	20	200	A	44.8025	*	*	
4	33	4	1	1	20	150	A	43.2365	0.2800	8	
5	64	5	1	1	50	200	B	38.8697	*	*	
6	47	6	1	1	20	200	B	47.2578	2.0003	8	

FIGURE 9-25 • Yieldstdev.MTW with added columns for variation analysis.

responses across rows. If the replicated measurements are all in one column, as they are here, choose Compute for replicates in each response column. If the standard deviations and counts of runs in each standard deviation are already listed in the worksheet, choose Standard deviations already in worksheet.

After doing this, the worksheet will contain two added columns, SDYield with the standard deviations and NYield with the counts, as shown in Fig. 9-25. These columns only have eight values, one for each distinct combination of factor values.

To analyze variation as a response, Austin selects Stat > DOE > Factorial > Analyze Variation. This dialog works in much the same way as the Analyze Factorial Design dialog. Here are the steps to follow:

- In the Analyze Variation dialog, select SDYield in the Response (Standard deviation) field. In this example, this should be the only column listed in the column selector box.
- Click the Terms button and select all available terms with the >> button.
- Click the Graphs button and select the Pareto effects plot, or another format if you prefer, and also select the Three in one residual plot.

After clicking OK, the report and graphs appear as requested. With the full model, only factors A and B appear to be significant. When reducing the model for standard deviation, it is particularly important to remove only one term at a time. Here are the steps to reduce the model:

- Return to the Analyze Variation – Terms dialog, and remove the highest-level interaction ABC from the model. The result has only factors A and B as significant.

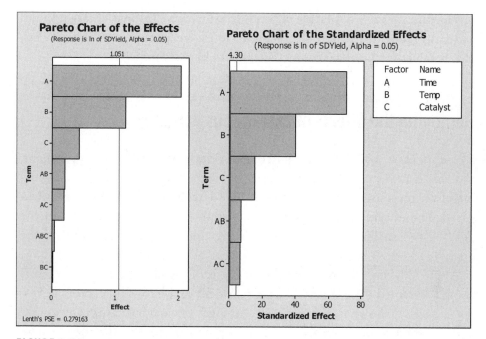

FIGURE 9-26 · Effects Pareto chart for variation—full model (left) and reduced model (right).

- Return to the Analyze Variation – Terms dialog, and remove the least-significant two-factor interaction term, BC from the model. The resulting analysis finds all remaining model terms to be significant.

Figure 9-26 compares the effects Pareto chart of the full model on the left to the reduced model on the right.

Here are some suggested next steps for this example:

- Fit a model to the mean of Yield using Analyze Factorial Design.
- Remove insignificant terms from the model, one at a time, always respecting hierarchy.

In the reduced model for the mean, Time is significant with a very low p-value. Also, Temp may be significant with a p-value of 0.078. There is 92.2% confidence that the effect of Temp seen in this data is not caused by random variation. Most analysts would probably leave it in the model.

- Use the Response Optimizer to find process settings that simultaneously maximize yield and minimize variation of yield.

The final optimized solution depends heavily on the settings of target values and limits provided to the optimizer. If you were in charge of this process, which values for Time, Temp, and Catalyst would you choose?

9.4   Removing the Effects of Extraneous Variables

Experimenters would like to control every variable during the experiment, but this is never possible. Sometimes variables have a known or suspected effect on responses, and they cannot be controlled, but they can be measured. The effects of these extraneous variables can be removed from the data by measuring them and then listing them as covariates during the analysis.

Abbie is trying to maximize the strength of injection molded insulators using a designed experiment. This experiment will have four factors at two levels each, as shown in Fig. 9-27. The strength of each insulator is measured and recorded by an electronic system. The temperature in the room where testing occurs varies throughout the day, and strength is known to vary as a function of temperature. Temperature cannot economically be controlled during the experiment, but it is easy to measure. Abbie records the temperature for each measurement.

The Minitab sample data file InsulationStrength.MTW contains the results from Abbie's experiment. Abbie ran six complete replications of the full factorial design, for a total of 96 runs. Columns named **Strength** and **Temp** contain the measurements for each trial.

First, try analyzing this data without considering the effect of temperature. Select Stat > DOE > Factorial > Analyze Factorial Design. Select Strength as the response variable. Click Terms and select all terms through the fourth-order interaction. Click Graphs and select a Pareto chart or the effects chart of your choice. After clicking OK, the following report appears:

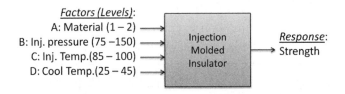

FIGURE 9-27 · Insulation strength experiment.

Factorial Fit: Strength versus Material, InjPress, InjTemp, CoolTemp

Estimated Effects and Coefficients for Strength (coded units)

Term	Effect	Coef	SE Coef	T	P
Constant		29.425	0.2168	135.72	0.000
Material	6.796	3.398	0.2168	15.67	0.000
InjPress	5.152	2.576	0.2168	11.88	0.000
InjTemp	4.326	2.163	0.2168	9.98	0.000
CoolTemp	-3.951	-1.975	0.2168	-9.11	0.000
Material*InjPress	0.053	0.027	0.2168	0.12	0.903
Material*InjTemp	-0.778	-0.389	0.2168	-1.79	0.076
Material*CoolTemp	-1.259	-0.630	0.2168	-2.90	0.005
InjPress*InjTemp	0.048	0.024	0.2168	0.11	0.913
InjPress*CoolTemp	0.191	0.096	0.2168	0.44	0.660
InjTemp*CoolTemp	1.915	0.957	0.2168	4.42	0.000
Material*InjPress*InjTemp	0.424	0.212	0.2168	0.98	0.331
Material*InjPress*CoolTemp	1.838	0.919	0.2168	4.24	0.000
Material*InjTemp*CoolTemp	0.397	0.198	0.2168	0.91	0.363
InjPress*InjTemp*CoolTemp	-0.092	-0.046	0.2168	-0.21	0.833
Material*InjPress*InjTemp*CoolTemp	0.463	0.232	0.2168	1.07	0.289

S = 2.12422   PRESS = 519.819
R-Sq = 88.60%   R-Sq(pred) = 83.58%   R-Sq(adj) = 86.46%

Now, for comparison, return to the same Analyze Factorial Design dialog. Click the Covariates button, and select Temp to be a covariate. Here is the report including the covariate:

Factorial Fit: Strength versus Temp, Material, ...

Estimated Effects and Coefficients for Strength (coded units)

Term	Effect	Coef	SE Coef	T	P
Constant		20.887	6.01892	3.47	0.001
Temp		0.126	0.08882	1.42	0.160
Material	6.803	3.402	0.21546	15.79	0.000
InjPress	5.196	2.598	0.21600	12.03	0.000
InjTemp	4.336	2.168	0.21547	10.06	0.000
CoolTemp	-3.944	-1.972	0.21545	-9.15	0.000
Material*InjPress	0.072	0.036	0.21555	0.17	0.867
Material*InjTemp	-0.943	-0.471	0.22312	-2.11	0.038
Material*CoolTemp	-1.240	-0.620	0.21555	-2.88	0.005
InjPress*InjTemp	0.146	0.073	0.21823	0.34	0.738
InjPress*CoolTemp	0.261	0.130	0.21683	0.60	0.549
InjTemp*CoolTemp	1.907	0.954	0.21546	4.43	0.000
Material*InjPress*InjTemp	0.302	0.151	0.21972	0.69	0.494
Material*InjPress*CoolTemp	2.014	1.007	0.22422	4.49	0.000
Material*InjTemp*CoolTemp	0.398	0.199	0.21544	0.92	0.358
InjPress*InjTemp*CoolTemp	-0.066	-0.033	0.21563	-0.15	0.878
Material*InjPress*InjTemp*CoolTemp	0.372	0.186	0.21780	0.86	0.395

S = 2.11087   PRESS = 513.541
R-Sq = 88.88%   R-Sq(pred) = 83.78%   R-Sq(adj) = 86.63%

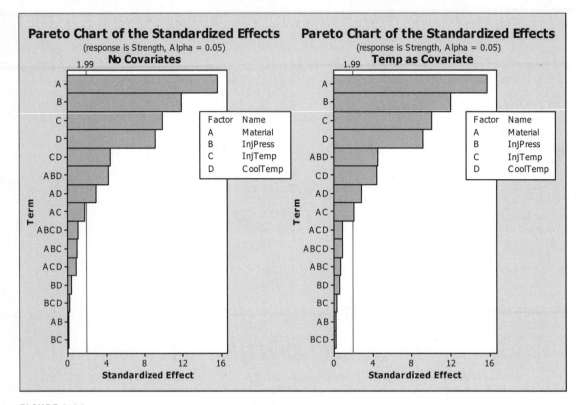

FIGURE 9-28 · Pareto charts of effects without and with covariate.

After removing the effects of `Temp` from the response, the residual standard deviation `S` is slightly reduced, and the `R-Sq(adj)` is slightly increased. These are both indicators of an improved model.

Figure 9-28 is a comparison of Pareto charts without and with `Temp` as a covariate. Adding the covariate to the model changes some of the estimated effects. As a result, one of the effects, the **AC** interaction, is significant at the 0.05 level, when it was not significant without the covariate.

With six replications, this InsulationStrength.MTW dataset is also a good example for analyzing the variation in strength as a second response variable, as discussed in the previous section. This dataset already includes **Std** and **N** columns with the standard deviations and counts of strength values, but these were calculated without considering the covariate.

When analyzing variation in the presence of covariates, the covariates must be listed in both steps of the process, as follows:

- In the Pre-Process Responses for Analyze Variability dialog, list any covariate variables in the Adjust for covariates field.

- In the Analyze Variability dialog, click the Covariates button to specify covariates.

Going through these steps is left as an exercise for the reader. In this example, specifying Temp as a covariate has a similar effect on the variation analysis as it does on the mean analysis.

9.5   Planning an Experiment with Many Factors and Few Runs

Every experimenter works with limited resources. While learning DOE, it is easy to play with free data provided by Minitab or a simulator, but real experiments cost real money, and there is never enough. Advance planning and consideration of alternatives are the keys to working within limited resources. Minitab offers many options to experimenters who need to learn the most information in the least experimental runs. By weighing the available options against the goals of the experiment, the best compromise can be found.

To understand these compromises, one must understand the advantages of having more runs. Suppose an experiment has N total runs, or N measurements of each response variable. This provides N pieces of information, usually called degrees of freedom. When analyzing the experiment, Minitab uses the N degrees of freedom for different purposes:

- One degree of freedom is used to estimate the overall mean.
- Every term in the model requires one degree of freedom, allocated as follows:
  - Every two-level factor requires one degree of freedom. If a factor has k levels, this requires $k - 1$ degrees of freedom.
  - Every interaction requires the product of the degrees of freedom required by each main effect in the interaction. Interactions of two-level factors require one degree of freedom each.
  - Center points, if used, require one degree of freedom.
  - Blocks require one fewer degree of freedom than the number of blocks.
- The count of replicated trials, excluding the first replication, is the degrees of freedom used to estimate "pure error." Pure error is the variation between multiple experimental units when the same levels of all factors are applied to each unit.

- All remaining degrees of freedom are used to estimate "lack of fit." Lack of fit represents variation between units that is not pure error, and is not explained by the model. If the lack of fit is significantly larger than pure error, this indicates that more terms could be added to the model. When possible, Minitab reports a p-value for lack of fit. If this p-value is small, this is evidence that the model needs more terms.

For example, consider a full factorial experiment with three factors at two levels, and four replications. This experiment has $2^3 \times 4 = 32$ total runs, and 32 total degrees of freedom. After running the experiment and fitting a model, suppose the model is reduced to have only four terms, A, B, C, and AB. Here is how the 32 degrees of freedom are allocated:

- 1 degree of freedom to the mean
- 4 degrees of freedom for the model
- 24 degrees of freedom for pure error, calculated as 32 total runs less 8 runs for the first replication
- 3 degrees of freedom for lack of fit, which is $32 - 1 - 4 - 24$

In a replicated experiment, pure error degrees of freedom are available. In this case, Minitab tests all the factor and interaction effects against pure error to determine which are significant. If there are also degrees of freedom for lack of fit, Minitab tests this against the pure error to determine if there is evidence of an inadequate model.

An experiment with only one replication is usually called an unreplicated experiment. In this case, there is no pure error. The degrees of freedom that would have been lack of fit, now become the only estimate of error. Minitab uses this to test the factors and interactions for significance.

When the number of terms in the model, plus the mean, equals the total number of runs, the experiment is said to be saturated. In this case, there is no information to estimate the error, and there are no residuals, since the model fits the data perfectly. With no error term, Minitab uses a method published by Lenth (1989) to separate the significant from insignificant effects in the Pareto, half normal, and normal effects plots.

Statistics provides options, but no free lunch. Pure error through replication is best, and more degrees of freedom for pure error gives the test more sensitivity to smaller changes. Without pure error, lack of fit is an acceptable alternative, if the model is in fact the correct model. With no error term at all, the

Lenth method is better than nothing, and it is effective in identifying the very large effects, but it may give incorrect results.

On the Minitab Pareto chart, the red line is the same shade of red however it is calculated. The analyst needs to keep in mind how the reliability of the red line varies by calculation method.

In the planning of an experiment with limited resources, Minitab offers many options, including these:

- **Fractional factorial designs** require fewer runs than full factorial designs. The penalty for fewer runs is that potential effects are aliased, so they cannot be separated in the analysis. Minitab offers the 2-level factorial (default generators) option which minimizes the impact of this penalty by aliasing main effects and lower-level interactions with higher-level interactions to the extent possible. With all factors at two levels, fractional factorial designs always require a number of runs which is a power of 2. Minitab offers two-level fractional factorial designs with 4, 8, 16, 32, 64, and 128 runs.

- **Plackett–Burman designs**, first published by Plackett and Burman (1946), are popular designs for screening a few significant factors from many candidates. These designs may have any multiple of 4 runs. Minitab offers Plackett–Burman designs of 12, 20, 24, 28, 36, 40, 44, and 48 runs.

- **Center points** may be added to any experiment where some factors are quantitative. When the corner points have only one replication, adding replicated center points provides a way to estimate pure error with only a few added runs. Center points are also commonly used to test for curvature. If there is significant evidence of curvature, the experiment may be augmented into a response surface design, which fits a curved model, by adding a few more runs. This process of sequential experimentation is illustrated later in this chapter.

- **Optimal designs** are the best available designs with a specified number of runs that can estimate a specified list of main effects and interactions.

To see how these options work out, consider the case of Cal, whose team is designing a new fuel control valve for aircraft applications. Cal's team plans to measure accuracy and several other variables as a response of six factors, as shown in Fig. 9-29. Of the six factors, five are continuous numerical variables (A-E), and one is categorical with only two possible values (F).

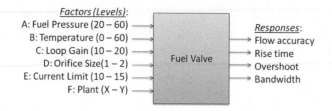

Factors (Levels):
A: Fuel Pressure (20 – 60) →
B: Temperature (0 – 60) →
C: Loop Gain (10 – 20) →
D: Orifice Size (1 – 2) →
E: Current Limit (10 – 15) →
F: Plant (X – Y) →

Fuel Valve

Responses:
→ Flow accuracy
→ Rise time
→ Overshoot
→ Bandwidth

FIGURE 9-29 • Fuel valve experiment.

Each test involves a lot of work and money with a very expensive test system. Considering the budget and conflicting demands on the test system, only 16 total runs can be performed. How should the experiment be designed? The answer depends on the objectives of Cal's team for the experiment. Each of the options above is worth considering for its merits and drawbacks. There is no definitive answer about which design is best. A skilled experimenter will consider all available options before selecting one to follow.

Option 1: 16-Run Fractional Factorial Design, 1 Replication

To view a table of available two-level factorial designs in Minitab, select Stat > DOE > Factorial > Create Factorial Design, and then click the Display Available Designs button. An informative dialog appears as shown in Fig. 9-30.

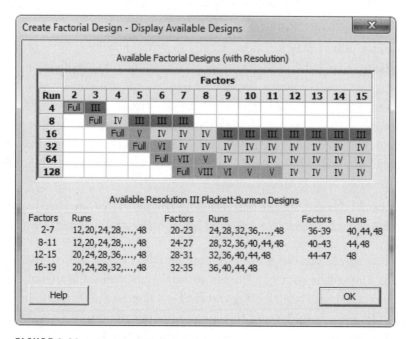

FIGURE 9-30 • Table of two-level designs.

To use this color-coded table, look up the number of factors in the column headings. Then look down that column to the row for the number of runs. Inside each cell in the table is a Roman numeral indicating the resolution of the best available design.

Resolution is a measure of the degree of aliasing in a design. Effects are aliased when they cannot be separately estimated by an experiment. Resolution is the smallest sum of the orders of two aliased effects in the design. Here are the color-coded values:

- Resolution III or R_{III} designs have main effects aliased with two-factor interactions. This is generally regarded as the lowest acceptable resolution, and it is only acceptable when main effects are expected to be much larger than two-factor interactions. When interactions are expected, this is a risky strategy. These designs are color-coded red in the Minitab table.

- Resolution IV or R_{IV} designs have main effects aliased with three-factor interactions and two-factor interactions aliased with each other. If only a few two-factor interactions are expected to be present, Resolution IV designs may be acceptable. These designs are color-coded yellow in the Minitab table.

- Resolution V or higher resolutions are generally regarded as safe because all main effects and two-factor interactions are free of aliasing with each other. These designs are color-coded green in the Minitab table.

- Full resolution designs have no aliasing. All possible interactions are estimable. These designs are also color-coded green in the Minitab table.

For Cal's example, with 6 factors and 16 runs, this is a Resolution IV design. To see specifically what this means, Cal creates the design in Minitab. In the Create Factorial Design dialog, he selects 6 in the Number of Factors dropdown box. He clicks the Designs button and selects the ¼ Factorial design with 16 runs. After creating this design, the alias table appears in the Session window as follows:

Fractional Factorial Design

```
Factors:    6   Base Design:        6, 16   Resolution:    IV
Runs:      16   Replicates:             1   Fraction:     1/4
Blocks:     1   Center pts (total):     0

Design Generators: E = ABC, F = BCD
```

```
Alias Structure

I + ABCE + ADEF + BCDF

A + BCE + DEF + ABCDF
B + ACE + CDF + ABDEF
C + ABE + BDF + ACDEF
D + AEF + BCF + ABCDE
E + ABC + ADF + BCDEF
F + ADE + BCD + ABCEF
AB + CE + ACDF + BDEF
AC + BE + ABDF + CDEF
AD + EF + ABCF + BCDE
AE + BC + DF + ABCDEF
AF + DE + ABCD + BCEF
BD + CF + ABEF + ACDE
BF + CD + ABDE + ACEF
ABD + ACF + BEF + CDE
ABF + ACD + BDE + CEF
```

According to the alias table, each of the six main effects is aliased with two three-factor interactions. Two-factor interactions are aliased with each other by twos, and in one case, by three. The last two estimable effects consist of four aliased three-factor interactions.

If Cal's team expects few factors to interact with each other, this design could work. For example, if Cal expects to see AB, AC, and BC interactions but no others, all these three will be free of aliasing.

The main drawback of this design is the inability to estimate pure error. The significance tests will be based on a few degrees of freedom for lack of fit. How well will this work?

To find out, Cal runs a power and sample size calculation for this design. If the final model includes six main effects and three interactions, this leaves six degrees of freedom for lack of fit. Cal selects Stat > Power and Sample Size > 2-Level Factorial Design. In the dialog, he enters 6 for Number of factors and 16 for Number of corner points. He enters 1 for Number of replications and 0.9 for Power values. As a planning value, Cal enters 1 for Standard deviation.

Cal clicks the Designs button and enters 6 in the Number of terms removed from the model box. It is critical here to estimate how many of the 16 possible model terms will not be used for the model. Subtracting 1 constant, 6 main effects, and 3 interactions from 16 leaves 6, the number of terms removed from the model. Here is the power and sample size report:

Power and Sample Size

```
2-Level Factorial Design

Alpha = 0.05  Assumed standard deviation = 1

Factors:    6   Base Design: 6, 16
Blocks:  none

Number of terms omitted from model: 6
```

```
Center        Total
Points   Reps  Runs  Power   Effect
     0      1    16    0.9  1.95631
```

This potential design has a 0.9 power of detecting an effect of 1.96 standard deviations in size. This can be compared with other design options.

Option 2: 8-Run Fractional Factorial Design, 2 Replications

It is possible to experiment with six factors in only eight runs. According to the table of available designs, this is a Resolution III design, which is risky. Cal creates this design in Minitab, and here is the report in the Session window:

Fractional Factorial Design

```
Factors:    6   Base Design:        6, 8   Resolution:  III
Runs:      16   Replicates:            2   Fraction:    1/8
Blocks:     1   Center pts (total):    0

* NOTE * Some main effects are confounded with two-way interactions.

Design Generators: D = AB, E = AC, F = BC

Alias Structure

I + ABD + ACE + BCF + DEF + ABEF + ACDF + BCDE

A + BD + CE + BEF + CDF + ABCF + ADEF + ABCDE
B + AD + CF + AEF + CDE + ABCE + BDEF + ABCDF
C + AE + BF + ADF + BDE + ABCD + CDEF + ABCEF
D + AB + EF + ACF + BCE + ACDE + BCDF + ABDEF
E + AC + DF + ABF + BCD + ABDE + BCEF + ACDEF
F + BC + DE + ABE + ACD + ABDF + ACEF + BCDEF
AF + BE + CD + ABC + ADE + BDF + CEF + ABCDEF
```

In this eight-run design, each main effect is aliased with two-factor, three-factor, and higher-order interactions. If this design is run, any interaction between factors will be mixed together with main effects. This may be successful, if the main effects are much larger than interactions. But if strong interactions exist, the results could also be confusing and misleading.

However, the benefit of this design over the first option is the second replication, providing eight degrees of freedom of pure error. Using Stat > Power and Sample Size > 2-Level Factorial Design, Cal generates this report for this design:

Power and Sample Size

```
2-Level Factorial Design

Alpha = 0.05   Assumed standard deviation = 1

Factors:     6    Base Design: 6, 8
Blocks:   none

Center           Total
Points   Reps    Runs   Power    Effect
    0       2      16    0.9    1.85622
```

According to this report, the eight-run design with two replications will detect an effect of 1.86 standard deviations, with a power of 0.9. This is a slightly smaller effect than the previous design can detect. At the price of more aliasing, this replicated design offers greater power to detect smaller effects.

? Still Struggling

Aliasing is a confusing yet accurate way to describe statistical confusion. When signal A looks exactly the same as signal B, we have no way to know which signal is real and which is fake. It could be that both signals are active, but we can only see the combined effect of both signals. If signals A and B are aliased, they might add or subtract, perhaps even canceling each other out. When signals must be aliased, the usual remedy is to design the experiment so that one signal is more likely to occur than others. In all the examples used here, one main effect is aliased with interactions. This strategy assumes that interactions are less likely to occur than main effects, and if they occur, they are smaller than main effects. Maximizing the resolution of an experimental design minimizes the probability of being confused by aliased signals.

Option 3: 12-Run Plackett–Burman Design with 4 Center Points

The 12-run Plackett–Burman design is a popular choice for experiments with between five and eight factors. Instead of aliasing, this design has an unusual property called partial confounding. If an interaction exists, the effect of the interaction is partially confounded with all the main effects not involved in the interaction. For example, if A and B interact, the effect of the AB interaction will be split up between the main effects of C, D, E, and F. When interactions are few and small, the Plackett–Burman design may provide results that are less confusing than a fractional factorial design with aliasing.

Technically, all Plackett–Burman designs are Resolution III, but some experts feel that they are better than Resolution III fractional factorial designs.

To create a Plackett–Burman design for this problem, Cal selects Stat > DOE > Factorial > Create Factorial Design and chooses the Plackett–Burman designs option. He selects 6 in the Number of factors dropdown box, then clicks the Designs button and selects 12 in the Number of runs dropdown box.

Center points are slightly tricky for this problem. If all factors were continuous, the center point would be a run at the middle or center value for each factor. But here, one factor (F) is categorical. To maintain balance in the design, Minitab will add center points at each level of the categorical factor.

In the Create Factorial Design – Designs dialog, Cal enters 2 in the Number of center points per replicate box. This instructs Minitab to add two center points for each level of the categorical factor. Cal also enters 1 in the Number of replications box. After clicking OK, Cal sees the finished design in a new worksheet, with 12 runs for the Plackett–Burman design and four center point runs.

But how large an effect can this design detect with a power of 0.90? To find out, Cal selects Stat > Power and Sample Size > Plackett–Burman Design. He fills out the dialog for 6 factors, 12 corner points, 1 replicate, 0.9 power, 4 center points, and a standard deviation of 1. Here is the resulting report:

Power and Sample Size

```
Plackett-Burman Design

Alpha = 0.05   Assumed standard deviation = 1

Factors:            6    Design: 12
Center pts (total): 4

Including a term for center points in model.

Center          Total
Points   Reps   Runs   Power   Effect
    4      1      16    0.9   2.14338
```

This design has a power of 0.9 to detect an effect of 2.14 standard deviations. This effect is larger than either of the two earlier options, so this design is the least powerful option considered so far. However, the benefit to this design is that interactions, if they exist, will create fewer problems, because they are partially confounded with main effects, instead of fully aliased.

? Still Struggling

Confounding is yet another term for statistical confusion. A good way to think of confounding is a scale with two ends. At one end of the scale is aliasing, where signals are totally confounded and inseparable. At the other end of the scale are orthogonal experiments, where every effect can be estimated independently. Between aliasing and orthogonality exists a wide continuum of experiments with partial confounding, such as the Plackett–Burman design featured here. Many of these experiments are useful compromises, balancing the need to evaluate many factors in few runs with the risks of confounded effects. The next option in this example presents another way to design an experiment that can estimate specific effects and interactions, with the least possible confounding.

Option 4: 16-Run Optimal Design

Optimal designs provide a flexible and powerful alternative to the catalog of traditional experimental designs, especially when resources are limited. Statisticians disagree on how to measure the optimality of a design, and many metrics have been proposed. Minitab produces what are called D-optimal designs, the most commonly used family of optimal designs. A design is D-optimal if the maximum variance of all regression coefficients is the lowest among all other designs.

There are two steps in the process of creating an optimal design in Minitab:

- First, use Minitab to create a general full factorial design, response surface design, or mixture design containing all the runs to be considered as possible runs in the optimal design. This can be created from scratch using the Create function, or an existing design can be defined with the Define Custom function.

- Next, click the Select Optimal Design tool in the appropriate DOE menu, and enter the number of runs for the optimal design. Click the Terms button, and specify which terms must be estimated by the model.

After clicking OK, an optimal design will appear in a new worksheet, with a report about that design in the Session window. The Select Optimal Design functions also have the capability to augment an existing design to have more runs, or to evaluate the optimality of an existing design.

For Cal's example, he and his team decide in advance which effects must be estimable. They consider each pair of the six factors, and decide that two-factor interactions AB, AC, AE, BC, BE, and CE are most likely to be present. They feel that factors D and F are unlikely to interact with any other factors. The aliasing table for the standard 16-run fractional factorial design shows those six interactions aliased together in three of the estimable terms in the model. If all six interactions are significant, it will be impossible to know which is which if the standard design is run.

To create the base design with all possible runs to be considered, Cal creates a general full factorial design with six factors at two levels. This will have $2^6 = 64$ runs. This could be defined as a two-level factorial design, but the optimal design selector requires a general full factorial design.

Cal selects Stat > DOE > Factorial > Create Factorial Design or clicks the ◻ button in the Factorial Designs toolbar. He selects the General full factorial design option with 6 factors. Cal clicks the Designs button and selects 2 levels for each factor. Back in the main dialog, he clicks the Factors button and enters names and levels for the six factors. Naming factors and levels could be done later, using the Modify Design function.

After clicking OK Cal sees a new worksheet with the 64-run design, and this report in the Session window:

Multilevel Factorial Design

```
Factors:          6     Replicates:      1
Base runs:       64     Total runs:     64
Base blocks:      1     Total blocks:    1

Number of levels: 2, 2, 2, 2, 2, 2
```

Now that the list of candidate runs is available, Cal proceeds to select the optimal subset of those runs for this experiment. He selects Stat > DOE > Factorial > Select Optimal Design or clicks the ◻ button in the Factorial Designs toolbar. In the Select Optimal Design dialog, Cal enters 16 in the Number of points in optimal design field.

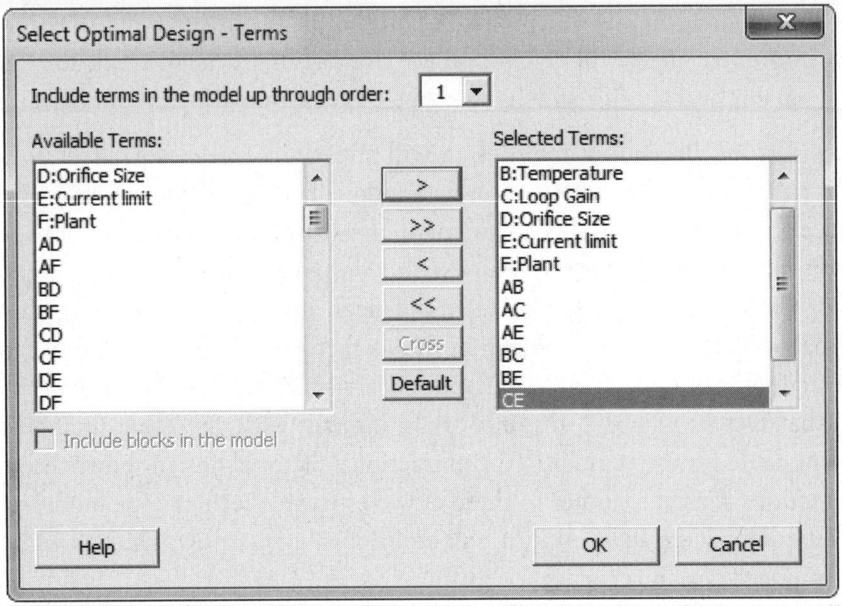

FIGURE 9-31 • Selecting estimable terms for the optimal design.

Next, Cal clicks the Terms button to select the terms which must be estimated by the optimal experiment. He removes all interactions by selecting 1 in the Include terms in the model up through order dropdown box. Then, he selects these interactions individually: AB, AC, AE, BC, BE, and CE. At this point, the Terms dialog looks like Fig. 9-31.

After Cal clicks OK, Minitab selects the best 16-run design that can estimate the required effects, and places this design in a new worksheet. The worksheet with the 64-run base design now has a new column OptPoint containing 1 for the runs selected for the optimal design and 0 for the other runs. Here is the report in the Session window:

Optimal Design: Fuel pressur, Temperature, Loop Gain, Orifice Size, Current lim

```
Factorial design selected according to D-optimality

Number of candidate design points: 64
Number of design points in optimal design: 16

Model terms: A, B, C, D, E, F, AB, AC, AE, BC, BE, CE

Initial design generated by Sequential method
Initial design improved by Exchange method
Number of design points exchanged is 1
```

```
Optimal Design

Row number of selected design points: 1, 8, 11, 14, 18, 32, 36, 58,
                                     19, 29, 47, 53, 33, 51, 46, 64

Condition number:                                   3.5
D-optimality (determinant of XTX):          2.46291E+15
A-optimality (trace of inv(XTX)):              0.898214
G-optimality (avg leverage/max leverage):      0.880077
V-optimality (average leverage):                 0.8125
Maximum leverage:                              0.923214
```

D-optimal designs are not unique, and there might be other subsets of 16 runs which are just as optimal for this situation.

How good is this design compared to the other options considered here? Minitab does not provide any tool to evaluate the power and sample size for optimal designs, but we can surely say that this design is less powerful than the three options considered above. Here are some reasons why:

- The 16-run optimal design has eight runs at the low level and eight runs at the high level of each factor. In this respect, it is quite similar to the 16-run fractional factorial design considered as Option 1. However, the optimal design may not be orthogonal. This tends to inflate the standard error of the regression coefficients, giving the design less power to detect an effect of the same size.

- For the fractional factorial design, Cal assumed that six model terms were not needed and could be used to estimate error. For the optimal design, Cal would have to assume that six main effects and six interactions would be included in the model. This leaves only three degrees of freedom for error, reducing the power of the experiment.

The advantage of the optimal design is that the six interactions predicted to exist by Cal's team can all be estimated by this design. This is a feature none of the other experiments considered here can provide.

By offering four similar options with no clearly superior choice, this example may be confusing, but it reflects the subtle real-life decisions facing experimenters. Each option considered here is a compromise between the ability to estimate effects and the ability to estimate residual variation, or error. With more degrees of freedom to estimate error, an experiment will have more power to detect smaller effects; on the other hand, if an experiment allows multiple active effects to alias each other, the results will be confusing or misleading.

The key is for the statistical experts and the subject matter experts to work together. Statistical experts can offer multiple options, explaining the tradeoffs. Subject matter experts can assess which design is most likely to be effective based on their prior knowledge of the system. As a team, they can choose the best possible experiment to meet their objectives, within the limitations of available resources.

9.6   Experimenting with Hard-to-Change Factors

Experiments measure not only the effects of having factors at certain levels, but also the process of setting factors. Setting a factor to a level creates variation, and this variation is reflected in the measured response values. One of the benefits of randomization is to induce variation from the process of setting factors to a random sequence of values.

Many experimenters make the mistake of running an incompletely randomized experiment and then analyzing it as if it is completely randomized. As a result of this mistake, the rate of type I errors, where a factor that has no effect is falsely called significant, is typically much higher than it should be.

In real experiments, some factors are hard to change for reasons of time or cost. In an experimental garden, it is not practical to irrigate each plant at a different level, but one row of plants could be irrigated at the same level. If the temperature of a furnace takes half a day to stabilize, no one will want to change the oven temperature for every run of a 32-run experiment.

A natural way to run an experiment with hard-to-change factors is to perform all the runs at one level at the same time, before changing to a new level. But this strategy goes too far. If each level is applied only once, there are no replications to measure the variation induced by setting that factor.

A good compromise is called the split-plot design. The split-plot design is planned and executed at two levels:

- The **whole plot** is a set of experimental units that will be run together with the same levels of hard-to-change factors. The effects of hard-to-change factors will be estimated from the mean responses from the whole plots.

- The **subplot** is one experimental unit run with other subplots within a whole plot.

In earlier versions of Minitab, split-plot designs were arduous to set up and to properly analyze. Now in Minitab 16, split-plot designs with up to seven factors may be quickly designed, appropriately randomized, and correctly analyzed with no more trouble than any other factorial design.

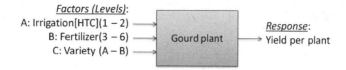

Factors (Levels):
A: Irrigation[HTC](1 – 2)
B: Fertilizer(3 – 6)
C: Variety (A – B)

Gourd plant

Response:
Yield per plant

FIGURE 9-32 • Gourd experiment.

For example, Geno grows award-winning *Cucurbita foetidissima*, or stinking gourd. Wanting to improve the yield from each plot, Geno decides to experiment with irrigation, fertilizer, and two varieties of seedlings. Figure 9-32 shows the factors for this experiment.

With an experimental garden large enough for 48 plants, Geno could run six full replications of the $2^3 = 8$ run full factorial experiment. But this experiment cannot be completely randomized. Irrigation is controlled by a drip system, and it is not practical to vary irrigation plant by plant. However, it is practical to vary irrigation by row of plants. With six rows of eight plants in each row, three rows could be at each irrigation level. This is a split-plot experiment where a whole plot is a row in Geno's garden, and a subplot is one plant.

To set up this experiment, Geno selects Stat > DOE > Factorial > Create Factorial Design or clicks the ⊡ button in the Factorial Designs toolbar. He selects the 2-level split-plot option with 3 factors.

To see the available split-plot designs supported by Minitab, click the Display Available Designs button with the split-plot option selected. A table appears as shown in Fig. 9-33. This table has three tabs for one, two, or three hard-to-change (HTC) factors.

For this example, Geno has one HTC factor, irrigation. Minitab offers designs with 2 , 4, 8, or 16 whole plots (WP). These are levels of the HTC factor, and do not consider replications. Geno has two levels of irrigation, so the correct choice is 2 WP. Geno also has two easy-to-change (ETC) factors. At the intersection of the 1 HTC, 2 WP column, and the 2 ETC row is this cell ▢. This cell indicates 4 subplots (SP), with full resolution. Any full factorial design or Resolution V or higher is shaded green.

To specify this design, Geno clicks the Designs button from the main dialog. Here, he selects 1 in the Number of hard-to-change factors dropdown box. Full factorial is the only option for this case. Geno selects 3 in the Number of whole plot replicates and 2 in the Number of subplot replicates. This will create a design with 3 replicates times 2 levels of the HTC factor, for 6 whole plots. Within each whole plot, the 4 combinations of the 2 ETC factors will be replicated 2 times, for 8 subplots. This is a total of $6 \times 8 = 48$ runs.

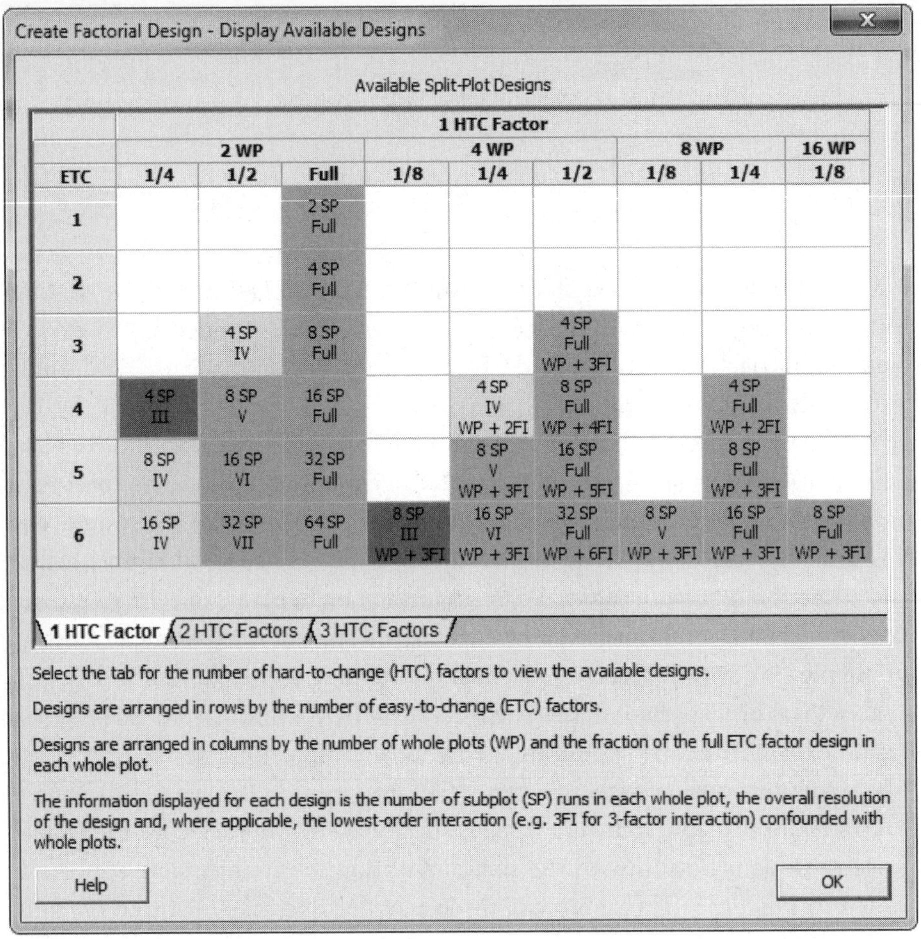

Create Factorial Design - Display Available Designs

Available Split-Plot Designs

	2 WP			4 WP			8 WP		16 WP
ETC	1/4	1/2	Full	1/8	1/4	1/2	1/8	1/4	1/8
1			2 SP Full						
2			4 SP Full						
3		4 SP IV	8 SP Full			4 SP Full WP + 3FI			
4	4 SP III	8 SP V	16 SP Full		4 SP IV WP + 2FI	8 SP Full WP + 4FI		4 SP Full WP + 2FI	
5	8 SP IV	16 SP VI	32 SP Full		8 SP V WP + 3FI	16 SP Full WP + 5FI		8 SP Full WP + 3FI	
6	16 SP IV	32 SP VII	64 SP Full	8 SP III WP + 3FI	16 SP VI WP + 3FI	32 SP Full WP + 6FI	8 SP V WP + 3FI	16 SP Full WP + 3FI	8 SP Full WP + 3FI

1 HTC Factor / 2 HTC Factors / 3 HTC Factors /

Select the tab for the number of hard-to-change (HTC) factors to view the available designs.

Designs are arranged in rows by the number of easy-to-change (ETC) factors.

Designs are arranged in columns by the number of whole plots (WP) and the fraction of the full ETC factor design in each whole plot.

The information displayed for each design is the number of subplot (SP) runs in each whole plot, the overall resolution of the design and, where applicable, the lowest-order interaction (e.g. 3FI for 3-factor interaction) confounded with whole plots.

| Help | | OK |

FIGURE 9-33 · Available split-plot designs.

Next, Geno clicks the Factors button from the main dialog to specify factor names and levels. After clicking OK, Geno sees a randomized 48-run split-plot design in a new worksheet, with this report in the Session window.

Full Factorial Split-Plot Design

```
Factors:            3    Whole plots:              6
Hard-to-change:     1    Runs per whole plot:      8
Runs:              48    Whole-plot replicates:    3
Blocks:             1    Subplot replicates:       2

Hard-to-change factors: A

Whole Plot Generators: A

All terms are free from aliasing.
```

In the worksheet, besides the usual four columns all experiments have, StdOrder, RunOrder, PtType, and Blocks, this split-plot design also has a WP column, containing the numbers 1, 2, 3, 4, 5, and 6 for the six whole plots. The HTC factor is named Irrigation[HTC], including [HTC] as a reminder that it is hard to change.

Minitab has randomized the experiment at two levels. In Geno's worksheet, the whole plots are randomized in order 3, 2, 5, 6, 4, 1. The first eight rows for WP 3 have two replications of the ETC factors, in random order. Each whole plot has a different random ordering of the same eight subplots.

Geno creates a map, shown in Fig. 9-34, showing how the plant varieties, fertilizer levels, and irrigation levels will be laid out in his garden, based on the randomized ordering calculated by Minitab.

After the growing season, when Geno analyzes the weight of gourds from his garden, Minitab will use the information about HTC and ETC factors to correctly analyze the experiment. Minitab will use the mean yield for each row, to analyze the HTC factor Irrigation. For Irrigation, this is a 6-run experiment with 3 replications at each level. Minitab analyzes all other main effects and interactions at the subplot level. In earlier versions of Minitab, this was a difficult, manual process, but Minitab 16 handles it behind the scenes without any extra effort by the experimenter.

Sadly, Geno's data was unavailable at publication time, since it requires a whole growing season to collect. To see an example of the analysis of a different split-plot experiment, load the Minitab sample data file Strength.MTW.

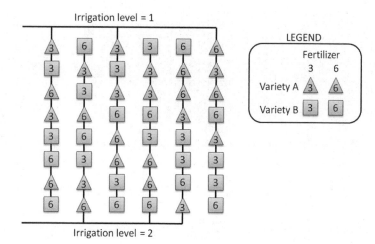

FIGURE 9-34 • Garden layout for gourd experiment.

This worksheet contains one HTC factor, Temp, and three ETC factors, Add, Rate, and Time. This experiment has four whole plots, representing two replications of the two-level HTC factor. Within each whole plot are eight subplots, comprising a full factorial combination of the three ETC factors. The total experiment has 32 runs.

To analyze this experiment, select Stat > DOE > Factorial > Analyze Factorial Design, or click the  toolbar button. Select Strength in the Responses field. Click Terms and select 2 in the Include terms in model up through order dropdown box. Click Graphs and choose a Pareto effects plot or one of the others.

Figure 9-35 is a Pareto chart of subplot effects for the Strength.MTW experiment. Several main effects and interactions are significant. Notice that the HTC factor A is not shown on this chart. Since the HTC factor is analyzed separately, it is not comparable to these subplot effects, and the significance of HTC factor A cannot be determined by the same red line as the other effects.

Referring to the Session window report, not shown here, the p-value for Temp[HTC] is 0.343, so there is no significant effect of temperature in this experiment.

To see why it is important to design and analyze split-plot experiments correctly, try analyzing the Strength.MTW experiment incorrectly. To do this, copy

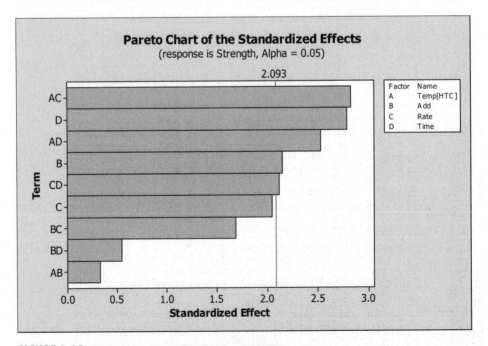

FIGURE 9-35 • Pareto chart from strength split-plot experiment.

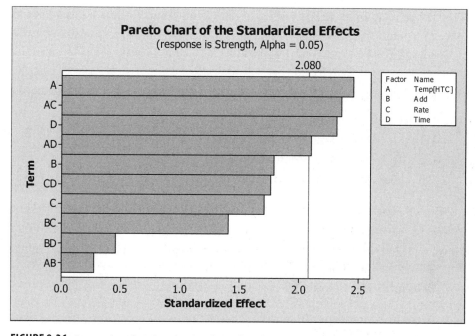

FIGURE 9-36 · Pareto chart from incorrect analysis of a split-plot experiment as completely randomized.

all columns into a new worksheet. Then use the Define Custom Factorial Design function to define a regular factorial experiment without any HTC factors.

The incorrect analysis of this data produces a Pareto chart as shown in Fig. 9-36. Comparing this to the correct Pareto chart in Fig. 9-35, notice that the HTC factor shows up as significant, when it is not significant in the correct analysis. Also, some of the lesser effects are not significant in the incorrect analysis, when they are significant, if analyzed as a split-plot experiment.

In the author's experience, the incorrect analysis of split-plot experiments as if they were completely randomized is one of the most common mistakes made by industrial experimenters. The new split-plot design features of Minitab 16 represent a huge advance in convenience and should become very popular.

9.7 Designing and Analyzing Response Surface Designs

Response surface designs are a family of experiments used to model and optimize systems of all kinds. Factors in a response surface design are assumed to be numeric variables, where it is possible to set each factor to any value between the high and low levels. There are several situations which call for response surface designs, including these:

- When a factorial design with a center point shows evidence of curvature, a response surface design can identify which factors are responsible for the curvature.

- When it is important to maximize a variable, a response surface model can be used to find a maximum or to point the direction toward a maximum, along a path of steepest ascent.

- When it is important to reduce variation, a response surface model can identify a flatter area of less slope, at which point variation in the factors will cause less variation in the responses.

Minitab separates Response Surface designs from Factorial designs in different menus, because both the design and analysis tools are different. In the design phase, Minitab offers two families of response surface designs, central composite and Box–Behnken designs. Figure 9-37 illustrates two types of central composite designs and a Box–Behnken design with three factors.

- A **central composite design** (CCD) combines corner points, from a two-level factorial or fractional factorial design, with a center point and axial points in which one factor is set at an extreme value while all other factors are held at their center values. Often, the axial points are outside the cube defined by the corner points. If the corner points have coded values of -1 and $+1$, the axial values are set at coded values of $-\alpha$ and $+\alpha$, where $\alpha \geq 1$. In Minitab, the Default alpha option results in a design with the desired property of rotatability, where the prediction variance is the same in all directions from the center. When extreme values outside the cube defined by the corner points are impractical, the face-centered option sets $\alpha = 1$, so all axial points are on the faces of the cube.

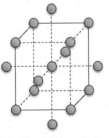
Central composite design
(default alpha)

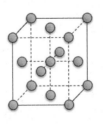
Central composite design
(face centered)

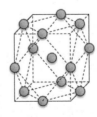
Box–Behnken design

FIGURE 9-37 · Response surface designs for three factors.

- A **Box–Behnken design** (BBD) sets two variables at a time to their extreme values, while holding other variables at their center values. These runs are combined with a center point run to complete the design. For many systems, the experimenter may have concerns about the feasibility of taking all factors to their extreme values in the same run. Box–Behnken designs avoid this problem by only taking some factors to their extreme values, avoiding the corners of the experimental space.

Both CCD and BBD typically have many more replications of center point runs than any other runs in the design. This is important for two reasons. First, many response surface experiments are not replicated because of limited resources. In these cases, replications of the center point may provide the only measurement of residual variation, also known as error. Second, most CCD and BBD designs are not orthogonal, which means that some of the regression coefficients are correlated. This results in inflated variation for the coefficients and also may cause confusing results. Including more center points reduces these problems by bringing the CCD and BBD closer to orthogonality.

Figure 9-38 shows a table of available CCD and BBD options in Minitab, for between two and ten factors. The numbers in the table represent the number of runs in the experiment, including a suggested number of replicated center point runs. When an experiment is defined, the actual number of center point

Create Response Surface Design - Display Available Designs

Available Response Surface Designs (with Number of Runs)

Design		Factors								
		2	3	4	5	6	7	8	9	10
Central Composite full	unblocked	13	20	31	52	90	152			
	blocked	14	20	30	54	90	160			
Central Composite half	unblocked				32	53	88	154		
	blocked				33	54	90	160		
Central composite quarter	unblocked							90	156	
	blocked							90	160	
Central Composite eighth	unblocked									158
	blocked									160
Box-Behnken	unblocked		15	27	46	54	62		130	170
	blocked			27	46	54	62		130	170

Help   OK

FIGURE 9-38 • Response surface designs available in Minitab.

runs can be changed. To see this table, select Stat > DOE > Response Surface > Create Response Surface Design and click the Display Available Designs button.

In addition to these built-in designs, any design may be analyzed as a response surface design by first using the Define Custom Response Surface Design function.

In the analysis of a response surface design, Minitab fits a typical model with main effects, two-factor interactions, and quadratic effects. The model looks like this for an experiment with two factors:

$$Y = b_0 + b_1X_1 + b_2X_2 + b_{12}X_1X_2 + b_{11}X_1^2 + b_{22}X_2^2$$

If any of the higher-order terms are not significant in the first analysis, they can be removed from the model until all remaining terms are significant or are required to maintain hierarchy. Then, using the Minitab Response Optimizer, factor settings to maximize, minimize, or hit a target value are easy to identify.

Minitab offers a Response Surface toolbar, providing one-click access to all the functions in the Stat > DOE > Response Surface menu. To enable this toolbar, right-click in the toolbar area and select the Response Surface option. The Response Surface toolbar looks like this:

Ben grows butterbeans. Wanting to improve the yield of his butterbean crop, Ben decides to experiment with fertilizer components. Ben mixes his own fertilizer, and he can precisely control the nitrogen, phosphorous acid, and potash that he delivers to each plant. He decides to experiment with these three fertilizer components, using the levels shown in Fig. 9-39.

To set up this experiment, Ben clicks the ▦ button to create a new response surface design. Despite the alliterative potential of a Box–Behnken design, Ben selects the Central Composite with 3 factors. He clicks the Designs button and selects a full factorial, 20-run design with the default Number of center points and the default Value of alpha.

Back in the main dialog, Ben clicks the Factors button and enters factor names and levels as shown in Fig. 9-40. Note that this dialog offers two options for the CCD. With the Cube points option selected, the levels will be used for the corner points, but the axial points will have values outside this range. The experimenter should evaluate these axial points to see if they are practical.

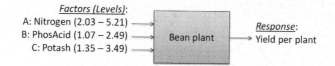

Factors (Levels):
A: Nitrogen (2.03 – 5.21)
B: PhosAcid (1.07 – 2.49)
C: Potash (1.35 – 3.49)
Bean plant
Response:
Yield per plant

FIGURE 9-39 • Bean yield experiment.

Create Response Surface Design - Factors
Levels Define
Cube points
Axial points
Factor
Name
Low
High
A
Nitrogen
2.03
5.21
B
PhosAcid
1.07
2.49
C
Potash
1.35
3.49
Help
OK
Cancel

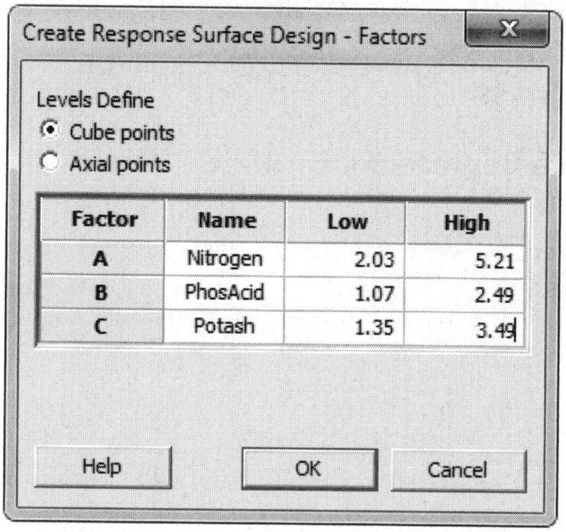

FIGURE 9-40 • Response surface design factors dialog.

Another option is to select Axial points in this dialog and then enter axial point values. With this option, the cube points will have values inside the range specified.

After clicking OK in all dialogs, Ben sees a randomized 20-run central composite design in a new worksheet, with this report in the Session window:

Central Composite Design

```
Factors:         3    Replicates:      1
Base runs:      20    Total runs:     20
Base blocks:     1    Total blocks:    1

Two-level factorial: Full factorial

Cube points:               8
Center points in cube:     6
Axial points:              6
Center points in axial:    0

Alpha: 1.68179
```

To see Ben's butterbean dataset, open the Minitab sample data file Ccd_ex1.MTW. To analyze the dataset, click the ▦ button or select Stat > DOE > Response Surface > Analyze Response Surface Design. Select BeanYield in the Responses field. In the Terms dialog, verify that the Full quadratic model is selected with all available terms. In the Graphs dialog, Minitab does not offer effects plots for response surface designs, but a Four in one residual plot is always a good idea.

After clicking OK, the analysis of Ben's data appears in the Session window. Here is part of the report:

Response Surface Regression: BeanYield versus Nitrogen, PhosAcid, Potash

```
The analysis was done using coded units.

Estimated Regression Coefficients for BeanYield

Term                    Coef   SE Coef        T       P
Constant             10.4623    0.4062   25.756   0.000
Nitrogen             -0.5738    0.2695   -2.129   0.059
PhosAcid              0.1834    0.2695    0.680   0.512
Potash                0.4555    0.2695    1.690   0.122
Nitrogen*Nitrogen    -0.6764    0.2624   -2.578   0.027
PhosAcid*PhosAcid     0.5628    0.2624    2.145   0.058
Potash*Potash        -0.2734    0.2624   -1.042   0.322
Nitrogen*PhosAcid    -0.6775    0.3521   -1.924   0.083
Nitrogen*Potash       1.1825    0.3521    3.358   0.007
PhosAcid*Potash       0.2325    0.3521    0.660   0.524


S = 0.995984    PRESS = 59.6070
R-Sq = 78.61%   R-Sq(pred) = 0.00%   R-Sq(adj) = 59.37%
```

Most effects in this model are statistically significant, but some are not. The model can be simplified, in steps. For a second model, remove the BC or PhosAcid*Potash interaction from the model, since this effect has the largest p-value. Here is part of the regression report from this second model:

```
S = 0.970112    PRESS = 48.5596
R-Sq = 77.68%   R-Sq(pred) = 0.00%   R-Sq(adj) = 61.45%
```

This change increased R-Sq(adj) and reduced S, so it is a good change to make.

The next highest p-value is the main effect of PhosAcid, but the rule of hierarchy says that this main effect cannot be removed from the model while it is still involved in interactions or quadratic effects.

The next highest *p*-value is the quadratic effect `Potash*Potash` or `CC`. This quadratic effect can be removed without violating hierarchy. After removing this effect, here is part of the report for this third model:

```
S = 0.975938    PRESS = 40.6394
R-Sq = 75.36%  R-Sq(pred) = 12.39%  R-Sq(adj) = 60.99%
```

Even though `Potash*Potash` had a high *p*-value, removing it from the model took `R-Sq(adj)` and `S` in the wrong direction. Opinions will vary about what to do at this point. For the purpose of this example, Ben puts the `Potash*Potash` effect back into the model and decides to use the second model for optimization.

To discover how to maximize bean yield, select Stat > DOE > Response Surface > Response Optimizer or click the 🔲 toolbar button. Select BeanYield as the response to optimize. In the Setup dialog, set a goal to Maximize the response, with a Goal of 15 and a Lower limit of 5.

Figure 9-41 shows the results of these settings, predicting maximum yield at low nitrogen, high phosphorous acid, and low potash. But Ben should be cautious about this recommendation, since the limits of the three factors use

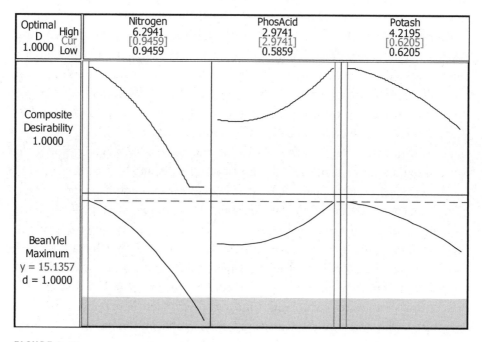

FIGURE 9-41 • Response surface optimization plot.

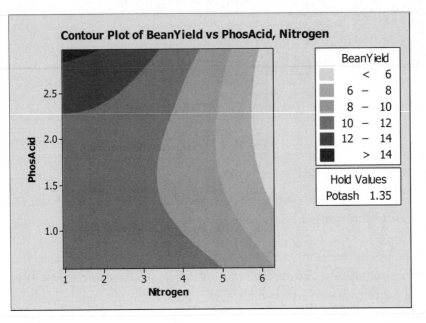

FIGURE 9-42 • Contour plot of yield with potash = 1.35.

the axial values, not the cube values. As a result, the recommended settings represent an extrapolation outside the range of the experiment.

Another way to visualize these results is with a contour plot, prepared by clicking the ⬚ button or selecting Stat > DOE > Response Surface > Contour / Surface Plots. This function can prepare either contour or surface plots based on the most recently fitted response surface model. Figure 9-42 is a contour plot of yield as a function of nitrogen and phosphorous acid, with potash held at 1.35, at the lower level of the cube corner points.

To conclude this example, Ben decides to run more trials to verify that yield is maximized at low nitrogen, high phosphorous acid, and low potash.

Sequential experimentation, where a simpler experiment leads into a more complex experiment only if needed, has become a popular strategy for systems with all continuous factors. Figure 9-43 is a flow chart illustrating this process. Sequential experimentation starts with a two-level design, which could be factorial, fractional factorial, or Plackett–Burman, depending on the number of factors. It is important to include some center point runs in the first experiment. Minitab uses the center point runs to test whether there is any significant curvature in the system. If the curvature is not significant, the linear model with

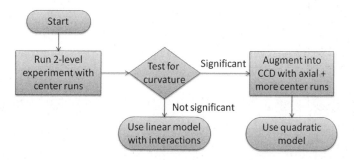

FIGURE 9-43 · Flow chart for sequential experimentation.

interactions fit from the two-level design is sufficient, and no quadratic terms are required.

If the center points indicate significant curvature, the factorial design can be augmented into a CCD by adding axial runs and a few more center points in a second block. Without redoing the whole experiment, the combination of the two-level corner points from the first block, the axial points from the second block, and the center points from both blocks can generate an effective quadratic response surface model. Having center points in both blocks allows Minitab to test whether the system changed between the first block and the second block.

For an example of sequential experimentation, consider a simple example from Andy's kitchen. Andy loves oatmeal raisin cookies, but whenever he bakes them he has trouble gauging the right time and temperature for baking. Andy decides to experiment with this, providing an excuse to bake a lot more cookies, all in the name of science.

Figure 9-44 is a diagram of Andy's cookie experiment with only two factors. To control variation in the batter, Andy uses a frozen batter from a commercial source. To measure a response value, Andy defines a quality

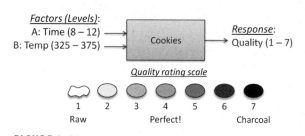

FIGURE 9-44 · Cookie experiment.

Cookies1.MTW ***

↓	C1	C2	C3	C4	C5	C6	C7	C8
	StdOrder	RunOrder	CenterPt	Blocks	Time	Temp	Quality	
1	1	8	1	1	8	325	2.5	
2	2	7	1	1	12	325	4.5	
3	3	2	1	1	8	375	2.5	
4	4	6	1	1	12	375	6.5	
5	5	5	1	1	8	325	2.0	
6	6	4	1	1	12	325	4.5	
7	7	1	1	1	8	375	3.0	
8	8	9	1	1	12	375	7.0	
9	9	3	0	1	10	350	3.5	
10	10	10	0	1	10	350	3.0	
11								

FIGURE 9-45 · First cookie experiment in standard order.

scale where 1 is raw, 4 is perfect, and 7 is a charcoal briquette. The scores will be assigned by a panel of expert tasters randomly selected from Andy's household.

For his first experiment, Andy chooses a 2^2 factorial experiment with two replications of the corner points, plus two center point runs for a total of 10 runs. This dataset is not available in the Minitab sample data files, but Fig. 9-45 shows the data window for the worksheet, sorted by the StdOrder column. Analyzing this data produces the following report:

Factorial Fit: Quality versus Time, Temp

Estimated Effects and Coefficients for Quality (coded units)

```
Term        Effect    Coef  SE Coef      T      P
Constant            4.0625   0.1118  36.34  0.000
Time        3.1250  1.5625   0.1118  13.98  0.000
Temp        1.3750  0.6875   0.1118   6.15  0.002
Time*Temp   0.8750  0.4375   0.1118   3.91  0.011
Ct Pt              -0.8125   0.2500  -3.25  0.023


S = 0.316228    PRESS = 3.38776
R-Sq = 98.11%   R-Sq(pred) = 87.17%   R-Sq(adj) = 96.59%
```

All terms are significant in this model, with low *p*-values. But the center point test, labeled `Ct Pt` in this table, also has a very low *p*-value of 0.023. This indicates strong evidence of curvature. Notice that this analysis cannot say which factor is causing the curvature. It could be `Time`, `Temp`, or some combination of both of them.

To stop the experiment now and use the linear model would be inaccurate because of the curvature. Therefore, Andy decides to augment this experiment into a CCD by adding axial points and more center points.

In Minitab, this is easy to do by selecting Stat > DOE > Modify Design or by clicking the 🔲 toolbar button. Depending on the type of design in the current worksheet, this tool offers different options. For factorial designs, these options are available:

- **Modify factors** allows the user to change the names or levels of any factor. Click the Specify button to specify the changes.

- **Replicate design** will add more runs to the design to replicate it. Click Specify.

- **Randomize design** generates a new random run order. Click Specify for options, including whether to display the randomized design in run order or standard order.

- **Renumber design** simply assigns sequential run orders to the runs in the worksheet.

- **Fold design** is used to augment a fractional factorial design into a larger design to remove aliasing. Click Specify.

- **Add axial points** is used to augment a two-level design into a CCD by adding axial points and optionally more center points in an additional block. Click Specify for options.

Andy chooses the Add axial points option. In the Specify dialog, he selects the default alpha and 2 center points in the axial point block. After completing this operation, Minitab changes the augmented design from factorial to a response surface design.

The experiment now has six more runs, four axial and two center points. Andy completes baking and testing on these six batches of cookies, and Fig. 9-46 shows the data from these additional runs. Analyzing the combined 16-run experiment with the Analyze Response Surface Design function yields this report:

Cookies2.MTW ***								
↓	C1	C2	C3	C4	C5	C6	C7	C8
	StdOrder	RunOrder	CenterPt	Blocks	Time	Temp	Quality	
11	11	11	-1	2	6.6364	350.000	2.5	
12	12	12	-1	2	13.3636	350.000	7.0	
13	13	13	-1	2	10.0000	307.955	2.5	
14	14	14	-1	2	10.0000	392.045	5.5	
15	15	15	0	2	10.0000	350.000	3.5	
16	16	16	0	2	10.0000	350.000	3.5	
17								

FIGURE 9-46 • Augmented runs in cookie experiment.

Response Surface Regression: Quality versus Block, Time, Temp

The analysis was done using coded units.

Estimated Regression Coefficients for Quality

```
Term            Coef  SE Coef        T      P
Constant     3.38919  0.15140   22.386  0.000
Block       -0.04230  0.07974   -0.530  0.609
Time         1.46945  0.08283   17.741  0.000
Temp         0.77217  0.08283    9.323  0.000
Time*Time    0.47828  0.09175    5.213  0.001
Temp*Temp    0.21311  0.09175    2.323  0.045
Time*Temp    0.43750  0.10822    4.043  0.003


S = 0.306091    PRESS = 3.34916
R-Sq = 98.03%   R-Sq(pred) = 92.16%  R-Sq(adj) = 96.71%
```

All terms in this model are statistically significant, except for blocks. If blocks are significant, this would indicate a shift between the initial factorial design and the augmented runs. Such a shift would cast doubt on the entire experiment. It is a good thing here that blocks are not significant. Therefore, Andy accepts this model and decides to use it to find the best time and temperature to bake perfect cookies.

The contour plot in Fig. 9-47 is a good way to visualize this model. To make this contour plot, Andy clicked the Contours button and entered contour levels 1 2 3 4 5 6 7, and he also selected the Contour lines and Symbols at design points options to make the plot more informative.

The contour line representing perfect cookies with a quality level of 4, runs from Time = 11.6 and Temp = 325 up to Time = 9.5 and Temp = 375.

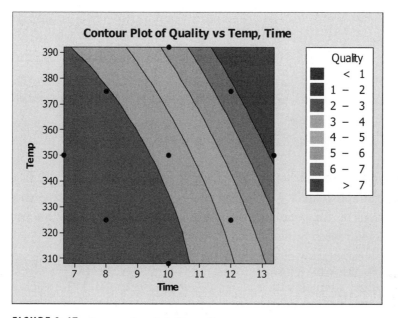

FIGURE 9-47 · Contour plot of cookie quality.

According to the model, any settings along this line will produce perfect cookies. As always, it is good practice to validate these conclusions and make many more cookies.

9.8   Designing and Analyzing Experiments with Mixtures

All the experiments illustrated so far in this chapter have factors that may be varied independently. By contrast, the proportions of various components in a mixture are linked together by the requirement that they sum to one. Whenever a response variable depends on the relative proportion of components in a blend, rather than on the total amount of the components, a mixture experiment is the appropriate choice.

Minitab offers many choices both for mixture designs and mixture models. Additional non-mixture process variables may be combined with a mixture design, in a full or fractional factorial arrangement. Any combination of mixture components and process variables must be defined as a mixture design in Minitab.

In a mixture, the proportions of all components must sum to one. For q components, the component values are constrained to a q-simplex. Figure 9-48 shows that a 2-simplex is a line segment, a 3-simplex is a triangle, and a

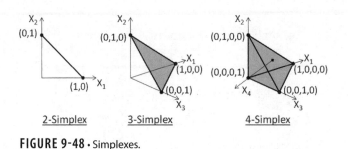

FIGURE 9-48 · Simplexes.

4-simplex is a tetrahedron. In general, a q-simplex is a polytope with facets that are $(q\text{-}1)$-simplexes. For convenient viewing by us three-dimensional people, the locations of design points in a mixture are typically plotted in a triangular simplex plot, representing mixtures with three components.

Minitab can quickly design three families of mixture designs:

- A **{q, m} simplex lattice** design divides the range $(0, 1)$ for each component into $m + 1$ equally spaced levels:

$$x_i = \left\{0, \frac{1}{m}, \frac{2}{m}, \ldots, 1\right\}, \qquad \text{for } i = 0, 1, \ldots, m+1$$

The simplex lattice design contains all possible combinations of levels for all components. The number of design points in a {q, m} simplex lattice design is $\dfrac{(q+m-1)!}{m!(q-1)!}$. Figure 9-49 shows simplex design plots for {3, 3} and {3, 4} simplex lattice designs, with 10 and 15 design points, respectively.

- A **simplex centroid** design with q components combines all q single-component blends $(1,0,\ldots,0)$ ... $(0,0,\ldots,1)$; all $\dbinom{q}{2}$ two-component blends $(\frac{1}{2},\frac{1}{2},\ldots,0)$, $(\frac{1}{2},0, \frac{1}{2},\ldots,0)$, ... $(0,0,\ldots, \frac{1}{2},\frac{1}{2})$; all $\dbinom{q}{3}$ three-component blends $(1/3,1/3,1/3,\ldots,0)$ ... $(0,\ldots, 1/3,1/3,1/3)$; and so on, through the q-component blend $(1/q, 1/q,\ldots, 1/q)$ at the centroid of the simplex. Here, $\dbinom{q}{k} = \dfrac{q!}{(q-k)!k!}$, the number of combinations of k items chosen from a set of q items. The simplex centroid design contains a total of $2^q - 1$ design points. All the design points are on the boundaries of the simplex except for the one centroid. To learn more about the interior, it is common to add axial points halfway between the single-component blend points and the centroid. Figure 9-49 shows a three-component simplex centroid design with and without axial points.

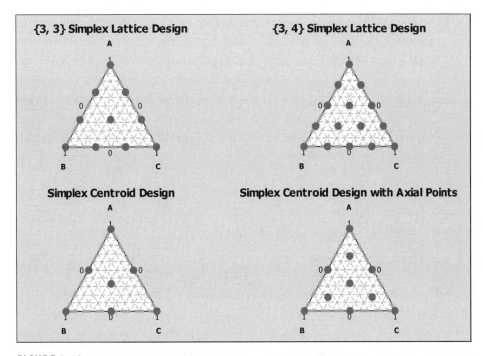

FIGURE 9-49 · Simplex lattice and centroid designs with three components.

- **Constrained mixture designs** have a minimum proportion $L_i \geq 0$ for each component. Almost every real mixture design has constraints, since single-component blends may not be practical. When components have a lower limit, the resulting design space is still a simplex. In Minitab, either a simplex lattice or a simplex centroid design can be specified with constraints. To reduce numerical problems in the analysis, each component x_i is rescaled into a pseudocomponent x_i^*, which varies from 0 to 1, as follows:

$$x_i^* = \frac{x_i - L_i}{1 - \sum_{j=1}^{q} L_j}$$

- **Extreme vertices mixture designs** are used when there are additional constraints on components or linear combinations of components. Constraints may cause the design space to become irregular in shape. Minitab will set design points at the extreme vertices of the design space. If degree 2 or 3 is selected, design points will include extreme values of 2-component or 3-component blends. Optionally, the centroid or axial points may be added to the design.

- **D-optimal mixture designs** use a subset of design points, selected to minimize the maximum variance of any of the regression coefficients. With many components, this is a good strategy to minimize the cost of an experiment to fit a specified model. To generate a D-optimal mixture design in Minitab, first use one of the other options to define a complete set of candidate design points. Then use the Select Optimal Design function to identify the optimal subset of those design points.

For one-click access to mixture design functions, Minitab provides a Mixture Designs toolbar. To show this toolbar, right-click in the toolbar area and select Mixture Designs. The toolbar looks like this:

To create a new mixture design, click the ▲ button, or to set up a custom mixture design from an existing design table, click the ▲ button. To create a simplex design plot, of the type seen in Fig. 9-49, click the ▲ button. To analyze a mixture design, click the ▲ button. The remaining functions are all similar to those seen earlier in this chapter for other families of designs. All of these functions can be accessed through the Stat > DOE > Mixture menu. Since these functions are very similar to corresponding functions in the Factorial and Response Surface menus, they will not be described in detail here.

For an example, consider the blending of two sweeteners, glucose and fructose, in iced tea. If the total amount of sweetener per volume of tea is held constant, what blend of glucose and fructose tastes sweetest?

Figure 9-50 shows a worksheet with a two-component mixture design to answer this question. This is a {2, 4} simplex lattice design, with five design points. The options to add centroid and axial points were turned off. There are two replications, for ten total runs. For each of ten batches of sweetened tea, the tea was tasted by five tasters, who rated sweetness on a scale of 0–10. The worksheet lists the average score from five tasters. The worksheet for this design is not available in the Minitab example files, but it is easy to create from scratch.

Analyze this design by selecting a quadratic model including A, B, and AB terms. Here is the analysis report:

↓	C1	C2	C3	C4	C5	C6	C7
	StdOrder	RunOrder	PtType	Blocks	Glucose	Fructose	Sweetness
1	1	5	1	1	1.00	0.00	3.6
2	2	4	2	1	0.75	0.25	4.8
3	3	9	0	1	0.50	0.50	6.4
4	4	3	2	1	0.25	0.75	6.0
5	5	10	1	1	0.00	1.00	4.8
6	6	7	1	1	1.00	0.00	4.0
7	7	1	2	1	0.75	0.25	4.6
8	8	6	0	1	0.50	0.50	6.0
9	9	8	2	1	0.25	0.75	6.2
10	10	2	1	1	0.00	1.00	5.2
11							

sweetener.MTW ***

FIGURE 9-50 • Sweetener experiment.

Regression for Mixtures: Sweetness versus Glucose, Fructose

Estimated Regression Coefficients for Sweetness (component proportions)

```
Term               Coef    SE Coef      T       P     VIF
Glucose            3.600   0.2535       *       *   1.661
Fructose           5.120   0.2535       *       *   1.661
Glucose*Fructose   6.400   1.1520    5.56   0.001   2.429

S = 0.380976     PRESS = 2.03896
R-Sq = 87.88%    R-Sq(pred) = 75.68%   R-Sq(adj) = 84.42%
```

Analysis of Variance for Sweetness (component proportions)

```
Source             DF   Seq SS   Adj SS   Adj MS      F       P
Regression          2   7.3680   7.3680  3.68400  25.38   0.001
   Linear           1   2.8880   2.8880  2.88800  19.90   0.003
   Quadratic        1   4.4800   4.4800  4.48000  30.87   0.001
      Glucose*Fructose  1  4.4800  4.4800  4.48000  30.87   0.001
Residual Error      7   1.0160   1.0160  0.14514
   Lack-of-Fit      2   0.7360   0.7360  0.36800   6.57   0.040
   Pure Error       5   0.2800   0.2800  0.05600
Total               9   8.3840
```

In the Regression Coefficients table, this analysis lists the variance inflation factor (VIF) for each coefficient. Mixture designs are not orthogonal, and there is some intentional correlation between regression coefficients. VIF provides a measure of the degree of correlation. If VIF exceeds 5 or 10, depending on the expert, this would raise concerns about the validity or usefulness of the model. VIF is discussed in more detail in Chapter 8.

In this analysis, the nonlinear blending term `Glucose*Fructose` is significant with a p-value of 0.001. By hierarchy, none of the three terms may be removed from the model. In a factorial design, this would be called an interaction, but in a mixture design, this effect is more properly called nonlinear blending.

Figure 9-51 shows two ways to visualize this dataset. At the top is a scatterplot of sweetness versus fructose. A the bottom is a response trace plot, made by clicking the button or selecting Response Trace Plot from the Mixture menu. The response trace plot shows how the fitted model predicts the response variable for each of the mixture components. Starting from a reference point, typically at the centroid, this plot traces the response versus each component.

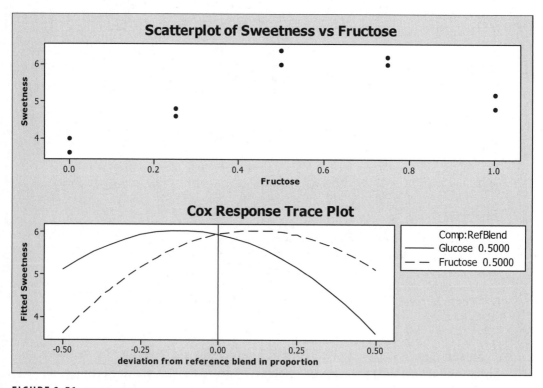

FIGURE 9-51 · Scatterplot and response trace plot.

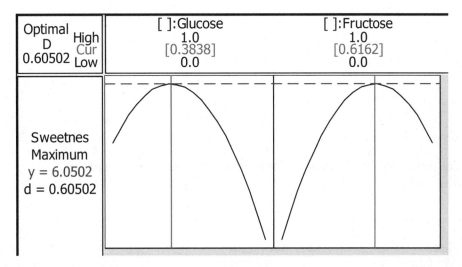

Optimal High D Cur 0.60502 Low	[ ]:Glucose 1.0 [0.3838] 0.0	[ ]:Fructose 1.0 [0.6162] 0.0

Sweetnes
Maximum
y = 6.0502
d = 0.60502

FIGURE 9-52 · Optimized sweetness.

Based on this model, the Minitab response optimizer predicts maximum sweetness at a blend of 38.38% fructose and 61.62% glucose. Figure 9-52 shows the optimization plot.

There is concern that this model may not be adequate. In the regression table above, Minitab reports that Lack-of-Fit has a *p*-value of 0.040. Since this is a small *p*-value, adding another term or two to the model might result in a better fit.

Regression models for mixture designs are typically different from those used for factorial or response surface designs. One key difference is that the constant term is not included in the model. Because proportions of all components sum to one, this constraint can be used to remove the constant term from the model. The following types of models are available for mixture designs of three or more components. In this list, A, B, and C represent components as they appear in the Analyze Mixture Design – Terms dialog:

- Linear: A B C
- Quadratic: Linear plus AB AC BC
- Special cubic: Quadratic plus ABC
- Full cubic: Special cubic plus AB(A-B) AC(A-C) BC(B-C)
- Special quartic: Quadratic plus AABC ABBC ABCC
- Full quartic: Special quartic plus AB(A-B) AC(A-C) BC(B-C) AB(A-B)^2 AC(A-C)^2 BC(B-C)^2
- Inverse: 1/A 1/B 1/C (terms available with lower bounds > 0)

For a mixture design with three components, open the Minitab sample data file Deodoriz.MTW. This worksheet contains the results of an acceptance test on a fragrance blended from three components: rose, neroli, and tangerine. This is a simplex centroid design with axial points, as shown in the lower right portion of Fig. 9-49.

For a first model, analyze this dataset using a quadratic model. Here is the report:

Regression for Mixtures: Acceptance versus Neroli, Rose, Tangerine

Estimated Regression Coefficients for Acceptance (component proportions)

Term	Coef	SE Coef	T	P	VIF
Neroli	5.856	0.4728	*	*	1.964
Rose	7.141	0.4728	*	*	1.964
Tangerine	7.448	0.4728	*	*	1.964
Neroli*Rose	1.795	2.1791	0.82	0.456	1.982
Neroli*Tangerine	5.090	2.1791	2.34	0.080	1.982
Rose*Tangerine	-1.941	2.1791	-0.89	0.423	1.982

S = 0.490234   PRESS = 11.4399
R-Sq = 73.84%   R-Sq(pred) = 0.00%   R-Sq(adj) = 41.14%

Analysis of Variance for Acceptance (component proportions)

Source	DF	Seq SS	Adj SS	Adj MS	F	P
Regression	5	2.71329	2.71329	0.54266	2.26	0.225
Linear	2	1.04563	1.56873	0.78437	3.26	0.144
Quadratic	3	1.66766	1.66766	0.55589	2.31	0.218
Neroli*Rose	1	0.15963	0.16309	0.16309	0.68	0.456
Neroli*Tangerin	1	1.31728	1.31109	1.31109	5.46	0.080
Rose*Tangerin	1	0.19075	0.19075	0.19075	0.79	0.423
Residual Error	4	0.96132	0.96132	0.24033		
Total	9	3.67461				

In this model, some of the nonlinear blending terms appear not to be significant, because they have high p-values. After removing the Neroli*Rose and Rose*Tangerine terms, one at a time, the remaining nonlinear term is significant. The three linear blending terms cannot be independently tested, so the best choice is to leave them all in.

After reducing the model, Fig. 9-53 is a response trace plot and Fig. 9-54 is a contour plot, both good ways to visualize how acceptance varies as a function of the three components. Contour and surface plots are easy to make from the most recent mixture model by clicking the 🔲 button.

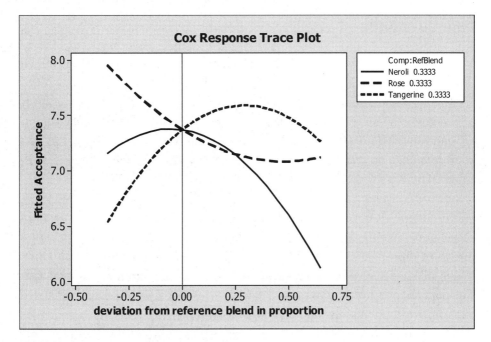

FIGURE 9-53 · Response trace plot for Deodriz.MTW dataset.

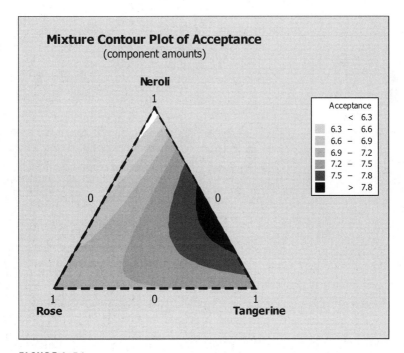

FIGURE 9-54 · Contour plot for reduced model.

9.9   Find Out More

Many excellent and very practical books have been written on experimental design, in particular, Montomery (2008) and Box, Hunter, and Hunter (2005) are standard references for students and professionals alike. The Montgomery book, now in its seventh edition, has a Minitab companion book by Montgomery and Kowalski (2010). Myers, Montgomery, and Anderson-Cook (2008) is a good reference on response surface methodology, and Cornell (2002) is dedicated to mixture designs.

With modern DOE tools, applied statistics has helped to advance all areas of science, engineering, and business. The Minitab tools introduced in this chapter provide a thorough and accessible interface for DOE applications of all kinds. While all experiments rely on measurements, not all measurements are reliable. The next chapter introduces measurement systems analysis, a set of specialized experiments used to assess and diagnose measurement systems. It is a good idea for all experimenters to understand measurement systems analysis, and to apply those tools before relying on measurement systems for critical experiments.

QUIZ

1. To experiment with five factors at two levels each, in 16 runs, which of the following experimental designs is most appropriate?
   A. Full factorial design
   B. Fractional factorial design
   C. Plackett–Burman design
   D. Central composite design

2. A central composite design can be best described how?
   A. Vary two factors at a time while holding all other factors at their center values, and combine these design points with a center point.
   B. Combine a two-level factorial design with a center point.
   C. A good tool for screening a few important factors from many factors.
   D. Combine a two-level factorial design with a center point and axial points, where one factor is varied to extreme values while holding other variables at their center values.

3. Suppose you have planned a completely randomized experiment with 20 runs, but the team objects to the randomization, because one of the factors requires many hours to change levels and stabilize at the new level before any runs can be performed. What is the best course of action?
   A. Insist that the team run the experiment according to the randomized plan.
   B. Allow the team to change the run order to be more convenient for them.
   C. Redesign the experiment with fewer runs so it can be completed on time.
   D. Redesign the experiment as a split-plot design, and then analyze the data as a split-plot design.

4. What is the benefit of adding a replicated center point run to a factorial design where all factors are continuous?
   A. It provides a way to test for curvature of the response function.
   B. It provides a measure of pure error.
   C. If the corner points are not replicated, replicating the center point provides a better way to test the effects for significance.
   D. All of the above.

5. A simplex centroid design with four components has how many design points?
   A. 10
   B. 15
   C. 16
   D. 20

6. Suppose you are designing an experiment with four factors, at two levels each, and the experiment must have no more than 24 runs. List at least two ways to design this experiment in 24 total runs. Specify the resolution for each.

7. Use Minitab to print out an alias structure for a two-level fractional factorial design with seven factors and 16 runs.

8. Open the Minitab sample data file Tiretread.MTW. What kind of experiment is this? Describe the experiment in enough detail that you could create the same experiment from scratch.

9. Analyze the experiment in the Tiretread.MTW worksheet with four response variables, Abrasion, Modulus, Elongation, and Hardness. Use a full quadratic model. Do not remove any terms from the model. Create an overlaid contour plot of all responses versus Mat A and Mat B, with the following contour settings:

Abrasion	Low: 50	High: 150
Modulus	Low: 500	High: 1000
Elongation	Low: 400	High: 800
Hardness	Low: 50	High: 70

Leave Mat C set at its middle value for this plot.

Is there any region that puts all four responses within their limits?

10. For the same model fit to the Tiretread.MTW, use the response optimizer to find the optimum factor settings, with the following setup:

Abrasion	Minimize	Target: 100	Upper: 200
Modulus	Minimize	Target: 800	Upper: 2000
Elongation	Maximize	Lower: 200	Target: 600
Hardness	Minimize	Target: 60	Upper: 80

chapter 10

Assessing Measurement Systems

All measurements are wrong. This unspeakable truth is surely known by all, but few like to talk about it. But now that it has been stated, what can we do about it? Advancement in all fields of work and study rely on measurements, so this question is vitally important.

To determine if a measurement system is "good enough" requires asking and answering two questions. First, is it accurate enough, or close enough to the truth? In place of the truth, which can never be known, we substitute a better reference measurement. With a hierarchy of standards of increasing accuracy, traceable back to national standards, it is possible to calibrate most measurement systems within known bounds of accuracy.

Second, is it precise enough? In other words, if measurement of the same item is repeated by the same person, or reproduced by many people, is the variation between those measurements small enough? With a simple experiment, analyzed by Minitab, the precision of any measurement system can be quantified, within bounds of known confidence.

Two types of measurement systems require different gage studies. Numerical measurements, sometimes called variable measurements, generally require gage repeatability and reproducibility (R&R) studies. Attribute measurements, in which an item is classified into two groups, such as pass or fail, require attribute gage studies.

CHAPTER OBJECTIVES

Here's what you'll learn in this chapter:

- How to quickly measure repeatability of variable measurement systems
- How to design, analyze, and interpret a gage repeatability and reproducibility (R&R) study
- How to measure bias and linearity of variable measurement systems
- How to assess destructive measurement systems
- How to assess agreement in attribute measurement systems
- How to assess bias and repeatability in attribute measurement systems

Figure 10-1 illustrates several components of measurement variation which can be assessed using Minitab gage tools. All of these functions can be found in the Stat > Quality Tools > Gage Tools menu, except for the attribute agreement study, which is in the Stat > Quality Tools menu.

- A **type 1 gage study** involves taking many repeated measurements of one part, by one operator. Combining these measurements with an accepted reference value, Minitab can quantify the bias, a measure of accuracy, and the repeatability of the measurement system. Without a reference value, the type 1 gage study only measures repeatability. This is frequently performed as a preliminary step, before a more elaborate gage R&R study.

- A **gage linearity and bias study** involves repeated measurements of several different parts with different values. Accepted reference values must be provided for all parts tested. From this information, Minitab tests for significant bias for each part, and whether the bias changes from part to part.

- A **gage R&R study** involves measurements of several parts, repeated multiple times by the same operator, and reproduced by multiple

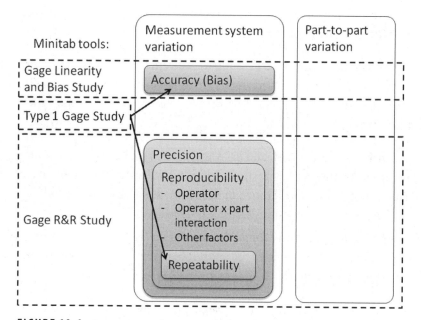

FIGURE 10-1 · Components of measurement variation and Minitab gage tools.

operators. With this information, Minitab separates the variation into components:

- Part-to-part variation is separated from the data, and the remaining variation is attributed to the measurement system.

- Repeatability is the variation between repeated measurements of the same part by the same operator. Repeatability can be considered the "smallest" component of measurement system variation, because it is an inseparable part of other components of variation.

- Reproducibility is the variation between operators when measuring the same parts. Every gage R&R study provides estimates of both repeatability and reproducibility.

- Reproducibility may also include an interaction between operators and parts, if some operators tend to measure parts differently from other operators. A gage R&R study can detect this interaction only if analyzed with the ANOVA method, which is the default.

- Reproducibility may also include the effects of other factors. In Minitab, the Gage R&R Study (Expanded) function, new in Minitab 16, can incorporate additional factors in a gage R&R study. This function can also analyze gage R&R studies with missing data, and in many other complicated scenarios. This powerful new tool greatly expands the capabilities of Minitab in gage studies.

The above tools are applied to variable measurement systems, which provide a numerical value for each measurement. Minitab also offers the following tools for attribute measurement systems, which classify tested items into two or more categories.

- An **attribute agreement study** is used to measure how often assessors agree with each other and with themselves when testing the same item more than once. When a reference or master assessment is available, the study also measures agreement with the reference.

- An **attribute gage study (analytic method)** is used to evaluate the bias and repeatability of an attribute gage used in place of a more costly numerical measurement system.

Now in Minitab 16, select Assistant > Measurement Systems Analysis (MSA) to start the new MSA assistant. This provides quick access to the two most popular gage tools, gage R&R studies and attribute agreement studies. For each tool, the assistant provides advice for conducting an effective study, a quick way to create a data collection worksheet, and an informative report in graphical format.

10.1   Conducting a Simple Gage Study

A type 1 gage study is a simple study that can measure both the bias and the repeatability of a variable measurement system, based on a number of repeated measurements of the same part. In Minitab, the Type 1 Gage Study function produces a standardized report in the form of a graph. This may be used as a preliminary to a full gage R&R study, although in some cases, a type 1 gage study may be enough.

Richard supervises the Freshman Chemistry lab at his university. One lab project involves a titration, which is a process of measuring an unknown acid concentration in a sample of solution. Richard has carefully prepared the solution in advance, so he knows from theory that the correct answer should be 0.1105. The titration results, reported by 37 students, are listed in the Minitab sample data file Acid2.MTW.

Richard selects Stat > Quality Tools > Gage Study > Type 1 Gage Study to analyze the data. He selects the data column Acid2 in the Measurement data field, and enters 0.1105 for Reference. To enter a tolerance, Richard selects Upper spec – Lower spec and enters 0.022. This represents a ± 10% tolerance on the measured acid concentration.

Figure 10-2 is the graphical report from the type 1 gage study. The graph shows the measured data plotted with three horizontal lines. The middle, green line is the reference value. The outer, red lines represent limits that a "good" measurement system should stay within almost all the time. By default, a "good" measurement system has its process width, represented by six standard deviations, smaller than 20% of the tolerance width, represented here by two red lines. In this example, several students had trouble staying within these limits.

Below the graph are some analytical results. On the left is a list of basic statistics, including the standard deviation of 0.0018442. Since these measurements represent titrations of one solution, the standard deviation is entirely measurement system variation.

In the middle is a statistical test for bias. Minitab finds that the mean of the measurements is below the reference value by 0.000851. The p-value for the test is 0.008, representing the probability that random variation could cause a bias as large as this. Since the p-value is very small, less than 0.05, this indicates a statistically significant bias.

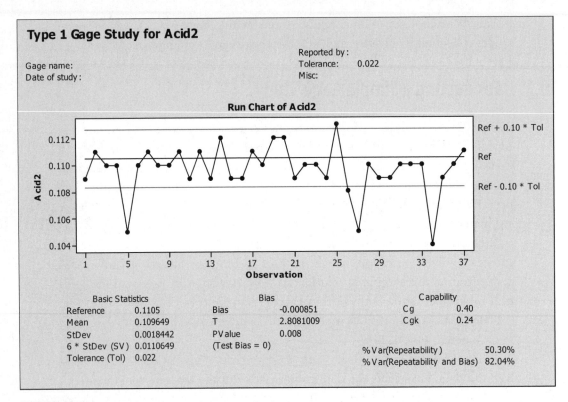

FIGURE 10-2 • Type 1 gage study for acid titration results.

The bias worries Richard, because it could be a problem in mixing the master solution, or it could be a systematic problem in the equipment or procedures used by the students. He expected the mean results from the students to be closer to the reference value. Diagnosing this problem will require additional work.

On the right are some additional metrics to summarize the measurement system as a whole. Cg and Cgk are intended to be functional equivalents of the process capability metrics Cp and Cpk, but applied to gage studies. Process capability metrics are discussed further in Chapter 12.

- **Cg** is the ratio of 20% of the tolerance width to 6 standard deviations of measurement variation:

$$Cg = \frac{0.20 \times Tolerance}{6\sigma_{gage}}$$

If **Cg** > 1, this indicates that the gage precision is good enough that measurements will almost always fall within 10% of the mean of measurements. This metric only measures repeatability, not bias.

- **Cgk** combines 10% of the tolerance with any bias, and divides this by 3 standard deviations:

$$Cgk = \frac{0.10 \times Tolerance - \left| \overline{X} - Reference \right|}{3\sigma_{gage}}$$

If Cgk > 1, this indicates that the gage accuracy and precision are good enough that measurements will almost always fall within 10% of the reference value.

- **%Var (Repeatability)** measures how much of the tolerance is consumed by measurement system repeatability:

$$\%Var\ (Repeatability) = \frac{6\sigma_{gage}}{Tolerance} \times 100\% = \frac{20\%}{Cg}$$

If %Var (Repeatability) < 10%, this indicates a good level of repeatability.

- **%Var (Repeatability and Bias)** measures how much of the tolerance is consumed by measurement system repeatability and bias:

$$\%Var\ (Rep.\ and\ Bias) = \frac{3\sigma_{gage} \times 20\%}{0.10 \times Tolerance - \left| \overline{X} - Ref. \right|} = \frac{20\%}{Cgk}$$

If %Var (Repeatability and Bias) < 10%, this indicates a good level of both repeatability and bias.

In some cases the constants used to define these four metrics may need to be changed. They can be changed by clicking the Options button in the Type 1 Gage Study dialog. In the Options dialog, the Percent of tolerance for calculating Cg has a default value of 20.0, corresponding to the usual rule of thumb that a good measurement system shouldn't vary more than ± 10%. If a looser criterion of ± 30% is allowed, this value could be increased to 60.0. It is also possible to change the assumed "width" of the measurement system distribution from 6σ to some other number of standard deviations. Some companies prefer to set the process "width" to 5.15σ which contains approximately 99% of the values.

For this Acid2.MTW data file and the given tolerance width, all the metrics are in the unacceptable range. If this measurement system were to be used for a product with a tolerance width of 0.022, there would be a high risk of significant measurement errors and misclassification of products. If the metrics were in the acceptable range, almost all the dots should be within the red lines in the plot.

The type 1 gage study can be applied to analyze any dataset where one thing is measured many times, either by one person or by many people. In this example, 37 students produced 37 different measurements. Therefore, the component of variation labeled repeatability is actually a combination of repeatability and reproducibility.

If we need to separate repeatability from reproducibility, each operator must measure the same item many times, and this process is reproduced for many operators. This scenario calls for a gage R&R study, the topic of the next section.

10.2   Setting Up and Analyzing a Crossed Gage R&R Study

The standard, crossed gage R&R study involves a selection of parts and a selection of operators. During the study, each operator will measure each part multiple times. The adjective "crossed" refers to the arrangement where every operator measures the same parts. In a good gage study, the order of measurement is randomized, usually so that each operator measures the same parts in a different randomized order.

Depending on the goals of the gage R&R study, the parts can be a random sample of typical parts, or they can be a carefully selected sample, representing many different values, some inside and some outside tolerance limits. To properly interpret the study requires knowing whether a random or a selected sample was chosen. The operators involved in the gage R&R study are assumed to be a random sample of the operators who will measure the same parts in production.

Minitab assists with gage R&R studies in two ways, first by setting up the data collection worksheet, and later by analyzing the data and preparing informative graphs and reports. Minitab 16 offers two distinctly different ways to perform each of these tasks. The MSA assistant, a new feature of Minitab 16, creates data collection worksheets and analyzes the results, producing a color-coded graphical report. The traditional Minitab functions offer more options to customize these functions and a report in text form. The traditional menus also offer a sixpack plot which has become a familiar format for visualizing gage R&R results without the interpretations provided by the assistant.

To explore the new MSA assistant, click Assistant > Measurement Systems Analysis (MSA). A flow chart appears as shown in Fig. 10-3. The first diamond-shaped decision box asks about data type. For continuous, numerical

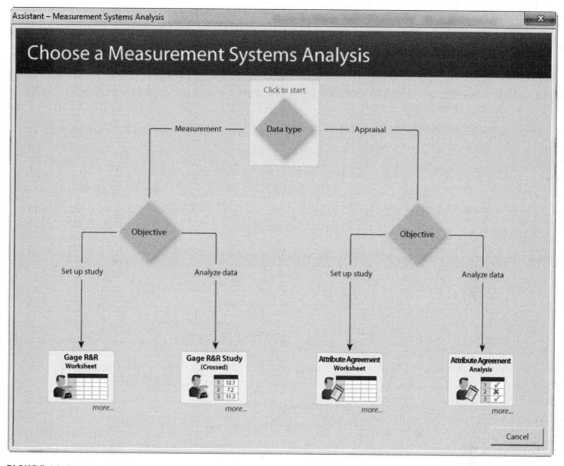

FIGURE 10-3 · MSA assistant.

measurements, use the left, Measurement branch. This branch leads to a standard gage R&R study. For pass/fail, attribute data, use the right, Appraisal branch for an attribute agreement study. Each branch offers two functions, one to set up a data collection worksheet, and the other to analyze the collected data.

To learn more about each of these choices, with examples, click directly on the decision box. For a list of advice about using each tool effectively, click the *more...* link below the box for each tool.

In the automotive industry and in many others, it is common to perform a gage R&R study with 10 parts, 3 operators, and 3 replicated measurements of each part by each operator, for a total of 90 measurements. To set up a data collection worksheet for this test, click the Gage R&R Worksheet box from the MSA assistant.

Create Gage R&R Worksheet

Operators and replicates

Enter your own operator names or use the defaults.

Number of operators: 3

Number of replicates: 3

(Number of times operators measure each part)

	Operator Name
1	Alvin
2	Theodore
3	Simon

Parts

Enter your own part names or use the defaults.

Number of parts: 10

	Part Name
1	101
2	102
3	103
4	104
5	105
6	106
7	107
8	108
9	109
10	110

OK   Cancel

FIGURE 10-4 · Setting up a gage R&R worksheet.

In the Create Gage R&R Worksheet dialog, seen in Fig. 10-4, select any number of operators, replicates, or parts to be measured. Names can be provided for the operators and the parts to customize the worksheet and make data collection easier.

After the user clicks OK, Minitab sets up a worksheet to hold the gage R&R data, and makes a one-time offer to print data collection worksheets. Figure 10-5 shows the dialog offering this choice. Clicking Yes will send nine pages to the printer of your choice, one page for each combination of operator and replicate.

The worksheet produced by the assistant randomizes the parts to be measured within each operator and replicate, but the operators and replicates are not randomized. This is a common and practical randomization choice.

Many more randomization options are offered by the traditional Minitab menus. To see these options, select Stat > Quality Tools > Gage Study > Create Gage R&R Study Worksheet. This dialog is a rearranged version of the dialog seen in Fig. 10-4, but with an Options button. Click Options, and a dialog appears as

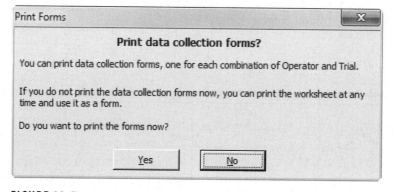

FIGURE 10-5 · Option to print forms.

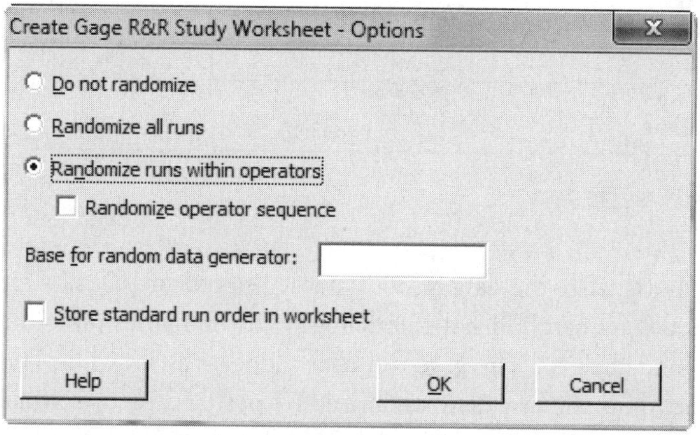

FIGURE 10-6 · Randomization options.

shown in Fig. 10-6. Options include no randomization, complete randomization, and randomization within operators, with or without randomized order of operators. The option to include a standard order in the worksheet is helpful to sort a randomized worksheet into standard order.

For an example of gage R&R data collected using this scheme, open the Minitab sample data file Gageaiag.MTW. The Automotive Industry Action Group (AIAG), a consortium of the big three American automobile companies, publishes informative manuals on many topics, including measurement systems analysis. This dataset appears as an example in AIAG (2002). The measurements listed represent the difference between the actual measurement and a nominal value, so some are negative and others are positive. The tolerance for this measurement is ± 4 units.

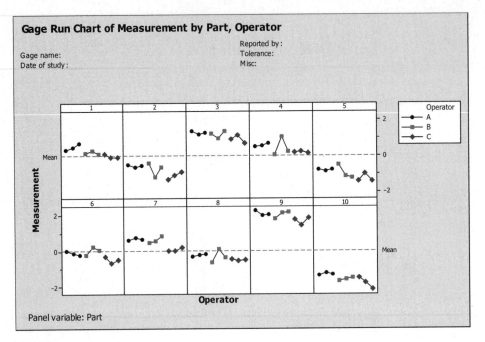

FIGURE 10-7 · Gage run chart.

To quickly visualize the data in this dataset, select Stat > Quality Tools > Gage Study > Gage Run Chart. Fill out the dialog with the names of columns in the worksheet, and click OK. The gage run chart appears as shown in Fig. 10-7.

This chart plots the raw data, organized by part and by operator. What can be seen in this chart? First, the variation between parts is much more than the variation of measurements within each part. This is a good thing, because it indicates that the measurement system can reliably distinguish between different parts. But other patterns are more concerning. For some parts, Operator B seems to have more variation between measurements than the other operators. Also, Operator C seems to have lower measurement values than the other operators. But are these findings significant? To answer this question requires further analysis.

To analyze this dataset with the assistant, select Assistant > Measurement Systems Analysis (MSA) from the menu, and then click the Gage R&R Study (Crossed) button. Fill out the dialog as shown in Fig. 10-8.

Besides specifying the variable names in the worksheet, this dialog asks some important questions. The first question concerns Process variation, which is the variation between parts. If the parts in the gage R&R study are a random sample of typical production, then it may be appropriate to use the Estimate from parts

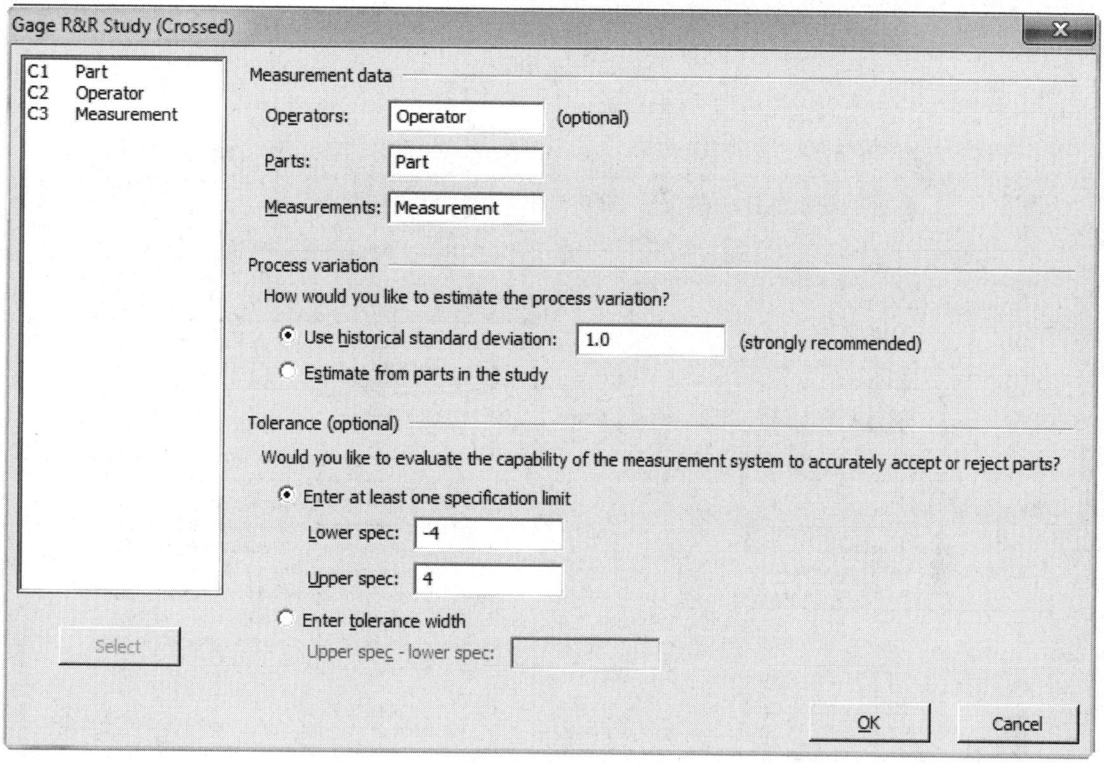

FIGURE 10-8 · Analyzing a gage R&R study with the MSA assistant.

in the study option. However, if the parts in the gage R&R study were selected to include both good and bad parts, this option will bias many of the metrics from the study, producing an unrealistically good assessment of the measurement system.

It is almost always a better idea to select Use historical standard deviation and enter a value from a separate capability study or some other external source. Even if the parts used in the gage R&R study are from regular production, a sample of ten parts is not enough to get a reliable estimate of process variation. For this example dataset, use a historical standard deviation of 1.0. The second question concerns the tolerance limits. Here, enter the upper limit, lower limit, or both limits, as appropriate.

After the user clicks OK, Minitab analyzes the data and prepares a report in the form of three graphs. Two of these graphs are shown in Figs. 10-9 and 10-10.

The Summary Report, Fig. 10-9, provides an overall summary with color-coded graphics and interpretive text. At the top left is a scale labeled, Can

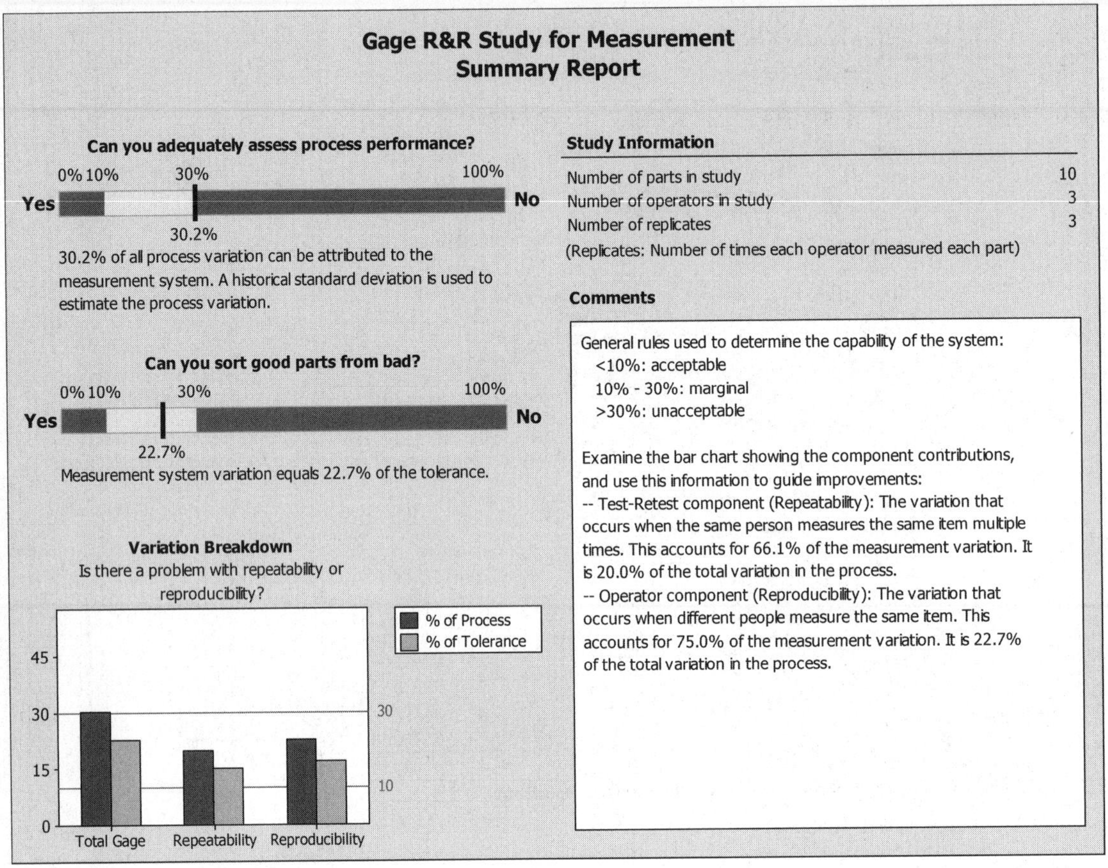

Gage R&R Study for Measurement
Summary Report
Can you adequately assess process performance?
0% 10% 30% 100%
Yes
No
30.2%
30.2% of all process variation can be attributed to the measurement system. A historical standard deviation is used to estimate the process variation.
Can you sort good parts from bad?
0% 10% 30% 100%
Yes
No
22.7%
Measurement system variation equals 22.7% of the tolerance.
Variation Breakdown
Is there a problem with repeatability or reproducibility?
% of Process
% of Tolerance
45
30
15
0
30
10
Total Gage
Repeatability
Reproducibility
Study Information
Number of parts in study 10
Number of operators in study 3
Number of replicates 3
(Replicates: Number of times each operator measured each part)
Comments
General rules used to determine the capability of the system:
<10%: acceptable
10% - 30%: marginal
>30%: unacceptable
Examine the bar chart showing the component contributions, and use this information to guide improvements:
-- Test-Retest component (Repeatability): The variation that occurs when the same person measures the same item multiple times. This accounts for 66.1% of the measurement variation. It is 20.0% of the total variation in the process.
-- Operator component (Reproducibility): The variation that occurs when different people measure the same item. This accounts for 75.0% of the measurement variation. It is 22.7% of the total variation in the process.

FIGURE 10-9 • Gage R&R summary report.

you adequately assess process performance? This graph displays a ratio of the measurement system variation to process variation. Here, the ratio is 30.2%, which is on the borderline of being unacceptable, according to typical criteria. Mouse over this graph to see a lengthier explanation of the metric and how to interpret it.

The second graph on the left is labeled, Can you sort good parts from bad? This is the ratio of six standard deviations of measurement system variation to the tolerance width. Here, the ratio is 22.7%, which is in the marginal, yellow range, again according to typical criteria.

The bar chart on the bottom left shows gage variation as a percentage of tolerance and as a percentage of process variation. The bar chart also shows how gage variation breaks down into repeatability and reproducibility.

On the right side of the Summary Report is a table listing the size of the gage R&R study, and a Comments block listing a text interpretation of the results

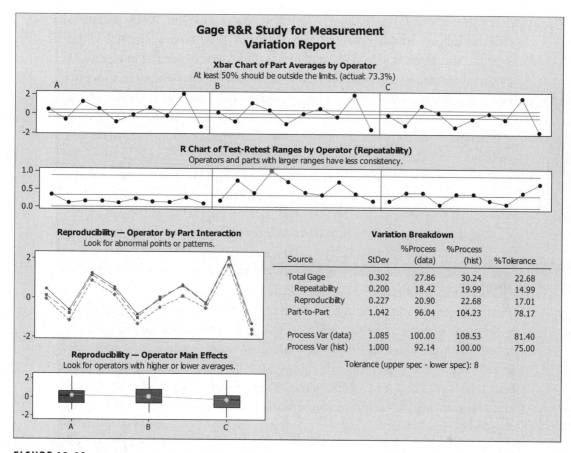

Gage R&R Study for Measurement Variation Report

Xbar Chart of Part Averages by Operator
At least 50% should be outside the limits. (actual: 73.3%)

R Chart of Test-Retest Ranges by Operator (Repeatability)
Operators and parts with larger ranges have less consistency.

Reproducibility — Operator by Part Interaction
Look for abnormal points or patterns.

Variation Breakdown

Source	StDev	%Process (data)	%Process (hist)	%Tolerance
Total Gage	0.302	27.86	30.24	22.68
Repeatability	0.200	18.42	19.99	14.99
Reproducibility	0.227	20.90	22.68	17.01
Part-to-Part	1.042	96.04	104.23	78.17
Process Var (data)	1.085	100.00	108.53	81.40
Process Var (hist)	1.000	92.14	100.00	75.00

Tolerance (upper spec - lower spec): 8

Reproducibility — Operator Main Effects
Look for operators with higher or lower averages.

FIGURE 10-10 · Gage R&R variation report.

prepared by Minitab. To edit these comments for a report or presentation, double-click on the **Comments** block.

Figure 10-10 shows the **Variation Report**, with more detailed information about the measurement system and components of variation.

At the top of the **Variation Report** is an Xbar Chart of Part Averages by Operator. Below the title of the report is this helpful advice: **At least 50% should be outside the limits.** In this graph, the dots represent the mean measurements of each part measured by each operator. The outer, red lines on the plot represent the bounds of measurement system variation. It is good for dots to be outside the red lines on this plot, because this means that the measurement system can reliably distinguish parts from each other. If all the dots were inside the lines, this would mean that the measurement system is unable to tell them apart.

The second graph is an R Chart of Test-Retest Ranges by Operator (Repeatability) with this helpful advice: Operators and parts with larger ranges have less consistency. For this chart, it would be good to see all the dots inside the lines, indicating that variation is consistent for all operators and for all parts. Here, Operator B clearly has more variation than Operator A, with Operator C somewhere in the middle. This important information may indicate a difference in techniques or procedures used by the three operators. Training, perhaps by Operator A, could help to reduce this variation for all operators.

The bottom two graphs illustrate reproducibility. The third graph, labeled Operator by Part Interaction shows means by operator and part, with the three lines drawn on top of each other. If these lines are parallel, as in this case, there is no significant interaction. If one of the lines were not parallel to the others, this would indicate either a data recording error or an operator who has serious trouble measuring and classifying parts in the same way as other operators.

The fourth graph, labeled Operator Main Effects shows any difference in mean measurements by operator. In this example, Operator C produces consistently lower measurements than the other operators. This also shows up in the interaction graph, although in this book, without the color coding, it is impossible to tell which line represents which operator. The symbols in this graph are boxplots, first introduced in Chapter 2. These boxplots show the distribution of measurements for each operator, making it easy to see differences between operators.

The table on the bottom right lists the standard deviations of various components of variation, including total gage variation, repeatability, reproducibility, and part variation. Each of these standard deviations is also expressed as a percentage of process variation and of the tolerance. For this example, the total gage variation as a percentage of historical process variation and of the tolerance are used to create the color-coded metric plots on the Summary Report.

? Still Struggling

Statistics are often expressed as percentages in an attempt to make them less confusing. In this case, percentages can have the opposite effect. The first row, Total Gage, and the fourth row, Part-to-Part should combine to equal the fifth row, Process Var (data). But the numbers don't add up. In the %Process (data) column, 27.86% and 96.04% clearly do not sum to 100%. These percentages are calculated from standard deviations of variation components. Standard deviations do not add up, but variances, the squares of standard deviations, do add up. From the first column, labeled StDev, $0.302^2 + 1.042^2 = 1.085^2$, showing that component variances add up properly. Also, variances of Repeatability and Reproducibility add up to the Total Gage variance: $0.200^2 + 0.227^2 = 0.302^2$. The key to using these statistics is to find the percentage that means the most for you, for instance, that total gage variation is 22.68% of tolerance, and not worry about whether the percentages add up or not.

A third graph not shown here, labeled **Report Card** provides a text interpretation of sample size, the Xbar chart, and the R chart.

To summarize this example, the gage R&R study provides important information to diagnose and improve the measurement system:

- As it stands, the measurement system is marginal to unacceptable, based on the metrics on the **Summary Report**.

- Some operators (Operator B) have significantly more variation between replicated measurements than other operators. This is clearly shown on the R chart. If the causes of this variation could be reduced, and all operators were as repeatable as Operator A, the measurement system would be much improved.

- Some operators (Operator C) have consistently lower measurements than the other operators. This is shown on the interaction plot and the operator main effects plot. Diagnosing and correcting this disparity will also improve the measurement system.

The same data can also be analyzed with the traditional menus by clicking Stat > Quality Tools > Gage Study > Gage R&R Study (Crossed). In the dialog, not shown here, identify the columns for Part numbers, Operators, and Measurement data. To specify the tolerance and the historical standard deviation, or to choose other options, click the Options button.

One important choice is between the ANOVA and the Xbar and R methods, which is on the main Gage R&R Study (Crossed) dialog. The ANOVA (analysis of variance) option is better for many reasons. First, the ANOVA can test for an interaction between operator and part. Second, ANOVA is more sensitive to smaller effects. Third, confidence intervals are available for the ANOVA method.

The anachronistic range-based method is a relic from earlier days when manual calculations where the rule and computers were rare. But since it is codified in the AIAG manual and in the procedures of many companies, Minitab continues to offer this inferior procedure as an alternative.

The ANOVA produces a text report and a sixpack graph. Here is the report:

Gage R&R Study - ANOVA Method
Two-Way ANOVA Table With Interaction

Source	DF	SS	MS	F	P
Part	9	88.3619	9.81799	492.291	0.000
Operator	2	3.1673	1.58363	79.406	0.000
Part * Operator	18	0.3590	0.01994	0.434	0.974
Repeatability	60	2.7589	0.04598		
Total	89	94.6471			

Alpha to remove interaction term = 0.25

Two-Way ANOVA Table Without Interaction

Source	DF	SS	MS	F	P
Part	9	88.3619	9.81799	245.614	0.000
Operator	2	3.1673	1.58363	39.617	0.000
Repeatability	78	3.1179	0.03997		
Total	89	94.6471			

Gage R&R

Source	VarComp	%Contribution (of VarComp)
Total Gage R&R	0.09143	7.76
Repeatability	0.03997	3.39
Reproducibility	0.05146	4.37
Operator	0.05146	4.37
Part-To-Part	1.08645	92.24
Total Variation	1.17788	100.00

Process tolerance = 8
Historical standard deviation = 1

Source	StdDev (SD)	Study Var (6 * SD)	%Study Var (%SV)	%Tolerance (SV/Toler)	%Process (SV/Proc)
Total Gage R&R	0.30237	1.81423	27.86	22.68	30.24
Repeatability	0.19993	1.19960	18.42	14.99	19.99
Reproducibility	0.22684	1.36103	20.90	17.01	22.68
Operator	0.22684	1.36103	20.90	17.01	22.68
Part-To-Part	1.04233	6.25396	96.04	78.17	104.23
Total Variation	1.08530	6.51180	100.00	81.40	108.53

Number of Distinct Categories = 4

At the top of the report, the first section is an analysis of variance (**ANOVA**) including the Part * Operator interaction. In this analysis, the *p*-value for the interaction is 0.974. Since this is larger than 0.25, an adjustable value, Minitab decides that the interaction is not significant and removes it from the analysis.

In a gage R&R analysis, removing the interaction effect changes the rest of the analysis, so the second ANOVA table repeats the analysis without the interaction. In this table, the *p*-value for Operator is 0.000, indicating that Operators have a significant difference in their mean measurements of the same parts.

The next table lists the variance of each component of variance: repeatability, reproducibility, and part-to-part. Because these are variances, these components do add up to 100%, as one would expect.

The final table converts the same components of variation into standard deviations, and expresses them in different ways, in different columns:

- The **StdDev (SD)** lists the square roots of the variance components in the previous table

- The **Study Var (6 * SD)** simply multiplies standard deviation by 6 to represent the width of the distribution of variation. The constant 6 can be changed in the Options dialog to 5.15 or to another value, if required.

- The **%Study Var (%SV)** column divides the (6 * SD) column by the total on the bottom. These values will not add together correctly, unless they are squared first. A typical rule of thumb is that the total gage R&R expressed as a percentage of study variation should be less than 10%, with 10–30% representing marginal performance. But this metric is only meaningful if the parts used in the gage R&R study represent typical production variation. Otherwise, this metric can be misleading.

- The **%Tolerance (SV/Toler)** divides study variation by the tolerance width, if the tolerance is specified. A typical rule of thumb is that the total gage R&R expressed as a percentage of tolerance should be less than 10%, with 10–30% representing marginal performance. This provides a measure of how well the measurement system can distinguish between acceptable and unacceptable parts.

- The **%Process (SV/Proc)** divides study variation by 6 times the historical standard deviation, if provided. A typical rule of thumb is that the total gage R&R expressed as a percentage of variation should be less than 10% with 10–30% representing marginal performance. This provides an assessment of how well the measurement system can distinguish between different parts in the process, without considering the tolerance.

- Below the table, Minitab reports the **Number of Distinct Categories**. This is the standard deviation of parts divided by the standard deviation of the gage, multiplied by 1.41, and then truncated to the next lower integer. This metric, often called NDC, is intended to represent the number of bins into which the parts could reliably be sorted. NDC is a recalculated version of gage variation in the %SV column. Some have proposed acceptability criteria for NDC, but these rarely line up with equivalent criteria applied to the %SV column. Because this incongruity is confusing, no criteria for NDC are listed here.

The gage R&R analysis also produces a sixpack of plots, shown in Fig. 10-11. Unlike the graphs produced by the MSA assistant, this sixpack has no interpretations or text comments, leaving that to the human viewer.

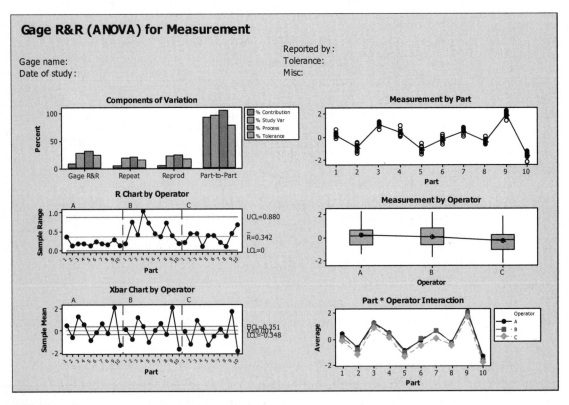

FIGURE 10-11 · Gage R&R sixpack plot.

Here are the components of the sixpack:

- The **Components of Variation** plot, top left, is a graphical version of percentages in the report above. It shows total gage variation, repeatability, reproducibility, and part variation as a percentage of contribution (based on variance), study variation (based on standard deviation), historical process variation, and tolerance.

- The **R Chart by Operator**, middle left, shows the ranges of repeated measurements of each part, by each operator. If some operators have more variation than other operators, it will show up on this graph. In this example, one point is outside the red lines, indicating significantly more variation for that part and operator than for the dataset as a whole.

- The **Xbar Chart by Operator**, bottom left, shows the means of repeated measurements of each part, by operator. The outer, red lines on this plot represent measurement system variation. On this plot, dots outside the red lines represent a good measurement system that can distinguish between the different parts in the study.

- The **Measurement by Part** plot, top right, shows the mean measurement for all parts in the study, with symbols indicating the variation of measurements around the mean.

- The **Measurement by Operator** plot, middle right, is a box plot of measurements by operator, with a line connecting the means. This plot shows when one operator measures parts consistently higher or lower than other operators.

- The **Part * Operator Interaction** plot, bottom right, has one line for each operator, connecting symbols for the mean measurements for each part. If the lines are parallel, there is no interaction. Deviations from parallel lines could represent a data error, or they could represent a serious discrepancy in measurement process or procedure between operators.

The analysis of a gage R&R study provides powerful and detailed information about how well the measurement system is performing and how it can be improved. But this analysis does not quantify the risk involved with small sample sizes. All the graphs and reports above are based on ten parts, three operators, and three replications. The true value of metrics like gage variation as a percentage of tolerance could be much higher or much lower than the values reported here.

 For the first time, Minitab 16 now provides optional confidence intervals for the various calculated values and metrics in a gage R&R report. To select this option, click the Conf Int button in the Gage R&R Study (Crossed) dialog.

For the Gageaiag.MTW dataset, suppose we want to calculate a 90% two-sided confidence interval. The upper bound of this interval can be taken as a 95% upper confidence bound. With this option selected, here is a portion of the resulting report:

```
                                            Study Var
Source               StdDev (SD)     90% CI  (6 * SD)         90% CI
Total Gage R&R           0.30237 (0.235, 1.033)  1.81423 (1.411,  6.200)
  Repeatability          0.19993 (0.177, 0.231)  1.19960 (1.061,  1.383)
  Reproducibility        0.22684 (0.128, 1.014)  1.36103 (0.765,  6.083)
    Operator             0.22684 (0.128, 1.014)  1.36103 (0.765,  6.083)
Part-To-Part             1.04233 (0.759, 1.717)  6.25396 (4.553, 10.302)
Total Variation          1.08530 (0.816, 1.811)  6.51180 (4.897, 10.867)


                     %Study Var               %Tolerance
Source                  (%SV)     90% CI      (SV/Toler)         90% CI
Total Gage R&R          27.86 (16.32, 70.40)     22.68 (17.63,  77.50)
  Repeatability         18.42 (10.98, 25.51)     14.99 (13.27,  17.29)
  Reproducibility       20.90 (10.19, 68.89)     17.01 ( 9.57,  76.03)
    Operator            20.90 (10.19, 68.89)     17.01 ( 9.57,  76.03)
Part-To-Part            96.04 (71.02, 98.66)     78.17 (56.91, 128.78)
Total Variation        100.00                    81.40 (61.21, 135.83)
```

In the bottom right section of this report, the total gage R&R has a point estimate which is 22.68% of tolerance. The 90% confidence interval for this metric is between 17.63% and 77.50%. For this gage R&R study, the marginal metric value of 22.68% could be as bad as 77.50%, or as good as 17.63%, with 90% confidence.

The gage R&R studies featured in this section measure the precision of the measurement system, but they provide no information about accuracy. A typical industrial environment combines a gage R&R study to assess precision with a calibration and metrology system to assess accuracy. In some cases a linearity and bias test, described next, provides a quick check of accuracy.

10.3   Assessing Linearity and Bias

When accepted reference values are available, it is easy to evaluate whether a measurement system has a significant bias between the reference values and the measured values, and whether the system is linear in its response to different values of parts. These are both aspects of accuracy, not precision, which was assessed in the previous section.

For an example, Mike is designing a probe that can quickly measure the thickness of microscopic metallic films created during the processing of integrated circuits. To test the probe, Mike prepares five test samples with metallic films of 2, 4, 6, 8, and 10 μm. He calculates these thicknesses from a theoretical understanding of the deposition process. Later, after doing the test, he sections and inspects the samples with electron microscopy, verifying that the films are within 0.1 μm of their intended thickness.

Mike tests each sample ten times with a prototype measurement probe. Mike's data is listed in the Minitab sample data file Gagelin.MTW. In the worksheet, column C2 Master contains the reference values of the five parts, and column C3 Response contains the measurements reported by the probe.

Mike selects Stat > Quality Tools > Gage Study > Gage Linearity and Bias Study. In the dialog, he selects Part in the Part numbers field, Master in the Reference values field, and Response in the Measurement data field.

The report from this function is entirely in the form of a graph, seen in Fig. 10-12. The plot on the left side tells a clear story. The dashed horizontal line represents zero bias. For smaller values, the probe reads values too high, and for larger values, the probe reads too low. Clearly, the probe does not have acceptable linearity. It is also notable that for reference values of 4 and 6, some measured values are significantly higher than the rest.

On the right side of the graph is a statistical report. Minitab uses linear regression to fit a line through the dots in the plot. If there were no bias and perfect linearity, both the constant and the slope for this line would be zero. Here, the p-values for both constant and slope are 0.000, providing strong evidence that both coefficients are non-zero.

The table in the lower right corner is a set of tests for significant bias for the overall average, and for each reference value. p-values smaller than 0.05 indicate significant bias, with 95% confidence. This dataset provides evidence of significant bias at 2, 8, and 10 μm.

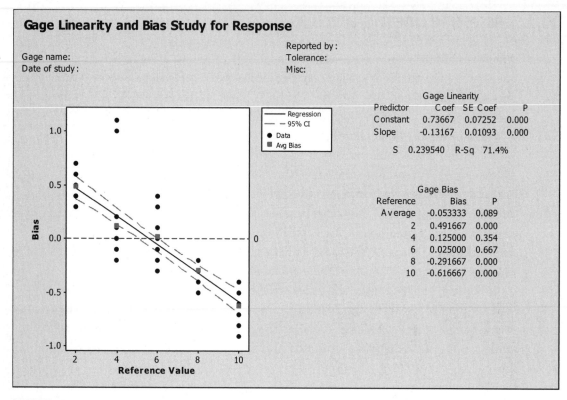

Gage Linearity and Bias Study for Response

FIGURE 10-12 • Linearity and bias report.

Clearly, Mike has some work to do on this probe, but this simple linearity and bias study provides very specific information on how the probe performs, and on what must be done to improve it.

10.4   Gage R&R Studies for Destructive Testing

Many types of measurements involve the destruction or alteration of the test sample, which makes repeated measurements of the same item impossible. Examples include measurements of stress required to break a piece of metal, the torque required to loosen a fastener, or any kind of food tasting. After the metal is broken, the fastener is loosened, and the food is eaten, the same item cannot be measured again. How can repeatability be estimated when measurements cannot be repeated?

Statistical tools provide many great benefits, but no free lunch. There is no magic way to calculate a pure estimate of repeatability without repeated measurements.

The dilemma can be resolved in the design of the study itself. If a batch of pieces can be defined so that we can assume that every piece in the batch is actually the same piece, then the variation of measurements within the batch can be attributed to repeatability.

In the example of breaking a piece of metal, each piece can be cut into smaller pieces so that the smaller pieces are assumed to break under the same stress. Similarly, a homogenous food sample can be subdivided for multiple tastings. Fasteners may be impossible to subdivide; instead of a fastener, perhaps something else of known torque, like a spring, can be substituted for an actual fastener. Many successful gage R&R studies measure surrogates, which are completely unlike the actual parts to be measured.

This process often leaves small batch sizes inadequate for a typical gage R&R study. This calls for a nested gage R&R study, instead of the usual crossed arrangement.

- In a **crossed** gage R&R study, every part is measured by every operator.
- In a **nested** gage R&R study, every part is measured by only one operator, and each operator measures a different set of parts. Parts are nested within operators. In Minitab reports, this is described as `Part (Operator)`.

For example, Joy is evaluating a device that measures the breaking stress for a polymer window used on a cell phone. The tester grips the window in the middle, with the two ends sticking out. Then another jaw grips the end and torques it until it breaks, measuring the applied force. Each window can only be tested two times, once for each end. Joy decides to assume that the breaking force for each part is the same on each end, so any difference in measured force can be attributed to the measurement system.

For this gage R&R study, Joy selects three operators and 15 parts. Each operator is randomly assigned a set of five parts. Then each operator will test, and break, both ends of each part. The result will be a total of 30 measurements.

Joy's data is available in the Minitab sample data file Gagenest.MTW. With this worksheet loaded, Joy selects Stat > Quality Tools > Gage Study > Gage R&R Study (Nested) to analyze the data. She enters Part in the Part or batch numbers field, Operator in the Operators field, and Response in the Measurement data field. To enter the tolerance width of 10, Joy clicks Options, selects Upper limit – Lower limit and enters 10 in the appropriate field.

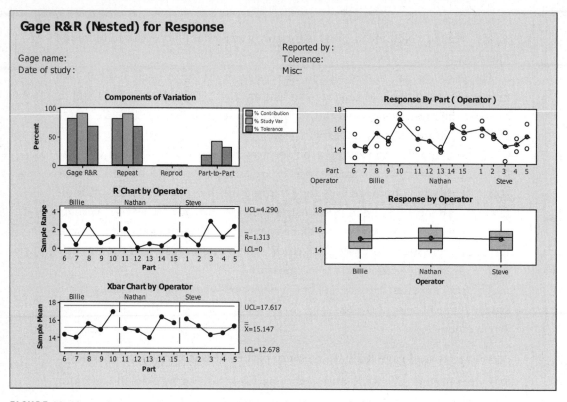

FIGURE 10-13 • Nested gage R&R report.

After clicking OK, Joy sees a graphical report as in Fig. 10-13. From the **Components of Variation** chart in the top left, Joy notes that the gage R&R as a percentage of study variation, and as a percentage of tolerance, are way over 30%. So far, this is not good. Also, the **Xbar Chart** in the bottom left has no points outside the limits. This means that either the parts tested are nearly identical, or the gage repeatability is so much that it overwhelms any difference between parts. On the good side, there is no apparent difference in mean measurements between operators.

Here is the report from the Session window:

Gage R&R Study - Nested ANOVA
Gage R&R (Nested) for Response

Source	DF	SS	MS	F	P
Operator	2	0.0142	0.00708	0.00385	0.996
Part (Operator)	12	22.0552	1.83794	1.42549	0.255
Repeatability	15	19.3400	1.28933		
Total	29	41.4094			

Gage R&R

Source	VarComp	%Contribution (of VarComp)
Total Gage R&R	1.28933	82.46
Repeatability	1.28933	82.46
Reproducibility	0.00000	0.00
Part-To-Part	0.27430	17.54
Total Variation	1.56364	100.00

Process tolerance = 10

Source	StdDev (SD)	Study Var (6 * SD)	%Study Var (%SV)	%Tolerance (SV/Toler)
Total Gage R&R	1.13549	6.81293	90.81	68.13
Repeatability	1.13549	6.81293	90.81	68.13
Reproducibility	0.00000	0.00000	0.00	0.00
Part-To-Part	0.52374	3.14243	41.88	31.42
Total Variation	1.25045	7.50273	100.00	75.03

Number of Distinct Categories = 1

The analytical report confirms the above findings. Total Gage R&R consumes 90.81% of study variation and 68.13% of tolerance, both unacceptable metrics. The analysis detects no difference between operators, and reports 0 for Reproducibility. The last line of the analysis notes that Number of Distinct Categories = 1 indicating that this data shows no evidence that the measurement system can detect any differences between these parts.

All of these findings depend on the correctness of the assumption that the breaking force is equal on both sides of the same part. If this assumption is not true, then there is no way in this experiment to separate repeatability from part-to-part variation. This is an essential, and perhaps untestable assumption behind all gage R&R studies, when applied to destructive measurement systems.

10.5   Analyzing More Complex Gage R&R Studies

Real gage studies can be far more complicated than the examples presented here, often because of additional factors. Caution is advisable here. Trying to accomplish too much in one experiment can lead to wasted resources and nothing accomplished. In particular, gage studies should focus on the measurement system. It is unwise to use a gage study to assess and diagnose the process that creates the parts being measured. First fix the gage, then in a separate step, use the gage to fix the process. But there are often factors that may make the measurements system better or worse. How can these factors be incorporated into the gage study?

 A new feature in Minitab 16 is the Gage R&R Study (Expanded) tool. This tool can handle up to eight additional factors in a gage study in addition to part and operator. These factors may be fixed or random, crossed or nested. This tool can also analyze an unbalanced gage R&R study, which the other functions cannot do.

Before using this tool, any additional factors must be correctly classified as fixed or random. Also, the arrangement of the factors in the gage study must be correctly classified as crossed or nested. Here is more information on these choices:

- A factor is **fixed** if the only values of interest are the levels tested in the experiment. A numerical factor is fixed if the only values of interest are within the range of the levels tested. Most designed experiments have only fixed factors. The examples analyzed with the DOE menu in Chapter 9 had fixed factors. A model for a fixed factor predicts mean response values for factor values of interest.

- A factor is **random** if the values tested are a random sample of some larger population. In a gage R&R study, part and operator are random factors. A model for a random factor predicts the variation in response values created by variation in the random factor. Variation caused by a random factor is measured as a variance or a standard deviation.

- Factors are **crossed** if the experiment may include all combinations of values of the factors. In a typical factorial experiment, all factors are crossed. In a crossed gage R&R study, all operators measure all parts.

- Factor A is **nested** within factor B if each level of factor B is tested with different levels of factor A. In a nested gage R&R study, each operator measures a different set of parts, so parts are nested within operator. In Minitab, this is described by Part (Operator).

For an example dataset, load the Minitab sample data file Gagegeneral.MTW. This gage study involves 10 parts and 3 operators, in a crossed configuration. The part being measured has one of two subcomponents, A or B. Does having one subcomponent or the other have an effect on the measurements? To find out, subcomponent can be included in the model as a fixed factor. Each operator will measure each part two times with subcomponent A, and two times with subcomponent B.

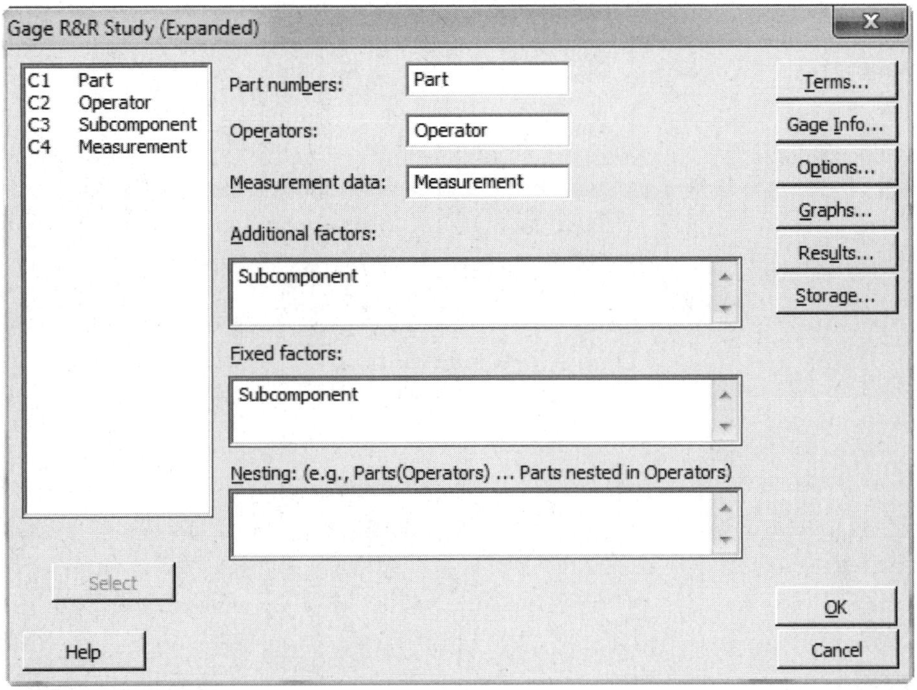

FIGURE 10-14 · Expanded Gage R&R dialog.

Fill out the dialog as shown in Fig. 10-14. Notice that additional fixed factors must be listed twice, in Additional factors and Fixed factors. Factors not listed as fixed are assumed to be random. If any factors are nested, this must be noted in the Nested factors field. As with the other Gage R&R dialogs, click Options to specify the tolerance. For this example, Gagegeneral.MTW, the Upper limit – Lower limit is 8.

The Gage R&R Study (Expanded) produces a sixpack graph very similar to the one produced by the Gage R&R Study (Crossed) function. Here is the analysis report:

Gage R&R Study: Measurement versus Part, Operator, Subcomponent

```
Factor Information

Factor        Type     Levels  Values
Part          random       10  1, 2, 3, 4, 5, 6, 7, 8, 9, 10
Operator      random        3  A, B, C
Subcomponent  fixed         2  A, B
```

```
ANOVA Table with All Terms

Source            DF     Seq SS    Adj SS    Adj MS        F       P
Part               9    97.8123   97.8123   10.8680   373.38   0.000
Operator           2     3.7413    3.7413    1.8706    64.27   0.000
Subcomponent       1     1.7160    1.7160    1.7160    58.96   0.000
Repeatability    107     3.1144    3.1144    0.0291
Total            119   106.3841
```

```
Alpha to remove interaction term = 0.25
Variance Components

                                    %Contribution
Source              VarComp         (of VarComp)
Total Gage R&R      0.089446              9.01
  Repeatability     0.029107              2.93
  Reproducibility   0.060339              6.08
    Operator        0.046038              4.64
    Subcomponent    0.014300              1.44
Part-To-Part        0.903244             90.99
  Part              0.903244             90.99
Total Variation     0.992689            100.00
```

```
Process tolerance = 8

Gage Evaluation
```

```
                                  Study Var   %Study Var   %Tolerance
Source             StdDev (SD)    (6 * SD)       (%SV)      (SV/Toler)
Total Gage R&R       0.299075      1.79445       30.02        22.43
  Repeatability      0.170608      1.02365       17.12        12.80
  Reproducibility    0.245639      1.47384       24.65        18.42
    Operator         0.214566      1.28739       21.54        16.09
    Subcomponent     0.119583      0.71750       12.00         8.97
Part-To-Part         0.950391      5.70235       95.39        71.28
  Part               0.950391      5.70235       95.39        71.28
Total Variation      0.996338      5.97803      100.00        74.73
```

```
Number of Distinct Categories = 4
```

According to the ANOVA Table, the Subcomponent has a very small p-value of 0.000. Therefore, the choice of subcomponent A or B does make a significant difference in the mean measurement. The final table notes that Subcomponent is responsible for a standard deviation of 0.1196, which is 12.00% of study variation and 8.97% of tolerance.

Another important feature of the expanded gage R&R analysis is the ability to handle unbalanced gage R&R studies. Typically, gage R&R studies are not designed to be unbalanced, but if one of the measured values is recorded incorrectly, corrupted, or lost, the remainder of the measurements become unbalanced. It is often impractical to retake a bad measurement, but analyzing the unbalanced dataset without the bad measurement is a practical alternative.

To see how this works, take any of the examples used in this chapter, delete one observation, and then analyze it again using the Gage R&R (Expanded) tool. The report is usually quite similar.

The expanded gage R&R analysis cannot calculate confidence intervals. But its capabilities to add variables to the model and to analyze unbalanced datasets are enormous benefits for practitioners.

10.6   Analyzing Agreement in Attribute Measurement Systems

From a statistical point of view, continuous, quantitative measurements are always better than attribute measurements because they provide more information. It is valuable to know that a part is comfortably inside tolerance limits, rather than just barely inside the limits. But does that value outweigh the added cost of a quantitative measurement?

Pass-fail or other attribute measurements are widely used in all industries because of cost and speed. In many cases, a quantitative measurement is simply not possible, while a functional gage can quickly indicate go or no-go status.

For attribute measurements, accuracy is measured by agreement with a master or reference measurement, and precision is measured by agreement between and within operators. An attribute agreement analysis assesses all aspects of agreement with a simple experiment.

To perform an attribute agreement analysis, select a large number of test items, including acceptable, unacceptable, and marginal cases. For measurements with more than two nominal or ordinal categories, choose some test items from each category. Test items should be approximately evenly divided between categories.

It is essential to establish a master or reference category for each test item. This is necessary to assess the accuracy of the measurement system. This can be established by a master inspector or by using some more expensive or elaborate measurement system.

Then, select a representative set of operators or appraisers to measure each part. Each appraiser will measure each test item at least two times, to provide measures of agreement between and within appraisers. The order of testing should be randomized, with items presented to each appraiser by someone else, so the appraiser does not realize when they are measuring the same item multiple times. All measurements ought to be performed under typical conditions, using the same people, equipment, environment, and procedures to be used in production.

 Minitab offers two options to set up and analyze an attribute agreement analysis. The MSA assistant, new in Minitab 16, offers simplified functions to prepare an attribute agreement worksheet in randomized order, and then to analyze the collected data in a predefined graphical format. These functions in the MSA assistant can handle any two-valued attribute system, such as pass/fail or go/no-go gaging. As an alternative, the Stat > Quality Tools menu has functions to prepare the data collection worksheet and analyze the study with more options. These functions can handle measurement systems with more than two categories for each test item.

As an example, Ruth works in a textile factory where she is investigating complaints with color and texture variations in cotton fabric. Each lot of fabric is visually assessed by a trained appraiser who judges the fabric for uniformity of color and texture before deciding "go" or "no-go." Before investigating how to improve uniformity, she is wisely checking the performance of the measurement system with an attribute agreement study.

For this study, she has selected 20 fabric swatches to use as test items, of which 9 are "go" and 11 are "no-go" according to a master inspector and company standards. Ruth randomizes the set of 20 swatches, so that items 1, 4, 6, 7, 10, 12, 14, 17, and 19 are "go" and the rest are "no-go."

To set up the worksheet for this study, Ruth selects Assistant > Measurement Systems Analysis (MSA) from the Minitab menu, and then selects Attribute Agreement Worksheet from the assistant. She then fills out the dialog as shown in Fig. 10-15. There are two options for specifying the number of test items and their reference values. Figure 10-15 illustrates the Enter in a table option. The other option is to enter item numbers and reference values in a worksheet, and then select Get from current worksheet in the dropdown box.

After clicking OK, Ruth sees a worksheet ready for data collection, with the order of measurements randomized. Ruth also has the one-time option to print data collection forms. The worksheet can be printed at any time to use for data collection.

The data collected by Ruth are in the Minitab sample data file Cotton.MTW. With this worksheet as the current worksheet, Ruth analyzes it by selecting Assistant > Measurement Systems Analysis (MSA) and then clicking the Attribute

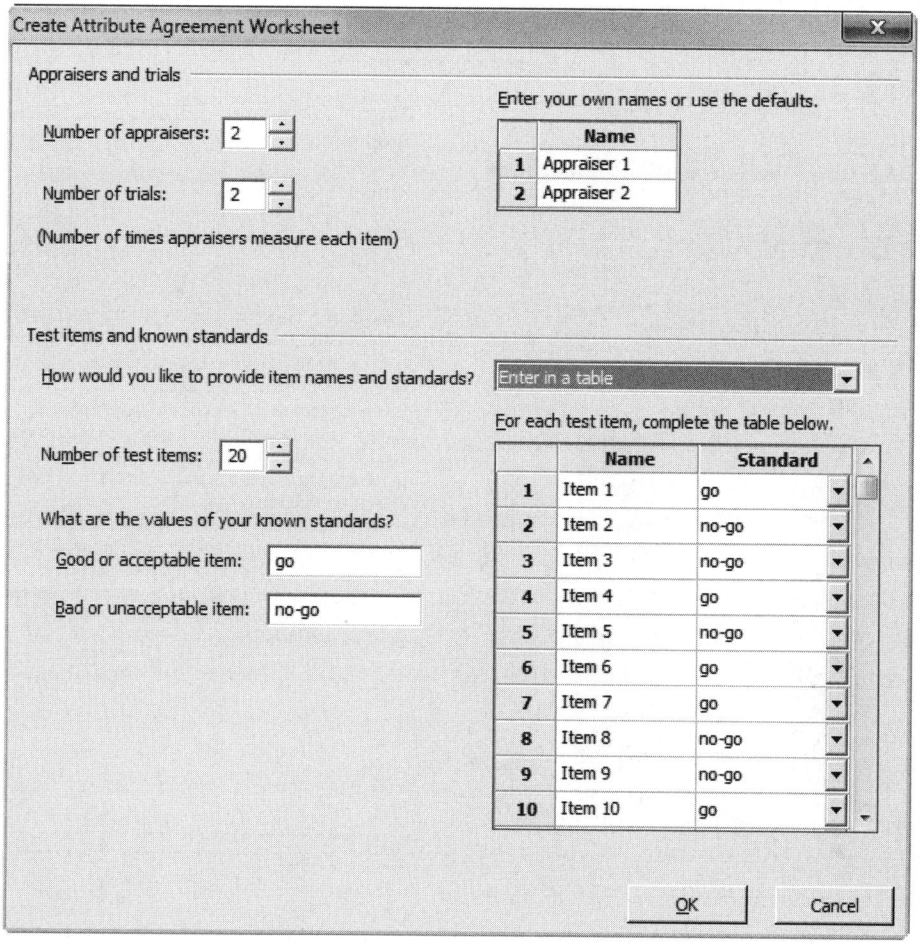

FIGURE 10-15 · Creating a worksheet for attribute agreement analysis.

Agreement Analysis option. She fills out the dialog with the following options:

- Appraisers: Appraiser
- Test items: Samples
- Appraisal results: Response
- Known standards: Standard
- Value of good or acceptable items: go

The report for this analysis is in the form of four graphs. The **Summary Report** is shown in Fig. 10-16. In the top left of this report, the overall accuracy is

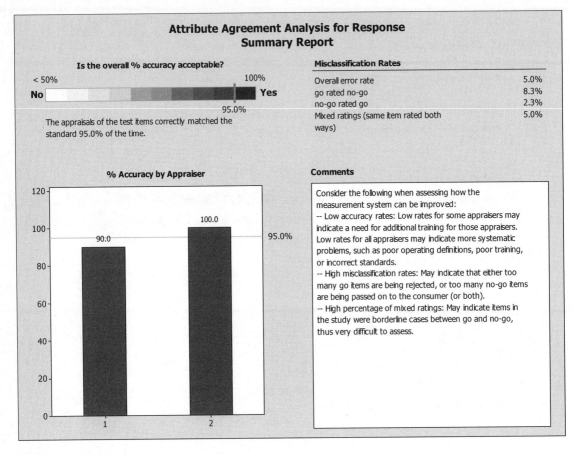

FIGURE 10-16 · Attribute agreement analysis summary report.

reported at 95%. The report explains this metric with these words: **The appraisals of the test items correctly matched the standard 95.0% of the time.** Below that, the graph shows that the two appraisers agreed with the standard 90% and 100% of the time. On the right is a table of misclassification rates and a block of comments. The **Comments** block may be edited by double-clicking on it.

The other three graphs are not shown here for space reasons, but they contain some important information for diagnosing and improving the measurement system. The **Accuracy Report** contains graphs of confidence intervals of the agreement percentages by appraiser and by go or no-go. The **Misclassification Report** shows graphically which items are most often misclassified, and which appraisers most often misclassified them. The **Report Card** contains informative comments about the mix of items and how accuracy and error rates are calculated.

Many attribute measurement systems use more than two categories, either nominal or ordinal. Here is the difference:

- **Nominal** data have no natural ordering of categories. In an animal shelter, one of the jobs is to assign a breed to each of the arriving stray dogs. Breed is a nominal characteristic with many categories.

- **Ordinal** data have categories with an order. In a dairy, eggs are sorted into size categories such as medium, large, and extra large. Since size categories have an order, this is an ordinal characteristic.

To analyze agreement in an attribute measurement system with more than two categories, use the functions in the Stat > Quality Tools menu instead of the MSA assistant.

Duncan manages a group of employees at an educational testing service whose job is to grade essays written by students taking the test. Each essay receives a grade of +2, +1, 0, –1, or –2. This is an ordinal scale with five categories. To assess agreement in the grading of essays, Duncan selects a set of 15 essays from last year and asks a panel of university English professors to assign a master grade based on written criteria of the testing service.

To perform the agreement study, Duncan will submit the essays in random order to five graders, including himself, and compare the assigned grades to the master grade. Since graders will remember essays they have seen before, it is not informative to have repeated grading of the same essay by the same grader. Therefore, this attribute agreement study will have a total of $15 \times 5 = 75$ grades.

To set up the worksheet for the study, Duncan selects Stat > Quality Tools > Create Attribute Agreement Analysis Worksheet. This dialog is very similar to the assistant dialog in Figure 10-15, except that this one allows any number of numeric or text values to be specified as a reference or standard value for each test item.

Grades and master grades are contained in the Minitab sample data file Essay. MTW. To analyze this data, Duncan selects Stat > Quality Tools > Attribute Agreement Analysis and fills out the dialog this way:

- Attribute column: Rating
- Samples: Sample
- Appraisers: Appraiser
- Known standard / attribute: Attribute
- Check the box labeled Categories of the attribute data are ordered

After clicking OK, Duncan sees a lengthy report in the Session window, with three sections: **Each Appraiser vs Standard, Between Appraisers**, and **All Appraisers vs Standard**. Here is a part of the report:

Each Appraiser vs Standard

```
Assessment Agreement
```

Appraiser	# Inspected	# Matched	Percent	95% CI
Duncan	15	8	53.33	(26.59, 78.73)
Hayes	15	13	86.67	(59.54, 98.34)
Holmes	15	15	100.00	(81.90, 100.00)
Montgomery	15	15	100.00	(81.90, 100.00)
Simpson	15	14	93.33	(68.05, 99.83)

Matched: Appraiser's assessment across trials agrees with the known standard.

```
Fleiss' Kappa Statistics
```

Appraiser	Response	Kappa	SE Kappa	Z	P(vs > 0)
Duncan	-2	0.58333	0.258199	2.25924	0.0119
	-1	0.16667	0.258199	0.64550	0.2593
	0	0.44099	0.258199	1.70796	0.0438
	1	0.44099	0.258199	1.70796	0.0438
	2	0.42308	0.258199	1.63857	0.0507
	Overall	0.41176	0.130924	3.14508	0.0008
Hayes	-2	0.62963	0.258199	2.43855	0.0074
	-1	0.81366	0.258199	3.15131	0.0008
	0	1.00000	0.258199	3.87298	0.0001
	1	0.76000	0.258199	2.94347	0.0016
	2	0.81366	0.258199	3.15131	0.0008
	Overall	0.82955	0.134164	6.18307	0.0000
Holmes	-2	1.00000	0.258199	3.87298	0.0001
	-1	1.00000	0.258199	3.87298	0.0001
	0	1.00000	0.258199	3.87298	0.0001
	1	1.00000	0.258199	3.87298	0.0001
	2	1.00000	0.258199	3.87298	0.0001
	Overall	1.00000	0.131305	7.61584	0.0000
Montgomery	-2	1.00000	0.258199	3.87298	0.0001
	-1	1.00000	0.258199	3.87298	0.0001
	0	1.00000	0.258199	3.87298	0.0001
	1	1.00000	0.258199	3.87298	0.0001
	2	1.00000	0.258199	3.87298	0.0001
	Overall	1.00000	0.131305	7.61584	0.0000
Simpson	-2	1.00000	0.258199	3.87298	0.0001
	-1	1.00000	0.258199	3.87298	0.0001
	0	0.81366	0.258199	3.15131	0.0008
	1	0.81366	0.258199	3.15131	0.0008
	2	1.00000	0.258199	3.87298	0.0001
	Overall	0.91597	0.130924	6.99619	0.0000

```
Kendall's Correlation Coefficient

Appraiser       Coef    SE Coef         Z        P
Duncan       0.87506   0.192450   4.49744   0.0000
Hayes        0.94871   0.192450   4.88016   0.0000
Holmes       1.00000   0.192450   5.14667   0.0000
Montgomery   1.00000   0.192450   5.14667   0.0000
Simpson      0.96629   0.192450   4.97151   0.0000
```

Attribute agreement analysis involves some statistics with unusual names. The easiest way to look up the meaning and interpretation of these statistics is to click somewhere in the report in the Session window and then visit the StatGuide by clicking the ▣ button.

At the top of the report, the `Assessment Agreement` table lists the percentage of assessments where each appraiser agrees with the standard, with a confidence interval. Only Holmes and Montgomery had perfect agreement in this study.

In the middle section of the report, `Fleiss' Kappa Statistic` is a measure of agreement between each appraiser and the standard. A value of 1 indicates perfect agreement, while a value of 0 corresponds to a totally random assignment of grades. The p-value indicates whether there is significant evidence that an appraiser is any better than simply assigning a random grade. If the p-value is small, less than 0.05, this indicates strong evidence that the grader is better than no grader. For this dataset, Duncan and Hayes have a concerning amount of disagreement with the standard for some grade levels.

At the bottom of the report is a table of `Kendall's Correlation Coefficients`. A correlation coefficient of 1 indicates perfect agreement with the standard, across all grade levels. If the p-value in the right column of the table is small, this indicates strong evidence that the appraiser is better than randomly assigning grades. In this case, all five appraisers pass this test. The p-value does not indicate how good the appraisers are, only that they are not bad.

Minitab also prepares a graph showing how well each appraiser agrees with the standard, with 95% confidence intervals. This graph is seen in Fig. 10-17.

Whether the graders are performing acceptably is a decision for the manager of the department, who happens to be Duncan. He laughs off his own poor performance by quoting the old adage: "Those who can't do, manage!"

10.7   Bias and Repeatability of Attribute Measurements

Go/no-go gaging is frequently used because it is fast, inexpensive, and easy. In a machine shop, hole diameters are measured with plug gages, one at the lower limit, which should fit, and one at the upper limit, which should not fit. To

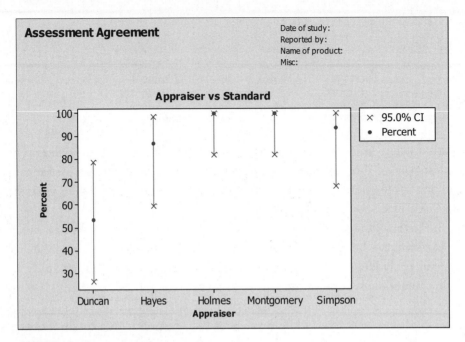

FIGURE 10-17 · Assessment agreement plot.

qualify an attribute gage used in place of a variable measurement, one needs to know if the attribute gage is biased, and if the gage is repeatable enough. This form of attribute gage study has been described in AIAG (2002) and is familiarly known as the "analytic method."

To measure the bias and repeatability of an attribute gage requires measuring a set of test items with a range of closely spaced reference values. The test items should include at least one which is always accepted by the gage, at least one which is always rejected, and several intermediate values. Each test item must have a reference value established as accurately as possible. The attribute gage is used to test each test item many times, preferably at least 20 times. As always, randomization is best, with a second person presenting test items to an appraiser who does not know which test item is which.

The Minitab sample data file Length.MTW is an example of results from an attribute gage study. This example involves eight test items with reference values listed in column C2 Reference. Column C3 Length contains the number of times, out of 20 replications, that the attribute gage accepted the test item. The lower tolerance limit for this characteristic is 0.7020.

To analyze this dataset, select Stat > Quality Tools > Gage Study > Attribute Gage Study (Analytic Method). Fill out the dialog as follows:

- Part numbers: Part
- Reference values: Reference
- Summarized counts: Length
- Number of trials: 20
- Attribute label: "Acceptance"
- Lower limit: .7020

The entirely graphical report from this analysis appears in Fig. 10-18. The two graphs plot the probability of acceptance versus reference value. The graph on the left has a nonlinear scale chosen so the points should line up along a straight line. The graph on the right plots the fitted model along a linear scale.

In the text on the right side is a report from a hypothesis test for significant bias. The p-value for this test is 0.11. Because this is greater than 0.05, there is not strong evidence of a significant bias.

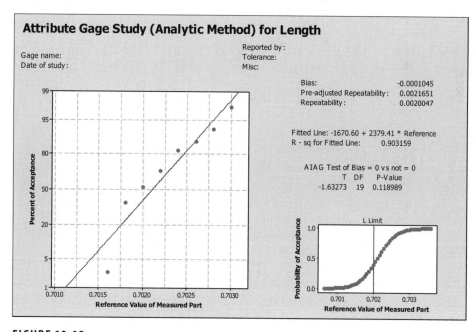

FIGURE 10-18 · Attribute gage study by analytic method.

The repeatability of this attribute gage is estimated to be 0.0020047. This may or may not be a good value. It would have to be interpreted in light of either process variation or the tolerance width to know whether this is acceptable.

10.8 Find Out More

Not as many authoritative books have been written about measurement systems analysis as about other Minitab application areas. The most widely respected is Wheeler (2006). The author of this book, Don Wheeler, has long been an influential figure in all areas of statistical tools for quality control. A recent column by Wheeler (2011) expresses some strong opinions about which MSA metrics are appropriate and which are not.

This chapter illustrated Minitab tools for assessing the accuracy and precision of measurement systems for a variety of common applications, and even a few uncommon ones. The next chapter continues the discussion of quality control applications of Minitab tools with control charts, a fundamental set of tools to assure the ongoing control and stability of process performance.

QUIZ

1. The variation between operators when measuring the same parts is called what?

    A. Repeatability

    B. Reliability

    C. Reproducibility

    D. Replicability

2. Suppose a gage R&R study involves 8 parts and 4 operators, where each operator measures the same 8 parts 3 times for each part. What type of gage R&R study is this?

    A. Crossed

    B. Nested

    C. Expanded

    D. AIAG

3. Which metric in a gage R&R analysis report is the best indication of how well the measurement system can distinguish between acceptable parts and unacceptable parts?

    A. Gage R&R as a % of study variation

    B. Gage R&R as % contribution

    C. Gage R&R as a % of tolerance

    D. Number of distinct categories

4. Suppose solder joints are determined to be acceptable or unacceptable using a visual inspection. Which Minitab tool(s) can be used to determine how well the inspectors agree with each other and with a master inspector?

    A. Attribute agreement analysis in the Stat > Quality Tools menu.

    B. Attribute agreement analysis in the MSA assistant.

    C. Either A or B will work.

    D. Attribute gage study (analytic method).

5. The brewmaster at Ruby's Root Beer measures the "rootiness" of the product on a scale with 7 categories from 1 to 7. What type of measurement is this?

    A. Variable

    B. Ordinal

    C. Nominal

    D. Ratio

For questions 6 and 7, perform a type 1 gage analysis on the data in the Minitab sample data file Shaft.MTW. For this analysis, the reference value is 12.300, and the tolerance upper limit – lower limit is 0.15.

6. Is there a significant bias in the measurements? How do you know?

7. What percentage of the tolerance width is consumed by repeatability and bias of the measurement system? According to typical rules of thumb, is this measurement system acceptable according to this metric?

For questions 8–10, perform a gage R&R analysis on the data in the Minitab sample data file Thickness.MTW. For this analysis, the tolerance limits are 0.0 and 2.0. No historical information is available regarding the standard deviation.

8. Is gage R&R variation as a percentage of tolerance in the good, marginal, or unacceptable range?

9. Do the Xbar or R charts provide any reasons for concern with this measurement system?

10. Does this measurement system have a significant interaction between parts and operators? How do you know? What graph best illustrates this interaction? (Hint: This question cannot be answered from the reports generated by the MSA assistant.)

chapter 11

Control Charting

Statistical process control (SPC) is the application of statistical tools to control variation in all kinds of processes. Control charts are the predominant statistical tool used in SPC. A control chart is a type of run chart or time-series chart with horizontal lines that allow the viewer to rapidly detect when the process changes its mean or standard deviation. Control charts are easy to create and easy to interpret by people with no other statistical training. Because of their simplicity and the wide availability of SPC software, control charts are among the world's most popular statistical tools.

CHAPTER OBJECTIVES

Here's what you'll learn in this chapter:

- How to select, create, and interpret control charts for subgrouped data
- How to select, create, and interpret control charts for individual data
- How to select, create, and interpret control charts for attribute data

Minitab offers two routes to create control charts. The Stat > Control Charts menu contains functions to create all kinds of commonly used control charts, plus several uncommon charts. A new feature of Minitab 16 is the control charts assistant, which provides an interactive flow chart for selecting the most appropriate control chart, plus informative reports in graphical format. The control charts assistant includes the most commonly used control charts, and will be sufficient for most Minitab users.

Another new feature of Minitab 16 is the DMAIC menu, available if the DMAIC profile is active. Most of the commonly used control charts are available through the Control menu of the DMAIC toolbar in addition to the Stat > Control Charts menu.

Control charts fall into two general families. One family is for continuous, numerical measurement data, sometimes called variables data. The other family is for attribute data, specifically counts of events. Before introducing specific control charts, the first section of this chapter discusses general rules and guidelines applicable to all control charts.

11.1   Making Decisions with Control Charts

Traditionally, a process is judged to be acceptable based only on tolerance or specification limits. If an item produced falls outside tolerance limits, the process must be corrected somehow so that all items are within tolerance limits.

When SPC is implemented, a process is judged based on its history of process performance. A control chart detects when the process mean or standard deviation changes significantly. When there is no change, the process is said to be in control. When the process mean or standard deviation changes, the process is said to be out of control.

For an example, Fig. 11-1 is a control chart prepared by Minitab. This type of chart is called an Xbar-S Chart, because the top part charts the mean, and the bottom part charts the standard deviation. The upper and lower horizontal lines on each chart are called control limits, which are set at three standard deviations on either side of the mean of plotted values. The middle line is a center line, at the mean of plotted values. Minitab draws control limits in red, and the center line in green.

In Fig. 11-1, the process is in control for first half of the chart, with all points inside the control limits. Then, point 17 is above the upper control limit on the Xbar Chart, indicating that the process mean has increased. Later,

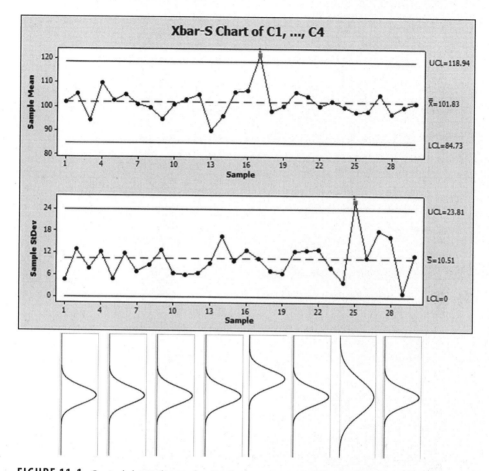

FIGURE 11-1 · Control charts detect changes in the process mean and standard deviation.

point 25 is above the upper control limit on the S Chart, indicating that the process variation has increased. The distribution curves drawn at the bottom of Fig. 11-1 are not part of the control chart. These curves represent the process distribution over time, showing when it is stable, and when it changes.

By default, Minitab highlights points outside the control limits with a red, square symbol, with a tiny 1 next to the symbol. The 1 indicates an out-of-control condition according to test 1 out of 8 tests which Minitab can apply to the control chart. To see a list of these eight tests, select Tools > Options to bring up the Options dialog. Click Control Charts and Quality Tools and then Tests to see all the tests, as shown in Fig. 11-2. Each of the tests is controlled by a parameter K, which may be adjusted in this dialog.

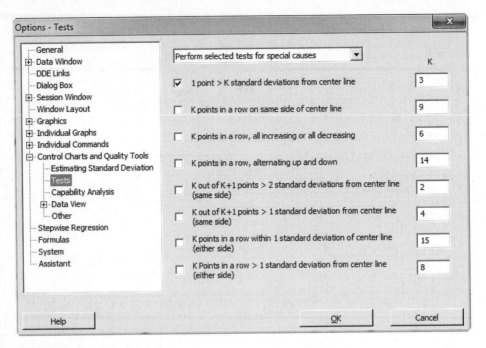

FIGURE 11-2 • Tests for control charts.

When a control chart shows an out-of-control condition, this indicates a significant shift of some kind in process performance. It is a sign that some action is needed to identify the root cause of the shift. Usually, the shift is a bad thing, when it increases variation or shifts the mean closer to a tolerance limit; this kind of shift needs to be diagnosed quickly and the root cause eliminated to return the process to a state of control. Sometimes, the shift is a good thing, when it decreases variation or shifts the mean in a good direction; this kind of shift needs to be diagnosed quickly and the root cause made a permanent part of the process. In either case, an appropriate control chart indicates an out-of-control condition as soon as it becomes statistically significant.

Control limits are generally based on the first 20 to 30 points plotted on the chart, and the limits remain the same as more points are added to the plot. When the plot becomes crowded and a new plot is started, the same control limits are carried forward onto the new plot. If the process changes, intentionally or otherwise, and the change is permanent, new control limits are calculated 20 to 30 points after the change. For every Minitab control chart, one can choose whether to calculate control limits from the data provided, or to enter previously calculated control limits.

Sometimes, one or more points among the first 20 to 30 points are outside the calculated control limits. Minitab offers the option to exclude these points from the calculation of control limits. If the out-of-control points represent a special cause of variation, and that cause of variation has been eliminated, it is fair to exclude those points from the calculation of control limits.

Like all Minitab tools, data for a control chart must be arranged in columns of a Minitab worksheet before creating the control chart. If the computer with Minitab is placed at the work station where measurements are recorded, the worker who makes the measurements can key them directly into the worksheet. All Minitab control charts can be set to automatically update when new measurements are available.

Some measurement systems automatically record data in a database or file of some other format. If these files are ODBC-compliant, and most are, Minitab can extract a copy of selected data from the database and place the data in a worksheet. To do this, select File > Query Database (ODBC) from the Minitab menu. To automatically query an ODBC database requires writing a Minitab macro to perform this operation either when Minitab is started or when requested. Macros are beyond the scope of this book, but the Minitab help file and the www.minitab.com Web site are good resources for those who want to develop macros.

Implementing SPC with control charts on all critical process parameters and following the operational guidelines in this section provides many benefits. Where control charts are used to monitor processes, variation decreases over time, and customer satisfaction improves. When the process distribution is comfortably inside specification limits, control charts can identify shifts in the process so they can be corrected, before the shifts cause any unacceptable parts to be produced.

11.2   Creating Control Charts for Subgrouped Data

A subgroup is a set of parts manufactured consecutively, and taken to represent the performance of the process at one point in time. When a process creates many parts, it is common to implement SPC by collecting and measuring one subgroup of several parts at regular intervals. This strategy is called rational subgrouping. If done properly, the variation within a subgroup represents the short-term variation of the process, and the interval between subgroups is chosen so that shifts are detected by the control chart before creating major problems.

Subgrouping is not appropriate for all processes. If the process produces only one measurement per day, or per batch of material, then it is more appropriate to use a control chart for individual data. These are discussed in the next section.

When subgroups are appropriate, a control chart for subgroups provides benefits over a control chart for individuals. The greatest benefit is more power to detect smaller shifts in the process. A secondary benefit is greater robustness to nonnormal distributions. Standard control charts are designed for normally distributed data. If the distribution is not normal, the chart may have a much larger or smaller rate of false alarms than is desirable. However, subgroups of nonnormal data behave much more like normal data than do individual values. Because of the central limit theorem, control charts for subgroups work well for nonnormal data, especially as the subgroup size increases.

The two most commonly used control charts for subgrouped data are the Xbar-R chart and Xbar-S chart. The difference between these charts is the bottom, variation graph, in which the points represent either subgroup ranges or subgroup standard deviations. Minitab offers other types of charts which are used less often.

For example, Bob works in an injection molding plant where he is monitoring the manufacture of a new part. Bob measures a critical dimension on five consecutively manufactured parts every two hours. The Minitab sample data file InjectionMolding.MTW contains Bob's measurements for 20 subgroups, which is a total of 100 parts.

To create a control chart, Bob selects Assistant > Control Charts from the Minitab menu. The control charts assistant displays a flow chart, as seen in Fig. 11-3. In the flow chart, click on any diamond-shaped decision box for an explanation of each decision. If you know which type of chart you want, simply click on that chart at the bottom of the chart. For a list of practical advice on collecting data and interpreting the chart, click the *more...* hyperlink below the box for each type of chart.

For this example, the first decision is between continuous and attribute data. These injection molding measurements are continuous. The second decision is between subgrouped and individual data. This dataset is organized into subgroups of five measurements each. The third decision concerns the size of subgroup. Since these subgroups are of size 5 which is less than 8, the Xbar-R chart is recommended.

After Bob selects the Xbar-R Chart button, he fills out the dialog this way:

- He selects Data are in one column for all subgroups in the first dropdown box.

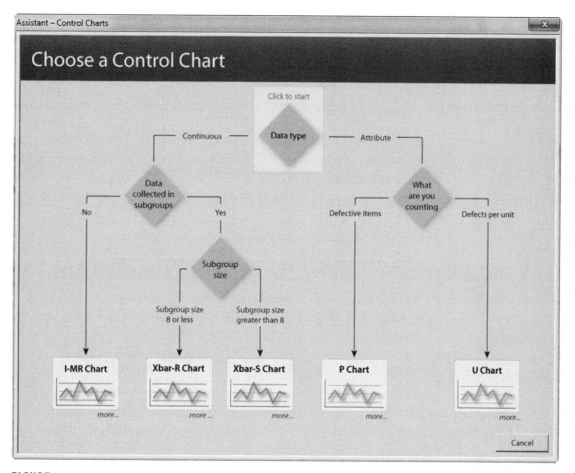

FIGURE 11-3 · Control charts assistant.

- Data column: Parts.
- Subgroup size: 5.
- In the How will you determine the control limits and center line? dropdown box, Bob selects Estimate from the data.

At this point, Minitab does a preliminary test of the dataset and finds that three of the points will be outside control limits. These are listed in a table in the dialog, as shown in Fig. 11-4.

At this point, Minitab offers the option to omit any of these three subgroups from the calculation of the control limits and center line. Since Bob does not know what might be causing these points to be out of control yet, he does not omit any of these for the first control chart. If later he decides that any of these

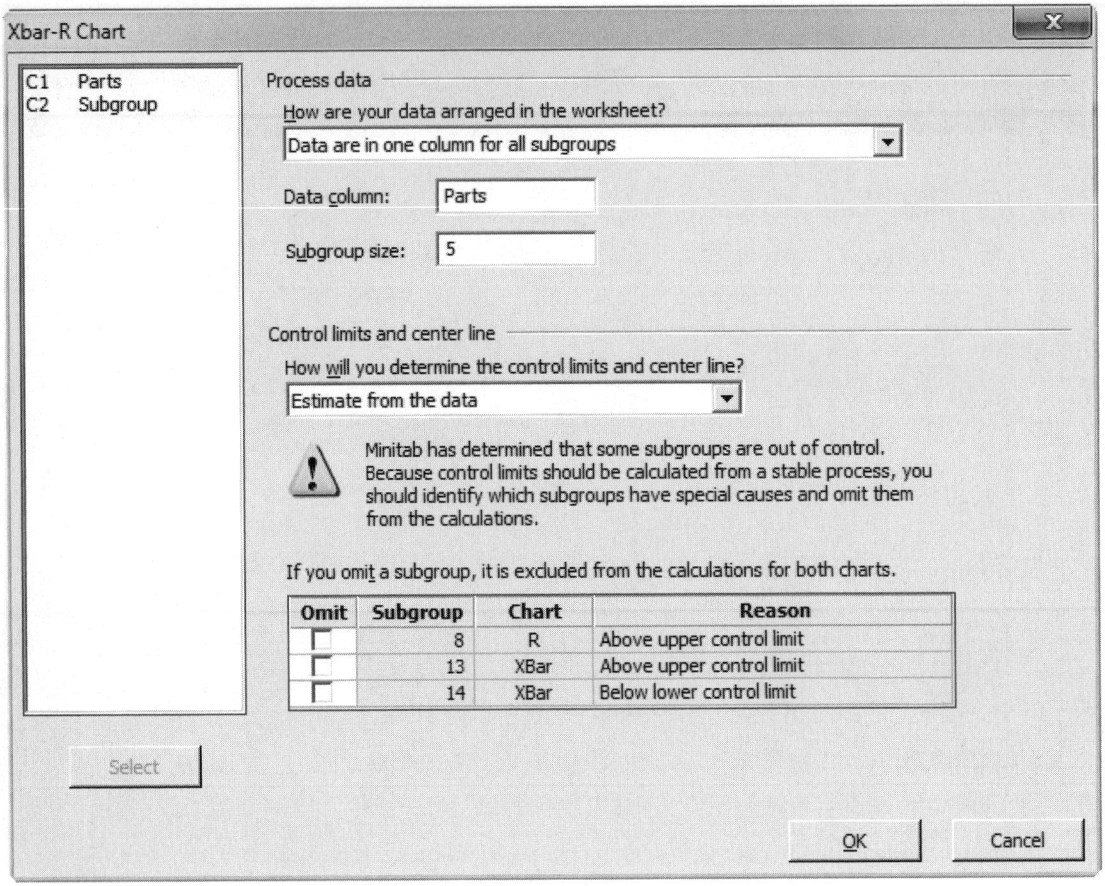

Xbar-R Chart

C1   Parts
C2   Subgroup

Process data

How are your data arranged in the worksheet?

Data are in one column for all subgroups

Data column: Parts

Subgroup size: 5

Control limits and center line

How will you determine the control limits and center line?

Estimate from the data

⚠ Minitab has determined that some subgroups are out of control. Because control limits should be calculated from a stable process, you should identify which subgroups have special causes and omit them from the calculations.

If you omit a subgroup, it is excluded from the calculations for both charts.

Omit	Subgroup	Chart	Reason
☐	8	R	Above upper control limit
☐	13	XBar	Above upper control limit
☐	14	XBar	Below lower control limit

Select

OK   Cancel

FIGURE 11-4 · Xbar-R Chart assistant dialog.

points represent special causes of variation and should be removed, he can easily create another control chart.

After Bob clicks OK, Minitab creates three new graphs. The top graph, labeled Summary Report, is shown here as Fig. 11-5. The two parts of the control chart are shown on the right side of the report with the Xbar Chart on top and the R Chart on the bottom. Two of the 20 points are outside the control limits on the Xbar Chart, as is one point on the R Chart. The top left portion of this report shows that 10% of the points on the Xbar Chart are outside the control limits. For a process in control, this percentage should be much smaller, theoretically 0.27% on average. The bottom left section of the Summary Report is a comment box with automatically written comments. Double-click on this box to edit its contents.

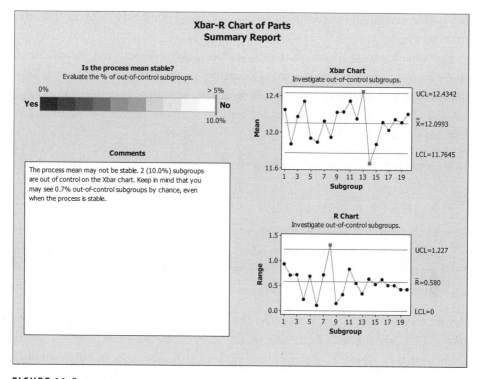

FIGURE 11-5 • Xbar-R Summary Report.

The Stability Report graph, not shown here, contains a more traditional presentation of the Xbar Chart and R Chart, filling the width of the graph. Below the control chart is a list of points which are outside the control limits.

The Report Card graph, not shown here, provides advice and warnings specific to this dataset. In this example, the Report Card contains a warning about points outside the control limits, but it also notes that the sample size is adequate, and there is no evidence of correlation between data points. This correlation test is automatically performed by the control charts assistant, but it is unavailable in the Stat > Control Charts menu. To estimate the correlation of a dataset with itself, known as autocorrelation, use Stat > Time Series > Autocorrelation.

In Minitab 16, the control charts assistant provides many benefits, including the pre-screening of points outside the control limits, automatic correlation testing, and an informative report. But the assistant does not offer a lot of options. The Stat > Control Charts menu provides more options to handle a wider variety of situations.

For example, suppose Bob wanted to apply more tests for out-of-control conditions. Minitab can apply eight different tests, as listed in Fig. 11-2. Only the traditional menu functions can apply any out of control tests other than the first one.

Bob decides to prepare an Xbar-S chart to compare with the Xbar-R chart made by the assistant. He selects Stat > Control Charts > Variables Charts for Subgroups > Xbar-S. If the DMAIC profile is active, he could also select Control > Variables Data > Data in Subgroups > Xbar-S Chart from the DMAIC toolbar. He fills out the dialog as follows:

- Bob selects All observations for a chart are in one column: in the dropdown box.
- He then enters Parts in the box below the dropdown box.
- In the Subgroup sizes box, Bob enters Subgroup. Unlike the assistant, this dialog provides the option to either enter a number or use a column with identifiers for each subgroup. This option allows for the possibility of subgroups with different sizes.

Before creating the chart, Bob clicks the Xbar-S Options button. In the Options dialog, he clicks the Tests tab, and selects Perform all tests for special causes in the dropdown box. Figure 11-6 shows the finished chart. The sizes and styles of lines and symbols in this chart and many others have been changed for legibility.

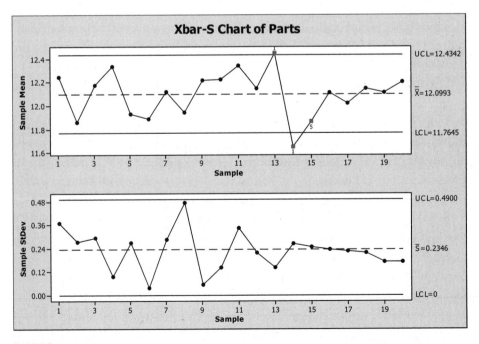

FIGURE 11-6 · Xbar-S chart.

With all tests enabled, Minitab identified three points out of control. Why? These details are printed in the Session window:

Test Results for Xbar Chart of Parts

```
TEST 1. One point more than 3.00 standard deviations from center line.
Test Failed at points:   13, 14

TEST 5. 2 out of 3 points more than 2 standard deviations from center
       line (on one side of CL).
Test Failed at points:   13, 15

TEST 6. 4 out of 5 points more than 1 standard deviation from center
       line (on one side of CL).
Test Failed at points:   13

* WARNING * If graph is updated with new data, the results above may no
          * longer be correct.
```

In addition to the two points outside of control limits (TEST 1), Minitab found that 2 out of 3 points are more than 2 standard deviations from the center line on one side of the center line (TEST 5). This test failed at point 13, because both points 11 and 13 are beyond 2 standard deviations above the center line. This test also failed at point 15, because both points 14 and 15 are beyond 2 standard deviations below the center line. Also, TEST 6 failed at point 13. On the chart, Minitab adds labels indicating the test number. When a point fails multiple tests, only the first test failed is listed on the chart.

Still Struggling

With eight tests, each of which is adjustable, the choice of tests can be bewildering. The eight tests in Minitab are based on the Nelson rules, listed by Lloyd Nelson (1984) in the *Journal of Quality Technology*. Generally it is unwise to use all these rules at the same time. Each rule has some probability of false alarms, that is, indicating changes when nothing changed. Enabling too many rules leads to frequent false alarms and disrespect for the control chart. Each author has their own advice about which rules to follow on which charts. Rather than adding another minority opinion to the mix, here is a simple approach: Always use the first rule, and none of the others. After you see the chart, if you suspect a non-random pattern, then enable the appropriate rule for that pattern. If the rule signals an out-of-control condition, this validates your suspicion.

After a control chart has been created, Minitab can automatically update it as new data becomes available. To enable this feature, right-click anywhere on the control chart and select Update Graph Automatically. This automatic update feature is only available for control charts created using the Stat > Control Charts menu, not the control charts assistant.

To try out automatic updating on Bob's InjectionMolding.MTW dataset, enter any five numbers at the bottom of the Parts column, for instance: 11, 11, 12, 12, 12. If the Subgroup column is used to identify subgroups, you must also enter 21, 21, 21, 21, 21 at the bottom of that column. Now the Xbar-S Chart will contain a twenty-first point. Using the values listed here, this new point should be outside the control limits on both the Xbar Chart and the S Chart.

If you followed the steps in this example, you will also note that the control limits changed with the addition of new points. Inconveniently, there is no way to change the way control limits are calculated after the chart is created. This option must be specified before creating the chart.

Suppose Bob wants to change his chart to calculate control limits from subgroups 1–12 and 16–20, omitting the problematic subgroups 13–15 and the new data in subgroup 21. To do this, he recalls the Xbar-S Chart dialog by clicking the 🖳 button. He clicks the Xbar-S Options button. In the Estimate tab, Bob selects Use the following subgroups when estimating parameters in the dropdown box, and then enters 1:12 16:20 in the box below the dropdown box. Now the completed chart will have control limits that do not change as new points are added to the chart.

Comparing Figs. 11-5 and 11-6, it is easy to see that subgroup 8 is above the upper control limit on the R Chart but not on the S Chart. The range and standard deviation are different statistics, so the two charts have slight differences. Which one is more appropriate?

The decision between an Xbar-R chart and an Xbar-S chart is often framed as dependent on sample size, as it is in the Minitab control charts assistant. However, opinions vary on this point. In particular, Sleeper (2006) argues that the range chart is an anachronism from the days before computers. When the subgroup size is 2, the R chart and the S chart are identical. With any subgroup size greater than 2, the S chart always has more power to detect a shift in standard deviation than the R chart.

Creating both R and S charts from the same dataset frequently leads to different conclusions. For the InjectionMolding.MTW dataset, subgroup 8 is out of control on the R chart, but inside the control limits on the S chart. For other datasets, points may be in control on the R chart and out of control on the S chart. Both charts are estimates based on incomplete information, so either chart could be wrong.

The range reflects only two numbers in the subgroup, while the standard deviation uses all the values in the subgroup and is the best estimate of short-term process variation at that time. For this reason, Sleeper argues that the S chart is always preferable.

Rational subgrouping is based on the idea that the variation within a subgroup represents short-term process variation. Control charts for subgrouped data usually use within-subgroup variation to establish control limits for the Xbar Chart. For some processes, this practice is neither practical nor appropriate. Short-term process variation is supposed to represent the behavior of a stable process over a short time. For many reasons, variation within subgroups may include too little or too much variation to fairly represent short-term variation.

One such situation occurs when tool wear causes an intentional drift in the process until a tool is changed to reset the process. In this situation, within-subgroup variation will be too small, the control limits on the Xbar Chart will be too narrow, and out-of-control conditions will be signaled too often. A different situation occurs when multiple process streams with different means are combined into each subgroup. In a manufacturing context, one usually wants multiple process streams to behave the same, and this situation must be corrected. Sometimes, correcting this variation between process streams is not possible. Having too much variation in each subgroup causes control limits on the Xbar Chart to be too wide, and real process shifts are never indicated.

For these situations, Minitab offers a specialized chart, called an I-MR-R/S chart, which separates within-subgroup from between-subgroup variation. In this chart, the control limits on the mean section of the chart are based on the variation between subgroup means, not the variation within a subgroup.

To see how this works, open the Minitab sample data file Bloodsugar.MTW. This file contains daily measurements of blood glucose for 9 patients over 20 days. Try first making an Xbar-S chart using the measurements in the Glucoselevel column, with subgroups specified by the Reading column. None of the subgroups are outside control limits on either chart.

But this chart is inappropriate for a process like this. Different people have different metabolisms, so it is reasonable to expect a wide variation between people. Unlike a manufacturing scenario, it is not possible to adjust the people to have the same glucose. Therefore, it is not appropriate to use a traditional control chart, which uses within-subgroup variation to detect significant changes between readings.

Instead, select Stat > Control Charts > Variable Charts for Subgroups > I-MR-R/S (Between/Within). In the dialog, select All observations for a chart in one column:

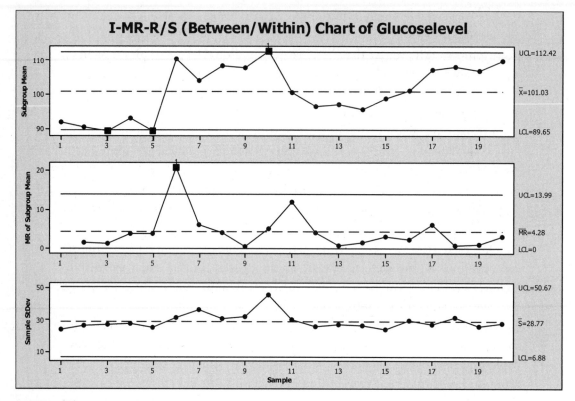

FIGURE 11-7 • I-MR-R/S chart.

and enter Glucoselevel in the box below the dropdown box. Enter Reading in the Subgroup sizes box. The finished chart is shown in Fig. 11-7.

With three parts, this chart has an unfamiliar appearance. The top part charts the process mean, and the bottom two parts chart two aspects of variation. Here are some more details:

- The **Subgroup Mean** chart plots the subgroup means over all 20 subgroups. The control limits for this chart are set by the between-subgroup variation, instead of the usual within-subgroup variation. If the process is stable over days, almost all points should be within control limits. In this example, three days are outside control limits, indicating significant day-to-day shifts in mean glucose.

- The **MR of Subgroup Mean** chart plots the moving range of subgroup means, which is the absolute difference between consecutive subgroup means. This chart expresses the variation between subgroups, or between days in this case. One day, day 6, saw a very significant shift from the previous day.

- The **Sample StDev** chart plots the subgroup standard deviations, which is the within-subgroup variation. Depending on subgroup size and options set in the Estimate tab, Minitab plots either range or standard deviation on this third graph.

This I-MR-R/S (Between/Within) control chart provides a powerful tool to detect changes in processes where subgroups are not as homogenous as one would like.

11.3   Creating Control Charts for Individual Data

Many processes do not produce parts fast enough to be practical candidates for subgrouping. In these situations, the standard control chart is the I-MR or Individuals – Moving Range chart. Like the Xbar-R and Xbar-S charts, the I-MR chart has two parts, with the top part representing the process mean and the bottom part representing variation. Unlike the subgrouped charts, the I-MR chart estimates short-term variation using moving ranges of the individual values. Moving range is the absolute difference between consecutive values, which is the best available estimate of short-term process variation.

For example, Frieda is a chemist at a plant manufacturing dishwasher detergent. She measures and monitors the pH of each batch of detergent. Large batches are produced once every four hours, and each batch provides only one measurement of pH. Subgroups are not practical for this situation, so Frieda decides to prepare an I-MR control chart.

Frieda's data is stored in the Minitab sample data file Detergent.MTW. With this worksheet open and current, Frieda uses the control charts assistant to select an I-MR chart.

In the I-MR Chart dialog, Frieda enters pH in the Data column field. In the How will you determine the control limits and center line? dropdown box, she selects Estimate from the data. The assistant presents a warning that one point is outside control limits, but for now, Frieda ignores this warning and creates the control chart as is, using all points to calculate control limits. Figure 11-8 shows the I-MR Chart Summary Report from the control charts assistant.

Like other assistant summary reports, this report shows the control chart on the right, along with an overall metric on the top left, and a comment block on the bottom left. The two other graphs created at the same time include a Stability Report with the chart by itself, and a Report Card with advice and warnings.

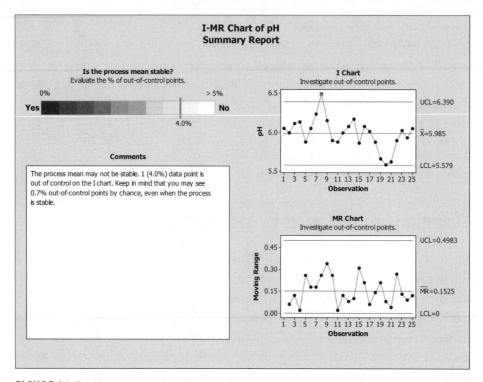

FIGURE 11-8 • I-MR Chart Summary Report.

This control chart shows Frieda that batch 8 had an unusually high pH. Since no points are outside control limits on the MR Chart, there is no strong evidence of changes in variation.

Because of its simplicity and applicability to an enormous class of processes, the I-MR chart is surely the most common type of control chart in the world. But this chart does not offer any protection from nonnormal distributions as do the charts for subgrouped data. If the natural process distribution is skewed, perhaps with a physical lower boundary of zero, the I-MR chart will not work well.

When normally distributed values are plotted on an I-MR chart, approximately 0.27% of the points, or 1 out of 370 points, will naturally be outside one of the control limits on the I chart. But a skewed distribution will generally result in many more points outside the control limits and an excessive rate of false alarms.

When a distribution is skewed, it is critical to decide whether the skewness represents natural process variation or an out-of-control condition. If the skewness is a sign of a problem, the problem must be recognized and corrected; using a control chart designed for skewed data will hide the problem so it can never be solved. If the skewness is a natural part of process variation, then the chart should be modified to deal with skewness without signaling an out-of-control condition.

Typically skewed datasets include measurements of time, money, and geometric characteristics that are defined to be non-negative. For an example of the latter category, open the Minitab sample data file Tiles.MTW. This file contains 100 measurements of warping in floor tiles. Warping is defined to be the distance between the highest point and the lowest point on the surface of the tile, so it can never be negative. Figure 11-9 is a histogram of this dataset, showing its obvious skew to the right.

Suppose we decide that this process is naturally skewed, so a control chart should not signal too many out-of-control conditions just because of this skew. A normal I-MR chart made from this data, not shown here, finds two points above the upper control limit on the Individual Value chart and two points above the upper control limit on the Moving Range chart. If this 4% false alarm rate is too high, than an alternative control chart is required.

First introduced in Chapter 4, the Box–Cox transformation is a family of transformations which are often used to transform skewed data into approximately normally distributed data. Box–Cox transformations are power transformations of the form $Y = X^\lambda$, when $\lambda \neq 0$ and $Y = \ln(X)$ when $\lambda = 0$.

Minitab offers a Box-Cox Transformation function in the Control Charts menu. This function is designed to handle either subgrouped or individual data and to find the most appropriate transformation.

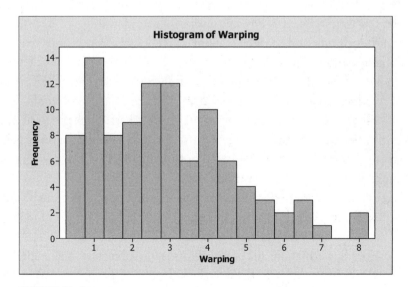

FIGURE 11-9 · Histogram of tile warping.

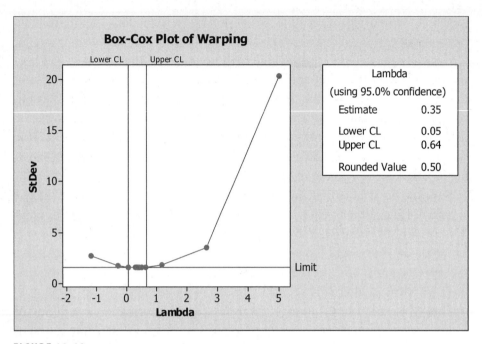

FIGURE 11-10 · Box–Cox transformation of warping data.

To find the best Box–Cox transformation for the Tiles.MTW dataset, select Stat > Control Charts > Box-Cox Transformation. Enter Warping as the data column and 1 for the Sample size. Click OK and a plot appears, as shown in Fig. 11-10.

Based on this analysis, Minitab reports a 95% confidence interval for λ of between 0.05 and 0.64. It is typical to select a rounded value of λ somewhere between these limits, and Minitab suggests 0.50, which corresponds to a square root transformation.

To make an I-MR chart with a Box–Cox transformation, select Stat > Control Charts > Variables Charts for Individuals > I-MR. Or, from the DMAIC toolbar, select Control > Variables Charts > Subgroup Size = 1 > I-MR Chart. Click the I-MR Options button and the Box-Cox tab. Check the Use Box-Cox transformation checkbox, and select the Lambda = 0.5 (square root) option. Figure 11-11 is the completed I-MR chart of the transformed warping data.

After the transformation, this data appears very much in control, except perhaps for point 7 which exceeds the upper control limit on the Moving Range chart. This could be a real signal, or it could be a false alarm.

The use of transformations in control charts is the subject of significant controversy among quality experts. But here is the key point: A properly applied control chart identifies significant deviations from the stable common-cause process

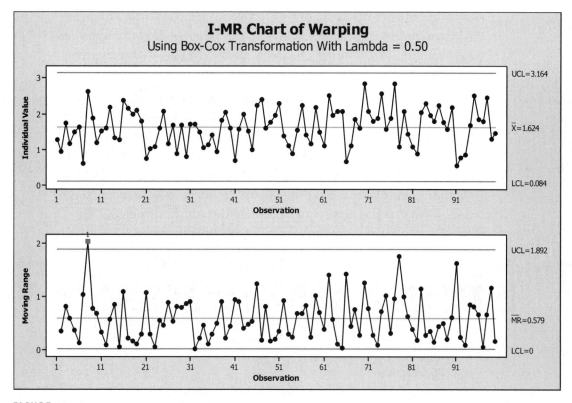

FIGURE 11-11 • I-MR chart of transformed warping data.

distribution, while not identifying too many false alarms. When a process displays a nonnormal distribution, one must decide whether the distribution shape is a special cause to be acted upon, or just a natural part of the process. Either way, Minitab can set up appropriate control charts based on that decision.

11.4   Creating Control Charts for Attribute Data

When continuous, numeric measurements are unavailable, attribute control charts are used to track the level of defects or defective units produced by a process. There are four common types of control charts for attributes, based on these two probability models:

- The **binomial** model applies to situations where every item tested is either defective or not, as a whole. When counting defective items, the Minitab control charts assistant recommends a P Chart. The P Chart plots the probability that each unit is defective. An alternative control chart available from the Control Charts menu or the Control > Attributes Data menu in the DMAIC toolbar is the NP chart, which plots the count of defective units per subgroup. Either the P or NP chart can handle datasets with either constant or varying subgroup sizes.

- The **Poisson** model applies to situations where every item tested can possibly have more than one defect. When counting defects, the Minitab control charts assistant recommends a U Chart. The U Chart plots the number of defects per unit tested, and it can also handle datasets with either constant or varying subgroup sizes. An alternative control chart available from the Control Charts menu or the Control > Attributes Data menu in the DMAIC toolbar is the C chart, which plots the counts of defects. The C chart can only handle datasets with constant subgroup sizes.

Table 11-1 lists key information about these four attribute control charts.

TABLE 11-1	Attribute Control Charts in Minitab			
Chart	Plots What?	Probability Model	Sample or Subgroup Size	In Control Charts Assistant?
P	Probability that a unit is defective	Binominal	Constant or varying	Yes
NP	Count of defective units	Binomial	Constant or varying	No
C	Count of defects	Poisson	Constant	No
U	Defects per unit	Poisson	Constant or varying	Yes

For example, the Minitab sample data file BulbDefect.MTW lists the counts of defective light bulbs found in each lot of 576 bulbs. Since each bulb is either defective or not, the binomial model applies here. Does this set of 24 counts of defectives represent a stable process?

To find out, load the worksheet file, and then select Assistant > Control Charts. Following the flow chart, select the recommended P Chart to plot the probability of a defective item. Fill out the dialog as follows:

- Enter Defectives in the Number of defective items column box.
- Enter the constant subgroup size of 576 where indicated.
- Select Estimate from the data for the control limits and center line.

Ignore the warning about the point outside of control limits, and click OK to finish the control chart and report, in the form of three new graphs. Figure 11-12 shows the Summary Report with the P Chart, editable Comments block, and an overall metric

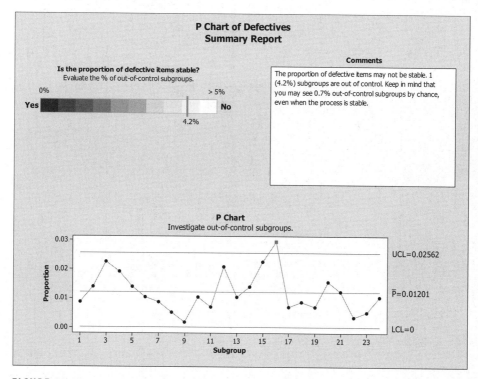

FIGURE 11-12 • P Chart Summary Report.

based on the percentage of points out of control. In this control chart, batch 16 appears to have significantly more defective bulbs than the other batches.

The NP chart is an alternative control chart for defectives, which may be created from the Control Charts menu. Figure 11-13 shows an NP chart made from the same BulbDefect.MTW dataset. The chart looks identical to the one made by the assistant. What is different is the vertical axis. The P chart plots probabilities, so the axis is labeled 0.01, 0.02, etc. The NP chart plots counts, so its axis is labeled 2, 4, etc. Many people find counts easier to understand than probabilities, and therefore prefer the NP chart.

The BulbDefect.MTW example has a fixed sample size for every subgroup. Very often this is not possible or practical with attribute control charts.

For example, the Minitab sample data file Transcription.MTW lists the number of typographical errors contained in 25 court documents transcribed from audio recordings. The worksheet lists the pages in the document in column C1 and the typos in column C2.

Since each page could possibly contain many typos, this is a case where defects and not defectives are counted. For this situation, the control charts assistant recommends the U Chart. Figure 11-14 shows the Stability Report created by using the

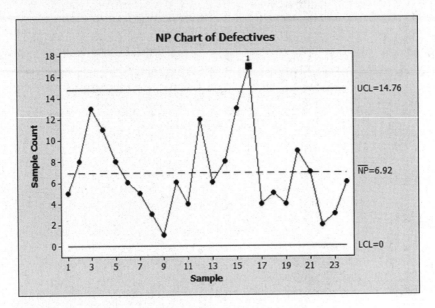

FIGURE 11-13 · NP chart created from the control charts menu.

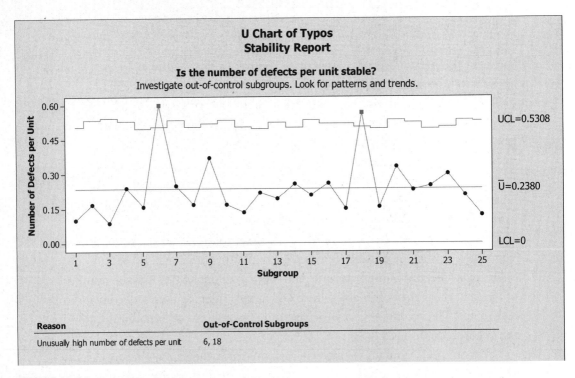

FIGURE 11-14 · U Chart Stability Report.

control charts assistant. The Stability Report presents the control chart and a list of points outside the control limits. In this case, documents 6 and 18 had an unusually large number of typos, significantly more than the others in the dataset.

Notice that the varying sample size in this dataset causes the upper control limit to vary up and down as the sample size changes.

To save space, the C chart is not shown here, but many people prefer it to the U chart because of its simplicity. If the size of each subgroup is the same, the C chart plots the count of defects, which is easier to understand than defects per unit on the U chart. In Minitab, the C chart is only available in the Stat > Control Charts > Attributes Charts menu.

11.5 Find Out More

Many excellent books are available on the use of control charts and other SPC tools. These include Montgomery (2008a), Wheeler (2010), and the classic Grant and Leavenworth (1996). AIAG (2005) is a widely used SPC reference manual written by and for the automotive industry, with forms, formulas, and practical advice.

This chapter raised the controversial issue of control charts for nonnormal processes. Wheeler (2000) wrote a book on the premise that transformations are not needed, and that normal-based control charts are always appropriate. Wheeler (2009, 2009a, 2009b) and Breyfogle (2009, 2009a) published a series of dueling online editorials on QualityDigest.com to debate the issue. However you feel about the controversy, Minitab has control charts for almost every situation and viewpoint. If you accept Breyfogle's claim that transformations are often necessary and valuable to stabilize error rates, Sleeper (2007) discusses many variations on control charts adapted to different process distributions with controlled error rates.

This chapter presented many tools for visualizing, testing, and controlling the variation of a process. The next chapter combines this process knowledge with customer specifications to measure the capability of the process to satisfy the customer.

QUIZ

1. **On a standard control chart, how are control limits calculated?**

    A. Control limits are calculated so that 95% of the plot points will stay within the control limits, unless there is a special cause of variation

    B. Control limits are two standard deviations of the individual values on either side of the mean.

    C. Control limits are three standard deviations of the individual values on either side of the mean.

    D. Control limits are three standard deviations of the plotted values on either side of the mean.

2. **What would be the most appropriate subgroup of size four to use for a control chart on a process that manufactures 50 parts per hour?**

    A. One part each hour for four hours

    B. The first, fifth, ninth, and thirteenth parts manufactured in one hour

    C. The first four parts manufactured in one hour

    D. A random selection of four parts from all parts manufactured in one hour

3. **Which of the following is an advantage of an Xbar-R chart over an I-MR chart?**

    A. The Xbar-R chart has more power to detect smaller shifts in the process.

    B. The Xbar-R chart is more robust for nonnormal distributions.

    C. The Xbar-R chart requires fewer measurements for each point plotted on the chart.

    D. Answers A and B are both correct.

4. **How does the standard I-MR chart estimate short-term process variation from a set of individual measurements?**

    A. Short-term variation is estimated from the moving average of two measurements.

    B. Short-term variation is estimated from the moving range of two measurements.

    C. Short-term variation is estimated by calculating the standard deviation of two consecutive measurements.

    D. Short-term variation is estimated from the moving range of three measurements.

5. **A connector plant tracks the number of connectors rejected out of each batch of 100 connectors. Which control chart(s) are most appropriate for this count of connectors rejected?**

    A. Xbar-R or Xbar-S charts

    B. P or NP charts

    C. C or U charts

    D. I-MR chart

6. The Minitab sample data file Camshaft.MTW contains measurements of 20 sub-groups of 5 camshafts in each subgroup. Create an appropriate control chart of the Length measurements in column C1 and interpret. Is there any evidence of instability in camshaft length?

7. In the same file Camshaft.MTW, create an appropriate control chart of the Supp1 measurements in column C2 and interpret. Is there any evidence of instability in this characteristic?

8. Here are the measurements of Supp1 for the next five camshafts in subgroup 21: 598.4, 599.0, 600.6, 598.0, 601.0. Using only the first 20 subgroups to calculate control limits, is subgroup 21 in control or not?

9. Open the Minitab sample data file Cap.MTW, and create an I-MR chart of the Torque measurement in column C1, using a Box–Cox transformation with optimal lambda. Which points, if any, are outside control limits?

10. The Minitab sample data file Accident.MTW lists the accidents per week at one dangerous intersection. Using a Poisson model for this data, prepare an appropriate control chart to see if this is a stable Poisson process.

chapter 12

Measuring Process Capability

Process capability is a measure of how well a process can satisfy customer requirements, by keeping characteristics within specification limits. To estimate process capability requires a stable process distribution, as demonstrated by an appropriate control chart, and specification limits representing customer requirements. From this basic information, Minitab provides a range of standard capability metrics, plus informative graphical reports.

CHAPTER OBJECTIVES

Here's what you'll learn in this chapter:

- How to create a quick capability snapshot
- How to analyze process capability for normal processes
- How to analyze process capability for continuous but nonnormal processes
- How to analyze process capability for binomial or Poisson processes
- How to compare process capability before and after an improvement project

NEW IN 16 Minitab offers a wide range of capability analysis tools for different situations. These are located in the Stat > Quality Tools menu. If the new DMAIC profile is active, most capability tools are also available in both the Measure > Establish Baseline menu and the Improve > Evaluate Capability menu of the DMAIC toolbar.

The Assistant menu, another new feature of Minitab 16, contains a capability analysis assistant providing access to the most commonly used capability tools. The capability analysis assistant also offers tools to compare capability before and after a process improvement. These comparison tools provide a useful set of graphs and statistics for comparing two process distributions. All reports generated by the capability analysis assistant are graphical, include appropriate tests for distribution and stability, and explain the analysis results in plain language.

There is an important reason why Chapter 11 on control charts comes before this chapter on capability metrics. Capability metrics are only useful for a stable process. People expect capability metrics to represent future process behavior. If the process is unstable today, capability metrics calculated from today's data will be useless to predict tomorrow's performance. Minitab will happily calculate all kinds of capability metrics, regardless of process stability, but the wise user should ignore these metrics when the process is unstable. Always check stability with an appropriate control chart before reporting or publishing process capability metrics.

12.1   Capability Metrics

Hundreds of capability metrics have been proposed, and many have become popular. But most people only need two of them. Which two they need varies between industries, companies, and the individual situation. Therefore, Minitab capability analysis reports offer an often bewildering bevy of metrics, leaving the reader to choose the few ones of interest. Adding to the confusion is the wide range of often contradictory adjectives used to describe classes of capability metrics. Here is a quick definition of the adjectives Minitab uses to describe capability metrics, in three broad categories:

- **Potential capability** metrics are based on an estimate of short-term or common-cause process variation, which usually is estimated by variation within subgroups. The rationale for the word "potential" is that if all process shifts and drifts were eliminated, the potential capability would be realized for all units manufactured.* In Minitab, potential capability metrics include Cp, CPL, CPU, and Cpk. In some other books, this class of metrics may be called capability metrics or short-term capability metrics.

- **Overall** or **actual capability** metrics are based on an estimate of long-term process variation, which is the overall variation of all available data. In Minitab, overall capability metrics include Pp, PPL, PPU, Ppk, and Cpm. In some other books, this class of metrics may be called performance indices or long-term capability metrics.

- Other metrics may be based on either short-term or long-term variation, depending on the context. These include Z.LSL, Z.USL, Z.Bench, % < LSL, % > USL, % Total, PPM < LSL, PPM > USL, and PPM Total. Minitab will generally list these under a heading such as "Potential" or "Overall." Sometimes potential metrics are labeled "Within" or "Between/Within" depending on how potential variation was estimated.

Following is a list of conceptual definitions for each of these metrics, in alphabetical order. The formulas used to calculate them vary based on the situation, and are best looked up in the Minitab Methods and Formulas file. In the definitions below, the phrase "natural process width" refers to 6 standard deviations, and "half natural process width" refers to 3 standard deviations of a normal distribution.[†]

- **% < LSL** is the percentage of units which are predicted to be below the lower specification limit. Smaller is better.

- **% > USL** is the percentage of units which are predicted to be above the upper specification limit. Smaller is better.

- **% Total** or **% Out of spec** is the total percentage of units which are predicted to be outside either specification limit. Smaller is better.

---

*In some books, potential capability metrics refer to Cp and Pp, because these are based on variation only and not the mean. Sleeper (2006) and Bothe (1997) use this terminology. Metrics like Cpk or Ppk which use both variation and mean are called actual capability metrics by Sleeper and performance capability by Bothe. Almost always, the same symbol refers to the same metric, whoever is writing about it.

†The 6, which defines a natural process width as 6-sigma, can be changed in Minitab. In the Options dialog in the Tools menu, in the Capability Analysis section, the setting is labeled Use tolerance of K*sigma for capability statistics. It is unwise to change this setting, because people generally expect capability metrics to be based on a 6-sigma process width.

- **Cp** is the specification width divided by the natural process width, short-term. Larger is better.

- **CCpk** is like the more familiar Cpk, except with the process mean replaced by the target value, if provided. CCpk represents how good Cpk might be if the process mean were equal to the target value. This metric is rarely used, and it will not appear unless enabled in the Options dialog, Capability Analysis section.

- **Cpk** is the difference between the mean and the closest specification limit, divided by the half natural process width, short-term. Larger is better. Cpk is the minimum of CPL and CPU. If the mean is centered between specification limits, Cpk = Cp, otherwise Cpk < Cp.

- **CPL** is the difference between the mean and the lower specification limit, divided by the half natural process width, short-term. Larger is better.

- **Cpm** is the specification width divided by 6 times the square root of the mean square deviation from the target. Larger is better. Compared to all the other metrics in this list, Cpm rewards consistency around the target value, rather than staying inside the specification limits.

- **CPU** is the difference between the upper specification limit and the mean, divided by the half natural process width, short-term. Larger is better.

- **Pp** is the specification width divided by the natural process width, long-term. Larger is better.

- **Ppk** is the difference between the mean and the closest specification limit, divided by the half natural process width, long-term. Larger is better.

- **PPL** is the difference between the mean and the lower specification limit, divided by the half natural process width, long-term. Larger is better.

- **PPM < LSL** is the parts per million predicted to be below the lower specification limit. (PPM < LSL) = (% < LSL) × 10,000. Smaller is better.

- **PPM > USL** is the parts per million predicted to be above the upper specification limit. (PPM > USL) = (% > LSL) × 10,000. Smaller is better.

- **PPM Total** or **PPM (DPMO)** is the parts per million predicted to be outside either specification limit. (PPM Total) = (% Total) × 10,000. Smaller is better. Some reports call this DPMO (Defects Per Million Opportunities).

- **PPU** is the difference between the upper specification limit and the mean, divided by the half natural process width, long-term. Larger is better.

- **Z.Bench** is the Z.LSL metric of a normal distribution with the same PPM Total as this data. Z.Bench is used as a benchmark to compare processes of different types, even to compare attributes with variables. Companies implementing

Six Sigma often want a "sigma level" which is 6 for a really good process. Z.Bench is the closest metric to a "sigma level" provided by Minitab.

- **Z.LSL** is the difference between the mean and the lower specification limit, divided by the standard deviation. Larger is better.

- **Z.USL** is the difference between the upper specification limit and the mean, divided by the standard deviation. Larger is better.

The above descriptions are based on an assumed normal distribution. Capability metrics for nonnormal distributions have different formulas, but are intended to behave the same way. These issues are discussed later in this chapter.

12.2   Measuring Capability for Normally Distributed Processes

Minitab offers many tools for capability analysis, for the usual situation when the normal distribution is an accepted assumption. Each of these tools has strengths and weaknesses.

- The capability analysis accessed by selecting Assistant > Capability Analysis provides these options:

  - **Capability snapshot**: This tool provides a quick analysis in the form of two graphs. One graph displays a capability plot, normality test, and summary of key statistics and capability metrics. The other graph offers text interpretation of the results and warnings of possible inadequacy in the data. All metrics are overall metrics, since this tool does not attempt to estimate short-term variation within the dataset. If the data fails a normality test, an optional transformation is offered.

  - **Complete capability analysis**: This tool provides a more thorough analysis in four graphs. In addition to the information provided by the snapshot, this report includes a control chart to test stability and an analysis of both potential and overall process capability.

  - **Capability comparison**: This tool compares process capability of two datasets, which are typically collected before and after a project to improve capability. The report includes hypothesis tests to identify significant improvements in the process, and charts to visually compare data before to data after.

- **Stat > Quality Tools > Capability Analysis > Normal** produces a capability graph surrounded by tables of statistics and metrics, including both potential and overall metrics. Options include a wide range of metrics, normalizing transformations, and confidence intervals.

- **Stat > Quality Tools > Capability Analysis > Between/Within** produces the same type of report as the Normal capability analysis, with one important difference. In the Between/Within analysis, all potential capability metrics are calculated using a combination of within-subgroup variation and between-subgroup variation. This is appropriate when the common-cause process variation includes variation between subgroups, and this needs to be considered in the calculation of capability metrics.

- **Stat > Quality Tools > Capability Sixpack > Normal** creates one graph containing a matrix of six graphs. These include a control chart, individual value plot, capability histogram, probability plot, capability plot, and a few selected statistics and metrics. A Between/Within sixpack is also available.

- **Stat > Quality Tools > Capability Analysis > Multiple Variables (Normal)** creates capability plots and probability plots for several variables with the same specification limits.

For example, Byron works at a digital camera factory. Byron has measured a critical thickness of a new plastic part on a first lot of 259 parts. This dataset is available in a Minitab sample data file Camera.MTW. All measurements have been coded by subtracting the lower specification limit and dividing by the specification width, so the specifications for this data are 0 and 1. The target value is 0.5.

With Camera.MTW loaded and current, Byron selects Assistant > Capability Analysis to display the capability analysis flow chart as seen in Fig. 12-1. The first diamond-shaped decision block selects between a capability analysis of one sample, and a comparison of before and after data. The second and third decisions choose between normal, binomial, and Poisson probability models.

For examples and explanations of any of the decisions in the flow chart, click directly on the diamond. For a list of helpful advice relating to collecting data and completing any of the capability analysis tools, click on the *more...* hyperlinks below the tools on the bottom row.

Byron selects the (normal) Capability Analysis block at the bottom left of the flow chart. He then selects a Snapshot analysis, and fills out the dialog as follows:

- Data are in one column in the dropdown box
- Column: Thickness
- Lower spec: 0
- Upper spec: 1
- Target: 0.5

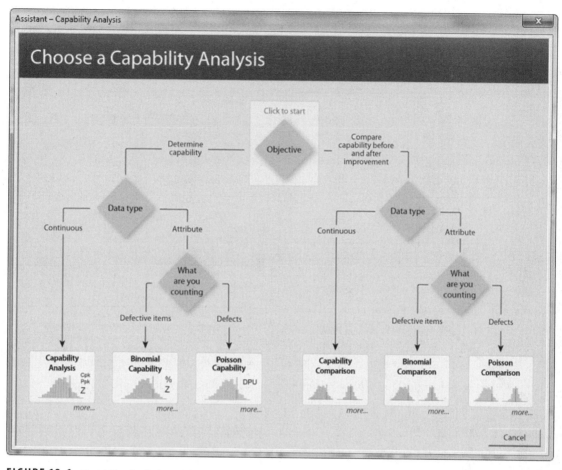

FIGURE 12-1 • Capability Analysis assistant.

After Byron clicks OK, two new graphs appear. The Summary Report is shown in Fig. 12-2. The capability graph in the top left is a histogram of the data, with a fitted normal distribution and vertical lines representing the specification limits and target. Below that is a probability plot and a report from an Anderson–Darling normality test. Since the p-value is greater than 0.05, Minitab notes that the normality test is passed.

On the right side of the Summary Report is a summary of the specification and a table of process characteristics. This table includes the overall capability metrics Pp and Ppk, since the snapshot does not estimate any form of short-term variation. With a small dataset, be careful about interpreting these metrics as an authoritative estimate of long-term capability. These metrics are only valid estimates of Pp and Ppk if the parts tested truly represent long-term variation.

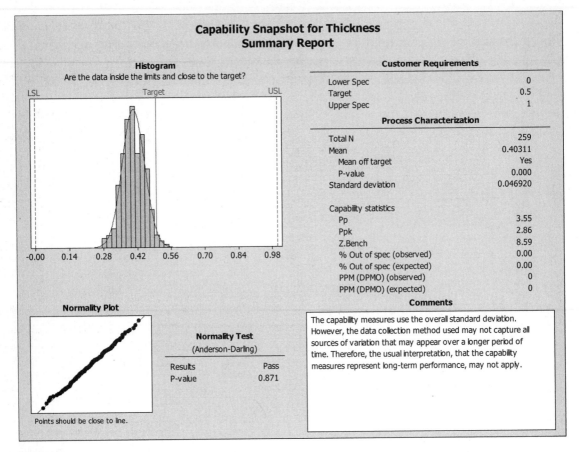

FIGURE 12-2 • Capability Snapshot Summary Report.

In the table, the % Out of spec and PPM (DPMO) metrics are labeled (observed) or (expected). The observed metrics reflect the actual parts in the sample outside of specification limits. The expected metrics are calculated based on a normal probability model.

All the metrics for this process are very good, indicating a very high capability level. The Z.Bench of 8.59 can be interpreted by saying "This is an 8.59-sigma process," which is far better than a Six Sigma initiative would typically require.

The Comments block is automatically written by Minitab. Double-click this block to edit its contents.

The Report Card graph, not shown here, lists comments and advice about normality, sample size, and how to interpret this report.

The capability snapshot is useful to provide a quick summary of a dataset, but it does not evaluate process stability, nor does it provide any potential capability metrics. If the time order of the data is unknown, then this is the only analysis possible. In the above example, if Byron received all 259 parts jumbled together in a box, with no way to determine which was manufactured first, there would be no way to determine short-term variation.

But now, consider a change in the example. Suppose Byron found in the box a list of measurements of all 259 parts, recorded in the order of manufacture. Also, suppose that the parts are produced by a mold with seven cavities, so that each set of seven measurements represents a subgroup of one part from each cavity. Then Byron can treat the dataset differently by analyzing it as 37 subgroups of size seven.

To do this, Byron uses the same capability analysis assistant, but this time he selects a Complete analysis, and specifies a Subgroup size of 7. This time, Minitab creates a report in four new graphs. Figure 12-3 shows the Summary Report.

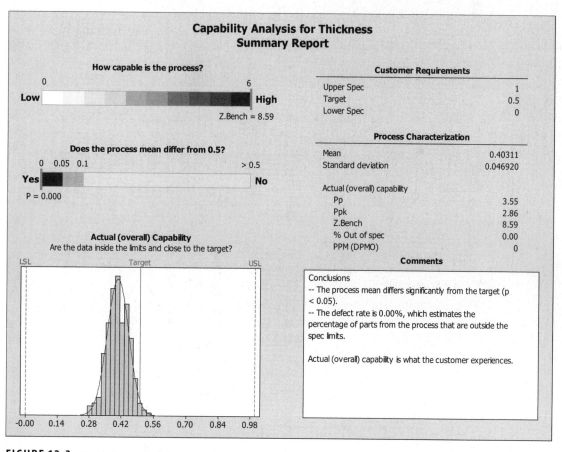

FIGURE 12-3 • Capability Analysis Summary Report.

In the top left of the Summary Report, Minitab displays two color-coded metric graphs. The first one plots Z.Bench, which, at 8.59, is better than the high end of the chart. Below that is a report of a hypothesis test to check whether the mean is on target. With a very small *p*-value, there is very strong evidence that the population mean is NOT 0.05. This conclusion should be visually apparent from the histogram at the bottom left. The tables and Comments block on the right side of the report are similar to those in the capability snapshot.

The Diagnostic Report, shown in Fig. 12-4, includes a control chart, an Xbar-R Chart in this case, a normal probability plot, and a normality test report. These charts show no evidence of instability or nonnormality, both of which are good things.

A third graph, the Process Performance Report, not shown here, includes another capability histogram, and a table listing both potential and overall capability metrics.

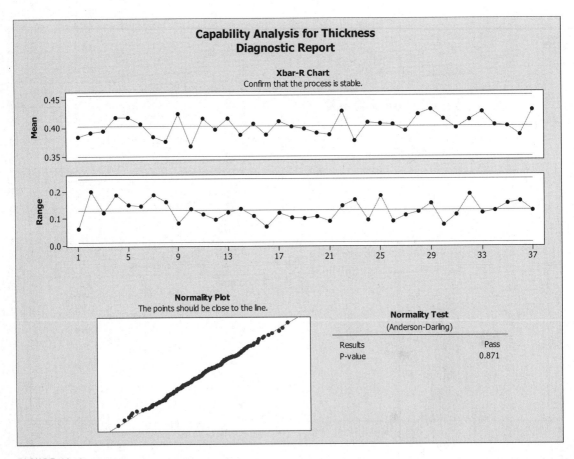

FIGURE 12-4 · Capability Analysis Diagnostic Report.

A fourth graph, the Report Card, provides a text summary of any potential issues with the dataset, along with advice on interpretation.

For new Minitab users, or for those unfamiliar with statistical tools and terminology, the capability analysis assistant is an invaluable aid, which provides not only a simplified interface, but also a thorough analysis of the data with a presentation-ready report.

Some people with more statistical experience may not want Minitab to advise them or to interpret the data for them. There are also legions of Minitab users who are familiar and comfortable with the opinion-free capability graphs and capability sixpacks. These popular tools are still available in the Stat > Quality Tools menu.

Figure 12-5 is a capability sixpack of Byron's Thickness data already analyzed by the assistant. To match Fig. 12-5, click the Options button in the Capability Sixpack (Normal Distribution) dialog, and enter the target value of 0.5 in the appropriate space. This allows the calculation of the target-based capability metric Cpm.

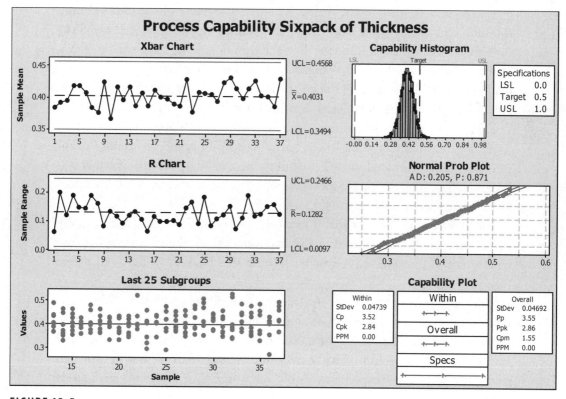

FIGURE 12-5 • Process capability sixpack.

At this point, most parts of this sixpack should be self-explanatory, except perhaps for the Capability Plot at the bottom right. This capability plot compares the width of the specification limits, labeled Specs, with the 6-sigma natural process width, estimated Within subgroups and Overall. The Within and Overall intervals shown are both much narrower than the specification width, which indicates a high-capability process.

The capability sixpack is heavy on graphs and light on statistics, and this combination of a few selected metrics with all the key graphs makes it a popular choice for analysts. But there are still options which are unavailable in the capability analysis tools seen so far.

In the example above, Byron should be very happy with the high capability metrics. But he knows that these metrics are only estimates, and the true capability of the population could be much worse than or better than these estimates. To quantify this risk, Byron wants to calculate a 95% lower confidence interval for all capability metrics.

Confidence intervals for capability metrics are available in the Capability Analysis menu. To perform this analysis, Byron selects Stat > Quality Tools > Capability Analysis > Normal. In the dialog, he enters the name of the data column, the subgroup size of 7, the lower spec of 0 and the upper spec of 1. He clicks the Options button. In the Options dialog, Byron enters the target value of 0.5, and then he selects the Include confidence intervals option. He selects a confidence level of 95.0 and Lower bound in the Confidence intervals dropdown box. Figure 12-6 shows the completed capability analysis.

In Fig. 12-6, to the right of the graph, is a table of both potential and overall capability metrics, including lower confidence bounds, labeled Lower CL. For example, Ppk is estimated to be 2.86, but Byron can be 95% confident that it is 2.65 or larger. Cpm, the target-focused metric, is estimated at 1.55, with a 95% lower confidence bound of 1.48.

For most businesses, a capability study involving 259 units is unusually large. These confidence bounds are quite close to the point estimates, because of the size of the dataset. A smaller sample size leads to wider confidence intervals.

Here is another example of an analysis that cannot be performed properly by the process capability assistant. Rollie works in a paper mill where he supervises the deposition of a critical film on rolls of paper to be used in inkjet labels. The film thickness should be between 47 and 53 μm. To evaluate the process capability, Rollie measures film thickness in 3 spots

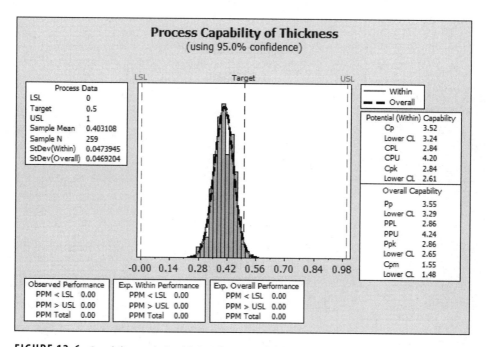

FIGURE 12-6 • Capability analysis with 95% lower confidence bounds.

on each of 25 rolls. Rollie's data is available as a Minitab sample data file Film.MTW.

Rollie first analyzes this using the capability analysis assistant, specifying a subgroup size of 3. The Summary Report, not shown here, lists a Ppk of 1.15 and a Z.Bench of 3.36. These metrics are not great, but other than that, the Summary Report reveals no signs of trouble in this dataset.

On the other hand, the Diagnostic Report in Fig. 12-7 shows a control chart with numerous points outside the control limits. This looks bad, but is it?

In this dataset, each subgroup of three measurements is taken from a different roll of paper.

This is a natural choice of subgroup, but it creates the appearance of a problem. Rollie knows that because the properties of the paper change between rolls, the thickness of the film also changes between rolls. This is a well-known and accepted fact, and not much can be done to reduce the variation between incoming paper rolls. The control limits on the Xbar Chart are based on variation within subgroups, or within rolls of paper. This process will never appear to be in control on this standard control chart.

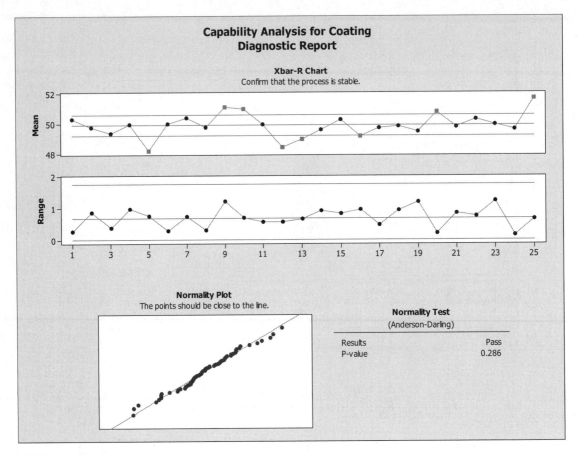

FIGURE 12-7 · Diagnostic Report with control chart and normality plot.

Minitab offers an alternative capability analysis and control chart, called Between/Within. Using this alternative method, potential variation is estimated by combining variation within subgroups with variation between subgroups.

To use this technique, Rollie selects Stat > Quality Tools > Capability Sixpack > Between/Within. He fills out the dialog specifying Coating as the data column, and Roll as the subgroup size. The column Roll contains numbers identifying each roll of paper. In the Capability Analysis or Sixpack, a column like this may be specified instead of a number for subgroup size. Rollie also enters the specification limits of 47 and 53, and clicks OK. Figure 12-8 shows the completed capability sixpack.

This graph has a three-part control chart, with the process mean at top left, the between-subgroup variation at middle left, and within-subgroup variation at bottom left. None of the three show signs of process instability.

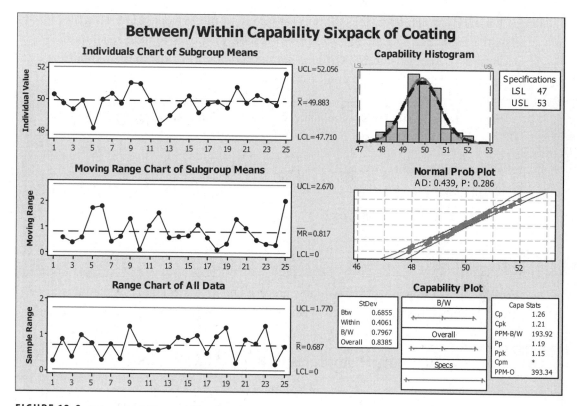

FIGURE 12-8 • Between/within capability sixpack.

Comparing the Xbar Charts from Figs. 12-7 and 12-8, the Between/Within chart has wider control limits, based on a combination of between-subgroup and within-subgroup variation.

At the bottom right of Fig. 12-8 are the predicted capability metrics. The overall metric of Ppk is the same, 1.15, by either analysis method. But the potential capability metric Cpk is 1.21 by the between/within method, a more realistic value than 2.37, which was based only on within-subgroup variability.

If Rollie uses the Capability Analysis > Between/Within function, he can calculate a wider variety of metrics with optional confidence intervals.

A common requirement is to compare the distributions and capabilities of many different processes. Minitab makes this easy with two different tools. In the traditional menus, the Stat > Quality Tools > Capability Analysis > Multiple Variables (Normal) will create capability graphs and probability plots for several variables at once. The new capability analysis assistant has a tool for comparing before and after distributions.

For an example, open the Minitab sample data file Mncapa.MTW. This file lists the measured weight of frozen food loaded into bags by two machines, indicated by 1 or 2 in column C2. This dataset has 50 individual measurements from each machine, recorded in time order, without any subgrouping. The specification is 27– 35.

Select Stat > Quality Tools > Capability Analysis > Multiple Variables (Normal) and fill out the dialog as follows:

- Variables: Weight
- Subgroup sizes: 1
- Check the By variables checkbox, and enter Machine
- Lower spec: 27
- Upper spec: 35

After clicking OK, you will see two new graphs. The first one, Fig. 12-9, contains two capability histograms, each with Within and Overall normal probability

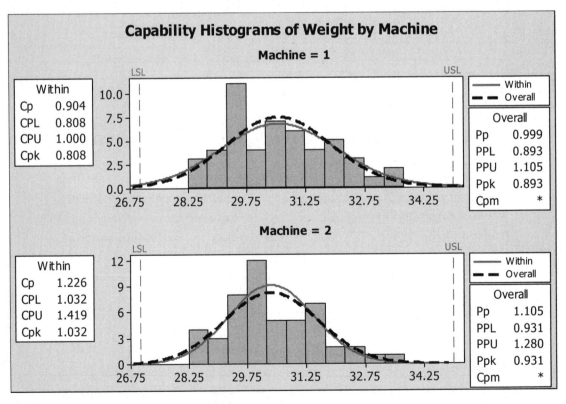

FIGURE 12-9 • Comparing two capability plots.

curves. The Overall capability metric Ppk is 0.893 for machine 1, and 0.931 for machine 2. Machine 2 looks slightly better, but neither machine has what any company would call good process capability.

A second graph, not shown here, contains two normal probability plots for the two distributions. These graphs list Anderson–Darling normality test statistics and p-values. The p-values for these two distributions are 0.158 and 0.349. Since both p-values are greater than 0.05, there is no reason to reject the assumption of normality.

To see how the comparison feature of the capability analysis assistant works, open the Minitab sample data file Camshaft2.MTW. In this worksheet, columns Supp1 and Supp2 list measurements of the length of 100 camshafts from two different suppliers, collected in 20 subgroups of size five. Although this dataset is not ideal for this demonstration, it will work. Suppose that the "Before" dataset is Supp2 and "After" dataset is Supp1.

From the capability analysis assistant, select the Capability Comparison, and fill out the dialog as follows:

- Baseline process data
  - How are your data arranged? Data are in one column
  - Column: Supp2
  - Subgroup size: 5
- Improved process data
  - How are your data arranged? Data are in one column
  - Column: Supp1
  - Subgroup size: 5
- Lower spec: 595
- Upper spec: 605
- Target: 600

After OK is clicked, Minitab creates the comparison report in four new graphs. Figure 12-10 is the Summary Report. At the top left of the report is the encouraging conclusion that the After dataset is 100% better than the Before dataset. Below that are two color-coded graphs displaying the results of hypothesis tests for changes in the standard deviation and mean. For this example, both p-values are very small, indicating strong evidence of significant changes in both standard deviation and mean. The Summary Report also contains before and after capability plots, a table of statistics, and an editable Comments block.

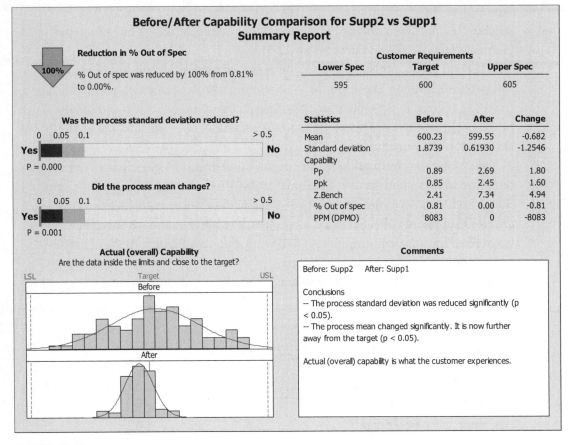

FIGURE 12-10 · Capability Comparison Summary Report.

Figure 12-11 is the Diagnostic Report, with Before and After control charts, probability plots, and normality tests. Since the control charts have the same scale, it is easy to see how variation decreased in the After data. There is no other single graph in Minitab that displays information about the stability and normality of two datasets side by side on the same graph. This should be quite useful in situations other than before-after comparisons. The labels on the graphs can be changed from Before and After to Supplier 1 and Supplier 2 or to whatever else might be appropriate.

The third graph created by the assistant, the Process Performance Report, not shown here, is a comparison of potential and overall capability metrics between the two datasets, with histograms. The fourth graph is the Report Card with a set of advice and warnings about potential problems with the data.

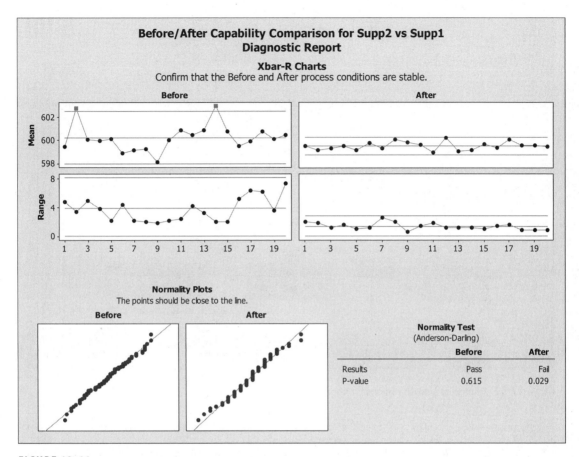

FIGURE 12-11 · Capability Comparison Diagnostic Report.

12.3   Measuring Capability for Nonnormal Processes

This section discusses the techniques and issues relating to capability analysis for continuous but not normal distributions. Discrete, attribute data following the binomial or Poisson distributions are discussed in the following section.

Almost all of the reports shown in the previous section include a normality test. What happens when the dataset fails the normality test and has a significantly nonnormal distribution? The analyst has many options, as illustrated by the flow chart in Fig. 12-12.

The first decision is the hardest decision, because no statistical tool is available to help answer it. Does the fact of nonnormality mean that the process is in control or out of control? To help answer this question, look at the histogram

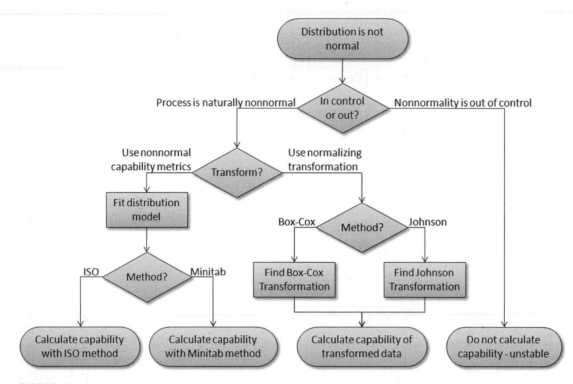

FIGURE 12-12 • Capability analysis options for nonnormal data.

of the data, and consider whether the process has natural forces or boundaries causing the distribution to be nonnormal. For example, a measurement which by definition is always a positive number has a zero boundary on the left, which may cause a skew to the right. There are other processes with a screening or filtering causing a boundary on the right, or on both sides. If these boundaries or other forces are natural parts of the process and will always be there, it is appropriate to consider the nonnormal process to be in control.

On the other hand, nonnormality can also be a signal of something seriously wrong or in need of improvement. If several processes mix their products together, the resulting combined distribution may be bimodal or multimodal. A very long tail on the histogram may indicate a sporadic problem causing excessively high or low values. These cases present improvement opportunities that need investigation before calculating any capability metrics. Applying nonnormal capability methods to these datasets could mask a problem that needs fixing and prolong the delivery of inferior quality products to the customer. Therefore, if nonnormality represents an out-of-control condition, the appropriate course of action is not to calculate any capability metrics, and instead to work to improve the process variation.

The decision just described stirs passionate debate among gurus and practitioners, but no one answer is always correct. The wise practitioner is prepared for both scenarios, because both do happen.

Suppose we decide that the process is naturally nonnormal. The next decision is what to do about it. One popular choice is to use a normalizing transformation. If we can find a function that transforms the data into an approximately normal distribution, then we can apply all the normal-based control charts and capability analysis tools to the transformed data. In this process, the specification limits and target value must also be transformed through the same function before calculating capability metrics.

Minitab offers two families of normalizing transformations, Box–Cox and Johnson. The Box–Cox transformation is a family of power transformations, including the log transformation. Box–Cox transformations can effectively normalize many right-skewed or left-skewed unimodal distributions. The Johnson transformation is a more flexible family of functions that can normalize a wide range of distributions. The Johnson transformation includes three families of functions for unbounded distributions, left-bounded distributions, and left- and right-bounded distributions. Chapter 4 has more details on both these families of transformations.

In Minitab, the normal capability analysis functions have options to select either a Box–Cox or a Johnson transformation before applying the normal capability tools to the transformed data. The Stat > Quality Tools menu also has a Johnson Transformation function to explore that option separately from any capability analysis.

The Box–Cox and Johnson transformations do not always find an effective normalizing transformation. Even when they do, it is not always a good idea to use them. Some Box–Cox transformations are quite simple, like $Y = \ln(X)$ or $Y = \sqrt{X}$. By comparison, Johnson transformations can be much more complicated formulas. A good and effective normalizing transformation will work not only for the initial capability study, but throughout the operational life of the process. It is more likely that a complicated function will not work in the long-term, so caution is advisable here.

An alternative to transformations is to fit a specific distribution model to the data, and then to use that model to calculate nonnormal capability metrics. Sometimes, theory or historical process knowledge suggests one family of distributions over another. In other situations, viewing probability plots for different distribution families can help select one particular family. In the Minitab menu, Stat > Quality Tools > Individual Distribution Identification is a quick way to generate probability plots and goodness-of-fit statistics for many different distribution families. The list of distributions includes Box–Cox and Johnson transformation options, providing an easy way to compare all available distributions and transformations in one step.

After selecting a distribution family, how should the nonnormal capability metrics be calculated? Minitab offers two options, nicknamed ISO and Minitab.

- The ISO option is based on the fact that for the normal distribution, the $\pm 3\,\sigma$ natural process width runs from $X_{0.00135}$, the 0.135th percentile, to $X_{0.99865}$, the 99.865th percentile. For the selected distribution model, the natural process width is represented by $X_{0.99865} - X_{0.00135}$, resulting in formulas like these:

$$Pp = \frac{USL - LSL}{X_{0.99865} - X_{0.00135}}$$

$$Ppk = Min\left\{ \frac{USL - X_{0.5}}{X_{0.99865} - X_{0.5}}, \frac{X_{0.5} - LSL}{X_{0.5} - X_{0.00135}} \right\}$$

- The Minitab option predicts the probability of defective units outside the specification limits, and then calculates the Pp and Ppk metric values which would have the same probability of defects for a normal distribution.

The ISO method is a nice idea, but it was not well thought out. It is very important that a statement like "Ppk = 1.5" refers to the same probability of defects, regardless of the distribution model. The Minitab method has this property for all values of Pp and Ppk. Using the ISO method, a statement like "Ppk = 1.5" could refer to hugely different defect rates, depending on the distribution.

A controversial aspect of the Minitab method is that it cannot calculate any metrics when the specification limit is beyond the range of possible values under the selected distribution model. In this situation, the predicted defect rate for that limit is zero, and if the distribution model is correct, some capability metrics are infinite. If the probability of values outside specification limits is really zero, then Pp and Ppk are really infinite.

For these reasons, the Minitab method is recommended over the ISO method. Oddly, this is not the default setting for Minitab. To change the setting, select Tools > Options from the menu. Expand the Control Charts and Quality Tools branch of the tree on the left side of the dialog, and select Capability Analysis. Then select Minitab method in the Nonnormal Capability Statistics section.

The new capability analysis assistant does a good job of finding and using an appropriate transformation, if this does in fact normalize the distribution.

For an example, open the Minitab sample data file Tiles.MTW. This file contains measurements of warping of 100 floor tiles, with an upper specification limit of 10. Warping is defined so that it is always a positive number, with a lower boundary of zero.

With Tiles.MTW as the current worksheet, select Assistant > Capability Analysis, and choose the Snapshot option to analyze this dataset with an upper specification limit of 10. After OK is clicked, Minitab displays a warning of nonnormality, as in Fig. 12-13.

This dialog offers the same choice as the first decision block in Fig. 12-12. Clicking No will analyze the data with an assumed normal distribution. The nonnormality will most likely cause points outside the control limits on a control chart. The nonnormality is a more important indicator than the capability metrics, since any capability metrics calculated by this method may not be reliable.

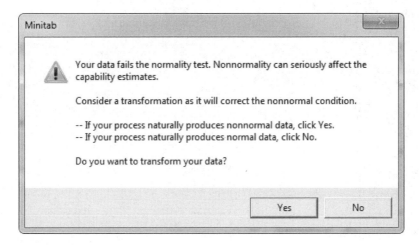

FIGURE 12-13 • Warning of nonnormality from assistant.

Clicking Yes will ask Minitab to look for a Box–Cox transformation that normalizes the data. If one is found, capability analysis will be performed on the transformed data. If the Box–Cox transformation fails, the original data is analyzed with a warning about the nonnormality.

Figure 12-14 shows the snapshot report generated by the assistant for the Tiles.MTW dataset. The top left histogram shows the original data with a badly-fitting normal distribution. The bottom left histogram shows the transformed data after the recommended Box–Cox transformation with lambda (λ) = 0.50, which is a square-root transformation. The probability plot shows a straight diagonal line, indicating that the transformed data fits a normal distribution well. The table on the right reports that Ppk = 0.95 and Z.Bench = 2.86, based on the transformed data.

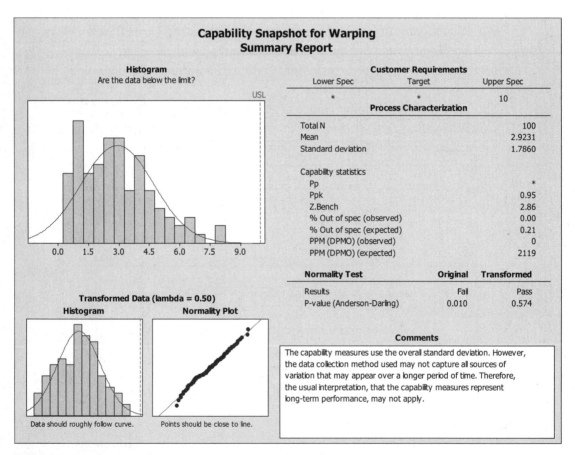

FIGURE 12-14 · Capability snapshot report with transformation.

Starting from the capability analysis assistant, performing a Complete analysis also provides a Diagnostic Report with a control chart of the transformed data and a Process Performance Report with a full analysis of potential and overall capability.

To use the capability analysis tools in the traditional menus with a Box–Cox or Johnson transformation, select either Capability Analysis > Normal or Capability Sixpack > Normal from the Stat > Quality Tools menu. Then, click the Transform button to select the desired transformation.

The Tiles.MTW example illustrates another important concept in capability analysis. The lower boundary of zero is a boundary, not a specification limit. If zero is entered as a lower specification limit, capability metrics like Cpk and Ppk will be worse as the data values get closer to zero. This is inappropriate, since being close to zero is a good thing. Instead, check the Boundary checkbox, as shown in Fig. 12-15. This alerts Minitab to treat the zero boundary appropriately. Capability metrics will be based only on the upper specification limit, but the zero boundary will appear on the histogram.

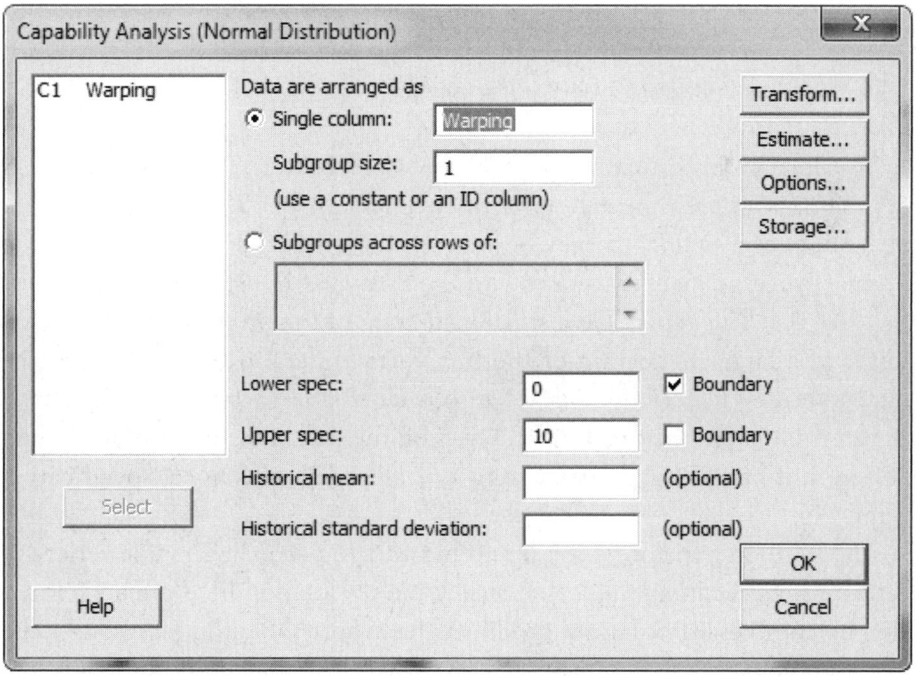

FIGURE 12-15 · Capability Analysis dialog with boundary.

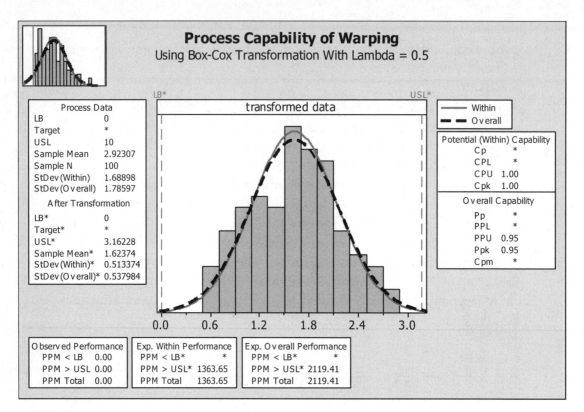

FIGURE 12-16 • Normal capability analysis with Box–Cox transformation.

To select a transformation, click the Transform button. The Transform dialog offers Box–Cox transformations with optimal λ, $\lambda = 0$, $\lambda = 0.5$, or any other value between –5 and +5 may be entered directly. Figure 12-16 shows the normal process capability report with the Box–Cox transformation and optimal λ of 0.5. This report has a small histogram of the original data in the top left, and a larger histogram of the transformed data in the center. On the histogram, the lower boundary of zero is labeled LB* where * denotes after transformation. In the capability metrics on the right side of the plot, CPL and PPL are not calculated, because zero is a boundary and not a specification limit.

The Johnson transformation is another way to normalize a wide variety of distributions. Running the Stat > Quality Tools > Johnson Transformation function on the Tiles.MTW dataset produces the report shown in Fig. 12-17. The best normalizing function is of type SB, which is bounded on both ends. For this dataset with a natural lower bound only, a lower bounded transformation of type SL might be preferred, but Minitab does not offer the option to

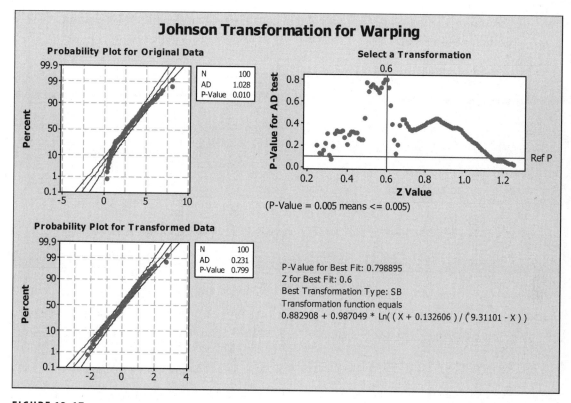

FIGURE 12-17 · Johnson transformation.

choose one of the three Johnson families. The SB function produced the highest Anderson–Darling *p*-value, and this is the best normalizing function:

$$Y = 0.882908 + 0.987049 \times \ln\left[\frac{X + 0.132606}{9.31101 - X}\right], \text{ for } -0.132606 < X < 9.31101$$

Obviously, this function is much more complicated than the Box–Cox $Y = \sqrt{X}$ transformation. Since the Box–Cox option works well, it would be preferred to the Johnson transformation in this case.

A different approach is to fit a distribution model to the available data, and then to use that model with nonnormal capability analysis. Minitab offers an Individual Distribution Identification tool which simultaneously tests 14 different distribution families, along with Box–Cox and Johnson transformations. This is conveniently located in the Stat > Quality Tools menu, just above the capability analysis function.

Running the Individual Distribution Identification tool on the Tiles.MTW dataset produces this report:

Distribution ID Plot for Warping

```
Descriptive Statistics

  N  N*     Mean     StDev   Median   Minimum   Maximum   Skewness   Kurtosis
100   0  2.92307  1.78597  2.60726   0.28186   8.09064   0.707725   0.135236


Box-Cox transformation: Lambda = 0.5

Johnson transformation function:
0.882908 + 0.987049 * Ln( ( X + 0.132606 ) / ( 9.31101 - X ) )


Goodness of Fit Test

Distribution                AD        P    LRT P
Normal                   1.028    0.010
Box-Cox Transformation   0.301    0.574
Lognormal                1.477   <0.005
3-Parameter Lognormal    0.523       *    0.007
Exponential              5.982   <0.003
2-Parameter Exponential  3.660   <0.010    0.000
Weibull                  0.248   >0.250
3-Parameter Weibull      0.359    0.467    0.225
Smallest Extreme Value   3.410   <0.010
Largest Extreme Value    0.504    0.213
Gamma                    0.489    0.238
3-Parameter Gamma        0.547       *    0.763
Logistic                 0.879    0.013
Loglogistic              1.239   <0.005
3-Parameter Loglogistic  0.692       *    0.085
Johnson Transformation   0.231    0.799
```

The table above lists statistics and p-values from the Anderson–Darling normality test for all distribution families tested. The AD column is the test statistic, which measures how badly the distribution fits the dataset. Generally, the lowest AD statistic indicates the best fit. However, a distribution or transformation with more parameters will often have a lower AD statistic, but the added complexity of the model may not be justified.

The P column lists the p-values for the Anderson–Darling test. If the p-value is small, less than 0.05, this indicates strong evidence that the model does not fit. Generally, the largest p-value indicates the best fit. But for various technical

reasons, p-values are not always available. Some distribution families have an *
indicating a missing p-value. Others indicate >0.250 or <0.010 when the exact
value is unknown.

The LRT P column lists the p-value for a likelihood ratio test (LRT). This
test is only used for some distribution families with an extra threshold parameter. If the LRT P value is small, less than 0.05, this means that adding the extra
threshold parameter significantly improves the fit of the distribution model. In
this example, the 3-Parameter Lognormal model is significantly better than
the Lognormal model, and the 2-Parameter Exponential model is significantly better than the Exponential model.

For the Tiles.MTW dataset, which model is best? The smallest AD statistic
belongs to the Johnson Transformation. With four parameters, the Johnson
Transformation is the most complicated model in this list. The Box-Cox
model has only one parameter, and its AD statistic is almost as good. Between the
two transformation models, Box–Cox is preferred because of its simplicity.

But the two-parameter Weibull model has a smaller AD than the Box-Cox
transformation. It may have a higher P value, but since it says >0.250, there is
no way to know for sure. Among all the distribution models, Weibull looks like
the best choice.

After selecting a Weibull model, the nonnormal capability can be analyzed
using either Stat > Quality Tools > Capability Analysis > Nonnormal or Stat > Quality
Tools > Capability Sixpack > Nonnormal. Figure 12-18 is a nonnormal capability
sixpack for the dataset, using a subgroup size of 5 and an upper specification
limit of 10. The Weibull-based analysis reports a Ppk of 1.00, which is quite
close to the 0.95 reported after the Box–Cox transformation.

The ISO and Minitab methods of nonnormal capability analysis typically
return different values of Ppk, except when Ppk = 1. For the Tiles.MTW example
and an upper specification limit of 10, either method will return essentially the
same metric values. However, if the upper specification is changed to 15 or 20,
the two calculation methods return very different values of Ppk. Only the
Minitab method maintains the same relationship between PPM defect rates and
Ppk, regardless of the distribution. This is the main reason why the Minitab
method ought to be preferred.

To summarize the capability analysis of the Tiles dataset, several options are
available:

- Ignore the nonnormality, and use normal based control charts and capability metrics. Since this process will never be normal, this approach will

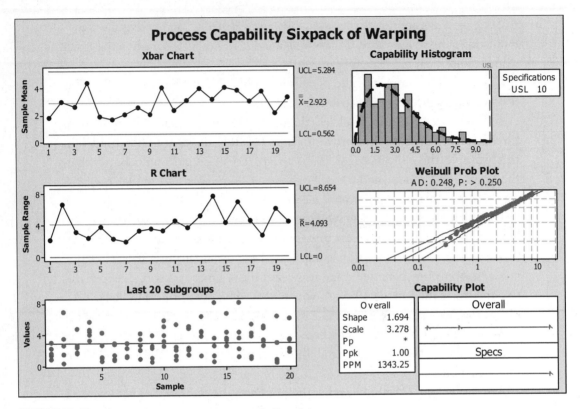

FIGURE 12-18 · Process capability sixpack using Weibull model.

lead to a frustratingly large number of false alarms on the control chart, and a defect rate much larger than the calculated Ppk would typically indicate.

- Use the square root transformation, the optimal Box–Cox transformation. This is an effective normalizing transformation for this distribution, so both the control charts and capability metrics should be reliable.

- Use the Johnson transformation. This method also would work, except that it is needlessly complicated for this dataset.

- Use nonnormal capability analysis with the Weibull model. Using this method, capability results match the Box–Cox option. This approach also has the advantage that control charts are labeled in the actual units of measurement, rather than in square roots of units. This may be more understandable and acceptable to those who must use and interpret it in the long run.

Still Struggling

If you are confused by the large number of capability metrics and optional calculation methods, you are not alone. Most managers and other consumers of capability metrics will never want to know the complexities discussed in this chapter. Here are the main points to remember:

- Is the process stable? For an unstable process, avoid the publication of any capability metrics, as they are not reliable predictors of future performance.
- Which capability metrics are best? Most people only need two capability metrics, but which two? The most popular choices are Cp and Cpk, followed by their long-term counterparts Pp and Ppk. Other metrics can be used to answer specific questions as needed.
- How should the metrics be calculated? The standard formulas are used most often, but Minitab provides options to deal with special cases. The analyst needs to choose a method that allows metrics to be interpreted consistently. "Cpk = 1.5" ought to mean the same thing in all cases. For some processes, methods and formulas must be changed to meet this goal, as illustrated by the examples above.

12.4   Measuring Capability for Attributes

Minitab offers capability tools for attribute data following either the binomial or Poisson models. These models were first introduced in Chapter 4, and further explained in Section 11.4 on attribute control charts. Please refer to Section 11.4 for an explanation of the binomial and Poisson models in these applications.

If an upper limit on defective units or defects is specified, Minitab capability tools can analyze how well the process is meeting that limit, calculate defect rates, and estimate Z levels for comparison to other processes.

The new control charts assistant provides easy access to binomial and Poisson capability analysis. The assistant also offers tools to compare before and after capability for either binomial or Poisson processes. In the Stat > Quality Tools > Capability Analysis menu, the Binomial and Poisson functions offer similar analyses to the assistant, with a few more options and without the helpful interpretive advice.

Continuing with an example from Section 11.4, the Minitab sample data file BulbDefect.MTW lists the counts of defective bulbs in each lot of 576 bulbs. Suppose management imposes an upper limit of 2% on bulbs tested defective, which must be met to avoid material shortages and to maintain shipment schedules. Since each bulb is either defective or nondefective, the binomial model is appropriate for this situation. How well does this process meet the 2% goal?

To find out, select Binomial Capability from the capability analysis assistant, and fill out the dialog as follows:

- Number of defective items column: Defectives

- Constant size for all subgroups: 576

- What is the maximum % defective you are willing to accept? Maximum: 2

Figure 12-19 shows the Summary Report generated by the assistant. In the top left, a color-coded graph answers this question: Is the % defective at or below 2?.

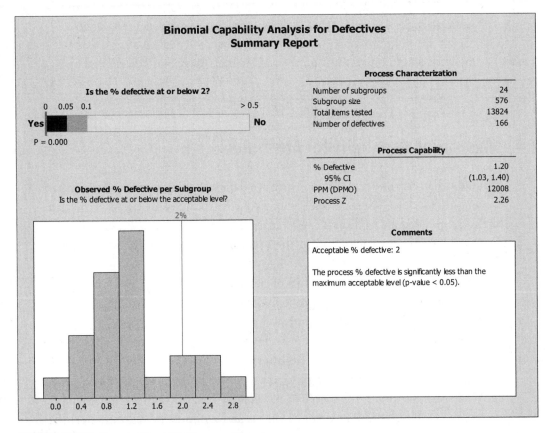

FIGURE 12-19 • Binomial Capability Summary Report.

Since the *p*-value from a hypothesis test is 0.000, the answer is a very strong yes. Since this test applies only to the mean % defective, it is still possible that some lots will have more than 2% defective.

The histogram in the bottom left reveals that some lots do in fact have more than 2% defective. The table on the right reports a defect rate of 12,008 PPM or DPMO, which is 1.2%. This equates to a Process Z value of 2.26, which could be compared to Z.bench from other reports.

Figure 12-20 is the Diagnostic Report from this analysis. The top graph is a P Chart to show whether this process is stable. It appears that batch 16 had significantly more defective bulbs than the rest. If the cause for problems in batch 16 could be eliminated, the process would have fewer defects in the long run.

The lower graph plots Cumulative % Defective over the 24 batches included in this dataset. The cumulative curve seems to be settling down to the overall

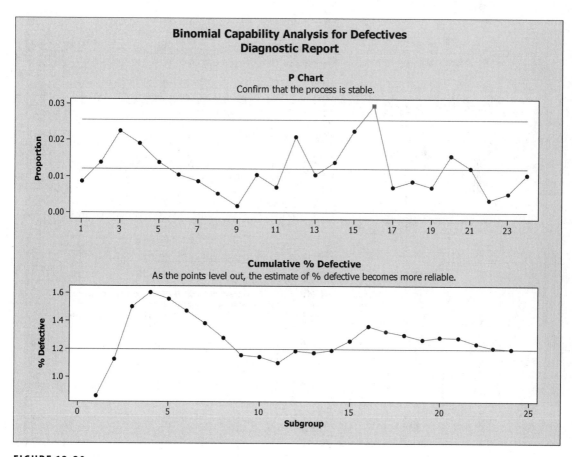

FIGURE 12-20 • Binomial Capability Diagnostic Report.

mean of 1.2% defective. The third graph created by the assistant, the Report Card is not shown here, but it includes text advice and warnings about stability, the number of subgroups, and the amount of data.

For another example, open the Minitab sample data file Transcription.MTW, which contains the number of typographical errors per pages of transcribed documents. Each document has a different number of pages, so the pages are listed in a second column. Since each page may contain many typos, the Poisson model should be used to model the counts of typos.

Suppose that the desired standard of transcription quality is to have fewer than 0.2 typos per page of transcription. To find out whether the transcription process meets the quality goal, use the capability analysis assistant, and select the Poisson Capability tool. Fill out the dialog as in previous examples. Figure 12-21 shows the Summary Report from this analysis.

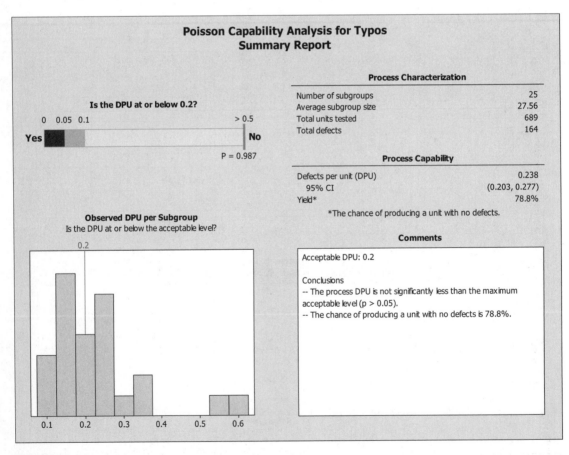

FIGURE 12-21 · Poisson Capability Summary Report.

Does the process meet the goal of 0.2 typos per page? According to the color-coded graph in the top left corner, the answer is a strong no. The histogram tells the story. Not only is the mean for typos per page more than 0.2, but some documents have as many as 0.6 typos per page. The right side of this graph reports that, with 95% confidence, the defect rate is somewhere between 0.203 and 0.277 typos per page. It is also interesting to note that the first-pass yield, which is the chance of transcribing one page with zero defects, is 78.8%. For a ten-page document, the yield would be reduced to $0.788^{10} = 0.0923$ or 9.23%. This means that the probability of a ten-page document being free of typos is only 9.23%.

For an example of capability comparison, open the Minitab sample data file Accident.MTW. This file lists the number of accidents per week at one dangerous intersection. Suppose a traffic engineer were assigned the responsibility to reduce the accident rate to below 1.5 accidents per week. After studying the alternatives, the city approves the engineer's plan to install cameras at the intersection which will automatically photograph those who either run the red light or exceed the speed limit as they pass through the intersection.

We do not have the data after the changes were made. To demonstrate the capability comparison tool of the assistant, let's simply generate some random numbers. Using Calc > Random Data > Poisson, generate 52 rows of random data with a mean of 1, and store them in a column called After. This will represent the accidents per week at the intersection after installing the cameras.

Now, using the capability analysis assistant, select Poisson Comparison. Fill out the dialog by entering Accidents for the Baseline process data and After for the Improved process data. Both will have a constant sample size of 1, representing 1 week. Enter 1.5 for the maximum defects per unit.

Figure 12-22 shows the Summary Report for the Poisson Capability Comparison. Since the After data were randomly generated, your results may vary. In the upper left corner, a big green down arrow notes an impressive 57% reduction in the accident rate. Below that are results of hypothesis tests showing that the original accident rate was significantly above 1.5, but now it is significantly below 1.5.

The Diagnostic Report, not shown here, contains two U Charts and two Cumulative DPU (defects per unit) graphs illustrating the significant improvement.

12.5   Find Out More

The references cited in Chapter 11 are good for process capability as well. Besides these works, Bothe (1997) and Kotz and Lovelace (1998) are entirely devoted to the subject of measuring process capability. Of these, Bothe is

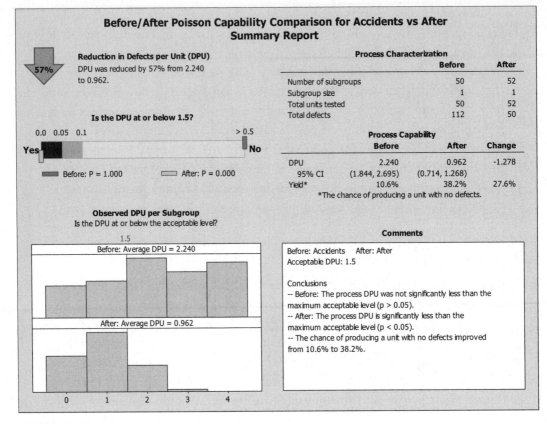

FIGURE 12-22 · Poisson Capability Comparison.

written from the perspective of a practitioner, while Kotz and Lovelace's book is more academic. Both are very readable and useful.

This chapter presented a variety of capability analysis tools, which quantitatively measure how well a process keeps its individual units inside specification limits or close to a target value. In Minitab, the capability analysis assistant provides a simplified interface to powerful capability reports, including automatic testing for stability and normality. The capability analysis functions in the Stat > Quality Tools menu include the popular sixpack graphs and alternative capability tools for many situations. Once a process is stable and capable, the next challenge is to keep it that way. Sometimes, acceptance sampling is used to audit and measure ongoing process performance. The next chapter shows how Minitab helps plan and analyze acceptance sampling test plans for both variables and attributes.

QUIZ

1. **Which of the following best describes the relationship between process stability and process capability?**

   A. A process should be capable before any process stability metrics are reported.

   B. A process should be stable before any process capability metrics are reported.

   C. Both stability and capability can be visualized with a control chart.

   D. There is no relationship between stability and capability.

2. **In Minitab, which of the following are called overall or actual capability metrics?**

   A. Cp, Cpk, and Cpm

   B. Ppk and Cpk

   C. Pp, Ppk, and Cpm

   D. PPM Total and Z.bench

3. **Which of the following metrics is usually calculated with the standard deviation within subgroups?**

   A. Cpk

   B. Ppk

   C. Z.bench

   D. Cpm

4. **Which of the following is the best choice for capability analysis of a nonnormal process distribution?**

   A. Box–Cox transformation

   B. Johnson transformation

   C. Fit a distribution model, then use the "Minitab" method to calculate nonnormal capability metrics.

   D. Any of the above might be the best choice, depending on the situation.

5. **Which tool does the capability analysis assistant recommend to determine the capability of counts of defective items?**

   A. Capability Analysis

   B. Binomial Capability

   C. Poisson Capability

   D. Capability Comparison

6. **The Minitab sample data file Antacid.MTW lists the minutes before 16 test subjects reported relief from heartburn symptoms. The brand tested advertises relief within 15 minutes, so 15 is the upper specification limit, and there is no lower limit. What is Ppk?**

7. **For the same dataset analyzed for question 6, what percentage of people with heartburn are expected to NOT feel relief from heartburn symptoms within 15 minutes?**

8. The Minitab sample data file Acid.MTW contains ion concentration measurements for a chemical product, with specification limits of 0.100 – 0.120. The first column Acid1 contains the initial or baseline data. After a project reduces variation in these concentrations, the improved results are listed in the second column Acid2. Treat this as individual measurements, with subgroup size of 1. What are the before and after estimates of Ppk?

9. For the data file Acid.MTW, and the second column Acid2 in that worksheet, calculate a 95% confidence interval on Ppk.

10. The Minitab sample data file Plating.MTW contains counts of parts with at least one plating defect, out of a lot size of 50 parts. The process has a goal of less than 10% defective parts. Your boss asks you for a "process sigma level" based on this data. What is the best answer?

chapter 13

Acceptance Sampling

How can we determine whether a population or a lot of parts has acceptable quality? Using acceptance sampling methods, a random sample of the lot is inspected. Based on the performance of the sample, the lot is either accepted or rejected. This sounds simple, but important questions must be answered: How large should the sample be? What sample criteria must be met to accept the lot? What will inspection cost in the long run? How good or bad will the quality of parts be, after the inspection process? Complex statistical theory is required to answer these questions, but Minitab can answer them quickly and easily.

CHAPTER OBJECTIVES

Here's what you'll learn in this chapter:

- How to create, compare, and analyze attribute sampling plans

- How to create, compare, and analyze variables sampling plans

- How to predict the economic impact of sampling

Two families of acceptance sampling plans are available. Attributes sampling is used when counting defective units or when counting defects within units. Variables sampling is used when measuring a quantitative, numerical characteristic of each unit. When it is possible to measure a characteristic quantitatively, it is often less expensive to perform go/no-go attributes sampling. The disadvantage of attributes sampling is that much larger sample sizes are required for the same quality goals and risk levels. When both attributes and variables sampling are possible, Minitab can quickly design sampling plans for both choices, so an educated business decision can be made.

For decades, military and industrial standards have been used to select sampling plans. The current incarnations of these standards are ANSI/ASQ Z1.4-2008 for attributes sampling plans and ANSI/ASQ Z1.9-2008 for variables sampling plans. These are useful recipe books, but as standards, they offer very little flexibility. Minitab provides opportunities to adjust risk levels and parameters beyond the values used in the standards. Minitab also provides graphs and analysis of sampling plans which are difficult to extract from the written standards.

13.1   Creating and Comparing Attributes Sampling Plans

To explain the acronyms and terminology associated with attributes sampling, consider an example of a sampling plan from MIL-STD-105, the now-obsolete predecessor of ANSI/ASQ Z1.4. A shorthand description of this sampling plan is $(n, c) = (80, 2)$. This means the sample size n is 80, and the acceptance number c is 2. After testing 80 parts, if 2 or fewer parts are found to be defective, the lot will be accepted. If 3 or more parts are found to be defective, the lot will be rejected. This could be a recommended sampling plan for a lot size of 1000 and an acceptable quality level (AQL) of 1.0%.

The best way to illustrate this example is with an illustration. To make a graph like the one shown in Fig. 13-1, select Stat > Quality Tools > Acceptance Sampling for Attributes, and fill out the dialog this way:

- Select Compare User Defined Sampling Plans from the dropdown box.
- Measurement type: Go / no go (defective)
- Units for quality levels: Percent defective
- Acceptable quality level (AQL): 1
- Rejectable quality level (RQL or LTPD): 4

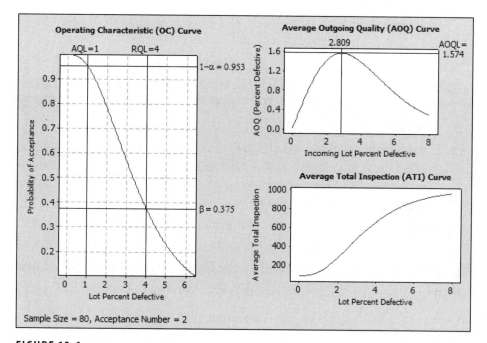

FIGURE 13-1 · Attribute sampling analysis with (n, c) = (80, 2).

- Sample sizes: 80
- Acceptance numbers: 2
- Lot size: 1000

With these settings, Minitab creates a three-part graph. Figure 13-1 is based on this graph, with some additional reference lines and labels to illustrate the following important concepts. The key graph is the Operating Characteristic (OC) curve on the left side of Fig. 13-1. The horizontal scale represents the Lot Percent Defective, the unknown percentage of defective items in the lot. The vertical scale represents the Probability of Acceptance for any percentage of defective units. For this example, the OC curve represents the probability that the sample of size 80 will contain 0, 1, or 2 defective units and be accepted by the sampling plan.

All OC curves have a similar shape to this one. When the lot contains zero defectives, the probability of acceptance is one. As the number of defectives increases, the probability of acceptance declines. The reference lines in this graph illustrate two important points on the curve with special names:

- The **acceptable quality level (AQL)** is the level of defects that should be accepted most of the time by the sampling plan. AQL can be expressed as a proportion (0–1), a percentage (0–100), or defectives per million units. In Fig. 13-1, AQL is 1%.

- **Producer's risk** or **alpha (α)** is the probability that a lot with AQL defectives will be wrongly rejected by the sampling plan. Producer's risk is also called **type I error**. In Fig. 13-1, $\alpha = 0.047$, so the probability of accepting the AQL lot is $1 - \alpha = 0.953$.

- The **rejectable quality level (RQL)** is the level of defects that should be rejected most of the time by the sampling plan. Like AQL, RQL can be expressed as a proportion, percentage, or defectives per million units. Lot tolerance percent defective (LTPD) is an older, alternate term for RQL, which is used in some references and standards. In Fig. 13-1, RQL is 4%.

- **Consumer's risk** or **beta (β)** is the probability that a lot with RQL defectives will be wrongly accepted by the sampling plan. Consumer's risk is also called **type II error**. In Fig. 13-1, $\beta = 0.375$.

To summarize this example so far, a sampling plan where a sample of size $n = 80$ and an acceptance number of $c = 2$ has an $\alpha = 0.047$ probability of wrongly rejecting a lot with AQL = 1% defective units, and it also has a $\beta = 0.375$ probability of wrongly accepting a lot with RQL = 4% defective units.

The terminology of sampling is fairly standardized, but it causes much confusion. For example, AQL and RQL do not measure quality, they measure un-quality. Also, how can any level of defective units be "acceptable?" It is more important to learn what these terms mean, than to worry about their odd names. The key point is that AQL maps to 1-α and RQL maps to β through the OC curve.

The two curves on the right of Fig. 13-1 describe the economic impact of the sampling plan, under some additional assumptions. These graphs assume that every rejected lot is screened 100%, so that every unit in that lot is tested and the defective parts are removed. In accepted lots, if any defective units are found in the sample, these defective units are also removed.

Under these assumptions, the Average Outgoing Quality (AOQ) Curve graphs the percentage of defective units leaving the inspection process, plotted against the percentage of defective units coming into the inspection process. In other words, this graph shows outgoing quality versus incoming quality. When zero defectives come in, zero defectives go out. When many defectives come in, the lot is almost certainly rejected, so few defectives go out. In the middle is a defective level where the AOQ reaches a maximum point. The maximum AOQ is called average outgoing quality limit (AOQL). For the example in Fig. 13-1, AOQL is 1.574%, which occurs when 2.809% defective units come in.

The Average Total Inspection (ATI) Curve graphs the average number of parts inspected against the incoming lot percent defective. When zero defectives come in, ATI equals the sample size, 80 in this example. When many defectives come in, ATI approaches the lot size, 1000 in this example, because almost every lot must be 100% screened.

To supplement the graph, this report appears in the Session window:

Acceptance Sampling by Attributes

```
Measurement type:  Go/no go
Lot quality in percent defective
Lot size:  1000
Use binomial distribution to calculate probability of acceptance


Acceptable Quality Level (AQL)             1
Rejectable Quality Level (RQL or LTPD)   4


Compare User Defined Plan(s)

Sample Size          80
Acceptance Number    2

Accept lot if defective items in 80 sampled <= 2;  Otherwise reject.


  Percent   Probability  Probability
Defective    Accepting    Rejecting    AOQ     ATI
      1          0.953                 0.047  0.877   122.8
      4          0.375                 0.625  1.379   655.2

Average outgoing quality limit (AOQL) = 1.574 at 2.809 percent defective.
```

How can this information be used to make economic decisions? The last part of the report above includes AOQ and ATI for 1% and 4% defective units. By default, this table includes calculations only for AQL and RQL. Additional quality levels may be specified in the Options dialog. These calculations can be used in the economic analysis of sampling.

Suppose the cost of inspecting one part is $2, but the cost of accepting a defective part is $100. If zero defective units come in, every lot of 1000 parts costs $2 \times 80 = $160 for inspection. If incoming quality is 1%, AOQ = 0.877%, so the cost of accepted defective parts is $1000 \times 0.877\% \times $100 = $877. ATI = 122.8, so inspection will cost $2 \times 122.80 = $245.60. When incoming quality is 1%, the total cost is $877 + $245.60 = $1,122.60.

Suppose we had a no-inspection policy, simply accepting every lot. With 1% incoming defective units, the cost per lot of this policy will be the cost of accepting 1% defective units, which is $1000 \times 1\% \times \$100 = \$1,000$. If, instead, we inspected every part in all lots, the cost per lot will be $2,000 for inspection only. At 1% defective units, inspection costs a little more than the cost of no inspection.

But instead, suppose incoming quality is 4% because of some big problem. At this quality level, AOQ = 1.379%, so the cost of accepted defective parts is $1000 \times 1.379\% \times \$100 = \$1,379$; ATI = 655.2, so inspection will cost $1,310.40. Total cost is $1,379 + \$1,310.40 = \$2,689.40$.

With the no-inspection policy, the cost of 4% incoming quality would be $4,000. If 100% of every lot is inspected, the cost would $2,000. At this quality level, the cost of the sampling inspection is between the two extreme values.

Well-planned acceptance sampling is a hedge on quality risks. We cannot know in advance how many units will be defective, or how that quality level will vary between lots. As the level of defective units varies in this example, the acceptance sampling plan reduces the overall costs, compared to the extreme alternatives of zero inspection or 100% inspection.

A real-life problem would include other costs, such as the cost of selecting a random sample of every lot, and the cost of processing and returning rejected units. Whatever the cost model may be, the calculations provided by Minitab enable an educated decision to be made about whether to sample, screen, or not inspect at all.

The example above had an acceptance number $c = 2$, which means that a lot of 1000 parts may be accepted, even after finding two defective units in the sample of 80. Many people and companies find this concept problematic, and prefer to use only $c = 0$ sampling plans.

Comparing OC curves can help to understand the differences between sampling plans. Figure 13-2 shows two sets of OC curves for two families of sampling plans. The top set of OC curves all have $c = 0$, where no lot can be accepted after finding even one defective in the sample. The bottom set of OC curves all have $n = 75$, with acceptance numbers of 0 through 5. These graphs are easy to make in Minitab with the Acceptance Sampling by Attributes function, by entering multiple values in the Sample sizes or Acceptance numbers fields.

Suppose it is important to reject a lot with 5% defective units, so RQL = 5%. An $(n, c) = (25, 0)$ sampling plan has a probability of approximately 0.28 of accepting a lot with 5% defective units. The OC curve for this sampling plan is the top line in the top part of Fig. 13-2. In Minitab, mouse over any of the OC curves to see a table of calculated values used to plot the curve. In the bottom

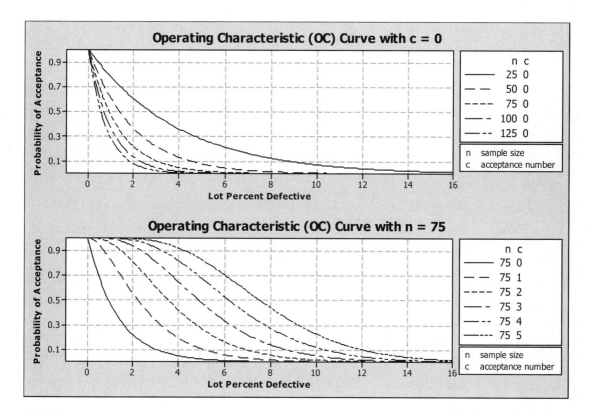

FIGURE 13-2 • Comparison of OC curves.

graph, a (75, 2) sampling plan has approximately the same probability of accepting a lot with 5% defective units.

Apparently, inspecting $n = 25$ units with $c = 0$ is just as good as inspecting $n = 75$ units with $c = 2$, at one-third the cost. Or is it? One benefit of the (75, 2) sampling plan comes at higher levels of defects. When the lot is 10% defective, the (25,0) plan has a 7.1% probability of accepting the lot, but the (75,2) plan has only a 1.6% probability of accepting the lot.

Another benefit of the (75, 2) sampling plan occurs at low defect levels. The ATI curves for the same sampling plans are shown in Fig. 13-3. If the incoming lots have 1% defective units, the (25, 0) plan has an ATI of about 250, while the (75, 2) plan has an ATI of only 115. Compared to the (25, 0) plan, the (75, 2) plan requires less total inspection at lower defect levels, because fewer lots are rejected and screened.

There are situations where it makes economic sense to have a sampling plan with $c > 0$. However, there may be a political cost based on how the sampling

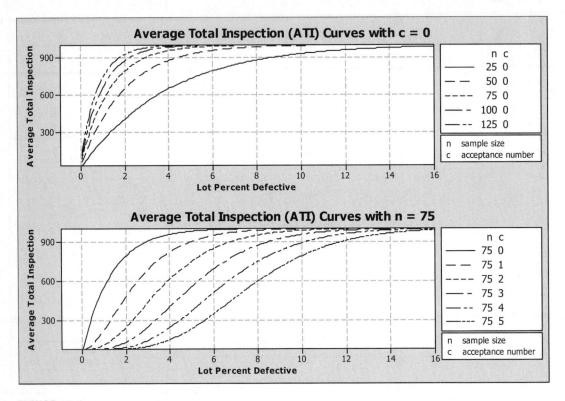

FIGURE 13-3 • Comparison of ATI curves.

plan is perceived. Regardless of the political and managerial concerns, Minitab provides the statistical analysis necessary for a dispassionate discussion of the issues.

As another example, consider the case of Cable by Ed, a company providing cable TV, internet, and telephone services to the town of Edburg. Recently, Ed purchased a pallet of set-top boxes from a new supplier in Elbonia. Ed never performed incoming inspection on boxes from the old supplier. Ed's installers and customers have reported 18 boxes out of 150 that have failed to boot properly, for a rate of 12% defective units.

Ed can create a sampling plan by selecting Stat > Quality Tools > Acceptance Sampling by Attributes and selecting Create a sampling plan in the first dropdown box. Then he selects Go/no go measurement type and Percent defective.

Now Ed must specify goals for the sampling plan. What he really cares about is to be very sure of rejecting a lot with 12% defective units. So, Ed specifies an RQL of 12 and a β of 0.01. This will give Ed 99% confidence of rejecting a lot with 12% defectives.

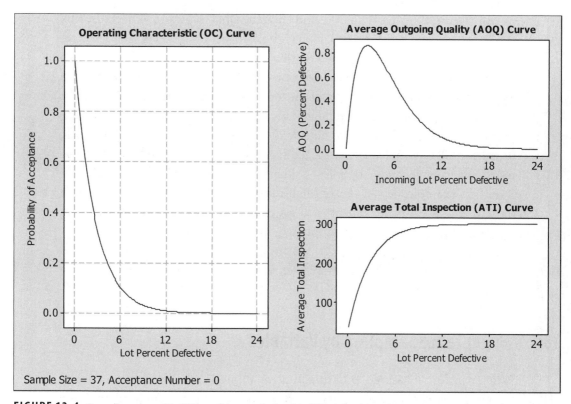

FIGURE 13-4 · Sampling plan with 99% confidence of rejecting 12% defective units.

But Ed really doesn't care about AQL. There is NO level of defective units that Ed wants to accept most of the time. He wants NO defects. Minitab does not like a value of 0 in the AQL field, so Ed enters 0.01, and an α of 0.05. Finally, Ed enters the Lot size of 300 and clicks OK.

Figure 13-4 illustrates the sampling plan specified by Ed. Minitab recommends $(n, c) = (37, 0)$. For each lot of 300 boxes, Ed should now inspect 37 boxes. If none in the sample are defective, he will accept the lot. If even one box in the sample is defective, Ed will either test 100% of the lot, or return the lot to the Elbonian supplier.

Minitab offers another option worth considering for this example. Based on the above calculations, the sample size of 37 is more than 10% of the lot of 300. Minitab does not consider the lot size in the calculation of the sample size. To test this, repeat the same calculation with a lot size of 37. The same sample size of 37 is calculated. Lot size is used for AOQ and ATI calculations, but not for sample size calculations.

Now return the lot size to 300, and click the Options button. Check the box labeled Use hypergeometric distribution for isolated lot. With this option selected, a sample size of $n = 34$ is required, with $c = 0$.

The hypergeometric distribution is a probability model for situations where a sample is selected from a finite lot. If the lot is more than ten times as large as the sample, this option makes little difference. However, it is an appropriate choice when no inference will be drawn outside the one lot being tested. In other words, if each lot will be sampled and inspected separately, or if there is only one lot to be tested, the hypergeometric option should be selected to reduce the sample size.

In Ed's example, he can satisfy the business goals for set-top box inspection by testing only 34 boxes out of each lot of 300. If Ed ever orders a larger lot size as Edburg grows, a larger sample size may be required.

Minitab reports that the AOQL for this plan is 0.860%. In the long run, this sampling plan assures that no more than 0.860% of Ed's set-top boxes will be defective when installed.

13.2   Acceptance Sampling by Variables

When parts are measured with quantitative, numeric measurements, variables sampling is used to create, compare, and analyze sample data. In Minitab, Stat > Quality Tools > Attribute Sampling by Variables is a menu containing two tools. The Create/Compare tool is very similar to the attribute sampling tool illustrated in the previous section. The Accept/Reject Lot tool analyzes a set of variable measurement data and recommends whether to accept or reject the lot.

All the terminology applicable to sampling by attributes also applies to sampling by variables. In addition to the terms defined in the preceding section, a variables sampling plan is defined by one additional parameter:

- The **critical distance** or **k value** is the minimum number of sample standard deviations between the sample mean and either specification limit for the lot to be acceptable.

A variables sampling plan is specified by the sample size n, the critical distance k, and the specification limits LSL and USL. After measuring all n parts, calculate the sample mean $\overline{X}$, and sample standard deviation s. If $\overline{X} + ks \leq$ USL and $\overline{X} - ks \geq$ LSL, then the lot is accepted. Otherwise, the lot is rejected.

It is worth mentioning that all the variables sampling plans supported by Minitab assume that the distribution is normal. The probability of parts being outside the specification limits is based on normal tail probabilities. If the distribution of parts is not normal, the decisions made by these variables sampling plans can be inaccurate.

As an example of variables sampling, Herb works at a canning factory, where he supervises packaging. Herb wants to design a sampling plan for outgoing inspection of the net weight of packaged products. It would be impractical and too expensive to weigh every package. Instead, Herb decides to weigh the contents of a random sample of packages in a lot of 2,000 packages. But how many should be measured?

Herb establishes the following goals for the sampling plan:

- If AQL = 0.5% of packages are outside specification limits, the producer's risk (α) is 0.05 that the lot will be rejected.
- If RQL = 1.8% of packages are outside specification limits, the consumer's risk (β) is 0.10 that the lot will be accepted.

For the product being tested, the specification limits are from 2.9 to 3.1, and the lot size is 2000.

In Minitab, Herb selects Stat > Quality Tools > Acceptance Sampling by Variables > Create/Compare and fills in the dialog with the above information. After Herb clicks OK, he sees the four-part graph shown here as Fig. 13-5. In this graph, the OC Curve, AOQ Curve, and ATI Curve are the same curves seen in the analysis of attribute sampling plans in the previous section.

The top right part of Fig. 13-5, the Acceptance Region Plot is used only for variables sampling plans. This graph has the Sample Mean on the horizontal scale, and Sample StDev on the vertical scale. If the sample mean and standard deviation are anywhere below the ∧-shaped curve, the lot will be accepted. If the sample mean and standard deviation are above the ∧-shaped curve, the lot will be rejected. The horizontal line at the top of the graph represents the maximum sample standard deviation which could be acceptable.

A note at the bottom of Fig. 13-5 states that Herb's goals would be met by a sample size of 137, with a critical distance (k) of 2.30665. The maximum sample standard deviation is 0.03910.

For good measure, Herb rounds the sample size up to 150. Herb conducts random selection and weighing of 150 packages from the next lot of 2000. These measurements are listed in the Minitab example data file Canning.MTW.

To analyze this data, Herb selects Stat > Quality Tools > Acceptance Sampling by Variables > Accept/Reject Lot from the Minitab menu. In the dialog, Herb

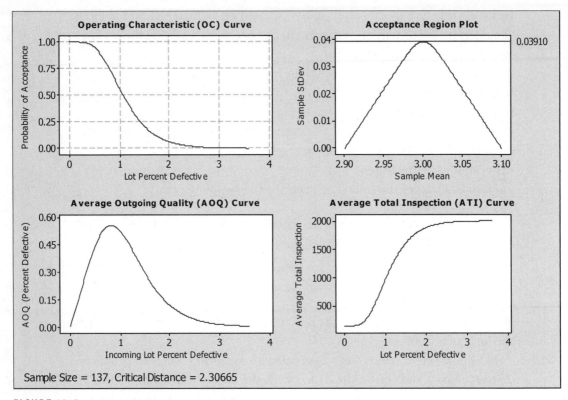

FIGURE 13-5 • Analysis of variables sampling plan.

specifies the column name, Weight, the Crticial distance (k value) of 2.30665, the Lower spec of 2.9, and the Upper spec of 3.1. After clicking OK, this report appears in the Session window:

Acceptance Sampling by Variables - Accept/Reject Lot

```
Make Accept or Reject Decision Using Weight

Sample Size                           150
Mean                                  3.03864
Standard Deviation                    0.0268681
Lower Specification Limit (LSL)       2.9
Upper Specification Limit (USL)       3.1

Z.LSL                                 5.16004
Z.USL                                 2.28372
Critical Distance (k Value)           2.30665
Maximum Standard Deviation (MSD)      0.0390979

Decision:  Reject lot.
```

Minitab finds that the sample mean is only $\text{Z.USL} = 2.28372$ sample standard deviations inside the upper specification limit of 3.1. Since this is less than the critical distance of 2.30665, the correct decision is to reject the lot.

The minimum weight in the sample is 2.9549, and the maximum weight is 3.0971. Every package inspected is inside the specification limits. Even so, this variables sampling plan correctly rejected the lot. Figure 13-6 shows why. This is a capability snapshot prepared with the capability analysis assistant, introduced in Chapter 12. The histogram shows the distribution of weights off target and very close to the upper specification limit. Visually, it appears risky to assume that a lot with this distribution will stay within specification limits.

At the bottom of the Process Characterization table is the bottom line. PPM (DPMO) (observed) is 0, meaning that no values were outside the specification limits. But PPM (DPMO) (expected) is 11,194. This is a prediction that 11,194 packages per million, or about 1.1% of packages will be outside the specification

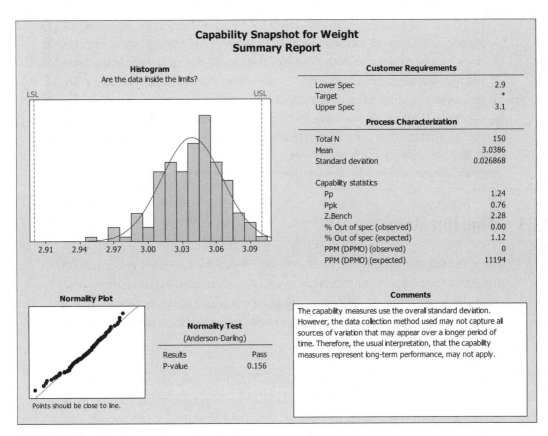

FIGURE 13-6 · Capability snapshot of weight data.

limits. Based on Herb's goals for the sampling plan, it is appropriate to reject this lot.

Since this is outgoing inspection, this test provides vital information to Herb. By working to adjust and improve the packaging process, the mean product weight can be reduced to be closer to the target value of 3.0. This will save a significant amount of money by reducing the amount of product required.

? Still Struggling

Which is better, attributes or variables sampling? As with every business decision, it all boils down to money. When either a pass/fail or quantitative measurement is possible, the quantitative measurement almost always costs more per unit tested. However, variables sampling plans with quantitative measurements usually require fewer measurements than attributes sampling for the same levels of risk. The sampling plan with lower total cost will vary depending on the situation, and Minitab calculations of AOQ and ATI can help with these calculations. Harder to quantify is the value of the knowledge obtained. In the final example above, suppose Herb had chosen an attributes sampling plan. With zero defective units in the sample, Herb would have accepted the lot. More significantly, Herb would not have recognized the opportunities to improve his process that can only come from quantitative measurements. In Herb's example, variables sampling is clearly superior.

13.3   Find Out More

The standards for sampling procedures, ANSI/ASQ Z1.4-2008 and Z1.9-2008 provide some additional information about sampling methods and offer options unavailable in Minitab, such as double or multiple sampling. Schilling and Neubauer (2008) is a thorough, modern text on acceptance sampling by noted experts in the field.

This chapter showed how to use Minitab tools to select, design, and analyze sampling plans for both attributes and variables. Next, the final chapter covers the analysis and prevention of failures over the lifetime of a product, through reliability and survival analysis.

QUIZ

1. **What is the most correct interpretation of AQL = 1.0%?**
   A. No more than 1.0% defective items are acceptable.
   B. Acceptance sampling should be designed so that a lot with 1.0% defective items is accepted most of the time.
   C. Each lot should contain at least 1.0% defective items.
   D. Acceptance sampling should be designed so that a lot with 1.0% defective items is rejected most of the time.

Questions 2 and 3 refer to the following section of a Minitab report:

```
Percent   Probability  Probability
Defective   Accepting    Rejecting    AOQ    ATI
        2       0.950        0.050    1.559   22.1
       20       0.099        0.901    1.625   91.9

Average outgoing quality limit (AOQL) = 3.764 at 8.567 percent
defective.
```

2. **If lots have 2% defective items, and all rejected lots are screened 100%, how many units will be tested per lot, on average?**
   A. 20
   B. 22.1
   C. 91.9
   D. There is no way to tell from the information available.

3. **What is the maximum level of defects which will remain in the lots after inspection, assuming that rejected lots are either returned to the supplier or 100% screened?**
   A. 3.764%
   B. 8.567%
   C. 1.559%
   D. There is no way to answer the question with the information provided.

4. **Which of the following situations calls for acceptance sampling by variables?**
   A. When the sample size varies from lot to lot.
   B. When inspecting the exterior of a household appliance and counting cosmetic defects.
   C. When deciding whether to accept a lot of machined shafts by measuring the diameters of a sample of shafts.
   D. When measuring 100% of parts in all lots.

5. Suppose castings are received in lots of size 100. A sample of castings needs to be tested for porosity, which is an attribute. If AQL = 2%, RQL = 20%, α = 0.05, and β = 0.10, what is the recommended sampling plan?

   A. Randomly inspect 18 castings. If 1 or more defective castings are found, reject the lot.

   B. Randomly inspect 18 castings. If 2 or more defective castings are found, reject the lot.

   C. Randomly inspect 18 castings. If 3 or more defective castings are found, reject the lot.

   D. There is no acceptance sampling plan available to meet these criteria.

6. A frequently cited measure of "Six Sigma quality" is 3.4 defects per million units (DPM). Suppose you want to apply acceptance sampling to a very large lot of 1,000,000 items, and you want to have a probability of 0.05 of rejecting a lot with 3.4 DPM. What is the minimum sample size required?

7. Does a (10, 0) or a (25, 1) attribute sampling plan have a higher probability of rejecting a lot with 10% defective units?

8. Does a (10, 0) or a (25, 1) attribute sampling plan have a smaller average outgoing quality limit (AOQL), with a lot size of 500?

9. What sample size and critical distance are required for a variables sampling plan meeting these requirements:

   A. The sampling plan should have a 0.05 probability of rejecting a lot with 1% defective units.

   B. The sampling plan should have a 0.90 probability of rejecting a lot with 5% defective units.

   C. The specification limits are 590 – 610.

   D. The lot size is 200.

10. Apply the specification limits and critical distance calculated in question 9 to analyze the measurements in the file Camshaft.MTW and the first column, named Length. Based on this sample dataset, should the lot be accepted or rejected?

chapter 14

Reliability Analysis

Everyone dies. But when? Nobody knows in advance when an individual will die. However, the probability distribution of life expectancy is well-known. Knowledge of this distribution is the key to pricing and profitability for life insurance products.

So it is with products of all kinds. It is impossible to predict when an individual product will fail, but the distribution of failure times can be estimated and predicted. This knowledge is critically important for improving customer satisfaction and profitability.

Reliability engineering merges physics, engineering, and statistical tools into a growing discipline based on the predicted distributions of failure times. Although numerous specialized reliability software products are available, the Stat > Reliability/Survival menu provides a rich and powerful set of tools for reliability analysis. This chapter introduces a few of these tools.

CHAPTER OBJECTIVES

Here's what you'll learn in this chapter:

- How to estimate reliability from life tests
- How to estimate reliability from warranty failure and sales data
- How to plan sample sizes for reliability tests
- How to estimate reliability as functions of other variables

Many tools featured in this chapter are improved or specialized versions of tools covered earlier in this book. For example, Chapter 4 introduced probability plots, goodness-of-fit tests, and the Individual Distribution Identification tool for selecting distribution models. The Reliability/Survival menu contains very similar tools with the added flexibility of dealing with censored data. Confidence intervals, hypothesis tests, and p-values have been featured in many chapters before; here, these same tools enable engineers and managers to assess reliability data and make more informed decisions.

This chapter shows how to fit probability models to survival data, using examples from the field of product reliability. After these models are fitted to the data, they can be used to predict survival probabilities and many other measures of life.

In these examples, time is always the measured quantity. In a more general sense, survival can be measured by many other quantities, such as force, cycles, voltage, or power. The same statistical techniques are used, whatever variable is used as a proxy for time.

14.1   Estimating Reliability from Failure Data

When measurements of failure times are available, there are three steps to process the data into a form suitable for making decisions:

- Arrange the data in a format that Minitab can analyze. Two formats are available, called Right Censoring and Arbitrary Censoring. These formats are described in more detail below. A special option is available for warranty data, discussed later.

- Select a distribution model for time to failure. If a specific distribution family has not already been selected by prior work, the Distribution ID Plot tool can compare the fit of several distribution families for failure times. As an alternative to parametric distribution models, Minitab offers nonparametric analysis of reliability data, which assumes no particular family of distribution models.

- Create graphs, and calculate metrics and predictions as required. Probability, survival, and hazard plots are standard tools for visual reliability analysis. For quantitative work, the mean time to failure (MTTF) or various percentiles of the failure time distribution are commonly used. Confidence intervals are usually used to quantify the uncertainty of a small sample size.

It is highly unusual for a set of failure time data to contain the exact failure times of every unit tested. Such a dataset is called complete. A distribution model can be fit to a complete dataset using any of the techniques in Chapter 4.

Most often, the dataset is said to be censored, because the exact failure times are not known. In Minitab, each time measurement in a dataset may have a different type of censoring, chosen from this list of four options:

- An **exact** failure time is the time at which the unit failed.

- A **right-censored** failure time is a measured time before the unit failed. Typically, a life test ends when some, but not all test units have failed. The units which did not fail during the test are right-censored. The time recorded is the last time at which the unit is known to be working.

- A **left-censored** failure time is a measured time after the unit failed. If units are tested occasionally, but not continuously, the exact times of failure cannot be known. A unit which is already failed at the first test is left-censored. The time recorded is the first time at which the unit is known to be failed.

- An **interval-censored** failure time is actually two times, one before and one after the unit failed. If units are tested occasionally, but not continuously, any unit that failed between test times is interval censored.

Minitab can analyze failure time data organized in either of two formats. The Right Censoring format can handle any combination of exact and right-censored failure times. The Arbitrary Censoring format can handle any combination of exact, right-, left-, and interval-censored failure times.

To set up a dataset for Right Censoring, the failure times must be in one column. Usually, a second column of the same length, with two numeric or text values, indicates censoring. By default, Minitab uses the lowest numeric value or the first text value in alphabetic sequence to identify right-censored data, and the other value identifies exact data. The user can specify which value identifies a censored time in the dialog.

In two special cases, the censoring column is not needed. If the test ended at a set time, the user can enter that time directly in the dialog, and Minitab will assume that all times greater than or equal to that time are censored. If the test ended after a certain number of failures occurred, the user can enter that number directly in the dialog. With failure censoring, the specified number of sorted failure times are exact, while the rest are censored.

As an example of right-censored data, Reid designs windings for industrial generators. Reid has tested several test windings at excessive temperatures of 80°C and 100°C. Reid's data is available in the Minitab example data file Reliable.MTW. In this worksheet, columns Temp80 and Temp100 contain the test times for every unit tested. Columns Censor80 and Censor100 contain numeric values 0 for right-censored data or 1 for exact data.

This dataset is already arranged for Minitab Right Censoring analysis. Reid does not have any historical information to suggest one family of distributions over another, so he needs to select a family now. To do this, Reid selects Stat > Reliabiliy/Survival > Distribution Analysis (Right Censoring) > Distribution ID Plot from the Minitab menu. Reid fills out the dialog as shown in Fig. 14-1.

To specify the censoring information, Reid clicks the Censor button and enters Cens80 Cens100 in the Use censoring columns field.

In the Distribution ID Plot dialog shown in Fig. 14-1, Reid selects the Specify option which allows him to select 1–4 specific distributions to test. The Weibull, Lognormal, Exponential, and Normal distributions are a good set of families to try. If Reid leaves the default Use all distributions option selected, the tool will try eleven families of distributions.

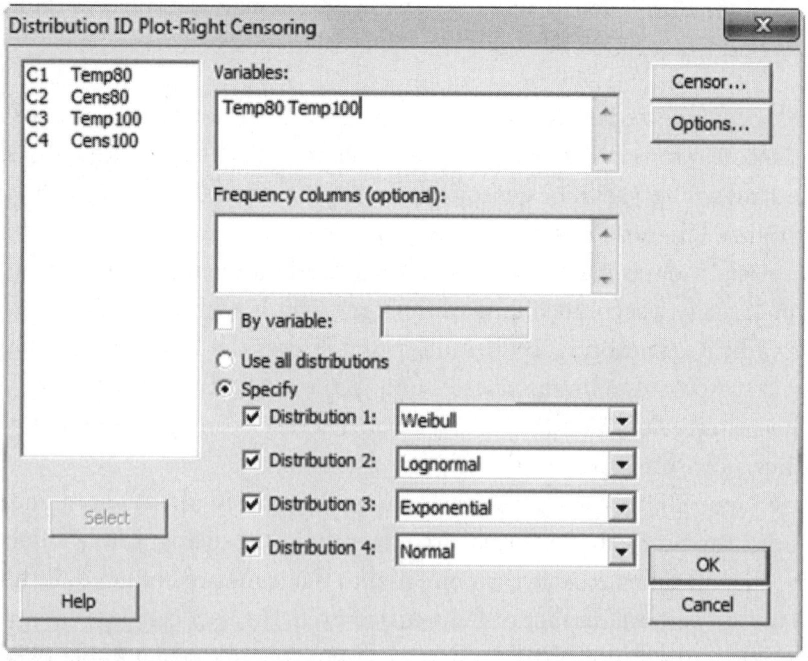

FIGURE 14-1 · Distribution ID plotdialog.

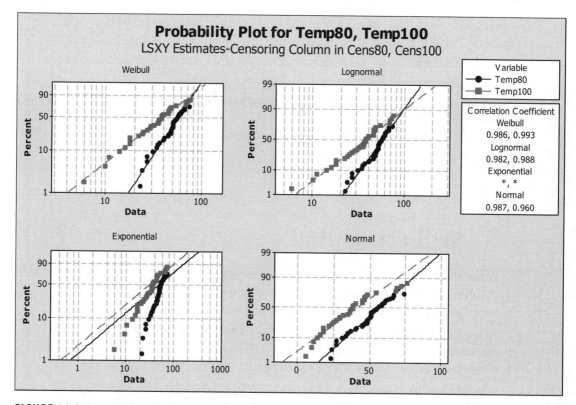

FIGURE 14-2 · Distribution ID plot.

After clicking OK, Reid sees a set of four probability plots, as shown in Fig. 14-2. Each plot contains two sets of dots and two lines, for the two datasets tested.

This figure is similar to the ones generated by the Individual Distribution Identification tool in the Stat > Quality Tools menu, with some important differences for reliability data. One difference is the method used to fit the distribution models. By default, the Distribution ID Plot uses a least squares regression approach to fit the failure times against the transformed percentages. Also, instead of a traditional goodness-of-fit test, this plot reports Pearson correlation coefficients that measure how well the distribution models fit the available data. A higher value of correlation coefficient represents a better fit.

In the Options form, the user can select maximum likelihood estimation, which also changes the correlation coefficients to Anderson–Darling statistics. When this option is selected, the Anderson–Darling statistic measures how bad the fit is, so a smaller value indicates a better fit. Which option works better depends on the situation, but many reliability engineers prefer the default, least squares approach. The least squares method is often more accurate than the maximum likelihood method, especially for small or heavily censored samples. For more information on the differences between these two methods, search the Minitab knowledgebase at www.minitab.com for ID 767 and ID 1331.

With the least squares method and correlation coefficients, the Weibull distribution family looks like the best choice for Reid's Reliable.MTW dataset. But, if Reid chooses the maximum likelihood option, the lognormal distribution family looks best. For this example, Reid decides to use the Weibull family.

Still Struggling

Which distribution model is best? The strongest argument for a reliability distribution model is based on theories about how things fail. If failures occur because the weakest link of some hypothetical chain breaks, statistical theory suggests that either the Weibull or the smallest extreme value distribution is reasonable. The next best argument is that the model fits the available data better than other models. The Distribution ID Plot tool helps support this argument, as illustrated in Fig. 14-2. The weakest argument is that "we always use it." Most reliability engineers habitually use nothing but the Weibull distribution over their entire career, and it often works well. Even so, the ability to select and properly apply a wider variety of models can be a significant career advantage.

After selecting the Weibull distribution, Reid has two Minitab tools to finish up the analysis, one mostly graphical, and the other mostly analytical. The more graphical approach is the Distribution Overview Plot in the Distribution Analysis menu. Reid completes the dialog for this tool in the same way as for the Distribution ID Plot, by specifying the failure times in the main dialog and the censoring columns in the Censor dialog.

Figure 14-3 is the distribution overview plot for this dataset. The four graphs in this plot provide four different views of the fitted distribution models.

- The Probability Density Function (PDF), top left, shows the relative probabilities of failures vs. the age of the units.
- The Weibull probability plot, top right, shows how well the Weibull distribution fits the available data.

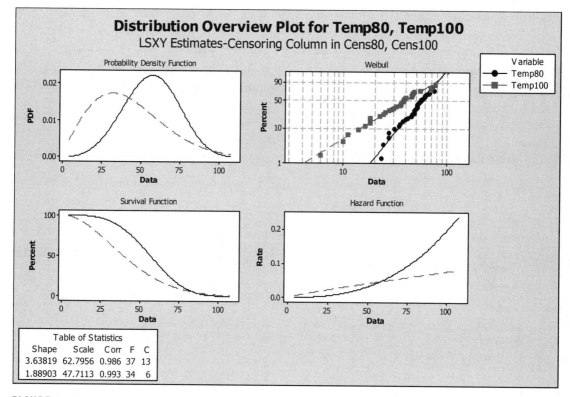

FIGURE 14-3 · Distribution overview plot.

- The Survival Function, bottom left, is the probability of surviving to a certain age.

- The Hazard Function, bottom right, is the ratio of the PDF to the survival function. The hazard function is the relative probability of failing at time t, given that a unit has survived up to time t.

Reliability engineers often use the slope of the hazard function to characterize different situations. A flat hazard function indicates an exponential distribution, under which model failures occur randomly at any time with the same hazard rate. A decreasing hazard function is typical of infant mortality, when failures become less likely as a unit ages. An increasing hazard function is typical of wearout, when failures become more likely over time. In the Reliable.MTW dataset, the hazard rate increases over time for both temperatures tested.

   In the same menu, the Parametric Distribution Analysis function offers many
more options, including confidence intervals, hypothesis tests, analyzing distributions of different failure modes, and more. Running this function on the
Reliable.MTW dataset produces, by default, a probability plot with confidence
intervals, plus a lengthy report in the Session window. Here is the first part of
that report:

Distribution Analysis: Temp80

```
Variable: Temp80

Censoring Information  Count
Uncensored value          37
Right censored value      13

Censoring value: Cens80 = 0

Estimation Method: Least Squares (failure time(X) on rank(Y))

Distribution:   Weibull

Parameter Estimates

                           Standard    95.0% Normal CI
Parameter  Estimate         Error      Lower     Upper
Shape       3.63819       0.296611   3.10091   4.26856
Scale      62.7956        2.84080   57.4674   68.6177

Log-Likelihood = -202.258

Goodness-of-Fit
Anderson-Darling (adjusted) = 67.606
Correlation Coefficient = 0.986

Characteristics of Distribution

                                 Standard    95.0% Normal CI
                      Estimate     Error      Lower     Upper
Mean(MTTF)             56.6179    2.73936   51.4955   62.2497
Standard Deviation     17.3032    0.872053  15.6757   19.0996
Median                 56.7777    2.90747   51.3558   62.7720
First Quartile(Q1)     44.5866    3.00877   39.0629   50.8914
Third Quartile(Q3)     68.6941    2.78798   63.4415   74.3817
Interquartile Range(IQR) 24.1075  1.27922   21.7263   26.7498
```

This report summarizes the counts of uncensored and censored values, the
parameters of the best-fitting Weibull distribution, with confidence intervals,

and finally, a table of key statistics for the distribution. For the Temp80 failure times, the mean time to failure (MTTF) is 56.6179 with a 95% confidence interval of between 51.4955 and 62.2497.

Following this part of the report is a table of percentiles, not shown here, and the same analysis for the Temp100 column of failure times.

One more alternative is worth exploring. If Reid does not want to choose any family of distribution models, Minitab offers a Nonparametric Distribution Analysis tool which makes no assumption about the distribution. This tool is in the same Distribution Analysis menu, right below the Parametric Distribution Analysis. This tool uses the widely accepted Kaplan–Meier method, or an alternative actuarial method.

By default, the Nonparametric Distribution Analysis tool produces no graphs. However, by clicking the Graphs button, any of three graphs are available. Figure 14-4 shows a nonparametric survival plot for the Reliable.MTW dataset, with 95% confidence intervals. This plot shows the probability of survival versus age.

One characteristic of a nonparametric analysis is the stair-step nature of the probability models. Since the observed data provide the only information available, there is no smoothing of the data by a continuous probability function. More significantly, the nonparametric model is limited to the range of the observed data. For the Temp80 variable, the maximum failure time observed

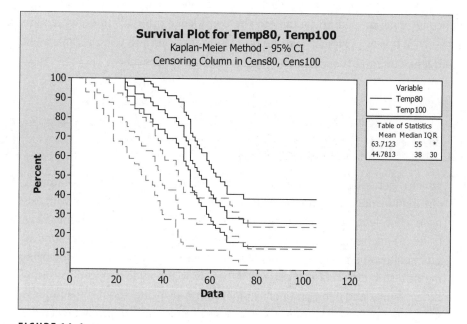

FIGURE 14-4 • Nonparametric distribution analysis.

is 105, so the nonparametric model ends at 105. Also, 13 out of 50 observations (26%) are censored, so the survival function ends at 0.26.

In the text box in Fig. 14-4, the nonparametric method predicts an MTTF of 63.7123 for Temp80, but the interquartile range (IQR) is not available, since the third quartile, which is also the 75th percentile, cannot be estimated.

Suppose Reid's company typically uses the b_{10} life, which is the 10th percentile, to set goals for product reliability. What is the b_{10} life for the windings tested at 80°C? Here is a selected portion of the Parametric Distribution Analysis report:

```
Table of Percentiles


                      Standard    95.0% Normal CI
Percent  Percentile    Error    Lower    Upper
    10     33.8299    2.97051  28.4812  40.1830
```

Using the Weibull distribution, Minitab predicts the b_{10} life to be 33.8299, with a 95% confidence interval of between 28.4812 and 40.1830.

Using the Kaplan–Meier nonparametric method, percentiles and confidence intervals can be estimated directly from the graph or read from the Session window. In Minitab, hover the mouse over the plot to display the values of plotted points. The b_{10} life corresponds to the survival probability of 0.90. When survival is 0.90, the survival line is horizontal, going from a time of 31 to a time of 34. The mean of these two values, 32.5, is an estimate for b_{10} life. To find the confidence interval, move horizontally to the confidence intervals lines, which are at 27 and 45. It is very typical that the nonparametric method will produce a wider confidence interval than a parametric method, as in this case.

? Still Struggling

Which is better, a parametric or a nonparametric model? The correct parametric distribution model provides benefits, including more precise estimates with narrower confidence intervals. Since most life tests end when only a few units have failed, a parametric distribution model allows extrapolation to predict survival probabilities at times much longer than the test. But how do we know the parametric distribution model is correct? If there is no theory to support one distribution family, and if the probability plot is not convincing about the goodness of fit, a nonparametric model provides a valid alternative to predict reliability metrics without relying on a questionable distribution model.

When a dataset includes left-censored or interval-censored data, the Distribution Analysis (Arbitrary Censoring) menu must be used to analyze it. To enter failure times in a Minitab worksheet for arbitrary censoring requires two columns, a start column and an end column. These two columns have numbers indicating the start and end of the interval during which a failure occurred.

- For exact failure times, the start time equals the end time.
- A right-censored failure time is entered in the start column, with * in the end column.
- A left-censored failure time is entered in the end column, with * in the start column.
- For interval censoring, enter the start time and end time of the interval in the two columns.

For an example of arbitrary censoring, open the Minitab example data file Cassette.MTW. This dataset was compiled by a company who services and repairs X-ray cassettes used by doctors and hospitals. The Start and End columns record an estimate of cycles, rather than a time to failure. This file also illustrates two other optional features of Minitab reliability datasets, a Freq column with the frequency of failures, and a Failure column with a description of the failure modes.

In the Cassette.MTW dataset, the first row describes 7 cassettes with Window failures occurring at some point before 2500 cycles. The second row describes 5 cassettes with Window failures occurring between 2500 and 5000 cycles. The final row describes 18 cassettes with no failures up to 32,500 cycles.

The Weibull distribution family is popular for modeling multiple failure modes, because it includes distributions with decreasing, flat, and increasing hazard functions, depending on the shape parameter. To use the Weibull distribution to analyze the Cassette.MTW dataset, select Stat > Reliability/Survival > Distribution Modeling (Arbitrary Censoring) > Parametric Distribution Analysis. In the dialog, enter Start, End, and Freq into the appropriate fields, and select Weibull for the Assumed distribution. Click the FMode button, and enter Failure into the Use failure mode columns box.

Completing this analysis produces two new graphs, shown in Figs. 14-5 and 14-6. Figure 14-5 shows three Weibull probability plots, one for each of the three failure modes listed in the dataset. When analyzing data with multiple failures modes, Minitab treats failure modes of one type as censored observations for the other failure modes.

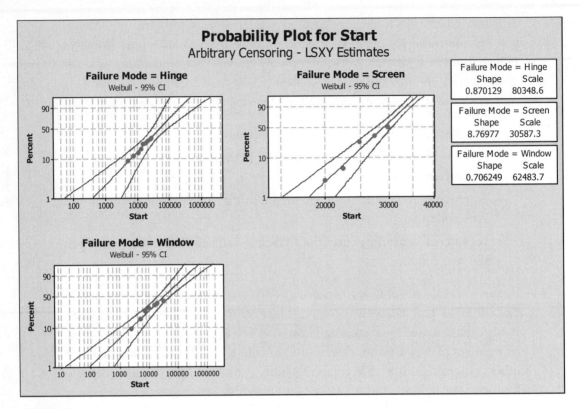

FIGURE 14-5 · Weibull analysis of multiple failure modes.

In Fig. 14-5, each failure mode generates a reasonably straight pattern of dots, with the dots inside the confidence interval lines, indicating a good fit for all three failure modes. The text boxes, at the right side of the graph, list the fitted parameter values for the three Weibull distributions. For Hinge and Window failure modes, the shape parameter is less than 1, indicating a decreasing hazard function. For Screen failures, the shape is far greater than 1, indicating an increasing hazard function for that failure mode.

Figure 14-6 is a combined probability plot produced by combining the three Weibull distribution models together into one composite distribution. This results in a curved line on the probability plot.

Here is the first part of the report from this analysis:

Distribution Analysis, Start = Start and End = End

```
Variable Start: Start  End: End
Frequency: Freq
```

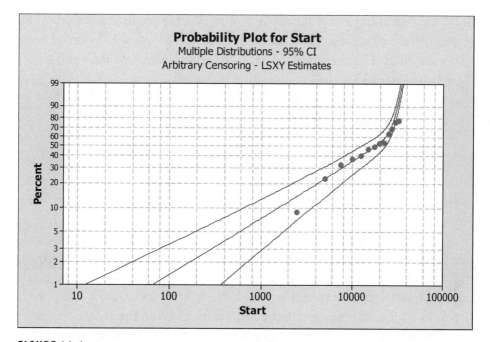

FIGURE 14-6 • Combined probability plot with multiple failure modes.

```
Failure Mode: Failure = Hinge, Screen, Window

Censoring Information    Count
Right censored value       18
Interval censored value    55
Left censored value         7

Estimation Method: Least Squares (failure time(X) on rank(Y))

Distribution:   Weibull, Weibull, Weibull

Table of Percentiles

                         95.0% Normal CI
Percent   Percentile    Lower     Upper
      1      66.6804   12.0802   361.778
      2     170.785    40.4778   711.083
      3     296.135    81.7034   1061.51
      4     437.967   134.295    1414.64
      5     593.807   197.395    1771.13
      6     762.126   270.437    2131.35
      7     941.899   353.023    2495.59
      8    1132.40    444.866    2864.09
      9    1333.08    545.756    3237.06
     10    1543.57    655.537    3614.71
```

Based on the bottom line of the above report, Minitab predicts that the b_{10} life, at which point 10% of the cassettes will have failed, occurs at 1544 cycles, with a 95% confidence interval of 655–3615 cycles. This estimate incorporates all three failure modes into one composite distribution.

14.2   Estimating Reliability from Warranty Data

Many companies who sell complex, repairable products spend a lot of money on warranty service. It is important for these companies to analyze their warranty data both to identify costly failure trends and to find ways to improve the reliability of present and future products.

But warranty analysis is not straightforward, for many reasons. When products have serial numbers identifying the month in which they were shipped, the serial number of returned items can be used to estimate the time the product was in service. But it is usually impossible to know exactly when the product was first used, or how much it has been used before the failure occurred. Products which are never returned are assumed to be still working, but this assumption cannot be verified.

Minitab cannot fix most of these problems, but it can help to solve another inconvenience. Most warranty datasets have a triangular shape. Products shipped last month have one month of failure data. Products shipped two months ago have two months of failure data, and so on. For months further in the past, more failure data becomes available. Minitab can process these triangular matrices of failure data into start, end, and frequency columns suitable for analysis in the Arbritrary Censoring format.

For an example, open the Minitab example data file Compressor.MTW. An appliance company collected this data on compressor failures in a new model of refrigerator. The first column, Sales, lists sales volume of 1000 units per month. The next 12 columns, Month1 through Month12, list the compressor warranty failures processed in each month, separated by the month of shipment.

To understand what this means, column Month5 contains five values, 0, 0, 1, 1, and 0. During month 5, the company processed 1 warranty on a compressor shipped in month 3, and 1 warranty on a compressor shipped in month 4.

Analyzing this data is a two-step process. The first step is to convert this triangular matrix into start, stop, and frequency columns. To do this, select Stat > Reliability/Survival > Warranty Analysis > Pre-process Warranty Data from the Minitab menu. Select Shipment values in a column from the dropdown box, which corresponds to the arrangement of this worksheet. The other option is Shipment values are in first row of return columns. Enter Sales in the Shipment (Sales) column field, and enter Month1-Month12 in the Return (Failure) columns field.

After OK is clicked, Minitab adds three new columns to the worksheet, Start time, End time, and Frequencies. These columns are set up correctly for reliability analysis with Arbitrary Censoring.

Instead of using the regular tools for Arbitrary Censoring, select Stat > Reliability/ Survival > Warranty Analysis > Warranty Prediction. Enter the Start time, End time, and Frequencies in the appropriate fields. To set up some optional features of this analysis, enter 12 as the Length of warranty and 1000 as Average cost per failure. Also, click the Predict button, and enter 1000 in the Production quantity for each time period field. Here is the finished report:

Warranty Prediction: Start = Start time and End = End time

```
* NOTE * 22 cases were used; 2 cases contained missing values or zero
         frequencies.

Using frequencies in Frequencies

Distribution: Weibull with shape = 1.31962, scale = 328.914
Estimation method: Least squares (failure time(X) on rank(Y))

Summary of Current Warranty Claims

Total number of units                          12000
Observed number of failures                    69
Expected number of failures                    71.2094
95% Poisson CI                                 (55.6367, 89.7905)

Number of units at risk for future time periods  10931
Warranty limit                                   12

Production Schedule

Future time period       1      2      3      4      5
Production quantity    1000   1000   1000   1000   1000

Table of Predicted Number of Failures and Cost
```

Future Time Period	Potential Number of Failures	Predicted Number of Failures	95% Poisson CI Lower	95% Poisson CI Upper	Predicted Cost of Failures	95% Poisson CI Lower	95% Poisson CI Upper
1	11931	12.5718	6.6117	21.6884	12571.8	6611.7	21688.4
2	12931	25.1272	16.2810	37.0567	25127.2	16281.0	37056.7
3	13931	37.6974	26.6367	51.8076	37697.4	26636.7	51807.6
4	14931	50.2648	37.3390	66.2199	50264.8	37339.0	66219.9
5	15931	62.8368	48.2679	80.4211	62836.8	48267.9	80421.1

```
Average cost per failure = 1000
```

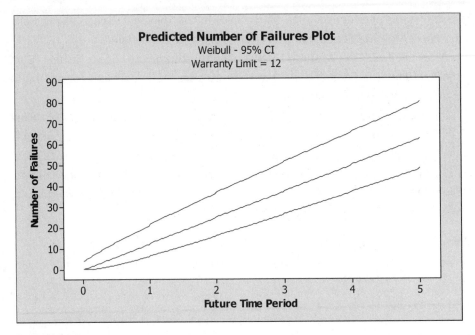

FIGURE 14-7 • Predicted warranty failures over five months.

The top part of this report provides the parameters of a fitted Weibull distribution model and some statistics on the 12 months of data provided. At the end of month 12, the first month of production goes out of warranty, so the number of units at risk in month 13 is 11,000 less the 69 already failed units, which is 10,931 units.

The production schedule is assumed to be 1000 per month for the next five months. The final table predicts the number of warranty failures over the next 1–5 months. Each row in this table is cumulative. The bottom row reports a total of 15,931 units at risk during the next five months, although not all of these are in warranty at the same time. Of these 15,931 units, Minitab predicts 62.8 warranty failures, with the confidence interval and cost projection provided.

Figure 14-7 shows a graph which plots the cumulative number of warranty failures over the next five months, with a 95% confidence interval. Minitab also provides a very similar graph of the cost of predicted warranty failures.

14.3   Calculating Sample Sizes for Reliability Tests

Sample size calculations for many types of statistical procedures were described in Chapter 7. These calculations are always tricky, because they require advance knowledge of the results of the test being planned. In practice, we make an educated guess about the results, specify planning values based on that guess, and plan the test based on the planning values. This process is a practical way to estimate resources required in advance.

With reliability tests, which are always complicated and expensive, it is common to plan tests for the best outcome. Planning to meet the specified reliability goals keeps the tests as short as possible. If the test is passed, all is good. If the test is failed, then some action is generally required to address the discovered problem, probably followed by more testing. From a management point of view, allocating more than the minimum time and resources is a good idea to handle some unexpected problems.

Minitab offers three tools in the Stat > Reliability/Survival > Test Plans menu:

- The Demonstration test plans tool calculates the sample size and length of test required to prove that a specified reliability goal is met to a specified confidence level.

- The Estimation test plans tool is used when the primary goal of a reliability test is to estimate a parameter like MTTF, survival rate, or percentile to within a certain precision. Compared to the Demonstration tool, the Estimation tool has more flexibility to plan for right-censoring and interval-censoring.

- The Accelerated Life Testing planning tool calculates sample sizes for a test where an environmental variable, like temperature, is raised above normal levels to accelerate the rate of failures. Accelerated life testing is controversial and rarely used, so it is not covered further in this introductory book. However, if desired, Minitab can both plan and analyze accelerated life tests.

As an example, Barry makes bearings. A new bearing designed for a wind turbine application needs to have high reliability. Barry's marketing department has established a reliability goal that no more than 5% of all bearings may fail in the first one year of continuous use, which is 8760 hours. Based on past experience with bearings of similar size, Barry expects bearing failure times to follow a Weibull distribution with a shape parameter of 3. The marketing goal, combined with the prior expectation of a Weibull shape of 3, are the planning values required to plan this test.

Barry has designed a test fixture which will simultaneously test 20 bearings at full speed and loading. Each bearing will have an accelerometer connected to a monitoring system which will continuously check the bearings and log any failures. Will Barry need 1, 2, or 3 of these test fixtures?

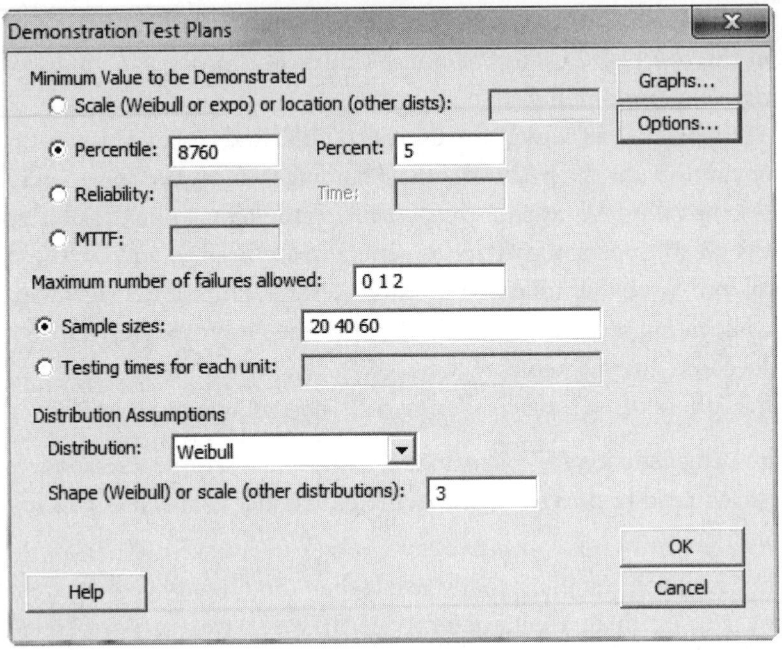

FIGURE 14-8 · Sample size for reliability demonstration.

To find out, Barry selects Stat > Reliability/Survival > Test Plans > Demonstration, and fills out the dialog as shown in Fig. 14-8.

The top part of the dialog, under the label Minimum Value to be Demonstrated specifies the reliability goal. The dialog offers four options to do this, by specifying a scale parameter, a percentile, a reliability, or MTTF. In this case, the 5th percentile of 8760 hours is the specified goal.

The second part of the dialog asks for test details. The Maximum number of failures is required, and this is usually 0. In this case, 1 and 2 are added for comparison. The user has the option to calculate a test time for a given sample size, or to calculate a sample size for a given test time. In this case, Barry has a test fixture for 20 bearings, so he enters 20 40 60 in the Sample sizes field.

The final part of the dialog asks for information on the family of distribution models. In this case, a Weibull distribution with a shape parameter of 3 is specified. One more option is helpful to make the graphs look better. Click the Graphs button, and select the Show different test plans overlaid on the same graphs. Here is the report that appears in the Session window:

Demonstration Test Plans

```
Reliability Test Plan
Distribution: Weibull, Shape = 3
Percentile Goal = 8760,  Actual Confidence Level = 95%
```

Failure Test	Sample Size	Testing Time
0	20	12521.1
0	40	9938.0
0	60	8681.6
1	20	14722.2
1	40	11633.0
1	60	10147.7
2	20	16327.8
2	40	12839.9
2	60	11183.7

According to this report, Barry needs to run 20 bearings for 12,521 hours with zero failures to prove that the reliability goal has been met with 95% confidence. With 60 bearings, the test time is reduced to 8682 hours. The table provides helpful information to examine the tradeoffs between time and cost.

The table also answers the question, "What if a failure occurs?" If one or two failures occur, the testing time is longer, but perhaps not as much longer as one might think.

Minitab also makes plots like Fig. 14-9 for the planned tests. This graph shows the probability of passing the test versus what is labeled the **Ratio of Improvement**. This is the ratio of actual reliability to the reliability goal. In this example, the goal is for the 5th percentile of failure time to be 8760 hours, or one year. If the 5th percentile is two years, twice as good as the goal of one year, the ratio of improvement is 2.

If the product is only as reliable as the goal, and the ratio of improvement is 1, the likelihood of passing the test is only 5%. This is 100% – 95%, where 95% is the confidence required that the goal is met, once the test is passed. If the reliability is better than the goal, the probability of passing the test increases significantly.

Barry is surprised by the long length of the test necessary to demonstrate reliability. According to the project schedule, the maximum test length is 6000 hours. How many bearings must be tested to prove the reliability requirements in only 6000 hours?

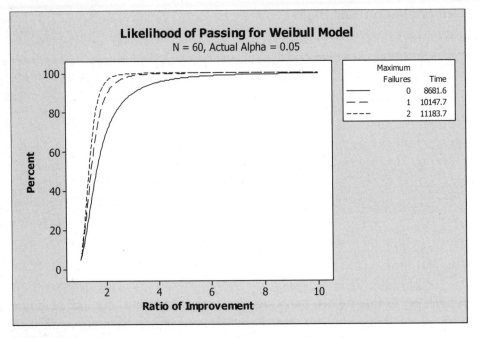

FIGURE 14-9 · Likelihood of passing the planned test vs. reliability.

To find out, Barry recalls the same dialog. This time, he selects Test times for each unit and enters 6000. To further reduce the test size, he clicks Options and changes the confidence level required from 95 to 90. Here is the report:

Demonstration Test Plans

```
Reliability Test Plan
Distribution: Weibull, Shape = 3
Percentile Goal = 8760, Target Confidence Level = 90%
```

			Actual
Failure	Testing	Sample	Confidence
Test	Time	Size	Level
0	6000	140	90.0484
1	6000	237	90.0649
2	6000	324	90.0085

If 140 bearings are tested with zero failures for 6000 hours, this will prove with 90% confidence that the 5th percentile of reliability is at least 8760 hours.

As an example of reliability estimation, consider the case of Richard, who designs living hinges for plastic food packaging. The hinge needs to survive until the food is gone, but not much longer. To design hinges effectively, Richard needs to estimate the distribution of cycles to failure. From previous tests, Richard expects that cycles to failure follow a smallest extreme value (SEV) distribution. Testing hinges is tedious, because failure cannot be automatically detected. A machine can cycle the hinge, and then stop at intervals for the hinge to be visually inspected. In this example, cycles takes the place of time in the reliability dialogs and reports.

Based on some earlier testing, Richard expects the SEV distribution to have a location parameter of 150 cycles and a scale parameter of 15 cycles. Richard wants to estimate the 25th percentile to within 10 cycles. To do this, Richard will use a machine to exercise each hinge 20 cycles, inspect, and then repeat until either the hinge fails or 200 cycles is reached. How many hinges are required?

To calculate the sample size, Richard selects Stat > Reliability/Survival > Test Plans > Estimation from the Minitab menu, and fills out the dialog as shown in Fig. 14-10. Since the data will be interval censored at 20 cycle intervals, he clicks the Interval Cens button and fills out that dialog, also shown in Fig. 14-10.

The top section of the Estimation dialog asks for the Parameter to be Estimated, which could be either a percentile or a reliability.

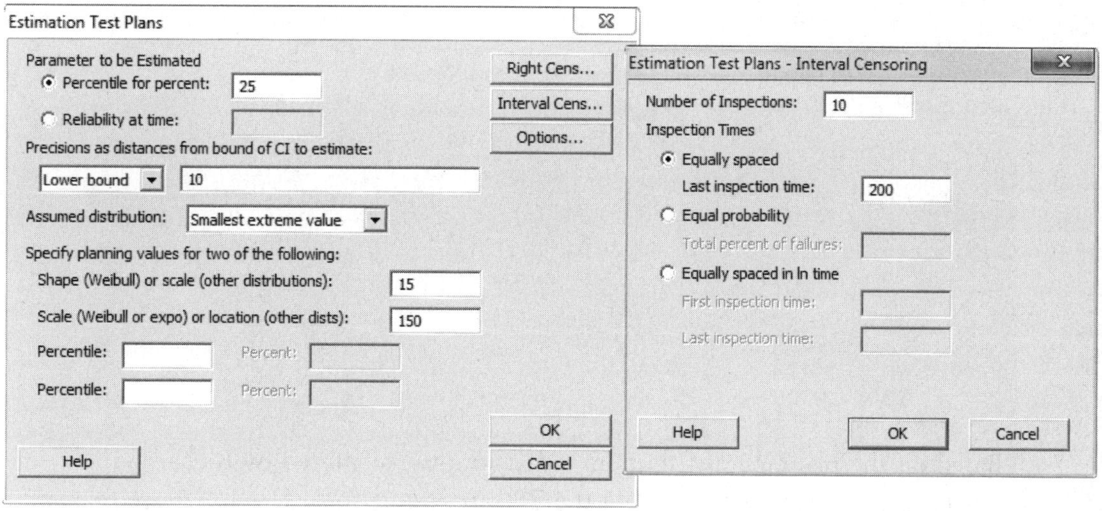

FIGURE 14-10. Calculating sample size for reliability estimation.

The second section asks for the required precision, expressed as the distance between the lower confidence bound and the estimate, or from the upper confidence bound and the estimate. In this example, Richard wants to estimate the 25th percentile so that the lower confidence bound is 10 cycles or less from the estimate.

The third section asks for the Assumed distribution family, for planning purposes. In this case, Richard selects the Smallest extreme value distribution.

The fourth section asks for information to specify the planning distribution within the selected family. Two of the four items listed are required. In this case, the location parameter of the SEV distribution is 150 and the scale is 15.

Finally, the Interval Censoring dialog asks about the inspection scheme. Richard specifies 10 inspections equally spaced up to 200 cycles. Here is the sample size report:

Estimation Test Plans

```
Inspection data
Equally Spaced Inspection Times
Last inspection time = 200

Estimated parameter: 25th percentile
Calculated planning estimate = 131.312
Target Confidence Level = 95%
Precision in terms of a one-sided confidence interval that gives
a lower bound
      for the parameter.

Planning distribution: Smallest Extreme Value
Location = 150, Scale = 15

Calculated Inspection Times

Time index        1    2    3    4    5    6    7    8    9   10
Inspection Time  20   40   60   80  100  120  140  160  180  200

                    Actual
          Sample  Confidence
Precision  Size     Level
      10    19    95.2921
```

Based on the planning distribution and assumptions entered by Richard, 19 hinges must be tested to estimate the 25th percentile of cycles to failure to within 10 cycles, with 95% confidence. If desired, the confidence level can be adjusted in the Options dialog.

14.4   Estimating Reliability as a Function of Other Variables

A project to improve product reliability is challenging from both engineering and statistical viewpoints. To explore potential reliability improvements requires a combination of the tools explored in this book, including the design of experiments, regression, and reliability analysis. To analyze an experiment where the response variable is a measure of reliability or survival, Minitab offers a powerful Regression with Life Data tool. This tool estimates reliability, with right or arbitrary censoring, as a function of either numeric variables or factors.

The generic model used by the Regression with Life Data tool looks like this:

$$Y = \beta_0 + \beta_1 X_1 + \beta_2 X_2 + \cdots + \beta_k X_k + \sigma\varepsilon$$

Where:

- Y is time to failure for normal, logistic, or extreme value distributions; otherwise, Y is the natural log of failure time for lognormal, loglogistic, or Weibull models.

- β_0, β_1, ... , β_k are the regression coefficients, which will be fitted to the data by Minitab.

- X_1, ..., X_k are the predictor variables. Factors are converted into suitable predictor variables, as they are in ordinary regression or DOE analysis.

- σ is a scale parameter for most distribution models, or 1/shape for the Weibull model.

- ε is the error term. The distribution of the error term depends on the distribution model. For normal or lognormal, ε is standard normal; for logistic or loglogistic, ε is standard logistic; for extreme value or Weibull, ε is standard smallest extreme value.

Before applying the Regression with Life Data tool, it is a good idea to select a distribution model using either theory or previous reliability tests. Once this is done, all that remains is to select the factors and variables, and then to let Minitab handle the complexities of the analysis.

To see how this works, consider an example about jet engines. Bird strikes pose a serious danger for all aircraft. Orville Wright was the first to report a bird encounter in 1905, and the problem continues today with occasionally spectacular and tragic crashes. Annual damages to the aviation industry are estimated in the billions of dollars. Aircraft and engine manufacturers continue to investigate design changes to improve bird strike survivability.

Julie is a turbine design engineer who is evaluating a proposed change to the compressor case. To test this design change, she will have a compressor fan running at full speed, within either the standard or the new compressor case. This is the front part of the turbine where the bird would contact. Then, Julie will shoot a frozen bird out of a cannon, into the engine. The size of the frozen bird is carefully selected to be 5.0, 7.5, or 10.0 pounds. The key to engine survival is for the engine to continue running safely after the strike. Julie measures the time after the strike until a catastrophic failure occurs, or if no failure occurs after several hours, the test of that unit is right-censored.

Julie's data is recorded in the Minitab example data file Jet.MTW. The first four columns of this worksheet list the minutes until failure, censoring (**Censored** or **Exact**), design (**Standard** or **New**), and the weight of the bird. For the censoring column, Minitab selects the first value, in alphabetic order, to represent the censored case. Since "Censored" comes before "Exact," this works well. If, instead of "Exact," Julie entered "Actual," she would have to enter "Censored" in the Censoring value field of the Censor dialog. When entering a text value in this field, the double quotes are required.

From previous work, Julie chooses to fit a Weibull distribution to this failure time distribution. Also in the Jet.MTW worksheet are two columns **NewDesign** and **NewWeight**. These values will be used to predict reliability for all combinations of design and bird weight.

To analyze this data, Julie selects Stat > Reliability/Survival > Regression with Life Data and fills out the form this way:

- She selects Responses are uncens/right censored data.
- In the Variables/Start variables: field, Julie enters Failure.
- In the Model field, she enters Design Weight.
- In the Factors field, Julie enters Design.
- In the Assumed distribution dropdown box, she chooses Weibull.

Next, Julie clicks the Censor button and enters Censor in the Use censoring columns field.

Back in the main dialog, Julie clicks the Estimate button and enters NewDesign NewWeight in the Enter new predictor values field.

Again, back in the main dialog, Julie clicks the Graphs button and selects all the options.

Here is the report from Julie's analysis:

Regression with Life Data: Failure versus Design, Weight

Response Variable: Failure

Censoring Information Count
Uncensored value   22
Right censored value   26

Censoring value: Censor = Censored

Estimation Method: Maximum Likelihood

Distribution: Weibull

Relationship with accelerating variable(s):   Linear

Regression Table

Predictor	Coef	Standard Error	Z	P	95.0% Normal CI Lower	Upper
Intercept	6.89652	0.263259	26.20	0.000	6.38055	7.41250
Design						
Standard	-0.711064	0.0968197	-7.34	0.000	-0.900827	-0.521301
Weight	-0.0780575	0.0286737	-2.72	0.006	-0.134257	-0.0218581
Shape	4.42326	0.851564			3.03298	6.45083

Log-Likelihood = -144.194

Anderson-Darling (adjusted) Goodness-of-Fit

Standardized Residuals = 55.536
Cox-Snell Residuals = 55.536

Table of Percentiles

Percent	Design	Weight	Percentile	Standard Error	95.0% Normal CI Lower	Upper
50	Standard	5.0	302.570	35.7685	239.994	381.462
50	Standard	7.5	248.929	18.1378	215.802	287.142
50	Standard	10.0	204.798	17.0370	173.986	241.067
50	New	5.0	616.080	76.5149	482.971	785.874
50	New	7.5	506.859	38.2122	437.235	587.570
50	New	10.0	417.001	32.8873	357.278	486.708

In the middle of the report, the Regression table contains the answers to Julie's questions about the new design. Does the new design improve reliability or not? In the Design section of the table, the Standard design has a very significant *p*-value of 0.000, meaning that the standard and new designs are very different. In the Coef column, the coefficient for the Standard design is less than zero, meaning that the standard design has worse reliability, and the new design has improved reliability.

Also, Julie notes that the Weight row of the Regression table has a very significant *p*-value and a negative coefficient, meaning that a heavier bird decreases reliability. This is no surprise, but it is good that the experiment is consistent with prior expectations.

The final part of the report is a table of predicted 50th percentiles, with confidence intervals for all combinations of design and bird weight. A different percentile can be selected in the Estimate dialog. Comparing the percentiles shows that the new design doubles the survival time of the engine after the bird strike. This improvement has enormous practical significance.

As a final check of model adequacy, Minitab also prepares two forms of probability plots of residuals. Figure 14-11 shows the plot of standardized residuals. A second plot, not shown here, plots Cox–Snell residuals. Both plots show the dots close to a straight diagonal line, and within the confidence interval lines.

If either residual plot veered significantly away from the straight line, this would cast doubt on the assumption of a Weibull distribution model. The

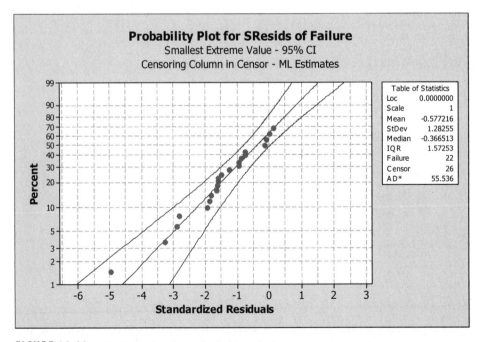

FIGURE 14-11 · Probability plot of standardized residuals.

Regression with Life Data tool fits seven different distribution families, offering tremendous flexibility for analyzing the toughest reliability problems.

14.5   Find Out More

Minitab offers other powerful tools in the Reliability/Survival menu for specialized applications. As always, the Minitab Help files, StatGuide, and Methods and Formulas files have other examples and helpful information on how to use these tools.

O'Connor (2002) is an excellent general reference and textbook on reliability engineering. Also, Wayne Nelson's books on life data analysis (2004) and accelerated testing (2004a) are practical, well-written, and highly recommended.

QUIZ

1. **Which of the following situations results in a right-censored failure time at 1000 hours?**

   A. When the test ends at 1000 hours, and a unit is still working.

   B. When the test ends at 1000 hours, and a unit is discovered to have failed, but the exact failure time is unknown.

   C. When a unit failed at some point between 900 and 1000 hours.

   D. When a unit fails at exactly at 1000 hours

2. **A batch of calculators is tested in an oven at high temperature. Every 24 hours, the calculators are removed from the oven for testing. After one week, 168 hours, the test ends, with some calculators failed and other calculators still working. Which Minitab menu or tool is most appropriate to analyze the distribution of failure times?**

   A. Stat > Quality Tools > Individual Distribution Identification

   B. Stat > Reliability/Survival > Distribution Analysis (Right Censoring)

   C. Stat > Reliability/Survival > Distribution Analysis (Arbitrary Censoring)

   D. Graph > Probability Distribution Plot

3. **Which of the following is an advantage of nonparametric distribution analysis for reliability data, compared to parametric distribution analysis?**

   A. Nonparametric models allow prediction or extrapolation beyond the maximum observed failure time.

   B. Nonparametric models are more accurate.

   C. Nonparametric models have narrower confidence intervals.

   D. Nonparametric models do not require an assumption of a particular distribution family.

4. **When each failure is recorded with one of four different failure modes, which** Distribution Analysis **function can be used to fit models to each failure mode separately?**

   A. Distribution ID Plot

   B. Distribution Overview Plot

   C. Parametric Distribution Analysis

   D. Any of the above may be used.

5. **Which Minitab tool is most appropriate to calculate the required sample size for a life test intended to demonstrate that the MTTF exceeds 1000 hours, with high confidence?**

   A. Stat > Power and Sample Size > Sample Size for Estimation

   B. Stat > Reliability/Survival > Test Plans > Demonstration

   C. Stat > Reliability/Survival > Test Plans > Estimation

   D. Stat > Reliability/Survival > Test Plans > Accelerated Life Testing

6. Suppose, for planning purposes, that a product has an MTTF of 1000 hours, with an exponential distribution of failure times. How many units must be tested in a 1000 hour life test, with zero failures, to demonstrate that the MTTF is more than 1000 hours with 95% confidence?

For questions 7–10, use the Minitab example dataset Tirewear.MTW. This contains observations of the miles until tires fail, arranged for Minitab analysis.

7. The first row in the worksheet contains the values * 10000 8. What does this first row represent in terms of the tires tested?

8. Test this dataset against all the available distribution models in Minitab. Which model(s) fit best? Which one model would you choose?

9. Using your chosen distribution model, estimate the probability that a tire will survive to 60,000 miles, with a 95% confidence interval. Hint: click Estimate and enter 60000 in the Estimate probabilities for these times field.

10. Now answer question 9 without using or assuming any particular family of distribution models.

Final Exam

1. If a Minitab project contains one worksheet, list three ways another data-set can be added into the project file.

Questions 2–5 ask about the Minitab example data file* Breakdowns.MTW and the Complaints column in that file.

2. Calculate the mean, median, and standard deviation of Complaints.

3. Calculate a 95% confidence interval for the mean of Complaints. What does this confidence interval mean?

4. For the Complaints data, assume that the measurements are recorded in time order. Create a graph that shows how the data changes in time order. Does the graph show evidence of an increasing or decreasing trend?

5. Is there any evidence that the distribution of Complaints is not normal? How do you know?

Questions 6–12 ask about the Minitab example data file Glucose.MTW, which contains the blood glucose measurements of several patients, measured by two methods, standard and new.

6. Create a display of the distribution of the New variable, formed entirely of text.

---

*To access any of the Minitab example data files, select File > Open Worksheet from the Minitab menu, then click the 🗐 icon labeled Look in Minitab Sample Data Folder.

7. What is the correlation coefficient between the two variables? Is there significant evidence of a non-zero correlation? How do you know?

8. Create a plot that illustrates the correlation, if any, between the two variables.

9. Now create a single graph including a scatterplot and histograms of both variables on the same graph.

10. What simple linear equation New = A + B×Standard best fits this data?

11. How much of the variation in the dataset is accounted for by the model fitted in Question 10?

12. In the model fitted in Question 10, is there strong evidence that the constant term (A) is non-zero?

Questions 13–16 ask about the Minitab example data file Beds.MTW. This file lists the number of vacant beds per night, for three hospitals, over 11 nights.

13. Is this data file in stacked or unstacked format?

14. Create a single graph showing the individual values for each hospital and confidence intervals for the means, on the same plot.

15. Is there a significant difference in the mean vacant beds by hospital? If so, which hospitals are different?

16. Is there a significant difference in the variation of vacant beds by hospital? If so, which hospitals are different?

17. A boxplot has been called a five-number summary. What are the five numbers?

18. Open the Minitab example data file Vseat.MTW. Is the distribution of the values in the Days column skewed, and if so, which way? Answer this question both by creating an appropriate graph and calculating a statistic.

19. Use the Calc > Make Mesh Data tool to create X, Y, and Z columns in a new worksheet, where both X and Y range from –5 to +5, and Z follows the "Cowboy Hat" function. Cowboy Hat is one of the options in the Use function example dropdown box. Then create an appropriate 3D plot to display the Cowboy Hat function.

20. Suppose you want to change the scale of a Minitab graph so that the ticks are between 500 and 700, at intervals of 25. Besides entering 500 525 550 ... 700 into the Positions of ticks field, what shorthand notation can be used instead?

21. Which of the following methods is the easiest way to change fonts and font colors used in all Minitab graphs?
    A. Select the text items in every graph you create, and edit them to change the fonts and colors.
    B. Click Tools > Customize and change the default settings for all graphs.
    C. Click Tools > Options and change the default settings for all graphs.
    D. Click Graph > Options and change the default settings for all graphs.

22. You notice that a friend of yours has a Minitab toolbar you have never seen before, containing icons for graphs and hypothesis tests he uses frequently. Not wanting to be outdone, you are determined to make an even better toolbar. How do you start creating a new Minitab toolbar?
    A. Right-click in the toolbar area and select New Toolbar.
    B. Click Tools > Options, and go to the toolbars settings.
    C. Click Tools > Customize, click the Toolbars tab, and click New.
    D. Custom toolbars require advanced programming techniques.

23. A Minitab profile stores which of the following information:
    A. All the options settings
    B. All the options and customization settings, including customized toolbars
    C. All the customization settings, but not option settings
    D. All of the above, plus the data in the current project

24. In Minitab, besides the Assistant menu, tools to make graphs are found in which menu(s)?
    A. Only in the Graph menu
    B. In the Graph and Calc menus
    C. In the Graph and Stat menus
    D. In the Graph, Stat, and Data menus

25. You would like to use the DMAIC toolbar: Define▾ Measure▾ Analyze▾ Improve▾ Control▾ , but in the Tools > Toolbars menu, there is no DMAIC toolbar listed. What must be done to show the DMAIC toolbar?

26. Suppose you want to populate two columns of a worksheet with all 100 combinations of the integers 1 to 10. Describe two ways to do this other than directly typing in the numbers.

27. Suppose that a production line is producing products that are 1% defective, and a sample of 100 units is tested. What is the probability that 0 units out of 100 will test defective? (Hint: the number of defective units out of 100 should follow the binomial distribution.)

28. For the same situation described in question 27, with a sample of 100 units, each of which has a 1% probability of failure, what is the probability that the sample will contain 3 or more defective units?

29. Suppose a computer power supply has a failure time with a Weibull distribution with a shape of 2, a scale of 15,000 hours, and a threshold of 0. What is the probability that the power supply will fail before 2,000 hours?

30. For the same power supply as in question 29, before what time will 10% of the power supplies fail?

Questions 31–33 and 35 concern the data in the Minitab example data file Boxcox.MTW

31. What is the best Box–Cox transformation to normalize this distribution? Specify the transformation by its lambda (λ) and the function $Y = f(X)$ represented by λ.

32. What is the best Johnson transformation to normalize this distribution? Specify the function $Y = f(X)$

33. Between the Box–Cox and the Johnson transformation, which better normalizes this distribution? How do you know?

34. Suppose you have a sample of data, and you want to calculate an interval which contains 90% of the individual values, with high probability. What kind of interval is this?

35. Based on the BoxCox.MTW data, calculate an appropriate interval which contains 90% of the population of values with 95% confidence.

Questions 36–39 concern the data in the Minitab example data file Wallpaper. MTW.

36. Calculate a 95% confidence interval for the mean. Use this confidence interval to decide if there is strong evidence that the mean is different from 30.

37. Now use a hypothesis test to answer the same question. If there is a significant shift from 30, how confident are you that the shift is real?

38. How large could the standard deviation be, with 90% confidence?

39. Is there strong evidence that the standard deviation is less than 12?

40. Suppose you are doing a 2-sample t-test with null hypothesis $H_0: \mu_1 = \mu_2$ and alternative hypothesis $H_A: \mu_1 \neq \mu_2$. Minitab reports a p-value of 0.024. If your false alarm rate $\alpha = 0.05$, what should you conclude?

41. Oklahoma sees 53.1 tornadoes per year, as a historical mean. In 2008, 77 tornadoes were reported. If tornadoes are independent events, is 77 tornadoes in 2008 a significant increase?

Questions 42–43 concern the Minitab example data file WineJudge.MTW, which lists the judged Aroma and Oakiness for wines from three Regions.

42. Is mean Aroma significantly different between regions? If so, which regions are different from which others?

43. Is mean Oakiness significantly different between regions? If so, which regions are different from which others?

44. In the fictional city of Megalopolis, the Purple party candidate received 20% of the vote in the last election. Now, the Purple party wants to conduct a poll of 400 likely voters to see how popular their new candidate is. What is the power of a survey of 400 voters to detect an increase in

support from 20% to 25%, with $\alpha = 0.05$? The survey should look for either an increase or a decrease in popularity.

45. A new lathe is supposed to cut the standard deviation of parts in half. How large a sample size on the new lathe is required to have 90% power to detect a reduction of standard deviation to half its historical level, with $\alpha = 0.05$? This test will only look for a decrease in standard deviation, not an increase.

Questions 46–47 concern the Minitab example data file Cereal.MTW. This file contains selected nutritional information for breakfast cereals.

46. Which subset of the variables Protein, Carbo, and Fat form the best model to predict Calories? How do you know?

47. For the best model chosen in 46, how much of the variation is explained by the model?

Questions 48–50 concern the Minitab example data file Biomass.MTW.

48. With Biomass as response, and Area2 as predictor, is a linear, quadratic, or cubic model best for this data?

49. What is the best fitting model from question 48? Write it out as a function in the form Biomass = f(Area2).

50. In this analysis, do any of the rows of data have unusually large residuals? Which ones?

Question 51 and 52 concern the Minitab example data file Dye.MTW. This file contains the design and collected data for an experiment with six factors (Index – Temp) and three responses (Strength – Brightness).

51. This experiment has 6 factors at 2 levels, with 1 replication in 64 runs. What is this type of experiment called? Is there any aliasing in this experiment?

52. Analyze this experiment, including all terms in the model up through order 2. That is, the model should include all main effects and all 2-factor interactions. Which of these main effects or interactions are significant in one or more of the responses, with $\alpha = 0.05$?

Questions 53–56 concern the Minitab example data file Cleaning.MTW.

53. **This worksheet contains an experiment already designed. Is this a factorial, response surface, mixture, or Taguchi experiment?**

54. **Analyze this experiment with response CleanEff, and these effects: A B C AA BB AB, where A = Pressure, B = Time, C = Conc. Write out the model fitted by Minitab.**

55. **By inspecting the model fitted in the previous question, decide what level of Conc gives the maximum CleanEff. Then, create a contour plot showing CleanEff as a function of Pressure and Time, with Conc held at the value that maximizes CleanEff.**

56. **What values of the three variables maximize CleanEff?**

Questions 57–60 concern the Minitab example data file Thickness.MTW containing the results of a crossed gage R&R study. The specification limits are 0.0 and 2.0.

57. **What is the total gage R&R, expressed as a percentage of the tolerance?**

58. **The gage R&R can be expressed as a percentage of tolerance, study variation, and contribution. Which of these is the most appropriate metric for a measurement system primarily used to detect which parts conform to the specification limits?**

59. **How many distinct categories can the measurement system reliably sort the parts into?**

60. **To improve this measurement system, which component of variation should be investigated first?**

Questions 61 and 62 concern the Minitab example data file Calico.MTW. This file contains the results of an attribute agreement analysis with 4 appraisers, 30 test samples, and 2 replications. The attribute rating is on a five-level scale from 1 to 5. The file contains the standard rating in column C5 and the appraisers rating in column C2.

61. **Perform an appropriate analysis. Is there a difference in agreement between the four appraisers? Which appraisers have the best and the worst agreement scores?**

62. What is a 95% confidence interval of the overall agreement between all the appraisers and the standard?

63. Open the Minitab example data file AssemblyPlant.MTW. The Length variable contains measurements of length of 100 shafts, collected in 25 subgroups of size 4. Create an appropriate control chart, and apply all tests for out-of-control conditions offered by Minitab. What are the out-of-control conditions, if any? For each out-of-control condition found in this dataset, describe what this means in terms of the process mean and/or variation?

Questions 64–66 concern Minitab example data file Bwcapa.MTW. This file lists a coating thickness three times for each roll of paper. Column Coating lists thickness, and Roll lists roll number. Treat each roll as a subgroup.

64. Create an Xbar-S chart, using the usual technique of estimating variation by within-subgroup variation. Are there any out-of-control conditions?

65. Now create a different control chart that estimates short-term variation with a combination of between- and within-subgroup variation. Are there any out-of-control conditions?

66. Now, using the same technique described in the previous question, estimate potential (short-term) and overall (long-term) process capability, with LSL = 45 and USL = 55.

67. Open the Minitab example data file Telephone.MTW. This file lists the counts of unanswered calls in each subgroup of calls. Subgroup sizes vary, and are listed in column C1. Create an appropriate control chart. Is the rate of unanswered calls stable or not?

68. Open the Minitab example data file Cable.MTW. The measurements in this file have specification limits of 0.500 to 0.600. Calculate a 95% confidence interval for overall capability index Ppk.

For questions 69–71, consider a proposed attribute sampling plan for percentage defective, with AQL = 1%, RQL = 5%, sample size n = 50, acceptance number c = 1, and lot size = 2000.

69. **Using this sampling plan, a sample of 50 units is inspected, and 1 unit out of 50 is found to be defective. Is the lot accepted or rejected?**

70. **If the lot is 5% defective, what is the probability that this sample plan will reject the lot?**

71. **If every rejected lot is 100% inspected, what is the maximum percentage of defective units outgoing from the sampling inspection? What incoming percentage of defective units produces this maximum outgoing percentage of defective units?**

72. **For a cable with a critical characteristic with specification limits of 0.500 – 0.600, design a variables sampling plan with these parameters: AQL = 0.1% with producer's risk of 0.05, RQL = 0.8% with consumer's risk of 0.10, and lot size = 1000. Specify the sample size and critical distance for this sampling plan.**

73. **Now consider the data in Cable.MTW as the results of an incoming inspection of 100 cables in a lot of 1000. Using the critical distance calculated in the preceding problem, should the lot be accepted or rejected?**

Questions 74–77 concern the Minitab example data file Ironcord.MTW which lists the results from reliability tests on power cords on electric irons. These are pull tests where the cord is pulled with increasing force until either the cord fails (**Exact**) or the test is suspended without a failure (**Censored**).

74. **Is this dataset set up for the Right Censoring or the Arbitrary Censoring analysis tools in Minitab?**

75. **Analyze the failure data in columns StdCord and StdCens to select a distribution model. Which two families of distribution models fit the data best?**

76. **Using the normal distribution model, what is the estimated mean force to fail a cord, with a 95% confidence interval?**

77. This dataset compares a standard cord with a new cord. The tests on the new cord are recorded in columns NewCord and NewCens. Analyze both datasets at once to compare the standard and new cords. Using the Test options, choose the option to test for equal location parameter. This option is labeled Test for equal scale (Weibull or expo) or equal location (other distributions). Is there a significant difference between the standard cord and the new cord? Which one is better?

Questions 78–80 concern the Minitab example data file Electronic.MTW. During a high-temperature test, a set of electronic control modules were operated at temperatures of 125°C, 150°C, and 175°C. Modules were tested every two hours, and the number of failed modules was recorded in this file.

78. Use the Regression with Life Data tool to analyze the reliability of this module as a function of temperature, with a Weibull model. Does higher temperature affect reliability? Is it better or worse at higher temperatures?

79. Predict the median time to failure at 125°C, 150°C, and 175°C.

80. Does the residual plot indicate any reason to doubt the Weibull model for this dataset?

Answers to Quizzes and Final Exam

Chapter 1

1. **B.** Session window
2. **D.** Assistant menu
3. **B.** The  button displays information about columns in the current worksheet.
4. **A.** *** means that Shaft.MTW is the current worksheet in the project.
5. **D.** A file created by Minitab with the .MPJ extension is a Minitab project file, which may contain many worksheets with data, many graphs, a report, session reports, history, and other information.
6. See Fig. A-1.
7. Here is the report:

Descriptive Statistics: Diameter

Variable	N	Mean	StDev	Median	Skewness	Kurtosis
Diameter	50	12.303	0.00363	12.303	-0.46	-0.17

8. See Fig. A-2.
9. The outlying tree in the diameter versus weight scatterplot is on row 15 of the file.
10. The Pearson correlation between diameter and weight is 0.838.

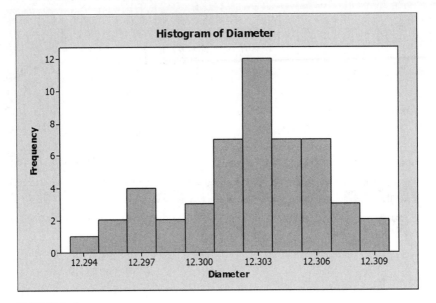

FIGURE A-1 • Histogram of diameter.

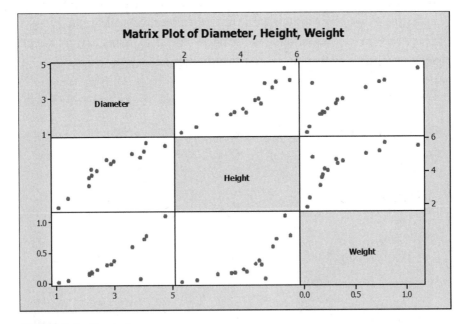

FIGURE A-2 • Matrix plot.

Chapter 2

1. **B.** Individual value plot. Another similar plot, the dotplot, does not always use one dot for every value, if the dataset is too large.

2. **D.** A boxplot represents the distribution of a variable by plotting the following five numbers: minimum, first quartile, median, third quartile, and maximum.

3. **D.** The graphical summary is a single graph containing all the elements listed in a single graph. This summary can be created from the Stat > Basic Statistics menu, but not from the Graph menu. In Minitab 16, the graphical summary is also available in the graphical analysis assistant.

4. **A.** The interval plot shows confidence intervals for the mean of each variable, and this can be used to compare the means for the four sections. If the intervals for two sections do not overlap, then the means are significantly different.

5. **C.** Contour plots represent Z values with shades of color, over a rectangular grid of X and Y values.

6. Many graphs are possible, but the graph shown in Fig. A-3 may be the best. This is an individual value plot of the four variables, combined with confidence intervals for the mean of each group, mean symbols, and a

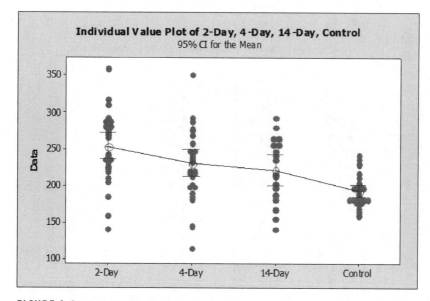

FIGURE A-3 • Individual value plot with intervals.

mean connect line. The fastest way to make this graph is to use the graphical analysis assistant and select an Individual Value Plot. The graph can also be created by selecting Graph > Individual Value Plot from the Minitab menu, and then selecting optional features in the Data View dialog.

7. Yes, there is a significant difference in mean cholesterol between the 2-Day and Control variables. The intervals plotted in the graph are 95% confidence intervals for the mean of each group. We can be 95% sure that the population mean of each group is within that interval. Since the confidence intervals for those two groups do not overlap, we can be at least 95% sure that the population means of those two groups are not the same. In this graph, other pairs of variables have overlapping confidence intervals. When confidence intervals overlap, the means may be the same or they may not, but the plot does not answer this question.

8. Figure A-4 is a bar chart of the standard deviation of the four variables in Cholest.MTW.

9. There are many possible graphs to answer this question, and there is no single best answer. Figure A-5 shows a wireframe-style surface plot made from the data. This dataset could also be a good application for a multi-vari chart, such as Fig. A-6.

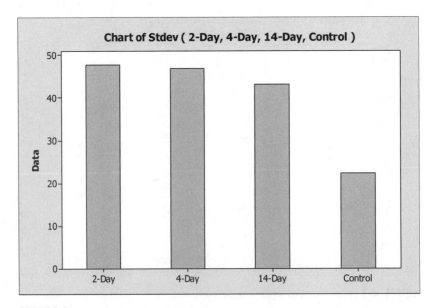

FIGURE A-4 • Bar chart of standard deviations.

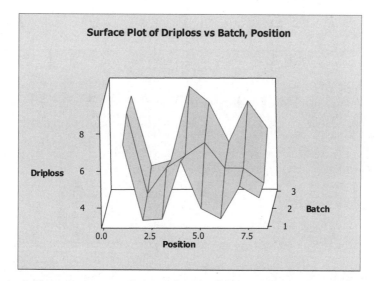

FIGURE A-5 • Surface plot of drip loss by batch and position.

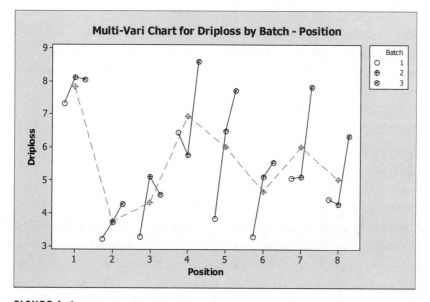

FIGURE A-6 • Multi-vari chart of drip loss.

10. There are many ways to add two columns, Row and Column, to the work-sheet as required. One way is to enter formulas for these columns, so that Row = Ceiling(Position/4,0) and Column = mod(Position-1,4)+1. Another way is to use the Calc > Make Patterned Data > Simple Set of Numbers command in the Minitab menu. After these rows are added, many graphs are possible. Figure A-7 shows a contour plot.

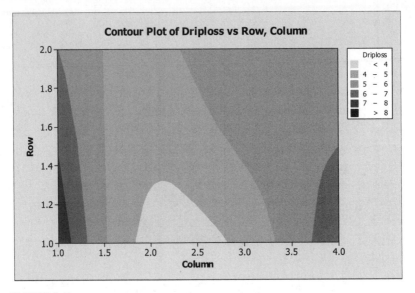

FIGURE A-7 • Contour plot of drip loss by row and column.

Chapter 3

1. **D. C1** has text format, as denoted by **C1-T** in the ID field. There are only three data types in Minitab, numeric (no suffix), date/time (-D suffix) and text (-T suffix).

2. **C.** Minitab recognizes this as a date and assigns date/time data type. Minitab also assigns a display format to display other dates entered in the same format as "October 12."

3. **D.** All of the above.

4. **B.** The values returned by the Excel formulas will copy into Minitab, but the formulas will not copy into Minitab.

5. **A.** All of the answers given to this question would work for databases of reasonable size. However, using ODBC is the most direct method because it directly queries only the required data, without having to make copies of the whole database to be filtered down. Also, for very large databases, ODBC will still work, but some of the other methods may not work.

6. **D.** In Minitab session commands, and in certain dialog box fields, a:b is shorthand for "start with a, and count up to b by ones."

7. **B.** In Minitab, constants are scalar or single-valued variables, and are assigned IDs of K1, K2, etc.

8. **C.** .MTW (MiniTab Worksheet) files contain all variables, formulas and formatting in one file. .XLS or .TXT files can hold some but not all this information. Also, .MTP (MiniTab Project) files contain all the information in all worksheets in the project, in one file.

9. **A.** The Data menu
10. **D.** Any of the above methods work.

Chapter 4

1. **B.** This sort of problem confuses many people, and the easiest way to avoid that confusion is to make a graph. First, recognize that this is a binomial distribution problem, with $n = 5$ and $p = 1/6 \approx 0.16667$. Create a probability distribution plot for this distribution, selecting the View probability option. In the Shaded area tab, select X value, Right tail, and enter 3. Figure A-8 shows this plot. Another way to answer this question is to use the Calc > Probability Distributions > Binomial calculator, and calculate the cumulative probability of 2 or fewer sixes. This answer is 0.96451. Subtract this from 1 to get 0.03549, the probability of 3 or more sixes.

2. **A.** 0.2636

   There are at least two ways to solve this with distribution models. One way is using the binomial model, with $n = 50$ and $p = 0.026316$. Calculate the probability of 0 wins using the Calc > Probability Distributions > Binomial calculator:

   ## Cumulative Distribution Function

   ```
   Binomial with n = 50 and p = 0.026316

   x    P( X <= x )
   0       0.263573
   ```

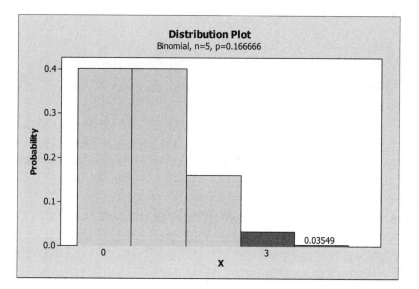

FIGURE A-8 • Binomial distribution plot.

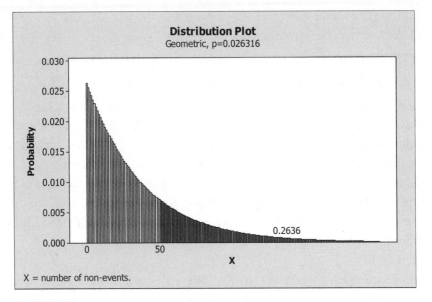

FIGURE A-9 • Geometric distribution plot.

Another method is to use the geometric distribution to model the number of losses before the first win. The probability of 50 or more losses before the first win is highlighted in Fig. A-9.

3. **A.** 0.00135

Here is the calculation report from Minitab:

Cumulative Distribution Function

```
Normal with mean = 250 and standard deviation = 10

  x  P( X <= x )
220    0.0013499
```

4. **B.** 224.242

This question asks for a strength value that is less than 99.5% of the population. The answer is provided by the inverse CDF of the normal distribution, with the probability of $1 - 0.995 = 0.005$. Here is the calculation report from Minitab:

Inverse Cumulative Distribution Function

```
Normal with mean = 250 and standard deviation = 10

P( X <= x )        x
    0.005   224.242
```

5. **D. 0.0283**

   Minitab can calculate the probability of 120 seconds or less between calls:

   Cumulative Distribution Function

   ```
   Exponential with mean = 30

     x   P( X <= x )
   120     0.981684
   ```

   Therefore, the probability of 120 or more seconds between calls is
   $1 - 0.9817 = 0.0283$.

6. **C.** The best fitting model is indicated by the lowest AD statistic and/or the highest p-value.

   Like all goodness-of-fit tests, the Anderson–Darling test statistic measures how badly the model fits the data, so a lower statistic value indicates a better fit. The p-value is the probability that a set of data from the hypothesized distribution would fit at least as badly as the data tested. If the p-value is higher, this indicates a better fit.

7. **A.** Normal

   Figure A-10 shows the results of the Minitab individual distribution identification for these four models. The p-values for all four models are very small, indicating that none of these is a perfect fit. But the best fitting model, or the least badly fitting model, is indicated by the smallest AD statistic. Between these four models, the normal model has the lowest AD statistic of 1.056.

8. The easiest way to make this graph is with Graph > Probability Distribution Plot. Select Vary Parameters from the gallery. Specify Gamma, Shape = 1:5 (shorthand for 1 2 3 4 5), Scale = 1, and Threshold = 0. Figure A-11 shows the result.

9. Figure A-12 is the normal probability plot of data in Train.MTW, with Days selected as the graph variable, and Type selected as the categorical variable.

10. The Box–Cox transformation suggests an optimal transformation of $\lambda = 0$, which is a natural log transformation. Clicking the Options button allows you to calculate and store the transformed data in a new column. After doing this, a histogram like Fig. A-13 is easy to create.

11. (extra credit) Lognormal. Fun fact from Section 4.6: If the log of X has a normal distribution, then X has a lognormal distribution. Minitab already proved this with the Box–Cox analysis. Triple extra points for you!

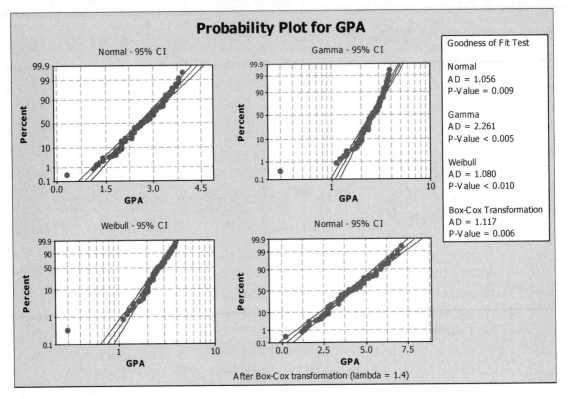

FIGURE A-10 • Individual distribution identification.

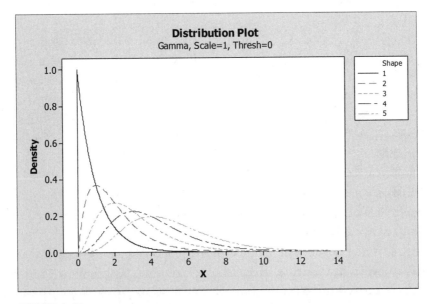

FIGURE A-11 • Gamma density functions.

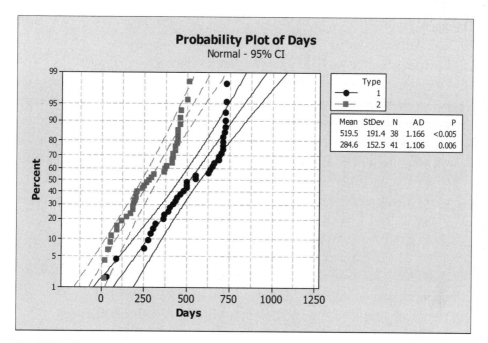

FIGURE A-12 • Probability plot.

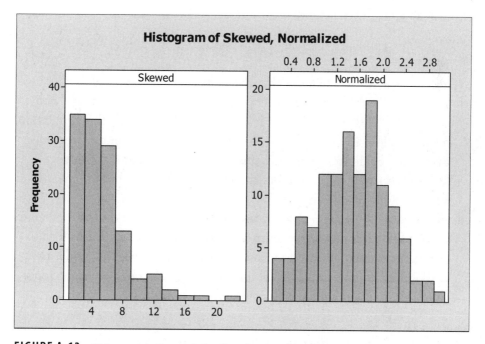

FIGURE A-13 • Histograms before and after Box–Cox transformation.

Chapter 5

1. **D.** Tolerance interval
2. **C.** Upper confidence bound on standard deviation
3. **D.** Wider; Lower
4. **B.** Confidence interval for the population mean. If you answered A, keep in mind that confidence intervals and hypothesis tests in the next chapter are ways to learn about the population. We already have the sample, so we don't need to do a lot of fancy math to learn about it. This is a common tricky test question.
5. **C.** 4.64 failures per year. The first challenge is to recognize that this question calls for a Poisson rate confidence interval. Key words that often point to a Poisson model are "rate" and "per." Select the 1-Sample Poisson Rate tool. Fill in the dialog with a sample size of 2 and 5 occurrences. In the Options form, select 90% confidence and Less than to generate an upper bound on the rate.
6. Here is the report from the 1-Sample t function with confidence set to 90%:

One-Sample T: Pin length

Variable	N	Mean	StDev	SE Mean	90% CI
Pin length	100	14.9923	0.0267	0.0027	(14.9879, 14.9967)

The 90% confidence interval for the population mean is (14.9879, 14.9967).

7. Yes, there is strong evidence that the population mean is below 15.00. The 90% confidence interval calculated in problem 6 does not contain 15.00. This provides at least 90% confidence that the population mean is below 15.00. The 90% confidence may or may not be regarded as "strong" evidence. Repeating this analysis with higher confidence levels shows that we have more than 99% confidence that the mean is below 15.00.
8. An Anderson–Darling normality test applied to the data returns a p-value of 0.014, suggesting that the normal distribution is not a good fit for this population. The Minitab Stat > Basic Statistics > 1 Variance function is used to calculate a confidence interval for standard deviation. Here is the report from this function, set for 90% confidence:

Test and CI for One Variance: Pin length

```
Method

The chi-square method is only for the normal distribution.
The Bonett method is for any continuous distribution.


Statistics

Variable       N    StDev  Variance
Pin length   100   0.0267  0.000715


90% Confidence Intervals

Variable     Method         CI for StDev       CI for Variance
Pin length   Chi-Square   (0.0240, 0.0303)   (0.000574, 0.000919)
             Bonett       (0.0245, 0.0296)   (0.000602, 0.000878)
```

Since the normal distribution may not be a good fit for this data, the Bonett method is preferred over the Chi-square method. The best answer here is (0.0245, 0.0296).

9. Below is the report from the tolerance intervals function for this data:

Tolerance Interval: Pin length

```
Method

Tolerance interval type          Two-sided
Confidence level                 95%
Percent of population in interval  99%


Statistics

Variable       N    Mean   StDev
Pin length   100  14.992   0.027


95% Tolerance Interval, Using Normal Method

Variable     Lower    Upper
Pin length  14.914   15.071


95% Tolerance Interval, Using Nonparametric Method

                                 Achieved
Variable     Lower    Upper    Confidence
Pin length  14.940   15.050       26.4
```

There is doubt about the normality of this data, which would ordinarily favor the nonparametric method for tolerance intervals. However, the achieved confidence for this tolerance interval is only 26.4%, far below the desired 95%. Therefore, this method simply fails for this case. The best available tolerance interval for this data is the normal-based interval of (14.914, 15.071).

10. This question requires the PREDINT macro from www.minitab.com to be installed, as described in this chapter. Here are the commands and the report from the Session window:

```
MTB > %predint c1;
SUBC> conf 99.
Executing from file: C:\Program Files\Minitab\Minitab 16\
English\Macros\predint.MAC
```

Prediction Interval for a Single Future Observation

```
Future Sample Size:        1
Estimated Value:           14.9923
99% Prediction Interval:   (14.9217, 15.0629)
```

The macro reports with 99% confidence that the next single observed value from this population will be between 14.9217 and 15.0629.

Chapter 6

1. **A.** H_0: The population follows a normal distribution.
2. **B.** Alpha is the probability that H_0 is rejected in favor of H_A, when H_0 is true.
3. **D.** When the p-value is less than α, there is strong evidence to reject H_0 and accept H_A.
4. **D.** The Summary Report contains an overall summary of the test, including a text interpretation of the results and comments.
5. **B.** When the report offers both an (approximate) p-value and an exact p-value, the exact one is preferred. The best interpretation is this: Since $0.032 < 0.05$, there is strong evidence to reject H_0.
6. This question asks for a one-sample test of the mean. Doing this test with the hypothesis tests assistant produces the summary report shown in Fig. A-14. The p-value is very small, indicating strong evidence that the mean is not 15.00, and in fact, it is below 15.00.
7. The question asks whether the % of students who pass a test is greater than 75%, based on a sample of 30 who take the test, 24 of whom pass. This is a 1-sample proportion test. Since we are only looking for evidence

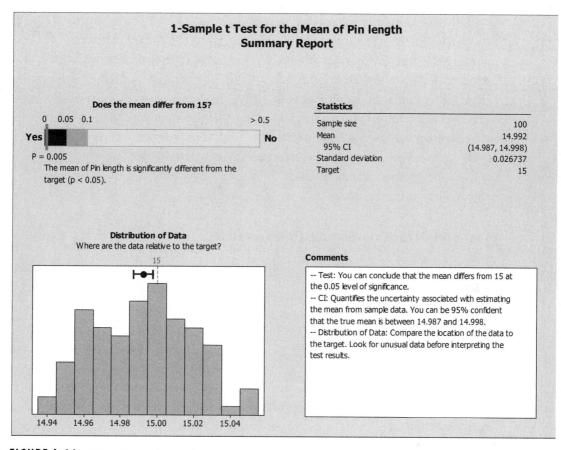

FIGURE A-14 • 1-Sample *t* test summary report.

that the proportion is greater than 75%, this is also a one-sided test. Using the hypothesis tests assistant, this is the 1-Sample % Defective test, but "Defective" in this case refers to "Passing the physical fitness test." After running the test, the *p*-value is 0.348, indicating there is not enough evidence from this sample of 30 to conclude that the overall freshman class meets this goal.

8. With three groups, the appropriate test to look for a difference between means is the one-way ANOVA. In the ANOVA dialog from the hypothesis tests assistant, for Y data column, enter Elastic. For X values column, enter Additive. After performing this test, the Summary Report contains this information: P = 0.000 Differences among the means are significant (p < 0.05). All three groups have significantly different means, with additive 2 having the lowest elasticity and additive 1 having the highest.

9. With three groups, the appropriate test to look for a difference between standard deviations is available in the hypothesis tests assistant. After performing this test, the Summary report lists P = 0.464 Differences among standard deviations are not significant (p > 0.05). The additive did not change the standard deviation of elasticity.

10. The hypothesis tests assistant has no test for this situation. Use the Stat > Basic Statistics > 1-Sample Poisson Rate test. Select Summarized data, and enter Sample size: 3 and Total occurrences: 5. Select Perform hypothesis test and enter Hypothesized rate: 3. Click Options and select the Less than alternative. Here is the report:

Test and CI for One-Sample Poisson Rate

```
Test of rate = 3 vs rate < 3
```

Sample	Total Occurrences	N	Rate of Occurrence	95% Upper Bound	Exact P-Value
1	5	3	1.66667	3.50434	0.116

```
"Length" of observation = 1.
```

With $\alpha = 0.05$, there is not yet significant evidence that the accident rate has been reduced.

Chapter 7

1. **B.** Stat > Power and Sample Size > Sample Size for Estimation. Since the goal of the survey is to estimate a proportion, not to test it or make a decision about the proportion, the Sample Size for Estimation is appropriate here.

2. **D.** Stat > Power and Sample Size > 1-Sample Poisson Rate. The count of events per unit time is often modeled as a Poisson rate. This is a testing, not an estimation problem, because the goal is to decide whether the rate has been reduced.

3. **C.** If the margin of error is 5 units, this means that the difference between the estimate and one limit of a 95% confidence interval is 5 units. In situations with a symmetric confidence interval, the confidence interval is ± 5 units. If you answered A, you are almost right, except that the statement is only true with a probability of 0.95.

4. **B.** To specify $\alpha = 0.10$, click Options and enter 0.10 in the Significance level field.

5. **D.** In the Power and Sample Size for 1-Sample t dialog, enter "10:30/10" or "10 20 30" in the Sample sizes field and "0.80 0.90" in the Power values field. Leave the Differences field blank.

6. Using the Minitab Sample Size for Estimation tool, a sample size of 18 is required to have a 95% two-sided margin of error of 5 units, when the standard deviation is 10 units.

7. 70 units in each sample. The key to this problem is to identify the correct sample size calculation. First, this is a test, not an estimation, since we will look for significant evidence that the new is better than the old. Second, the 2-sample t test is used to look for a difference in the means of two populations. Here, the hypothesis tests assistant can be helpful to identify the correct test, if you are not sure. Third, this is a one-sided test, since we already expect new to be better than old. If they are the same, or if the new is worse than the old, this is a failure of the new design. In Minitab, select Stat > Power and Sample Size > 2-Sample t. Enter 50 for Differences, 0.9 for Power values, and 100 for Standard deviation. Click Options and select a Greater than Alternative. The report lists a required sample size of 70 in each sample.

8. In the same dialog, enter 20 in the Sample sizes field and clear out the Power values field. Enter "50 93" in the Differences field. The power of this test is 0.46 at a difference of 50, and 0.89 at a difference of 93. Figure A-15 is the power curve with these points highlighted. In this case, it is quite important to choose a one-sided hypothesis test, because a two-sided test will reduce the power for the same sample size.

9. 200 in each sample. Power = $1 - \beta$, so if $\beta = 0.36$, power = 0.64. All three curves in the figure compare probabilities to 0.20. With the second probability = 0.30, the middle curve, representing a sample size of 200 (in each sample) passes through a power of approximately 0.64.

10. The probability is 0.88. Power, the vertical scale on the power curve, is the probability that the test will reject the null hypothesis. The lowest curve represents a sample size of $n = 100$. This curve passes through 0.88 with a comparison probability of 0.40.

Bonus: There are many correct answers. How you answer depends on who is asking and other factors. In general, avoiding the phrase "null hypothesis" is a good idea. Here are a few points you could make:

- If there is no difference in proportions, the test still has a 0.05 probability of detecting a difference just from random variation or sampling error.

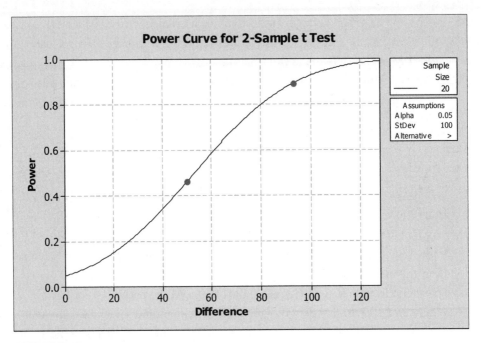

FIGURE A-15 • Power curve.

- Using a 0.05 risk here means that if there are no differences, we will incorrectly detect a difference about one time out of 20.
- The gap below the curve represents the probability of a "false positive" error.
- This risk, 0.05, can be changed to trade off the risk of "false positives" against sample size or power.

Chapter 8

1. **D.** Any of the Minitab functions listed can fit a cubic polynomial model.
2. **C.** Only the Fitted Line Plot produces a plot with the observed data, a fitted model line, and optional confidence or prediction intervals.
3. **C.** Sure, this question is a little tricky, because different criteria may be more important in different situations. Option A is wrong, because the best model will have lower S. The three models listed have different numbers of parameters, so it is important to use adjusted R^2, which is R-Sq(adj) in the Minitab Session window, instead of the unadjusted R^2. Predicted R^2 measures the predictive value, which is less often used than adjusted R^2. Overall, C is the best answer.

4. **B.** The model listed is not a linear regression model, because it is not a linear function of the unknown parameters a and b. In Minitab 16, this can only be fitted using the Nonlinear Regression tool.

5. **D.** All of the problems listed are potential effects of multicollinearity.

6. When the response variable has only two values, Binary Logistic Regression must be used to fit regression models.

7. When outliers are identified, the analyst should evaluate them for possible data errors or for some other identifiable reason why those cases do not represent the population which needs to be studied. There are a wide range of correct answers to this question, but it is wrong to always remove outliers from the data, just as it is wrong to never remove outliers. The proper response to outliers depends on the situation.

8. Using Minitab's Stepwise tool, with the default settings, here is the report:

Results for: Winearoma.MTW
Stepwise Regression: Aroma versus Cd, Mo, ...

```
   Alpha-to-Enter: 0.15  Alpha-to-Remove: 0.15


Response is Aroma on 17 predictors, with N = 37
```

Step	1	2	3	4
Constant	6.516	7.264	7.143	6.496
Sr	-1.93	-1.78	-1.67	-1.48
T-Value	-7.80	-7.17	-7.21	-6.22
P-Value	0.000	0.000	0.000	0.000
Ca		-0.0114	-0.0177	-0.0202
T-Value		-2.00	-3.09	-3.61
P-Value		0.054	0.004	0.001
Mo			2.9	3.4
T-Value			2.69	3.19
P-Value			0.011	0.003
B				0.126
T-Value				2.09
P-Value				0.045
S	0.656	0.629	0.579	0.551
R-Sq	63.46	67.30	73.19	76.41
R-Sq(adj)	62.42	65.38	70.76	73.47
Mallows Cp	10.1	7.6	2.7	0.9

The best four predictors are, in order, Sr, Ca, Mo, and B. There are undoubtedly other correct answers to this question.

9. With the four predictors identified above, and fitted using General Regression, here is the report:

General Regression Analysis: Aroma versus Sr, Ca, Mo, B

```
Regression Equation

Aroma  =   6.49609 - 1.48446 Sr - 0.020192 Ca + 3.35578 Mo +
0.126015 B
```

```
Coefficients

Term           Coef  SE Coef        T      P      VIF
Constant    6.49609  0.49377  13.1560  0.000
Sr         -1.48446  0.23871  -6.2188  0.000  1.31783
Ca         -0.02019  0.00559  -3.6102  0.001  1.37791
Mo          3.35578  1.05294   3.1870  0.003  1.25454
B           0.12601  0.06027   2.0908  0.045  1.18518
```

```
Summary of Model

S = 0.551082      R-Sq = 76.41%        R-Sq(adj) = 73.47%
PRESS = 12.9517  R-Sq(pred) = 68.57%
```

```
Analysis of Variance

Source       DF   Seq SS   Adj SS   Adj MS        F            P
Regression    4  31.4851  31.4851   7.8713  25.9186  0.0000000
  Sr          1  26.1488  11.7446  11.7446  38.6729  0.0000006
  Ca          1   1.5830   3.9581   3.9581  13.0333  0.0010323
  Mo          1   2.4257   3.0847   3.0847  10.1572  0.0032033
  B           1   1.3276   1.3276   1.3276   4.3714  0.0445744
Error        32   9.7181   9.7181   0.3037
Total        36  41.2032
```

```
Fits and Diagnostics for Unusual Observations


No unusual observations
```

The report identifies no concerns with extreme unusual residuals or high leverage X values. The VIF statistics are quite small, so there is no concern

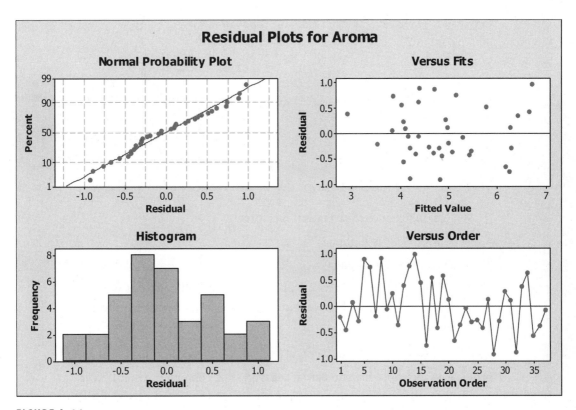

FIGURE A-16 • Residual plots.

with multicollinearity. The residual plot is shown as Fig. A-16. There are no significant reasons to be concerned with this residual plot.

10. The least significant *p*-value is 0.045, assigned to predictor B. Removing this predictor leaves a three-term model. Here is a portion of the report for this model:

```
Coefficients

Term          Coef    SE Coef         T      P      VIF
Constant   7.14268    0.40412   17.6749  0.000
Sr        -1.67271    0.23209   -7.2072  0.000  1.13032
Ca        -0.01772    0.00574   -3.0872  0.004  1.31616
Mo         2.91582    1.08312    2.6920  0.011  1.20444


Summary of Model

S = 0.578548    R-Sq = 73.19%       R-Sq(adj) = 70.76%
PRESS = 13.9477  R-Sq(pred) = 66.15%
```

```
Fits and Diagnostics for Unusual Observations

Obs   Aroma      Fit    SE Fit   Residual   St Resid
  7     4.8   5.00129  0.339184  -0.20129   -0.42948   X
 12     3.3   2.81709  0.333196   0.48291    1.02103   X
 14     7.7   6.44818  0.209844   1.25182    2.32184   R
 32     3.3   4.45621  0.141203  -1.15621   -2.06079   R

R denotes an observation with a large standardized residual.
X denotes an observation whose X value gives it large leverage.
```

There are several reasons to favor the 4-term model, including these:

- Residual standard deviation S is lower.
- Adjusted R^2 is higher.
- Predicted R^2 is higher.
- With the three-term model, Minitab identified concerns with high residuals and high leverage X values, which were resolved by adding the fourth term.

Note: This Winearoma.MTW dataset is used in the Minitab help file to provide an example for the Partial Least Squares regression tool. If you are curious about this, you may want to dig into this tool to see if it can fit a better predictive model than the one fit by standard least squares regression.

Chapter 9

1. **B.** Fractional factorial design
2. **D.** A central composite design combines a two-level factorial design with a center point and axial points, where one factor is varied to extreme values while holding other variables at their center values.
3. **D.** When one or more factors are hard to change, a split-plot design is the most appropriate way to design and analyze the experiment.
4. **D.** All of the above are potential benefits of center points.
5. **C.** A simplex centroid design with q factors has $2^q - 1$ design points. When $q = 4$, the design has 15 design points.
6. With four factors at two levels and 24 runs, design options include these, but other options are also possible:

- 16-run full factorial design, 1 replication, plus 8 center points. Full resolution.

- 8-run fractional factorial design, 3 replications. Resolution III.
- 12-run Plackett-Burman design, 2 replications. Resolution III.

7. The easiest way to calculate an alias structure is to create a new design. Minitab will automatically print out the alias structure in the Session window. Here it is:

Fractional Factorial Design

```
Factors:    7   Base Design:        7, 16   Resolution:   IV
Runs:      16   Replicates:             1   Fraction:     1/8
Blocks:     1   Center pts (total):     0

Design Generators: E = ABC, F = BCD, G = ACD

Alias Structure

I + ABCE + ABFG + ACDG + ADEF + BCDF + BDEG + CEFG

A + BCE + BFG + CDG + DEF + ABCDF + ABDEG + ACEFG
B + ACE + AFG + CDF + DEG + ABCDG + ABDEF + BCEFG
C + ABE + ADG + BDF + EFG + ABCFG + ACDEF + BCDEG
D + ACG + AEF + BCF + BEG + ABCDE + ABDFG + CDEFG
E + ABC + ADF + BDG + CFG + ABEFG + ACDEG + BCDEF
F + ABG + ADE + BCD + CEG + ABCEF + ACDFG + BDEFG
G + ABF + ACD + BDE + CEF + ABCEG + ADEFG + BCDFG
AB + CE + FG + ACDF + ADEG + BCDG + BDEF + ABCEFG
AC + BE + DG + ABDF + AEFG + BCFG + CDEF + ABCDEG
AD + CG + EF + ABCF + ABEG + BCDE + BDFG + ACDEFG
AE + BC + DF + ABDG + ACFG + BEFG + CDEG + ABCDEF
AF + BG + DE + ABCD + ACEG + BCEF + CDFG + ABDEFG
AG + BF + CD + ABDE + ACEF + BCEG + DEFG + ABCDFG
BD + CF + EG + ABCG + ABEF + ACDE + ADFG + BCDEFG
ABD + ACF + AEG + BCG + BEF + CDE + DFG + ABCDEFG
```

8. The easiest way to describe the experiment is to click the ⊞ button. This description appears:

```
Factors:  3   Blocks:     none   Center points in cube: 6
Runs:    20   Alpha:   1.68179   Center points in star: 0

Display Order: Standard Order
Display Units: Uncoded

Factors and Their Uncoded Levels

Factor  Name   Low  High
A       Mat A  0.7   1.7
B       Mat B   40    60
C       Mat C  1.8   2.8
```

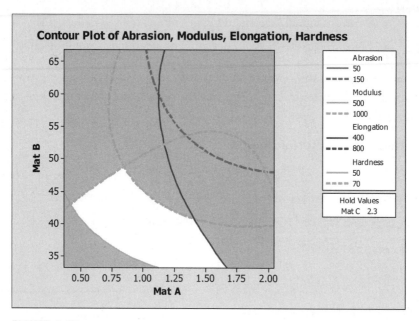

FIGURE A-17 • Overlaid contour plot.

This is a response surface design, specifically a central composite design. All necessary information required to duplicate the experiment is contained in the report above.

9. The overlaid contour plot is shown in Fig. A-17.
10. The optimization plot with the optimum settings of three factors is shown in Fig. A-18.

Chapter 10

1. **C.** Reproducibility
2. **A.** Crossed
3. **C.** Gage R&R as a % of tolerance is a measure of how well the measurement system can distinguish between good parts and bad parts.
4. **C.** Attribute agreement analysis is the correct tool. In this case, with only two categories for each inspection, either the MSA assistant or the traditional menus may be used.
5. **B.** Ordinal. This is a type of attribute measurement.
6. The type 1 gage study report is shown in Fig. A-19. The bias is significant because the p-value is small, 0.000.

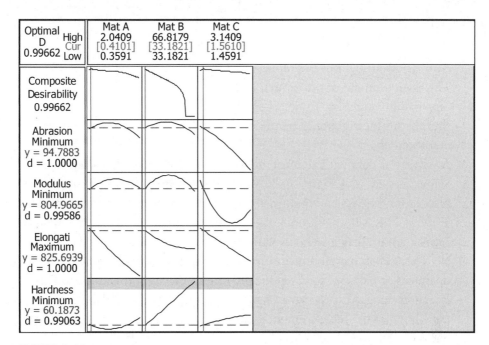

FIGURE A-18 • Optimization plot.

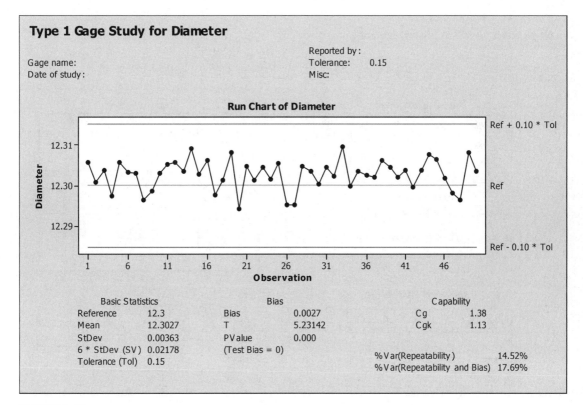

FIGURE A-19 • Type 1 gage study.

525

7. At the bottom right of the report is %Var(Repeatability and Bias) of 17.69%. This is an estimate of how much of the tolerance width is taken up with repeatability and bias. To be acceptable according to typical rules of thumb, this metric should be under 10%, so this measurement system is not acceptable.

8. Analyze this data with the Stat > Quality Tools > Gage Study > Gage R&R Study (Crossed) tool. Figure A-20 shows the resulting gage R&R sixpack plot. From the Session window, gage R&R as a percentage of tolerance is 19.98%. This is in the middle of the marginal range of 10% – 30%. The MSA assistant may also be used to analyze this dataset.

9. No. The R Chart has all dots inside the limits, meaning that none of the operators or parts showed significantly more variation than others. This is a good thing. Also, the Xbar Chart has a lot of dots outside the limits, meaning that the measurement system can successfully distinguish between different categories of parts. This is also a good thing.

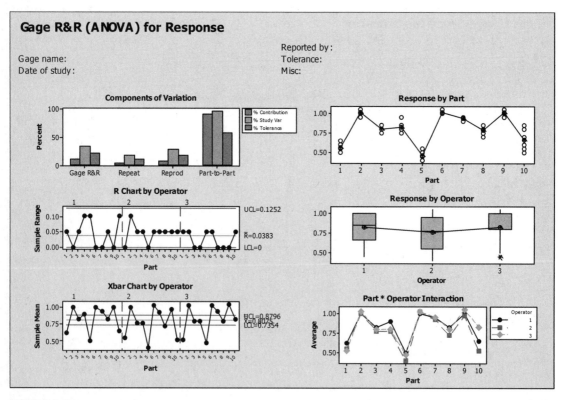

FIGURE A-20 • Gage R&R study sixpack plot.

10. If the dataset is analyzed from the traditional menus, here is the ANOVA table from the report:

Two-Way ANOVA Table With Interaction

Source	DF	SS	MS	F	P
Part	9	2.05871	0.228745	39.7178	0.000
Operator	2	0.04800	0.024000	4.1672	0.033
Part * Operator	18	0.10367	0.005759	4.4588	0.000
Repeatability	30	0.03875	0.001292		
Total	59	2.24913			

The Part * Operator term has a very small p-value of 0.000, therefore, the interaction IS significant. This bit of information is not available from the MSA assistant. The lower right plot in Fig. A-20 shows three lines, one for each appraiser. Any departure from parallel lines is an interaction. In this example, part 10 has a much larger variation between operators than the other parts.

Chapter 11

1. **D.** Control limits are usually drawn at three standard deviations of the plotted values on either side of the mean, or center line.
2. **C.** The most appropriate subgroup would be the first four parts manufactured per hour.
3. **D.** Control charts for subgroups are better than control charts for individuals because of both A) more power to detect smaller shifts and B) more robustness to nonnormality.
4. **B.** Short-term variation is estimated from the moving range of two consecutive measurements.
5. **B.** Each connector is either rejected or not, so the count of rejects is a count of defective units. Either P or NP charts may be used.
6. Figure A-21 is an Xbar-S chart of camshaft length. Subgroup 8 shows a significant decrease in mean length.
7. There are no out of control conditions in the Supp1 column.
8. This question must be answered using the traditional menus, not the assistant. Add the measurements for subgroup 21 to the bottom of the worksheet. Choose either Xbar-S or Xbar-R. Click Options, go to the Estimate tab, and specify to calculate control limits from subgroups 1:20. The finished control chart will show the new subgroup out of control with a significant increase in variation.

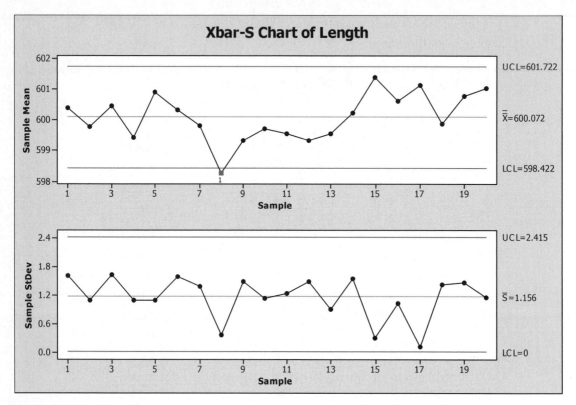

FIGURE A-21 • Xbar-S chart.

9. The optimal lambda for this dataset is –0.5, representing an inverse square-root transformation $Y = 1/\sqrt{X}$. The I-MR chart with this transformation shows that observation 52 is outside the control limits on both parts of this chart.

10. Either a C chart or a U chart of this data shows no out-of-control conditions. This is a stable Poisson process.

Chapter 12

1. **B.** A process should be stable before reporting capability metrics.
2. **C.** Pp, Ppk, and Cpm are overall or actual capability metrics.
3. **A.** Cpk is almost always calculated with within-subgroup variation.
4. **D.** Alternatives for nonnormal capability analysis include all of the above.
5. **B.** Binomial capability
6. Ppk = 0.55
7. % Out of spec (expected) = 5.00%
8. Before Ppk = 0.73; After Ppk = 1.74. This is an excellent opportunity to use the capability comparison tool in the assistant.

9. A 95% confidence interval for Ppk is (1.33, 2.16). The assistant does not provide confidence intervals. Instead, use Capability Analysis > Normal, and click Options to select the confidence interval option.
10. A P chart from the process shows two lots (20 and 21) well above the upper control limit. The level of defective units is not stable. Therefore, the best answer is to report that the process is unstable and needs to be stabilized before any "sigma level" or other capability metric can be reported. After the process is stabilized, Z.Bench is the closest Minitab metric to a "sigma level."

Chapter 13

1. **B.** Acceptable quality level (AQL) is a level of defects or defective items which should be accepted most of the time by the acceptance sampling plan.
2. **B.** ATI = Average Total Inspection, the average number of parts inspected per lot, assuming rejected lots are screened.
3. **A.** The average outgoing quality limit (AOQL) is the maximum level of defective parts which will pass through this acceptance sampling plan, assuming that rejected lots are 100% screened.
4. **C.**
5. **B.** Minitab recommends a sample size $n = 18$ and an acceptance number $c = 1$. If 1 or fewer defective castings are found, accept the lot. Therefore, if 2 or more defectives are found, reject the lot.
6. 2,302. To find this, create an attributes sampling plan for defective units, measured as defectives per million. Enter 3.4 in the AQL field and 0.05 in the alpha field. Since RQL was not specified, enter a large number, like 1000 for RQL, so the acceptance number $c = 0$. If $c = 1$ or more, a much larger sample size will be required.
7. The (25, 1) sampling plan has a higher probability of rejecting a lot with 10% defective units. To compare these two plans visually, make an OC curve using the Acceptance Sampling by Attributes tool. Select Compare User Defined Sampling Plans in the dropdown box. Enter 10 25 in the Sample sizes field and 0 1 in the Acceptance numbers field. The finished plot is shown in the top part of Fig. A-22. The OC curve plots the probability of acceptance. At 10% defective, the (25, 1) plan has lower probability of acceptance, and therefore, a higher probability of rejection.
8. The (25, 1) sampling plan has the lower AOQL. The bottom part of Fig. A-22 shows the AOQ curves made using the same procedure as for question 7, with Lot size set to 500. AOQL is the maximum value of the AOQ curve, which is lower for the (25, 1) plan.

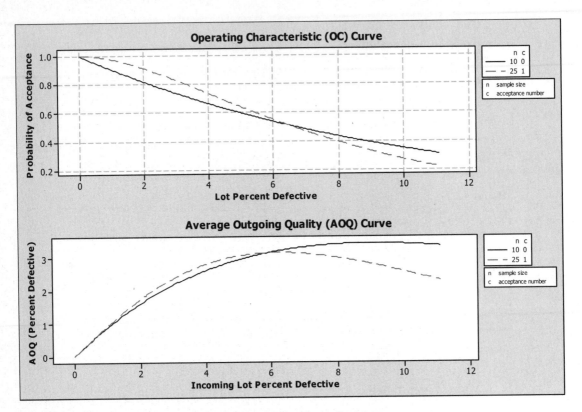

FIGURE A-22 • OC curves and AOQ curves for (10, 0) and (25,1) sampling plans.

9. Sample size = 54 and critical distance = 1.94330. Fill out the dialog with AQL = 1, RQL = 5, Alpha = 0.05, and Beta = 0.10.

10. Accept the lot. Here is the report from Minitab:

Acceptance Sampling by Variables - Accept/Reject Lot

Make Accept or Reject Decision Using Length

```
Sample Size                          100
Mean                                 600.072
Standard Deviation                   1.33501
Lower Specification Limit (LSL)      590
Upper Specification Limit (USL)      610

Z.LSL                                7.54454
Z.USL                                7.43668
Critical Distance (k Value)          1.9433
Maximum Standard Deviation (MSD)     4.49163

Decision:  Accept lot.
```

Chapter 14

1. **A.** A failure time is right-censored when the failure occurs at some unknown, later time.

2. **C.** This dataset contains right-censored and interval-censored data. To analyze this data requires the tools in the Arbitrary Censoring menu.

3. **D.** Nonparametric models do not require an assumption of a particular distribution family; but they do not allow extrapolation beyond the range of observed failure data, and they typically have wider confidence intervals.

4. **C.** Of the tools listed, only the Parametric Distribution Analysis tool can properly analyze multiple failure modes. The Nonparametric Distribution Analysis tool can also do this.

5. **B.** Key word in the question: demonstrate

6. Only 3. The trick is that if MTTF really is 1,000 hours, there is a 95% probability of failing the test. MTTF must be a lot better than 1,000 hours to have a high probability of passing. Here's the Minitab report:

Demonstration Test Plans

```
Reliability Test Plan
Distribution: Exponential
MTTF Goal = 1000, Target Confidence Level = 95%
```

Failure Test	Testing Time	Sample Size	Actual Confidence Level
0	1000	3	95.0213

7. The data in this worksheet is set up for analysis using the Arbitrary Censoring features of Minitab. The first row means that 8 tires were failed before the time of their first inspection at 10,000 miles.

8. Using the Distribution ID Plot tool in the Arbitrary Censoring menu, with all the distribution models selected, returns a lengthy report. Here is the section of the report dealing with goodness-of-fit:

```
Goodness-of-Fit
```

Distribution	Anderson-Darling (adj)	Correlation Coefficient
Weibull	2.387	0.948
Lognormal	2.960	0.880
Exponential	6.411	*
Loglogistic	2.831	0.911
3-Parameter Weibull	2.321	0.998
3-Parameter Lognormal	2.602	0.975
2-Parameter Exponential	6.034	*
3-Parameter Loglogistic	2.591	0.987
Smallest Extreme Value	2.325	0.998
Normal	2.600	0.975
Logistic	2.592	0.987

The best model is indicated either by the lowest Anderson–Darling statistic or the highest Correlation Coefficient. By either measure, the 3-Parameter Weibull and the Smallest Extreme Value models are better than the others, and they are essentially equally good. Either model would be a correct choice. For simplicity, the SEV distribution with only 2 parameters might be preferred.

9. Using the SEV model, the estimate of survival at 60,000 miles is 0.7416, with a 95% confidence interval of 0.7143 – 0.7667. Using the also correct 3-parameter Weibull model, the estimate of survival at 60,000 miles is 0.7410, with a 95% confidence interval of 0.7136 – 0.7661. The difference in the two models is trivial in this case.

10. Using the nonparametric approach, survival at 60,000 hours is estimated to be 0.7658, with a 95% confidence interval of 0.7360 to 0.7957.

Final Exam

1. A new dataset can be added to the file by (a) opening a Minitab worksheet file containing the data; (b) copying and pasting from Microsoft Excel or another spreadsheet application; (c) opening an Excel workbook file with File > Open Worksheet; or, (d) querying a database with ODBC.

2. Mean = 19.933; Median = 19.5; Standard deviation = 3.039.

3. 95% confidence interval for the mean is 18.798 to 21.068. Based on the available data, the probability that the population mean is between these limits is 95%.

4. Figure A-23 is a time series plot, which shows no evidence of a trend.

5. The Anderson–Darling normality test has a p-value of 0.226. Since this p-value is larger than 0.05, there is no strong evidence of nonnormality.

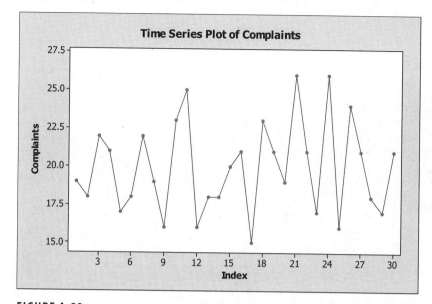

FIGURE A-23 • Time series plot of complaints.

6. The question asks for a stem-and-leaf display, which looks like this:

Stem-and-Leaf Display: New

```
Stem-and-leaf of New  N  = 36
Leaf Unit = 1.0

   4    7    0023
   9    7    56669
  12    8    122
  (9)   8    566667888
  15    9    3
  14    9    556
  11   10    024
   8   10    569
   5   11    23
   3   11    7
   2   12
   2   12    8
   1   13
   1   13    5
```

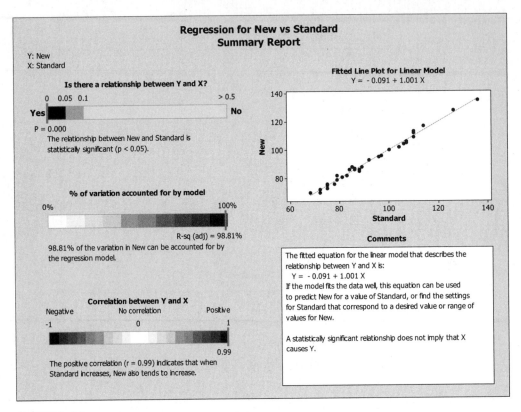

FIGURE A-24 • Regression Assistant Summary Report.

7. The correlation between data in columns **New** and **Standard** is 0.994 with a *p*-value of 0.000. Since the *p*-value is small, this is strong evidence that the correlation is non-zero.

8. A simple scatter plot would answer this question. Figure A-24 is the **Summary Report** from the regression assistant, which includes the scatter plot and more information to answer the following questions.

9. The best way to do this is with a Marginal Plot, found in the Graph menu. See Fig. A-25.

10. New = −0.091 + 1.001 Standard

11. The adjusted R^2 is 98.81%. This is the percentage of variation in the data accounted for by the model.

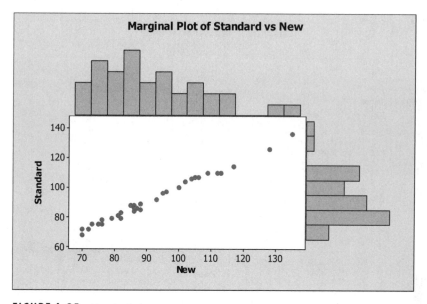

FIGURE A-25 • Marginal plot.

12. No. This question cannot be answered by the regression assistant. Use Stat > Regression > Regression to fit the simple linear model. Here is a part of the report:

Regression Analysis: New versus Standard

```
The regression equation is
New = - 0.09 + 1.00 Standard

Predictor      Coef   SE Coef      T      P
Constant     -0.091     1.730   -0.05  0.958
Standard    1.00100   0.01859   53.85  0.000
```

In the regression table, the Constant term has a high p-value of 0.958, so there is no evidence that this term in the model is non-zero.

13. Stacked format

14. See Fig. A-26. This plot may be made from the graphical analysis assistant, or from the Graph menu, starting either with an Individual Value Plot or an Interval Plot.

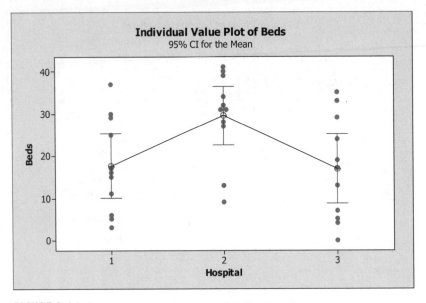

FIGURE A-26 • Individual value plot with confidence intervals.

15. The one-way ANOVA performed by the hypothesis testing assistant reports a significant difference with a *p*-value of 0.023. Hospital 2 has significantly more mean vacant beds than 1 and 3, but there is no difference between 1 and 3.

16. The test for equal variances in the Stat > ANOVA menu finds no significant difference in variance, by either Bartlett's or Levene's method.

17. The boxplot shows the minimum, first quartile, median, third quartile, and the maximum.

18. The coefficient of skewness is –0.81, so the distribution is skewed to the left. Many graphs display this effectively, including a graphical summary, histogram, individual value plot, or a boxplot.

19. Many plots are possible, including Fig. A-27.

20. 500:700/25

21. **C.** Graphical font settings are found in the Tools > Options dialog.

22. **C.** Custom toolbars are created through the Tools > Customize dialog. They are easy to make and definitely do not require any programming.

23. **B.** Minitab profiles store all the options and customization settings.

24. **C.** Most graph types are found in the Graph menu, but many specialized graphs are accessed through submenus of the Stat menu.

25. The DMAIC profile must be active. To do this, select Tools > Manage Profiles, and move the DMAIC profile to the Active Profiles box.

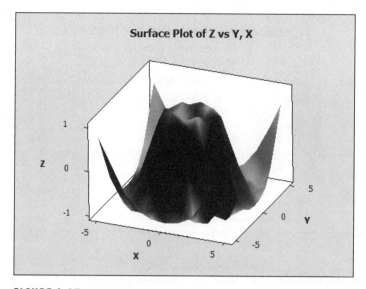

FIGURE A-27 • Surface plot of cowboy hat function.

26. At least three ways: (a) Calc > Make Patterned Data > Simple Set of Numbers
for each column; (b) Calc > Make Mesh Data; and, (c) using session commands as follows:
```
MTB > set c1
DATA> (1:10)10
DATA> end
MTB > set c2
DATA> 10(1:10)
DATA> end
MTB >
```

27. 0.366032

28. 0.079373. The probability of 2 or fewer defective units is 0.920627.
Therefore, the probability of 3 or more defective units is $1 - 0.920627 =$
0.079373

29. 0.0176207

30. 4868.89 hours

31. $\lambda = 0$, corresponding to $Y = \ln(X)$

32. $Y = 2.95594 + 1.33769 * \text{Ln}((X - 0.0225681)/(45.6736 - X))$

33. Johnson is better, with an AD statistic of 0.198. The AD statistic of the
Box–Cox transformed data is 0.282, indicating a worse fit. The p-value is
lower for the Box–Cox, also indicating a worse fit. The easiest way to calculate both of these in one step is with the Individual Distribution Identification tool.

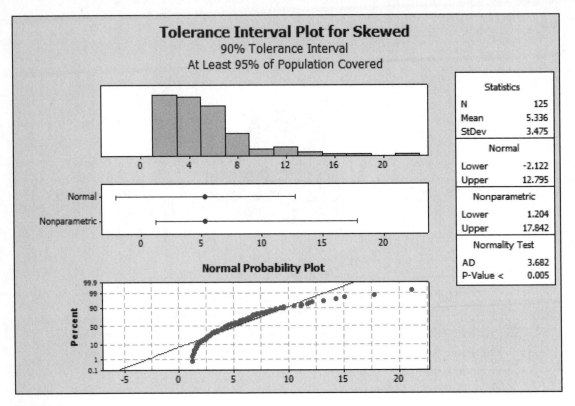

FIGURE A-28 • Tolerance interval graph.

34. Tolerance interval
35. Figure A-28 shows a tolerance interval graph for the BoxCox.MTW dataset, with 90% containment and 95% confidence. From the histogram, probability plot, and AD test, the normal distribution clearly does not fit. Here is a portion of the Session.MTW window report with the nonparametric tolerance interval:

```
90% Tolerance Interval, Using Nonparametric Method

                             Achieved
Variable  Lower   Upper   Confidence
Skewed    1.204   17.842       95.2
```

Since the nonparametric tolerance interval has a confidence of more than 95%, as required, the nonparametric tolerance interval of (1.204, 17.842) is the best answer.

36. The 95% confidence interval is from 32.394 to 40.966. Since the test value 30 is outside the interval, there is strong evidence that the mean is different from 30.

37. A 1-sample t-test returns a p-value of 0.004. Subtracting this from 1, this data provides 99.6% confidence that the mean is not 30.

38. Using the Bonett method, the 90% upper confidence limit on standard deviation is 12.5. The chi-square method returns a value of 12.9. Either answer is acceptable for this data.

39. The p-value for a hypothesis test is 0.157 (Bonett) or 0.195 (chi-square). Either way, there is no strong evidence that standard deviation is less than 12.

40. Since the p-value is less than α, the correct conclusion is to reject H_0 and conclude that $\mu_1 \neq \mu_2$.

41. If tornadoes are independent events, then the count of tornadoes per year should follow a Poisson distribution, with mean 53.1. A 1-sample Poisson rate test with sample size = 1, total occurrences = 77, and hypothesized mean = 53.1 returns a p-value of 0.002. (This is a two-sided test, with the Not equal alternative. If we are only interested in testing for an increase, not a decrease, click Options and select a Greater than alternative. This reduces the p-value to 0.001) The very small p-value means that 77 tornadoes is a significant increase. It could also mean that individual tornadoes are not really independent events, but happen in groups or outbreaks.

42. This question calls for a one-way ANOVA test with response = Aroma and factor = Region. The p-value is 0.000 so there is a significant difference. The means comparison chart shows that the mean Aroma for region 3 is significantly higher than for 1 and 2, but there is no difference between 1 and 2.

43. The p-value is 0.872, so there is no significant difference in Oakiness by region.

44. Power = 0.691. Use the power and sample size tool for the 1-sample proportions test.

45. A sample of size 12 has power of 0.925 to detect a standard deviation ratio of 0.5.

46. The best subset of the three variables is Protein and Carbo. This can be determined by either Best Subsets or Stepwise regression. The best model has the largest R-Sq(adj), the adjusted R^2, and also the smallest S, the residual standard deviation.

47. R^2 is 94.1%, meaning that 94.1% of the variation in Calories is explained by Protein and Carbo.

The easiest way to answer Questions 48–50 is with the regression assistant.

48. Using default settings, the assistant recommends a linear model.
49. Best fitting model: Biomass = 48.09 + 2.116 Area2
50. Rows 3 and 4 have unusually large residuals.
51. With every combination of levels, this is called a "full factorial" experiment. It has no aliasing, since every main effect and every interaction can be estimated independently.
52. Factors A (Index), D (Time), and F (Temp) are significant in one or more of the responses. None of the other main effects or interactions are significant. The easiest way to answer this question is to select Pareto charts, in the Graphs dialog. Then, look for which bars extend to the right of the red, vertical line.
53. The easiest way to answer this question is to click the the ⊞ button in the Project Manager toolbar. In the left pane of the Project Manager window, under the Cleaning.MTW folder, is this helpful clue: ⊞ Response Surface Design.
54. The coefficients for the model can be read from the `Coef` column of the regression table: `CleanEff = 69.6650 - 0.1829*Pressure + 15.28*Time + 0.9111*Conc + 0.001*Pressure*Pressure - 1.402*Time*Time - 0.0158*Pressure*Time`.
55. Since the coefficient of Conc (+0.9111) is positive, increasing Conc to its maximum value (7) will maximize CleanEff. Figure A-29 is the contour plot.

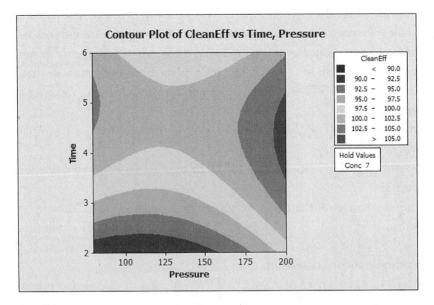

FIGURE A-29 • Contour plot of CleanEff versus Time and Pressure.

56. Using the optimizer, maximum CleanEff is predicted at Pressure = 200, Time = 4.303, and Conc = 7.0.

57. 19.98% (This is listed in the report in the %Tolerance (SV/Toler) column.)

58. When the primary goal is to measure parts against the tolerance limits, the percentage of tolerance is most appropriate.

59. According to the report, Number of distinct categories = 4.

60. The report lists three components of variation: repeatability (10.78% of tolerance), reproducibility between operators (9.06% of tolerance), and operator by part interaction (14.18% of tolerance). The interaction is the largest component of variation, and needs to be investigated first.

61. With more than two levels, this data cannot be analyzed with the MSA assistant. Figure A-30 is a graph summarizing the analysis.

62. The answer is at the end of the report, under the All Appraisers vs Standard heading. Overall assessment agreement is 80.00%, with a 95% confidence interval of from 61.43% to 92.29%.

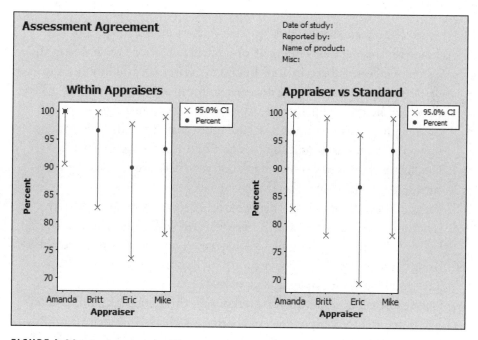

FIGURE A-30 • Attribute agreement analysis.

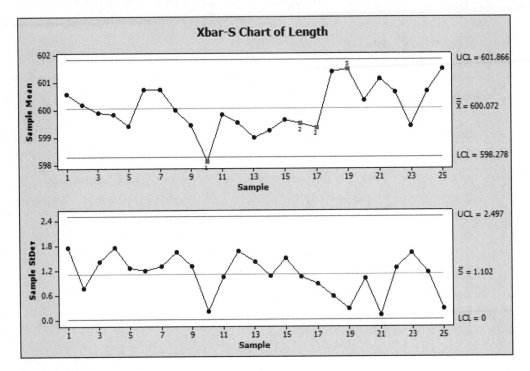

FIGURE A-31 • Xbar-S chart.

63. Figure A-31 is an Xbar-S chart. An Xbar-R chart is also an appropriate choice for this dataset. Three out-of-control conditions are noted in the Session window. Subgroup 10 is below the lower control limit on the Xbar chart, indicating a significant decrease in mean. Also, subgroups 8–17 are all below the center line on the Xbar chart, indicating a significant decrease in mean. Subgroups 18–19 are more than 2 standard deviations above the center line, indicating a significant increase in mean.

64. The Xbar-S chart is not shown here, but yes, there are many subgroups outside the control limits on the Xbar chart.

65. Use the I-MR-R/S (Between/Within) control chart to estimate short-term variation using a combination of between and within subgroup variation. Figure A-32 shows the completed chart, with no out-of-control conditions.

66. Using the Between/Within Capability tool, short-term capability Cpk = 2.04 and long-term capability Ppk = 1.94.

67. Since each call is either unanswered or not, this data is a count of defective units, and the proper control chart is a P chart. This chart (not shown here) finds five subgroups either above the upper or below the lower control limit. This process is not stable.

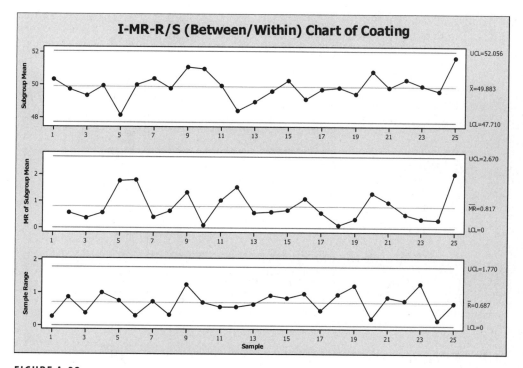

FIGURE A-32 • I-MR-R/S (Between/Within) control chart.

68. Ppk is estimated to be 0.80, with a 95% confidence interval of 0.67 to 0.93.
69. Accept. The acceptance number of 1 means that if 0 or 1 defectives are found, accept the lot. If 2 or more are found, reject the lot.
70. 0.721
71. Average Outgoing Quality Limit (AOQL) = 1.628% which occurs at an incoming rate of 3.179% defective.
72. Sample Size = 87, Critical Distance = 2.70728
73. Reject the lot. Z.LSL is only 2.4.
74. The dataset is set up for the Right Censoring analysis tools.
75. Using the Distribution ID Plot tool, the lowest Anderson–Darling statistics belong to the 3-parameter lognormal and the normal distributions.
76. Using parametric analysis with a normal distribution, the estimated mean force to failure is 118.516, with a 95% confidence interval of 103.582 to 133.451.
77. There is a significant difference, with a *p*-value of 0.000. The new cord is estimated to be 44 units worse than the standard cord.

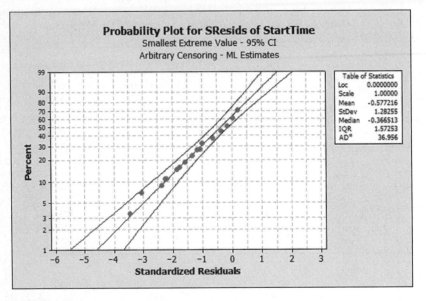

FIGURE A-33 • Residual probability plot.

78. The regression table reports that the `Temp` term in the model is very significant, with a *p*-value of 0.000. Yes, temperature does affect reliability. Since the `Coef` is negative, higher temperature makes reliability worse.

79. To answer this question, enter 125, 150, 175 into a column of the worksheet, then use the Estimate dialog to estimate the 50th percentile at those temperatures. Median times to failure are 88.5, 26.7, and 8.1 hours, respectively.

80. Figure A-33 shows the probability plot of residuals. Since all the dots follow the line nicely, there is no reason to be concerned about this model.

Further Reading

Agresti, A. and B. A. Coull. (1998) Approximate is better than 'exact' for interval estimation of binomial proportions. *The American Statistician* 52:119–126.

Anscombe, F. J. (1973) Graphs in statistical analysis. *The American Statistician* 27:17–21.

ANSI/ASQ Z1.4. (2008) Sampling Procedures and Tables for Inspection by Attributes. American National Standards Institute.

ANSI/ASQ Z1.9. (2008) Sampling Procedures and Tables for Inspection by Variables for Percent Nonconforming. American National Standards Institute.

Automotive Industry Action Group (AIAG). (2002) *Measurement Systems Analysis Reference Manual*, 3d ed. Chrysler, Ford, General Motors Supplier Quality Requirements Task Force. www.aiag.org, Southfield, MI.

Automotive Industry Action Group (AIAG). (2005) *Statistical Process Control (SPC)*, 2nd ed. www.aiag.org, Southfield, MI.

Barnett, V. and T. Lewis. (1994) *Outliers in Statistical Data*, 3d ed., Chichester, Wiley.

Bonett, D.G. (2006) Approximate confidence interval for standard deviation of nonnormal distributions. *Computational Statistics & Data Analysis* 50:775–782.

Bothe, D. R. (1992) A capability study for an entire product. 46th ASQC Annual Quality Congress Transactions, Nashville, TN, May, 1992, 172–178.

Bothe, D. R. (1997) *Measuring Process Capability*, McGraw-Hill, New York.

Box, G. E. P. and D. R. Cox. (1964) An analysis of transformations. *J R Stat Soc, Ser B*, 26:211–243.

Box, G. E. P., J. S. Hunter, W. G. Hunter. (2005) *Statistics for Experimenters*, Wiley-Interscience, New York.

Breyfogle, F. (2009) Non-normal data: To transform or not to transform. www. QualityDigest.com 8/24/2009.

Breyfogle, F. (2009a) NOT transforming the data can be fatal to your analysis. www.QualityDigest.com 9/16/2009.

Cornell, J. A. (2002) *Experiments with Mixtures*, 3d ed. Wiley, New York.

Chou, Y. M., A. M. Polansky, and R. L. Mason. (1998) Transforming non-normal data to normality in statistical process control. *J Qual Tech* 30(2):133–141.

Clopper, C. and E. S. Pearson. (1934) The use of confidence or fiducial limits illustrated in the case of the binomial. *Biometrika* 26:404–413.

D'Agostino, R. B. and M. A. Stephens. (1986) *Goodness-of-Fit Techniques*, Marcel Dekker, New York.

Draper, N. R. and H. Smith. (1998) *Applied Regression Analysis*, 3d ed. Wiley, New York.

Evans, M., N. Hastings, and B. Peacock. (2000) *Statistical Distributions*, 3d ed. Wiley, New York.

Grant, E. and R. Leavenworth. (1996) *Statistical Process Control*, McGraw-Hill, New York.

Johnson, N. L. (1949) Systems of frequency curves generated by methods of translation. *Biometrika* 73:149–176.

Johnson, N.L., S. Kotz, and N. Balakrishnan. (1994) *Continuous Univariate Distributions*, Volume 1, 2nd ed. Wiley, New York.

Johnson, N.L., S. Kotz, and N. Balakrishnan. (1995) *Continuous Univariate Distributions*, Volume 2, 2nd ed. Wiley, New York.

Johnson, N. L., A. W. Kemp, and S. Kotz. (2005) *Univariate Discrete Distributions*, 3d ed. Wiley, New York.

Kotz, S. and C. R. Lovelace. (1998) *Process Capability Indices in Theory and Practice.* Arnold, London.

Kutner, M. H., C. Nachtsheim, J. Neter, and W. Li. (2004) *Applied Linear Statistical Models*, 5th ed. McGraw-Hill/Irwin, New York.

Lenth, R.V. (1989) Quick and easy Analysis of unreplicated factorials. *Technometrics* 31:469–473.

Minitab Inc. (2010) *Meet Minitab 16*, Release 16.1.0. www.minitab.com.

Minitab Inc. (2010) Minitab Statistical Software, Release 16 for Windows, State College, Pennsylvania.

Minitab Inc. (2010) Methods for Minitab 16 Assistant (White Papers for Assistant Menu), http://www.minitab.com/en-US/support/answers/answer.aspx?id=2613.

Montgomery, D. C., G. C. Runger, and N. F. Hubele. (2010) *Engineering Statistics*. Wiley, Hoboken, NJ.

Montgomery, D. C. (2008) *Design and Analysis of Experiments*. Wiley, New York.

Montgomery, D. C. (2008a) *Introduction to Statistical Process Control*. Wiley, New York.

Montgomery, D. C. and E. A. Peck. (1982) *Introduction to Linear Regression Analysis*. Wiley, New York.

Montgomery, D. C. and S. M. Kowalski. (2010) *Design and Analysis of Experiments: MINITAB Companion*. Wiley, New York.

Myers, R. H., D. C. Montgomery, and C. Anderson-Cook. (2008) *Response Surface Methodology: Process and Product Optimization Using Designed Experiments*, 3d ed. Wiley, New York.

Nelson, Lloyd S. (1984) Technical aids: the Shewhart control chart—tests for special causes, *Journal of Quality Technology* 16, 4:237–239.

Nelson, W. (2004) *Applied Life Data Analysis*. Wiley, Hoboken, NJ.

Nelson, W. (2004a) *Accelerated Testing: Statistical Models, Test Plans, and Data Analysis*. Wiley, Hoboken, NJ.

O'Connor, P. (2002) *Practical Reliability Engineering*, 4th ed. Wiley, Chichester.

Ott, R. L. and M. Longnecker. (2010) *An Introduction to Statistical Methods and Data Analysis*. Brooks/Cole, Belmont, CA.

Plackett, R.L. and J.P. Burman. (1946) The design of optimum multifactorial experiments. *Biometrika* 34:255–272.

Ross, T. D. (2003) Accurate confidence intervals for binomial probabilities and Poisson rate estimation. *Computers in Biology and Medicine* 33:509–531.

Schilling, E. G. and D. V. Neubauer. (2008) *Acceptance Sampling in Quality Control*, 2nd ed. Chapman and Hall/CRC, Boca Raton, FL.

Sleeper, A. D. (2006) *Design for Six Sigma Statistics: 59 Tools for Diagnosing and Solving Problems in DFSS Initiatives*. McGraw-Hill, New York.

Sleeper, A. D. (2007) *Six Sigma Distribution Modeling*, McGraw-Hill, New York.

Taguchi, G. (1987) *The System of Experimental Design: Engineering Methods to Optimize Quality and Minimize Costs.* UNIPUB/Kraus, White Plains, NY & American Supplier Institute, Dearborn, MI.

Tufte, E. R. (2001) *The Visual Display of Quantitative Information*, 2nd ed. Graphics Press, Cheshire, CT.

Wheeler, D. J. (2000) *Normality and the Process Behavior Chart.* SPC Press, Knoxville, TN.

Wheeler, D. J. (2006) *EMP (Evaluating the Measurement Process) III Using Imperfect Data.* SPC Press, Knoxville, TN.

Wheeler, D. J. (2009) Do you have leptokurtophobia? www.QualityDigest .com 8/05/2009.

Wheeler, D. J. (2009a) Transforming the data can be fatal to your analysis. www.QualityDigest.com 9/03/2009.

Wheeler, D. J. (2009b) Avoiding statistical jabberwocky. www.QualityDigest .com 10/07/2009.

Wheeler, D. J. (2010) *Understanding Statistical Process Control*, 3d ed. SPC Press, Knoxville, TN.

Wheeler, D. J. (2011) "Problems with gage R&R studies. Quality Digest, http:// www.qualitydigest.com/inside/quality-insider-column/problems-gauge-rr-studies.html.

Index

Note: Bold page numbers indicate primary references.